Napoléon Coste: Composer and Guitarist in the Musical Life of 19th-Century Paris

Ari van Vliet

Napoléon Coste - Disdéri, 1867

Translation and elaboration of the biography in the PhD dissertation in the graduation to doctor at Utrecht University on Wednesday, May 27, 2015.

DGA Editions catalog number: 203
ISBN-13: 978-0-9883876-8-3

Copyright © 2018 by DGA Editions, a division of Digital Guitar Archive.
All rights reserved. No part of this document may be reproduced or transmitted in any form or by any means, electronic, mechanical, photocopying, recording, or otherwise, without prior written permission of the Publisher.
This edition contains new and original material. Photocopying is ILLEGAL.

More information on DGA Editions may be obtained at the Digital Guitar Archive website:
http://www.DigitalGuitarArchive.com

This biography is the biographical part of the first full scholarly edition: Biography, Thematic Catalogue, Compact Disc Cumuli foundation, Zwolle, The Netherlands, 2015
ISBN 978-90-808625-2-4; NUR 661.
Website: www.cumuli.nl
Compact Disc: Cumuli Guitar Recital CGR 1204
Translation and proofreading: Dr Leston Buell
Cover: Kresse heptacorde 2010, copy Lacôte 1856

CONTENTS

Prélude - Biography	v
I *Introduction* – Preliminary History 1754-1805	1
II *Caprice* – Birth and Childhood 1805-1814	7
III *Thème Varié* – Youth 1815-1828	15
Intermezzo I – Paris, Musical Life Around 1828	25
IV *Aux Parisiens* – The Early Period, Paris 1829-1839	45
V *Souvenirs* – Development, Paris 1840-1855	83
VI *Grande Sérénade* – The Makaroff Competition, Brussels 1856	137
Intermezzo II – Paris, Musical Life Around 1856	159
VII *Études de Genre* – Composer and Guitarist, Paris 1857-1872	171
VIII *Divagation* – The Final Years, Paris 1873-1883	203
IX *Finale* – Conclusion	233
Appendices	251
Bibliographies	275
Illustrations	307
Index	311
The Author	318
CD Notes	319

dedicated to
Ina
my loving wife

Prélude

As people generally do not have their own judgement, let alone being capable of accurately assessing eminent and complicated achievements, they always rely on the authority of others, such that for 99 per cent of those expressing their approval the praise of a higher order depends exclusively on faith and credulity.[1]

INTRODUCTION: BIOGRAPHY, SEARCHING OR FINDING?

Since Josef Zuth published his study on the guitar and guitar music in 1920[2] – François Fétis dedicated some words to the history of the instrument in 1831[3] – the initial scant number of publications dedicated to the subject by the millennium has nearly grown to what one could call an abundance of books. Many articles on the history and literature of the guitar have also come to light.[4] As a rule, these publications concern the history of the Classical guitar, the history and morphology of the instrument, case studies of types of guitars and guitar playing, guitar construction and luthiers or composers and their music. As a musical prelude to this biography, it is interesting to show the relation in numbers as reflected in my library of guitar books, of which just those from Allorto to Zuth number some 250 items. The majority of these concern instruments and luthiers, a minority of them music and players, and a few in which the lives of guitar composers are described.[5] The latter include only a few scholarly biographies of composers regarded as great names in the world of the Classical guitar.[6] Specifically these are biographies of Mauro Giuliani, Fernando Sor and Dionisio Aguado in the beginning of the 19th century, written by Thomas Heck, Brian Jeffery, Wolf Moser, William Sasser, and Pompeyo Pérez-Díaz, respectively.[7] Other books and articles on them and their music are not of a very musicological or scholarly historical nature, method and structure, leading to the consequences one might expect: in monographs and reviews contained in manuals one finds assumptions that are either undemonstrable or unresearched, false references or unsupported claims, which moreover suffer from the bad tradition of being handed down from author to author. Biographical data, for instance, are unreliable: in regard to Napoléon Coste I found eight different dates of birth and seven dates of death, which alone gives reason enough to approach Napoléon Coste's life in a scholarly fashion. As a rule, the dates of particular events, concerts and compositions in the time that Coste lived are difficult to ascertain; the correct information is hard to establish. Magazines often list the wrong dates, an incorrect day and at times no date at all. This is why I have brought together different sources for verification. The spelling of names, places and streets is also not uniform in the 19th-century sources. To prevent confusion, here I have chosen to standardize on the present-day custom in the text: 'Lizst' remains Liszt, 'Scizepanowski'

---

[1] Schopenhauer, Arthur: 'Aphorismen zur Lebensweisheit', in: *Parerga und 1 Paralipomena*, Berlin, Hayn, 1851, repr. Leipzig, Insel Verlag, 1917, p. 112: 'Denn da die Menschen in der Regel ohne eigenes Urtheil und zumal hohe und schwierige Leistungen abzuschätzen durchaus keine Fähigkeit haben; so folgen sie hier stets fremder Auktorität, und der Ruhm, in hoher Gattung, beruht bei 99 unter 100 Rühmern bloss auf Treu und Glauben.'

[2] Zuth, Josef: *Simon Molitor und die Wiener gitarristik*, Wien, Goll, 1920.

[3] Fétis, François: 'Instrumens [sic] à cordes pincées', in: *Revue musicale*, Vme année, no. 3, 19 II 1831, p. 17-19.

[4] Lyons, David B.: *Lute, vihuela, guitar to 1800: a bibliography*, Detroit, Information Coordinators, 1978; Rezits, Joseph: *The Guitarist's Resource Guide*, San Diego, Pallma Music Co., 1983. Schwarz, Werner: *Guitar Bibliography*, München, Saur, 1984; McCutcheon, Meredith Alice: *Guitar and Vihuela, An Annotated Bibliography*, New York, Pendragon Press, 1985.

[5] Allorto, Enrico: 'L'organologia' in: Chiesa, Ruggiero, ed.: *La Chitarra*, Torino, Edizioni di Torino, 1990, p. 3-96; Zuth, Josef: *Handbuch der Laute und Gitarre*, Wien, Doblinger, 1926-28, repr. Hildesheim, Olms, 1978.

[6] Chiesa, Ruggiero: 'La diteggiatura', in: Chiesa, Ruggiero ed.: *La Chitarra*, Torino, Edizioni di Torino, 1990, p. 179.

[7] Sasser, William Gray: *The guitar works of Fernando Sor*, PhD University of North Carolina, Ann Arbor, Michigan, 1960; Heck, Thomas Fitzsimmons: *The Birth of the Classic Guitar and its Cultivation in Vienna, reflected in the Career and Compositions of Mauro Giuliani (d.1829)* (with) vol II: *Thematic Catalogue of the complete works of Mauro Giuliani*, PhD Yale University, 1970, Ann Arbor, Michigan, 1977; Jeffery, Brian: *Fernando Sor, Composer and Guitarist*, Tecla, London, 1977; Jeffery, Brian: *Dionisio Aguado*, biography and bibliography, Chanterelle, Heidelberg, 1994; Moser, Wolf: *Fernando Sor: Versuch einer Autobiografie und gitarristische Schriften*, [translation in German of Ledhuy], Köln, Saint-Georges, 1984; Pérez-Díaz, Pompeyo: *Dionisio Aguado y la guitarra clásico-romántica*, Madrid, Alpuerto, 2003.

remains Szczepanowski, and 'boulevart' remains boulevard, for instance. As Coste bears the name of Napoléon Bonaparte, the latter always is mentioned with his two names.

Being a guitarist I have not only been occupied with studying and practicing the music of the great composers in guitar history, but also with reading and studying the historical background of the composers, their life story, the analysis of their style and the description of their technique, as well as the instrument they played. Historical performance practice adds experience to our understanding of the music. To learn how their music can be played on a contemporary instrument, I had copies of those instruments made by luthiers, only because original instruments are only rarely available: a vihuela for the Renaissance, a Stradivarius for Baroque music and a Panormo for Classical music. In every style period the instrument underwent a metamorphosis. This is also the case in Romantic music. Coste can be seen in what for a long time was the only photograph of him, made by Disdéri, with four guitars, including a seven-string Lacôte guitar. This instrument was acquired by the Musée de la Musique in Paris in 1995.[8] It turns out that more of these have been made. Luthier Bernhard Kresse, in possession of an original copy, has made a similar instrument for me, which I used to conduct my research on interpretation and playing technique. The results of this interpretation can be listened to on the compact disc which is available separately from this biography and which includes the most important of Coste's works – *Souvenirs, Sept Morceaux Épisodiques* opus 17-23, *Fantaisie symphonique* opus 28[b] and *Le Passage des Alpes* opus 27, 28 & 40 – performed by me on the aforesaid copy of the Lacôte heptacorde. In making this recording, I was surprised to find such a great discrepancy between the many musical compositions by Coste and the few historical data that could be found on him as a person. For me, this was my motive start conducting research into this matter as a musicologist, so that I could use the results to write his biography.

Next to and after the aforesaid 'great three' among the Classics, there are three composers/guitarists around the middle of the 19th century, in the Romantic period of the guitar, who can be considered great names: J. K. Mertz, Marco Aurelio Zani de Ferranti and Napoléon Coste.[9] Astrid Stempnik has already published a thesis on Mertz. Simon Wynberg has also published the biography of Zani de Ferranti in his edition of his music, while another biography of Zani de Ferranti appeared in 2005 by Marcus Van de Cruys.[10] But until now, no scholarly biography of Coste has appeared, giving me reason to fill the void. After the Romantic period, at the end of the 19th century, attention turns to the so-called 'School of Francisco Tárrega', with Miguel Llobet and Emilio Pujol, later also to Andrés Segovia, whose importance as a guitarist, it must be said, is greater than as a composer.[11]

Similar to the development from the Classic to the Romantic generation, Coste may have had an influence on the 'School of Tárrega'. I will shed some light upon this matter, but the main goal is to contribute to the knowledge of – and understanding of – guitar music of the 19th century, by way of Napoléon Coste. Here, the term Romantic is used in three ways: as a historical style period in the 19th century, as a musical style with formal features and style elements, and as an aesthetic attitude towards life, in the way it emerges from literary sources. The wording is in all cases the same; the meaning is explained by the literary context. Apart from his biography, Coste's compositions also deserve attention. Only Sasser and Stempnik report their musical analysis of Sor and Mertz, whereas Jeffery and Heck are mainly occupied with biographical matters and aspects concerning the catalogue. In writing the biography of this composer my point of departure is to relate, if possible, his life and work to each other, as is so important for the Romantic period, in which composers themselves refer to biographical or

---

[8] Sinier, Daniel & Françoise de Ridder: *La Guitare, Paris 1650-1950*, Cremona, Il Salabue, 2007, p. 56.
[9] Chiesa, Ruggiero: 'La diteggiatura', in: Chiesa, Ruggiero, ed.: *La Chitarra*, Torino, Edizioni di Torino, 1990, p. 208-210.
[10] Stempnik, Astrid: *Caspar Joseph [sic birth name] Mertz, Leben und Werk...*, Frankfurt am Main, Lang, 1990; Wynberg, Simon: *Marco Aurelio Zani de Ferranti*, a biography, Heidelberg, Chanterelle, 1989; Cruys, Marcus G.S. Van de: *The King's guitarist: The life and times of Marco Aurelio Zani de Ferranti*, Wijnegem, Homunculus, 2005.
[11] Hofmeester, Theodorus M.: 'Is There a School of Tárrega', in: *The Guitar Review*, New York, The Society of the Classic Guitar, vol. I no. 1, October-November 1946, p. 4-6, (reprint 1974/1975 vol. I); Pujol, Emilio: *Tárrega, Ensayo biográfico*, Lisboa, Ramos, 1960, p. 239-245; Moser, Wolf: *Francisco Tárrega, Werden und Wirkung*, Lyon, Saint - Georges, 1996, p. 359-372.

Prélude vii

contextual elements: program music. This is why I wanted my research to be accompanied by a musical analysis of Coste's works for guitar solo, to reveal any interaction between his life and work, as well as to stimulate this aspect of musicology for the guitar. In general, little analysis is being done. Napoléon Coste starts publishing his works in 1830, after having established himself in Paris a year earlier. Soon his compositions are being published by editors like Richault, Challiot, Girod and Schonenberger, but, this aside, he also publishes many works himself, 'chez l'auteur', a practice that is quite usual for the time. His works contain 53 opus numbers, apart from works without opus number and arrangements of works by other composers. Most of these works are composed for guitar solo, but there are also some duets for guitar and for a melody instrument (oboe, violin, flute, cello) and guitar or piano.

I also found songs, both original and arranged (Schubert), for voice and guitar or piano, which are a valuable addition to the composer's works that are already known. His music for guitar, both solo and duet, have already been published – and republished – in facsimile from first editions by Chanterelle.[12] For other works I had to search in libraries in Paris, London, Brussels, Stockholm and Copenhagen. First editions and copies thereof were available in the Bibliothèque nationale in Paris, in the library of the Royal Academy of Music in London, the Koninklijke Bibliotheek in Brussels, the Statens Musikbibliotek in Stockholm, and most of all in the Kongelige Bibliotek in Copenhagen, where these can be found in the Rischel & Birket-Smith collection.[13] Almost all of Coste's musical works are available in either published or manuscript form, largely thanks to Simon Wynberg. Much of Coste's music has already been released on CD by several performers, but one of his most important compositions still was missing: the one he wrote for the Makaroff competition in 1856, the *Fantaisie symphonique* opus 28[b]. I immediately took on the challenge to record this – unperformed – work, but being a musician I first turned to his *Études* opus 38 for a better understanding of his style. These *Études* are the most renowned of his works. They show many aspects of his style, and in a way they can be regarded as key works in his oeuvre. Then there are his *Souvenirs* opus 17-23: *La Vallée d'Ornans, Les Bords du Rhin, Delfzil, Le Zuyderzée, Les Cloches, Meulan* and *Les Soirées d'Auteuil*, seven compositions, two of whose titles especially appealed to me as a Dutchman for adding to my repertoire. In doing so, I could experience his work in performance practice, an aspect not to be underestimated when trying to understand a composer in a time when professional players of musical instruments mostly played their own work. Playing the works of a composer with one's own hands enhances and deepens one's understanding of this music; an empathic approach based on experience that supports the musicological analysis. This can be heard on the compact disc accompanying this biography. The publications of Roman Jaworski and Noël Roncet were important in providing biographical information on Coste.[14] I contacted both authors for further information. This aside, the fluctuation in the number of publications was striking. Around 1980, when the facsimile edition of Coste's work for guitar was published by Chanterelle, many articles could be found, when Simon Wynberg wrote about Coste, Brian Jeffery did research in Coste's youth and Matanya Ophee took a second look at the Makaroff's memoirs of his composition competition.[15] Around 1970 some articles appeared in which Coste was mentioned, but from there on I had to go back to around 1925 to find any more relevant information about him, in *Der Gitarrefreund*, articles by Erwin Schwarz-Reiflingen and Thorvald Rischel, who had an active interest in Coste and his work at the time.[16] Finally, there was a biographical article by Richard Läpke

---

[12] Wynberg, Simon: *The Guitar Works Napoléon Coste*, facsimile edition, vol. I-IX, Monaco, Chanterelle, 1981, 1983, 2ᵉ ed. 2007.
[13] Torpp Larsson, Jytte: *Catalogue of the Rischel and Birket-Smith Collection*, Columbus, Orphée, 1989.
[14] Jaworski, Roman: 'Napoléon Coste 1805-1883, une histoire perdue', in: *Valentiana*, Valenciennes, Association Valentiana, 1992, no. 10; Roncet, Noël: *Napoléon Coste, Compositeur - 1805-1883*, Amondans, 2005.
[15] Wynberg, Simon: '...zur Rettung Napoléon Costes', in: *Gitarre und Laute*, Köln, vol. III, 1981, no. 5, p. 29-32; Jeffery, Brian: 'Napoléon Costes Jugend', in: *Gitarre und Laute*, Köln, vol. IV, 1982, no. 5, p. 253-256; Ophee, Matanya: 'The Memoirs of Makaroff, A Second Look', in: *Soundboard*, the journal of the Guitar Foundation of America, vol. IX, No. 3, 1982.
[16] Schwarz-Reiflingen, Erwin: 'Napoléon Coste', in: *Die Gitarre*, Berlin, 1927, Jahrgang VIII, Heft 7/8, [Coste-Heft] p. 43-47; Rischel, Thorvald: 'Bibliographische Notizen zu den Gitarrenwerken von Napoléon Coste', in: *Die Gitarre*, Berlin, 1927, Jahrgang VIII, Heft 7/8, [Coste-Heft] p. 47-51.

in 1884 in the *Internationale Gitarre-Zeitung*, my investigation into which produced nothing more than a transcript which agreed with what Coste himself wrote and what others wrote about him.[17]

Contemporary sources are of utmost importance for gathering information about Coste, his life and his work. In Paris I found personal data, such as birth, marriage and death certificates in the Archives de Paris. The Archives nationales contain vast volumes of the register of musical publications, in which those of Coste are recorded, along with the publication date. I visited the Département de la musique of the Bibliothèque nationale de France, where I found many of Coste's published works, consulted magazines and collected photographic material. Photos of Paris around 1871 of the addresses where Coste lived emerged from the Bibliothèque historique de la Ville de Paris. The Service historique de la Défense in the Château de Vincennes gave a wealth of information on Coste's father, and, surprisingly, a reference to Coste's visit to Holland in 1813 as an eight-year-old boy, the connection to his 'Dutch' compositions: eureka! I have numbered the items in the file 'Coste, Jean-François' in the order in which I found them to make them more accessible; an annotated bibliography has been added as an appendix. In the Bibliothèque municipale of Besançon and Ornans I found biographical and pictorial material concerning Coste's compositions, and in the Bibliothèque municipale of Valenciennes I found information about his youth in that town in the local newspaper *Petites affiches* and its successor *L'écho de la frontière*, as well as in *Mon histoire*, a less reliable source of clippings. In 2002 and 2005 I visited Amondans in the département of Doubs in France, Coste's place of birth, where, the second time I was there, I found an exposition made by Roncet on the occasion the bicentennial of Coste's birthday in the mairie of the small village of 300 inhabitants. I bought the colorful booklet about Coste by the same author. Visiting locations where Coste lived and worked, Amondans, Ornans, Delfzijl, Valenciennes, Paris and Brussels, with a biographical study as a goal, also has an emotional value: this is where he walked, where he lived, and where he gave concerts – the empathic approach. In this I found another reason to illustrate a biography. For instance, when Coste takes second prize in the Makaroff competition in 1856, it is relevant to illustrate the story with portraits of the members of the jury, even if this makes research more intensive considering that photography had just been invented at the time.

Research in the Koninklijke Bibliotheek in Brussels brought articles to light from 1856 in *L'Écho de Bruxelles*, *L'Observateur Belge* and *Le Guide musical*, most of the time using the very same words, and photographs of the members of the jury of the Makaroff competition there, as well as a number of Coste's works (arrangements of songs). The Utrecht University library is where the reprint of the *Bibliographie de la France* was located, with a survey of publications for guitar by Coste and many others. Apart from this I consulted a great deal of historical and theoretical literature and many musical editions there. In the Nederlands Muziek Instituut in the Koninklijke Bibliotheek in The Hague I found a great deal of new information about Coste and musical life in Paris in contemporary magazines, such as the *Revue musicale*, the *Gazette musicale*, the *Revue et Gazette musicale de Paris*, *Le Ménestrel*, *Le Dilettante*, *Le Pianiste*, *La France musicale* and *La Mélodie*, among which only the first three and *Le Pianiste* are included in the *Répertoire international de la presse musicale*. Mostly I found information confirming matters that came from other sources, but I also found many new pieces of information, such as dates of concerts and publications. What's more, I discovered a list of the concerts of the *Société académique des Enfants d'Apollon*, of which Coste was a member. This allowed me to double the number of known concert dates. The University of Amsterdam library houses volumes of the *Handbuch des musikalischen literatur:...* by Whistling, which did not list any of Coste's publications, however. I discovered the dates of Coste's concerts in the Bibliothèque nationale of Paris in the Gallica on-line database in the digitized 19th-century magazines *La France musicale*, *Le Ménestrel* and *L'Univers musical*. Research via modern media in the Kongelige Bibliotek in Copenhagen, apart from finding digitized editions and manuscripts of Coste in the Rischel & Birket-Smith collection, resulted in an unknown photographic portrait, which had nevertheless already been published in the book by Erling Møldrup, along with two

---

[17] Läpke, Richard: 'Biographie Napoléon Coste' in: *Internationale Gitarre-Zeitung*, Jahrgang I, no. 4 (Jan.1884), no. 5 (Febr.1884), Leipzig, unp. transcr. Eduard Fack, 'Die Meister'.

personal letters by Coste to Søffren Degen, in a Danish translation.[18] Prints from the originals emerged from the Statsbiblioteket Århus, which raises the question for the remaining correspondence of the composer, that must be in Marseille, Genua and Livorno, for instance, as he mentioned these cities himself. As far as is known to date – at least this is what Rischel writes in 1927 in *Die Gitarre* – Coste's works were in the possession of his Danish friend Søffren Degen, who bequeathed his collection to Rischel, material that was in this way transferred to the Rischel & Birket-Smith collection in the Kongelige Bibliotek of Copenhagen; but no letters could be found there.[19] According to Møldrup, Coste had correspondence with Schult in Stockholm, a merchant who posed with his guitars in a photograph in the same way Coste did, but the libraries in Sweden did not turn up any of these letters, nor did those in Germany, Austria, Italy or France.[20] And then there are also the 35 letters Coste wrote to Hallberg, tracked down by Andreas Stevens, letters that survived in the hands of Georg Meier and are now owned by his heirs in Hamburg, who eventually made the contents available for this biographical research. I was able to make use of them, along with another seven letters from Coste to Schult. Also thanks to Stevens' mediation, six short notes from Coste addressed to Gruel appeared, acquired by Norbert Fischer, who voluntarily made them available. This brought the number of letters to 50, a valuable source of information. Still the question of Coste's remaining correspondence remains unanswered. He had many international contacts with friends and pupils. He dedicated his *Livre d'Or* opus 52 to the Club des Guitaristes in Leipzig, a publication that must have resulted in letters back and forth. Coste was made an honorary member, but no archive of this association could be found. Perhaps this correspondence was lost during the wars. Anyway, many questions can be asked that will only be possible to answer after the publication of this biography, perhaps as the result of further research.

My search for information was accompanied by a search for his personal acquaintances. Many names emerged: those of his pupils to whom he dedicated works, those of composers whose themes he used in his works, those of fellow guitarists/composers, publishers, critics, luthiers, teachers, members of the jury, friends, family, composers whose compositions he performed. I was able to use this indirect information regarding our protagonist to describe his place in the musical life of Paris. Establishing his position as a composer entailed devoting a great deal of attention to the social-cultural context. The position of an artist in society can be explained in the same way that the altar gives meaning to a cathedral and vice versa. In this case it is a guitar composer among the bourgeoisie, with the understanding that a development from a musical elite towards popularization can be observed. Among the things that surface is a difference between more serious and shallow music. Coste lived and worked in a time when Berlioz, Chopin and Liszt dominated the musical world, Cherubini was director of the Conservatoire, and Nicolò Paganini achieved his major artistic (and financial!) impact. The salons and theatres were determining musical life. This development was followed critically by Fétis, a trendsetter and founder of musical criticism and musicology, in the *Revue musicale*, which he founded, later called the *Revue et Gazette musicale de Paris*, and in which the guitar often took a hard beating.[21] In sketching the social-cultural context, primarily in the two intermezzos, I turned to musicologists like Hans Erich Bödeker (et al.), Jeffrey Cooper, James Johnson and William Weber, who enabled me to observe the developments in detail as well as in general.[22]

---

[18] Møldrup, Erling: *Guitaren, et eksotisk instrument i den danske musik*, Kopenhagen, Kontrapunkt, 1997, p. 134-137.
[19] Rischel, Thorvald: 'Bibliographische Notizen zu den Gitarrenwerken von Napoléon Coste', in: *Die Gitarre*, Berlin, 1927, Jahrgang VIII, Heft 7/8, [Coste-Heft] p. 48; Torpp Larsson, Jytte: *Catalogue of the Rischel and Birket-Smith Collection*, Columbus, Orphée, 1989, p. i.
[20] Møldrup, Erling: *Guitaren, et eksotisk instrument i den danske musik*, Kopenhagen, Kontrapunkt, 1997, p. 197-198.
[21] *Revue musicale de Paris*, tome VII, 3 IV 1830, p. 267, 'instrument ingrat!'
[22] Bödeker, Hans Erich, Patrice Veit et Michael Werner, ed.: *Les sociétés de musique en Europe 1700-1900*; *Organisateurs et formes d'organisation du concert en Europe 1700-1920*; *Espaces et lieux de concert en Europe 1700-1920*, Berlin, Berliner Wissenschafts Verlag, 2007-2008. Cooper, Jeffrey: *The rise of instrumental music and concert series in Paris, 1828-1871*, Ann Arbor, UMI Press, 1983. Johnson, James H.: *Listening in Paris: a cultural history*, Berkeley, University of Berkeley Press, 1995. Weber, William: *Music and the Middle Class, The Social Structure of Concert Life in London, Paris and Vienna between 1830 and 1848*, Ashgate, Aldershot, 1975, 2nd ed. 2004; *The Great Transformation of Musical Taste*, Cambridge, Cambridge University Press, 2008.

Music publishers come and go, and the life of Coste is no exception. A publisher is not a philanthropist. While some of them are no doubt altruistic, a publisher still has to make a profit or he will go bankrupt, and many examples of this can be found in Paris. I described the sometimes difficult relation between Coste and his publishers, just to put the image of Coste publishing his own works by lack of a publisher into context, a phenomenon that was quite common in the 19th century. Sufficient literature was available on this issue, and Coste was also mentioned there. It was possible to date his works according to the edition numbers, among other things. I have contacted people who gave me advice in this research, such as Thomas Heck, Roman Jaworski, Brian Jeffery, Jan de Kloe, Erling Møldrup, Matanya Ophee, Marco Riboni, Noël Roncet and Erik Stenstadvold, who I wish to thank here. Andreas Stevens made an important contribution to this research with his efforts to provide me with literature and sources that were very hard to find, and Bernhard Kresse made it possible for me to play Coste's works on the copy of the Lacôte heptacorde he made for me and to perform the compositions in concert and for audio recordings. Structural indications were given by prof. dr Emile Wennekes and prof. dr Louis Grijp, both from Utrecht University. I received linguistic advice from Evert van den Berg. I obtained support and stimulation from Michiel Verhagen. Others helped me with translations, such as Gerrit Berveling from Italian, Herbert van Vliet from Danish, Carine van Vliet from Spanish and Arne van Vliet and Jenneke van der Wal into English. The proofreading and a substantial part of the translation, *Intermezzo II, Chapter VII, VIII,* and *Works Chapter 5, 6, 7*, was done by dr Leston Buell. All other translations from French, Dutch and German I was able to do myself. Finally, my deepest recognition goes to the person who has supported me on my path on this project for years, through my deviations and wandering: my spouse Ina van Vliet-Voordouw.

As explained above, the decision to write the biography of Napoléon Coste was based on my desire to fill a void. My approach in this endeavor as an author is historically descriptive, musicologically analytic, musically empathetic and social-culturally explanatory. In this biography I have related Coste's life to his works. Interweaving these matters I have produced a description of his life and works in chronological order, discussing his works separately in the descriptive analysis as addenda to the [not included] relevant chapters and placing the conclusion (résumé) of the analysis in the chapter itself. Each chapter is titled with the name of a work that either is reviewed in the chapter or is relevant for the content. The division into chapters has been made on the basis of crucial years in Coste's life, with two intermezzos that describe the social-cultural context and musical life. As already mentioned, each chapter is followed by the descriptive analysis of Coste's works, the conclusion of which is inserted into the relevant chapter. The appendices include a list of concerts in which Coste participated and that were reviewed in the musical press, as well as other guitar concerts, relevant events, the dedications Coste made and copies of some letters and official certificates. Concerning the footnotes, I have chosen to follow the Chicago Manual of Style to show the reader the reference on the same page. I do not use abbreviations like 'op. cit.' and 'ibid.' to prevent unnecessary page-turning. This method also makes it possible to provide the footnotes with annotations from magazines which are quoted often, or the original text of a translated quotation. The reference usually is put at the end of a paragraph. The bibliography to which the footnotes refer is divided into several categories: literature, musical editions, sources, annotated letters, magazines with annotation, the J.F. Coste dossier in my own department, websites and a discography. Bibliographic information about the illustrations is listed in an appendix. An index of names and works mentioned in the biography and a word about the author have also been included. Justification for the way the [not included] thematic catalogue has been structured is provided in the first three chapters.

PRINCIPLES: BIOGRAPHY, WRITING OR ANALYSIS?

For a better understanding of the Romantic character of his musical work, I first determined what is thought about the music in the Romantic era in terms of its stylistic characteristics in general. Using things written about Romantic music by renowned musicologists as a starting point, such as Ian Bent,

Prélude xi

Friedrich Blume, Carl Dahlhaus, Alfred Einstein and Charles Rosen,[23] and more specifically using Wolfgang Bötticher, Wolfgang Dömling and Rey Longyear,[24] the results of the analysis of Coste's works could be related to those of his contemporaries Franz Liszt, Hector Berlioz and Frédéric Chopin. The way the historical and systematic musicology should be approached and possibly relativized is discussed in the book by David Beard and Kenneth Gloag.[25] New paths that could be taken by music studies are reviewed in John Neubauer's book.[26]

In the beginning of the 19th century the Romantic style is finding increasing expression in music. First of all, the Classical composers Haydn, Mozart and Beethoven come to be appreciated in a new way. Their music does not change, but it is interpreted in a Romantic way, so to speak.[27] Moreover, composers living in the period itself, Coste's contemporaries, also create works that are the expression of the dawning Romantic notion of music. The Romantic style does not only concern the interpretation of music; no, indications can be found in music itself of the new, Romantic idea of music's content and meaning. These are well described in the following review of musical literature and music theory. An obvious way to acquaint oneself with the Romantic style in the music of Coste is to review of the writings of the aforesaid authors on this subject to acquire a general orientation. Aside from the relativization of the concept Romanticism, as proposed by Dahlhaus, who wants to nuance the stereotypical concept of Romanticism as a distinguishable style and period, it is still the case that also he thinks that concepts like exoticism, historicism and folkloricism can be employed in this complex matter.[28]

Longyear writes that the movement arises at the height of Classicism, in about 1800, in literary circles in Germany and Austria around E.T.A. Hoffmann. The Romantic concept originates in German literature in this way. Ernst Theodor Amadeus Hoffmann (1776-1822) considers Bach, Haydn, Mozart and above all Beethoven to be Romantic; instrumental music is the most Romantic of the arts, more so than vocal music. But music does not play such an important role with the writers in French Romantic literature, and in this way French Romanticism comes into existence later than its German counterpart. Among these writers Stendhal (Henri Beyle 1783-1842) is the one most interested in music, while Honoré de Balzac's (1799-1850) interest is limited to Italian and French opera.[29] The Romantic style is identifiable in Liszt, Berlioz and Chopin, to mention three influential composers in Paris as an example of an initial technical description of the elements of this musical style. With Liszt, who is in Paris from 1823 on, Romanticism is expressed in virtuosity and the transformation of themes, such as in the *Etudes d'exécution transcendante*, in the use of altered chords in contrast to modal harmony, unresolved dissonances, in his 'Paganini showmanship', and his extensive use of chromatics and use of the augmented triad, as in the *Grand galop chromatique*. The music of Berlioz, in Paris from 1824 on, is notable for its original harmony, diminished seventh chords, modal progressions and long delayed resolution of suspensions, as well as the flat submediant harmony and reharmonization of melody, such as in *Harold en Italie* II the 'Marche des Pèlerins', cross-rhythms and the famous idée fixe, in the *Symphonie fantastique*. In the music of Chopin, in Paris from 1831 on, harmonic freedom, as in the *Polonaise-Fantaisie* opus 61, has a great deal of figuration and passage work, ornamentation and vocal

---

[23] Bent, Ian, ed.: *Music theory in the age of Romanticism*, Cambridge University Press, 1996; Blume, Friedrich: *Classic and Romantic Music, A Comprehensive Survey*, Norton, New York - London, 1970; Dahlhaus, Carl & Norbert Miller: *Europäische Romantik in der Musik*, Bd. 2, Metzler, Stuttgart, 1999/2007; Einstein, Alfred: *Music in the Romantic Era, a history of musical thought in the 19th century*, New York - London, Norton, 1947, repr.1975; Rosen, Charles: *The Romantic Generation*, Harvard University Press, Cambridge, Massachusetts, 1995.

[24] Bötticher, Wolfgang: *Einführung in die musikalische Romantik*, Darmstadt, Wissenschaftliche Buchgesellschaft, 1983; Dömling, Wolfgang: *Hector Berlioz. Symphonie fantastique*, München, Fink, 1985; Longyear, Rey M.: *Nineteenth-century romanticism in music*, Englewood Cliffs, New Jersey, Prentice-Hall, 1969.

[25] Beard, David & Kenneth Gloag: *Musicology: the key concepts*, London, Routledge, 2005.

[26] Neubauer, John, et al: *New Paths: aspects of music theory and aesthetics in the age of romanticism*, Leuven, Leuven U.P., 2009.

[27] Dahlhaus, Carl: 'Die Musik des 19. Jahrhunderts' in: Carl Dahlhaus ed.: *Neues Handbuch der Musikwissenschaft*, vol. VI, Wiesbaden, Athenaion, 1980-1995, p. 15-16.

[28] Dahlhaus, Carl: 'Die Musik des 19. Jahrhunderts' in: Carl Dahlhaus ed.: *Neues Handbuch der Musikwissenschaft*, vol. VI, Wiesbaden, Athenaion, 1980-1995, p. 13-14, 21.

[29] Longyear, Rey M.: *Nineteenth-century romanticism in music*, New Jersey, Prentice-Hall, 1969, p. 3, 6, 7.

portamento, such as in the *Ballade* in f-minor; the raised fourth and lowered second degree in harmony and modal harmony are important, as in *Mazurka* opus 56 no. 2 and 3, as well as passing dominants and flexible rhythms.[30]

Romanticism, writes Bötticher, is the expression of the fantastic, extraordinary in art and world image. He describes the changes this brings on with the examples from Schubert, Chopin and Liszt. With Schubert, Romanticism is expressed by means of the new altered chords with the raised fourth and lowered fifth tone of the chord when images of fright and confusion are concerned, and increasing chromatics and the new phrasing as an unusual differentiation of the expression in relation to older formal structures, aspiring for an arioso, recitative style. The piano accompaniment abandons the neutral arpeggio of chords and acquires greater sound volume and intensity. His modulatory coloring is characteristic, apart from his unusual way of clinging to an ostinato, an extreme climactic effect and enharmonic contrasts around a pivot tone. In musical form the lyrical piano piece stands opposite the colossal sonata form, the chain form becomes liberated from the cyclical form and the chain structure, the variation. Instrumental solo music, especially for piano, is becoming dominant. The songs of Schubert, above all, become very popular in Paris. With Chopin there is the Romantic principle of solely instrumental piano music with specific upper voice melodics in the nocturnes, chains of arpeggios in the *Études*, dance rhythms and lashing motives of Polish origin, and the modern whole-tone relation between chains of motifs. Coloratura has a substantial importance in his music, cascades of sequences in sixths and thirds passages in his piano concertos. He is a master of chromatic modulation. With Liszt the volume of sound increases, including with chromatic 32nd runs; his modifications of themes and alienation are the expression of his strong imagination. Huge blocks of themes and hammering entry motifs are juxtaposed with trivial melodies. The Romanticism in his sacred works is expressed in ongoing Gregorian-like melodics, which are theatrical and colorful.[31]

In 1830 the Romantic concept also makes an entry in symphonic music in Paris as shown in the *Symphonie fantastique* by Berlioz, a model of Romanticism manifesting itself, according to Dömling. The idée fixe in it points forward to the changing way thematics are handled; later this is a reminiscence motif.[32] Berlioz's music is programmatic, compared to the words of an opera, which makes the instrumental work to drama. The autobiographical element plays a role now, apart from literary references, such as the 'Dies irae' in the witches sabbath, referring to Goethe's Faust, and the 'Ronde du Sabbat' which is a title of a ballad by Victor Hugo also, but there is no direct connection in this case, an indirect one is. By the 'fantastic' mixture of the very different elements it is a really Romantic work, the dark side of Romantics in special, which finds its German literary representative particularly in E.T.A. Hoffmann with 'Rausch und Traum', unchained fantasy, tendency towards the pathological, the bizarre, changes of moods, irony and parody, in which distortion and deformation are means of artistic expression.[33] Hoffmann was an important philosopher on music, which emerges in his review of the fifth symphony of Beethoven, the upbeat for the shaping of the canon in the Classical repertoire. These more general notions are made tangible in the changing way of composing in the Romantic era, the Romantic characteristics of style given concrete expression in music itself. In this way it is possible to make clear that there are formal characteristics and style elements that can be interpreted as Romantic, and it becomes important to point them out by means of analysis of Coste's music. These views on the Romantic style in music give enough cause, when considering the music of Coste, to formulate a number of characteristics, to describe the way they occur in his music, to clarify what their exact contents are in his works, and how they are anchored in or connected to more general

---

[30] Longyear, Rey M.: *Nineteenth-century romanticism in music*, New Jersey, Prentice-Hall, 1969, p. 90-94, 98-99, 104-114.

[31] Bötticher, Wolfgang: *Einführung in die musikalische Romantik*, Darmstadt, Wissenschaftliche Buchgesellschaft, 1983, p. 25, 31-42, 113, 115, 121, 165, 168-169; Erpf, Hermann: *Form und Struktur in der Musik*, Schott, Mainz, 1967, p. 152-154.

[32] The term 'Leitmotif' is introduced in 1871 by Jähns; Warrack, Johns: 'Leitmotif', in: Sadie, Stanley, ed.: *The New Grove Dictionary of Music and Musicians*, London, Macmillan, 1980, vol.10, p. 644; the term is first used c. 1865 by Ambros, Whittall, Arnold: 'Leitmotif', in: Sadie, Stanley, ed.: *The New Grove Dictionary of Music and Musicians*, second edition, London, Macmillan, 2001, vol. 14, p. 527.

[33] Dömling, Wolfgang: *Hector Berlioz. Symphonie fantastique*, München, Fink, 1985, p. 18, 57, 65, 67.

Prélude

developments that take place in music in Paris. However, to do so it is necessary to first come to a more complete definition of Romanticism, before proceeding to a formulation of the tangible characteristics and style elements that can be understood as intentionally Romantic.

In this endeavor the connection can be made with what Friedrich Blume writes in his essays on this subject, as translated in his *Classic and Romantic Music: A Comprehensive Survey*, because his explanation is clear and because in a certain way he also succeeds in making concrete the content of musical Romanticism. At the same time this is the occasion to organize the above-mentioned characteristics into a clear structure. First of all, according to Blume, the Classical and Romantic styles are two aspects of one and the same phenomenon and of one and the same period in history. There is no clearly definable line separating Classicism and Romanticism, he says. In the 19th century the word 'Classical' came to refer to the music of 'old' composers, in opposition to the contemporary ones. The word 'Romantic' is used only later for the aesthetic norm of continuously intensified overexcitement of musical means and exaggerated individualization of the experience. Classical music, then, is the sublime form of what moves the composer and what he wants to express in symbols. Interpretation of the symbol is the private and inalienable right of the listener. In this sense music becomes autonomous, 'l'art pour l'art', symbolism for the ear, as Goethe said, with truthfulness and wholeness, as Herder said, and released from the imitation of nature, from the diversion of mind and wits, from being the handmaiden of theology. In this sense, music becomes the highest of all the arts because it alone possesses the capacity to lift man above himself, as Herder puts it. Romantic music, in contrast, has individual feeling, free fantasy, imitation and pictorialization, associative through-composition, giving music concrete content, condemning the listener to passivity.[34]

The words Schiller used for Romantic, in a letter to Goethe in 1796, are: unusual, knightly, archaic, naive, folk, surprising, distant, miraculous and strange, as well as nightly, ghostly, horrifying – words with an emotional and fanciful meaning. The problem with this music is that not all these elements always have to be present to recognize a piece as being Romantic; it is sufficient if only a few of them are present. The Romantic style is expressed in music by deviation from the principle of the eight-bar period, the application of varied rhythms and the declamatory style in anti-metrical figures, interchanging of tempo and exaggerated use of effects and many indications for character. In the harmony, remote tonalities occur, minor keys equal major keys, gliding modulations, sometimes deceptive progressions, harmony becomes modulating, cadences are used to change the mood, instead of structural principles. There is a preference for the song type melody with a lyrical character, melody and harmony are more or less integrated. In the Romantic period the Classical form is subject to amplification and modification, most genres remain custom, and new ones, especially dance forms, are introduced. A speciality of the 19th century is the lyric character piece, the impromptu and the rhapsodic form. Music takes on virtuoso character and exceeds the capacities of the dilettante by the diminutions in melody. The search for the 'lieto fine' changes in the open ending, programmatic music stands in opposition to absolute music.[35]

Typically Romantic, Alfred Einstein adds to this, is the veneration of the folk song. In 1852 a study in popular chansons and poetry instigated by Fortoul, minister of education, shows the general interest there was in folk music.[36] Furthermore, indications of this can be found in literature, such as in *Le Meunier d'Angibault* from 1845 by Georges Sand (Amandine Dupin, 1804-1876) where she writes:

> *The sound of the cornemuse, united with that of the fiddle, scrapes the ear from up close, but from afar this rural voice, which sometimes sings such gracious motifs, which are made even more original by a barbaric harmony, has a charm that penetrates the simple soul... That violent vibration of the musette, both rough*

---

[34] Blume, Friedrich: *Classic and Romantic Music, A Comprehensive Survey*, New York - London, Norton, 1970, p. vii, viii, 8-15; translation Blume, Friedrich: *Musik in Geschichte und Gegenwart*, Kassel, Bärenreiter, 1948-1986.
[35] Blume, Friedrich: *Classic and Romantic Music, A Comprehensive Survey*, New York - London, Norton, 1970, p. 95, 132-157.
[36] Coeuroy, André: *La musique et le peuple en France*, Paris, Stock, 1941, p. 59.

and nasal, that sour chirping and that nervous staccato of the fiddle are meant for each other and correct one another.[37]

The 'origin' of the distinction between folk music and art music lies in the 18th century already. When James McPherson publishes the work of the presumed 3rd-century Celtic bard Ossian early in the years 1760, this makes Scotland to the original connection of the primitive and the civilized in the intellectual circles and the reading public in Europe. Along with this Scottish music is going to play a similar role in the musical world.[38] The difference between art music and folk music gradually becomes more manifest during the 19th century. In 1795 already an essay insists on the reservation of music belonging to the people. The Revolution chooses to enforce the folk notion with hymns that adjust to folklore music. After the Restauration, 1830, the folk element enters choir music, followed by instrumental music, in a process of 'democratization' of 'great music'. The attention for and the discussion on this proceeds during the middle of the 19th century, when music which is called folk appears in travelling stories, correspondence of writers and literary works.[39] From 1860 on this music becomes the object of musicological research. This suits the general idea composers do not only use elements of musical content in their compositions, like modal harmony, but also are going to employ folk genres, such as the barcarolle, the Ländler, the mazurka, the polonaise. As this phenomenon also arises in pictoral art, for instance, where Gustave Courbet, contemporary and fellow countryman of Coste, makes folk life to the subject of his pictures and brings Realism into pictoral art, in this same way, taking a folk element, which does not occur in art music, as a theme for a composition, can be called a kind of realism in art music. Then the question still is if taking a realistic subject in art is really Romantic. The paradox here is: 'What if Realism is a metaphor?'[40]

In literature as well as in music there is an interest in folk music, its sound and instruments, its sincerity and simplicity. In the growing gap between the artist and the public in this period, composers try to find a way out of this increasing isolation by meeting the listener halfway in music containing aspects of folklore.[41] In this way Dahlhaus's phenomena – exoticism, historicism and folkloricism – can be described in musical terms and be pointed out in music. In considering the symphonic poems of Liszt he discusses the independence of the phrase, the way it is poeticized where improvisation is concerned, the inspiration of the performance and programmaticism in music. Thus the aesthetics of sentiment found in Liszt around 1830 is rooted in the aesthetics of the artist's interpretation and its reception by the listener.[42]

The aesthetical approach of music comes from several points of view. In the opinion of Neubauer its origin lies in Goethe's review of music, his ideas on organic metamorphosis and morphology, as a Romantic metaphor opposite the more mechanistic notions of the Enlightment. This metaphor can only be applied to absolute music, which is instrumental music. Here the paradox is that the term energetic is taken from biology and aesthetics by musical theory around 1800. The principle has had influence on the ideas of a artists biography; at present there is a much broader approach.[43] In the

---

[37] Coeuroy, André: *La musique et le peuple en France*, Paris, Stock, 1941, p. 43-44: 'Le son de la cornemuse, uni à celui de la vielle, écorche un peu les oreilles de près; mais de loin cette voix rustique qui chante parfois de si gracieux motifs, rendus plus originaux par une harmonie barbare, a un charme qui pénètre les âmes simples... Cette forte vibration de la musette, quoique rauque et nasillarde, ce grincement aigre et ce staccato nerveux de la vielle sont faits l'un pour l'autre et se corrigent mutuellement.'

[38] Gelbart, Matthew: *The Invention of "Folk Music" and "Art Music"*, Cambridge, Cambridge University Press, 2007, p. 11.

[39] Gumplowicz, Philippe: 'Le rêve et la mission. La Musique et le peuple en France 1789-1848' in: Bödeker, Hans Erich, Patrice Veit et Michael Werner, red.: *Les sociétés de musique en Europe 1700-1900*, Berlin, Berliner Wissenschafts Verlag, 2007, p. 373-379.

[40] Bajou, Valérie: *Courbet*, Parijs, Biro, 2003, p.160-167.

[41] Einstein, Alfred: *Music in the Romantic Era, a history of musical thought in the 19th century*, New York - London, Norton, 1947, repr. 1975, p. 32, 37, 40.

[42] Dahlhaus, Carl: 'Die Musik des 19. Jahrhunderts' in: Carl Dahlhaus ed.: *Neues Handbuch der Musikwissenschaft*, vol. VI, Wiesbaden, Athenaion, 1980-1995, p. 21; Dahlhaus, Carl & Norbert Miller: *Europäische Romantik in der Musik*, Bd2, Stuttgart, Metzler, 1999/2007, p. 639, 641, 643, 927, 939.

[43] Neubauer, John, et al: *New Paths: aspects of music theory and aesthetics in the age of romanticism*, Leuven, Leuven U.P., 2009, p. 11, 16, 18-19, 27.

Prélude xv

opinion of Beard and Gloag the division in historic and systematic musical science has its origin in Adler, already in the 19th century. His line of approach in musical aesthetics concern the literary and linguistic aspects of the musical experience. The starting point in this approach produces a description of a linear ongoing development in music, but has no attention to the phenomena which do occur, but does not fit in this premises.[44] An example of this esthetical interpretation can be found with Koechlin in 1929, who describes Berlioz's *Scène aux Champs* from a sentimental starting point, and wants to avoid any analysis that would not add any value.[45] According to Beard and Gloag the term absolute music in Romanticism comes from Hoffmann and Hanslick. The latter criticize extra-musical references, music should be aesthetically autonomous. Enlarged subjectivity and more intensive meaning are the philosophical principles of Kant and Hegel and they are supported by Nietsche and Schopenhauer. A more critical approach is coming into vogue more and more in the 20th century. The diversity of music leads to a new aesthetical interpretation of music. It consists of several elements, which are the foundation of the hermeneutics, like narrativity, semiotics, periodization, genre, rhetorics, and also historicity, sociopolitics, humanism. The musicological approach is very various and does not lead to a single purpose anymore. Analysis cannot be based on a single principle, but has to lead to a multifaceted explanation.[46]

To give concrete form to the Romantic style in the consideration of the music of Coste, one must distinguish between formal characteristics and style elements. The historic aspect aside, this study is directed at the Romantic aspect, as can be found in his works in formal characteristics as phrasing, ornamentation, tonality, meter, tempo, dynamics and articulation, and at the way it occurs in style elements like cadenza, figuration, idée fixe, chromatics, dissonance, modulation, four-voice progressions, open endings, arpeggio, rhythm, rests, story, folklore and onomatopoeia. Here it will suffice to just mention these qualities; descriptions of them can be found in Chapter IV of the [not included] Thematic Catalogue, along with a schematic outline, provided with musical examples. The way they occur in the music of Coste is described when considering the works themselves. Where they are found is indicated by several appendices and can easily be looked up.

The Romantic style, as it develops in music in Paris, is reflected in the guitar music of Napoléon Coste. In this study this is investigated by way of the model of analysis explained above, which is laid out in further detail in the thematic catalogue. Many of Coste's compositions have a programmatic title, but does that necessarily mean they are programmatic in nature? In the world of the guitar, what is the difference between music that is called Classical and what is called Romantic? The descriptive analysis of those works of Coste for solo guitar that can be dated will shed light upon this matter. The data concerning his style of phrasing, the form and structure of his music were provided by an analysis of melody, used themes and their development, brought in relation with the harmony he applied. In the same way, an analysis of his use of rhythm, in relation with the meter and tempo he applied, provided data concerning the character of his works. An analysis of the harmonic structure resulted in information about the way he utilized the Classical notions concerning this matter and about how he developed his own way of doing so, as well as about the musical taste in his time. To show all this, the dissertation needed to include a descriptive analysis of these works, which is not included in this edition. The conclusions drawn from them were illustrative enough to make the phenomena that occurred in them clear, while sometimes a reference could be made to their occurrence in other works of Coste and other guitarists, such as Sor. As a rule, it is the constellation of characteristics that makes up the Romantic character, it is the intensity of its occurrence which shapes the image. Many of these style characteristics are already foreshadowed with his predecessors, aren't they? The works Coste himself considered to be of high enough quality to enter them in the Makaroff competition in

---

[44] Beard, David & Kenneth Gloag: *Musicology: the key concepts*, London, Routledge, 2005, Introduction.
[45] Koechlin, Ch.: 'Les tendances de la musique moderne Française', in: Lavignac, Albert: *Encyclopédie de la musique...*, Paris, Delagrave, 1925, p. 63.
[46] Beard, David & Kenneth Gloag: *Musicology: the key concepts*, London, Routledge, 2005, p. 3, 5-6, 10-12.

1856 are central in this dissertation. I have used the combination of the analytical measuring rod and the experience in playing technique to interpret the soundscape of the works, as well as the historical, sociological and cultural approaches for sketching an image of the time in which the composer lived, its musical tradition and conventions, and the musical reception. In the discussion of the works a review is also given of the way they have been discussed in publications after Coste's death, the historiography. I found 26 citations on the *Méthode* Coste-Sor and the *Études* opus 38. Other works are hardly discussed in the period between 1902 and 2005. This is why this historiography is rather limited, but I still found it important enough to warrant including it in the biography. To make the information that was found easy to handle, I compiled the thematic catalogue of all his works, with incipit, dates, references and concordances, which has been added to this biography as a second volume, which is separately available. The considerations made regarding the premises for the biography and how it was compiled are described in it. The analytical model is also described which has been used for the [not included] descriptive analysis in the biography, consisting of 21 criteria in terms of formal features and style elements, provided with musical examples. The tables show the occurrence and numbers of incidence of these phenomena.

THEORY AND METHOD: BIOGRAPHY, FORM OR CONTENT?

After considering the essence of biography I came to the conclusion that this biography of Napoléon Coste should be approached using the interweaving of biographical and musical data as a point of departure, to show his life and work in relation to one another: the programmatic aspect of his works give enough cause for this. The choice to marry the biographical-historical aspect to the description of the works in their genre, seen in their relation to artistry and originality seems appropriate. I see the development of his musical work in the social-cultural context, and I use this to determine his place in the musical world of Paris in a large part of the 19th century. His style is described in examples, against the background of the means of style that were in use in the musical world of Paris in this period, in relation to the 'great Romantic music.' This development in his career can be followed in chronological order with short characterizations of his main works, and the place occupied by the guitar in this musical world. To show the view upon picture and sound, practice and theory in the best way possible, contemporaries are quoted as much as possible, either in translation and the original text in footnotes, with citations from magazines and theoretical works, apart from reviews in contemporary musical journals. This approach is attractive for its possibilities for verification. The structure is that of a historiographical biography, with analysis as a background, supporting the dissertation, in chapters as an addendum to the main text, but being an integral part of it, along with a thematic catalogue, supplemented with bibliographies, illustrations, a chronology with addenda and an index. With respect to the matters that are described – biographical data, social-cultural context, musical works – the author is a historical-objective academic writer, an interpretative-analytic narrator and a musical-empathic guitarist, making the dissertation to become a chronological artistically pictorial analytic biography.

QUESTIONS: BIOGRAPHY, QUESTIONS AND ANSWERS.

Finally I would like to review the questions that will be answered in this study into the life, works, times and places of Napoléon Coste. The main question is in what way the relation between the guitar and its music, on the one hand, and music and musical life in Paris in the Romantic era on the other hand, emerge in the life and works of Napoléon Coste. This question can be divided into the following subquestions.

As far as the *social-cultural context* is concerned, there are three questions to be answered:
- What *cultural-artistic circles* was Coste active in as a guitarist, composer and teacher?
- What *social-political developments* influenced Coste's life?
- What *status* did the composer/guitarist Coste have in 19th-century Paris?

Prélude

Musical life in Paris in the 19th century raises the following questions:

- What is *Coste's role* in it as far as concert practice, musical reception, publishing, teaching, amateur music, home music and salons are concerned?
- How does the *position of the guitar* as an instrument influence Coste's musical development?

Musical traditions have an influence on Coste and his music, and there the question arises as to the way in which the tradition of the *classics* among the guitar composers affected Coste and his works. Aside from this, there is the question of the significance of the tradition of *musical theory* for Coste's Romantic style. Coste lives and works in the period of the Romantics. The Romantic way of life is playing an important role here, aside the music itself. Here the first question is the *relation* Coste had with Romantic music in Paris.

Then the issue is discussed as to which characteristics of the Romantic style are to be found in Coste's compositions, especially with regards to *form, melody, harmony, meter, expression and Romanticism* in his works, classified in a taxonomy of 21 formal characteristics and style elements, as can be found in the Thematic Catalogue which is separately available. Then finally, the question is how the results of this study could influence the way of the music's *interpretation*, as expressed in the compact disc which is part of this dissertation, but also is separately available to this edition.

The main question and the subquestions are discussed and described with an open eye for future contributions based on new evidence. They are answered in the conclusion.

This theory and method touch on the philosophical problem Schopenhauer posed in 1851 in his *Contemplations of Worldly Wisdom*. This study may also add something to the discussion of this problem concerning appreciation. The premises and results of the study can be employed for further investigation in the comparison of the works of Zani de Ferranti and Mertz, in which the importance of Coste for the Romantic guitar music can be made even more evident. Working on this biography I set about searching and interpreting data concerning Coste's life and work. I analyzed the dated works for solo guitar in relation to relevant theories applied to works by other composers, in chronology order, and I have made references to the spirit of the Romantic era. Also I have performed nine of Coste's most important works in concert and on compact disc, striving to remain as close as possible to his notions of music, and I have related this experience to Coste and his era.

STRUCTURE: BIOGRAPHY AND [NOT INCLUDED] THEMATIC CATALOGUE

The [not included] descriptive analyses are parallel to the discussion of the compositions in the Biography itself and can be regarded as support for the argumentation there, where reference is made to this survey. The three-way references between the Biography, the descriptive analysis and the Thematic Catalogue in the first scholarly edition from 2016 are made apparent in:

- explanations, genres, style and tables of formal characteristics and style elements in the Thematic Catalogue [not included], chapter II-IV and appendix;
- descriptive analysis in Works addendum [not included] to chapter IV-VIII in Biography;
- résumé of works in history, social-cultural context in Biography.

The schematic report here makes it easy to search for these supporting thoughts. The discussions in the chapters Works in the original edition of the Biography are provided with relevant musical examples, in any case the incipit or a reference to the type of style element, to explain the relation with the Thematic Catalogue, which is separately available.

This *Prélude* is an elaborated version of the 2016 edition.

Dr. Ari van Vliet
Huizen, February 2018

I
Introduction

We, members of the administrative council, declare that citizen J. François Coste, geometrist, is chosen to be captain, the 12th of August 1792. Of which we put up the certificate for him today, in the camp near Mayenne, the 7th Prairéal of the 3rd year of the French Republic.[1]

SURROUNDINGS

Through the high table-land of the Jura the small river of the Loue winds along villages such as Ornans [1] and Cléron [2] in the Franche-Comté in the east of France. Further away it flows into the Doubs, the river that gives its name to this *département* since the French Revolution, with Besançon as its capital. This valley of Ornans, geographically the Vallée de la Loue, wooded with forest, has been brought into cultivation with grasslands and grain agriculture, as well as vineyards that produce the white wine of Arbois [3] that even Jacques Brel sang of, only available in this area. The climate provides ample showers of rain, alternated with a summer sun, and cold and snow in winter. It is this region where Napoléon Coste is born in Amondans [4] in 1805 and where he lives in his childhood, where his contemporary Gustave Courbet finds inspiration to paint his realistic art. Further to the south the Source du Lison [5] can be found. There, a small stream with the same name jumps away from the mountain cave, now a tourist attraction. Once there was a watermill. After a cascade with the Conche this water joins the Loue.

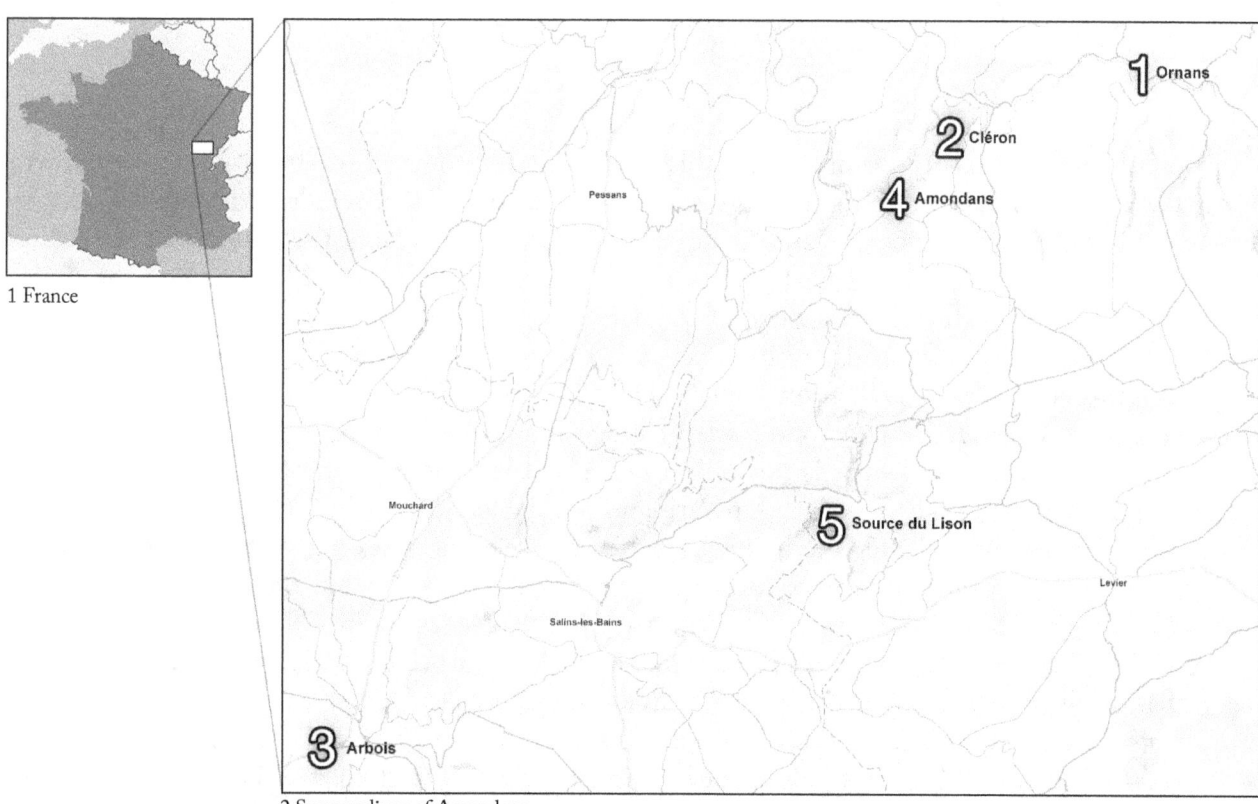

1 France

2 Surroundings of Amondans

Coste refers to these places in his compositions *La Vallée d'Ornans* opus 17 (1852), *Souvenir(s) du Jura* opus 44 (1876) and *La Source du Lyson* opus 47 (1878). At distance to the north-east are the banks

---

[1] Dossier J.F. Coste, Château de Vincennes, 24e 815 [Item 02]: 'Nous membres du conseil d'administration certifions que le citoyen, J. Francois Coste, Géomètre a été élus Capitaine le 12 août 1792. Ensoi de quoi nous lui avons délivré le présent, au camp près Mayenne, le 7 Prairéal 3me année de la République française.'

of the Rhine, to the south-east, much further, the Alps. These also are places the composer refers to in *Les Bords du Rhin* opus 18 (1852) and *Le Passage des Alpes* opus 27, 28 & 40 (1856 and 1876). Natural landscapes like these are a source of inspiration to him, and to many other Romantic composers in this era. Along with cities, history, sentiments, death, and even folklore, nature is a distinguishing characteristic of Romanticism in 19th-century music. This short outline of the surroundings where Coste passes his early youth is directly connected to his works in this way.

3 'La Vallée d'Ornans' - Vallée de la Loue, 2005

Era

As a result of the rational economic politics of king Louis XVI, France attains some prosperity in the second half of the 18th century, and this reasonably long period of stability leads to growth in agriculture. The potato is introduced, grasslands are expanded and scientific inventions lead to technological progress with the arrival of steam engines and the growth of the industry in textile and chinaware, and even to the first balloon flight in 1783.[2] The revolution of 1789 changes the whole structure of society. War breaks out, France is under siege by the Prussians; on September 20, 1792 the French Convention is signed, the Prussians withdraw and on September 21 the proclamation of the First Republic follows. Then on January 21, 1793 Louis XVI is decapitated and a period of terror ensues which extends far beyond Paris. In the Vendée, for instance, a royalist rebellion leads to thousands of executions. But it is not only trouble and affliction. In the field of culture several initiatives are taken: the Louvre is opened in Paris and on August 3, 1795 the Conservatoire is founded by surveyors Gossec, Méhul and Cherubini. The latter becomes the first director.[3] However, the costs of daily life are high. The old monetary unit *livre* is transferred to *franc*, but the old coins remain in circulation, with much confusion as a result. Prices rise, poverty increases. In 1793 the Convention fixes the salaries for handcraft and wages and establishes a maximum price for basic necessities. The rate of high inflation also strikes the price of bread, on which the republicans levy a tax: in June 1795 a loaf of bread costs 12 livres, and already in July it has risen to 15. Between 1790 and 1795 the price of a pair of socks rises from 3 to 100 livres, a pair of shoes costs 1500 livres.[4] The father of the composer, captain Coste, is involved In the coalition wars waged by Prussia, Bohemia and Hungary, later Naples, Austria and Russia against the French Revolution.

---

[2] Michelin, *The Green Guide: France*, Watford, Hannay House, 2000, p. 30.
[3] Planque, *Agenda musical pour l'année 1836*, Paris, 1836, repr. Genève, Minkoff, 1981, p. 13: 'Conservatoire de musique [...] Gossec, Méhul et Chérubini; [...]'.
[4] 'Les assignats et les prix pendant la Révolution française' in: *Correspondance familiale*, vie économique, http://correspondancefamiliale.echess.fr.

I — Introduction

Family

Apart from landscape as an inspiration for his music, his family, in a different way, has an influence on Napoléon Coste. The father of the composer, Jean-François Coste, is the son of Étienne-François Coste and Jeanne-Françoise Brion, farmers by profession, who live in Clairon (now Cléron), a little village on the Loue.

4 Cléron Château, 2002

He is born there April 23, 1754.[5] In his family there is a nephew Germain, an officer in the army, decorated with the Croix de St. Louis, a certain Mr. Coste, former vicar of Besançon, another Mr. Coste, vicar of Quingey, one Mr. Varoux, a priest, a nun, Madame Magdeleine Varoud, a niece Germaine, abbess of the Abbey of Mirecourt, etc. etc., all names, the etcetera's inclusive, that Jean-François produces in 1794 to obtain the Croix de St. Louis for himself.[6] So, a family with clerics and a decorated soldier, in the service of church or state, or a selection to impress the minister; other parts of the family are less impressive, as the archives in Besançon show under the name of Coste.[7] Nothing is known about his training, but he must have had some as a member of such a family from the civil middle class, also because a thorough education must have been necessary in his later career as an engineer-officer. Jean-François Coste marries his first wife Claudine Pretet on November 8, 1774 in the town hall of Besançon. It is certain that the couple has two daughters, Julie in 1783 and Jeanne-Étienne in 1785.[8] There might also be a third daughter, Jeanne-Pierrette in 1787, the birth certificate is not clear on that: the name of the father is incomplete, but he is married to Claudine Pretet, and

---

[5] Dossier J.F.Coste, Château de Vincennes, 24ᵉ 815 [Item 03]: 'Extrait des régistres [...] né le vingt trois avril de l'année mil sept cent cinquante quatre, [...]'.
[6] Dossier J.F.Coste, Château de Vincennes, 24ᵉ 815 [Item 22]: 'Valenciennes, (2p) le 26 juin 1816, Coste à Ministre Secrétaire [...]'; [Item 74]: '[...] Dans la famille du supliant [...]'
[7] Besançon, Archives municipales, *Actes de Naissance, Baptêmes, Mariages, Décès, Sépultures*.
[8] Roncet, Noël: Expositiion Napoléon Coste, Amondans, 21-26 VI 2005,[no. 6], Généalogie.

another couple with the same name in the same place is very unlikely.[9] The year of birth also is probable. According to the information provided by Noël Roncet[10] there is a letter from father Coste to the ministry of war on September 18, 1800 in which he writes about three children. This supports the theory. Also, from the certificate it can be concluded that father Coste is the principal of a school, a post that cannot be obtained without schooling.

In 1789, the year of the revolution, he joins the army and on August 5, 1792, the year of the Marseillaise,[11] at the age of 38, he becomes a captain of the fifth battalion of the Doubs, a part of the tenth regiment light infantry.[12] With his wife and children at home in Besançon Coste makes a career as a soldier, but not without injuries. After a promotion to *adjudant général chef de brigade* in 1793 he is considered incapable of fulfilling this rank and is demoted again.[13] Whereas Napoléon Bonaparte makes a grand career in the revolutionary army and is in command of the most important military campaigns to Italy and Austria, Jean-François Coste takes part in several revolutionary wars as a captain of infantry. In Germany he serves the army in the battles of Rhine and Moselle under general Bruneleau Ste Suzanne. At the withdrawal from Mayenne he is injured on November 10, 1795. At Klinkheim, near Radstadt, he is hurt again on July 9, 1796.[14] Then he is promoted to *capitaine de première classe* and earns a salary of 2400 fr. a year. He joins the army in the battle of Limath, near Zurich, under general Gazan and is injured there too on September 25, 1799. He also fights near Constance where he is injured on October 7, 1799. This time he is shot in the face, the bullet passes through his upper jaw, he cannot have solid food and also cannot speak clearly, later. With a painful right eye that is partly functioning, he is unable to continue his career as a soldier.[15] The French military administration, settled in the Château de Vincennes in Paris today, is very accurate in these turbulent times. From that a picture can be drawn of the composers father: a dedicated soldier of rank and many injuries which are mentioned time and again in his record of service. After this last injury, at the advice of army doctor Pénotet,[16] Coste returns home to recover with his family in Besançon. But adversity catches up with him. In 1800 his wife dies after a long period of illness[17] and he is left behind with his three daughters, of 17, 15 and 12 years of age. He asks for a pension, is appointed to captain-reporter and functions as an administrator in Besançon in that way.

On January 18, 1801 Jean-François Coste marries his second wife Anne Pierrette Dénéria at the town hall of Clairon. She is 34 years old and he is 48, according to the certificate of marriage.[18] Her social background is comparable to that of Jean-François. For instance, in her family there is an uncle who is captain, who holds the Croix de St. Louis, an uncle Mr. Giraud who is a doctor in medicine, another uncle Giraud who is an engineer, and a Monseigneur Baliet, bishop of Babilone, (probably the church in rue Babylone in Paris), etc. etc. Here also we have a respectable family that serves state and church.[19] From September 25, 1801 on, father Coste earns a salary of 1366 fr. 88 a year,[20] but, as it appears later, his military career is not over yet. In Besançon his daughter Cathérine-Françoise is born on January 24, 1802.[21] Now Jean-François is not part of the campaigns of Napoléon Bonaparte who

---

[9] Besançon, Archives municipales, *Baptêmes*, GG 305 Fo 21, 18 V 1787.
[10] Roncet, Noël: *Exposition Napoléon Coste*, Amondans, 21-26 VI 2005, [no.6], Généalogie.
[11] Pistone, Danièle: *La musique en France de la Révolution à 1900*, Paris, Honoré Champion, 1979, p. 11.
[12] Dossier J.F.Coste, Château de Vincennes, 24e 815 [Item 27]: 'État de services Lille (4p) le 16 septembre 1814 & Feuille individuelle.'
[13] Dossier J.F.Coste, Château de Vincennes, 24e 815 [Item 80]: 'Rapport ecrit le 7 Germinal (2p) le citoyen Coste nommé adjudant général chef de brigade à l'armee du Rhin [...] absolument incapable d'occuper [...]'.
[14] Dossier J.F.Coste, Château de Vincennes, 24e 815 [Item 53]: '[...] Coste à General chef de service - blessé [...]'.
[15] Dossier J.F.Coste, Château de Vincennes, 24e 815 [Item 56]: 'Officier de santé ... Coste a reçu un coup d'armes à feu qui a traversé les os maxillaires supérieures [...]'.
[16] Dossier J.F.Coste, Château de Vincennes, 24e 815 [Item 55]. '[...] à cause de blessure, [...]'.
[17] Besançon, Archives municipales, *Acte de sépulture* E 174 Fo 7 Vo, 25 Germ. An 8, i.e. 15 IV 1800.
[18] Dossier J.F.Coste, Château de Vincennes, 24e 815 [Item 11]: 'Extrait des régistres des actes civils [...]'.
[19] Dossier J.F.Coste, Château de Vincennes, 24e 815 [Item 22]: '[...] sort d'une famille respectable [...]'; [Item 74]: 'Valenciennes le 2 décembre 1815 Coste a ministre secretaire [...]'.
[20] Dossier J.F.Coste, Château de Vincennes, 24e 815 [Item 13]: '[...] solde 1366 fr 88 [...]'.
[21] Roncet, Noël: Exposition Napoléon Coste, Amondans, 21-26 VI 2005, [no. 6] - Généalogie.

I — Introduction 5

on December 2, 1804 crowns himself Emperor of the French in the Notre Dame in presence of Pope Pius VII. Napoléon 'Bonaparte abandons the battle of Britain after his defeat at Trafalgar, but wins the battles of Ulm and Austerlitz. Militarism has an influence on the works of the composer. Later, apparent references to military music and events can be found in his works, such as in *Le Passage des Alpes* opus 27, 28 & 40 (1856 and 1876) where probably the story of the march of Napoléon Bonaparte across these mountains is told, with trumpet calls in the second part. According to Thorvald Rischel[22] in *Le Départ* opus 31 (1856) Coste has the army returning in a triumphal march on December 29, 1855!..., after the Crimean War. That war ends in 1856, however, here a number of divisions are concerned. The military career of his father also has a direct influence on the course of Napoléon Coste's life.

5 La Source du Lison, 2005

---

[22] Rischel, Thorvald: 'Bibliographische Notizen zu den Gitarrenwerken von Napoleon Coste', in: *Die Gitarre*, Berlin, 1927, Jahrgang VIII, Heft 7/8, [Coste-Heft] p. 50.

II
Caprice

We now number 5 soldiers, including my son, who, only eight years old, armed himself with a good saddle pistol and has \very well/ done the guard duty with us and is continuing.[23]

AMONDANS 1805-1809

The small village of Amondans is situated in the rural countryside along the river Loue, which flows through the town of Ornans, some ten kilometers further on. In present-day Europe, expressing this distance in kilometers is a matter of course, but the metric system that this unit of measurement is part of had only been introduced by the French revolutionists in 1798 in France and still new in the beginning of the 19th century. Today Amondans has some 100 houses, most of them in the town, some in the neighborhood.[24] At the time it would not have been very different. Here Napoléon Coste was born in 1805 as the first and only son of Jean-François Coste (1754-1835) and Anne Pierrette Dénéria (1766-1842). Coste's father is 51 years old now and a retired officer of the Napoleonic army. He is chosen mayor of Amondans in 1803 and he lives with his family in the *mairie*, the same town hall whose present tenant (in 2005) says it still is functioning in this way. Other members of the family are 3-year-old daughter Cathérine-Françoise and the three daughters from Coste's first marriage with Claudine Pretet (1752-1800), Julie, 22 years of age at this point, Jeanne-Étienne, 20 years and Jeanne-Pierrette, 16 years.

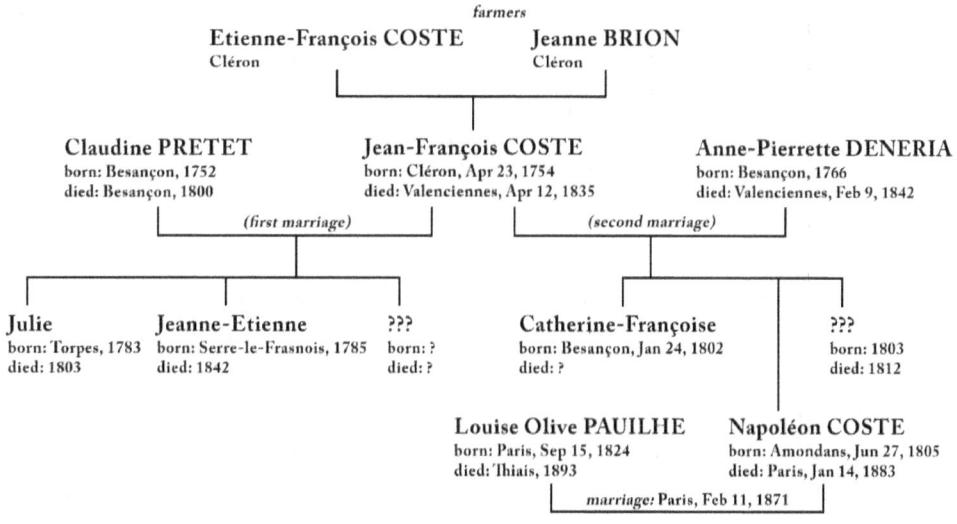

6 Genealogy Napoléon Coste (based on Roncet, exhibition Amondans, 2005)

This presentation of the genealogy of Coste seems well-ordered, but in reality it is more complex. It might be the case that Julie dies in Amondans November 20, 1803. In that case there are four children in 1805, a fact that concurs a letter dated May 16, 1810 from Coste's father to the ministry in which he writes of 'a wife and four children.'[25] But when he mentions 'the death of one of my daughters' in a letter to the ministry dated July 28, 1812, requested to be transferred away from Rochefort, where he is stationed at the time,[26] the question remains open which daughter this can be. In 1835 Jeanne-Étienne

---

[23] Dossier J. F. Coste, Château de Vincennes, 24e 815 [Item 28]: 'Nous sommes alors au nombre de 5 Combattants y compris mon fils qui, agé de 8 ans seulement, s'est armé d'un bon pistolet d'arçon et a \ fort bien / fait avec nous le service de surveillance et il continue.'
[24] The author visited Amondans and Ornans in 2002 and in 2005.
[25] Dossier J.F. Coste, Château de Vincennes, 24e 815 [Item 50]: '[...] avec une femme et quatre enfants [...]'.
[26] Dossier J.F. Coste, Château de Vincennes, 24e 815 [Item 34]: '[...] la mort d'une de mes filles [...]'.

lives with him in Valenciennes,[27] therefore it may concern Jeanne-Pierrette from his first marriage, or Cathérine-Françoise from his second. There are three children left, then. When he mentions 'a family of 5 persons' in a letter from Valenciennes dated February 28, 1817 that must include himself.[28] This matter of genealogy still is under research, because there may be another child from the second marriage, born in 1803 or 1809 and deceased in 1812.[29] For the time being, the available information in the sources must be taken as a starting point. In another way oral information can be of some importance. The *mairie* is located across from the castle of Amondans. That could be the place where possibly Napoléon Coste was born, for hygienic reasons, so tells the mayor in 2005. In that year an exhibition is held for the bicentennial of the birth of Coste, by father Noël Roncet, who is conducting research in Coste and published a booklet on him for this occasion.[30]

7 Mairie Amondans, 2002

There is much confusion about Napoléon Coste's correct date of birth June 27, 1805 among authors of articles, handbooks and histories of the guitar in which Coste is mentioned. Most of them give June 28, 1806 as his date of birth,[31] but this alternates with others ranging from February 17, 1806[32] to as early as 1803.[33] Some only give a wrong year, 1806. These numerous dates of birth persist until 1981, when Simon Wynberg, editor of the facsimile edition of the complete works of Coste, is the first to publish the correct date of birth,[34] informed on that point by Brian Jeffery. The wrong date can

---

[27] Bibliothèque Municipale Valenciennes, *Acte de décès Jean François Coste*, 13 IV 1835, VAL fonds modernes, série E: État civil, E1, R53.
[28] Dossier J.F. Coste, Château de Vincennes, 24ᵉ 815 [Item 16]: '[...] une famille de 5 personnes [...]'.
[29] Roncet, Noël: *Exposition Napoléon Coste*, Amondans, 21-26 VI 2005, [no. 6], Généalogie.
[30] Roncet, Noël: *Napoléon Coste, Compositeur, 1805-1883*, Amondans, 2005; *Exposition Napoléon Coste*, Amondans, 21-26 VI 2005.
[31] Bone, Philip J.: 'Coste, Napoleon', in: *The Guitar and the Mandolin*, London, Schott, 2ⁿᵈ ed. 1954, repr. 1972, p. 84-85, 97 (plate); Buek, Fritz: *Die Gitarre und ihre Meister*, Berlin, Robert Lienau, 1926, 2ⁿᵈ ed 1935, p. 104-109; Cooper, Jeffrey: 'Coste, Napoléon', in: Stanley Sadie, ed: *The New Grove Dictionary of Music and Musicians*, London, Macmillan, 1980, vol. 4, p. 824; Powroźniak, József: 'Coste, Napoléon', in: *Gitarrenlexikon*, Berlin, Verlag Neue Musik, 1979, p. 36; Prat, Domingo: *Diccionario biografico, bibliografico, critico, de Guitarras, Guitarristas y Guitarreros*, Buenos Aires, Fernando Romero, 1934, repr. 1986, Columbus, Orphée, p. 96-98; Radke, Hans: 'Coste, Napoléon', in: *Die Musik in Geschichte und Gegenwart*, ed. Blume, Kassel, Bärenreiter, 1956, ed. 1973, vol. XV, supplement 1, Kol. 1616-1617; Sharpe, A.P.: *The Story of the Spanish Guitar*, London, Clifford Essex, 1954, 4ᵗʰ ed. 1968, p. 18-19, 27, 61; Zuth, Josef: 'Coste, Napoléon', in: *Handbuch der Laute und Gitarre*, Wien, Doblinger, 1926, repr. Hildesheim, Olms, 1978, p. 72-73.
[32] Wynberg, Simon: '...zur Rettung Napoleon Costes...', in: *Gitarre und Laute*, Köln, vol. III, 1981, no. 5, p.29-32.
[33] Tonazzi, Bruno: *Liuto, Vihuela, Chitarra e Strumenti similari nelle loro Intavolature*, Trieste, Bèrben, 1971, 2ⁿᵈ ed. 1977, p. 142.
[34] Wynberg, Simon: 'Napoleon Coste', in: *Gitarre und Laute*, Köln, vol. IV, 1982, no. 1, p.51.

II — Caprice

already be found in 1902,[35] but strikingly enough also with Coste himself in 1843. In his registration as a member of the Freemasons' lodge *Les Frères Unis Inséparables* of that year the date of birth June 28, 1806 is recorded, possibly a date he offered himself.[36] In this way the assumption can be justified that he himself was not aware of the right date at the time, as the certificate of marriage in 1871 gives the correct date. The question is whether this confusion comes from taking the date of baptism for the date of birth. As newborn children in the Roman Catholic tradition are baptized without delay,[37] like Coste's father was the following day when he was born on April 23, 1754,[38] that is unlikely. The cause of this confusion more probably lies in the revolutionary calendar. The French Revolution wants to install a new society of liberty, equality and fraternity for the citizens, the *citoyens*. A part from the draft the universal declaration of human rights and the introduction of the metric system in 1798, a new calendar is introduced. The poet Fabre d'Églantine is commissioned to create new names for the months: the month of June now is called 'Messidor'. In a decree from October 5, 1793 the revolutionists declare that the first Year of the Revolution will commence at midnight on September 22, 1792.[39] While the system might be clear to everyone in France in this era, it can also cause confusion, moreover where it only lasted until the 15th Year of the Revolution, 1807. The birth certificate was found in assignment of Brian Jeffery by M. François Lassus of the 'Institut d'Études Comtoises et Jurassiens' and published by Jeffery in 1982. The certificate states that Coste was born on the eighth of Messidor of the thirteenth Year of the Revolution. It reads as follows:

> *The 13th Year of the Revolution, the eighth of Messidor, we, Jean-François Coste, retired captain of the light infantry, mayor of Amondans, officer of civil registration of the aforementioned town, hereby gives notice of a child of male sex, born on the aforementioned day at noon, on behalf of us and Anne-Pierrette Dénéria, our legal spouse, in her name, whom we hereby give the names Claude, Antoine, Jean, George, Napoléon, the said declarations and notices given in presence of gentleman Jean-Antoine Ordinaire master in surgery and gentleman Claude-François Laurent adjoint of the town hall of the aforesaid town of Amondans and have signed with the mentioned father and witnesses the present certificate after reading. C.F. Laurent, J.F. Coste, J.A. Ordinaire.*[40]

This date of birth can be converted to the Gregorian calendar that still is in use in Europe. Converted to the Gregorian calendar, the month of Messidor of the 13th Year of the Revolution starts June 20, 1805 and Claude Antoine Jean Georges Napoléon Coste is born on the 8th, which means June 27, 1805. With this all doubt is set at rest. Apart from the name of the father and the names of three other people, perhaps members of the family, the child is given the name of Napoléon Bonaparte, once a general, now emperor of France, possibly as a tribute. The name of Jean was already in the family, that of Napoléon too, now.

As a mayor Coste's father knows how to turn his hand to matters, he issues orders to have a map made of Amondans and takes the initiative to build a parish church which still stands including the stone commemorating this fact, which must be placed later, after the end of the Republican calendar.

---

[35] Stockmann [Shtokman], J.: 'Napoléon Coste', in: *Der Gitarrefreund*, München, 1902, 3. Jahrgang, Heft 5, p. 55.
[36] http://www.mvmm.org/m/docs/coste.html.
[37] Dossier J.F. Coste, Château de Vincennes, 24e 815 [Item 03]: '[...] extrait des régistres de baptême [...] a été baptésé le jour suivant [...]'.
[38] Sasser, William Gray: *The guitar works of Fernando Sor*, PhD dissertation, University of North Carolina, 1960, Ann Arbor, Michigan, 1975, p. 34.
[39] Cherpillod, André: *La kalendaro tra la tempo, tra la spaco*, Cournegard, Blanchetière, 2002, p.152-155.
[40] Besançon, Archives départementales, *acte de naissance Napoléon Coste*, État Civil, Amondans, N, 1793-1872, 5 Mi 177 [see appendix]: 'L'an treize de la République le huit Messidor nous Jean-François Coste, ancien Capitaine D'Infanterie Légère, maire de la Commune D'amondans, officier de L'État Civil de la ditte Commune, déclarons présenter un Enfant du Sexe Masculin né le dit Jour huit Messdor à Midy, de nous Déclarant et de anne-Pierrette Denéria, notre Épouse Légitime, et auquel nous déclarons donner les prénoms de Claude, antoine, Jean, George, Napoléon, les dittes Déclarations et présentations faites en présence de Monsieur Jean Antoine Ordinaire Maître en Chirurgie et de Monsieur Claude-François Laurent adjoint à la Mairie de la susditte commune D'amondans et avons lesdits père et témoins signé le présent acte de naissance après lecture. C.F. Laurent; J.F. Coste; J.A. Ordinaire.'; Jeffery, Brian: 'Napoleon Costes Jugend', in: *Gitarre und Laute*, Köln, vol. IV, 1982, no. 5, p. 255.

But then he is accused in using 857 fr. in community funds for his own purposes. This he paid back by pawning his pension, but he is nevertheless dismissed in 1807.[41]

ORNANS 1809-1812

In 1809 Coste's father lives with his family in Ornans, so the young Napoléon Coste just lived for four years in his village of birth and therefore has little or no memories of this time; he does not write a musical composition referring to this little town, for sure. In fact, he does just that for his new residence, the valley in which it is located, in his composition *La Vallée d'Ornans* opus 17 (1852) from his *Sept Souvenirs*. Gustave Courbet (1819-1877), the painter, created a canvas with the same title as the Coste's composition and painted his *Un enterrement à Ornans* in 1849. In view of the realism in his art, which is not restricted to subjects, but is extended to people,[42] even acquaintances of Coste might be present here, who are some forty years older in this painting.

8 Ornans, 2005

Napoléon Coste now lives in Ornans with his father, who is taken to court there by representatives of Amondans for the missing of money of the village,[43] with his mother and perhaps the three other children of the family, although both daughters from the first marriage of Jean-François are of marriageable age and may well already be married. His sister Catherine-Françoise is seven years old, Napoléon four. In a letter of August 10, 1809 to His Excellency Monseigneur le Comte de Lunebourg, minister of war, Jean-François Coste asks to be readmitted in active service: his sight has improved much; for the purpose of geometric operations he is able to see for 25 kilometers to locate the place of an object. A medical certificate supports his request and he is stationed in Antwerp on August 18, 1809 as a temporary attaché, but degraded to captain third rank with a salary of 1800 fr., whereas he had hoped for 2400 fr. as a captain first class; but still this is more than his pension of 1366 fr. 88 a year.[44] Apart from that, an income like that is not small compared with the annual budget of a family

---

[41] Jeffery, Brian: 'Napoleon Costes Jugend', in: *Gitarre und Laute*, Köln, vol. IV, 1982, no. 5, p. 254-256; Jaworski, Roman: 'Napoleon Coste 1805-1883, une histoire perdue', in: *Valentiana*, Valenciennes, Association Valentiana, 1992, no. 10, p. 68; Roncet, Noël: *Napoléon Coste, Compositeur, 1805-1883*, Amondans, 2005, p. 9.

[42] Bajou, Valérie: *Courbet*, Parijs, Biro, 2003, p. 61-79.

[43] Jaworski, Roman: 'Napoleon Coste 1805-1883, une histoire perdue', in: *Valentiana*, Valenciennes, Association Valentiana, 1992, no. 10, p. 68; Jeffery, Brian: 'Napoleon Costes Jugend', in: *Gitarre und Laute*, Köln, vol. IV, 1982, no. 5, p. 255; Roncet, Noël: *Napoléon Coste, Compositeur, 1805-1883*, Amondans, 2005, p. 9-10.

[44] Dossier J.F. Coste, Château de Vincennes, 24ᵉ 815 [Item 53: '[...] solde annuelle 2400 francs par an [...]'.

II — Caprice

of laborers, which is about 400 fr. in 1813.[45] There might have been financial reasons for him wanting to reenter the army, possibly professional pride as well, considering his many requests for a decoration. His family remains in Ornans, as is apparent from his application for a paid leave on May 16, 1810 to be with his family with four children that costs him 150 fr. a month to support; Jeanne-Etienne apparently still lives at home. He can get an unpaid leave, so he remains in Antwerp: without an income a family visit is too costly. Then he requests to be put on full duty, but preferably not in such a remote place. In his opinion he is underpaid, he even has to lend money.[46] His request is granted, but only partially.

ROCHEFORT 1810-1812

Jean-François Coste is appointed on October 25, 1810 to adjutant first class in Rochefort, the military harbor, south of La Rochelle at the mouth of the Charente, which is not exactly what he asked for.[47] In any case, from November 1811 on he is attached to Rochefort, but also there he is pursued by troubles. He is accused of stealing an inheritance, but the case against him is dropped by the court of Poitiers. He does not want to stay in Rocherfort, and in his letter of July 26, 1812 he requests a transfer. He wants to change places with captain Bessat in Langeoog, a Frisian Island way up North, near the East Ems.[48] As a reason for his request he raises the issue that the arrangement would allow Bessat to be with his family then, that he himself, in spite of his robust health, has been seriously ill for three months as a result of the bad air in Rochefort, that one of his daughters has deceased and that the rest of his family is repeatedly ill, which straps him with large expenses.[49] While first he asked for a leave in Antwerp to be with his family in Ornans, so far away, he now asks for a transfer from Rochefort, itself not so very close, to Langeoog. A more distant post is hardly possible. It looks like an escape, and he succeeds in it, because on September 24, 1812 he is appointed adjutant of Langeoog. How to get there is not as easy as it seems: the road has many obstacles, as he complains in a report upon his delay.[50] Travelling for a French officer probably means riding on horseback, a carriage is more likely for civilians. He is in Bois le Duc [1], ('s Hertogenbosch) for some time. He must have crossed the Rhine [2] and then pass the Zuiderzee [3], because on February 27, 1813 he is able to replace Captain Bessat on the Frisian island Langeoog [4], and starts to be engaged with the reinforcement of the local fortifications.[51] He has taken his son Napoléon Coste with him.

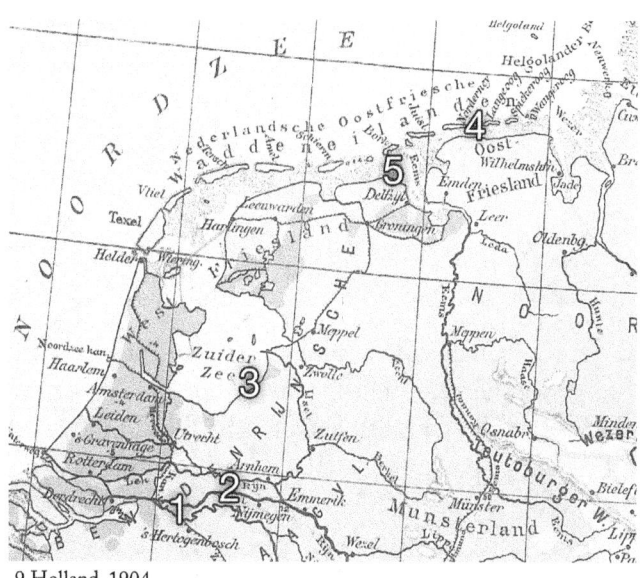

9 Holland, 1904

---

[45] Chevallier, Émile: *Les salaires au XIXe siècle*, Paris, Hachette, 1887, p. 32.

[46] Dossier J.F. Coste, Château de Vincennes, 24ᵉ 815 [Item 41]: '[...] je jouirais de la solde de retraite [...] emprunté 600 francs [...]'; [Item 50]: '[...] éloigné de ma famille, par un distance d'environ 78 miriamètres [...]'.

[47] Dossier J.F. Coste, Château de Vincennes, 24ᵉ 815 [Item 49]: 'Anvers le 21 9bre 1810 Coste à Ministre de la guerre - reçu la lettre nommé adjudant de 1ᵉʳᵉ classe de Rochefort [...]'.

[48] Dossier J.F. Coste, Château de Vincennes, 24ᵉ 815 [Item 34]: 'Rochefort le 28 juillet 1812 (2p) Coste à ministre de la guerre [...] changement de place capitaine Bessat de Langeroge occupe la place de Rochefort [...] et que j'occupe celle de Langeroge [...]'; Jeffery, Brian: 'Napoleon Costes Jugend', in: *Gitarre und Laute*, Köln, vol. IV, 1982, no. 5, p. 256; Roncet, Noël: *Napoléon Coste, Compositeur, 1805-1883*, Amondans, 2005, p. 11.

[49] Dossier J.F. Coste, Château de Vincennes, 24ᵉ 815 [Item 34]: '1ᵉ Rochefort etant un endroit très mal. - 2ᵉ Mais victime du mauvais air de ce pays ci, sav(?) trois mois de maladie la plus terrible, la mort d'une de mes filles du maladies réitéreér du restant de ma famille.'

[50] Dossier J.F. Coste, Château de Vincennes, 24ᵉ 815 [Item 33]: '[...] soit la longueur de la route, soit les obstacles qu'on y retrouve, je ne me trouve qu'à Bois le Duc [...]'.

[51] Dossier J.F. Coste, Château de Vincennes, 24ᵉ 815 [Item 31]: 'Place de Delfzil, le 21 mai 1814, Maufroy - - Mr le Capitaine Coste constamment occupé, comme adjoint a Mr le commdt du génie, aux travaux de construction pour la défense de la place - - levé et dressé la carte géometrique, representant fidellement les ouvrages d'attaque et de défense des assiéger et des assiégeants &c.'

HOLLAND 1813-1814

Influenced by the French Revolution the Batavian Republic comes into existence in 1795, until the country is incorporated into the Kingdom of Holland in 1806, with Louis Napoléon in power and French soldiers present to far in the North, even in Langeoog. From the 24th through the 30th of March 1813 the Frisian island lies under siege by the Britons. As the officer in charge in Langeoog, Captain Coste writes in his report of the defense of the island as follows:

'We now number 5 soldiers, including

10 Report J.F. Coste 1813, p. 2

[the next page there is different handwriting – the document is probably a copy in which the transcription has been continued by someone else, or else Coste dictated the report as an officer]

including my son, who, only eight years old, armed himself with a good saddle pistol and has done the guard duty \very well/ with us and is continuing.'[52]

[the last word of a page always is repeated on the next, to ensure that it is a continuous text].

11 Report J.F. Coste 1813, p. 3

As it concerns a military report by the commander of Langeoog here, signed by the father of Coste – who, as an engineer officer, makes a sketch in his signature of the way a fired shell passes by – this son, who almost is eight, must be Napoléon Coste. So, here is the connection with his later compositions *Delfzil* and *Le Zuyderzée* in his *Souvenirs* opus 19 and 20 which he publishes in 1852. Later, Commander Coste is praised for his courage.[53] The opinion that Coste's

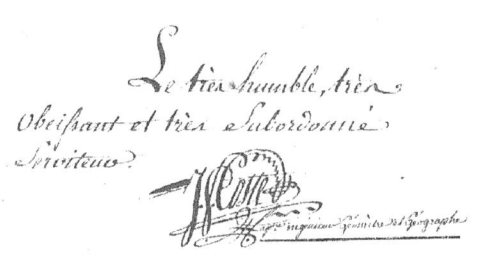

12 Signature J.F. Coste

father has a military career in mind for his son, is supported with this; he brings the boy along on a remote military mission and proudly reports his contribution to the defense. From January until November he is on the island. Napoléon Bonaparte's defeat in the battle of Leipzig of the 16th through the 19th of October 1813 ends his influence on the Netherlands. The Dutch rise in rebellion, supported by the English.[54] Not only is this threatening for the French, the Russian Cossacks approach the Eastern borders of Holland; Embden is conquered on November 13.[55] General Maufroy closes the

---

[52] Dossier J.F. Coste, Château de Vincennes, 24e 815 [Item 28], p. 2, 3: 'Nous sommes alors au nombre de 5 Combattants y compris / compris *mon fils qui, agé de 8 ans seulement, s'est armé d'un bon pistolet d'arçon et a* [inserted] \ fort bien / fait avec nous le service de surveillance et il continue.'
[53] Dossier J.F. Coste, Château de Vincennes, 24e 815 [Item 31]: '[...] Je ne puis, Monsieur, qu'applaudir à vôtre conduite dans cette circonstance [...]'.
[54] Bottema, Jaap: *Delfzijl, Schetsen uit de Franse Tijd (1795-1814)*, Bedum, Profiel, 2004, p. 48-51.
[55] Bottema, Jaap: *Delfzijl, Schetsen uit de Franse Tijd (1795-1814)*, Bedum, Profiel, 2004, p. 106.

II — Caprice

gates of Delfzijl [5] onNovember 3 and the fortress is besieged by the English and the Dutch. On November 11 Captain Coste gets the order from general Ambert from Groningen to evacuate the island of Langeoog and he arrives in Delfzijl on November 19, after eight days of storm.[56] In doing so he must have broken through the siege, or else have travelled from Langeoog to Delfzijl by boat, which is more likely.

There, during the siege, he is occupied with the defense works and he draws a geographical map with an accurate representation of it.[57] Of course, little Napoléon is with his father in this period. In Delfzijl he might be in contact with the local population and their musical culture. But the difference in language must have stood in the way: nothing later points to even a single word of Dutch. Tangible evidence of any influence of the Dutch musical culture is missing. Moreover, the Dutch do not have much reason to dance and sing in those years. They are not very fond of the French, who claim large quantities of food and numbers of cattle, they plunder the region and even rob houses in Delfzijl.[58] The fortress is under siege by the allies and General Maufroy threatens to open the floodgates and inundate the surrounding land; he is not even willing to believe Paris is already occupied on March 31, 1814 by the allies. After negotiations he is permitted to send a scout to The Hague ('s Gravenhage), who eventually returns with the message that indeed the Empire Français no longer exists. On April 20, 1814 Napoléon Bonaparte resigns and the French, who – from Dutch point of view – occupy Delfzijl, have permission, after negotiation, to leave in peace, but in battlearray and in full armament.[59] A painting by Tobias Roelfs van Streun (1795-1830) shows the withdrawal of the French from the fortress on 23 May 1814. 'Union is Strength', it says. Among them are Captain Coste and his son of eight years, Napoléon. On their journey they pass the Zuiderzee and the Rhine again and ultimately arrive at Lille.

13 Withdrawal of the French, Streun

---

[56] Dossier J.F. Coste, Château de Vincennes, 24ᵉ 815 [Item 16,]: '[...] ordre de l'evacuer [...] j'arrivai à Delfzil après huit jours de tempête, [...]'.
[57] Dossier J.F. Coste, Château de Vincennes, 24ᵉ 815 [Item 31]: '[...] Mr le Capitaine Coste constamment occupé, comme adjoint a Mr le commdt du génie, aux travaux de construction pour la défense de la place - - levé et dressé la carte géometrique, [...]'.
[58] Bottema, Jaap: *Delfzijl, Schetsen uit de Franse Tijd (1795-1814)*, Bedum, Profiel, 2004, p. 106-107.
[59] Bottema, Jaap: *Delfzijl, Schetsen uit de Franse Tijd (1795-1814)*, Bedum, Profiel, 2004, p. 119.

III
Thème varié

Last Saturday's concert deserves a separate mention, nevertheless. M. Coste had the good spirit to appeal to the legs as well as to the ears, and the announcement of a final ball did not make a little contribution to the raising of the box-office money.[60]

VALENCIENNES 1815-1828

From Holland Captain Coste and Napoléon, his son of eight years, eventually arrive at Lille on June 9, 1814. His wife and the other children go there too. The family is reunited and temporarily stays in Hôtel d'Angleterre. As an ex-commander the captain awaits new orders and meanwhile asks for the decoration he is keen on, apparently. Because he is out of active service, his salary is halved, which causes financial problems.[61] These are hard times for him and for his family, the future is uncertain, the political circumstances unstable. Then Napoléon Bonaparte's last action comes. He escapes from Elba in February 1815, lands in the south of France and marches north with a couple of followers. On the way he meets the French army in la Mure, which is searching for him, and he succeeds to win them to his side in a theatrical scene. In March he arrives at Paris. Captain Coste then is appointed adjutant first class in Valenciennes in the Douai district, département du Nord, where he arrives at the end of May 1815.[62]

14 Valenciennes, plan 19th C.

---

[60] *Petites Affiches*, Valenciennes: 6ᵉ Année, 28 III 1827, no. 556, p. 545: 'Le concert de samedi dernier mérite cependant une mention particulière. M. Coste a eu le bon esprit d'intéresser les jambes en même temps que les oreilles, et l'annonce d'un bal à la suite, n'a pas peu contribué à grossir la recette.'

[61] Dossier J.F. Coste, Château de Vincennes, 24ᵉ 815 [Item 68]: 'Lille le 25 juin 1814 [...] Coste a ministre de la guerre.'

[62] Dossier J.F. Coste, Château de Vincennes, 24ᵉ 815 [Item 17]: '[...] nommé adjudant de première classe pour la place de Valenciennes - Je me mettrai en route pour me rendre à mon poste au plutard le 22 du courrant [...]'.

He and his family first settle in rue Cardon [Capron] no. 23 [1], later in rue de l'Ormerie [2].[63] At the time, there must have been considerable movements of troops in the surroundings. From the south Valenciennes is situated at the way to Waterloo, some 80 kilometers away. So close to the big battle, these cannot have passed unnoticed by the young Coste. Then comes the renowned end of Napoléon, the battle in which Captain Coste at the age of 61 does not fight. And his great desire, to obtain the Croix de St. Louis, is not fulfilled. He is decorated, however, with the Fleur de Lys. He obviously does not find this satisfactory for his age, behavior, loyalty, wounds and important family, as he persists in his demands and continues to do so until 1824. He does not obtain it, as he was not of service to the king.[64] On January 1, 1816 he is back at half salary of 1366 fr. 88, after which he is demobilized on May 20, 1817 and put on pension on June 3.[65] When he dies in 1835 he is living apart from his wife on the dike near the Faubourg de Paris [3].

Guitar

The town of Valenciennes, where Watteau painted his rococo-scenes with baroque guitars a century earlier,[66] is located in 'notre ancienne Flandres,' the Flanders on which Coste later in 1835 musically models his memories in opus 5 *Souvenirs de Flandres*.[67] In the first part, a march, and in the third part, a waltz, evident references to military musical signals are audible. Little is known about Coste's youth, from age 12 to 23. In just one letter in 1878 to Hallberg, his friend in Sweden, he gives a brief retrospective on this period in his life:

> *At a very young age I learned mathematics. I did algebra and equations. Then a terrible illness deprived me of my intelligence for fifteen months. I had completely lost my memory. So there you have it, dear Sir, that is why I am a musician. Because if I hadn't forgotten the math I had learnt, I would have enrolled in a polytechnic and would have finished as a brilliant officer. That was the career my father had chosen for me. That is also why I became a composer so late. The intelligence compartment in my brain being emptied, It took me quite a few years to return to its primitive state. So this is why, after having explained the squares of the hypotenuse and the squaring of the circle, I now know nothing or practically nothing. But excuse me, dear Sir, for having bored you with these sad memories, instead of telling you things you might have found more interesting.*[68]

So, the reason he gave up a career in the military and chose to become a guitarist is to be found in his illness. The biographical sketches in handbooks and guitar histories concerning the period 1817-1825 contain a mix of fact and fiction, which can probably be attributed to the quotation above, but it cannot be denied that the authors also used their imagination. To date, the oldest secondary source for this information is Stockmann [Shtokman] in Der Gitarrefreund 1902. This publication had the following to say about the military career that Coste's father envisioned for his son:

---

[63] Jaworski, Roman: 'Napoleon Coste 1805-1883, une histoire perdue', in: *Valentiana*, Valenciennes, Association Valentiana, 1992, no. 10, p. 68, 73.
[64] Dossier J.F. Coste, Château de Vincennes, 24ᵉ 815 [Item 06]: '[...] ajourner sa demande de la Croix de St. Louis [...] aucun service au Roi [...]'.
[65] Dossier J.F. Coste, Château de Vincennes, 24ᵉ 815 [Item 04]: 'Retraite, Paris, le 19 juin 1817. Services'; [Item 08]: '[...] demi solde [...]'; [Item 16]: '[...] de 1814 ensuite mis à demi solde en 1814 et 1815 [...]'; [Item 22]: '[...] solde 1366 fr 88, [...]'.
[66] Ramade, Patrick et al.: *Watteau et la fête galante*, Valenciennes, Musée des Beaux Arts, 2004, p. 87. 153, 157, 195, 196-197, 220, 225; Bailey, Colin B. et al: *The Age of Watteau, Chardin and Fragonard*, New Haven, Yale University Press, 2003, p. 133, 141.
[67] *Petites Affiches*, Valenciennes: 5ᵉ Année, 20 V 1826, no. 467 p. 165: 'La *musicomanie* [...] notre ancienne Flandres.'
[68] Coste-Hallberg, 20 II 1878: 'Très jeune j'ai été initié aux mathématiques. J'ai fait de l'algèbre et des équations. Puis une affreuse maladie m'a privé pendant quinze mois de l'intelligence. J'avais complètement perdu la mémoire. Voilà, cher Monsieur, pourquoi je suis musicien. Car si je n'avais oublié ce que je savais en mathématiques, je serais entré à l'école polytechnique dont je serais sorti officier du génie. C'était la carrière que mon père me destinait. Voilà pourquoi aussi, de suis devenu compositeur si tard. C'est que la case de l'intelligence, s'étant vidée dans mon cerveau, il a fallu bien des années pour la remettre dans son état primitif. Voilà pourquoi enfin, après avoir expliqué les carrés de l'hypotenuse et la quadrature du cercle, je ne sais plus rien ou presque rien. Mais pardon, cher Monsieur, de vous avoir ennuyé de ces tristes souvenirs, au lieu de vous dire des choses qui auraient pu vous intéresser davantage.'

III — Thème varié 17

With that aim of his father's in mind, the boy was so excessively tormented with mathematics that at 11 years of age he became so seriously ill that even after his recovery it was inconceivable for him to continue this preparation. At the age of 16, for no apparent reason, Coste began to occupy himself with the guitar in secret, and he showed such musical aptitude that he was enthusiastically supported in his efforts by his mother, who also played the guitar well. In Valenciennes, where the family had settled permanently after the father's discharge, he was already giving lessons at the age of 18 and performed more than once for the local philharmonic association.[69]

The notion that mathematics made Coste ill is a curious conclusion to reach. This story is not at all improbable. The source dates from twenty years after Coste's death, but Coste himself does not mention his mother playing the guitar. From this source the same story – sometimes to the letter – is copied by Bone, 1914 and Zuth, 1920, who do not mention its origin.[70] On the contrary Schwarz-Reiflingen does mention the origin in 1927[71] and he refers on the one hand to Richard Läpke, who publishes a biography in the *Internationale Gitarre-Zeitung*, vol. I no. 4, January 1884 and no. 5, February 1884 in Leipzig – a source that appears to be impossible to find – while on the other hand he also refers to aforesaid Shtokman. He might also draw on this origin. Läpke's text is transcribed by Eduard Fack in *Die Meister*, p.118-119.[72] Other authors who fail the acknowledgement of their source are Buek in 1926, who relates the whole tale[73] and Gelas in 1927, who only states that Coste was a gifted mathematician, which was an advance in discerning distinct harmonic functions while composing.[74] Then one needs to wait until 1980 to take up the tradition of this biographical sketch with Cooper and Wynberg's edition of Coste's complete works for guitar in 1982:[75] here he teaches himself to play the guitar at the age of 6, encouraged by his mother, and he moves to Valenciennes at the age of 18, thus in 1823, where he starts his concert career – also the revised editions of 2006-7 do not correct of this.[76] Apart from his date of birth, there also is confusion on this subject. Then in 1993 Jaworski publishes an article on Coste, based on research into sources, in the *Valentiana*, but he too has to refer to Buek, because there is no tangible indication of Coste's serious illness, possible education or musical schooling. He does report, however, that Coste is named in the music teachers' review. So, Coste teaches music at an early age and to do so it is convenient to know how to play the piano.[77] It also is likely he did, because he composes 13 pieces with piano accompaniment for sure, and transcribes 16 pieces for piano to the guitar. Burzik tells the story again in 2000, as does Stenstadvold briefly in 2001.[78] Roncet recalls Buek in 2005 and attaches the year 1816 to the disease, without any reference, however.[79] In a document from that time, found by Jaworski, a personal description can be read, meant for military service, which seems to fit

---

[69] Stockmann [Shtokman], J.: 'Napoléon Coste', in: *Der Guitarrefreund, Mitteilungen des Internationalen Guitarristen-Verbandes*, München, 3. Jahrgang, 1902, Heft 5, p. 55: 'Dieser Absicht des Vaters entsprechend wurde der Knabe schon im frühendsten Alter so übermässig mit Mathematik geplagt, dass er im elften Lebensjahre gefärlich erkrankte und selbst nach erfolgter Genesung an eine Fortsetzung seiner Vorbereitung nicht mehr zu denken war. Mit 16 Jahren begann er heimlich und ohne jede Anleitung sich mit der Guitarre zu beschäftigen und verriet dabei eine so hervorragende musikalische Veranlagung, dass er von seiner Mutter, die glücklicherweise selbst eine gute Guitarrespielerin war, in seine Bestrebungen eifrig unterstützt wurde. In Valencienne, wo die Familie nach des Verabschiedung des Vaters sich bleibend niedergelassen hatte, erteilte Coste bereits im alter von 18 Jahren Unterricht und liess er sich auch mehrmals in der dortigen philharmonischen Gesellschaft hören.

[70] Bone, Philip J. : 'Coste, Napoleon', in: *The Guitar and the Mandolin*, London, 1954, reprint 1972, p. 84-85; Zuth, Josef: 'Coste, Napoléon', in: *Handbuch der Laute und Gitarre*, Wien, Doblinger, 1926-27, reprint Hildesheim, Olms, 1978, p. 72-73.

[71] Schwarz-Reiflingen, Erwin: 'Napoleon Coste', in: *Die Gitarre*, Berlin, 1927, Jahrgang VIII, Heft 7/8, [Coste-Heft] p. 44.

[72] Läpke, Richard: 'Biographie Napoleon Coste' in: *Internationale Gitarre-Zeitung*, Jahrgang I, no. 4 (Jan.1884), no. 5 (Febr.1884), Leipzig, transcr. Eduard Fack, 'Die Meister', unp. p. 118-119 [transcript obtained by Andreas Stevens].

[73] Buek, Fritz: *Die Gitarre und ihre Meister*, Berlin, 1926, 4th ed. >1935, p. 106.

[74] Gelas, Lucien: 'Biographische Notizen über Napoleon Coste', in: *Die Gitarre*, Berlin, 1927, Jahrgang VIII, Heft 11/12, p. 82.

[75] Cooper, Jeffrey: 'Coste, Napoléon', in: Sadie, Stanley, ed.: *The New Grove Dictionary of Music and Musicians*, London, Macmillan, 1980, vol. 4, p. 824.

[76] Wynberg, Simon: *The Guitar Works Napoleon Coste*, facsimile edition, vol. I-IX, Monaco, 1981, 1983; reprint 2006-7.

[77] Jaworski, Roman: 'Napoleon Coste 1805-1883, une histoire perdue', in: *Valentiana*, Valenciennes, Association Valentiana, 1992, no. 10, p. 68.

[78] Burzik, Monika: 'Coste, Napoléon', in: *Die Musik in Geschichte und Gegenwart*, (ed. Blume, Finscher), 4, Kassel, 2000, Kol. 1714-1717; Stenstadvold, Erik 'Coste, Napoléon', in: *The New Grove Dictionary of Music and Musicians*, Second edition, London, 2001, p. 534.

[79] Roncet, Noël: *Napoléon Coste, Compositeur - 1805-1883*, Amondans, 2005, p. 11.

the two photographs of him that exist; Coste is 1.60m tall, has brown hair, a high forehead, grey eyes, a medium-sized nose and mouth, a round chin, oval face, clear complexion and a small scar.[80] The last word is 'vérole' which means smallpox in French, and that might have been the disease the authors above write about.

Concerts 1826-1827

The progress made by the young Coste in his guitar-playing is apparent from a concert in the village of St-Amand, but a few kilometers away from Valenciennes, south of Arras. The local newspaper *Petites Affiches* of Valenciennes writes on May 20, 1826:

Musicomania is taking on really appalling proportions really in our ancient Flanders. Every city, one could almost say every village, now has a philharmonic society. Without speaking of St-Amand, which is not lagging behind in the present development of civilization, we have successively seen associations of musicians in the most smallest towns in our region, which dedicate multiple days a month to their mutual education. [...] ... the inhabitants of St-Amand [..] almost all refused to subscribe to the concert that was announced for the day of the fair at that place for the benefit of a young guitarist from Valenciennes. Despite the goodness of the local dilettants, the subscribers fell six people short ... of making a dozen. We have to say that the price of a ticket was set at 1 franc per person![81]

15 Petites Affiches, May 20, 1826

The name of Coste is not mentioned here, but it is most plausible to accredit this concert to him; the presence of another young guitarist in Valenciennes who wants to present himself in a concert like this is improbable. In this period the local press makes no mention of any guitarist other than

---

[80] Jaworski, Roman: 'Napoleon Coste 1805-1883, une histoire perdue', in: *Valentiana*, Valenciennes, Association Valentiana, 1992, no. 10, p. 68.
[81] *Petites Affiches*, Valenciennes: 5ᵉ Année, 20 V 1826, no. 467, p. 165: 'La *musicomanie* fait depuis quelques tems [sic] des progrès vraiment effrayaux, dans notre ancienne Flandres. Toutes les villes, on pourrait presque dire tous les villages ont maintenant des sociétés philharmoniques. Sans parler de St-Amand qui, sur ce point, n'est pas en arrière des progrès actuels de la civilisation, nous avons vu successivement naitre et se former autour de nous dans les plus petites communes des sociétés de musiciens qui consacrent quelques jours par mois à leur enseignement mutuel. [...] ..les St-Amandinois [...] ont presque tous refusé de souscrire à un concert proposé pour lundi dernier, jour de leur kermesse, au profit d'un jeune guitariste de Valenciennes. Malgré la bonne volonté de tous les *dilettanti* de l'endroit, il a manqué six souscripteurs pour compléter.... la douzaine. Il est vrai de dire aussi, que le billet était fixé au prix d'un franc par personne!' [The spelling of French in 19th-century papers is differs from modern standards].

III — Thème varié

Coste. From this newspaper report it can be concluded that the poorly attended concert took place on Monday, May 15, 1826. The tone of this piece is ironic. To show the contemporary opinion of the guitar and guitar music, it is important to make accurately quote the press of the time.

Almost a year later, on Saturday, March 24, 1827, Coste plays in a vocal and instrumental concert, with a ball at the end, in the Salon Chinois in Valenciennes, together with the amateurs and artists of the Société Philharmonique, established in 1823. Under the heading *Concert de M. Coste*, the local newspaper Petites Affiches writes:

> *Mr. Coste has had the good spirit to appeal to the legs as well as to the ears, and the announcement of a final ball did not make a little contribution to the raising of the box-office money. There were many visitors, and the applause and the cash also did satisfied the expectations of the beneficiary whose talent deserves more than this double award. Nevertheless the gentlemen Perriquet, G*** and Engebert also shared in the honors of the evening. The variations of M. Coste gave great pleasure, but the guitar always plays a sad role in a concert.*[82]

Here, a not very favorable judgement of the guitar as a concert instrument is demonstrated. In this and later critiques the tendency is visible to regard the guitar as an archaic musical instrument that has too weak a sound to compete with other musical instruments, of which musicians, luthiers, the public and reviewers expect an ever-increasing volume. This mixed concert is an example of a practice that was primarily in use in Paris: professional musicians and amateurs performed in a varied program of soloists, with or without accompaniment, and ensembles. To make it more attractive to the public, there is a dance at the end. At the time it is customary for soloists to play their own work; with ensemble music, that is different. Coste plays variations in this concert, and this passage taken literally, a work he himself composed. Therefore opus 2 is suitable, *Variations et Finale sur un motif favori de la famille Suisse de Weigl*, published around 1830, an assumption that puts this work in 1827. The Singspiel *Die Schweizerfamilie* by Joseph Weigl, from which Coste adopts the theme, is put on the stage as *Emmeline* in Paris in 1827,[83] which makes him follow the topic of the hour. Other 'Introduction et Variations' – being a set of theme and variations – that he might have had played in this concert are *Introduction et Variations sur la Cavatine favorite de l'Opéra Le Pirate* WoO 9 upon a motif of Bellini [not Rossini]. The opera seria *Il Pirata* had its opening performance on October 27, 1827 in Milan; so Coste could not have already heard this theme.[84] But he could well have heard Weigl's theme (motif), and the melody is so catchy that it even could have reached Valenciennes. As Zani de Ferranti also has devoted a 'Niaiserie' (a mere nothing) to the same theme, the motif was surely widely known. Other sets of theme and variations are published with the title *Fantaisie* and belong to the genre Fantaisie variée, like the fantasy on a motif of *Armide* by Gluck opus 4, published in 1832, a *Fantaisie de Concert* opus 6, published in 1837, an unpublished *Grand Solo* opus 24, dated circa 1840, and a *Fantaisie de Concert* for two oboes with piano accompaniment (ad libitum) opus 35. These pieces cannot be considered to have been played in the concert of March 24, 1827 in Valenciennes because of the title and the dates: Coste did not compose more than these two 'real' sets of theme and variations. In this way it can be assumed that it were the 'Weigl-variations', as the first work, that were played in this concert. This mixed concert has the young guitarist Coste as a beneficiary. This type of concert is apparently usual in Valenciennes also.

---

[82] *Petites Affiches*, Valenciennes: 6e Année, 28 III 1827, no. 556, p. 544-545: 'M. Coste a eu le bon esprit d'intéresser les jambes en même temps que les oreilles, et l'annonce d'un bal à la suite, n'a pas peu contribué à grossir la recette. La réunion était nombreuse, et les applaudissements et la caisse ont répondu également à l'attente du bénéficiaire dont le talent mérite bien cette double récompense. Cependant MM. *Perriquet*, G*** et *Engebert* ont eu également les honneurs de la soirée. Les variations de M. Coste ont fait un très-grand plaisir, mais la guitare joue toujours un triste rôle dans un concert.'

[83] Angermüller, Rudolph: 'Weigl', in: Sadie, Stanley, ed.: *The New Grove Dictionary of Music and Musicians*, vol. 1-20, London, Macmillan, 1980, vol. 20, p. 298.

[84] Lippmann, Friedrich: 'Vincenzo Bellini', in: Sadie, Stanley, ed.: *The New Grove Dictionary of Music and Musicians*,, London, Macmillan, 1980, vol. 2, p. 447-448, 452.

A full example can be found in the local newspaper *Petites Affiches* from April 14, 1827 in the announcement of a vocal and instrumental concert on Monday, April 16 in Condé, a village some 11 kilometers north-east of Valenciennes, and on Tuesday April 17, 1827 in the Salon Chinois in Valenciennes. Both times Miss Clorinde Moline is performing:

In Condé: Monday 6 [sic] April 1827, at six in the evening, this town's symphonic society, accompanied by [...] and Miss Clorinde Moline, the Italian solo singer, will give a vocal and instrumental concert in the main auditorium of the town hall [...] with a final ball.[85]

For the concert in the Salon Chinois the program is already given:

First part: 1. Harmony by the gentlemen musicians of the 14th regiment; 2. Air from Tancredi (O Patria), by Rossini, sung by Miss Clorinde; 3. Fantaisies for flute on the melodies from La Dame Blanche, performed by M. Boquet; 4. Della Tromba, great cavatine by Ponchita, sung by miss Clorinde; Second part: 5. Harmony by the gentlemen musicians of the 14th regiment; 6. Solo for guitar; 7. Grand air from Torbida by Pietre Romani, sung by Miss Clorinde with Mr. Hermann at the piano. Immediately after the concert there will be a ball. The orchestra is composed of the gentlemen musicians from the 14th regiment. The event will begin promptly at six thirty.[86]

16 Petites Affiches, April 14, 1827

This varied program centered around contributions of the Italian female singer, who is probably called Molino. Both parts are opened by the soldiers, who also play at civil concerts and accompany the closing ball. The heroic melodrama *Tancredi* by Rossini had its first performance in Venice in 1813; in 1827 he is already a celebrity in Paris.[87] The opéra comique *La Dame Blanche* by Boieldieu dates from 1825; from 1817 on he is a master of composition at the Conservatoire of Paris.[88] Nothing is known

---

[85] *Petites Affiches*, Valenciennes: 6ᵉ Année, 14 IV 1827, no. 561, p. 568: '*Ville de Condé* Lundi 6 [sic] avril 1827, a six heures du soir, la société symphoniste du dit lieu, secondée par [...] et Melle CLORINDE MOLINE, première cantatrice italienne [...] donnera, dans le grand salon de la mairie, UN CONCERT vocal et instrumental [...] suivie d'un BAL.'

[86] *Petites Affiches*, Valenciennes: 6ᵉ Année, 14 IV 1827, no. 561, p. 568: '*Première partie*. 1ᵉ Harmonie par MM. les musiciens du 14 regiment. 2. Air de Tancredi (O Patria), de Rossini, chant par Mlle Clorinde. - 3. Fantaisies pour flû e [sic], sur sur les airs de *la Dame Blanche*, exécutées par M. *Boquet* - 4. Della Tromba, grande cavatine de Ponchita, chantée pas Mlle Clorinde. *Deuxième Partie*. 5 Harmonie par MM. les musiciens du 14ᵉ regiment, - 6. Solo de guitare. - 7. Grand air de Torbida, de Pietre Romani, chanté par M. Clorinde. - M. *Hermann* tiendra le piano. UN BAL aura lieu immediatement apres le concert. L'orchestre sera composé de MM. les musiciens du 14ᵉ de ligne. [...] On commencera a six heures et demie precises.'

[87] Gossett, Philip: 'Rossini, Gioachino', in: Sadie, Stanley, ed.: *The New Grove Dictionary of Music and Musicians*, vol. 1-20, London, Macmillan, 1980. vol. 16, p. 229, 244.

[88] Devriès-Lesure, A.: 'Boieldieu', in: Fauquet, Joël-Marie: *Dictionnaire de la Musique en France au XIXe siècle*, Paris, Fayard, 2003, p. 156-158.

III — Thème varié 21

about the composer Ponchita, perhaps the vocalist brought along an Italian repertoire. Pietro Romani (1791-1877) is a conductor and composer in Florence.[89] Despite the fact that Coste is not explicitly mentioned, there is no other known guitarist in Valenciennes who might have played a solo in this concert. In Condé no guitar solo is mentioned in the concert, but Coste may have participated there as well. And if he performs there, it is still unknown what he plays. If that is a work of his own, it might be the 'Weigl-variations' again. If not, a work of Carulli is probable: according to the *Indicateur de Valenciennes* he teaches guitar with the Carulli method in rue Askièvre [4], and is thus informed about that composer's work.[90]

17 Valenciennes, rue Askièvre, 2007

Along with many other classic guitarists and composers, such as Diabelli, Giuliani, Carcassi, Legnani, Aguado and Sor, Carulli composed in the theme and variation genre; he wrote more than 50 of them. Ferdinando Carulli (Naples 1770 - Paris 1841) has been living in Paris since 1807. The 'method' may be his *Méthode complète* opus 27, which is published circa 1810 by Carli, or opus 247 from 1825.[91] Both methods contain scales, exercises and arpeggio's, arranged in order of key, pieces in first and second position, theme and variations, legatos and duets, and they are quite extensive for the beginning guitarist.

Sagrini 1828

In 1828 Luigi Sagrini (1809-1874), a travelling concert guitarist, visits the village in French Flanders.[92] He is announced, with a sneer to the guitar, in the *Petites Affiches* on Wednesday, February 20, 1828:

> *Mr. Sagrini, a famous guitarist, one of the virtuosos of Europe, who is a great champion of an instrument that is regarded unsuitable as well as worthless, will give a concert in Valenciennes in a few days.*[93]

---

[89] Loewenberg, Alfred: 'Romani, Pietro', in: Sadie, Stanley, ed.: *The New Grove Dictionary of Music and Musicians*, vol. 1-20, London, Macmillan, 1980. vol.16, p.127-128.

[90] Jaworski, Roman: 'Napoleon Coste 1805-1883, une histoire perdue', in: *Valentiana*, Valenciennes, Association Valentiana, 1992, no. 10, p. 70.

[91] Stenstadvold, Erik: *An Annotated Bibliography of Guitar Methods, 1760-1860*, Organologia: Musical Instruments and Performance Practice no. 4, London, Pendragon Press, 2010, p. 4, 5.

[92] Zuth, Josef: 'Luigi Sagrini', in: *Handbuch der Laute und Gitarre*, Wien, Doblinger, 1926-28, repr. Hildesheim, Olms, 1978, p. 238-239; Bone, Philip J.: Sagrini, Luigi', in: *The Guitar and the Mandolin*, London, Schott, 2nd ed, 1954, reprint 1972, p. 304-305; Chapalain, Guy: 'Luigi Sagrini', in: *Les Cahiers de la Guitare*, Boissy-St-Léger, Association Guitares et Luths, no. 68, 1998, p. 36; Coldwell, Robert: "Luigi Sagrini", in: *Soundboard*, Vol. XXXVII, No. 1, 2011, p. 51-52, date confirmed by Bernard Lewis, 9 August 2015.

[93] *Petites Affiches*, Valenciennes: 6e Année, no. 651, p. 59: 'M. *Sagrini*, célèbre *guitariste*, l'un des virtuoses de l'Europe qui tire le plus grand partie d'un instrument que l'on regarde mal-à-propos comme ingrat, se propose de donner un concert à Valenciennes dans un peu de jours.'

He meets Coste, the local talent. They practice together and give a concert on February 27, 1828.

18 Luigi Sagrini

The concert that was given on Wednesday by M. Sagrini did not escape the public's attention. Never we have heard so good a guitarist as this young artist and by the lightness of his playing as well as the certainty and ease he displayed, he did rightly deserve all approval. Our young and modest fellow-townsman M. Coste was a dignified competitor, and mister Perriquet gave the audience the greatest pleasure with the duo concertant for violin and guitar. [...] The youngsters have had the courteousness to offer the ladies, by way of improvisation, a ball at the end. In Valenciennes we will soon have the saying that there is no beautiful concert without a ball, just as in Paris they say that there is no good party without gendarmes.[94]

The review is favorable, Coste is a match for the younger Sagrini and the final ball seems to become usual. Another source, *Mon Histoire* of Valenciennes, does not give a review, but rather a program. This also is a mixed concert with singing, choir, flute, violin and guitar, but the main part is played by Sagrini, who performs own works, such as a *Concerto* for guitar and *Grandes Variations* for violin and guitar. Together with Coste he plays *Grandes Variations Concertantes pour deux guitares*.[95] This work, of which the composer is not mentioned in the review, might be opus 130 of Mauro Giuliani, according to Zuth, Bone and Chapalain.[96] However, that is not possible, because this work was published only in 1840, posthumously, unless Sagrini had a copy of the manuscript. Heck, in his biography, does not mention Sagrini's name at all, so that is improbable. Among the theme and variations sets only *Gran Variazioni Concertanti* opus 35 by Giuliani could be taken in consideration as a candidate for this work with the same title, published in Vienna in 1812 and later in Paris in 1828.[97] Coste writes later:

---

[94] *Petites Affiches*, Valenciennes: 7ᵉ Année, 1 III 1828 no. 654, p. 70: 'Le concert donné mercredi par M. Sagrini n'a pas été au dessous de l'attente du public. Nous n'avons jamais entendu de *guitariste* aussi fort que ce jeune artiste: et par la légéreté de son jeu autant que par l'aplomb et l'aisance dont il a fait preuve, il a enlevé, comme il a mérité tous les suffrages. Notre jeune et modeste concitoyen M. Coste a dignement rivalisé avec lui, et M. *Perriquet* a fait le plus grand plaisir dans le duo concertant de violon et guitare. [...] Les jeunes gens ont eu la galanterie d'offrir à ces dames, et par manière *d'impromptu* un petit bal *à la suite*. Il passera bientôt en proverbe à Valenciennes qu'il n'y a pas de beau concert sans bal, comme on dit à Paris qu'il n'est pas de bonne fête sans gendarmes.'

[95] *Mon Histoire*, Valenciennes, 27 II 1828, 'Concert donné par M. Sagrini.'

[96] Zuth, Josef: 'Coste, Napoléon', in: *Handbuch der Laute und Gitarre*, Wien, Doblinger, 1926-27, reprint Hildesheim, Olms, 1978, p. 238; Bone, Philip J.: 'Coste, Napoleon', in: *The Guitar and the Mandolin*, London, 1954, reprint 1972, p. 304; Chapalain, Guy: 'Luigi Sagrini', in: *Les Cahiers de la Guitare*, 1998 no. 68, p. 36.

[97] Heck, Thomas Fitzsimmons: *The Birth of the Classic Guitar and its Cultivation in Vienna, reflected in the Career and Compositions of Mauro Giuliani (d.1829)* (with) vol II: *Thematic Catalogue of the complete works of Mauro Giuliani*, Ph.D. Yale University, 1970, Ann Arbor, Michigan, 1977, vol. II, p. 41, 137, 216.

III — Thème varié

> *Long before 1828 I had contacts with Sagrini in the provinces (in Valenciennes). We performed Giuliani's grandes variations (35) for an audience. It was a very big success for me, because nobody knew me and because Sagrini's great reputation went before him. Sagrini was a brilliant performer and had a beautiful sound. But at the time when Sagrini was already giving concerts in all the capitals of Europe, I did not know that I myself would one day be a guitarist.*[98]

What is now clear is that the work of Giuliani referred to was his opus 35. This work, whose beginning also resembles opus 130, demands a high technical standard on the part of the performer. So, Coste must either have begun playing the guitar before he turned 16, thus comfortably before 1821, or have had exceptional talent. The former hypothesis is quite possible, the latter very probable. Coste himself writes that he played a great deal of Sor and everything by Giuliani in his youth, but he would not have had all 150 opus numbers in his possession:

> *Up to the age of 24 I played all the music by this composer. I didn't know anything better at the time, and as soon as Sor's music fell into my hands, I was able to see the hollowness and the paucity present in the Giuliani's works.*[99]

Giuliani could not hold a candle to Sor. On Sunday December 14, 1828 Coste gives his last concert in Valenciennes; it is announced on December 6 in *Petites Affiches*:

> *Next Sunday, 14 December, vocal and instrumental concert in the Salon Chinois, given by M. N. Coste, guitarist, assisted by the gentlemen amateurs of the Société Philharmonique of this city.*[100]

On December 10 in the same paper the time of the start time half past six in the evening is mentioned, and also that:

> *M. Coste will leave nothing undone to give the public a brilliant and dignified evening. Subscriptions are being taken by M. Boucher in the Rue Viéwarde.*[101]

Then on December 17 the review of the concert follows. Not a word on Coste, therein, instead the piece talks about the youth of both sexes who enjoyed themselves at the end of the evening with some quadrilles, but:

> *at the last bow it became dark. There was no lack of gas, as we are not at the level of new inventions yet, but it appeared that the oil lamps were simply extinguished at the order of ... the Chinese manager. He wants, is said, to punish the subscribers because there were so few of them. We do not think, however, that this is a way to have more flourishing concerts in the future.*[102]

After this concert Coste leaves this provincial town to pursue his artistic fortune in Paris, the city that is at the threshold of great developments in musical life. He is not the only one.

---

[98] Coste-Schult, 17 IV 1875: 'Longtemps avant en 1828 j'avais eu des relations en province avec Sagrini (à Valenciennes). Nous exécutons en public les grandes variations de Giuliani (35) J'y eus un très grand succès, parce que l'on ne me connaissait pas et que Sagrini arrivait précédé d'une grande réputation. Sagrini avait une brillante exécution et un beau son. Mais à l'époque où Sagrini donnait déjà des concerts dans toutes les capitales de l'Europe, je ne savais pas que je serais un jour guitariste.'

[99] Coste-Hallberg, 29 IV 1881: 'Jusqu'à l'age de 24 ans j'ai joué toute la musique de cet auteur. Je n'en connaissait pas meilleur alors, et aussitôt que la musique de Sor est tombée entre mes mains, j'ai pu juger du vide et de la pauvreté qui existe dans l'oeuvre de Giuliani.'

[100] *Petites Affiches*, Valenciennes: 7e Année, 6 XII 1828, no. 734, p. 480: 'Dimanche 14 décembre prochain, concert vocal et instrumental au Salon Chinois, donné par M. N. Coste, guitariste, aidé de MM. les amateurs de la Société philharmonique de cette ville.'

[101] *Petites Affiches*, Valenciennes: 7e Année, 10 XII 1828, no. 735, p. 486: 'Le Sr. Coste ne négligera rien pour rendre cette soirée brillante et digne d'être offerte au public. [...] On souscrit chez Sr. Boucher, rue de la Viewarde.'

[102] *Petites Affiches*, Valenciennes: 7e Année, 17 XII 1828, no. 737, p. 495: 'au dernier coup d'archet on s'est trouvé dans les ténèbres. Ce n'est pas que le gaz ait manqué, car nous ne sommes pas encore au niveau des nouvelles inventions, mais il parait qu'on avait tout simplement soufflé les quinquets, en vertu *d'ordres superieurs*, provenenant de l'administration.......... *chinoise*. On veut, dit-on, punir de ce que les signataires pour les redoutes n'ont pas été nombreux. Nous ne pensons pas que ce soit le moyen de rendre pour l'avenir les concerts bien florissans [sic].'

19 Valenciennes, Place d'Armes, 2007

Intermezzo I

In the past the guitar was a poor instrument, meant to accompany the singing of a romance or an ariëtte with some plucking. Since then the works of several distinguished artists have given it a greater importance in music, but in this endeavor no one has succeeded in making use of as many resources as M. Sor.[103]

INFRASTRUCTURE

Not only did the French Revolution upend the entire social status quo in France, it also is of importance to musical life in Paris, which had been dominated by the nobility. After 1789 it becomes increasingly structured and as regards contents also becomes subject to regulation by the new revolutionary state. After the revolution every person is equal to the law and titles of nobility vested by birth are abolished. However, in his *Code civil* of 1814 Napoléon Bonaparte states that some people may earn such a title by merit. As a result some 3,200 people receive titles of nobility, only 22.5% of them from the old nobility, a fact that makes the return to royalism impossible.[104] The influence of the Revolution clears the way to fast growth in public concert life. Private concert life is in the hands of the upperclass consisting of industrialists and practitioners of free professions, but of some of the nobility too. The new difference between light and serious music that comes into existence, brings citizens and aristocracy together in matters of musical taste, crossing boundaries of social class.[105]

When Coste arrives in Paris, at the end of 1828 or the beginning of 1829, the city is on the threshold of great developments. After the Restoration of 1814 Charles X rules France from 1824, but he gives way to Louis-Philippe I in the Revolution of July 1830. Coste writes a song on that subject, and Carulli also composes a guitar piece on 'Les Trois Glorieuses' [the three days of glory], the name under which this event entered history. The city then is far from being modelled by Baron Haussmann's radical changes, which take place between 1852 and 1870, and it still has the moderate suburban size in the center.[106] But by 1846 the population has grown from around 750,000 inhabitants to 1 million citizens. Moreover, there are many developments in infrastructure that change the daily life of the Parisians dramatically. Transport of passengers still is by diligence (public stagecoach) under the monopoly of Caillard. The omnibus appears in 1828 with 100 carriages for 14 passengers at 25c per seat for everyone. Paris has to wait until 1835 for its first railway station West; until 1846 the city has three railway stations only, Saint Lazare, Montparnasse and Jardin des Plantes. The Gare du Nord is opened in 1846, whereafter Gare de Lyon and Gare de l'Est follow in 1849, the last in Coste's neighborhood. At the end of 1828 Napoléon Coste will have travelled from Valenciennes to Paris by diligence. Traffic in the city always is difficult, with carriages, wheelbarrows, and pedestrians crowding each other out. The roads are paved with cobblestones until 1800, when Rambuteau replaces them by 'macadam', crushed stone. Water is supplied by canals and the Seine or drawn from wells. The food supply is arranged at the famous Halles and many marketplaces. For defense the city is surrounded by many walls, almost making Paris a prison: 'Le mur murant Paris rend Paris murmurant' [the wall that walls about Paris makes Paris murmur].

---

[103] *Revue musicale de Paris*, tome I, mars 1827, p. 124: 'La guitare était autrefois un pauvre instrument destiné à soutenir par quelques harpèges le chant d'une romance ou d'une ariette. Les travaux de plusieurs artistes distingués lui ont donné depuis une plus grande importance dans la musique; mais personne n'a su trouver autant de ressources que M. Sor.'

[104] Johnson, James H.: *Listening in Paris: a cultural history*, Berkeley, University of Berkeley Press, 1995, p. 229.

[105] Weber, William: *Music and the Middle Class, The Social Structure of Concert Life in London, Paris and Vienna between 1830 and 1848*, Ashgate, Aldershot, 1975, 2nd ed. 2004, p. 80-86; Weber, William: *The Great Transformation of Musical Taste*, Cambridge, Cambridge University Press, 2008, p. 90-91.

[106] Gaillard, Jeanne: *Paris, la ville, 1852-1870, l'urbanisme Parisien à l'heure d'Haussman...*[sic], Paris, Honoré Champion, 1977, p. 47-48.

20 Les Trois Jours, Carulli

To send letters and packages, a service often used by Coste for his correspondence, under the Restoration there are 205 postal boxes connected to eight post offices, apart from the central office, with five deliveries a day in winter and six in summer. In 1804 there are five telegraph offices.[107] The news of the world and the musical tidings from the many cities of Europe can reach the newspapers in Paris this way, as there are *Le Courrier français, Le Constitutionel, La Gazette de France, Journal des Débats, La Quotidienne, L'Universel, Le Correspondant, Le Figaro, Le National*, papers which also have a place for the musical critiques of Castil-Blaze, Sévelinges, Soulié, Miel, d'Ortigue and Berlioz.[108] On the other hand news from Paris can reach Valenciennes as well, where the local journal *Petites Affiches*, from 1829 on *L'Echo de la Frontière* features news items as well, such as a report on April 1, 1829 of one of Coste's concerts. In 1820 Castil-Blaze starts with his first regular column of musical reviews in the *Journal des Débats*.[109] Fétis launches the *Revue musicale* in February 1827, specialized in music, and edits it almost completely on his own until 1833, when he is appointed as the first director of the Brussels conservatory.[110] The infrastructure for communication and information is used intensively and undergoes great developments, as well as in musical life.

Musical life

During the years of the Revolution and the Directoire, 1789-1799, the Première République from 1792 on, a number of changes in musical life is established. Instruments from emigrants are sold or even destroyed in churches, trade is in decline, some entrepreneurs leave Paris, like piano manufacturer Érard, who flees to England, but returns in 1795.[111] Convents, abbeys, churches and chapels are

---

[107] Hillairet, Jacques: *Dictionnaire historique des rues de Paris*, Paris, Les Éditions de Minuit, 1963-1972, p. 29, 9-45.
[108] Lesure, François: *La musique à Paris en 1830-1831*, Paris, Bibliothèque Natonale, 1983, p. 8; Devriès-Lesure, Anik: 'Historical Sources', in: Rasch, Rudolf, ed.: *Music Publishing in Europe 1600-1900*, Berlin, Berliner Wissenschafts-Verlag, 2005, p. 54.
[109] Pistone, Danièle: *La musique en France de la Révolution à 1900*, Paris, Honoré Champion, 1979, p. 15-19.
[110] Liebaars, Herman: *François-Joseph Fétis en het muziekleven van zijn tijd*, Brussel, Koninklijke Bibliotheek, 1972, p. XXIVXXV.
[111] Pistone, Danièle: *La musique en France de la Révolution à 1900*, Paris, Honoré Champion, 1979, p. 10-11; Place, A. de: 'Érard', in: Fauquet, Joël-Marie: *Dictionnaire de la Musique en France au XIXe siècle*, Paris, Fayard, 2003, p. 429.

closed,[112] with which the musical education of the youth disappears. Musical education, mostly in the hands of the church before, is now democratized, especially with the foundation of the Conservatoire on the 16th of Thermidor Year III, which corresponds to August 3, 1795, and also with the profession of teacher in music that comes into existence for that purpose. Here, as regards content, a debate arises into the matter of teaching folk repertoire. Intellectual liberalism prevails, the Conservatoire should be occupied with training of the musical elite. Here the question is – in sociological terms – a conflict between the 'values of the community' which advocate the democratization of the arts, and the 'values of the individual' which give privilege to excellence, the elite, the rarity. These opposing opinions both have influence in Paris in the beginning of the 19th century, in musical periodicals, in institutes, in salons, in concert halls.

21 Salon Herz

The Conservatoire prefers excellence, the Orphéon of Wilhem the peoples education, from 1837 on.[113] There is a priority for music in the open air, music for the people, the short musical form and military music, which did not flourish that much before. Composers' rights are protected in 1791, after 1810 even for a period of ten years after they have died. Theatres, which were under a strict system of privilege, become free, and many new ones are founded, until the privilege system is reintroduced. As a result of the departure of the nobility, not only does musical taste change, but beneficence comes to an end. Musicians are no longer supported or favored by the nobility, they are obliged to turn to take on pupils to make a living. At the time of the Monarchy of July after 1830 the influence of the *bourgeoisie* is increasing, including on musical taste, and there is a growth in orchestral music. The many changes also give rise to nostalgia for the music of the past. Napoléon Bonaparte, during the years of the Consulat and the Empire (1799-1814) wants to make Paris to the capital of the artistic world and he has a preference for Italian music which he patronizes, as is shown by the growth and significance of the Théâtre-Italien. German music is not that well liked in general, it is not of great importance, except in instrumental music. Liszt has to commit himself to the music of Schubert, for instance, which becomes very popular afterwards, especially his songs. During the Restoration (1814-1830) Louis XVIII and Charles X do not interfere that much with musical life. As an instrument, the piano becomes more and more important and has its triumphs in the salons. Cherubini even is worried about the many piano players in the Conservatoire. The word 'piano-forte' falls out of use around 1820, and in 1822 Érard,

---

[112] Hillairet, Jacques: *Dictionnaire historique des rues de Paris*, Paris, Les Éditions de Minuit, 1963-1972, p. 10.
[113] Gumplowicz, Philippe: 'Le rêve et la mission. La musique et le peuple en France 1789-1848', in: Bödeker, Hans Erich, Patrice Veit et Michael Werner, ed.: *Les sociétés de musique en Europe 1700-1900*, Berlin, Berliner Wissenschafts Verlag, 2007, p. 384-386.

who has returned to Paris, invents the 'double-échappement'. Liszt arrives in Paris in 1823 and gives his first concert in the Théâtre-Italien on March 7, 1824. The opera enjoys a supreme reign in this period. Napoléon Bonaparte struck up the Italian taste in music, whereby the Italian opera flourished. After a great career in Italy, Rossini arrives in Paris, first in 1822 and then in 1824, where the public adores him in the Théâtre-Italien, the Opéra and the Académie Royale de Musique. His opera *Le Comte d'Ory* has its opening performance in 1828, *Guillaume Tell* in 1829.[114] Rossini has great influence and other Italian composers, such as Bellini and Donizetti take advantage of that as a consequence. Berlioz also is active in this period. In 1826 he takes lessons in composition at the Conservatoire with Lesueur and counterpoint and harmony with Reicha. The literary influence of Walter Scott on Berlioz is noticed by 1828 already in *Waverley*; the *Symphonie Fantastique* follows in 1830. Before, Scott's great poem *The Lady of the Lake* from 1810 is taken by Rossini for his opera *La Donne del Lago*. In 1819 Schubert dedicates a song cycle to it in 1825 with the famous *Ave Maria* in Ellen Douglas's hymn from the third canto, a song published by Coste in 1835 with guitar accompaniment. *The Bride of Lammermoor* from 1819 is set to music by Donizetti in 1835 as *Lucia di Lamermoor* [sic, Italian], to which Coste devotes his *Divertissement* opus 9 in 1841. Scott's *Ivanhoe* appears in 1820 and its heroicism resonates in Coste's *Le Tournoi* opus 15 in 1843.[115] With these historic novels Scott advocates the Romantic desire for the greatness of history, where in particular he models the action around real people in real places. Adolescents, who until then made a grand tour as a finale to their education, now travel to the Trossachs in Scotland, where *The Lady of the Lake* is situated. Scott's novels, in translation by Defauconpret, are most popular in France in this period. They mean an immense success for this illustrious author.[116]

INSTITUTIONS

Several institutions put their mark on musical life in Paris. Since 1795 the Conservatoire trains students to be instrumentalists, vocalists or composers. They are educated in counterpoint, harmony, solfeggio, singing and recitation; in 1822 there are 59 teachers and 317 students for the instruments piano, organ, harp, strings and wind-instruments, but not for guitar, a reality that has important consequences for the position of this instrument.[117] The institute is established in the rue du Faubourg Poissonnière no. 11, the street where publishers Richault and Schonenberger, important for Coste, are also located. La salle Chantereine, 'très jolie', built in 1817, organizes soirées and concerts, but after 1821 is forbidden to stage drama because of the presumed competition with the Opéra-Comique. It continues with concerts for pupils. Concerts are also given in the *salle* in the Rue de Cléry. The Société, founded in 1799, is already active before; the season includes eight concerts, a season-ticket is 48 fr. for gentlemen and 36 fr. for ladies. The *Gymnase musical*, founded in 1827 by the painter and amateur flutist Jean-Louis Decourcelle, offers programs with song, piano and other instruments, sometimes even small orchestras, conducted by Tilmant. In 1828 it moves to the salle Molière and gets permission to continue its activities in the salle St-Jean of the Hôtel de Ville, with the purpose of expanding public attention. Coste plays there in his first concert in Paris.[118] Then there are the large institutes for the theatre public, such as the Opéra-Comique, the Théâtre-Italien, the Société philharmonique, the Théâtre du Vaudeville and the Théâtre des Variétés, which, as a rule, focused on opera, symphony, ballet, or vaudeville and other entertainment. In the Théâtre de l'Opéra the ballet *Cendrillon*, based on music

---

[114] Gossett, Philip: 'Rossini, Gioachino', in: Sadie, Stanley ed.: *The New Grove Dictionary of Music and Musicians*, London, Macmillan, 1980, vol. 16, p. 238-239; id. in: Sadie, Stanley, ed.: *The New Grove Dictionary of Music and Musicians*, second edition, London, Macmillan, 2001, vol. 21, p. 748-751.

[115] MacDonald, Hugh: 'Hector Berlioz', in: Sadie, Stanley ed.: *The New Grove Dictionary of Music and Musicians*, London, Macmillan, 1980, vol. 2, p. 580-585, 602-603; id. in: Sadie, Stanley, ed.: *The New Grove Dictionary of Music and Musicians*, second edition, London, Macmillan, 2001, vol. 2, p. 384-385, 389.

[116] *Revue de Paris*, vol. VI, tome 11, novembre 1834, p. 319: 'Le Walter Scott de M. Defauconpret, [...] obtient un immense succès.'

[117] Pierre, Constant: *Le Conservatoire national de musique et de déclamation: documents historiques et administratifs*, Paris, Imprimerie nationale, 1900, p. 420.

[118] Lesure, François: *La musique à Paris en 1830-1831*, Paris, Bibliothèque nationale, 1983, p. 115; *L' Echo de la Frontière*, Valenciennes, 1829, 8e Année, merc. 1 IV 1829, no. 767; Fauquet, Joël-Marie: 'Gymnase musical', in: Fauquet, Joël-Marie: *Dictionnaire de la Musique en France au XIXe siècle*, Paris, Fayard, 2003, p. 551-552.

by Fernando Sor, is performed for years.[119] The democratization of the public comes to expression in Veron's approach in the Opéra. During the short period of his appointment – four years – he implements thorough and lasting changes. When he enters the institute as the new director in 1830 he immediately starts to popularize the Opéra. He invests capital, takes a high risk, but knows precisely what to do to interest the bourgeois audience, which wants to spend money on the opera by attending performances. He changes the programming, lowers the admission prices, tickets are even sold in the streets, and he renovates the interior to attract a more penny-wise and less ostentatious audience. The boxes lose their function putting members of the audience on display by darkening the hall and the adjusted way it is lit. Véron appoints the so-called claqueurs. Guided by Auguste Levoisseur, who attends rehearsals and studies the musical score, it is their task to give the right sort of applause at the right time in the performance of an opera, just like a tightly managed regiment of clappers and cheerers, to enhance the success of an opera with the public, a phenomenon which even Berlioz reports. So, Véron aims at the *juste milieu*, that can no longer be republican or royalist after the July-Revolution and his approach contributes to the popularization of the opera as well as the public.[120]

CONCERT WORLD

The public concert in the first half of the 19th century is a relatively new phenomenon. Between 1813 and 1848 a rapid expansion in number and importance can be observed. The kind of audience that takes part in musical life is influenced by movements in the social structure in Paris. The boundaries between different classes become weaker in this period. The Revolution brings a sharp discontinuity in the social roles of the middle class and in the composition of its members. The newness of the group poses great uncertainties for its members both economically and socially and it creates a sharp competitive atmosphere among them. After the Revolution of 1830 the nobility withdraws from political and social life outside its own ranks.[121] Between 1806 and 1815 the Conservatoire organizes the 'exercices publiques', conducted by Habeneck. The 'Arrêté ministériel' of February 15, 1828, signed by Vicomte de La Rochefoucauld, prescribes that students at the Conservatoire give six public performances a year. Together with Cherubini, the director of the Conservatoire, Habeneck, who is conductor of the orchestra of the Opéra from 1821 to 1824, founds the Société des Concerts du Conservatoire, with an orchestra of 88 instrumentalists and a choir of 79 vocalists. The concerts take place in the new hall with 1,078 seats which is built in 1806 in the area of the Menus-Plaisirs, today the Rue du Conservatoire. They give programs with great symphonic works, solo concerts, opera and oratoria of 'old' composers such as Bach, Haendel, Rameau, Haydn, Mozart and Beethoven. Along with that, a canonization of orchestral works gradually takes place from these programs, and reviews of them in musical periodicals adopt the term 'classical music'. Later, the contemporaries Berlioz, Meyerbeer, Mendelssohn and Bellini are adopted. The Société offers a flowering concert practice to soloists and virtuosi like the violinists Tilmant, Girard, Dancla, flutist Dorus and bass player Bottesini.[122]

Especially from 1820 on the most important piano manufacturers, such as the Érard brothers, are going to organize concerts in their salons for the promotion of their instruments, and in doing so they contribute to the development of the concert practice in Paris. They stand between the private salons and the public in the theatre. Fétis writes in 1828:

For some time now our most renowned piano manufacturers have adopted the custom of putting on musical soirées by invitation, which allows them to have their instruments heard, as played by the most gifted pianists.[123]

---

[119] Dell'Ara, Mario: 'La chitarra a Parigi negli anni 1830-1831', in: *Il Fronimo*, Milano, Suvini Zerboni, XVI, no. 63, apr. 1988, p. 19.
[120] Johnson, James H.: *Listening in Paris: a cultural history*, Berkeley, University of Berkeley Press, 1995, p. 240-247.
[121] Weber, William: *Music and the Middle Class, The Social Structure of Concert Life in London, Paris and Vienna between 1830 and 1848*, Ashgate, Aldershot, 1975, 2nd ed. 2004, p. 3,15.
[122] Dandelot, A.: *La Société des Concerts du Conservatoire de 1828 à 1897*, Paris, Delagrave, 1923, p. 1-9, 40-47.
[123] *Revue musicale de Paris*, tome III, jan. 1828, p. 40: 'Depuis quelque temps, nos facteurs de piano les plus renommés ont adopté l'usage de donner des soirées musicales par invitations, ce qui leur procure l'avantage de faire entendre leurs instrumens [sic] sous la main des pianistes les plus habiles.'

22 Berlioz in Cique Olympique, 1841

He points at Dietz's soirées, every Saturday evening, and there Fernando Sor performs a solo for guitar on January 29.[124] To mention some salons: in 1818 Érard holds two salons for a total of 300 people, in 1828 Pleyel has three salons for a total of 100 people and in 1838 Herz has a salle for 668 people, and there Coste plays 1840. The Pleyel Hall which is still famous even today, opens in 1838 with room for 700 people.[125] The halls are large for an instrument as small as the guitar. The public expects long, varied concerts. The number of concerts a year increases from 78 in 1827 to 373 in 1848.[126] A kind of standard program is developed, especially by Pierre Baillot, who was put on half salary by Véron as the first violinist of the Opéra, refused to accept this and started to become active in his own initiatives,[127] concerts in which opera pieces alternate with instrumental chamber music. These programs are an amicable collaboration of musicians who play in many different ensembles, alternating with solos, where many composers pass in revue. These are performances that last an entire afternoon or evening with many pieces and many genres. This eventually leads to a differentiation between the more popular music in café concerts, opera galas, promenade concerts and 'serious' Classical music with complete programs, the composer concert, the recital. It is a time when popular music is becoming distinct from the Classical music.[128] The concerts organized by institutions are mostly given in series,

---

[124] *Revue musicale de Paris*, tome III, jan. 1828, p. 40: '[...] solo de guitare, Sor.'
[125] Schnapper, Laure: 'Le rôle des facteurs de piano', in: Bödeker, Hans Erich, Patrice Veit et Michael Werner, *Organisateurs et formes d'organisation du concert en Europe 1700-1920*, Berlin, Berliner Wissenschafts Verlag, 2008, p. 245-250; Fauquet, Joël-Marie: 'salle de concert', in: Fauquet, Joël-Marie: *Dictionnaire de la Musique en France au XIXe siècle*, Paris, Fayard, 2003, p. 1113.
[126] Weber, William: *Music and the Middle Class, The Social Structure of Concert Life in London, Paris and Vienna between 1830 and 1848*, Ashgate, Aldershot, 1975, 2nd ed. 2004, p. 19-20, 42, 111.
[127] *Gazette musicale de Paris*, vol. II, no. 35, 30 VIII 1835, p. 286.
[128] Weber, William: *The Great Transformation of Musical Taste*, Cambridge, Cambridge University Press, 2008, p. 5, 118, 123, 130-133, 144, 148, 167.

Intermezzo I   31

where 'loose' concerts, organized by composers or the performing artist himself, have a mixed content, with additional players and family, teachers, pupils, sponsors of acquaintances as the audience. In the salons the musical taste is determined by the owner of the room, who organizes the concert at home. In these benefit-concerts the money collected goes to the musicians.[129] In this way three types of concerts can be distinguished. The first is the benefit-concert which is mostly organized by a participating musician to support himself. The audience consists mainly of pupils or acquaintances for whom he has played previously in a salon. The second type is the concert given by an organization of professional musicians, orchestras or ensembles, examples of which have been outlined above. Here the audience consists of listeners who have subscribed for a whole season, selected by the organization itself. The third type is the presentation of amateur musical organizations, musicians who play before family and friends. Still there is a difference between concerts with high status and low status. The salons of the nobility lose their importance, while the popular music, freed from the aristocratic dominance, now is liable to the commercialism of the middle-class. The program suits the taste of the host or hostess, and, of course, that of those invited.[130] In the void of musical taste and leadership the Concert du Conservatoire blossoms in the 1820s with Habeneck as a conductor. The 1,100 subscribers for the eight yearly concerts are probably selected by their influence and social class, an example of the high-status concert. The history of the low-status concert during the 1830s shows the modernization of the musical life even more than that of the high-status concert. The origin lies in household music-making, singing in the tavern, playing in an ensemble or singing in a choir, all this in a low degree of organization and negligible commercial intent. The admission is cheap and attracts a public that cannot afford to attend a high-status concert. The resources of this development lie in the enormous public it can potentially reach, the robust amateur music activity – along with the demand for musical training – and in the rising level of income and standard of living among this public.[131]

PUBLIC CONVENTION

The convention of the public also is going to change. Whereas music in the 18th century was played to the greater glory of the nobility, which put itself on grand display during the 'concert', made conversation with others, gave comment, or presented musicians to a smaller circle and interfered with the program, the bourgeois audience seats itself properly on chairs, and when the lights go out it listens attentively and in silence to the music performed. Turning out the lights is made possible with the new invention of the gaslight; candles cannot be extinguished and lighted again all together, apart from the regiment of servants that would be necessary to do so. In 1837 Liszt is one of the first to draw full attention to himself and to the music in a darkened hall in his performance of the *Sonata quasi una fantasia* opus 27 no. 2 by Beethoven, better known as the 'Mondschein sonate'. The effect is enormous, now the musician's person is subject to admiration by the public. In this Romantic experience the visitors are expected to be on time. In some cases they arrive hours early to secure a good seat, as in the Concert des Amateurs. They are not allowed to go in and out anymore between parts of the program. The attention fully is directed at the platform[132] This phenomenon also can be psychologically explained by the newly risen bourgeois public's relative ignorance in music. This new type of audience prefers the security of a dark hall to being in the full light to share its knowledge on music with the other audience members.[133]

In this way a kind of intellectual attitude arises in the first half of the 19th century among critics, teachers and managers of concerts, which play an important role in the diffusion of musical values and the interpretation of the classics. The public is influenced by the higher intellectual authorities, such as

---

[129] Cooper, Jeffrey: *The rise of instrumental music and concert series in Paris, 1828-1871*, Ann Arbor, UMi Press, 1983, p. 85-87.
[130] Cooper, Jeffrey: *The rise of instrumental music and concert series in Paris, 1828-1871*, Ann Arbor, UMi Press, 1983, p. 86-87.
[131] Weber, William: *Music and the Middle Class, The Social Structure of Concert Life in London, Paris and Vienna between 1830 and 1848*, Ashgate, Aldershot, 1975, 2nd ed. 2004, p. 21-22, 55, 91, 99.
[132] Johnson, James H.: *Listening in Paris: a cultural history*, Berkeley, University of Berkeley Press, 1995, p. 200-203, 270.
[133] Johnson, James H.: *Listening in Paris, a cultural history*, Berkeley, University of Berkeley Press, 1995, p. 199, 203, 228, 240.

the virtuoso, the critic, and is guided in what it should think and feel by program notes. The traditional benefit-concert owes its existence to big changes that took place between 1815 and 1840. The travelling virtuoso and the local performer usually set up the same kind of event for their own advantage or disadvantage. They experiment with programming, which leads to a recreation of the conventional practice. The alternation of vocal and instrumental pieces and the balancing of genres changes in a more homogeneous practice. Some concerts are mainly dedicated to ballads, opera selections, classical works or pieces by a single composer, sometimes a pianist is the only performer. In the mixed concerts arrangements of opera-themes or opera selections are often played. In this period many tunes from opera are 'domesticated': to perform an opera a theatre is needed, with soloists, a choir and an orchestra. If a soloist wants to perform parts of an opera, piano accompaniment is more efficient, and thus operas are often followed by a flood of arrangements for solo voice and piano or guitar accompaniment also for use in domestic circles. Weber speaks about 'republicanization', making opera accessible to a wide audience that could not attend to opera performances.[134] The programming balances between serious and light taste, as an expression of the tension between idealism and commercialism. The institutional monopolies give way to a freer market in the 1830s. Commercialism has an influence on music itself.[135]

METHODS

In the development from the private to the public concert, the transition from the elitist concert to democratization, or 'republicanization' of music itself, the appearance of methods for the musical practice, the professional training and the amateur musician is central. As citizens have become a major factor in musical life, the government aims at the musical education of the people by founding several institutes, such as the Conservatoire and the Gymnase musical. Along with this, many methods for musical instruments are published – piano, violin, guitar – to make playing accessible for everyone. Naturally, music publishers play an important role here. Methods for instrumental and vocal tuition are a new phenomenon in this period and they play a different role for the guitar than for other instruments. In the beginning of the 19th century, dilettantism springs up, amateur musicians begin to play in domestic circles and they need repertoire and above all training to do so. For many instruments and singing, methods are published. Systematic didactics is elaborated in methods, for violin, by Rode, Baillot and Kreutzer for instance,[136] and for piano, by Adam, Czerny, Kalkbrenner, Hummel, Fétis, Clementi and Moschelès, who publish a variety of pedagogical treatises. The publication of methods, for other instruments as well, will say that a well-considered musical pedagogy is in question, where not only technical aspects of playing an instrument are the matter. The method also has to contribute to one's understanding of music. From the idea that musical notation is not all there is to say about music, training in playing an instrument must lead to the free flow of music, through association to sentiment. At the Conservatoire of Paris the piano method of Louis Adam is taught. This *Méthode de piano du Conservatoire* from 1805 deals with theory of music as well as technique of playing. A new aspect here is the expanded treatment of fingering, worked out in the new genre of the study. Adam's method is the first of more than a hundred methods to appear in the next forty years. The pedagogy also is applied by Liszt, Chopin and Thalberg, who do not write a method themselves, but do teach with it.[137] The systematization also leads to far-reaching adaptation of the instrumental didactics. Accessories are made for the hands to play the keyboard, such as the 'chiroplast' by Hummel, a board with supports for the hands that can move parallel to the keyboard, or the 'guidemains' by Kalkbrenner with which the fingers can move along the keys without load of the underarm. Mechanical aids are also developed for the guitar. In 1827 in Vienna a *Méthode* opus 1 by Beilner is published by Diabelli, in the preface

---

[134] Weber, William: *The Great Transformation of Musical Taste*, Cambridge University Press, Cambridge, 2008, p. 144.
[135] Weber, William: *The Great Transformation of Musical Taste*, Cambridge, Cambridge University Press, 2008, p. 101, 141.
[136] Penesco, Anne: 'Le violon en France au temps de Baillot et de Paganini', in: Bailbé [et al]: *La musique en France à l'époque romantique (1830-1870)*, Paris, Flammarion, 1991, p. 205.
[137] Blasius, Leslie David: 'The mechanics of sensation and the construction of the Romantic musical experience', in: Bent, Ian, ed.: *Music theory in the age of Romanticism*, Cambridge, Cambridge University Press, 1996, p. 9-11, 18-20.

of which it is explained how the strings should be plucked with metal thimbles placed on the tips of the right hand fingers.[138] These do resemble the 'fingerpicks' steel-string guitarists use nowadays to play their folk guitars, metal plectrums shaped like a fingertip. Much later, it is true, but still anecdotal enough to mention, is the eight string pedal-guitar with an adjustable capotasto, developed in 1848 by a certain Johann Knaffl-Lenz, used by Eduard Bayer (1822-1908)[139] as well as the guitar with adjustable frets by Lacôte in 1852, a very special instrument.[140] 1830 also is the year when Aguado plays with a special guitar support, not the 'tripodison' yet, but for the moment simply a kind of plank the guitarist sets on his chair to put the guitar on. He applies for a 'brevet d'invention' on May 18, 1830.[141] In 1832 he is spotted with it in a concert and in 1835 he designs his 'tripodison'.[142] There are many experiments in holding the guitar, such as the one of Sor, who placed the guitar on the side of a table. He rejects the way the French and the Italians put the guitar on their left leg.[143]

Guitar

Along with the systematization of the instrumental didactics for piano, violin and other musical instruments is the development of didactics for the guitar, but there is an important difference. In France between 1758 and 1857 some 130 methods for guitar are published, among them that of Coste-Sor in 1851. Apart from a single one all of these are published in Paris, which attests to the popularity of the guitar in that city. In 1825 already De Marescot notices that 'there probably is no other instrument for which as many methods have been published as the guitar.'[144]

In the first thirty years of the 19th century the guitar enjoys unprecedented popularity in all of Europe, during the period where Giuliani, Carulli, Aguado, Sor and many others of the 'classic generation' are at the peak of their career.

23 Giuliani   24 Carulli   25 Aguado   26 Sor

The large number of methods for the guitar can probably be explained by the absence of an official and standardized method, as exists for the instruments that are taught at the Conservatoire in Paris. Those methods, of which the last appears in 1814, are authorized in that way and dominate the market in Paris for years. As guitar is not taught at the Conservatoire, an authorized method exists and every

---

[138] Bellow, Alexander: *The Illustrated History of the Guitar*, New York, Colombo, 1970, p. 154; Zuth, Josef: *Handbuch der Laute und Gitarre*, Wien, Doblinger, 1926-28, repr. Hildesheim, Olms, 1978, p. 33.

[139] Bellow, Alexander: *The Illustrated History of the Guitar*, New York, Colombo, 1970, p. 154; Zuth, Josef: *Handbuch der Laute und Gitarre*, Wien, Doblinger, 1926-28, repr. Hildesheim, Olms, 1978, p. 31-32.

[140] Ribouillault, Danielle: 'La "Guitaromanie": du salon à la salle de concert', in: *Instrumentistes et Luthiers Parisiens*, Florence Gétreau, red., Paris, La Ville de paris, 1988, p. 184-186; Lesure, François (préface): *Guitares, Chefs-d'oeuvre des collections de France*, Paris, La Flûte de Pan, 1980, p. 137, 314.

[141] Lesure, François: *La musique à Paris en 1830-1831*, Paris, Bibliothèque nationale, 1983, p. 355.

[142] *Revue Musicale de Paris*, VIme année, no. 7, 17 III 1832, p. 54: '[...] M. Aguado [...] mécanisme simple [...]'; Ledhuy, Adolphe & Henri Bertini: *Encyclopédie pittoresque de la musique...*, Paris, Delloye, 1835, Tome II 123-127, Tripodison Aguado; Ribouillault, Danielle: *La technique de guitare en France dans la première moitié du XIXe siècle*, thèse musicologie, Paris, Sorbonne, 1980, p. 81-83.

[143] Sor, Fernando: *Méthode pour La Guitare*, L'Auteur, Paris, 1830, repr. Genève, Minkoff, 1981, p. 11-12, Pl. II Fig. 7, Pl. III Fig. 8.

[144] Stenstadvold, Erik: *An Annotated Bibliography of Guitar Methods, 1760-1860*, Organologia: Musical Instruments and Performance Practice no. 4, London, Pendragon Press, 2010, p. xi.

ambitious guitarist publishes a method of his own. In the second half of the 18th century the guitar is already popular in Paris, and when Carulli arrives in 1808 it rises to a popularity previously unknown and in the years that follow the number of guitar music publications grows to a great extent. The appearance of guitar methods follows this wave of popularity, some 15 new ones in the first ten years of the century, and the same in the next ten years , and that number is nearly tripled to 50 in the twenties. In the thirties again some 15 methods are published, followed by only six in the forties. In no other country did so many methods appear.[145] The methods for guitar published in Paris start with Merchi in 1761 going up to Doisy in 1801, as predecessors of the great methods that appear thereafter. In the first half of the 19th century the last method for five-string guitar is published, as a part of the de *Nouvelle Méthode pour la Lyre ou Guitare à cinq et six cordes* by Aubert in 1810-13. This means that the six-string guitar has replaced its five-string counterpart completely, and that all methods are written for six-string guitar now, which coincides with the appearance of the lyre-guitar.

  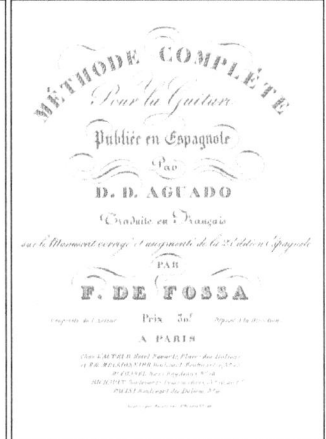 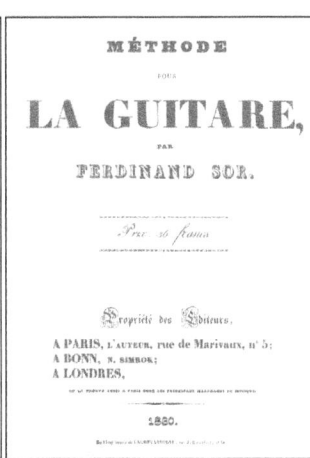

27 Méthode Giuliani, 1812   28 Méthode Carulli, 1825   29 Méthode Aguado, 1826   30 Méthode Sor, 1830

The many methods in this period, including those of Bédard, Gatayes, Lemoine, Lintant, Vidal and Doisy, just to mention some of the better-known ones, all concern several aspects of the playing technique, scales, arpeggio's, chords, whereby theory and practice are mixed, just as the methods for piano do, and different genres and all kinds of keys are discussed.

Notation in tablature gradually disappears; it develops from mixed tablature/mensural to solely mensural. In 1814 Sor makes an attempt to introduce the mensural notation at the actual pitch for guitar in his *Fantaisie* opus 7, but guitar music remains standardly notated an octave higher on a single staff.

31 Sor opus 7 ed. Pleyel 1814   32 Sor opus 7 ed. Oxford Guitar Music 1974

Then Carulli's methods appear, six different ones from 1809 to 1825, Molino comes out with eight editions from 1813 to 1840 and Aguado comes out with six in Paris from 1825 to 1846. Sor publishes his method in 1830, Carcassi in 1836, Giuliani's *Studio* appear in Vienna in 1812. The great methods are more expanded, they are concerned more in position and technique, again with a mixture of theory and practice, but aim at a much higher level of playing. The old-fashioned emphasis on the accompaniment of singing shifts to autonomous guitar playing. The disagreement between Carulli and Molino concerns Carulli's use of the left thumb for some bass notes and Molino's playing of the right

---

[145] Stenstadvold, Erik: *An Annotated Bibliography of Guitar Methods, 1760-1860*, Organologia: Musical Instruments and Performance Practice no. 4, London, Pendragon Press, 2010, p. xi-xiii, 3-6.

ring finger on the first string, as well as his advice to use a ribbon during the first months.[146] Apart from the almost complete treatise in methods in the first half of the 19th century, concerning many different playing techniques for scales, chords, arpeggios, barré, ornaments, tremolo, campanella, legatos, timbre, vibrato, sound effects and imitating other instruments, the mensural notation becomes more accurate. In 1875 Coste writes in retrospective that he arrived in Paris in 1830 and made the acquaintance of guitarists there:

When I arrived in Paris in 1830, Sor was the most distinguished [guitarist], followed by Aguado (played with his fingernails), Carcassi, Molino, Carulli (already old) and many others of a lesser order. Later came Legnani (played brilliantly), the young Regondi, who I forgot had some very big successes around 1838.[147]

33 Carcassi

That last year is not reviewed in the press of the time, but Regondi's concerts in 1830 and 1831 are. Coste is aware of the Parisian guitarists and notes that Aguado played with his nails, something he himself did not do at the time. In 1877 he notes of Carcassi:

Carcassi has also composed some rather pretty pieces, a bit incorrect, but brilliant and gracious.[148]

And later that year he adds:

I have met Carcassi, he was above all a talented performer who gets a beautiful sound out of the guitar. His compositions are light, but they are rather graceful and brilliant. They only lack depth, and the harmony is a bit neglected in them.[149]

Coste does not think very highly of Carcassi as a composer, but he does appreciate him as a guitarist.

On February 19, 1831 Fétis writes a review in his *Revue musicale* of Sor's *Méthode* and he takes the opportunity to publish an essay on the guitar in Paris. He writes as follows:

In the past the guitar was an instrument for accompaniment by amateurs of the lowest degree; [...] that's why what are called Méthodes de guitare in the last twenty-five or thirty years did not come any further than some elementary rules and exercises and that the rest in these methods only had small pieces that could serve the pupils as studies. This is the way that methods of Vidal, Pollet, Lintant, Lemoine and Doisy were written. Towards 1808 Carulli settled in Paris and he let hear things on the guitar that seemed to belong to a completely new art. I remember that his playing caused a very lively sensation among the artists, and that Dussek, who heard him at a certain occasion, took his hand and said: Monsieur, you are an extraordinary man. Carulli intended to spread his findings in France and to elevate the guitar to the rank of harmony instruments, but from the beginning he was opposed, because his way to approach and treat the guitar went too far in comparison with that of all other teachers of this instrument. Everything he wrote was found too difficult; editors of music did not dare to publish his work. [...] Nevertheless, while Carulli awoke the French guitarists from their apathy, in which they had languished before him, other guitarists,

---

[146] Carulli, Ferdinando: *Méthode complète* opus 241, 5e ed., Paris, Carl, 1825, repr. Genève, Minkoff, 1987, p. 6-7; Molino, François: *Grande Méthode Complète*, op. 33, Paris, Lemoine, Richaut [sic], ca 1823, p. 15-17; Dell'Ara, Mario: 'Metodi e Trattati', in: *La Chitarra*, Ruggiero Chiesa, red., Torino, Edizioni di Torino, 1990, p. 243-248.

[147] Coste-Schult, 17 IV 1875: 'Lorsque je suis arrivé à Paris en 1830, Sor était le plus distingué, puis Aguado (jouant des ongles), Carcassi, Molino, Carulli (déjà vieux) et beaucoup d'autres d'un ordre inférieur. Plus tard Legnani (jeu très brillant), le jeune Regondi que j'oubliais a eu de très beaux succès vers 1838.'

[148] Coste-Hallberg, 7 II 1877: 'Carcassi aussi a composé d'assez jolis morceaux, un peu incorrects, mais brillants et gracieux.'

[149] Coste-Hallberg, 1 V 1877: 'J'ai connu Carcassi, c'était surtout un exécutant de talent tirant un beau son de la guitare. Ses compositions sont légèrs, mais elles ont de la grâce et du brillant. Seulement elles manquent de fond et l'harmonie y est un peu négligé.'

with great talent such as Moretti, Giuliani, Carcassi, two Spaniards named Aguado and Arailza and, in particular Fernando Sor, made an immense progress for the guitar, which necessitated a new explanation of their principles. Each of these masters has compiled his experience in [...] methods [...] with as the most important goal to improve the brilliance of the performance. As far as Sor is concerned, he followed another direction. Being convinced that the guitar is first and foremost a harmony instrument, [...] he thought is necessary to revise the basic principles of the art of playing the guitar completely. [...] this means that the thumb is put at the backside of the guitar, and that the hand is posed at the front, bent, in such a way that all intervals and all positions can be played. One can understand that even this starting point alone already results in principles different from those of other guitarists: these are the principles that M. Sor has revealed in his Méthode pour la guitare.[150]

With these words Fétis displays a clear vision of, and a bright outlook on the situation of the guitar in this period. After describing the contents of the method by chapters and its importance for the guitar technique, he concludes:

The work of M. Sor may seem to be too serious for amateurs who want to learn to play a poor romance or accompaniment of a chansonnette in a few days: but those who really want to play the instrument, with all its potentials, and above all the teachers, can find in here a thorough and new instruction. The success may possibly not be popular, but it will be durable.[151]

With this he shows that Sor takes new paths, which go beyond those of his contemporaries. This development is continued by Coste, who revises, expands and publishes the method of Sor in 1851.

Publishers

Until 1830 most publishers are located in the 2nd and 3rd (nowadays 2nd, 3rd and 10th) arrondissement, around the rue de St-Eustache. Most music shops are in the neighborhood of the rue St-Honoré and are going to settle near the great boulevards, des Italiens, Montmartre and Poissonnière, where theatres, cafés, stores and bookshops draw a large public. Here also is the Opéra, the Opéra-Comique, the Théâtre-Italien, the Théâtre du Vaudeville, the Théâtre des Variétés. The Conservatoire de Musique is not far. The major publishing houses like Richault, Schonenberger, Challiot and Lemoine as well as less important ones such as Escudier, Latte, Colombier and Girod, are established in this *quartier*, publishers where Coste will later issue his works.[152] Richault, very important for Coste in his early period, started in 1805 and is located in the boulevard Poissonnière 16 from 1825 to 1841 and publishes

---

[150] *Revue musicale de Paris*, Vme année, no. 2, 12 II 1831, p. 12-13: 'La guitare était autrefois l'instrument d'accompagnement des amateurs du dernier ordre; [...] de là vient que ce qu'on appelait des *Méthodes de guitare*, il y a vingt-cinq ou trente ans, ne contenait qu'un petit nombre de préceptes et d'exemples élémentaires, et que le reste de ces méthodes était rempli de petits morceaux pour servir d'études aux élèves. C'est ainsi qu'étaient faites les méthodes de Vidal, de Pollet, de Lintant, de Lemoine et de Doisy. Vers 1808, M. Carulli vint se fixer à Paris, et fit entendre sur la guitare des choses qui parurent alors appartenir à un art tout nouveau. Je me souviens que son exécution fit parmi les artistes une assez vive sensation, et que Dussck [sic], l'entendant un jour, lui dit en lui prenant la main: *Monsieur, vous êtes un homme extraordinaire*. M. Carulli avait l'intention de propager ses découvertes en France, et d'élever la guitare au rang des instrumens [sic] d'harmonie; mais dès les premiers pas, il fut arrêté, parce qu'il y avait trop loin de sa manière de considérer et de traiter la guitare à celle de tous les autres professeurs de l'instrument. Tout ce qu'il écrivait était trouvé trop difficile; les marchands de musique n'osaient se charger de ses ouvrages. [...] Cependant, tandis que M. Carulli faisait sortir les guitaristes français de l'apathie où ils avaient langui jusqu'à lui, d'autres artistes d'un talent fort remarquable, tels que Moretti, Giuliani, Carcassi, deux espagnols nommés Aguado et Arailza et, dans un genre tout particulier, Ferdinand Sor, faisaient faire à la guitare d'immenses progrès qui exigeaient des exposés nouveaux de leurs principes. Chacun de ces maîtres a résumé ses recherches dans des [...] *Méthodes*; [...] dont l'objet principal est d'augmenter le brillant de l'exécution. Quant à M. Sor, il suivait une autre direction. Convaincu que la guitare est surtout un instrument d'harmonie, [...] il lui semblait nécessaire de refaire en entier les primiers principes de l'art de jouer de la guitare. [...] ce fut que le pouce qu'il appuye sur le dos de la guitare, et dès lors toute la main se trouva portée en avant et arrondie, de manière à pouvoir saisir tous les intervalles et toutes les positions. On conçoit que de ce seul préliminaire découlent des principes tous différens [sic] de ceux des autres guitaristes: ce sont ces principes que M. Sor vient d'exposer dans sa *Méthode pour la guitare*.'

[151] *Revue musicale de Paris*, Vme année, no. 2, 12 II 1831, p.13: 'L'ouvrage de M. Sor paraîtra peut-être trop sérieux aux amateurs qui veulent apprendre en quelques jours à jouer à peu près un maigre accompagnement de romance ou de chansonnette; mais ceux qui se proposeront de jouer réellement de l'instrument, avec toutes ses ressources, et surtout les professeurs, y trouveront une source d'instruction solide et neuve. Le succès pourra n'être pas populaire, mais il sera durable.'

[152] Devriès, Anik & François Lesure: *Dictionnaire des éditeurs de musique français*, vol. II, de 1820, Genève, Minkoff, 1979, p. 14-17.

eight works of Coste there.[153] The number of publishing houses greatly increases in the following years. Music publishing is about to flourish, partly due to the invention of the steam-press, which makes a production on a larger scale possible.[154] The sales of sheet music often go by way of subscription, where the buyer can get up to 50% discount. In Aguado's *Méthode* is a list of subscribers, which includes guitar teachers in and outside Paris, and even the publisher Richault.[155] Additionally the customer can contribute to the publisher's 'société', like that of Schlesinger in 1834, the 'Société pour la publication de musique classique à bon marché', and can get a discount to titles on a list with a moderate subscription rate. Some publishers are also composer, like Lemoine. Others are luthier, such as Challiot, who also makes harps and pianos.[156]

Many titles are published by the composer himself, *chez l'auteur* with his address on it, if not with the communication 'Chez tous les Marchands de Musique' and the price, for instance with *Fantaisie Armide* by Coste opus 4, prix 4.f 50.c. Of all 53 compositions by Coste 15 are self-published, 32 appear with other publishers ad 9 remain unpublished; some opus numbers belong together, while other are later separated in a, b and c. In this matter it can be noticed that only in 1891 is an 'Agence française du Copyright' founded in Paris, after the signing of the Bern convention in 1886: copyright did not exist in Coste's lifetime.[157]

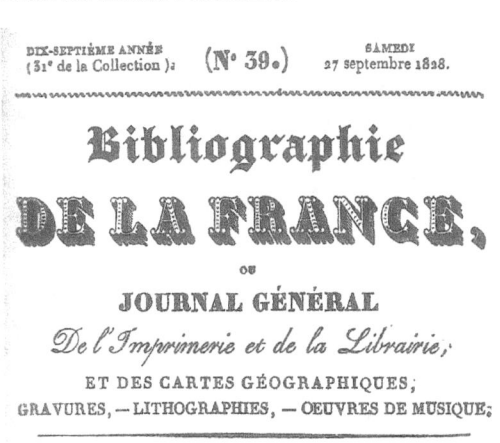

34 Bibliographie de la France, 1828

In 1828 the *Bibliographie de la France, ou journal général de l'imprimerie et de la librairie* reports an inscription for six new works for guitar by Sor, his *Douze Etudes* op. 29 are available for 9 fr. and his complete works for 48 fr. with Meissonnier, boulevard Montmartre, n. 25. The periodical *Bibliographie de la France* already appears from 1812 on, weekly on Saturdays, with records and reviews of French and translated literature and engravings. At the back there is a survey of new published music by editors or *chez l'auteur*. Digging in this periodical resulted in a precise date of the publication of nine works by Coste. The development of music editing can be followed in this magazine, which grows from a 16-page brochure with successive items in 1828 in to a 24-page booklet with advertisements and an overview of the contents. Here it is notable that the lists of published music become even longer and is eventually classed by genre and instrument. There are many chansons with guitar accompaniment, along with quadrilles and contredanses and titles like 'Regrets', 'Montagnard' and 'Le Départ', Coste definitely is not the only one to use these titles. Sor is present in some regularity with publications of his own. Sagrini turns up in September 1828 with two *Variations brillantes*;[158] he may have gone to Paris after his concert with Coste on February 28 in Valenciennes, to give concerts there and to

---

[153] Devriès, Anik & François Lesure: *Dictionnaire des éditeurs de musique français*, vol. II, de 1820, Genève, Minkoff, 1979, p. 274-282, 394-398; Hopkinson, Cecil: *A Dictionary of Parisian Music Publishers 1700-1950*, London, 1954, p. 66-68, 80-81, 104, 110.

[154] Weber, William: *Music and the Middle Class, The Social Structure of Concert Life in London, Paris and Vienna between 1830 and 1848*, Ashgate, Aldershot, 1975, 2nd ed. 2004, p. 20.

[155] Aguado, Dionisio: *Méthode Complète Pour la Guitare... Traduite en Français... par F. de Fossa*, Paris, Meissonnier, 1826, repr. Genève, Minkoff, 1980.

[156] Devriès, Anik & François Lesure: *Dictionnaire des éditeurs de musique français*, vol. II, de 1820, Genève, Minkoff, 1979, p. 98, 277.

[157] Devriès, Anik & François Lesure: *Dictionnaire des éditeurs de musique français*, vol. II, de 1820, Genève, Minkoff, 1979, p. 18.

[158] *Bibliographie de la France*, Paris, vol. XVI, no. 38, 20 IX 1828, p. 704: 'A Paris, chez Troupenas, rue de Ménars, n. 3. Variations brillantes sur un thème allemand, pour guitare, par Sagrini; Variantions brillantes sur un air de Rossini, pour guitare, par Sagrini Prix 3-75.'

make contact with the publisher. Little is known about his life. In 1829 several *methods, romances, valses, fantaisies, variations*, a *boléro* appear.

Then on November 21 *La Guitaromanie* appears by Charles de Marescot with six lovely – and comical – engravings of guitar life, which became most famous.[159]

35 La Guitaromanie, Montoux, 1829

Publishers also are going to publish special musical magazines: Romagnesi started his *L'Abeille musicale* in 1828, filled mainly with his own compositions, and Meissonnier *Le Troubadour des salons* in 1830, with guitar accompaniments and pieces for guitar. Others follow in this period, such as Massimino with *La Galerie musicale*, Troupenas with *La Mélodie, nouveau journal de chant*, Egrefeuille with *Le Dilettante*, and Chaulieu/Delacour with *Le Pianiste*, journals which do not last very long, especially intended to promote sheet music sales. That is not the case with L'Henry who started *Le Ménestrel* in 1833, which is continued by Meissonnier/Heugel, up to 1940. An important source of information on musical life in Paris, as far as magazines specialized in music are concerned, is the keynote *Revue musicale*, founded in 1827 by François Fétis, which joined Schlesinger's *Gazette musicale* in 1835, which started in 1834, into the *Revue et Gazette musicale de Paris*, published by Schlesinger until 1880.[160] The many magazines, now and later, show a great development in music publishing.

Press

The most important founders of the musical criticism in Paris beyond any doubt are Castil-Blaze and Fétis. The first writes in the *Journal des Débats*, but in there not a word on the guitar is to be found. The latter writes in the *Revue Musicale*, alongside his work as a teacher in composition since 1821

---

[159] *Bibliographie de la France*, Paris, vol. XVI, 1828 p. 231: 'Oeuvre XXIX. Douze études,Sor; p. 533: 'Deus quadrilles [...] Desvergnes', p. 643: 'Trois pièces [...] Sor'; p. 688: 'Ving-quatre exercices [...] Sor; p. 704: 'Variations brillantes [...] Sagrini'; p. 736: Méthode de guitare [...] Heu'; vol. XVII, 1829, p. 16: 'Méthode complète et extrèmement simplifiée pour la guitare [...] chez Richault'; p. 135: 'Deux quadrilles [...] Magnien', p. 356: 'Nouvelle méthode pour la guitare [...] Lemaire'; p. 608: 'Grand boléro [...] Croze'; p. 792: 'La guitaromanie, pas Marescot, oeuvre 46. Prix 12-0'; Marescot, Charles de: *La Guitaromanie*, Paris, chez l'auteur, 1829, repr. Firenze, Studio per Edizioni Scelte.

[160] Devriès, Anik & François Lesure: *Dictionnaire des éditeurs de musique français*, vol. II, de 1820, Genève, Minkoff, 1979, p. 310-312, 372-373; Ellis, Katharine: *Music criticism in nineteenth-century France: La revue et gazette musicale de Paris 1834-80*, Cambridge, Cambridge University Press, 1995, p. 33, 45-46; Fauquet, Joël-Marie: *Dictionnaire de la Musique en France au XIXe siècle*, Paris, Fayard, 2003, p. 1061-1063.

Intermezzo I

and as a librarian since 1826 at the Conservatoire.[161] Fétis is characterized as an intellectual and an ambitious critic and the influence of his work upon the French musical criticism is enormous in every aspect. He elevates the historical musicology to a higher level, as Castil-Blaze does with the opera criticism. To Fétis the culmination of musical art is Mozart, but he also loves renaissance and baroque music, especially of Bach, a love which comes to expression in the *Concerts historiques* he organizes and for which he was frequently criticized. The first of these concerts could not take place because the Société des Concerts opposed it.[162] He tries again a month later, then Sor plays in it, and in 1835 Aguado plays the lute![163] Anyhow, there was just a small audience in that concert in the Théâtre-Italien.[164] In the opinion of Fétis the past is a source of truth and renewal, inspired by the official philosophy of eclecticism during the Restoration: the new comes from a synthesis of the good things produced in the past. The origin of Fétis's antipathy to programmatic music is, in his opinion, that this was nothing more that the revival of the old ideas of imitation.[165] In Fétis's time the term 'classic' for old music generates the canonization of composers of from the past. Music by contemporaries becomes 'Romantic' and along with this the term 'popular' rises to designate music for everyone, which also includes opera. The public becomes fractioned in a group with knowledge of, and insight into 'difficult' music, as instrumental music is, and another group with a tendency towards entertainment.[166]

36 Revue musicale, 1827 37 Le Ménestrel, 1838 38 Gazette musicale, 1835 39 Revue et Gazette musicale, 1852

Fétis's opinion on the guitar as an instrument varies. He praises Sor's method, but criticizes his instrument, whose sound is underdeveloped in comparison to Joseph Anelli, a guitarist who lived in Paris from 1813 to 1815, 'who produces good sounds of a quality that exceeds everything he has heard before.'[167] In the hands of Sor the guitar has too little a sound, does not sound full enough, and later Sor produces a bad sound again from his instrument. 'It is a pity that he devotes his talent to such a bad instrument!'[168] On the other hand, other guitarists are praised; the cause might be in Sor's fingertip technique opposed to the nail technique used by the others.

---

[161] Liebaars, Herman: *François-Joseph Fétis en het muziekleven van zijn tijd*, Brussel, Koninklijke Bibliotheek, 1972, p, XII.
[162] *Revue musicale de Paris*, VIIme année, no. 2, sam. 9 II 1833, p. 12: 'concerts historiques de M. Fétis'; no. 3, sam. 16 II 1833, p. 21: Lle concert historique [...]'.
[163] *Revue musicale de Paris*, VIIme année, no. 8, lun. 25 III 1833, p. 60: '[...] concert historique [...] Sor'; IXme année, no. 15, dim.12 IV 1835, p. 116-117: 'Concert historique [...] Aguado luth [...]'.
[164] *Gazette musicale de Paris*,vol. II, no. 16, 19 IV 1835, p. 139: 'Le premier concert prétendu historique de M. Fétis, avait attiré fort peu de monde au Théâtre-Italien.'
[165] Ellis, Katharine: *Music criticism in nineteenth-century France: La revue et gazette musicale de Paris 1834-80*, Cambridge, Cambridge University Press, 1995, p. 33-36, 43-45.
[166] Johnson, James H.: *Listening in Paris: a cultural history*, Berkeley, University of Berkeley Press, 1995, p. 199-201.
[167] Sparks, Paul: 'The origins of the classical guitar' in: James Tyler and Paul Sparks: *The guitar and its music*, Oxford, Oxford University Press, 2002, p. 248-249.
[168] *Revue musicale de Paris*, tome III, 1828, p. 40: '[...] instrument trop peu sonore [...]'; p. 304: 'Sor a du talent [...] mauvais son'; tome VII, vol. I, 3 IV 1830, p. 267: '[...] instrument ingrat!.'

INSTRUMENTS

France's economic growth during the Napoleonic wars also has advantages for musical instrument manufacturers. In addition to 24 piano factories in 1805 there are 34 makers of string and plucked instruments, including guitars and still 30 makers of other musical instruments. Luthiers making plucked and bowed instruments outnumber makers of keyboard instruments, which also can be the expression of the musical taste in this period, where the piano pushed aside the cembalo. The guitar, in 1800 still regarded as a pre-eminent accompanying instrument, is gradually falling in disuse. In 1830 this situation is reversed: now there are 90 piano manufacturers as compared to 39 makers of string and plucked instruments, in a total of 288 instrument makers, a proportion also observed in the participation in the Expositions nationales. In 1800 an ordinary piano sells for 1000 fr. and a guitar for 35 fr. These are considerable prices compared to the salary of an agricultural laborer, who earns about 300 fr. a year.[169] A metronome even is more expensive than a guitar, costing 100 fr.; in Paris the device is taken in production by Maelzel, following the example of Winkel in Amsterdam in 1815.[170] The prescription of metronome numbers is not used by the classical guitar composers; Mertz and Zani de Ferranti do not apply these either, sticking to the familiar Italian and French terms for tempo and character. Coste indicates metronome numbers only in opus 50 in 1879 and opus 51 in 1880.

The democratization of prices of musical instruments starts with the July Monarchy, in parallel with the popularization of music and the aforementioned production of cheap sheet music by Schlesinger, for instance. In his essay 'Sur l'industrie musicale' in his *Revue musicale* of December 25, 1830 and January 1, 1831, Fétis draws a distinction between the direct musical industry such as manufacturers of pianos and bowed instruments divided in 25 professions, and the indirect musical industry such as suppliers of materials divided in 22 professions. Apart from insight in economics he gives a survey in numbers, with which he creates a reasonably clear image of this aspect of musical life in Paris.[171] In later articles on other subjects Fétis approaches his vision of musical life systematically too. The manufacturers of large musical instruments such as harps and pianos are located in Paris and innovate their production process, also thanks to the steam engine, in contrast with the constructors of bowed and plucked instruments, who are located mostly outside Paris – in Mirecourt in the Vosges – who

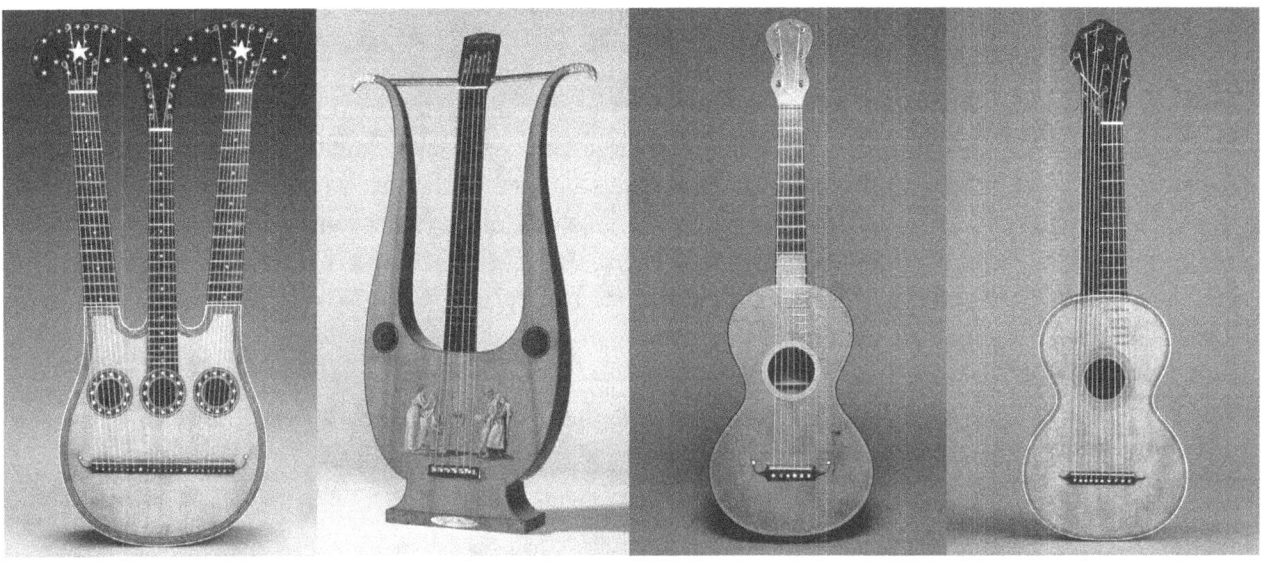

40 Harpolyre, Salomon, 1830   41 Lyre-guitare, Pleyel, 1809   42 Grobert, Paris, 1830   43 Dedacorde, Lacôte, 1830

---

[169] Chevallier, Émile: *Les salaires au XIXe siècle*, Paris, Hachette, 1887, p. 33.
[170] Richardson, E.G.: 'Metronome' in: Sadie, Stanley ed.: *The New Grove Dictionary of Music and Musicians*, London, Macmillan, 1980, vol.12, p. 222-223.
[171] *Revue musicale de Paris,* tome IV, 25 XII 1830, 1 I 1831: 'De l'industrie musicale.'

are not much concerned with industrial innovations.¹⁷² For the guitar the introduction of chlorine to bleach the sheep gut, which improves the sound, is important.¹⁷³

Technical changes in the construction of the guitar also take place in this period around 1830, such as Salomon's harpolyre. Pleyel makes a lyreguitar, Grobert makes a guitar with a larger resonance box, which is signed by both Paganini and Berlioz.¹⁷⁴ Lacôte already makes guitars and is very successful at expositions. He develops a decachord guitar in 1826.¹⁷⁵ Other luthiers working in Paris, like Fontaine, Franck, Husson, Lacoux and Levien are less well known.¹⁷⁶ Aguado first has his 'porte-guitare' which he first uses demonstrably in 1832 and again, somewhat later, his tripodison, to support the instrument.

Guitar mania

Paris is such an attractive city to guitarists, that it can be called the capital of the guitar in this period. Many settle here and pursue activities as soloists, composers, publishers and teachers. Sor is the first of these to be mentioned. He arrives in Paris in 1813, stays there until 1815 and leaves for London, where he writes the music for the ballet *Cendrillon* in 1822, which also is performed in 1823 in Paris and Brussels. In 1824 the ballet goes to Moscow, where he and his new spouse, prima ballerina Félicité Hullin, travel to. Then he goes to Berlin, Warsaw and St. Petersburg and returns to Paris in 1826/27, where *Cendrillon* in a choreography of Decombe still is performed in the Opéra, playing up to 1830 as a great success with 104 performances.¹⁷⁷ Together with his brother Charles (Carlos) he is named as a composer in Gardeton's *Almanach de la Musique* in 1819.¹⁷⁸ Like many other guitarist-composers Sor plays the piano, as can be seen in his original works and transcriptions for the instrument and accompaniments of chansons. Jeffery reports this playing the piano in connection with his promotion to lieutenant.¹⁷⁹ The technique of Sor's playing with fingertips may have something to do with this; long fingernails are difficult in playing the piano. If so, the dilemma concerning this aspect of guitar-playing with or without nails would be solved. Emilio Pujol sticks to the aesthetic choice for a certain quality of sound, and mentions that even a convinced nail-player like Aguado¹⁸⁰ is persuaded by Sor and tries to play without fingernails for a while.¹⁸¹ Apart from Sor, Pujol mentions Carcassi and Meissonnier as a fingertip-player and they both play the piano.¹⁸² Carcassi himself even declares in his method opus 59 that the contact of the fingernails with the string must be avoided.¹⁸³ Coste may also have played with short nails, but nothing is known about that. The issue of the nails is discussed extensively by Ribouillault, who gives a survey of the different right hand techniques in methods in the first half of the 19th century, the use of the ring finger, whether or not the little finger should be on the soundboard and the fingertip or fingernail technique.¹⁸⁴ The situation remains unclear, for sure.

---

172 Haine, Malou: 'Les facteurs d'instruments de musique à l'époque romantique' in: Bailbé, Joseph Marc: *La musique en France à l'"epoque romantique (1830-1870)*, Paris, Flammarion, 1991, p.108.
173 Haine, Malou: *Les facteurs d'instruments de musique à Paris au 19ᵉ siècle des artisans face à l'industrialisation*, Bruxelles, ed. Université de Bruxelles, 1985, p. 21-24, 47-48, 52-58, 65-92.
174 *Revue musicale de Paris*, tome VI, 1830, p. 277-279: 'Harpolyre, nouvelle guitare, inventé par Salomon'; VIme année no. 7, 17 III 1832, p. 54: 'Aguado [...] mécanisme simple'; Ribouillault, Danielle: 'La "Guitaromanie": du salon à la salle de concert', in: *Instrumentistes et Luthiers Parisiens*, Florence Gétreau, red., Paris, La Ville de Paris, 1988, p. 171-194.
175 Pierre, Constant: *Les Facteurs d'instruments de musique*, Paris, Sagot, 1893, p. 275.
176 Dell'Ara, Mario: 'La chitarra a Parigi negli anni 1830-1831', in: *Il Fronimo*, Milano, Suvini Zerboni, vol. XVI, no. 63, apr. 1988, p. 24.
177 Lajarte, Théodore de: *Bibliothèque Musicale du Théatre de l'Opéra*, Paris, Librairie des Bibliophiles, 1878, vol. 2, p. 104; Sinier, Daniel & Françoise de Ridder: *La Guitare, Paris 1650-1950*, Torino, Il Salabue, 2007, p. 40-49.
178 Gardeton, César: *Annales de la musique ou almanach musical pour l'an 1819 et 1820*, Paris, 1819, repr. Genève, Minkoff, 1978, p. 101.
179 Jeffery, Brian: *Fernando Sor, Composer and Guitarist*, London, Tecla, 1977; second edition 1994, p. 3, 33-37, 87, 170-186.
180 Aguado, Dionisio: *Méthode Complète Pour la Guitare... Traduite en Français... par F. de Fossa*, Paris, Meissonnier, 1826, repr. Genève, Minkoff, 1980, p. 4, no 21.
181 Aguado, Dionisio in: Jeffery, Brian: *The Complete Works for Guitar... Dionisio Aguado*, facsimile edition, Chanterelle, Heidelberg, 1994, p. 60 [146] n. 1.
182 Pujol, Emilio: *El dilema del sonido en la guitarra*, Buenos Aires, Ricordi, 1960, p. 42-47.
183 Carcassi, Matteo: *Méthode Complète op.59*, Paris, Carli, 1825, repr. Genève, Minkoff, 1988, p. 8.
184 Ribouillault, Danielle: *La technique de guitare en France dans la première moitié du XIXe siècle*, thèse musicologie, Paris, Sorbonne, 1980, p.125-141.

44 Discussion, Montoux, 1829

Other guitarists and composers in Paris, who are mentioned by Gardeton in his *Annales* of 1819-1820, include Carcassi, Carulli and Molino.[185] Molino's pedagogical activities are extensive and he is quite a rival to Carulli, as attested by the quarrel between the two musicians' followers in sources of the time, illustrated in picture and music in *La Guitaromanie* from 1829 by De Marescot.[186] Apart from the 'musicomanie' in Valenciennes there is the 'guitaromanie' in Paris. The cause of this *discussion*, here formulated here in greater detail, might lie in the difference in playing method and technique. Molino still works with a ribbon on the guitar, as with the baroque guitar, but does not use the left thumb to press the strings, as Carulli still does in 1823.[187] Molino has a way to determine the position of the left hand that Carulli rejects. Also he wants to hold the right hand still while the right little finger rests on the soundboard and only the fingers can move, a thing that Carulli thinks has a negative influence on the sound.[188] Even the model of the guitar even seems to be part of this controversy.[189] Dionisio Aguado comes to Paris around 1826, where he stays at Hôtel Favart at the Place des Italiens, where Sor also stays in the adjacent room from 1827 on. They become great friends.[190] Aguado's method is published 1826 in a translation in French by De Fossa.[191] They mutually dedicate works to each other and they also play duets in concerts. Matteo Carcassi is in Paris since 1820. His activities are giving

---

[185] Gardeton, César: *Annales de la musique ou almanach musical pour l'an 1819 et 1820*, Paris, 1819, repr. Genève, Minkoff, 1978, p. 52-55.

[186] Marescot, Charles de: *La Guitaromanie*, Paris, 1829, p. 3, 33. [BF no. 47, 21 XI 1829 p. 792]; Molino, François: *Grande méthode complète*, op.33, Paris, c. 1823, p. 16.

[187] Carulli, Ferdinando: *Méthode complète* opus 241, 5ᵉ ed., Paris, Carl, 1825, repr. Genève, Minkoff, 1987, p. 6-7; Molino, François: *Grande Méthode Complète*, op. 33, Paris, Lemoine, Richaut [sic], ca 1823, p. 15-17; Dell'Ara, Mario: 'Metodi e Trattati', in: *La Chitarra*, Ruggiero Chiesa, red., Torino, Edizioni di Torino, 1990, p. 243-248.

[188] Dell'Ara, Mario: 'Luigi, Valentino e Francesco Molino' in: *Il Fronimo*, Miano, Suvini Zerboni, no. 50, 1985, p. 32; Dell'Ara, Mario: 'Metodi e Trattati', in: *La Chitarra*, Ruggiero Chiesa red., Torino, Edizioni di Torino, 1990, p. 245-248; Ribouillault, Danielle: *La technique de guitare en France dans la première moitié du XIXe siècle*, thèse musicologie, Paris, Sorbonne, 1980, p. 70, 73, 89, 91, 100, 123, 140, 161; Ribouillault, Danielle: 'La "Guitaromanie": du salon à la salle de concert', in: *Instrumentistes et Luthiers Parisiens*, Florence Gétreau, red., Paris, La Ville de Paris, 1988, p. 179-183.

[189] Sinier, Daniel & Françoise de Ridder: *La Guitare, Paris 1650-1950*, Torino, Il Salabue, 2007, p. 58-60; Molino, François: *Grande méthode complète*, op.33, Paris, c. 1823, pl. 13.

[190] Jeffery, Brian: *Dionisio Aguado*, biography and bibliography, Heidelberg, Chanterelle, 1994, p. xv-xvi; Jeffery, Brian: *Fernando Sor, Composer and Guitarist*, London, Tecla, 1977; second edition 1994, p. 92-93, 104.

[191] Aguado, Dionisio: *Méthode Complète Pour la Guitare... Traduite en Français... par F. de Fossa*, Paris, Meissonnier, 1826, repr. Genève, Minkoff, 1980.

Intermezzo I

concerts and lessons, with a then already old-fashioned technique, with the right little finger resting on the soundboard, which hinders the mobility of the hand.

On the historicity of the pitch to which the guitar is tuned, the following remarks can be made. In the Opéra in Paris the standard pitch in 1810 is a'=423 Hz; it rises to a'=431-437 Hz in 1822, after which the singers, who really think this is too high, succeed in lowering it to a'=425-428 Hz. In 1830 the pitch is back to a'=430-438 Hz and it keeps rising. Finally, in 1859 the pitch is definitive fixed at a'=435 Hz to be the 'diapason normal' of the Lissajous-Halévy committee in the international congress in Paris. This even has the status of a law and legally approved tuning forks are distributed.[192] The meaning of this for the interpretation of the music of Coste and others is that the guitar must be tuned in the pitch of a'=435 Hz. The Romantic style, as it develops in music in Paris, is reflected in the guitar music of Napoléon Coste. The guitar plays a modest role in musical life, but Paris sparkles with musical activity, when Napoléon Coste arrives there at the end of 1828 or the beginning of 1829 and first settles in rue Bleue no. 28, then in rue du [Vieux] Colombier no. 25. In this musical life he has to earn a reputation for himself.

45 Rue Bleue, street sign, 2007

---

[192] Rhodes, J.J.K. & W.R. Thomas: 'Pitch class' in: Sadie, Stanley ed.: *The New Grove Dictionary of Music and Musicians*, London, Macmillan, 1980. vol.14, p. 785; Lloyd, Llewelyn: 'Pitch', in: Sadie, Stanley, ed.: *The New Grove Dictionary of Music and Musicians*, second edition, London, Macmillan, 2001, vol. 19, p. 799-800; Ribouillault, Danielle: *La technique de guitare en France dans la première moitié du XIXe siècle*, thèse musicologie, Paris, Sorbonne, 1980, p. 56.

IV
Aux Parisiens

In the province the guitar often is the instrument of the intimate music. The great progress it has made, prove that talented artists do not cease to be engaged with it. M. Coste walks with dignity in the tracks of the famous guitarists. He is distinguished by his excellent style, pure and with crisp. It is a very sublime musical sentiment that the guitar imputes him, and, in this respect, he has much in common with Sor: he approaches him as a performing artist and as a composer.[193]

CONTACTS 1829

Paris is a sparkling city, full of musical activities, when young Napoléon Coste, as an onrushing guitar talent, arrives there at the turn of the year 1828-1829, and settles in the rue Bleue no. 28. This street begins at the rue du Faubourg-Poissonnière no. 67 and ends at the rue La Fayette no. 72 in the 9th arrondissement of Paris. At the time it is 250 meters long and 10 meters wide. Rue Bleue is a continuation of the rue du Paradis and is therefore also called 'rue de l'Enfer.' Much later, in 1859 the rue La Fayette is widened, for which the last houses of rue Bleue had to give way, among them no. 28.[194] In 1818 Fétis lives in an apartment in rue Bleue no. 18 and in 1830 the office of the *Revue musicale de Paris* is located there, almost next to Coste's address.[195]

The Conservatoire in the rue du Faubourg Poissonnière no. 11 is around the corner, where Coste, according to a note on the title page of the issue, played his *Le Tournoi* opus 15, and his *Fantaisie 'Norma'* opus 16, but by then he already lives in the rue de l'Échiquier.[196] Richault, who publishes the first works of Coste, opus 2, 3, 5 and 7, is located at no.16. This publisher remains important to Coste, editing another ten works by him later.[197] According to Planque's *Agenda musical* in 1836 Coste lives in rue Bleue no. 28 as a *professeur de guitare*, which is curious because he lives in the rue du Vieux-Colombier no. 25 from 1832 on. Did Planque made a mistake, or has he copied old information? In this almanac Coste is in the company of Castellacci, Carulli, Huerta, Ledhuy, a party where the names of Aguado, Carcassi, Molino and Sor are strikingly missing. Lacôte is active as a luthier in the rue de Louvois.[198] In the 1837 edition Planque is far more extensive: the list of guitar teachers there includes 25 gentlemen and 7 ladies, for piano that is 144 and 173, both sexes being neatly distinguished. He also gives an indication of prices of instruments; a Mirecourt guitar costs 20 to 40 fr., but a guitar can be hired for 3 to 10 fr. a month.[199] Coste settles in a district that is important for Parisian musical life. One might expect that the young man, once arrived in Paris, tries to make contacts, on the one hand with people he knows, musicians who came from Valenciennes to Paris such as the Tilmant brothers, violinist Lecointe and female singer Dorus-Gras, and on the other hand with established

---

[193] *Revue et Gazette musicale de Paris*, vol. V, no. 18, 6 V 1838, Nouvelles, p. 190: 'La guitare est souvent en province l'instrument de la musique intime. Les grands progrès qu'elle a faits attestent que d'habiles artistes n'ont pas cessé de s'en occuper. M. Coste marche dignement sur les traces des guitaristes célèbres. Ce qui le distingue, c'est un excellent style, pur, gracieux et nerveux; c'est un sentiment musical plus élevé que la guitare ne le suppose, et, à cet égard, il a beaucoup d'analogie avec Sor: il se rapproche de lui comme exécutant et comme compositeur.'

[194] Leconte, André, ed.: *Plan de Paris par Arrondissement*, Paris, 1977, p. 16. plan O7.

[195] Hillairet, Jacques: *Dictionnaire historique des rues de Paris*, Paris, Les Èditions de Minuit, 1963-1972, p. 9-45, plan 1808, p. 202; *Revue musicale*, tome I, vol. 7, no. 7, 1830.

[196] Gardeton, César: *Bibliographie musicale de la France et de l'étranger*, Paris, 1822, repr. Genève, Minkoff, 1978, p. 530: 'Conservatoire de musique [...] rue du faubourg Poissonnière n. 11'.

[197] Devriès, Anik & François Lesure: *Dictionnaire des éditeurs de musique français*, vol. II, De 1820, Genève, Minkoff, 1979, p. 365, 395.

[198] Planque: *Agenda musical pour l'année 1836*, Paris, 1836, repr. Genève, Minkoff, 1981, p. 63: 'Professeurs de guitare: Castellacci, Carulli, Coste, rue Bleue, 28, Huerta.'; p. 158: 'Luthiers: Lacote, r. de Louvois, 10'; p. 186: 'Guitare: Aguado, Carcassi, Carulli, Castellacci'; p. 265: 'Guitare: Aguado, Carcassi, Carulli, Castellacci, Piano: Chopin'.

[199] Planque: *Agenda musical...3e Annèe, 1837*, Paris, 1837, repr. Genève, Minkoff, 1981, p. 279: 'Guitares à six cordes, 60 fr., Les guitares communes de Mirecourt varient de prix de 20 à 40 fr.'; p. 285: 'Location (au mois): Guitare, de 3 à 10 fr.'

guitarists he knows by name, like Carcassi, Carulli, Molino, Sor, Aguado. Théophile Alexandre Tilmant (1799-1878), born in Valenciennes, is a little older than Coste and studies the violin in Paris at the Conservatoire with Kreutzer, taking first prize in 1819. His brother Alexandre Théophile Tilmant (1808-1880), somewhat younger than Coste, is a violoncellist. He also studies at the Conservatoire and wins first prize in 1829.[200] Coste plays in a concert on 10 April 1838 in the salons Duport with these two brothers, together with violinist Eugène Joseph Lecointe (1817-1889), and female singer d'Hennin, about whom no other information can be found.[201]

46 Boulevard Poissonnière

A source in Valenciennes proudly mentions that they radiate a certain light on their town of birth with their success.[202] Soprano Julie Dorus also comes from Valenciennes. She studies at the Conservatoire, takes first prize for singing in 1823, and is heard in several salons on a regular basis, in the company of her younger brother, flutist Vincent-Joseph Dorus, in concerts in which Sor takes part.[203] So there is a total of five musicians from Valenciennes who came to Paris before Coste, and he joins them in the mixed concerts of that period, but only demonstrably so in 1838. As for the guitarists who are active in Paris, Coste makes contacts with Carulli in any case, who dedicates his *Duo Concertant pour deux guitares composé et dédié à Monsieur Coste*, opus 328 to Coste in 1831,[204] and he plays with Sor in three concerts in 1838.[205] Sagrini, with whom Coste played in Valenciennes a short while ago, might be in Paris, but little is known on his course of life In Paris there is a certain circle of musical acquaintances and a club of guitarists to which Coste is connected, a starting point for his career.[206]

---

[200] Fauquet, J.-M.: 'Tilmant, Alexandre', 'Théophile', in: Fauquet, Joël-Marie: *Dictionnaire de la Musique en France au XIXe siècle*, Paris, Fayard, 2003, p. 1218-1219.

[201] Pierre, Constant: *Le Conservatoire national de musique et de déclamation: documents historiques et administratifs*, Paris, Imprimerie nationale, 1900, p. 792.

[202] *La France musicale,*; vol. I, no. 14, 1 IV 1838, p. 7: 'Tilmant [...] Lecointe', no. 16, 15 IV 1838, p. 5: 'Lecointe [...] d'Hennin'; *Mon Histoire*, Valenciennes, extrait de mon Histoire fonds Goube, 19 IV 1838, p. 198: 'reflètent quelqu'éclat sur leur ville natale.'

[203] Colas, D.: 'Dorus-Gras, Julie', in: Fauquet, Joël-Marie: *Dictionnaire de la Musique en France au XIXe siècle*, Paris, Fayard, 2003, p. 398; Pierre, Constant: *Le Conservatoire national de musique et de déclamation: documents historiques et administratifs*, Paris, Imprimerie nationale, 1900, p. 442; *Revue musicale de Paris*, tome VII, 1833, p. 60, tome IX, 1835 p. 62.

[204] Torta, Mario: *Catalogo tematico delle opere di Ferdinando Carulli*, Lucca, Libreria Musicale Italiana, 1993, p. 635-636.

[205] *Revue et Gazette musicale de Paris*, vol. V, no. 18, 6 V 1838, no. 18, Nouvelles, p. 190: 'M. Coste marche'; *La France musicale*, vol. I, no. 4, 21 I 1838, p. 6, Concert Mll. Sardi...Sor & Coste Hôtel-de-Ville; vol. I, no. 16, 15 IV 1838, p. 5-7, Soirée Musicale [10 IV 1838] de M. Nap. Coste... duo avec Sor; vol. I, no. 19, 29 IV 1838, p. 6-7, Concert Mlle Mazel huit jours... M. Sor et M. Coste.

[206] *Bibliographie de la France*, Paris, vol. XVI, no. 38, 20 IX 1828, p. 704: 'A Paris, chez Troupenas, rue de Ménars, n. 3. Variations brillantes sur un thème allemand, pour guitare, par Sagrini; Variantions brillantes sur un air de Rossini, pour guitare, par Sagrini Prix 3-75.'

IV — Aux Parisiens 47

The guitar regularly figures in the usual mixed concerts in this period, which are generally divided in a vocal part and an instrumental part. In those in 1828 Sor is often present. He plays, as is mentioned before, a 'solo for guitar' in the salon Dietz on Saturday, January 26. On Sunday, April 13 he plays in the hall in the rue de Cléry,

Sor has talent [...] but he produces a bad sound on the instrument,

a concert where Listz [sic Liszt] also performs. That same week he already executed a 'piece for guitar' in the salle de la rue Chantereine, here with Liszt too. On Wednesday, May 7 he performs in a program in the salon Dietz with pianist Sowinski and singer Panseron. And on Sunday, May 18 Sor gives his first 'benefit' concert in a 'really astonishing performance.'[207] That year the Schultz brothers from Vienna, the 13-year-old Léonard on the terz guitar and the 15-year-old Eduard on the piano, play a concerto by Giuliani and Hummel. This work was created in around 1818 in Vienna in a collaboration between the two composers, but was lost afterwards, according to Kroll.[208] It might not have concerned a 'concerto', but rather Giuliani and Hummel's *Grand potpourri national* opus 93, for guitar and piano, the only work of the two together that could be considered to be that 'concerto', let alone where a terz guitar is involved. That it really is a terz guitar is apparent from the review, which says 'it is as if a *capotasto* is placed at the third fret.'[209] As a matter of fact, the potpourri is very popular in this era, but later it is more and more reviled for that popularity, when the musical ideal of classical music is defined more precisely in the musical reviews.[210] In the press the young Léonard with his terz guitar in the Pape salons is called the *Ajax des guitaristes;* outstanding musicians often receive a name of honor. In 1828 seven mixed concerts can be found in Paris with the guitar in the program, which is not many, but not all concerts are mentioned in the press.[211] A survey of the concerts with guitar that are found in the magazines in this period has been added as an appendix. The instrument occupies a modest place in musical life, despite the popularity of the amateur playing of accompaniments to song, particularly. That role seems hard to break.

Debut 1829

On Friday, March 27 young Coste, as far as is known now, gives his first concert in Paris, in the Gymnase musical. He is supposed to be 22 years, but is actually 23, unless then already his year of birth was presumed to be 1806. *L'Écho de la Frontière* of Valenciennes, the continuation of *Petites Affiches*, proudly quotes the Parisian *L'Observateur des beaux-arts*:

The variations of his own composition he executed were performed with a perfect precision. The young guitarist in question here is M. Coste from Valenciennes.[212]

Whether by way of the telegraph or by post, apparently there is contact between Paris and his former hometown. The above citation aside, the *Observateur des beaux-arts* itself, in the writing of Gyot de Fère, is more extensive in its review of the concert:

---

[207] *Revue musicale de Paris*, 1828, tome III, jan. p. 40-41 'solo de guitare joué par M. Sor', p. 304 'M. Sor a du talent [...] tire un mauvais son de l'instrument., p. 303 'morceau pour la guitare par M. Sor;', p. 336: 'Sor', 402-403 exécution vraiment étonnante;'.
[208] *Revue musicale de Paris*, 1828, tome III, p. 142-143; Kroll, Mark: *Johann Nepomuk Hummel, A Musician's Life and World*, Maryland, The Scarecrow Press, 2007, p. 62-63, 122-123, 159; Zimmerschied, Dieter: *Thematisches Verzeichnis der Werke von Johann Nepomuk Hummel*, Hofheim am Taunus, 1971.
[209] Heck, Thomas Fitzsimmons: *Mauro Giuliani: Virtuoso Guitarist and Composer*, Columbus, Orphée, 1995, p. 81, 91, 208; Giuliani, Mauro in: Jeffery, Brian: *The Complete Works..Mauro Giuliani*, facsimile edition, Vol. I-XXXIX, London, Tecla editions, 1988, vol 34, opus 93, preface; *Revue musicale de Paris*, 1828, tome III, p. 156 'c'est comme si le *capodastre* était placé sur la troisième case.'
[210] Weber, William: *The Great Transformation of Musical Taste*, Cambridge, Cambridge University Press, 2008, p. 98.
[211] *Revue musicale de Paris*, 1828, tome III, p. 40-41, 142-143, 155-157, 302-305, 336, 402-403; Jeffery, Brian: 'Fernando Sor, concert performer', in: *Guitar Review*, New York, The Society of the Classic Guitar, vol. XXXIX, summer 1974, p. 9.
[212] *L'Echo de la Frontière*, Valenciennes, 8ᵉ année, 1 IV 1829 no. 767, p. 111: 'Les variations de sa composition qu'il a exécuté ont été rendues avec une précision parfaite. Le jeune guitariste don't il est ici question est M. *Coste*, de Valenciennes.'

47 Gymnase musical

The soirées at this Gymnase are sometimes very brilliant, they please most of all by the variety in talent that is notable time after time. In last Friday's presentation we heard a young guitar virtuoso, who was astonishing in the way he knew how to play this instrument, which seems to offer few possibilities. The variations of his own composition that he executed on the guitar were performed with a perfect precision, despite the very great difficulty of some parts. His execution is sometimes studious, brilliant and pure, and we believe that M. Costes [sic Coste], not even 22 years of age, will have great success in the development of his art.[213]

With this good review Coste has an excellent debut in Paris. The variations mentioned practically must be those of opus 2, *Variations et Finale sur un motif favori de la Famille Suisse de Weigl*, which is also confirmed by Coste's letter of December 21, 1876 to his friend Hallberg:

[...] the first thing I had engraved (variations on an air of the Swiss family op. 2) composed in 1829 earned me some amazing successes upon my arrival in Paris, notably at the concert of the famous pianist Moschelès, where I played it between the Bohrer brothers and the singer Malibran. Not that the piece is worth anything. I composed it without having the slightest notion of counterpoint. But I played it with a lot of imagination and spirit, and then at the time I was full of youthful illusions.[214]

Maria Félicité Malibran is a beautiful, passionate brunette with beautiful eyes and above all an unbelievable voice, who turns up the public and admirers, including even Zani de Ferranti, with ladies copying her hairstyle, young girls imitating her gestures, and even her way of speaking – an idol, but unfortunately no review can be found of such a concert in Fétis's *Revue musicale de Paris* in this period, the only magazine dedicated to music and concerts at the time, aside from the *L'Abeille musicale* of Romagnesi.[215] Female singer Maria Malibran goes to London in the autumn of 1829, the brothers Max and Antoine Bohrer arrive in Paris in 1830 and the reviews of the concerts of Ignaz Moschelès do not mention Coste or even a guitar in the program.[216] It is possible that Coste correctly remembers that he played in concerts with these famous musicians, but whether this occurred in a single concert is unlikely. Anyhow, Coste broadens his circle of musical contacts. His remark that he composed the work in 1829 could mean that the work came into existence in Paris, not earlier in Valenciennes, as was presumed before. In that case Coste might not have played his opus 2 *Variations et finale La Famille*

---

[213] *L'Observateur des beaux-arts*, vol. I, 29 III 1829, p. 419: '*Gymnase musical*. Les soirées de ce gymnase sont quelquefois très brillantes, et elles plaisent sur-tout par la variété des talens qui s'y font tout-à-tour remarquer. Dans la séance de vendredi dernier, nous y avons entendu un jeune virtuose guitariste, qui a étonné par le parti qu'il sait tirer de cet instrument, lequel semble offrir peu de ressources. Les variations de sa composition qu'il a exécutées sur la guitare, ont été rendues avec une précision parfaite, malgré la difficulté très grande de plusieurs traits. Son exécution est à-la-fois savante, brillante et pure; et nous croyons que M. Costes [sic], à peine âgé de 22 ans, obtiendra de grands succès, en cultivant son art.'

[214] Coste-Hallberg, 21 XII 1876: '[...] le premier que j'ai fait graver (variations sur un air de la famille suisse op. 2) composé 1829 m'a valus à mon arrivée à Paris des succès étonnants notamment au concert de célèbre pianiste Moschelès où je l'ai joué entre les frères Bohrer et la cantatrice Malibran. Et ce n'est pas parce que le morceau a de la valeur, je l'ai composé n'ayant aucune notion de contrepoint. Mais je le jouais avec beaucoup de verve et d'entrain; et puis j'avais alors toutes les illusions de la jeunesse.'

[215] Cruys, Marcus G.S. van de: *The life and times of Marco Aurelio Zani de Ferranti*, Wijnegem, Homunculus, 2005, p. 39.

[216] *Revue musicale de Paris*, 1828, 1e série, tome IV, vol. 4 - 1830, 2e série, tome I, vol. 7.

IV — *Aux Parisiens* 49

Suisse de Weigl in the concert on Saturday, March 24, 1827. Which work he did play, remains unclear, as does the question of whether he performs it in the Gymnase musical in Paris on March 27, 1829.

OPUS 2, *VARIATIONS ET FINALE LA FAMILLE SUISSE DE WEIGL* 1830

This work is first published by Romagnesi around 1830, and only later by Richault, as can be concluded from the high serial number on that edition.[217] The theme on which Coste bases his composition 'und Lust, umgaukeln mich Freude…' is from no.7 Cavatine of the opera *Die Schweizerfamilie* by Joseph Weigl (1766-1846). How Coste does call it a motif indeed; the melody begins much earlier, does it not, with the words 'Ich hüpse und singe, ich tanze und springe, und immer umgaukeln mich Freude…' and after that the theme enters in the middle of the phrase, the upbeat of measure 19.[218] In the Parisian version of this opera this motif is the same, and Zani de Ferranti takes this same element as a motif for his *Niaiserie* opus 21. Coste, however, adds a refrain to the theme, of which the melody is probably taken from measures 46-47 of the Cavatine. Weigl's opera has its premiere in Vienna in 1809 and is staged in Paris in 1827 in translation as *Emmeline* in the 'Théatre De D'Odéon' [sic].[219] Fétis covers it in the February issue of the *Revue musicale de Paris*:

> *Weigl's music seems tasteful enough to perform the work several times. […] The composers after Mozart followed his way, but Weigl only followed his own inspirations in everything he wrote. […] Today, people like long developments and almost all of Weigl's pieces are short. Furthermore, there must be a great value in the music of Weigl, because it resists the bad performance to which it is subjected in the Odéon.*[220]

Fétis's language is lofty, fitting in the spirit of the age. He finds the music original, indeed, 'charming', but not at all great. There is a lack of uniformity in it. *Emmeline* is performed again in 1830, but the performance of 1827 already is a revival. As early as 1811 already a translation of *La Famille Suisse* is performed in the theatre of Saint-Cloud by the artists of the Opéra-Comique.[221] On June 5, 1830 Fétis writes in the *Revue musicale de Paris* about the performance. Where first Weigl has his own way, now he is apparently a follower of Mozart:

> *Among the followers and imitators of Mozart, Weigl has shared the honor with Winter of leaving behind dramatic works of which the audience in Germany, thirty years on, have not grown weary. […] Napoléon, who only loved soft and gracious music, was a great devotee of the work of Weigl. […] The singing is sweet, delicate with a waft of melancholy and sometimes with a movement that is not without charm, but other than that it is without many notable things: the harmony is pure and correct, but does not have that striking effects to which the new school has accustomed our ears. Finally, the instrumentation, which had some elegance at the time it was written, is weak and colorless for our time.*[222]

With this Fétis suggests that he finds the music and the instrumentation out of date: there is not enough innovative harmony in it, an important characteristic of the Romantic music. He probably

---

[217] Devriès, Anik & François Lesure: *Dictionnaire des éditeurs de musique français*, Genève, Minkoff, 1979-1988, vol. II, p. 369, 372.; Baillie, Laureen: *The Catalogue of Printed Music in the British Library to 1980*, London, Saur, 1982, p. 58.

[218] Weigl, Joseph: *Die Schweizerfamilie*, Oper in 3 Akten, 1809, vollständiger Klavierauszug ca 1809, no. 7 Cavatine m. 20-26.

[219] Wynberg, Simon: *The Guitar Works Napoleon Coste*, facsimile edition, Monaco, Chanterelle, vol. II, 1981, Introduction.

[220] *Revue musicale de Paris*, 1827, tome I, no. 1, février, p. 42-44: '[…] la musique de Weigl semble être assez goûtée pour procurer à l'ouvrage un certain nombre de représentations. […] Les compositeurs qui avaient succédé à Mozart avaient imité sa manière; mais Weigl n'a suivi que ses propres inspirations dans tout ce qu'il a produit. […] On aime d'ailleurs aujourd'hui les longs développemens, et presque tous les morceaux de la partition de Weigl sont courts. […] Au reste il faut qu'il y ait un grand mérite dans la musique de Weigl, puisqu'elle résiste à l'exécution déplorabe qu'on lui fait subir à l'Odéon.'

[221] *Revue musicale de Paris*, vol. VII, tome II, 5 VI 1830, p. 150-153: '*Emmeline ou la Famille Suisse*'; Lesure, François: *La musique à Paris en 1830-1831*, Paris, Bibliothèque nationale, 1983, p. 62, 92.

[222] *Revue musicale de Paris*, vol. VII, tome Il. II, 5 VI 1830, p. 152-153:'Parmi les successeurs et les imitateurs de Mozart, Weigl a partagé avec Winter la gloire de laisser des ouvrages dramatiques dont le public de l'Allemagne ne s'est point lassé depuis trente ans. […] Napoléon, qui n'aimait que la musique douce et gracieuse, goûta beaucoup l'ouvrage de Weigl. […] Les chants sont suaves, délicats, empreints d'une teinte de mélancholie, et quelquefois d'un certain vague qui n'est pas sans charme, mais il est dépourvu de traits saillants: son harmonie est pure et correcte, mais n'a point de ces effets piquants auxquels la nouvelle école a façonné nos oreilles; enfin, l'instrumentation, qui avait de l'élégance dans le temps où elle fut écrite, parait aujourd'hui faible et décolorée.

founds his expectations on *Waverley* from 1828 by Berlioz and on sketches of the *Symphonie Fantastique* that Berlioz began to compose in the beginning of 1830 and that had its opening night on December 5.[223]

Coste publishes his next work with variations opus 4 on *Armide* by Gluck in 1832, *chez l'auteur* and the other *Variations* WoO 9, opus 6 and opus 24, cannot be assumed to have been played by him in the Gymnase musical in Paris on March 27, 1829, for reasons that were already explained in chapter III. The qualification 'very great difficulty of some parts' in *L'Observateur des beaux-arts* can point at both works – in general the works of Coste are not that easy to play – but for reasons of date it is plausible that in this concert opus 2, the 'Weigl variations', is concerned. Anyhow, Coste fits in to the tradition of playing one's own work in a concert. With this work he seems to follow the existing practice of the domestication of popular tunes from opera, certainly also to make good sales of the piece, a *motif favori*. Nevertheless, using an opera theme to make a technically difficult piece for guitar solo is something quite different from making the arrangement of a melody for singing with guitar or piano. Opus 2 is dated as published in 1830, and in relation to the topicality of the programming of *Emmeline* in l'Odéon this is likely.[224] However, in Coste's letter of December 21, 1876 to his musical friend Hallberg in Sweden, his opinion about the work is not positive:

> *I have also found my fantasy on Gluck's gavotte l'Armide again (op. 4), which is a bit less bad, all the first works are quite mediocre, meaning that they are not worth much more than many others.*[225]

His opinion gives us cause to turn our attention to the music itself. From this letter it also becomes apparent that he later studied counterpoint. His opinion is reason to take a look at the music itself. Is the piece of musical value? The 'weakness' of the theme, as put into words above by Fétis, does not restrain Coste from making more of it than merely coloring in between the lines. It is a work in which almost all the characteristics of classical variation form can be distinguished, but where also the 'Sturm und Drang' – so to speak – of a young and talented composer starts to glimmer. Since Zani de Ferranti also wrote variations on exactly the same theme, it is worthwhile discussing this work here, for purpose of comparison.

The works of Coste and of Zani de Ferranti are very much on par, but Coste has a more elaborate harmony in three voices and a slight advantage in the variety in compositional and guitar-specific techniques; The addition of the little refrain is a lucky strike that gives the musical form a more diversified structure. Carcassi also wrote variations on one of Weigl's themes, but those have a different melody and are so short and shallow that they are not of any interest for this comparison.[226] As is mentioned in the chapter with the reviews of the works, with musical examples, here Coste launches virtuosity in passages, 'parachute-motifs', arpeggios with campanellas, trills, an ascending scale in alternating octaves. A sudden chromatic submediant F, varied with a descending chromatic scale in alternating octaves, a modulating movement in broken thirds and a confirmation of the tonic with dominant tonic chords, alternating with the rhythmic motif of the refrain, have a surprising effect. An ascending chromatic tremolo passage is striking. The whole piece is in 3/4 meter. Coste regularly gives signs for tempo, dynamics, and performance. All is conceived in three voices in melody, bass and inner voice. He eventually breaks through the rigid harmonic structure to put his own mark upon the composition even more, where the virtuosity increases.

---

[223] MacDonald, Hugh: 'Hector Berlioz', in: Sadie, Stanley, ed.: *The New Grove Dictionary of Music and Musicians*, London, Macmillan, 1980. vol. 2, p. 581-583; id. in: Sadie, Stanley, ed.: *The New Grove Dictionary of Music and Musicians*, second edition, London, Macmillan, 2001, vol. 2, p. 384-385, 389.

[224] Baillie, Laureen: *The Catalogue of Printed Music in the British Library to 1980*, London, Saur, 1982, p. 58.

[225] Coste - Hallberg, 21 XII 1876: 'J'ai retrouvé aussi ma fantaisie sur la gavotte l'Armide de Gluck (op. 4) qui est un peu moins mauvaise, tous les premiers ouvrages sont fort médiocres, c'est à dire qu'ils ne valent pas mieux que beaucoup d'autres.'

[226] Carcassi, Matteo: 'Variationen über ein Tema von Weigl aus dem Singspiel 'Die Schweizerfamilie' in: *Gitarre-Freund* vol. VIII, no. 2, 1907, Sk Boije 965:13.

IV — Aux Parisiens   51

48 Coste incipit Weigl-variations opus 2 1829

49 Zani de Ferranti incipit Niaiserie opus 21 c. 1832

Coste has composed a musically attractive and above all guitaristic piece. He dedicates his opus 2 to Madame Pascal née Valentin, but nothing is known about her. Coste adds a dedication to at least 45 of his works, mostly pupils of friends who have become a part of his social network in Paris with this. The circumstances around these dedications are discussed in Intermezzo II.

WoO 2, Chanson *Aux Parisiens des 27, 28 et 29 juillet 1830*

In July 1839 political disturbances arise in Paris around the four ordinations of Charles X, who is in power from 1824 on, in the period of the Restauration. These are in opposition to the Constitution. In Paris a revolution breaks out, leading to the flight of the Bourbons, after the skirmishes of July 27, 28 and 29, the 'three glorious days of July'. Louis-Philippe becomes king of the 'Monarchie de Juillet', the era of the Restauration is over.[227] The riots lead to the temporary closure of all theatres, which present an occasional repertoire afterwards. They leave their traces in musical life too, where Berlioz reports that, after finishing his cantata *La mort de Sardanapale*, he sneaks around in Paris on the 29th at night with a pistol in his hand, until the morning.[228] During the months after this July revolution numerous benefit concerts are organized to help the wounded, for instance by Berlioz in the Conservatoire on 5 December with a financial contribution of 300 fr. Under the new government, just as before, artists send the king an invitation to attend the benefit concerts; the king does not attend these, but sends money instead.[229] Coste writes a chanson on the occasion of this event and publishes it at the end of 1830 'chez l'auteur, Rue Bleue, no. 28', with the title *Aux Parisiens des 27, 28 et 29 juillet 1830*. It is a song for voice and piano, with lyrics by M. Harion on the *Trois Glorieuses* in July that year.[230] In his chanson Coste celebrates, with an effective melody like the Marseillaise, the courage of the people that chooses freedom over the tyrant. The piece is available in all music stores for the price of 2 fr. In the *Bibliographie de la France* it is announced on December 25, 1830, making it the second work whose date can be determined, one week after the *Deux quadrilles* opus 3.[231] The question arises as to whether this could be the lost opus 1 of Napoléon Coste. The chanson *Aux Parisiens* WoO 2 is written after July 1830 and is certainly not his first work. But he does publish it as one of the first of his works. The fact that Coste has written more chansons that he did not provide with an opus number is an argument against this assumption, considering *L'Enfant au Berceau* WoO 7, 1864, *Lolla* WoO 10, 1878, and *Le Petit Ange rose* WoO 11, also in 1878, all for voice and piano or guitar and published much later.[232]

---

[227] Michelin et Cie., ed.: *The Green Guide, France*, Paris, 2000, p. 32.
[228] Berlioz, Hector: *Mémoires 1803-1865*, ed. Callmann-Lévy, Paris, 1919, p. 153; Macdonald, Hugh: 'Hector Berlioz' in: Stanley Sadie, ed.: *The New Grove Dictionary of Music and Musicians*, London, Macmillan, 1980, vol. 2, p. 603; id. in: Sadie, Stanley, ed.: *The New Grove Dictionary of Music and Musicians*, second edition, London, Macmillan, 2001, vol. 2, p. 384-385, 389.
[229] Lesure, François: *La musique à Paris en 1830-1831*, Paris, Bibliothèque nationale, p. 2-3, 17-18, 28.
[230] Bibliothèque nationale, Département de la Musique, Paris, Mr. Coste: *Aux Parisiens des 27, 28 et 29 juillet 1830*, Paroles de Harion, Paris, chez l'auteur, In.fol., 2 ex. [Vm7 44.830 et 44831.
[231] *Bibliographie de la France*, vol. XIX, no. 52, 25 XII 1830, p. 834: '*Aux Parisiens des 27, 28 et 29 juillet 1830*, paroles de M. Harion, musique de M. Coste. A Paris, chez l'auteur, rue Bleue no. 28. Prix 2-0'; Lesure, François: *La musique à Paris en 1830-1831*, Paris, Bibliothèque nationale, 1983, p. 293.
[232] Bibliothèque nationale, Département de la Musique, Paris, Coste, Nap.: *L'Enfant au Berceau*, Paroles de Jules Adenis, Paris, Emile Chatot, 1864, In.fol., [Vm7 44.834; *Lolla*, Mélodie, Paroles de Pélan d'Angers, Paris, Katto, 1878, In.fol., [Vm7 44,835; *Le Petit Ange rose* - Berceuse. Paroles de Pélan d'Angers, Paris, Katto, 1878, In. fol., [Vm7 44.836.

50 Aux Parisiens, Napoléon Coste WoO 2, 1830

The missing opus 1 could then be a lost work for guitar solo, but no trace of it or even a reference to it can be found. Coste may have judged his first work to be of insufficient quality, leading him not to publish it, but opus 3 – see further below – cannot stand the test of criticism either, and it is published nevertheless. The indications are too scanty to name *Aux Parisiens* opus 1.

But the assumption that Coste plays the piano is obvious, the work is written for voice and this instrument. For a guitarist, just like Carcassi, Sor and Zani de Ferranti, this is not unusual, and as far as Coste is concerned it is very likely when he is mentioned as a music teacher in Valenciennes.[233] It is not only Coste who is concerned with the events of July 1830 in Paris. Carulli also presents an edition on this subject in his *Les Trois Jours, Pièce analogue aux événemens [sic] des trois journées 27, 28 et 29 juillet 1830*. The title speaks volumes. In this opus 331 for guitar solo, the revolutionary events pass in revue. In the music Carulli puts the inscriptions 'Resistance caused by despotism', 'Action by the people', 'The people are victor', where these events are put into music in sequential episodes.[234] The piece appears with Romagnesi and later with Schott. The work does not have any musical reference to the melody in Coste's *Aux Parisiens*, but Carulli tries hard to make non-musical things resonate in this music. It is program-music, just as the Coste's chanson. Carulli's sympathy for the revolution is also expressed in his *La Marseillaise Variée* opus 330 for solo guitar, which appears at the end of 1830.[235] Carulli is just as impressed with Napoléon Coste: he composes a *Duo concertant pour deux guitares* opus 328 in 1831 and dedicates it to him.[236] They are acquainted with each other and when Coste is taking part in musical life around the guitar in Paris, why shouldn't he have played this duet together with Carulli? Factual indications for this are missing. Carulli's works are numerous and moreover he publishes a composition

---

[233] Jaworski, Roman: 'Napoleon Coste 1805-1883, une histoire perdue', in: *Valentiana*, Valenciennes, Association Valentiana, 1992, no. 10, p. 68; Roncet, Noël: *Napoléon Coste, Compositeur - 1805 - 1883*, Amondans, 2005, p. 11.

[234] Carulli, Fernando: *Les Trois Jours...*, op.331. Schott, Mayence et Anvers, no. 3425, 1830, Kk RiBS 0216. Torta, Mario: *Catalogo tematico delle opere di Ferdinando Carulli*, Lucca, Libreria Musicale Italiana, 1993, p. 639-641.

[235] Carulli, Fernando: *La Marseillaise Variée...*, op.330. Schott, Mayence et Anvers, no. 3378, 1830, Kk RiBS 0217. Torta, Mario: *Catalogo tematico delle opere di Ferdinando Carulli*, Lucca, Libreria Musicale Italiana, 1993, p. 637-639.

[236] Torta, Mario: *Catalogo tematico delle opere di Ferdinando Carulli*, Lucca, Libreria Musicale Italiana, 1993, p. 635-636; Kk RiBS Ms. 248 mu 7910.2682.

La Parisienne opus 332 in 1830, a 'Marche nationale' to the three-colored flag.[237] *La Fayette à Paris* also fits into this framework , a 'cantata' with the lyrics of Hortensius de St-Albin and music by Carulli, performed in September 1830 in the presence of the National Guard, but this work was probably written by his son Gustavo, as it is not included in Torta's thematic catalogue.[238] Other composers also write works that refer to the July revolution – Marseillaises – and Coste is in their company with *Aux Parisiens*.[239] Still, it is remarkable that a young guitar composer makes his debut in Paris with a chanson with this title for voice and piano. He probably wants to follow the trend of the republican public first. In musical circles the 'juste milieu' is in question, the right middle course between the royalists and the republicans. Véron, as a director of the Opéra, also follows this commercial middle course Coste and Carulli clearly take the side of the republicans. The chanson *Aux Parisiens des 27 28 et 29 juillet 1830* tells the story of the heroism of the people in the 'Trois Glorieuses', who opposed the tyrant that shed their blood. In it, indications for Romantic musical characteristics can be found, such as the martial rhythm, a nice modulation, a 'stoptime' and an onomatopoeic cock-crowing motif, the programmatic content aside. Whether it is performed in a concert, is unknown, but this genre is practiced in the mixed concerts, which are still popular.

Concerts 1830

On Saturday March 27, 1830 Sor, who is of great importance to Coste, plays in Pape's salon, where pianist Sowinski also performs, in a mixed concert. On March 30, 1830 Sor and Panseron, the baritone singer and composer who teaches at the Conservatoire and later performs with Huerta, can be heard in salle Taitbout, which resulted in an unfavorable critique. Fétis does not like Sor's guitar very much:

51 Giulio Regondi

To mention M. Sor is to say that we have heard guitar playing with a rare perfection. What a pity that such a harmonious head has used so much talent and patience to master a worthless instrument![240]

In these lines also can be read that Fétis does respect Sor's control of harmony. Coste and Sor know each other and it is possible that Coste studies this subject with Sor. On Tuesday April 27, 1830 there is a special event in a concert in salon Dietz, a 'small three-foot tall artist' who plays the guitar: the child prodigy Giulio Regondi visits Paris. Regondi earns much admiration with the public and the critics, and apparently also with Sor who dedicates his opus 46 *Souvenir d'Amitié Fantaisie* to him that year.[241]

In the following years it is notable how many very young male and female guitarists appear in the salons. On May 8 the 7-year-old Regondi plays again, this time in the salons Chantereine, at 8:30 p.m. In July, clearly after the concert season, Sor and Hummel, among others, play in madame Farrenc's concert in the salons of Érard, this time to Fétis's great pleasure. In the new season, on October 26, 'professeur de guitare' Huerta plays with an admission

---

[237] Torta, Mario: *Catalogo tematico delle opere di Ferdinando Carulli*, Lucca, Libreria Musicale Italiana, 1993, p. 641-642.
[238] Lesure, François: *La musique à Paris en 1830-1831*, Paris, Bibliothèque nationale, 1983, p. 57.
[239] *Revue musicale de Paris*, vol. VII, tome III, décembre 1830, p. 190-191: 'Paer, Walkiers, Payer'.
[240] *Revue musicale de Paris*, vol. VII, tome. I, 3 IV 1830, p. 267: 'Citer M. Sor, c'est dire qu'on a entendu de la guitare avec une perfection rare. Quel dommage qu'une tête si harmonique ait employé tant de talent et de patience à vaincre un instrument ingrat!'
[241] Jeffery, Brian: *Fernando Sor, Composer and Guitarist*, London, 1977; second edition 1994, p. 164; Wynberg, Simon: *Giulio Regondi, Complete Works for Guitar*, Monaco, 1981, 6, 7.

charge of 10 fr. at 8 o'clock in the evening in the salons of Petzold. Again, seven concerts with guitar are reported in 1830,[242] but Fétis does not find Huerta very satisfying, as later becomes apparent in 1831. In mixed concerts the guitar still occupies a modest place, but when the development of the concert practice in the 19th century leads to the solo concert, or the recital, the guitar practically disappears from the stage.[243] The 'concerts with guitar' appendices show a sharp decline in the number of reported concerts over several periods. But this trend has not set in yet in the 1830's, when Sor becomes Coste's guiding leader in the salons. Along with the rise of the public mixed concert and the public's changing attitude towards concerts, discussed earlier, there is a remarkable parallel with a changing approach of dedications. Those to whom dedications are addressed now are well-to-do civilians, not the nobility as had earlier been the case, while the public concert shows a strong development and the private concert for nobility vanishes.[244]

OPUS 3, *2 QUADRILLES DE CONTREDANSES* 1830

The first entry of a composition by Coste can be found in the *Revue musicale de Paris* of December 18, 1830. In there the publication of *Deux nouveaux quadrilles de contredanses pour la guitare*' opus 5 by Napoléon Coste with Romagnesi is mentioned:

> *A collection of contredanses for the guitar, above all elegant and easy, was still lacking in the music shops. The amateurs of this instrument will be really happy with this new production of M. Coste.*[245]

Here, however, opus 3 is concerned and the notion 'new production' taken literally means that Coste already has published works before; no trace of that can be found in the press. The work originates from 1830 or 1829. Romagnesi first publishes his own compositions, in the rue Vivienne, close to the Conservatoire, but in 1830 he starts to publish works by other composers. In the review of the work in the *Bulletin d'Annonces* of the *Revue musicale de Paris* this ironic remark upon this edition is made. The small work costs 3 fr.75c., is of a normal size and is available at Romagnesi, rue Vivienne no. 21. The

52 La Contredanse, Montoux

---

[242] Lesure, François: *La musique à Paris en 1830-1831*, Paris, Bibliothèque Natonale, 1983, p. 137, 138, 143, 148-150.
[243] Bödeker, Hans Erich, Patrice Veit et Michael Werner, ed.: *Organisateurs et formes d'organisation du concert en Europe 1700-1920*, Berlin, Berliner Wissenschafts Verlag, 2008; Myriam Chymènes: 'Élites sociales et vie musicale parisienne sous la Troisième République: promotion, diffusion, création', p. 31-46; Bruno Moysan: 'Pratiques lisztiennes du concert', p. 133-134.
[244] Weber, William: *The Great Transformation of Musical Taste*, Cambridge, Cambridge University Press, 2008, p. 141-144; Johnson, James H.: *Listening in Paris: a cultural history*, Berkeley, University of Berkeley Press, 1995, p. 199-205.
[245] *Revue musicale de Paris,* vol. VI, tome III, 18 XII 1830, p. 191: 'Bulletin d'annonces, quadrilles et contredanses […] Napoléon Coste op. 5 […] 3 fr.75c. Romagnesi'; Un recueil de contredanses pour guitare, surtout élégantes et faciles, manquait également dans le commerce de la musique. Les amateurs de cet instrument auront lieu d'être satisfait de cette nouvelle production de M. Coste.; Lesure, François: *La musique à Paris en 1830-1831*, Paris, Bibliothèque Natonale, 1983, p. 293.

IV — Aux Parisiens 55

contredanse, danced in groups of 4, 6 or 8 couples, was very popular during the first Empire in Paris, as witnessed by Montoux's almost caricaturistic engraving in *La Guitaromanie* by de Marescot.[246] The Quadrille as a dance is critically reviewed by Lasalle, later in 1868:

> *When we think about it, for a moment, nothing is so crude, & totally bestial, & silly as the quadrille that is danced in the salons. That crowd of people who bump up against each other, going forward, then four steps backward, which they don't want to do! & that music that puts you to sleep with the monotony of its rhythm, were if not by the violence of its noise! ...*[247]

The series of dances are not taken very seriously by the critics, and is regarded as rather pedestrian. It is probably one of Coste's juvenile works, intended to be danced to in Valenciennes, and which he took the opportunity to publish it in Paris. The music consists of lively, rhythmic themes with a rigid 8- or 16-bar periodicity, in 2/4 meter, except for 'La poule' which has a 6/8 meter, a format that Coste applies unaltered. Despite the ornamental chromatics that appear from time to time, primarily augmented fourths, and the frequently occurring legato, this is certainly not a brilliant work at the beginning of the oeuvre of a talented guitar composer. Not a trace of Romanticism can be found in it. He reuses some parts in the, probably later, work *Deux Quadrilles* WoO 5, the transcript of which in the Kongelige Bibliotek in Copenhagen is dated 1844. In this way he composed two sets of quadrilles.

RELATIONS 1831

The question of Coste's study of counterpoint and harmony is discussed by many authors. It took him ten years, according to some of them.[248] However, none of them say with whom Coste studied. Did he take lessons with Sor, who he met soon after his arrival in Paris, with whom he became friends and who introduced him in the salons of Paris? Sor had a thorough musical education at the convent of Montserrat near Barcelona, when musical education still was in the hands of the clergy, and composed vocal works, works for piano and ballet, apart from his works for guitar, for which he became most famous.[249] In his works for guitar, Sor shows the command of a full harmony, a thorough voicing and knowledge of the potentials of the guitar as an instrument. It is quite possible that Coste studied counterpoint and harmony with Sor, but any proof is lacking. If Sor is the starting point, Coste makes a step forward, as will be shown later. Does Coste study these subjects at the Conservatoire, considering that the guitar is not taught there, and further considering that he – a guitarist playing the piano – does not have the requisite level to enter a study of the piano at the Conservatoire? Cherubini complains about the many pianists at the Conservatoire, which makes the selection harder. The name Napoléon Coste is not recorded in the annals of the Conservatoire in this period.[250] He could have had private lessons with one of the teachers. It is definitely established that, from the start, his compositions show a tendency to make full use of harmony, do not avoid polyphony for technical complexity and try to

---

[246] Marescot, Charles de: *La Guitaromanie*, Paris, Archivum Musicum, z.j. no. 16, Studio per Edizione scelte. Firenze, 1985, p. 17.

[247] Lasalle, Albert: *Dictionnaire de la musique appliquée à l'amour*, Paris, Librairie internationale, 1868, p. 225: 'Si on y réfléchissait une bonne fois, rien n'est grossier, & tout ensemble bestial & niais, comme le quadrille que l'on danse dans les salons. Cette foule composée de gens qui se heurtent pour faire en avant, puis en arrière, quatre pas qu'ils n'ont point envie de faire! & cette musique qui endormirait par la monotonie de son rhythme, n'était la violence de son bruit!...'

[248] Stockmann [Shtokman], J.: 'Napoléon Coste', in: *Der Guitarrefreund, Mitteilungen des Internationalen Guitarristen-Verbandes*, München, 3. Jahrgang, 1902, Heft 5, p. 56; Buek, Fritz: *Die Gitarre und ihre Meister*, Berlin, Robert Lienau, 1926, 2nd ed. 1935, p. 107 [ten years]; Zuth, Josef: 'Coste, Napoléon', in: *Handbuch der Laute und Gitarre*, Wien, Doblinger, 1926-28, repr. Hildesheim, Olms, 1978, p. 72 [musical theory]; Schwarz-Reiflingen, Erwin: 'Napoleon Coste', in: *Die Gitarre*, Berlin, 1927, Jahrgang VIII, Heft 7/8, [Coste-Heft] p. 45 [not composed for 10 years]; Prat, Domingo: *Diccionario biografico, bibliografico, critico, de Guitarras, Guitarristas y Guitarreros*, Buenos Aires, Fernando Romero, 1934, repr. Columbus, Orphée, 1986, p. 97 [profound study]; Bone, Philip J.: 'Coste, Napoleon', in: *The Guitar and the Mandolin*, London, Schott, 2nd ed, 1954, reprint 1972, p. 84 [ten years]; Radke, Hans: 'Coste, Napoléon', in: *Die Musik in Geschichte und Gegenwart*, ed. Blume, Kassel, Bärenreiter, 1956, ed. 1973, vol. XV (Supplement 1) Kol. 1616; Wynberg, Simon: '...zur Rettung Napoleon Costes', in: *Gitarre und Laute*, Köln, vol. III, 1981, no. 5, p. 29; Jaworski, Roman: 'Napoleon Coste 1805-1883, une histoire perdue', in: *Valentiana*, Valenciennes, Association Valentiana, 1992, no. 10, p. 73; Burzik, Monika: 'Coste, Napoléon', in: *Die Musik in Geschichte und Gegenwart*, ed. Blume, Finscher, Kassel, Bärenreiter, 2000, vol. 4, Kol. 1714.

[249] Jeffery, Brian: *Fernando Sor, Composer and Guitarist*, London, Tecla, 1977; p. 13-14.

[250] Pierre, Constant: *Le Conservatoire national de musique et de déclamation: documents historiques et administratifs*, Paris, Imprimerie nationale, 1900, p. 403-406, 420-431, 875.

find that complexity in opposing voices, either accompanying the melody or in counterpoint to it. In 1921 the suggestion is made that Coste studied with Berlioz. In a concert that Georg Meier gave with his son Willy Meier-Pauselius in Hamburg in 1921 the program includes the *Concertino* in E-moll, better known as *Grand Duo* WoO 8 by Napoléon Coste.[251] Meier is the German guitarist presumed to have obtained the double copies from the collection of Coste from Thorvald Rischel in Copenhagen.[252] According to him, Coste takes first place in guitar literature of 8,000 works for the instrument. Meier single-handedly wrote a *Handbuch über Guittar-Musik* in 1934, which includes a survey of Coste's works.[253] Because of their great value these works seem to have been put in a safe in a bank in Hamburg, which was bombed during the Second World War, when everything was lost, except for some 36 letters from Coste to Hallberg. In the program notes, Meier writes that Coste 'finished his theoretical study with Berlioz, to whom he dedicated his large work *Le Tournoi' Fantasie Chevaleresque opus 15*. This sounds plausible, all the more so since on the title page of the work it is mentioned that 'it was 'executed at the Conservatoire of music by the author.' However, in none of Berlioz's writings, memoirs or letters is the name of Coste ever mentioned. Berlioz does write that he gave lessons in guitar in Paris in 1825, when he studies with Lesueur at the Conservatoire and later, instructed by Cherubini, counterpoint and fugue with Reicha.[254] Berlioz does not teach at the Conservatoire. However, he serves there as a librarian for a long time, from 1839 to 1869.[255] So it is improbable that Coste studied counterpoint and harmony with Berlioz, the subjects that are in question in many biographical essays, despite the love of the guitar that the two men shared, Berlioz does mention the name 'Coste' in some of his letters in 1835, but there it is Amable Costes who is concerned – the bookseller – and his copy of 'l'Italie pittoresque.'[256] And if he wrongly writes Coste's name, wouldn't that lead him to make an association with a (former) pupil? He does not mention him at all. Coste dedicates his opus 15 to Berlioz and publishes it in 1844 with Challiot. The connection to Berlioz could also have been out of pure admiration. Berlioz is already famous then and has composed many great works, *Waverley* 1828, *Symphonie fantastique* 1830, *Le roi Lear* 1831, *Harold en Italie* 1834, *Roméo et Juliette* 1839 and *Grande symphonie* 1840.

Then the year 1831 arrives, the year when Paganini appears in the footlights of Parisian musical life in Paris in a spectacular way. A parenthetical note should be made about the expression 'footlights': in small theatres performances are still lit by candlelight or with oil lamps, with many fires as a result. The novelty of gas lighting is restricted to the major theatres, as is already noticed in the review of Coste's concert on December 14, 1828. Gas footlights have probably already been installed in the Opéra in Paris. It is in these years that Paris acquires its nickname of 'the city of light'. The gas streetlights illuminate the grand boulevards in the evening for the first time. This must have created a fairylike atmosphere in the city, especially in theatre season, from November to April. He agrees with the newly installed director of the Opéra, Veron, to give a series of eleven solo concerts in March and April 1831, a unique event in the history of the public

53 Paganini

---

[251] Meier, Georg, *Programm Konzert*, Hamburg, 1921, Archiv Andreas Stevens, Hilden.
[252] Rischel, Thorwald: 'Bibliographische Notizen zu den Gitarrenwerken von Napoleon Coste', in: *Die Gitarre*, Berlin, 1927, Jahrgang VIII, Heft 7/8, [Coste-Heft] p. 48 Red.; Buek, Fritz: *Die Gitarre und ihre Meister*, Berlin, Robert Lienau, 1926, 2nd ed. 1935, p. 108.
[253] Meier, Georg, *Handbuch über Guittar-Musik*, Hamburg, 1934, unp. MS, Archiv Andreas Stevens, Hilden.
[254] Berlioz, Hector: *Mémoires 1803-1865*, Paris, Callmann-Lévy, 1919, p. 53.
[255] Pierre, Constant: *Le Conservatoire national de musique et de déclamation: documents historiques et administratifs*, Paris, Imprimerie nationale, 1900, p. 422-428, 438.
[256] Berlioz, Hector: *Correspondance générale*, Paris, Flammarion, 1972, vol. II, p. 253, 262-265.

IV — *Aux Parisiens* 57

concert.[257] For Paris Paganini is representative for the public's taste for virtuosity and the popularity of the Italian repertoire of Rossini, Bellini, Donizetti.[258] With this he introduces a new concept for the travelling virtuoso and makes a good thing out of it. Liszt, who is in Paris from 1827 on, and who admires Paganini, takes full advantage of this idea later by applying his fantastic virtuoso technique to the piano.[259] Paganini enlists the sympathy of the Parisian public and earns a tidy sum of 130,000 fr. in box-office receipts, a fortune in those days, compared with Cherubini, who has an annual salary of 8,000 fr. as a director of the Conservatoire in 1830, and Fétis who earns 3,000 fr. a year as a librarian and teacher in counterpoint and fugue.[260] In 1838 Paganini famously donates 20,000 fr. to Berlioz, with reference to *Harold*, with the comment *je ne suis pas riche...*[261] Paganini is not the only one to enjoy such stardom. Maria Malibran is also blessed. She is engaged for the season 1835-36 at the Opéra of Milan for 100,000 fr., and in Paris they are happy that she returns there, if only for the moment.[262] The earnings are public knowledge, being published in musical magazines, and lead to jealousy, such as happens with a certain 'Paganini of the street', named Lefèvre, who plays in the street at the Bourse, at the continuation of rue Vivienne, in 1835. He complains that 'Paganini, maestro Paganini, earns 10,000 fr. a night. I need 30 sous for a supper. Don't you think, gentlemen, that I am worth 30 sous?' On May 11 the police ask him for his license. He hasn't got one, and it takes a month for this 'Paganini of the street' to obtain it.[263] The violin is not only on the great stage, but can also be found in the street scape of everyday life. In March and April 1831 Paganini gives the eleven concerts.[264] Two of these coincide, as for the guitar, with 'traditional' mixed concerts. The first of these is on March 27 with Sor and Aguado, who give a benefit concert in the salons Dietz with pianist Miró, the 'Spanish evening,' of which Fétis remarks:

> *Beyond any doubt the gentlemen Sor and Aguado show a remarkable talent for the guitar; yet, I must admit, the duet these gentlemen played gave to me only a weak impression.*[265]

The second of these concerts, given on April 17 with Coste in the salle Petzold, passes without a review in the *Revue musicale de Paris*.[266] Nevertheless, this is the second concert that is found in the sources. *Le Figaro* only makes the following announcement, without further information on the program:

> *M. Costes [sic], a young and distinguished guitarist, will give a concert next Sunday, at eight, in the salons of M. Petzold, in which several of our better artists will perform.*[267]

Later that year, in September, Chopin arrives in Paris and gives his successful first concert on February 28, 1832, of which Fétis writes with much enthusiasm that he finds great originality in the works, where the *Concerto in F-mineur* and the *Variations* opus 2 are concerned. Chopin associates

---

[257] Lesure, François: *La musique à Paris en 1830-1831*, Paris, Bibliothèque nationale, 1983, p. 53, 159.
[258] Pistone, Danièle: *La musique en France de la Révolution à 1900*, Paris, Honoré Champion, 1979, p. 21.
[259] Searle, Humphrey: 'Liszt, Franz', in: Sadie, Stanley ed.: *The New Grove Dictionary of Music and Musicians*, London, Macmillan, 1980, vol.11, p. 29-30; Walker, Alan: 'Liszt', in: Sadie, Stanley, ed.:*The New Grove Dictionary of Music and Musicians*, second edition, London, Macmillan, 2001, vol. 14, p. 755--760.
[260] Pierre, Constant: *Le Conservatoire national de musique et de déclamation: documents historiques et administratifs*, Paris, Imprimerie nationale, 1900, p. 420.
[261] Berlioz, Hector: *Mémoires de Hector Berlioz*, Paris, Calmann-Lévy, 1919, p. 301, 337: 'I am not rich...'.
[262] *Revue de Paris*, vol. VI, tome 6, juin 1834, p. 64-65: 'Mme Malibran [...] Opéra de Milan [...] 100.000 francs'.
[263] *Le Ménestrel*, vol. II, no. 29, 14 VI 1835, p. [4]: 'Paganini des rues'.
[264] Lesure, François: *La musique à Paris en 1830-1831*, Paris, Bibliothèque nationale, 1983, p. 53, 159.
[265] *Revue musicale de Paris*, Vme année, no. 9, 2 IV 1831, p. 71: 'Nul doute que MM. Sor et Aguado aient sur la guitare un talent remarquable; cependant, je dois l'avouer, le duo qu'ont joué ces messieurs ne m'a fait qu'une bien faible impression.'
[266] Dell'Ara, Mario: 'La chitarra a Parigi negli anni 1830-1831', in: *Il Fronimo*, Milano, Suvini Zerboni, XVI, no. 63, apr. 1988, p. 21; Lesure, François: *La musique à Paris en 1830-1831*, Paris, Bibliothèque natonale, 1983, p. 53, 166; *Le Figaro*, vol. VI, no. 105, 13 IV 1831, p. 4.
[267] *Le Figaro*: vol. VI, no. 105, merc. 13 avril 1831, p. 4: 'M. Costes [sic], jeune guitariste distingué, doit donner dimanche prochain, à huit heures, dans les salons de M. Petzold, un concert où se feront entendre plusieurs de nos meilleurs artistes.'

with the circle of Liszt, Berlioz, Bellini and Meyerbeer,[268] who, in turn, are related to Coste by way of concerts or compositions.

OPUS 4, *FANTAISIE ... SUR UN MOTIF DU BALLET D'ARMIDE* 1832

The work on a motif of Gluck is formally a set of theme and variations, preceded by an introduction and finishing with a coda. It is part of the tradition of the so-called 'domestication' of opera themes in that way. In the sense of not being an arrangement of an opera selection, but meant to be a serious work for guitar solo, it hardly can be classified as such, considering the difficulty of the composition. The publication of Coste's work is mentioned in the *Bibliographie de la France* of August 19, 1832, making it possible to date it.[269] Ferdinando Carulli, who has many activities in Paris, adds two variations on the same theme in his *Souvenirs Des Grands Auteurs* opus 286 no. 4 circa 1831,[270] but gradually the theme and variations genre disappears in the 19th century, including in the works of Coste. Here the composer already starts to diverge from the rigid classical form by inserting an *Andante* between variation 3 and 4, which is a character piece due to its tonal and metrical changes and its cadenza, and furthermore by its title.

54 Rue du Vieux Colombier c. 1876

The *Fantaisie* on *Armide* of Gluck opus 4 appears in 1832 and is for sale for 4 f. 50 c. with all music sellers and with the author himself in the rue du [Vieux] Colombier no. 25, close to the rue de Seine, as the title page reads. So Coste already moved from rue Bleue no. 28 in the 9th arrondissement to this address in the 6th. He lives here until 1837, close to the St-Sulpice and the Jardin du Luxembourg, south of the Seine, in the continuation of the rue de Grenelle, which is very convenient when he gives

---

[268] Hedley, Arthur & Maurice Brown: 'Chopin, Fryderyc Franziszek', in: Sadie, Stanley ed.: *The New Grove Dictionary of Music and Musicians*, London, Macmillan, 1980, vol. 4, p. 294; Kornel, Michalowski: 'Chopin', in: Sadie, Stanley, ed.:*The New Grove Dictionary of Music and Musicians*, second edition, London, Macmillan, 2001, vol. 5, p. 706-710; Laforêt, Claude (pseud. Flavien Bonnet-Roy): *La Vie musicale au Temps romantique*, Paris, Peyronnet, 1929, p. 151.

[269] *Bibliographie de la France*, vol. XXI, no. 33, 18 VIII 1832, p. 472: 'Fantaisie pour la guitare, composée sur un motif du ballet d'*Armide*, pas Nap. Coste, op. 4. Prix 4-50'.

[270] Torta, Mario: *Catalogo tematico delle opere di Ferdinando Carulli*, Lucca, Libreria Musicale Italiana, 1993, p. 579-581.

IV — *Aux Parisiens* 59

a concert in the Théâtre de Grenelle on February 21, 1835, at walking distance.²⁷¹ A photograph from around 1876 by amateur photographer Hippolyte Blancard, a druggist who made his fortune and lives at rue du Vieux Colombier no. 21, two houses away 40 years later, shows a street, shining by recent rain; Coste's apartment can be seen at the right edge.²⁷²

Coste now lives much further away from his first publisher Richault – of opus 3 and 7 – in the Boulevart [sic] Poissonnière no. 16. Coste self publishes his *Aux Parisiens* WoO 2 as well as opus 4 and opus 6. It is a widespread practice to publish one's own work. The professions of composer an publisher are not independent yet, they are combined very often. In concurrence with Buek and Schwarz-Reiflingen, for instance,²⁷³ Coste was later obliged, in a time of decreasing interest in the guitar and its music, to publish his own compositions. Until 1876, 32 of his compositions for guitar are issued with publishers, he published 15 himself, 6 are not published. Most of his self-published works run from opus 41 on. Only opus 47 is published by Katto in 1878. This means that his self-publishing mainly occurs from 1876 on, when the composer already has edited most of his works with publishers.²⁷⁴ Opus 4, just like opus 11, is dedicated to Monsieur P. Montigny, *directeur de l'Hôpital Militaire du Gros Caillou*, possibly the father or a relative of Mlle Caroline de Montigny, the pupil to whom Coste dedicates his opus 10 and *Étude* 19 opus 38. She must played considerably well, as this étude is among the most difficult in the collection. Furthermore, opus 4 can be considered to be very difficult and M. de Montigny must have had a good technical level of playing too, to be able to play this.

55 Armide, stage design Cambon

---

²⁷¹ Hillairet, Jacques: *Dictionnaire historique des rues de Paris*, Paris, Les Èditions de Minuit, 1963-1972, p. p. 642-643. Leconte, André, ed.: *Plan de Paris par Arrondissement*, Paris, 1977, p. 131, plan M11.
²⁷² Baronnet, Jean: *Regard d'un Parisien sur la Commune, Photographies inédites de la Bibliothèque historique de la Ville de Paris*, Paris, Gallimard, 2006, p. 6.
²⁷³ Buek, Fritz: *Die Gitarre und ihre Meister*, Berlin, Robert Lienau, 1926, 2ⁿᵈ ed 1935, p. 107; Schwarz-Reiflingen, Erwin: 'Napoleon Coste', in: *Die Gitarre*, Berlin, 1927, Jahrgang VIII, Heft 7/8, [Coste-Heft] p. 45.
²⁷⁴ Cooper, Jeffrey: 'Coste, Napoléon', in: Sadie, Slanley ed.: *The New Grove Dictionary of Music and Musicians*, London, Macmillan, 1980, vol. 4, p. 824; Stockmann-Kursk, J.: 'Napoléon Coste', in: *Der Gitarrefreund*, München, 1902, Jahrgang III, Heft 5, p. 56.

Gluck composed the opera *Armide* during his stay in Vienna in 1776 and the work had its premiere night in the Académie Royale in Paris on September 23, 1777.[275] In 1825 Hector Berlioz becomes incensed – in favor of Gluck – over the negative reviews by Castil Blaze, among others, of the performance in the Opéra, contending that some of the themes are just like *airs populaires*.[276] This concerns other themes than the one Coste chose for his opus 4. In 1831 the work is revived again, in a reduction to three acts, with a premiere on September 9, 1831 in the Opéra, where Coste might have seen and heard it. The Bibliothèque nationale has an engraving of a stage design by Cambon for a performance of Gluck's Armide at this time.[277]

In 1831 it is in the program of the series *exercices publiques* of the Concerts du Conservatoire side by side with that of Lully, for comparison.[278] The 'Ballett' 'Musette' from the fourth act must have had belonged to the reduction from five to three acts, as Coste selects this theme for his opus 4. This second set of theme and variations already bears the title *Fantaisie*. He does not use the complete title of the genre and only mentions variations in his opus 2 and WoO 9. This means that the genre is disappearing. It ceases to turn up in Coste's later works.

The most interesting movements in this work are the Introduction and the Andante. In this work, the known classical style elements aside, there are musical developments to be noticed that can be distinguished as Romantic. The use of keys that are 'strange' to the guitar, like C-minor and A-flat, a pivot tone modulation, a major-minor transition, several cadenzas and the regular use of chromatics all point to a budding Romanticism with the composer. The intensification of the theme and the harmony also can be interpreted in the same way. There is just one indication for dynamics – piano – in variation 3 measure 9. After this edition one must wait three years to hear anything more about Coste.

Guitarists 1831-1833

Meanwhile in Paris several concerts take place where the guitar can be heard. Bohemian Huerta dominates Paris as a guitarist in different salons, but he is subject to severe criticism.[279] Fétis writes about the benefit concert for a family of Spanish refugees on January 16, 1831 in salle Taitbout:

> *Among the artists that performed was M. Huerta, whose talent is even greater because he, it is said, hardly knows the elements of music. M. Huerta's compositions of are not so good, but it is quite something to compose without knowing anything about music.*[280]

His sneer puts Huerta in his place as a composer. Fétis keeps a critical eye on the guitarists and the guitar. The German guitarist Schmidt plays in salon Dietz on April 16, 1831, 'but he makes a mistake, I think, in playing the guitar'. Sor plays in salon Dietz on April 19 with 'renewed success.'[281] Huerta gives another five concerts in Paris, in Hôtel-de-Ville, salle Chantereine, Athenée musical, Hôtel Fesch and the salon of Kepper. Sor can be heard in salons Petzold on December 25. Sor, Aguado and Huerta perform in concerts in 1832 and 1833, where Huerta shows a 'remarkable dexterity' that leads to 'surprising excitement' in the salons Dietz.[282] Aguado introduces his tripodison, as mentioned above,

---

[275] Croll, Gerhard: 'Gluck, Christoph Willibald von', in: Sadie, Stanley ed.: *The New Grove Dictionary of Music and Musicians*, London, Macmillan, 1980, vol. 7, p. 465, 472.
[276] Berlioz, Hector: *La Critique musicale*, ed. H. Robert Cohen, Yves Gérard, Paris, 1996-..., vol. I, p. 9-11 Armide - Gluck, 229-231.
[277] Paris, Bibliothèque nationale, Département de la Musique, Photothèque, *Gluck, décor de Cambon pour Armide*, 2ᵉ tiers 19ᵉ s., Cliché: C 73716, B.N.Opéra.Esq.
[278] Lesure, François: *La musique à Paris en 1830-1831*, Paris, Bibliothèque nationale, 1983, p. 56, 222.
[279] Coldwell, Robert & Suàrez-Pajares, Javier: *A.T. Huerta, Life and Works*, DGA Editions, 2006, p. 4-5.
[280] *Revue musicale de Paris*, vol. VIII, tome IV, 22 I 1831, p. 330-331: 'Au nombre des artistes qui se sont fait entendre dans ce concert se trouvait M. Huerta, guitariste espagnol don't le talent est autant plus extraordinaire qu'il sait, dit-on, à peine les élémens [sic] de la musique. [...] Les compositions de M. Huerta ne sont pas très bonnes, mais c'est déjà beaucoup que de composer quand on ne sait pas la musique.'
[281] *Revue musicale de Paris*, Vme année, no. 12, 23 IV 1831, p. 96: '[...] mais il lui reste le tort, à mes yeux, de jouer de la guitare.'; '[...] nous n'avons donc aujourd'hui qu'à constater le nouveau succès que cet artiste a obtenu [...]'.
[282] *Revue musicale de Paris*, VIme année, no. 49, 14 I 1832, p. 394: 'merveilleuse agilité'; VIIme année, no. 8, lun. 25 III 1833, p. 61: 'excité l'étonnement'.

IV — *Aux Parisiens* 61

56 Trinidad Huerta

on March 21, 1832 in a duet with Sor,[283] and here the remark is made that Aguado's performance is elegant, pure and light, his compositions subtle and original.[284] Significant for the way the guitar is seen is a short story that appears in *Le Ménestrel* in August 1834 with the title *Jack le Guitariste*: one day a Romanticist meets a lonesome monkey on Ceylon who appears to have a guitar in his hand. The author plays and sings a Venetian barcarolle for him and teaches him to play *Ah! Vous dirais-je, maman... Malborough... Au clair de la lune*, etc.![285] Even monkeys can play the guitar. Later that year Castil-Blaze ironically says that the guitar can hardly be disdained more than it already is. He gives guitarists the advice:

> *to give their talent to accompaniment and to preserve the study of so-called sonata's, in which melodies can be found, lines, thrills, legatos, scales, cadences and pedal points that are just a reality on paper, and that are heard with believing ears, without being sure to have really heard them.*[286]

They have to limit themselves to accompaniment with chords. These two ways to approach the guitar as an instrument can be distinguished from a vision of the guitar as a symbol of a Romantic feeling. On the one hand, isn't the guitar the instrument of the poet who wanders around in search

---

[283] *Revue musicale de Paris*, VIme année, no. 7, sam. 17 III 1832, p. 54: 'M. Aguado vient d'inventer un mécanisme simple et ingénieux […]'.
[284] Bergadà, M.: 'Aguado, Dionisio', in: Fauquet, Joël-Marie: *Dictionnaire de la Musique en France au XIXe siècle*, Paris, Fayard, 2003, p.19.
[285] *Le Ménestrel*, vol. II, no. 36, 3 VIII 1834, p. [1, 4]: 'Jack le Guitariste.'
[286] *Le Ménestrel*, vol. II, no. 42, 14 IX 1834, p. [1]: La guitare n'est point à dédaigner. […] Nous conseillerons aux guitaristes de consacrer leur talent à l'accompagnement, et de réserver, pour les exercices de l'étude, de prétendues sonates, dans lesquelles on trouve des chants, des traits, des trilles, des coulés, des gammes, des cadences, des points d'orgue, qui n'existent réellement que sur le papier, et que l'on écoute avec *les oreilles de la foi*, sans acquérir la certitude de les avoir entendus.'

of inspiration and who accompanies himself in his poetry and songs on the guitar. In this symbolism the guitar does not need to be played in reality. On the other hand, there is the musical view of the instrument that has to be played with several appropriate techniques and in certain cases is put in a negative light in relation to, according to this view, more successful instruments, such as the piano and the violin, for instance. This dichotomy continues to play a role in the Romantic period, the instrument played artistically in reality against the Romantic image of the instrument in literature and the fine arts, yes, even in music itself. While the debate on the quality of the compositions and the instruments is proceeding in a critical way, Sor and Huerta practically dominate the concert life as far as the guitar is concerned. Coste has to carve out a place in musical life in Paris, and that is not easy.

Concert 1835

On Saturday February 21, 1835 a ball takes place in the Théâtre de Grenelle, preceded by a concert, organized by the third legion of the *banlieue*, the towns of Vaugirard and Grenelle, for the benefit of the poor in these two towns. This is a concert to the benefit of people other than the musicians themselves. After some works for choir, violin and ensemble Coste is in the program with a solo for guitar, performed by himself. Tickets are 6 fr for gentlemen and 3 fr. for ladies and are available at the office of *Le Pianiste* and at the entrance of the hall.

> *It was a very numerous audience, and the entire notability of the département and the arrondissement were seen there. The prefect of the Seine, the secretary-general of the prefecture, the sous-prefect of Sceaux, the colonel of the legion, several mayors and functionaries from the surroundings were pursued to add their contribution to that of the subscribers. They were well rewarded by the concert indeed [...] in which the gentlemen Fontaine, Benazet, Chaulieu, Coste, Castelli and madame Deligny were heard with new pleasure time and again, [...] The concert was followed by a ball that lasted all night.*[287]

So writes the critic of the concert in *Le Pianiste*, the piano magazine that appears monthly between 1833 and 1835. To give an impression of this musical company, here is a review of the participants. Nicolas-Marie Fontaine (1787-1866) is a violoncellist and a composer. He establishes the *Société philharmonique de Paris* in 1822. Charles Chaulieu (1788-1849) is a pianist and a prolific composer, having written many works for piano. He writes for *Le Pianiste* in 1834-35 and leaves for London in 1840. Nothing is known about Benazet, violoncello, Castelli, and madame Deligny.[288] Most of the time what the ladies do in a concert is sing, and with piano and cello there must have been works for ensemble. Due to the concert's charitable cause it is attended by an ample representation of the notability. In the concert and the ball Coste might have made contact with them, a circumstance that could have played a role when he accepts a job as an administrator at the *Caisse Municipale* of Paris, much later in 1855. This is a special example of a benefit concert where attendees are named by name, in addition to the performers.

Le Pianiste, usually dedicated to the piano, but now 'making an exception to entertain the reader with things that occur in the arts in general', reports the publication of a remarkable guitar method by Duverger with a preface by De Fossa, the translator of the Aguado method. The method, so writes the critic, is meant to simplify the accompaniment of romances, with careful drawings of the position of the hands and a musical shorthand with which the chords can be read at a glance. The title is *La guitare simplifiée et mise à la portée de tout le monde*,[289] possibly referring to Fétis's publication 'La musique

---

[287] *Le Pianiste*, 2ᵉ Année, no. 8, 20 II 1835, p. 66: '5ᵉ Solo de guitare, composé et exécuté par M. Coste.'; no. 9, 5 III 1835, p. 68: 'L'assemblée était fort nombreuse, et l'on y remarquait toutes les notabilités du département et de l'arrondissement. [...] M. le préfet de la Seine, M. le secrétaire général de la préfecture, M. le sous-préfet de Sceaux, M. le colonel de la légion, plusieurs maires et fonctionnaires des environs s'étaient emressés de venir joindre leur offrande à celle des nombreux souscripteurs. Ils en ont été, du reste, bien récompensés par le concert [...] dans lequel on a entendu, avec un plaisir toujours nouveau, MM. Fontaine, Benazet, Chaulieu, Coste, Castelli et mad. Deligny, [...] Le concert a été suivi d'un bal qui s'est prolongé toute la nuit.'

[288] Kocevar, É.: 'Chaulieu, Charles'; J.-M. Fauquet: 'Fontaine, Nicolas-Marie', in: Fauquet, Joël-Marie: *Dictionnaire de la Musique en France au XIXe siècle*, Paris, Fayard, 2003, p. 261, 480.

[289] *Le Pianiste*, 2ᵉ année, no. 17, 5 VII 1835, p. 107: 'La guitare simplifiée [...]'.

mise à la portée de tout le monde' in 1830.²⁹⁰ The remark is casually made that the author brings back the instrument to a role from which it could hardly escape. The guitar has to be within the reach of everyone, just like music itself. This does show that the guitar did not reach the high level of an artistic instrument.

Fétis organizes historical concerts in the Théâtre-Italien, where Aguado can be heard on the lute on April 14, 1835, together with other artists who perform a *Vilhancico* for six female voices and six guitars – a hit, which returns several times later, but:

> *with a small effect, as far as the instruments are concerned... The admirable Baillot plays La Romanesca, 'fameux air de danse de la fin du seizième siècle', with accompaniment of violins, bass violins and guitar,*

a popular romance that appears in different versions later.²⁹¹ And Sor and Liszt know each other from joint concerts, such as the one given on May 7, 1835 in the salons of Pleyel, it is a small world that is very accessible for Coste, following Sor's footsteps.²⁹² Later that year a new composition by Coste is published, he must have worked on it during this time.

Opus 5, *Souvenirs de Flandres* 1835

Coste's composition *Souvenirs de Flandres* opus 5 is announced in the July 11, 1835 edition of the *Bibliographie de la France* and is for sale for 5 fr. with the publisher Lacôte.²⁹³ The very same work is also published (later?) by Richault Editeur, boulevard Poissonnière 16, au 1ᵉʳ.²⁹⁴ The publications of works with Richault are generally hard to date, but the publisher can be found at this address between July 1825 and November 1841.²⁹⁵ Opus 6 through 12 have a later date, and then Coste lives at a new address. Here the first problems arise concerning the dating of Coste's works, which are discussed in the explanations of the thematic catalogue.

57 Coste Marche - Souvenirs de Flandres opus 5, measure 15

The first time he prescribes the seventh string in his works, or gives the advice to use one because he writes an octave sign, is in 1835 in opus 5, the Marche in measure 3 and measure 15. Coste himself later writes in his letter to Degen, his Danish guitar friend, on October 17, 1863 that he added a seventh string to the guitar in 1835:

> *I have not felt the necessity to augment the number of strings, other than the 7ᵗʰ that I added and that gives it almost the range of the violoncello.²⁹⁶*

And on February 7, 1877 he explains to Hallberg why he only added a seventh string to the guitar:

---

²⁹⁰ Liebaars, Herman: *François-Joseph Fétis en het muziekleven van zijn tijd*, Brussel, Koninklijke Bibliotheek, 1972, p. .XXIV.
²⁹¹ *Revue musicale de Paris*, vol. IX, no.15, 12 IV 1835 p. 117: '[...] *Aguado* sur le luth, [...] *La Romanesca*, fameux air de danse de la fin du seizième siècle [...]; 19 IV 1835, p. 125-126: 'Le *Vilhancico*, pour six voix de femmes et six guitares, a été faiblement rendu, quant à ces instruments. [...] Baillot, l'admirable Baillot, a joué la *Romanesca*;; *Le Ménestrel*, vol. II, 19 IV 1835, p. [4]: 'concert historique [...] *la Romanesca* [...] Baillot'.
²⁹² *Le Ménestrel*, vol. II, no. 23, 3 V 1835, p. [4]: 'Listz [sic], Sor'; no. 24, 10 V 1835, p. [4]: 'Listz [sic], Sor'.
²⁹³ *Bibliographie de la France*, vol. XXIV, no. 28, 11 VII 1835, p. 448: '*Souvenirs de Flandre*. Marche: quatre valses et un rondo pour la guitare, par Nap. Coste, op. 5. Prix 5-0 A Paris, chez Lacôte, rue de Louvois, no. 10.'
²⁹⁴ Kk Rischel 142 mu 6612.2287 U48, Lacôte, Kk Rischel 143 mu 6612.2185 (eks. 1) U48, Richault, Coste *Souvenirs de Flandres*; Wynberg, Simon: *The Guitar Works Napoleon Coste*, facsimile edition, Monaco, Chanterelle, vol. II,1981, Intr., p. 43, *Souvenirs de Flandres*.
²⁹⁵ Devriès, Anik & François Lesure: *Dictionnaire des éditeurs de musique français*, vol. II, De 1820, Genéve, Minkoff, 1979, p. 365.
²⁹⁶ Coste - Degen, 17 X 1863, Århus, Statsbiblioteket, Søffren Degens Papirer, Manuscript no.27b, p. 4: 'Je n'ai pas senti la nécessité d'augmenter le nombre des cordes, outre la 7ème que j'ai ajouté et qui lui donne à peu près l'étendue du violoncelle.'

I added a seventh string to complete the instrument's system, as I understood it. I strove above all to obtain evenness in the various registers in the entire range of the guitar and the vibration. Besides, the guitar, which has the same range as that of the cello, does not need to be extended in the bass. I am not criticizing these innovations, but I myself find them superfluous. In 1835 I added one string to the instrument. I found that satisfactory and left it at that.[297]

These circumstances might lead one to assume that Coste proposed to Lacôte that he should build this seven-string guitar. This is confirmed by comments made by Coste's pupil Petetin, to whom he dedicated his *Étude* 1 in the *Études* opus 38:

It is a name by Lacôte that won the said medal. M. Coste and Lacôte had a deal whereby Lacôte was to give 50 fr. to Coste for each heptacorde sold. Lacôte practically always disregarded this agreement. Later, Coste got very angry at the crook. – There might still be some heptacorde guitars around, unless ignorant people have gone and removed the seventh string to make the instrument more beautiful. – The first ordinary heptacorde was built in 1844 for 270 francs. M. Coste received 50 fr from Lacôte, who was only supposed to receive 220 fr. more. This is no doubt the reason why Lacôte felt a bit upset about how little profit he was making.[298]

But in the twenties René Lacôte had already made a seven-string guitar, with six strings over the fingerboard and one aside, theorboed, so that a similar idea had been implemented before. Indeed, in 1826 Lacôte registers a 'brevet d'invention' for a ten-stringed guitar, with four strings running to the side of the fingerboard, together with Carulli, who writes a method for it.[299] This is the *Méthode Complète* opus 293, published in 1826 by Carli. Lacôte did not publish any of Carulli's works.[300] In 1842 he is noticed with a seven-string guitar for the first time in a concert.[301] He gives an extended motivation for the necessity of a seventh string in the *Méthode* Coste-Sor.[302] It is remarkable Coste doesn't dedicate this work to his father. Jean François Coste dies on April 12, 1835 at the age of 81 years – an age he would have reached on April 23 – in Valenciennes where he lived as a retired captain of infantry, with his daughter Jeanne-Étienne, in the sixth house on the dike near the Faubourg de Paris, separated from his spouse Anne Pierrette Dénéria.[303] In spite of his ripe old age he still led the company of the National Guard in 1830.[304] The couple were not divorced officially, which would have cost Coste's mother her pension, which she asks from the Ministère de la guerre on May 12.[305] It is possible that Napoléon Coste received the sad message of his father's death either by post or by telegraph, perhaps even sooner on the occasion his father's possible illness. A visit to Valenciennes also is likely; the journey would have

---

[297] Coste-Hallberg, 21 XII 1876: 'J'ai ajouté une septième corde pour compléter le système de l'instrument tel que je l'ai compris. Je me suis appliqué par dessus tout à obtenir de l'égalité dans les différent régistres dans toute l'étendue de la guitare et de la vibration. D'ailleurs la guitare dont le diapason est le même que celui du violoncelle n'a pas besoin d'être étendue dans le grave. Je ne blâme pas ces innovations, mais je les trouve superflues pour moi. En 1835 j'ai ajouté une corde à l'instrument. Cela me satisfait et je m'en tiens là.

[298] Petetin, E: *heptacorde*, in: Coste, Napoléon: 'Méthode Complète pour la Guitare par Fernando Sor rédigée et augmentée... par N. Coste', Paris, Schonenberger S.No.1726 [1851] Lbl b.1169, p. 45::'C'est un nom de Lacôte qui fait accorder la dite médaille. M. Coste et Lacôte avaient un traité en vendu duquel Lacôte devait remettre 50 fr à M. Coste par heptacorde vendu. Lacôte s'est presque toujours soustrait à cet engagement. M. Coste devint apres sérieux griffe dérisiant le chevalier - On trouverait encore quelques guitares heptacordes si les ignorants ne l'empreinaient pour rendre l'instrument plus joli, de faire enlever la 7ème corde - La première guitare heptacorde ordinaire était en 1844, de 270 francs. M. Coste touchait 50 fr de Lacôte ne devait recevoir que 220 fr encore. C'est sans doute pour cette raison que Lacôte s'est mouché peu emprofi ce répendu'. [Thanks to Michael McMeeken for this edition].

[299] Lesure, François (préface): *Guitares, Chefs-d'oeuvre des collections de France*, Paris, La Flûte de Pan, 1980, p. 313; Chouquet, Gustave: *Le Musée du Conservatoire national de Musique. Catalogue raisonnée des instruments de cette Collection*, Paris, 1875, 2/1884, 3 suppls. 1894-1903, 1884, no. 280, p. 68; *Le Musée du Conservatoire de Musique, avec les Ier, IIe et IIIe suppléments*, Genève, Minkoff, 1993, p. 16, 17; Vannes, René: *Dictionaire Universel des Luthiers*, Paris, 1951, 3e ed. Bruxelles, 1988, p. 198.

[300] Torta, Mario: *Catalogo tematico delle opere di Ferdinando Carulli*, Lucca, Libreria Musicale Italiana, 1993, p. 694, 695, 707, 736, 765.

[301] *Le Ménestrel*, vol. IX, no. 18, 3 IV 1842, p. [2]: M. 'Coste, guitariste d'un grand mérite, qui se sert d'une guitare à sept cordes, a donné une soirée dans les salons de Duport où il a obtenu de beaux succès.'

[302] Sor, Fernando: *Méthode Complète pour la Guitare par Fernando Sor* rédigée et augmentée... par N. Coste, Paris, Schonenberger, 1851, p. 45: 'Septième corde.'

[303] Bibliothèque municipale Valenciennes, *Acte de décès Jean François Coste*, 13 IV 1835, VAL fonds modernes, série E: Etat civil, E1, R53.

[304] *L'Echo de la Frontière*, Valenciennes: 14e année, 14 IV 1835 no. 1533: 'Le capitaine Coste, [...]'.

[305] Roncet, Noël: *Napoléon Coste, Compositeur - 1805 - 1883*, Amondans, 2005, p. 16.

IV — *Aux Parisiens*   65

taken place by stagecoach, as Paris's first railway station is only established in 1837. During this period the composer might have had many thoughts in mind of his family in Valenciennes in the Flanders of Northern France, a probable reason to write his opus 5 *Souvenirs de Flandres*, which consist of six parts, a *March*, four *Valses* and a *Rondeau*. In these works a master guitarist 's command of the instrument is apparent, as can be seen by the many legatos in high positions with open strings, the broken chords, chord inversions and positions that are quite effective on the guitar. The cadenza, completely written in small notes, in the Valse no. 5 measure 25 also appears, as does a short one in the Rondo no. 6 measure 136. The cadenza as a stylistic element of Romanticism is first noticed in the Andante of the Weigl variations opus 2 and in the Introduction and the Andante of the Armide-fantaisie opus 4. A nice deviation from periodicity can be heard right away in the Marche no. 1, in the elaboration of which the primary joint motif appears in triplet movement, and somewhat further even in corresponding minor. In the second part of this, measure 56, comes a lengthened phrase of 6 measures and a shortened one of 3 measures. Some moments of sudden silence – the 'abruptio' characteristic of Burzik[306] – occur in the Rondo, at measures 4, 20, 32, 56, 99. In this work clear elements are found that can be called folkloristic, apart from onomatopoeia. As far as this work is concerned, many indications of Romantic intentions can be found by way of the descriptive analysis. Furthermore, here is the first time Coste prescribes the seventh string, in the Marche and Valse no. 2 and no. 5. The piece is dedicated to his mother, who, according to the story, lovingly taught him the basics of guitar playing. As this work is composed in the period of his father's death, it would have been more natural to dedicate the work to him. But the dedication could also have been intended as a sort of comfort to his mother. There is a possibility that this says something about his – probably detached – relationship with his father, who was, after all, 51 years older. Coste does not dedicate even a single work to him. In 1877 Coste reuses two of the waltzes, no. 4 and no. 5 in a new work, the *Valse favorite* opus 46.

SITUATION 1835

In 1835 F. Liszt writes an article in six parts in the *Gazette musicale de Paris*, which was founded a year earlier, on the subject of the situation of artists and their societal circumstances. In 1830-1831 Fétis already described the situation of the music industry in his article 'Sur l'industrie musicale.'[307] In the series, Liszt sketches the image of the societal circumstances musicians have, from the point of view of a renowned contemporary artist. Liszt describes the musician's position in this context at the time, which apparently does not seem to have lost any topicality. Just like Rousseau and others he divides artists in three classes: the performers, the composers and the teachers. He immediately sneers at this last group, they are a throng of individuals who cannot play or compose. Musical critics might be a fourth, higher class of musicians, at least some of them, because most of them don't have any knowledge beyond the seven notes of the scale.[308] In capital letters he posits as an important and preponderating FACT the musician's political, social and religious SUBORDINATION of the way, originating in two centuries of history of music and musicians. He reproachfully asks the optimistic drafters of the glorious proclamation of the 'Charte de 1830' *how* they perceive the role of the musician in their *aristocracy of intelligence*. He writes:

> *[...] the religious excommunication that still strikes many of us in France, [...] with Donizetti having the honor of being received by their Majesties the king and the queen of the French. [...] Another fact that can be regarded as a cause and effect of the subordination of the musician is the LACK of CONFIDENCE, the small-minded EGOISM and COMMERCIALISM found among many of them.*[309]

---

[306] Burzik, Monika: 'Coste, Napoléon', in: *Die Musik in Geschichte und Gegenwart*, ed. Blume, Finscher, Kassel, Bärenreiter, 2000, vol. 4, Kol. 1715.

[307] *Revue musicale de Paris*, vol. VII, tome IV, 25 XII 1830, vol. VIII, tome I, I 1831: 'Sur l'industrie musicale.'

[308] *Gazette musicale de Paris*, vol. II, no. 19, 10 V 1835, p. 158-159: 'De la situation des artistes et de leur condition dans la société.'

[309] *Gazette musicale de Paris*, vol. II, no. 20, 17 V 1835, p. 165-166: '[...] *l'excommunication religieuse* qui, en France, frappe encore une si notable portion d'entre nous, [...] que M. Donizetti *avait eut l'honneur d'être reçu* par leurs Majestés le roi et la reine des Français. [...] Un autre FAIT qu'on peut regarder à la fois comme *cause* et *effet* de la Subalternité *des musiciens*, c'est le MANQUE de FOI, - l'ÉGOISME *mesquin* et MERCANTILE d'un grand nombre d'entre eux.'

Here again Liszt puts the words in capital letters. In the fourth article he writes that his short exposition already led to heated debates, but that in this *quasi symphonic-cacophony* he does not hear any serious objections, other than faint and deceitful accusations.[310] Liszt believes in a free debate, and he answers questions and gives examples of the performing *artiste*, the teacher, the lack of welfare facilities:

> *Look at the young man with hollow cheeks, [...] who, out of fifty competitors [...] has had the honor of being admitted to the Conservatoire. [...] He is locked up in a small chamber, has lessons for three quarters of an hour per week, has to eat for 20 sous, [...] for lack of means he cannot visit great artists to listen to them, [...] After two, three or four years [...] his teacher tells him that there is nothing left for him to learn, now he [...] is an established artist... Ridiculous! ... There are a hundred, a thousand of these young people, [...] they are a class of their own, the performing artist. [...] Take another look, if you have the courage, at another class of musicians, the teachers, [...] Listen to their complaints [...] about their awful job, about the ignorance and incorrigible stupidity of their pupils, [...] Look on all the walls of Paris with the posters for benefit concerts for poor artists, that attest to the lack of any welfare provisions for them.[311]*

Liszt evidently speaks in plain terms. He, himself being in a different position as a renowned artist, stands up for his less endowed colleagues with subtle arguments and in his colorful use of language. Other people do the same, but with music. Luigi Legnani, who visits Paris as a travelling virtuoso, just like Paganini, and receives resounding applause in a concert on October 11, 1835 where he plays

58 Liszt - Noël, 1837

---

[310] *Gazette musicale de Paris*, vol. II, no. 30, 26 VII 1835, p. 245-246: '[...] cette *cacophonie quasi-symphonique* [...]'.
[311] *Gazette musicale de Paris*, vol. II, no. 30, 26 VII 1835, p. 247-248: '*Voyez* ce jeune homme aux joues creuses, [...] il l'ait emporté sur une cinquantaine de rivaux [...] fait le faveur de l'admettre au Conservatoire. [...] renfermé dans une mansarde [...] recevant trois quarts d'heure de leçon par semaine, dinant à 20 sous; [...] n'ayant pas [...] les moyens de voir et d'entendre les artistes supérieurs, [...] Après deux, trois ou quatre ans, [...] son professeur lui dira "qu'il n'a plus rien à apprendre, qu'il est [...] artiste achevé..."Dérision!... [...] c'est vingt, cent, mille jeunes gens [...] c'est tout une classe: c'est l'exécutant. [...] *Voyez* encore, si vous avez le courage, une autre *classe* de musiciens, les professeurs, [...] Écoutez leurs plaintes [...] sur le *chien de métier* [...] sur l'impéritie et l'incurable stupidité de leurs élèves; [...] *Voyez* de plus, sur tous les murs de Paris, ces affiches de concerts [...] au *bénéfice d'artistes malheureux*, qui témoignent de l'absence de toute prévoyance sociale à leur égard.'

IV — Aux Parisiens

a *Grande Fantaisie Originale*,[312] falls and breaks his arm getting out of a carriage and cannot play his next concert. Sor and Aguado offer to replace him, and the box office receipts from the concert they give on November 29, 1835 in the salle Chantereine are donated to him. Here musicians stand in for a misfortunate colleague and give a benefit concert for him.[313] On August 30 Liszt resumes his argument, this time on the subject of defraying the costs of musical life:

> *With one stroke of the pen Bonaparte cuts half of the teachers and students from the Conservatoire and reduces funds for maintenance by 100,000 francs. Immediately after the July Revolution his majesty the bourgeois king sacks the artists of the chapelle du roi, as an economy, as if they were some superfluous part of the household. [...] The illustrious champion of paté Regnault, becoming director of the Opéra, sacks Baillot, because our great violinist rejected the offer this intrepid Mr. Véron made him to set his salary at half of what it had been.*[314]

These are apparently awful times for the art of music in Paris in 1835. The guitar is not even mentioned. But Liszt does not persist in showing and analyzing a miserable situation. He formulates a concrete course of action in eight points:

> *In the name of all musicians, in the name of the arts and the social progression, we ask, we demand: First, the foundation of a competition held every five years for sacred, dramatic and symphonic music. [...] Second, the implementation of musical education in all primary schools and promotion in other schools. Third, the reintroduction of plainsong in the churches of Paris and the departments. Four, the establishment of assemblées générales of philharmonic societies, following the example of England and Germany. Five, a théâtre lyrique, concerts, performances of chamber music. Six, a progressive school in music, apart from the Conservatoire, directed by renowned artists. Seven, a professional chair in history and the philosophy of music. Eight, the publication of cheap editions of the most outstanding works of old and new composers, from the Renaissance to modern times. This publication [...] which concerns the complete development of the art, from popular song [...] to symphony, [...] could bear the title Panthéon Musical. [...] This is the program we suggest in summary [...] to all who are interested in art in France. We think we know all about the circumstances around the impossibility of putting this into effect, some people possibly would urge against it. F. Liszt.*[315]

Here Franz Liszt offers not only criticism, but also a proposition that cannot be declined, put in clear words, and stating a coherent view on the art of music. But of course Liszt is also aware that in Paris not much is done with these demands after 1835. However, Liszt's sketch shows a clear

---

[312] *Le Ménestrel*, vol. II, no. 37, 18 X 1835, p. [4]: 'M. Legnani, [...] grande fantaisie originale.'; Rossato, Daniela: 'Luigi Rinaldo Legnani' in: *Il Fronimo*, Milano, Suvini Zerboni, vol. VII, no. 27, 1979, p. 14; [*Grande Fantasia* opus 61].

[313] *Gazette musicale de Paris*, vol. II, no. 42, 18 X 1835, p. 336: 'Le guitariste Legnani'; no. 48, 29 XI 1835; p. 395: 'M. Lagnani [sic] [...] casser le bras [...] Aguado et Sor [...]'; no. 49, 6 XII 1835, p. 403: concert [...] au bénéfice de M. Lagnani [sic]'.

[314] *Gazette musicale de Paris*, vol. II, no. 35, 30 VIII 1835, p. 286: 'Bonaparte, d'un trait de plume, biffe la moitié des professeurs et des élèves du conservatoire, et réduit de 100.000 francs les fonds alloués à son entretien. Immédiatement après la révolution de juillet, sa majesté citoyenne renvoie, par économie, comme on renvoie une domesticité inutile, les artistes composant la chapelle du roi. [...] L'illustre propagateur de *paté Regnault*, devenu directeur de l'Opéra, congédia Baillot, parce que notre grand violon refusa le *demi-solde* que lui offrait intrépidement M. Véron!!!'

[315] *Gazette musicale de Paris*, vol. II, no. 41, 11 X 1835, p. 333: 'Au nom de tous les musiciens, au nom de l'art et du progrès social, nous demandons, nous réclamons: Premièrement, la fondation d'un concours quinquennal de musique religieuse, dramatique et symphonique. [...] Secondement, l'introduction de l'enseignement musical dans les écoles primaires; Sa propagation dans d'autres écoles, [...] Troisièmement, la réorganisation de la chapelle et la réforme du plain-chant dans toutes nos églises de Paris et des départemens. [sic] Quatrièmement, des assemblées générales des sociétés philharmoniques, à l'instar des grandes fêtes musicales de l'Angleterre et de l'Allemagne. Cinquièmement, un théâtre lyrique; des concerts; Des séances de *musique da Camera*, [...] Sixièmement une ÉCOLE PROGRESSIVE de musique, fondée en dehors du Conservatoire par des artistes éminens; [sic] [...] Septièmement, une chaire d'histoire et de philosophie de la musique. Huitièmement, la publication à bon marché des oeuvres les plus remarquables de tous les compositeurs anciens et modernes, depuis la renaissance de la musique jusqu'à nos jours. Embrassant dans son entier le développement de l'art, partant de la chanson populaire, pour arriver [...] à la symphonie [...] cette publication pourrait prendre le titre de PANTHÉON MUSICAL. [...] Tel est le programme que nous exposons sommairement [...] à tous ceux qui s'intéressent à l'art en France. Nous croyons connaître trop à fond la situation des choses pour admettre de prétendues *impossibilités d'exécution* qu'à tout hasard quelques personnes objecteront peut-être. F. Liszt.'

contemporary view of the circumstances in life and work of musicians in Paris. The points Liszt puts forward give occasion to compare with the situation of Coste himself. In the first place he participates in Makaroff's guitar competition of 1856, winning the second prize. This is the first competition in history for the instrument. Secondly, he contributed to musical education by giving lessons, not in primary schools, but in Valenciennes. Thirdly, Coste only composes chansons for voice with piano or guitar accompaniment for voice and arranges many other for voice and guitar, but he does not compose any sacred music. He does not betray the slightest trace of religiosity, apart from him joining the Freemasons' lodge. In the fourth place, he is not occupied with orchestral music and is not involved that way in any organization to that purpose. In the fifth place, he gives concerts himself in theatres and salons. In the sixth place, a progressive school of music, apart from the Conservatoire, would have been very attractive for him, with the intent to be a student first and a teacher later, which may have had a great influence on the development and position of the guitar in Paris and France, but that did not happen. In the seventh place, apart from in his letters and explanations in the *Méthode*, Coste expresses no reflections on his music or on music in general. In the eighth place he works on cheap editions of popular and classical music himself and gives 'old' works a place in his publications, as the first guitar composer. The conclusion can be drawn that Coste is surely devoted in developing his talent, in the spirit of Liszt, but that there is an insufficient basis to do so within the musical infrastructure available. An important issue here is that the guitar is not taught on the Conservatoire, and as a result no authorization is made for the instrument. The situation of the guitarists and guitar composers is strongly liable to erosion, with negative consequences for Coste's position as a young, onrushing guitar talent as a result.

Opus 19[b], *La Romanesca* 1836

The year 1836 brings no news about Coste, except by way of the presumable publication of his arrangement for guitar solo of *La Romanesca, Fameux Air de Danse de la Fin du 16ème Siècle*. The opus numbering is not given by Coste himself. It is Thorvald Rischel who gives this work the number 19. Why he did so, is not clear.[316] It is clear, however, that the edition has no opus number, the title page is missing in the known edition of Richault. The date is based on Richault's numbering, which is not very reliable. Still it is the only grounds for it. *La Romanesca* was played with the same title already in 1835 by violinist Baillot in an ensemble in the *concert historique*, organized by Fétis.[317] In 1836 it is published by Coste, in 1839 in an arrangement for piano by Burgmüller, in 1840 by Liszt and in 1843 in an arrangement for violoncello and piano by Servais. Sor also published it in 1835 for violin and guitar.[318] It is a very popular work with a nice melody, appealing to many people in the first half of the 19th century, and it was provided with words by Adolphe Larmande, published in *Échos du temps Passé* in an arrangement for voice and piano by Baptiste Wekerlin with publisher Durand, probably in the second half of the 19th century.[319] The explanatory note says that Rousseau in his *Dictionnaire de Musique* makes clear that it originated in Rome and therefore is called Romanesca.[320] Rischel's numbering is in conflict with the other opus 19, *Delfzil* from the *Sept Souvenirs*, the reason why Wynberg was obliged to adapt the number of the chanson to opus 19[b].[321] Wynberg gives 1843 as a date for the work, which might concur with the opus number, referring to the *Bibliographie de la France*, where *La Norma* opus

---

[316] Rischel, Thorvald: 'Bibliographische Notizen zu den Gitarrenwerken von Napoleon Coste', in: *Die Gitarre*, Berlin, 1927, Jahrgang VIII, Heft 7/8, [Coste-Heft] p. 47-51.

[317] *Revue musicale de Paris*, vol. IX, no. 15, 12 IV 1835 p. 116-117: 'Le *Concert historique* [...]'; no.16, 19 IV 1835, p. 125-126: 'Théatre-Italien. Concert historique [...] six guitares'; *Le Ménestrel*, vol. II, no. 21, 19 IV 1835, p. [4]: 'Le concert historique [...] la *Romanesca* [...] Baillot.'.

[318] *Bibliographie de la France*, vol. XXVIII, no. 7, 16 II 1839, p. 84, 'Burgmuller'; vol. XXIX, no. 29, 18 VII 1840, p. 410, 'Liszt'; vol. XXXII, no. 46, 18 XI 1843, p. 588, 'Servais'; Jeffery, Brian: *Fernando Sor, Composer and Guitarist*, London, Tecla, 1977; second edition 1994, p.174, Sor 1835.

[319] Devriès-Lesure, A.: 'Durand, Maison d'édition'; Gétreau, F.: 'Weckerlin, Jean-Baptiste', in: Fauquet, Joël-Marie: *Dictionnaire de la Musique en France au XIXe siècle*, Paris, Fayard, 2003, p. 413, 1312-1313.

[320] Wekerlin, J.B.: *Échos du Temps Passé*, vol. I, Paris, Durand, 1971, p.43.

[321] Wynberg, Simon: *The Guitar Works of Napoleon Coste*, facsimile edition, Vol. III, Monaco, 1981, reprint 2006-7.

IV — Aux Parisiens 69

16 is concerned, so this is not correct.[322] The work itself is an easy one to play, a quite literal arrangement of the melody supplied with accompanying chords, a didactic, commercial intended edition.

ZANI DE FERRANTI

This aside, no further information exists on Coste in 1836, but there is information on Marco Aurelio Zani de Ferranti, a contemporary of Coste already identified in this biography as the composer of the *Niaiserie* opus 21, who visits Paris as a travelling virtuoso. He is in Paris as early as 1820 when he is 19 years old. There he gives his first performance and probably meets Carulli and Carcassi. Then he goes to St. Petersburg, travels to Paris again via Hamburg in 1825, goes to Brussels, back to Paris, to Holland, and to Brussels, where he teaches Italian at the Royal Athenaeum in 1829, when Coste arrives in Paris.[323] In Paris again in 1836, he gives a concert in the salons Pleyel with other distinguished artists on Wednesday, March 16.[324] By that time he is already appointed 'guitarist to the king' in Belgium, a country which was founded in 1830 as a consequence of the July Revolution in Paris and the performance of Auber's *La Muette de Portici*. He achieves this appointment in 1834 through the mediation of Fétis, who calls him the 'Paganini of the guitar', and a letter by Paganini himself, declaring him to be 'superior to all guitarists.'[325] He participates in concerts of the *société musical*, which is founded in 1835 by the gentlemen Herz, Labarre, Bertini, etc.[326] Along with Coste and Mertz, Zani de Ferranti is one of the three great Romantic guitar composers.

59 Marco Aurelio Zani de Ferranti

WoO 9, INTRODUCTION ET VARIATIONS SUR LA CAVATINA FAVORITE DE L'OPÉRA LE PIRATE 1837

The opera *Il Pirata* by Vincenzo Bellini is a source of inspiration for Coste. The unpublished work Coste bases on it exists in four different manuscripts in the Kongelige Bibliotek in Copenhagen. Two of those, Ms. 24 and Ms. 28, are 20th century transcripts by Thorvald Rischel and Frederik Birket-Smith respectively, who gave the collection their name. Ms. 64a is a transcript by J.G. Holm, a friend of Coste from Copenhagen, to whom opus 38 no 7 and opus 39 are dedicated. These transcripts bear the title *Introduction et Variations sur la Cavatina favorite de l'opéra: Le Pirate*. Ms. 47, which according to Simon Wynberg is in Søffren Degen's handwriting with the date 15-4-1844, has the title as above, but the motif is wrongly ascribed to Rossini. This incorrect title is found again in modern editions since then. *Il Pirata* is Vincenzo Bellini's first opera, with which he founds his career. This work has its opening night in 1827 in Milan, and is performed in the Théâtre-Italien in autumn 1833, after his arrival

---

[322] *Bibliographie de la France*, vol. XXXII, no. 35, 2I X 1843, p. 452, '*Fantaisie Norma*, Nap. Coste, [op. 16] prix 5-0; Chez Challiot, rue Saint-Honoré, n. 336.'
[323] Wynberg, Simon: *Marco Aurelio Zani de Ferranti*, a biography, Heidelberg, Chanterelle, 1989, p. 7, 8,12-14.
[324] *Le Ménestrel*, vol. III, no. 15, 13 III 1836, p. [4]: '[...] soirée musicale [...] Ferranti [...]'.
[325] Cruys, Marcus G.S. van de: *The life and times of Marco Aurelio Zani de Ferranti*, Wijnegem, Homunculus, 2005, p. 20, 21, 30, 35, 41, 52-53; *Revue et Gazette musicale de Paris*, vol.III, no. 17, 24 IV 1836, p. 40.
[326] *Le Ménestrel*, vol. III, no. 11, 14 II 1836, p. [4]: '[...] réorganisation de la société musicale [...] Zani de Ferranti [...]'.

60 Bellini, 1835

in Paris.³²⁷ This is the reason to assume that Coste wrote this work between these dates, in any case before 1844. Coste wrote another work in which he uses a theme by Bellini, the *Fantaisie 'Norma'* opus 16, a composition he plays in a concert in 1838 and which is published in 1843. The opera *Norma* also has its premiere in Paris in 1833. Coste strongly deviates from the variation form, and the work also has more Romantic characteristics, such that it can be presumed he wrote *Il Pirata* first, hence, before 1838. The year 1838 shows many activities that Coste was engaged in, in his arrangements of Schubert songs and 16 waltzes by Strauss. Apart from that, the work can be dated to the time of *Fantaisie Armide* for stylistic and characteristic reasons. In this way a date around 1837 is likely for *Il Pirata*. The motif is taken from the second act number 15 *Scena ed Aria* where Gualtiero, after the chorale in measure 79, starts with 'Ah non fia sempre odiata...'. This aria has a refrain with a typical and catchy melody, which Bellini returns to several times in the finale of the opera, sometimes changed, sometimes unaltered, to satisfy the audience. That this principle works, also emerges from the choice for this theme by the guitar composer. The descriptive analysis of the work shows for certain that it has a number of characteristics that can be called Romantic, such as cadenza, figuration, ornaments, notable chromatics, harmony and modulation, apart from the open ending, chromatic third relation in key and nice arpeggio's, the latter typical for Coste's style. The reason why an opus number is missing probably lies in the fact that it remains unpublished. But how this came about remains incomprehensible: in spite of the theme and variations form it is a mature, early Romantic work that fits well in the development Coste goes through in this period.

Opus 6 *Fantaisie de Concert* 1837

Coste's next work in the consecutive opus numbers is his *Fantaisie de Concert* opus 6 on a theme of Meyerbeer, a theme that could not be specified as yet. It is dedicated to his pupil Mad'lle Albertine Douillez, whose last name coincides with that of a teacher of piano, harp and guitar at 20 Culture Ste-Catherine, mentioned by Planque in 1836.³²⁸ The edition is announced in the *Bibliographie de la France* on August 26, 1837³²⁹ as published by the author in the 'rue de l'Echiquier, n. 23'. The price is 5-7, in francs, of course. Coste has apparently moved from the rue du Colombier, close to the St-Sulpice, to his new address in the neighborhood of the rue du Faubourg Poissonnière and the St-Denis, on the other bank of the Seine, with the Conservatoire and his publisher Richault around the corner.³³⁰ The work is a *fantaisie variée* on a prominent 'Thème de Meyerbeer', which could not be traced back in any of his operas that could be considered for this question. After his successes in Italy with *Semiramide*

---

³²⁷ Lippmann, Friedrich: 'Vincenzo Bellini' in: Sadie, Stanley ed.: *The New Grove Dictionary of Music and Musicians*, Vol.1-20, Macmillan, London, 1980. Vol.2, p.447, 452; id. in: Sadie, Stanley, ed.: *The New Grove Dictionary of Music and Musicians*, second edition, London, Macmillan, 2001, vol. 2, p. 208.

³²⁸ Planque: *Agenda musical, 2ᵉ Année 1836*, Paris, 1836, repr. Genève, Minkoff, 1981, p. 268: 'Douillez, piano, harpe, guitare,'.

³²⁹ *Bibliographie de la France*, vol. XXVI, no. 34, 26 VIII 1837, p. 424: 'Fantaisie de Concert, composée pour la guitare, par Nap. Coste, op. 6. A Paris, chez l'auteur, rue de l'Echiquier, no. 23. Prix 5-0'.

³³⁰ Leconte, André, ed.: *Plan de Paris par Arrondissement*, Paris, 1977, G7 Xe Arr,; Halliard, Jacques: *Dictionary historic des rues de Paris*, Paris, Les Editions de Minuet, 1963-1972, plan 1808, p. 457.

IV — *Aux Parisiens* 71

in 1819 and *Margherite d'Anjou* in 1820, Giacomo Meyerbeer (1791-1864) wants to conquer a place in the Opéra of Paris, and he has Scribe take care of the libretto, as he is aware of the French public's taste. After negotiations and compromises with Véron he succeeds with the premieres in Paris of *Robert le Diable* in 1831 and *Les Huguenots* in 1836.[331] Coste could have taken his theme from one of these operas. There is some resemblance with the themes, the rhythm and the harmony of the 'Choeur des Baigneuses' no.8 of the latter, but the theme Coste has chosen is so characteristic, that it is not convincing he chose this one.[332] Apart from that, the central melody in *Les Huguenots* is the Luther-Lied 'Ein feste Burg ist unser Gott', which Coste does not use for his composition. The 'Thème de

61 Meyerbeer, 1836

Meyerbeer' remains unfound until this date, but it has a very typical character with the dotted rhythm, the melody, mostly in broken triads and the single I-V-I harmony, classical in structure and character. In the consecutive variations Coste uses figurations with many chromatics. Chords with tension, such as #IV2, I6#5 and even a #2 suspension with minor-major effect are recognizable as harmonically interesting, as well as a double diminished seventh chord and many diminished seventh chords as dissonant. Variation 3 has a cadenza, a variation, by the way, with many legatos and a glissando, written out in notes. Coste applies many dynamics in this piece, as well as prescriptions of tempo changes and articulation. A flageolet passage is to be found in the finale, though the latter is not called as such. This opus 6, which has the form of a theme and variations, preceded by an introduction and ending in an unannounced coda, has some fairly Romantic musical aspects. That is not so in his next opus, number 7, which appears in 1838.

Opus 7, *16 Walses favorites de Johann Strauss* 1838

The famous Johann Strauss (Vater) is one year older than Coste. He gives concerts in Vienna with his orchestra and writes compositions for piano and for orchestra with much success, in the genre of the Walzer, the Galopp, the Cotillon, but Marches also. His works are in great demand with editors and he becomes well known in Paris as well and an inevitable visit to the city eventually follows. After 1833 he tours with his orchestra, which includes 28 musicians, through Austria, Bohemia and Germany, and he visits Holland and France. His arrival in Paris in 1837, where he discovers the quadrille which he later introduces in Vienna, is an unprecedented hit, especially with Berlioz, who writes favorable critiques on his conducting and composing in *Le Journal des Débats*.[333] This visit has a positive effect

---

[331] Almanach musical pour 1854..., Paris, Houssiaux ed., 1854, p. 29: 'Meyerbeer (Giacomo).'; Becker, Heinz: 'Meyerbeer, Giacomo', in: Sadie, Stanley, ed.: *The New Grove Dictionary of Music and Musicians*, London, Macmillan, 1980. vol. 12, p. 247-249, 254; Brzoska, Matthias: 'Meyerbeer', in: Sadie, Stanley, ed.:*The New Grove Dictionary of Music and Musicians*, second edition, London, Macmillan, 2001, vol. 16, p. 566-569.

[332] Meyerbeer, Giacomo: *Les Huguenots*, facs. ed. score, New York, Garland, 1980, p. 261.

[333] Carner, Mosco & Max Schönherr: 'Strauss, (1) Johann', in: Sadie, Stanley ed.: *The New Grove Dictionary of Music and Musicians*, London, Macmillan, 1980, vol. 18, p. 207-208; Kemp, Peter: 'Strauss', in: Sadie, Stanley, ed.:*The New Grove Dictionary of Music and Musicians*, second edition, London, Macmillan, 2001, vol. 24, p. 475; Albert, K.: 'Strauss, Johann' in: Robijns, J. & Miep Zijlstra: *Algemene Muziek Encyclopedie*, Weesp, De Haan, 1983, vol.9, p. 274.

62 Strauss (Vater) 1835

on his popularity. Many people want to play his works for piano, apparently including guitarists, because Napoléon Coste provides them with an edition of 16 of Strauss's Waltzes in transcription for guitar solo, making his way again in the popular genre, after the Quadrilles. But Coste is genuinely fond of the Waltz. He himself composes eleven of them, either as a separate work or as a part of a larger one. This opus 7 *16 Walses favorites de Johann Strauss arrangées Pour la Guitare* appears with Richault, and from the number of the edition it can be concluded that the date must be 1838, one year after Strauss visited Paris. Ten of these waltzes are found in other piano editions, 4 are from a collection of Strauss waltzes opus 82 from 1835. Coste generally simplifies the arrangement of the pieces, so that they are quite easy to play: it is a didactic edition that we are dealing with here. In every way this is a competent transcription, which supports the presumption that Coste played the piano. A dedication is missing, but a mention 'dédiées aux Amateurs' would not be unsuitable. This opus 7 shows his interest in the work of other composers and another instrument for the first time, apart from taking a theme or a motif to write his own composition, an interest he will show later in other transcriptions, for instance in the *Méthode* and in opus 52, as well as in many arrangements of Schubert songs and the works of Sor. Here too his interest in 'old' music from the guitar world is striking, but this is in line with Fétis's initiative of the *Concert historique*. Apart from taking opera themes, composing a chanson with a political content and writing didactic music, Coste is present in the Romantic musical reality of the time. Strictly speaking, in relation to the opinion of Liszt, a distinction must be made between the more commercial activities with opera songs, current trends and didactics, and the more serious Romantic activities, such as the new interpretation of historical music and composing in the Romantic style. Coste starts making arrangements of chansons for voice accompanied by guitar.

CHANSON, *L'ESQUIF DU PÊCHEUR* - CONCONE [ARR. COSTE] 1838

The first known arrangement by Coste of a chanson for voice and guitar is that of M. L. Escudier and J. Concone. The cover of *L'Esquif du Pêcheur* shows the fisherman's little boat at the dramatic moment when it is almost swallowed up by the waves. The man himself looks up in despair. The chanson is dedicated to Mlle Elisa d'Hennin, perhaps the same female singer from Valenciennes with whom Coste already performed twice in 1838. The words of Léon Escudier are put to music by Giuseppe Concone; there is no date. As usual, publishers in this period start by publishing their own work, expanding their list later with works by others. Escudier is no exception to the rule. Together with his brother Marie he started the magazine *La France Musicale* in 1837.[334] Léon Escudier (1815-1881) probably wrote the words around 1838, when he was 25 years of age, but the chanson is published by Richault, who lives at Boulevard Poissonnière no.16 au premier between 1825 and 1841, in a list of twelve other titles by

---

[334] Devriès, Anik & François Lesure: *Dictionary des éditeurs de musique français*, Vol. II, De 1820, Geneva, 1979, p. 8; Laforêt, Claude (pseud. Flavien Bonnet-Roy): *La Vie musicale au Temps romantique*, Peyronnet, Paris, 1929, p. 172.

IV — *Aux Parisiens* 73

the same composer. The title page does not say whether these are for voice and guitar, in which case Coste may have collaborated in the edition. The music is by J. [Giuseppe] Concone (1801-1861), an Italian composer and voice teacher, who gives lessons in Paris from 1837 to 1848, plays the piano in a concert with Coste in 1838 and 1840, and apparently also writes chansons.[335] Coste knows all three people involved in this chanson.

63 L'Esquif du Pêcheur

The story by Escudier tells of a poor and misfortunate fisherman, who goes out in search of adventure with his boat as an unstable home, gets caught in by a storm and meets with disaster. In the music Concone pictures the rolling water with the swaying 6/8 time, but the drama of the storm and the sinking boat cannot be heard in the melody or accompaniment, which mainly remains in the key of C. Nevertheless, there are some moody chromatics in the introduction. Apart from a phrase of 5 measures the song is periodic. With the swallow in the first phrase the bass is omitted, which gives a floating effect, but this bears n no relation whatsoever to the words of the next two verses. With four ornaments, some legatos and some intervals the melody is quite tuneful. The minor chord in phrase 3 and the ♭6 'a-flat' in the last phrase are signs of a dawning Romantic sentiment. It is a simple chanson that will appeal to the amateur. The arrangement of this chanson, and perhaps the other 12 as well, is clearly one of Coste's commercial activities.

Schubert arrangements

The arrangements Coste makes of the songs of Schubert also can be counted among his more commercial activities. Singing these songs with lyrics in French is very popular in these years both in the salons and in the home. For the latter the guitar is a very suitable instrument: not everyone can afford a piano, and in that case his Schubert songs for voice and guitar are appealing. It is even supposed that Schubert himself composed the songs with the guitar as an instrument, as can be concluded from the sometimes very guitar-like accompaniments, which can be played from the piano score on the guitar without much effort.[336] Coste is very productive in this period, publishing fourteen chansons

---

[335] Forbes, Elisabeth: 'Concone, Giuseppe', in: Sadie, Stanley ed.: *The New Grove Dictionary of Music and Musicians*, London, Macmillan, 1980, vol. 4, p. 640.
[336] Duarte, John W.: *Songs by Schubert*, Ancona, Bèrben, 1973, p. 5.

in separate editions, which are announced in *La France musicale* on April 8, 1838 under 'Nouvelles Publications Musicales' as 'Mélodies de François Schubert.' 'Avec accompagnement de guitare, par Coste.' Between 1828 and 1840 Richault publishes many of the Schubert songs in various editions, separately or in collections, and now apparently in transcription for voice and guitar as well.[337] The conclusion is that there must be a great demand.

64 Ave Maria, Schubert, arr. Coste

Most of them are famous chansons, like *Ave Maria, La Jeune Mère, La Jeune Fille et la Mort, La Fille du Pêcheur, La Barcarolle, Marguerite, La Poste, La Sérénade*, provided with French lyrics and titles, but also less well-known ones, such as *La Berceuse, Les Plaintes de la Jeune Fille, Le Jeune Aveugle, Fais mes Amours* and *Amour et Mystère* also are mentioned in the list of editions 'chez Richault, Boulevard Poissonnière, 16, au Premier.' In his letter to Hallberg of June 25, 1877 Coste himself points out *Marguerite, Adieu, Les Plaintes de la Jeune Fille* and *La Sérénade* to be the best.[338] Some of these are considered here to find out if they show any Romantic characteristics and also to illuminate Coste's skills in making arrangements once more.

Schubert composed the *Schlummerlied* or *Schlaflied* of *Abendlied* D 527 on the words of Mayerhofer in January 1817. It was numbered opus 24/2 and published in 1832,[339] and subsequently in a French translation by Bélanger as *La Berceuse* in an arrangement for voice and guitar by Coste in Paris in 1838, published by Richault. The original song is in F, as is the arrangement for voice and guitar by Coste in the modern edition of Brian Jeffery also. To make the piece easier to play, the advice is to tune the sixth string to F. Sor also applied this scordatura once in Étude 12 opus 35 from 1828. Some early Romantic characteristics can be observed, the sort of open ending of the melody, the plagal cadence there, pointing to folk music harmony, and some passing chromatics. Schubert left this berceuse quite simple, but the chanson does have his mark: the harmonic urge in measure 9-10. Schubert composed *Das Fischermädchen* in 1828 to the words of Heine, as no. 10 of his *Schwanengesang* D 957.[340] In French translation by Bélanger and as an arrangement for voice and guitar the song appears with the title *La*

---

[337] *La France musicale*, vol. I, no. 15, 8 IV 1838, p. 8: 'Mélodies de François Schubert. *Avec accompagnement de guitare, par Coste.*'; Tunley, David: *Salons, singers and songs: a background to romantic French song, 1830-1870*, Ashgate, Aldershot, 2002, p. 230-249.
[338] Coste-Hallberg, 25 VI 1877: 'Les meilleurs sont ceux de Marguérite, Adieux, Les Plaintes de la Jeune Fille, La Sérénade.'
[339] Brown, Maurice J.E. & Eric Sams: 'Franz Schubert', in: Sadie, Stanley ed.: *The New Grove Dictionary of Music and Musicians*, London, Macmillan, 1980, vol. 16, p. 796; id. in: Sadie, Stanley, ed.: *The New Grove Dictionary of Music and Musicians*, second edition, London, Macmillan, 2001, vol. 22, p. 700-721.
[340] *La France Musicale*, vol I, no. 15, 8 IV 1838, p. 8: 'La Fille du Pêcheur.'; Brown, Maurice J.E. & Eric Sams: 'Schubert', in: Sadie, Stanley ed,: *The New Grove Dictionary of Music and Musicians*, London, Macmillan, 1980, vol. 16, p. 803-804.

Fille du Pêcheur. The introduction shows a quickened heartbeat, lively and smooth in meter and rhythm. Nature and love play a role here, the cloudless sky foretells happiness, the prophecy is love. Romantic characteristics here can be the sometimes interesting harmonic movements, a quasi-open ending, folk-like harmony and some chromatics. Apart from that the imagination of the words can be considered as programmatic. Some chord prolongations occur with Coste himself too.

Concerts 1838

1838 is also the year in which Coste, who is 33 years of age now, plays in some concerts together with Sor, who plays an important role in his musical life in this period. It is natural that his oft-mentioned study of counterpoint and harmony was under Sor's supervision. Sor dedicates his last work to him, *Souvenir de Russie* opus 63, and probably entrusts him with the republication of his *Méthode*. And they make music together. This is mentioned in *La France musicale*, the 'journal hebdomadaire' started by the brothers Marie and Léon Escudier as a weekly publication in December 1837,[341] in the column 'Revue des Concerts' on January 21:

> *The duet for guitar, executed by M. Sor and M. C., did not have great results. The guitar never should have left the salons, it is better suited to accompany songs than to reproduce serious compositions.*[342]

It is a concert by Mlle Sardi, a young female singer, which is given on January 15, 1838 in the salle Saint-Jean in the Hôtel de Ville and the critic apparently does not have a high opinion of the guitar duo, of which 'M. C.' is Monsieur Coste, at least, that is the assumption that can be made. According to Moser and Piris the date must be January 15, but they do not mention a source.[343] The critic will have none of the female singer and there was not a large audience for this still interesting concert, due to inclement weather. The duet is not mentioned by name. Around this year Sor composed his *Souvenir de Russie* opus 63, a memory of Russia where he travelled to in 1823 together with his spouse Félicité Hullin, prima ballerina of the Bolshoi Theatre in Moscow, and where he had great triumphs with the performance of his ballet *Cendrillon*.[344] He dedicates this work to his friend N. Coste. And in case this piece has already been composed, why shouldn't they have played it in this concert? Other, more likely works for this concert, as can be concluded from the lack of success, are recent works by Sor, such as *Trois petits Divertissements* opus 61, but this piece is far too easy, or perhaps *Divertissement* opus 62 from the same period. Of these then the latter is more likely: the Rischel & Birket-Smith collection in the Royal Library in Copenhagen has an edition of this work with the signature 'L'auteur à son ami N. Coste' and Sor's autograph on the title page.[345] If Sor has given Coste this copy so that they can play it together, it is via Søffren Degen and Thorvald Rischel that it found its way into this collection . Now his opus 63, Sor's last work, can be set aside for his last concert.

Sor's personal circumstances are dramatic in these years, when his daughter Caroline dies June 8, 1837, when his – former? – spouse Félicité Hullin, who stayed behind in Moscow, marries someone else in 1838, and when he himself falls ill around August 1838.[346] But first he plays in one of Coste's concerts.

---

[341] Devriès, Anik & François Lesure: *Dictionary des éditeurs de musique français*, vol. II, de 1820, Genève, Minkoff, 1979-1988, p. 10; Laforêt, Claude (pseud. Flavien Bonnet-Roy): *La Vie musicale au Temps romantique*, Paris, Peyronnet, 1929, p. 172.

[342] *La France musicale*, vol. I, no. 4, 21 I 1838, p. 6: 'Le duo sur la guitare, exécuté par M. Sor et M. C., n'a pas produit un grand effet. La guitare ne devrait jamais sortir des salons; elle est plutôt faite pour accompagner la voix que pour reproduire des compositions sérieuses.'

[343] Moser, Wolf: *Fernando Sor: Versuch einer Autobiografie und gitarristische Schriften*, Köln, 1984, p. 97; Piris, Bernard: *Fernando Sor, Une guitare à l'orée du Romantisme*, Arles, Aubier, 1989, p. 162.

[344] Jeffery, Brian: *Fernando Sor, Composer and Guitarist*, London, Tecla, 1977; second edition 1994, p. 75-76, 167-168; Moser, Wolf: *Ich, Fernando Sor, Versuch einer Autobiographie und gitarristische Schriften*, 2nd ed., Lyon, Saint-Georges, 2005, p. 128.

[345] Kk Rischel 784 mu 6706.2884 U74, Sor, *Divertissement op. 62*; Wynberg, Simon: *The Guitar Works Napoleon Coste*, facsimile edition, vol. I-IX, Monaco, Chanterelle, 1981, vol. VII, p. vii.

[346] Jeffery, Brian: *Fernando Sor, Composer and Guitarist*, London, Tecla, 1977; second edition 1994, p.107-108; Moser, Wolf: *Ich, Fernando Sor, Versuch einer Autobiographie und gitarristische Schriften*, 2nd ed., Lyon, Saint-Georges, 2005, p202; Piris, Bernard: *Fernando Sor, Une guitare à l'orée du Romantisme*, Arles, Aubier, 1989, p. 67.

65 Paris, Hôtel de Ville, salle St-Jean, 15 I 1838

That concert takes place on Tuesday April 10, 1838 in the salons Duport and it is already announced on April 1 in *La France musicale*. According to Léon Escudier, Coste is 'one of our best guitarists' when he plays in the instrumental part, where Sor is mentioned, together with the Tilmant brothers, Koken and Lecointe. François Coken (1801-1875) [i.e. Cokken] is mentioned here as 'Koken'. He plays the bassoon in the orchestras of the Théâtre-Italien and of the Opéra. It is not for certain whether he played in this concert, he is not mentioned again in the reviews, while Concone is.

In the same magazine Escudier sneers at the guitar on April 15:

The musical night was rather brilliant. M. Coste is certainly an outstanding guitarist. His duet with Sor pleased the audience; [...[they seem to have a part of the pleasure themselves by playing an instrument as ugly as the guitar. The audience took a fancy to a fantasy on a motif from Norma, performed by M. Coste. The piano was played by the gentlemen Burgmüller and Concone, who played the accompaniment with the methodical tact that can be expected from them.[347]

Apart from the fact that the guitar is judged as an ugly instrument and that the players are meritorious, Coste's *Fantaisie sur deux motifs de La Norma* opus 16 can be dated to the year 1838. It would be nice to know for sure that the duet that was played was *Souvenir de Russie* opus 63. After all, Sor dedicated it to Coste, but no evidence can be found for this. The vocal part is accompanied by Burgmüller and Concone on the piano. Coste knows them because he is the one who organizes the concert. In Valenciennes they are satisfied with the performance of their former compatriot in this concert, and other former locals were also present:

On 10 April M. Coste, a young guitarist from Valenciennes, gave a concert in Paris, in the salons of M. Duport, causing a considerable stir in the musical world. The young virtuoso, who has left venerable memories in Valenciennes, was assisted in the concert by other musicians belonging to our town. The

---

[347] *La France musicale*, vol. I, no. 14, 1 IV 1838, p. 7: 'M. Coste, un de nos meilleurs guitaristes, donnera, le 10 avril, un concert [...] Sor [...] Coste'; no. 19, 15 IV 1838, p. 5: 'La soirée musicale [...] a été assez brillante. M. Coste est certainement un guitariste très distingué. Son duo avec Sor a plu généralement; [...] une partie du plaisir qu'ils semblent prendre eux-mêmes à jouer d'un instrument aussi ingrat que la guitare. Une fantaisie sur un motif de *Norma*, exécuté par M. Coste, a été fort goutée de l'auditoire.'

IV — *Aux Parisiens*

Tilmant-brothers, violin and violoncello, M. Lecointe, violin, Mlle D'Hennin could be heard in this musical evening and have shared, with Coste, in the applause of the public.[348]

Sor is not mentioned here, he is not from Valenciennes, but the Tilmant-brothers are.[349] They play the violin and the violoncello, as mentioned.[350] The violinist Lecointe and female singer d'Hennin also come from this town in the North of France, Coste is an acquaintance in their circles. From this concert still another review is found:

In the province the guitar often is the instrument of the intimate music. The great progress it has made, prove that talented artists do not cease to be engaged with it. M. Coste walks with dignity in the tracks of the famous guitarists. He is distinguished by his excellent style, pure and with crisp. It is a very sublime musical sentiment that the guitar imputes him, and, in this respect, he has much in common with Sor: he approaches him as a performing artist and as a composer. So he made the right choice to begin with a duo together with this great master. After that, he played a concerto that was written by Hummel and Giuliani, and a fantasy he wrote himself, on the cavatine from Norma. These three works were favorably received by a remarkably brilliant and large audience. The rest of the concert was equally satisfactory in terms of choice and variety. M. Lecointe on the violin and the ladies D'Hennin and Boucher shared in the bravos, by the beauty of their voices, which blended together so well. [...] The beneficiary may be satisfied with this night.[351]

This review in the *Revue et Gazette musicale de Paris* of May 6, 1838 praises Napoléon Coste. It seems to be a little late, but the performers who are mentioned concur, including his compatriots Lecointe and D'Hennin from Valenciennes, as well as the program, about which even more is written. After the duet with Sor, which duet is not said, but *Souvenir de Russie* is an obvious candidate because the duets by Coste himself probably are written later, he plays a concerto written jointly by Hummel and Giuliani, and after that the fantaisie *Norma*. The review is very favorable, and the words 'he plays a concerto that Hummel and Giuliani wrote together' taken literally, this work is executed here once more, after the performance by the Schultz-brothers in 1828.[352]

The concerto in question is the *Grand Pot-Pourri National* which was published as Giuliani's opus 93, the only work of which Hummel is known to have arranged the 'Partie du Clavecin.'[353] In this

---

[348] *Mon Histoire*, Valenciennes, 19 IV 1838, p. 198: 'Le 10 avril, M. *Napoléon Coste*, jeune guitariste de Valenciennes, a donné un concert à Paris, dans les salons de M. Duport, qui a eu beaucoup de retentissement dans le monde musical. Ce jeune virtuose, qui a laissé d'honorables souvenirs à Valenciennes, a été aidé dans son concert par des exécutans [sic] qui appartiennent à notre localité. MM. *Tilmant* frères, violon et violoncelle, M. *Lecointe*, violon, Mlle *D'Hennin*, se sont fait entendre dans cette soirée musicale et ont partagé, avec M. Coste, les applaudissements du public.'; Dandelot, A.: *La Société des Concerts du Conservatoire de 1828 à 1897*, Paris, Delagrave, 1923, p. 47, Pierre, Constant: *Le Conservatoire national de musique et de déclamation: documents historiques et administratifs*, Paris, Imprimerie nationale, 1900, p. 859.

[349] Fauquet, J.-M.: 'Tilmant, Alexandre', 'Théophile' in: Fauquet, Joël-Marie: *Dictionnaire de la Musique en France au XIXe siècle*, Paris, Fayard, 2003, p. 1218-1219.

[350] *La France musicale*, vol. I, no. 16, 15 IV 1838, p. 5-6: '[...] Coste, Lecointe, d'Hennin, Walknaer, Bouchers, Tilmant frères, Burgmüller, Concone [...]'.

[351] *Revue et Gazette musicale de Paris*, vol. V, no. 18, 6 V 1838, Nouvelles, p. 190: 'La guitare est souvent en province l'instrument de la musique intime. Les grands progrès qu'elle a faits attestent que d'habiles artistes n'ont pas cessé de s'en occuper. M. Coste marche dignement sur les traces des guitaristes célèbres. Ce qui le distingue, c'est un excellent style, pur, gracieux et nerveux; c'est un sentiment musical plus élevé que la guitare ne le suppose, et, à cet égard, il a beaucoup d'analogie avec Sor: il se rapproche de lui comme exécutant et comme compositeur. Il a donc bien fait débuter par un duo avec ce maître distingué. Ensuite il a joué un concerto écrit par Hummel et Giuliani, et une fantaisie composée par lui-même sur la cavatine de *Norma*. Ces trois morceaux ont mérité l'accueil le plus favorable d'un auditoire singulièrement nombreux et brillant. Le reste du concert a satisfait aussi par le choixet la variété. M. Lecointe, sur le violon, mesdames Dhennin et Boucher, par la beauté de leurs voix, qui se marient fort bien ensemble, se sont partagé les bravos. [...] Le bénéficiaire a du être content de sa soirée.'

[352] *Revue musicale de Paris*, 1828, tome III, p. 142-143: 'Concerto Giuliani (accompagnement par M. Hummel), M. Léonard Schultz.'

[353] Kroll, Mark: *Johann Nepomuk Hummel, A Musician's Life and World*, Maryland, 2007, p. 62-63, 122-123, 159; Zimmerschied, Dieter: *Thematisches Verzeichnis der Werke von Johann Nepomuk Hummel*, Hofheim am Taunus, 1971; Heck, Thomas Fitzsimmons: *Mauro Giuliani: Virtuoso Guitarist and Composer*, Columbus, 1995, p. 81, 91, 208; 'Giuliani, Mauro' in: Jeffery, Brian: *The Complete Works.. Mauro Giuliani*, facsimile edition, Vol. I-XXXIX, Tecla editions, London, 1988, vol 34, opus 93, preface.

work a terz guitar is concerned and Coste could have used a capotasto, of course.[354] It is an outstanding company of musicians with which Coste is associated. Friedrich Burgmüller (1806-1874) is the well-known pianist and composer,[355] of the same age as Coste, and Giuseppe Concone (1801-1861) is the Italian composer, singing teacher and composer of *L'Esquif du Pêcheur*, who gives lessons in Paris and who plays the piano.[356] It is remarkable that in the review a parallel is drawn between Sor and Coste, as a guitarist and as a composer. According to the reporter they have much in common in their way of playing and composing. From this review alone the line from Sor to Coste already can be drawn.

Together, Coste and Sor play again in a concert of Mlle Mazel on Sunday, April 22, this time in the salons of M. Pape. Miss Mazel is a female singer on tour who accompanies herself on the piano in ballads from her album, such as *La Dorade, La Coquette* and *Pigeon vole*. This coquettish young lady garnered great applause, singing of gilthead bream and pigeons:

> *with a naive charm that suits this genre of composition. [...] The concert was remarkable because of the choice of works [...] The gentlemen Sor and Coste [...] combined their talent to make a complete success of this night.*[357]

What else is played in this concert remains obscure, but works that were performed in the first two concerts this year, such as *Divertissement* opus 62 and/or *Souvenir de Russie* opus 63 by Sor, are very likely. From this review the conclusion can also be made that music of popular taste can be combined with that of classical taste as well. In this way, in relation to the upper-class concert and the lower-class concert, the division between the vocal and the instrumental part, and the benefit concert for musicians or for charitable causes, the mixed concert is a very colorful phenomenon.

Opus 16, *Fantaisie sur deux motifs de La Norma* 1838

In the concert on 10 April 1838 in salons Duport, the piano manufacturer, Coste plays his *Fantaisie sur deux motifs de La Norma* opus 16, or an earlier version of it, because this work was not published before 1843 with Challiot, which is possibly the reason why it has been assigned such a high opus number. The opera *Norma* itself, by Vincenzo Bellini, has its opening night in 1831 in La Scala in Milan, with little success, to the disappointment of the composer. After his earlier great successes, with *Il Pirata*, for instance, in 1827, Bellini first goes to London in 1833, where his operas are received favorably, with among others Maria Malibran in a leading part, and then to Paris, where he fails to have his works performed, despite negotiations with the Opéra. After interference of Rossini he does succeed in the Théâtre-Italien, where *Il Pirata* and *I Capuletti e i Montecchi* are successful in the autumn of 1833. Bellini, who dies in 1835, is very popular in the Italian artistic circles of Cherubini and Rossini, and in that way makes contact with Chopin, who uses the melody of *Teneri figli* from *Norma* in his study opus 25/7, and with Liszt, who writes his *Réminescences de Norma* in 1841.[358] *Norma* is known in Paris, either partly or in its entirety but the opera is not staged there at that time. Coste takes two melodies and an instrumental accompaniment of a third melody as a starting point for his composition, and he is in good company, so to speak The title page of the Challiot edition which is mentioned in the *Bibliographie de la France* on September 2, 1843, says that the work was performed at the Conservatoire. This is also the case on the title page of *Le Tournoi* opus 15, also an edition of Challiot, dated in 1843. So, Coste played

---

[354] *Revue musicale de Paris*, 182,8 tome III, p. 156: '[...] MM. Schultz, guitare tierce plus haut, comme si le *capodastre* [...]'.
[355] Fauquet, J.-M.: 'Friedrich Burgmuller', in: Fauquet, Joël-Marie: *Dictionnaire de la Musique en France au XIXe siècle*, Paris, Fayard, 2003, p. 188.
[356] Forbes, Elisabeth: 'Concone, Giuseppe', in: Sadie, Stanley ed.: *The New Grove Dictionary of Music and Musicians*, London, Macmillan, 1980, vol. 4, p. 640.
[357] *La France musicale*, vol. I, no. 19, 29 IV 1838, p. 7: '[...] qu'elle a chantées avec l'esprit et la grace naïve qui conviennent à ce genre de composition. [...] Le concert a été remarquable par le choix des morceaux [...] MM. Sor et N. Coste, [...] avaient associé leur beau talent pou compléter le succès de cette soirée.'
[358] Lippmann, Friedrich: 'Vincenzo Bellini', in: Sadie, Stanley ed.: *The New Grove Dictionary of Music and Musicians*, London, Macmillan, 1980, vol.2, p. 447-448, 452; Pintér-Lück, Éva: 'Norma', in: Batta, András: *Opera*, Köln, Könemann, 1999, p. 28; Searle, Humphrey: 'Liszt, Franz, in: Sadie, Stanley ed.: *The New Grove Dictionary of Music and Musicians*, London, Macmillan, 1980, vol 11, p. 66.

these two works at the *Conservatoire de Musique* between 1839 and 1843.[359] In 1841 Coste becomes a member of the *Société académique des Enfants d'Apollon*, an organization of artists, assembling each month to make music. In 1843 Coste takes part in the yearly concert that is given on May 25. There he plays *Le Tournoi* opus 15 in the salle du Conservatoire. The program of the concert is published in 1881 by chairman Decourcelle.[360] This makes apparent what the entry on the title page of opus 15 means to say, but not that of opus 16, which does not appear in these annals, if it was not the 'Fantaisie et variations' which are mentioned in 1841.[361] The entry 'exécuté au Conservatoire Royal de Musique' on the edition of opus 16 *'Norma'* of Challiot can be explained by the republication, where it is said. The new edition of Wynberg then is the facsimile of the example in the Spencer Collection, which does not mention this.[362] On the other hand, the 'Concerts du Conservatoire' have a program for orchestra, but soloists and chamber musicians are also allowed to try out their performance in the 'Exercices des Élèves.' So, it is possible that Coste played on one of these occasions, but no sign of this can be found, and apart from that, he was not a student. One way or another, here the connection can be made with the Conservatoire; some room is made for the instrument. The contacts Coste has with several teachers at the Conservatoire, such as clarinet player Klosé, the singer Panseron, and with Berlioz, to whom he dedicated *Le Tournoi*, who is assistant librarian there in 1839, also point in this direction. And Fétis was librarian of the institute from 1830 to 1833, as well as a teacher in counterpoint and fugue. Could Coste have had private lessons with him in counterpoint and harmony? In 1830 they both live in rue Bleue, Coste at no. 28, Fétis at no.18.[363] This is the first work in which Coste applies the Romantic style element of free lyricism. Along with the chromatics, the ornamentation, the modulation, the dissonant chords, the arpeggios, changes in tempo and prescription of articulation, the lyrical melody belongs to the style elements that can give cause to the interpretation that this composition is Romantic.

CHANSON, *LE PERRUQUIER* - THOMAS [ARR. COSTE] 1838

66 Thomas

In the Opéra-Comique in Paris *Le Perruquier de la Régence* by Ambroise Thomas, with lyrics by Planard and Duport, has its first night, with much success, because in the eleventh performance on April 26, 1838 the audience is still as large as on the first night. As usual this success is followed by musical editions of opera selections, and in an advertisement in *La France musicale* it is announced on May 6 that twelve songs from the opera are going to be published on May 15, the same pieces for voice and guitar accompaniment also.[364] One of these editions can be found in the Royal Library in Brussels, and on the second page of this edition of Richault the first lines of the melodies are listed, making it more attractive for the amateur to purchase other favorite songs. In this case no. 3 *Si vous voulez un jour*, sung by M. Chollet, with guitar accompaniment by N. Coste is concerned. If Coste has arranged all these songs, and why would that not be the case if that is what's written, it is said so – an endeavor involving lot of work, but also

---

[359] Kk Rischel 149 mu 6701,0982 U48, Coste, *Norma* op. 16; Kk Rischel 148 mu 6612.2285, Coste, *Le Tournoi* op. 15.
[360] Decourcelle, Maurice: *La Société des Enfants d'Apollon (1741-1880): programmes des concerts annuels...*, Paris, Durand, 1881, p. 78: 'M. Coste *Le Tournoi*, fantaisie pour la guitare'.
[361] Decourcelle, Maurice: *La Société des Enfants d'Apollon (1741-1880): programmes des concerts annuels...*, Paris, Durand, 1881, p. 157: 'Fantaisie et variations pour la guitare, composées et exécutées par M. Coste.'
[362] Lam XX(159197.1) Spencer Collection, Coste: *Fantaisie 'Norma'* opus 16.
[363] Pierre, Constant: *Le Conservatoire national de musique et de déclamation: documents historiques et administratifs*, Paris, Imprimerie nationale, 1900, p.420, 422, 438, 444, 453, 457.
[364] *La France musicale*, vol. I, no. 20, 6 V 1838, p. 8, '*Les mêmes morceaux de chant avec accompgnement de guitare*'; Robinson, Philip: 'Ambroise Thomas' in: Sadie, Stanley ed.: *The New Grove Dictionary of Music and Musicians*, London, Macmillan, 1980, vol. 18, p. 776; Smith, Richard Langham: 'Thomas', in: Sadie, Stanley, ed.: *The New Grove Dictionary of Music and Musicians*, second edition, London, Macmillan, 2001, vol. 25, p. 403-407.

income if sales are good – there must be other songs as well. But this is the only one that has surfaced, come forward, just like *L'Esquif du Pêcheur*, which may be part of a series of thirteen songs. In these years Coste is very productive in making arrangements of works by Strauss, Concone, Schubert and Thomas, at least 35 pieces but perhaps as many as 64 in this period.

Sor's end

In the end of the year 1838, Dionisio Aguado leaves the musical capital of Europe and returns to Madrid, where he dies in 1849. In the period of the *Guitaromanie* he contributed his *études* and solo works to the guitar in a personal, but classical style that opened to Romanticism by exploring tension in harmony through modulation. His *Méthode* and his *Tripodison* are of importance for the guitar in Paris, as are his contacts with luthier Lacôte and of course his share in concerts and his friendship with Sor.[365] Sor dies in 1839:

> *The expert guitarist Sor has just died at the age of 59 years. This skillful musician, who has taken rank among the celebrities of our era, has ended his artistic career with a mass that the connoisseurs only could appreciate, and with a duet for two guitars, which was dedicated to M. Coste, his friend and emulator.*

This is how Escudier begins this obituary on July 15, 1839. He mentions Sor's successes in Russia and Germany, his ballets such as *Cendrillon*, and he continues with his importance for the guitar:

> *It is Sor who has broken through the routine in which the guitar was stuck in the musical genre for which it was used before him. Sor is the only one to develop a language to express the most artistic and most graceful musical ideas on the instrument.*[366]

In this way *La France musicale* succeeds in giving the treatment he deserves, where the *Revue et Gazette musicale de Paris* limits itself to: 'The famous guitarist Sor died in Paris.'[367] Mentioning the duet that is dedicated to Coste in *La France musicale*, the *Souvenirs de Russie*, published 'chez l'auteur', could lead to the conclusion that it is played in a concert, possibly on April 10, 1838. In his biography of Sor, Brian Jeffery writes more about the circumstances of his death. The guitarist suffers from cancer of the throat. He is been taken care of by an old woman, lives on a mere bit of soup, and dies on July 10, 1839. He is buried on July 12 in the Cimetière de Montmartre.[368] Considering Sor's celebrity many colleagues may have been present at the funeral, with Coste possibly among them. At present there is a monument placed on his tombstone. Sor had a great influence on the musical life of the guitar in Paris and can be considered one of the greatest composers for the guitar in the Classical period, along with Giuliani and Aguado. His friendship made him very important to Coste, who writes:

> *I made Sor's acquaintance a few years later. We did a lot of duos together. He made me his friend. I played two pieces with him at his last concert. He died a few months later of a throat cancer. He was a musician of a higher order, but one with a fantastic and bizarre character.*[369]

---

[365] Bergadà, M.: 'Aguado, Dionisio', in: Fauquet, Joël-Marie: *Dictionnaire de la Musique en France au XIXe siècle*, Paris, Fayard, 2003, p. 19; Fétis, François Joseph: *Biographie universelle des musiciens*, Brussels, 2ᵉ ed. 1860-1881, tome I p. 36; Jeffery, Brian: *Fernando Sor, Composer and Guitarist*, London, Tecla, 1977; second edition 1994, p. 104, 105; Jeffery, Brian: *Dionisio Aguado*, biography and bibliography, Heidelberg, Chanterelle, 1994, p.xv-xvii; Moser, Wolf: *Fernando Sor: Versuch einer Autobiografie und gitarristischen Schriften*, (translation in German of Ledhuy), Köln, 1984, p. 96,133; Pérez-Diaz, Pompeyo: *Dionisio Aguado y la guitarra clásico-romántica*, Madrid, Alpuerto, 2003, p. 110, 140-142, 360-361; Pujol, Emilio: *El dilema del sonido en la guitarra*, Buenos Aires, Ricordi, 1960, p. 20, 47, 71.

[366] *La France musicale*, vol. II, no. 45, 14 VII 1839, p. 390: 'Le savant guitariste Sor vient de mourir à l'age de cinquante-neuf ans. Ce grand musicien, qui a pris rang parmi les célébrités de notre époque, a terminé sa carrière artistique par une messe que les connaisseurs ont pu seuls apprécier, et par un duo pour deux guitares, dédiés à M. Coste son ami en son émule.' 'C'est Sor qui a fait sortir la guitare de l'ornière où l'avait plongée le genre de musique adopté avant lui. Sor est le seul qui ait créé une langue pour exprimer les idées musicales les plus savantes et les plus gracieuses sur cet instrument.'

[367] *Revue et Gazette musicale de Paris*, vol. VI, no. 31, 18 VII 1839, p. 247: 'Le célèbre guitariste Sor vient de mourir à Paris.'

[368] Jeffery, Brian: *Fernando Sor, Composer and Guitarist*, London, Tecla, 1977; second edition 1994, p. 112-115.

[369] Coste-Schult, 17 IV 1875: 'Je fis la connaissance de Sor quelques années plus tard. Nous fîmes beaucoup de Duos ensemble. Il m'avait pris en amitié. Je jouai deux morceaux avec lui à son dernier concert. Il mourut quelques mois après d'un cancer à la gorge. C'était un musicien d'un ordre supérieur, mais d'un caractère fantastique et bizarre.'

It appears that Sor and Coste played two works together in the concert given on April 22, 1838. And Coste made Sor's acquaintance a few years after coming to Paris, which must have been in 1829. And how different from Fétis in the *Revue musicale de Paris* is the director of *La France musicale* writing about the guitar as an instrument. On August 11, Leon Escudier writes the following under the heading 'The guitar of Fernando Sor':

> *This guitar, which has served to reveal one of the greatest geniuses of our era, was made by Ferd. Rada in Málaga in 1801. With this instrument Sor could be heard at the 'Menus-Plaisirs' when he arrived in Paris, and in his travels to London and to St. Petersburg. at the time of his great successes. This great guitarist left this guitar in his will to Napoléon Coste, who more than once has been mentioned with praise in our columns and with whom Sor had the pleasure of playing his admirable duets. It is a valuable memory and the last token of the highest esteem an artist like Sor can leave behind to a colleague.*[370]

It is in this way that the guitar of Rada's that is mentioned came into Coste's possession. This is confirmed by Coste himself:

> *This artist, you have been told, used a very small guitar. It was just nothing. And I know what I'm talking about, since he left his guitar to me in his will. It was a mediocre instrument made in Spain. (I) The body was very thick, the neck was wide, and I believe a bit longer than that of my own guitars. This is the guitar he played when he arrived in Paris, around 1817 or 18. [...] (I) When I was moving house in 1847, this poor guitar got broken in an irreparable way, along with some other items whose loss is regrettable.*[371]

This may also explain the criticism levelled at the instrument in the press. The quotations above make it clearer that Coste was highly appreciated as an artist by Sor. The feeling was mutual, but Coste is still critical about Sor in a letter, which is the only blemish on the relationship between the two guitarists. On September 30, 1877 he writes the following to Hallberg:

> *Sor had an admirable left hand, which, with its flexibility, lent itself to being stretched in some practically impossible ways. He relished in writing things that no one could play but himself. But ten years ago I played the grande fantaisie dedicated to Pleyel in public, which is his most difficult work (op. 7), but I used a terz sized guitar (I must tell you that I have a very small hand).*[372]

So Coste plays Sor's works in concerts and complains about his small hands that are not so well suited for playing them. A more substantial opinion can be deduced from Coste's letter to Hallberg dated November 16, 1877:

> *Generally his works, which contain things of great beauty, especially in their introductions, are brought to a mediocre end. Almost all his pieces contain some passages that are practically impossible. All in all, Sor has done more damage to the instrument than good. But nevertheless, his Études will remain the masterpiece of that genre.*[373]

---

[370] *La France musicale*, vol. II, no. 49, 11 VIII 1839, p. 451: 'La guitare de Ferdinand Sor. - Cette guitare, qui a servi à révéler un des plus beaux génies de notre époque, a été fabriquée à Malaga en 1801 par Ferd. Rada. C'est avec cet instrument que Sor se fit entendre aux Menus-Plaisirs lors de son arrivée à Paris, et dans ses différens [sic] voyages à Londres et à St- Petersbourg, à l'époque de ses plus brillans [sic] succès. Ce grand artiste vient de léguer cette guitare, par testament, au guitariste Napoléon Coste, qui a été plus d'une fois cité avec éloge dans nos colonnes, et avec lequel Sor se plaisait à exécuter ses admirables duos. C'est un précieux souvenir et la dernière marque d'estime la plus flatteuse qu'un artiste comme Sor pût laisser son confrère.'

[371] Coste-Hallberg, 30 IX 1877: 'Cet artiste, vous a-t-on dit, se servait d'une très petite guitare. Il n'en est rien. Et je puis en parler savantment, puisqu'il m'a légué sa guitare par testament. C'était un instrument médiocre fait en Espagne (I) Le Coffre était très épais, le manche large et je crois, un peu plus long que celui des miennes. C'est sur cette guitare qu'il jouait lorsqu'il est arrivé à Paris, vers 1817 ou 18. [...] (I) Dans un déménagement, que je fis an 1847, cette pauvre guitare fût brisé d'un façon irréparable avec d'autres objets dont la perte est bien regrettable.'

[372] Coste-Hallberg, 30 IX 1877: 'Sor avait une main gauche admirable qui, par sa souplesse, se trêtait à des extensions presque impossibles. Il se faisait un malin plaisir d'écrire des choses que personne que lui pouvait jouer. J'ai pourtant joué en public, il y a 10 ans, la grande fantaisie dédié à Pleyel, et qui est son oeuvre la plus difficile (op. 7); mais je me servais alors d'une guitare tierce (il faut vous dire j'ai la main très petite).'

[373] Coste-Hallberg, 15 XI 1877: 'Généralement ses oeuvres qui renferment des grandes beautés, surtout dans leurs introductions, finissant médiocrement. Presque tous ses morceaux renferment des passages presque impossibles. En définitive Sor a fait plus de mal que de bien à l'instrument. Mais ses études, néanmoins, resteront comme le chef d'oeuvre du genre.'

The *Études* remain Sor's most important work, according to Coste, earning him an honorable nickname:

> *I as well have an admiration for Sor, and in something I wrote some thirty years ago I gave him the title of the Beethoven of the guitar, and in 1856, when the Brussels context took place, I would not have competed had Sor still been alive.*[374]

Coste's relationship with Sor is significant for both Coste and his work. Coste knows how to bring Romanticism to life in the classical heritage. This already is expressed in the works he composed until now, opus 4 'Armide', opus 5 'Flandres', opus 6 'Meyerbeer', WoO 9 'Il Pirata' and opus 16 'Norma'. The way Coste develops himself as a Romantic guitar composer, emerges in the review of the compositions in the next chapter. With the end of Sor a new chapter begins, as it were, in the life of the now 34-year-old guitarist and composer Napoléon Coste.

67 Ru de l'Échiquier, street sign, 2007

---

[374] Coste-Hallberg, 7 XII 1877: 'Moi aussi, j'ai une admiration pour Sor, et dans un écrit il y a une trentaine d'années, je lui ai donné cette qualification de Beethoven de la guitare, et en 1856 lorsqu'eut lieu le concours de Bruxelles je n'eusse point concouru, si Sor avait vécu.'

V
Souvenirs

What to say about the concert given by M. Napoléon Coste. Despite the decline into which the guitar has fallen, this intrepid guitarist persists in the study of this instrument with a laudable perseverance. He has performed twice and was listened to with the greatest attention. If there aren't a great number of guitar amateurs, there is, nevertheless, a substantial audience to applaud this skillful guitarist, as a compensation. M. Coste is first class; he plays with an unbelievable speed and a perfect purity. [375]

REPUTATION 1840

In the years of his youth in Valenciennes a total of six concerts are found in the sources in which Coste played as a guitarist. In the early period in Paris, between 1828 and 1839, another six concerts are found in which it is almost certain Coste participated. Still, these are mixed concerts and there are not too many of them, but it is very likely Coste, as a budding talent, played in many more, of which there is no report in the early musical press. Sor, for instance, is known to have played in 27 concerts in Paris between 1828 and 1838, which is not very many for a celebrity like him.[376] The information available remains the starting point for sketching the situation concerning concerts in this period and the position that the guitar as an instrument – and Coste as a guitarist – has in them. Liszt continues the solo concert which was introduced by Paganini in 1831, but this was not a general practice. He starts with these in London in 1840, where his solo concerts are given the name 'recital', after the custom of reciting poems by heart.[377] In Paris he calls it a *solilogue musical* or *monologue de piano* on April 20, 1840.[378] There are no solo concerts for guitar, but 17 mixed concerts take place in the period between 1840 and 1855 in which Coste demonstrably participates. Another eight will come after this, which brings the total of concerts by Coste in Paris up to 31. This is very few for such a long period and it is therefore of great importance to discuss these and determine what he has played in them, first to draw the relation with his works and then to determine to which musical circles he is associated with. After the departure of Aguado and the death of Sor he now is on his own, so to speak. The only guitarists active in Paris are Carulli, Molino and Carcassi – from the Classic generation – and Castellacci and Huerta – from the Romantic generation – as far as a clear artistic distinction between the two generations can be made.

The first concert in which Coste plays in 1840 is an afternoon performance, organized by M. Laurelli, on clarinet and Mme Laurelli, on the piano, in Petzold's salon, on Sunday, February 16. *Le Ménestrel* writes:

> [...] *the musical matinee was very interesting.* [...] *The instrumental part consisted of a solo for guitar by M. Coste, an air varié for clarinet by M. Laurelli and a duet for harp and piano, in a perfect performance by M. La Rivière and Mme Laurelli.*[379]

---

[375] *La France musicale*, vol. V, no. 15, 17 IV 1842, p. 153: 'Que vous dire du concert donné par M. Napoléon Coste. Ce guitariste intrépide, malgré le dépérissement où est tombée la guitare, poursuit avec une louable persévérence l'étude de cet instrument. Deux fois il s'est fait entendre et il a été écouté avec le plus intérêt. S'il n'y a pas un grand nombre d'amateurs de guitare, il y a au moins un public nombreux pour applaudir l'habile guitariste, c'est là une compensation. M. Coste est de première force; il joue avec une incroyable agilité et une pureté parfaite.'

[376] Jeffery, Brian: 'Fernando Sor, concert performer', in: *Guitar Review*, New York, The Society of the Classic Guitar, no. 39, summer 1974, p. 8-10; *Revue musicale de Paris*, 1829 tome V, p. 115, 181, 240, 304, 351; 1831, tome IV, p. 71, 96, 1832, vol. VI, p. 21, 31, 60, 63, 150; 1835, vol. IX, p. 61-62; *La France musicale*, 1838, vol. I, no. 16, p. 5-7.

[377] Weber, William: *The Great Transformation of Musical Taste*, Cambridge, Cambridge University Press, 2008, p. 158-160.

[378] Eigeldinger, Jean-Jacques: 'Introduction'; Bailbé, Joseph Marc: 'La critique musicale au *Journal des Débats*' in: Bailbé [et al]: *La musique en France à l'epoque romantique (1830-1870)*, Paris, Flammarion, 1991, p. 12-13, 81.

[379] *Le Ménestrel*, vol. VII, no. 12, 16 II 1840, p. [4]: 'Aujourd'hui dimanche [...] Laurelli [..] matinée musicale [...] salons Petzold,'; no. 13, 23 II 1840, p. [4]: '[...] a été très intéressante. [...] La partie instrumentale a été remplie par un *solo* de guitare de M. Coste, un *air varié* pour clarinette. par M. Laurelli, et un *duo* de harpe et de piano, supérieurement exécuté par M. La Rivière et Mme Laurelli.'

There is singing as well, by the ladies Féron, Alesi, Caudron, who sing opera numbers and romances in this mixed concert with a varied content, as is usual. Coste plays in these sort of concerts, becomes acquainted with these musicians, in addition to those from Valenciennes and takes part in these musical circles, even if their names do not appear in modern reference books. From celebrities to amateurs, the spectrum of the musical world is wide, and the circumstances in which Coste finds himself are colorful. Which solo he played in the concert is uncertain: his most recent work is *Norma* opus 16 from 1838, but alternatively he could have performed a new piece.

On Sunday March 1, 1840 Léon Escudier, director of *La France musicale*, writes the following announcement in his journal:

M. Coste, guitarist, will give a concert in the salle of M. Herz on the 29ᵗʰ of this month.[380]

68 Salle Herz

This concert, which takes place in the hall that was built two years earlier near the piano factory of the famous pianist and composer Henri Herz at rue de la Victoire 48, is Coste's only one that is discussed so extensively in the press, with three announcements and three reviews. *Le Ménestrel* makes the announcement later, on March 22:

Monsieur Coste, the guitarist, gives a grand concert on the 29ᵗʰ of this month in the salle of M. Henri Herz.[381]

And in Valenciennes they have not forgotten him in the *Écho de la Frontière*:

We, in Valenciennes, do remember the young and modest guitarist Coste, the son of captain Coste, who died here; this is what a journal in Paris writes about the talent of our fellow-townsman: 'We announce a grand concert given by M. Coste, our famous guitarist, for Sunday 29 March in the salle of M. Herz. The artists who will participate in this event have long enjoyed the public's admiration. The pieces that may give M. Coste's concert a truly original appearance, include a major divertissement for guitar, violin and voice by

---

[380] *La France musicale*, vol. III, no. 9, 1 III 1840, p. 99: 'M. Coste, guitariste, donnera, le 29 de ce mois, un concert dans la salle de M. Herz.'
[381] *Le Ménestrel*, vol. II, no. 17, 22 III 1840, p. [3]: 'M. Coste, le guitariste, donnera le 29 de ce mois, un grand concert dans la salle de M. Henri Herz.'

Moschelès, Mayseder and Giuliani, and an unpublished work for guitar solo, with which M. Coste, as people say, will reveal still unknown possibilities.[382]

The wording of the announcement is rather stilted, but this has already been seen on more than one occasion. The local paper does not quote the *Revue et Gazette musicale de Paris*, because the concert is not announced in this magazine, and apparently not in the two other musical newspapers either. The reviews tell what is played in the concert. On April 5 *La France musicale* writes about the concert:

The concert of M. Coste, the guitarist, last Sunday in the salle of M. Herz, has been one of the most interesting of the season. This artist's reputation has long been established; this new proof will only confirm the respect he has in the musical world. The grand solo he has written with the title Rêverie has given the most pleasure. The concerto by Hummel and Jiuliani [sic], for guitar, resulted in well-deserved great applause, As a composer, M. Concone has played a major role in the success of this concert.[383]

The way this journal writes about guitar concerts is different from what the *Revue musicale* and the *Revue et Gazette musicale* are accustomed to doing. Here, Coste is an established artist and is of high esteem in the musical world. In this benefit concert he plays a grand solo he wrote himself with the title *Rêverie*, which had an excellent reception. Giuseppe Concone is the Italian composer and singing teacher who gives lessons in Paris and plays the piano, as he already did in the concert with Coste on April 10, 1838, and is now doing again with his own work. It is already known that he wrote the music of *L'Esquif du Pêcheur*. Coste may have been accompanied by Concone in Hummel and Giuliani's *Concerto*. It is likely that this work is the *Grand Pot-Pourri National* opus 93, for terz guitar and piano, which is apparently a rather popular concert piece.[384]

The same concert is reviewed in *Le Ménestrel*:

The very same day M. Henri Herz had opened his salle to a musical afternoon, which was given by Coste, the guitarist. This virtuoso performer played a concerto by Hummel and a grand solo of his own composition in an excellent performance. Mme Wideman sang an air by Rossini with much power and expression. Several other artists, including MM. Verroust, Grard, the young Dancla, have earned the public's applause. A duet for two guitars, the 'Souvenirs de Russie', Sor's last inspiration, was very successful. This piece was performed by M. Coste and one of his female pupils, whose early talent is an honor to the teacher.[385]

In this mixed concert Coste is in the company of more and less well-known musicians. Stanislas Verroust (1814-1863) is an oboist and teaches at the Gymnase musical militaire; M. Grard has left no trace in modern reference books; Jean-Pierre Dancla (1822-1895), the youngest brother of the

---

[382] *L'Echo de la Frontière*, Valenciennes, vol. XIX, no. 2307, 24 III 1840, p. 790: 'On se rappelle encore à Valenciennes le jeune et modeste guitariste *Coste*, fils du capitaine *Coste*, décédé ici; voici ce que proclame un journal de Paris sur le talent de notre compatriotte: "On annonce pour dimanche 29 mars un grand concert donné par M. Coste, notre célèbre guitariste, dans la salle de M. Herz. Les artistes qui doivent concourir à cette solennité sont depuis longtemps en possession de la faveur du public. Parmi les morceaux qui doivent donner au concert de M. Coste une physionomie vraiment originale, on cite un grand divertissement pour guitare, violon et chant, de Moschelès, Mayseder et Giuliani, et un morceau inédit pour guitare seule, dans lequel M. Coste nous révèlera, dit-on, des ressources encore inconnues."'

[383] *La France musicale*, vol. III, no. 14, 5 IV 1840, p. 147: 'Le concert donné dimanche dans la salle de M. Herz par M. Coste, le guitariste, a été un des plus intéressans [sic] de la saison. La réputation de cet artiste est faite depuis long-temps; cette nouvelle épreuve ne servira qu'à confirmer la haute opnion qu'on a de lui dans le monde musical. Le grand solo de sa composition, intitulé *Rêverie*, a fait le plus grand plaisir. Le concerto de Hummel et Jiuliani [sic], pour guitare, a valu au bénéficiaire des applaudissemens [sic] bien mérités. M. Concone a eu aussi, comme compositeur, une bonne part dans le succès de ce concert.'

[384] *Revue musicale de Paris*, 1828, tome III, p. 143 'Concerto pour la guitare, composé par M. Mauro Giuliani (accompagnement par M. Hummel); p. 156 'La guitare de M. Léonard Schulz est une tierce plus haute que les autres guitares;'.

[385] *Le Ménestrel*, vol. VII, no. 19, 5 IV 1840, p. [3]: 'Le même jour, M. Henri Herz avait ouvert sa salle à une matinée musicale donnée par le guitariste Coste. Ce virtuose a parfaitement exécuté un concerto de Hummel et un grand solo de sa composition. Mme Wideman a chanté un air de Bellini avec beaucoup de vigueur et expression. Plusieurs autres artistes, tels que MM. Verroust, Grard, Dancla jeune, ont su mériter les applaudissements du public. Un duo pour deux guitares, les *Souvenirs de Russie*, dernière inspiration du célèbre Sor, a produit beaucoup d'effet. Ce morceau a été exécuté par M. Coste et une de ses élèves dont le talent précoce fait honneur à son maître.'

aforementioned famous Charles, is a violinist and composer, just like his brother.[386] Coste meets the oboe here for the first time. He takes an interest in the instrument, for which he writes twelve works, mainly duets for oboe and piano. In this concert he may well have played one of them. The unknown Mme Wideman [sic] sings in another concert with Coste later this year. It is remarkable that Coste is playing the duet Sor dedicated to him as a friend together with a pupil. With this he follows the tradition of introducing pupils in mixed concerts. Sor's last work is an introduction and theme with variations, in which the second guitar serves as accompaniment, which is something very suitable for a duo consisting of a teacher and a pupil. The words 'early talent' mean that this must be one of Coste's younger pupils. Referring to the dedications works so far composed by Coste, this could be one of four ladies: Mlle Albertine Douillez, from opus 6, Mlle Clarisse Lelorin, from opus 12, Mlle Caroline Montigny, from opus 10, with whom Coste probably played that work on April 8, 1842, and Mlle Olive Pauilhé, from opus 13, who would later become his spouse. The *Revue et Gazette musicale de Paris* writes a short review of this concert on April 19:

> *M. Coste, guitarist, gave a grand concert in the salle of M. Herz on 29 March. This artist successfully performed several works, notably the grand solo entitled Rêverie, allegro martial et final. This work, written with purity, has shown the guitar's possibilities and the composer's performance in a remarkable way.*[387]

With this and the preceding positive reviews it might be possible to determine which work Coste has played in this concert. The piece in question is an as yet unpublished work with the title *Rêverie* in two parts, an allegro martial and a finale. There happen to be two works by Coste with this title. The first is *Andante sostenuto* from opus 53 no.1, with 63 measures in total which consists of one single part and cannot be called martial in character at all. The second is the *Rêverie nocturne*, an étude in flageolets in the *Méthode* Coste-Sor,[388] also consisting of a single part totaling 69 measures and lacking any martial character. Neither of the two are likely to have been played in this concert. And furthermore, all works published so far are out of the question, meaning that one has to search for a composition other than opus 2 to 7. The *Caprice* opus 8 is not published, but presumably came into existence around 1842.[389] The *Divertissement Lucia di Lammermoor* opus 9 appearing in 1839 or 1841 has five parts with themes by Donizetti and it certainly lacks military character as well. The *Scherzo et Pastorale* opus 10 is a guitar duet that also appears around these years. The *Grand Caprice* opus 11 has a part of opus 8 in it and is dated to around 1844. The *Rondeau de Concert* opus 12 appears around 1840, but also lacks martial character.[390] The *Caprice La Cachucha* opus 13, an arrangement of a popular dance, as by its very nature obviously not the piece in question, either. In this way, good candidates for this composition are the unpublished *Deuxième Polonaise* opus 14 and *Le Tournoi* opus 15, because the as yet unpublished *Fantaisie 'Norma'* opus 16 has already been played in 1838 and would have been recognized and mentioned in the reviews. Other compositions are of much later date. *Le Tournoi* indeed consists of two parts. A martial character is certainly discernable in this work in the allegro after the introduction, and in a beginning part, after an open ending, with finalizing effects. But the *Deuxième Polonaise* also has a martial character in the first part. later returning in *Le Passage des Alpes* opus 27, and a part with a very finalizing effect, the polonaise with a middle part, deriving from opus 8 which is called polonaise there too, such that this can be called a second polonaise to distinguish

---

[386] Badol-Bertrand, F., & J.-M. Fauquet: 'Verroust, Stanislas'; Penesco, A. & J.-M. Fauquet: 'Dancla, Charles, Philippe, Jean-Pierre'; in: Fauquet, Joël-Marie: *Dictionnaire de la Musique en France au XIXe siècle*, Paris, Fayard, 2003, p. 346-348, 1269.

[387] *Revue et Gazette musicale de Paris*, vol. VII, no. 32, 19 IV 1840, p. 277: 'M. Coste, guitariste, a donné le 29 mars un grand concert dans la salle de M. Herz. Cet artiste y a exécuté avec succès plusieurs morceaux, parmi lesquels on a remarqué le grand solo intitulé: *Rêverie*, allegro martial et final. Ce morceau, écrit avec pureté, a mis en relief d'une manière remarquable les ressources de la guitare et exécution de l'auteur.'

[388] Sor, Ferdinand & N. Coste: *Méthode complète pour la Guitare...*, Paris, Schonenberger, 1851, p. 43-44.

[389] Kk Rischel Ms. 48a mu 6701.1181, Paris 14-8-42?, Coste, *Caprice* opus 9 [sic i.e. 8].

[390] Devriès, Anik & François Lesure: *Dictionnaire des éditeurs de musique français*, Genève, Minkoff, 1979-1988, vol. II, p. 203, 259, 307-309, 365, 369.

between the two. To make things even more complicated, it has to be explained that part one of the *Grand Caprice* opus 11 also comes from opus 8, but this work has three parts with different tempo indications and has no indications of a martial character. But there is more to say on this. The *Revue et Gazette musicale de Paris* writes that this piece is written with a certain purity and shows the guitar's possibilities and the composer's performance in a remarkable way.[391] In Valenciennes the *Écho de la Frontière* cites a Parisian newspaper: 'M. Coste reveals to us unknown possibilities.'[392] *Le Tournoi* opus 15 really has no sign of any reverie, while it does manifest a thirst for battle and the work is published no earlier than 1844 by Challiot. To wait four years to publish it, is a rather long time. In this way it is probably the *Deuxième Polonaise* which is played in the concert. The title *Rêverie* may have been changed at a later point; a dreamy piece has a different character from an allegro martial and a finale. After all these considerations, a review in regards to contents may shed more light upon the matter and also determine its place in the chronology of Coste's works. The question is to determine which work consists of two parts like an allegro martial and a finale, which embodies dreaminess and purity, and which reveals unknown potentials of the guitar and the guitarist. Polonaise, the second part of *Caprice* opus 8, is reused in the first part of opus 14; the first part Allegro of opus 8 is inserted in the *Grand Caprice* opus 11. Opus 8 is dedicated to Monsieur P. Montigny, while opus 11 is dedicated to Monsieur Paul de Montigny, the very same person who could be the father of Mlle Caroline Montigny, to whom opus 10 is dedicated. Their names are almost the same and both of them are Coste's pupils. To make things clear, a small table shows the concordance between these works. The remark must be made that the parts are not copied as such, unchanged or shortened, but are rather inserted in and adapted to the new work.

Caprice opus 8	*Grand Caprice* opus 11	*Deuxième Polonaise* opus 14	*Le Passage des Alpes* opus 27
	I Introduction		
	II Andante maestoso		
I Allegro	III Allegro		
		I Introduction	I Maestoso
II Polonaise		II Polonaise	

OPUS 8, *CAPRICE* 1840

This composition has two parts, an Allegro moderato, which is reused as the third part of opus 11 and a Polonaise which returns and the central part in the second part of opus 14. It remains a puzzle why this work has not been published separately, not even as opus 11. The first part starts with a striking and identifiable chord motif, followed by a modulatory development. This strong harmonic development returns in several through-composed phrases, in which the rigid Classical periodicity clearly is broken. The chromatics are included in the modulating passages and the dissonant chords. The violent beginning is a determining factor for the mood of the whole piece because of the repetition, the positioning in the dominant and in a different voicing. It is a structural part of this composition, which is well worked out. The second part is preceded by a broken octave passage, figuring as a joint motif. This polonaise has a kind of idée fixe which returns twelve times in different places, harmonized and altered. This part in the key of A has many passing and suspending chromatics in the passages. The theme, or motif, is ornamented and many arpeggios and legatos are incorporated into it. The arpeggios and the passages lead to a passing dominant series, which goes into the parallel a minor via a joint motif sequence, after which the composer resumes the beginning and ends in A major. The composition shows no weaknesses or predictable elements, on the contrary, it demonstrates a great deal of 'Sturm und Drang' Romanticism, which is found mainly in the restlessness of the harmonic prolongations,

---

[391] *Revue et Gazette musicale de Paris*, vol. VII, no. 32, 19 IV 1840, p. 277: 'Ce morceau, écrit avec pureté, [...]'.
[392] *L'Echo de la Frontière*, Valenciennes, vol. XIX, no. 2307, 24 III 1840, p. 790.: '[...] et un morceau inédit pour guitare seule, dans lequel M. Coste nous révèlera, dit-on, des ressources encore inconnues.'

which also show some metrical shift in the beginning. These prolongations seem to become typical for his way of composing, as he also applies these in his *Fantaisie symphonique* opus 28[b]. That is why it is very likely that this is the piece which is played in the concert on March 29, 1840. The composition must therefore be dated before 1840.

Opus 11, *Grand Caprice* [1842?]

Just like opus 8, this work is dedicated to M. Paul de Montigny. It consists of a short Introduction, an Andante maestoso and an Allegro moderato which is almost similar to the allegro of opus 8, it is used here again. The first part is short: it is really a completely notated cadenza, which can be regarded as Romantic due to its structure and function. The second part is also short, 37 measures, but it has a moody, gripping, moving melody. Then a repeated short motif leads to the dominant by way of some passing dominants. After this an Amoroso melody with a triplet accompaniment creates a lyrical atmosphere, supported by some passing dominants harmony, whereby the possibilities of chromatics are used in a beautifully conceived arpeggio with campanella. The climax comes in the form of a diminished seventh chord, followed twice by a descending chromatic scale in octaves. This small part ends at the dominant. Then the Allegro of opus 8 follows, in which some cadenzas are inserted and a motif is further elaborated. These additions have 'parachute' arpeggios and some chromatics, and they evidently contribute to the meaning of the piece because the quite rigid metrical aspect breaks into free lyricism.

Opus 14, *Deuxième Polonaise* [1842?]

The work in two parts begins with an Andante Allegro, which Coste uses later almost identical as the first part of *Le Passage des Alpes* opus 27. The descriptive analysis of this work shows nine different Romantic features, that can be discerned: some extended phrases, two cadenzas, many structural embellishments and an idée fixe. In it, many chromatics are employed, from time to time dissonant chords are used, one time even including a remarkable diminished seventh chord on the tonic, as well as a modulation to relative minor. The many prescriptions given concerning dynamics and articulation also contribute to the Romantic impression given in this work. Like so many of Coste's works, this work is very guitaristic, perfectly adapted to the possibilities the instrument has to offer, but at the same time very demanding in regards to technique. In this way it fits the description given in the reviews, and this piece may well have been the one played in the program of the concert on Sunday, March 29, 1840 in the salle of Herz, were it not that opus 8 also has two parts and is written earlier, as indicated by the opus number. In opus 14 some differences or improvements of the reused Polonaise from opus 8 can be noticed and a cadenza is added before the reprise.

With regards to dreaminess alternating with combativeness and displaying the unknown possibilities of the guitar, it is not opus 8 or opus 11, but rather opus 14 which is the best candidate for the composition played in the concert of March 29, 1840. Concerning the date, it must have been composed after opus 8, because a part of the latter is reused. As such, in theory it is plausible to assign opus 8 a date before 1840 in regard to the concert. Then, opus 11 has a date before 1842 in regard to the manuscript[393] and opus 14 the same date, because of the opus number, as *Le Tournoi* opus 15 can be dated to 1843. Based on considerations to context as well as content, opus 8 remains the most suitable for the concert in the salle of Herz in 1840.

Harmony 1840

These and other works by Coste can be seen against the background of the general theory of music from the perspective of the period. In 1840 François Fétis is also working on his view of the musical world and all that takes place in it. Before this he already divided the various activities that take place in the economics of the musical world into instrumentalist, composer, teacher, publisher,

---

[393] Kk Rischel Ms. 48a mu 6701.1181 op. 9 [i.e. op. 8] [i.e. op. 11], Coste: *Caprice* opus 9 [sic i.e. 8].

theorist and critic, and had made a division of the criteria to which music must be reviewed and an outline of the music of the future. From 1821 to 1833 he is a master in counterpoint and fugue at the Conservatoire and in this connection he also studied the harmony of music.[394] Now he draws a sketch of the history of harmony in a series of lectures he gives in 1832. When he left for Brussels in 1833 to become the director of the conservatory, he publishes this in the *Revue et Gazette musicale de Paris*, which is continued by his son.[395] This sketch appears in 1840 as a series of articles with the title *Esquisse de l'histoire de l'harmonie* and contains not only a summary of how he believes the theory of chords came into being and is structured, but also a survey of the situation in that time and a vision on the way it could develop in the future. Fétis is in a large company as far as treatises on harmony are concerned; between 1830 and 1845 some forty of these publications appeared by authors such as Choron, Lemoine and Concone, as well as three by Fétis himself. Most of these are methods in theory of harmony.[396] In short, he divides the development of harmony into four stages.

69 François Fétis

The first stage is the 'ordre unitonique', the inevitable consequence of the plainchant tonality, which consists solely of triads. This is based on the diatonic scale with seven modes which differ in where the semitones occur. Here, no modulation is possible because there is no relation of tension between the different tonalities in this consonant harmony. These church modes lack tension in the tritone between the fourth and seventh tones. According to Fétis, this stage of *tonalité ancienne* existed until the end of the 16th century.[397] In guitar music this concerns the renaissance music of the vihuelists Milán, Narváez, Mudarra, Valderrábano, Pisador, Fuenllana and Daza. Coste probably does not know them, but he does know the music from their period, as he publishes some works from the 16th century in opus 52 *Le Livre d'Or du Guitariste*.

The second stage is the 'ordre transitonique', the first phase of the 'tonalité moderne'. This starts with the 'discovery' of the dominant seventh chord by Monteverdi, due to the crucial relation between the leading tone and the tonic. With the discovery of the natural dissonant harmony a transition from one tonality to another is made possible: modulation. With this a new art in music was created.[398] As far as the guitar is concerned, this is the baroque music by Granata, Roncalli, Sanz, Guerau, Visée and Campion, for instance. Coste certainly had knowledge of this music: he transcribes several works by Visée, which he publishes in the *Méthode* Coste-Sor, and music of Haendel, Visée, Couperin and Exaudet in opus 52 *Le Livre d'Or du Guitariste*.

---

[394] Pierre, Constant: *Le Conservatoire national de musique et de déclamation: documents historiques et administratifs*, Paris, Imprimerie nationale, 1900, p. 420.

[395] Fétis, François Joseph: 'Esquisse de l'histoire de l'harmonie', in: *Revue et Gazette musicale de Paris*, 1840, English translation Mary I. Arlin, Harmonologia series No. 7, Pendragon Press, Stuyvesant NY, 1994.

[396] Robert, F.: 'harmonie et tonalité en France, Traités d'Harmonie en France au XIXe s.', in: Fauquet, Joël-Marie: *Dictionnaire de la Musique en France au XIXe siècle*, Paris, Fayard, 2003, p. 570-572.

[397] Fétis, François Joseph: 'Esquisse de l'histoire de l'harmonie', in: *Revue et Gazette musicale de Paris*, 1840, English translation Mary I. Arlin, Harmonologia series No. 7, Pendragon Press, Stuyvesant NY, 1994, p. xxxii-xxxiv.

[398] Fétis, François Joseph: 'Esquisse de l'histoire de l'harmonie', in: *Revue et Gazette musicale de Paris*, 1840, English translation Mary I. Arlin, Harmonologia series No. 7, Pendragon Press, Stuyvesant NY, 1994, p. xxxiv-xxxv.

The third stage is the 'ordre pluritonique'. Here, modulation is realized using enharmonic relations, when a tone of a chord is used as the pivot tone between different scales. The value of the attraction of dissonance is in the diminished seventh chord and the German and Italian augmented sixth chords. because in the enharmonic resolutions of each chord several possible tonal relations are concerned. According to Fétis, Mozart was the first to notice this as a valuable means of expression.[399] In guitar music all these applications occur in the music of Giuliani and Sor. It should be evident that Coste has a solid knowledge of Classical guitar music. Apart from that, he makes transcriptions of works by Haydn, Mozart and Beethoven in opus 52 *Le Livre d'Or du Guitariste*.

The fourth and last stage of tonality is the 'ordre omnitonique', a stage now achieved by this art after developing in that direction for half a century. 'Ordre omnitonique' derives from the intervals of natural chords and the changing of tones by substitution. The main problem of intensive alteration and change by replacement of tones in the harmony is that the point of saturation in harmonic development is reached, from which point it is impossible to recognize the original chord. Fétis now foresees the chromaticism of the end of the 19th century and the end of tonality in the early 20th century. Liszt, who attends his lectures on this subject in 1832, writes to Fétis in 1859: 'I have had ceaseless benefit from your lessons, in particular those remarkable lectures on "ordre omnitonique."'[400] When Coste begins with his study of counterpoint and harmony after his arrival in Paris in the end of 1828 or at the beginning of 1829, it is even possible that he also attended to these lectures. If not, he may have taken notice of the course content via other people or the publication of the *Esquisse* in 1840. This makes it relevant to take a look at the aspects of harmony in Coste's music, and connect these with Fétis's view upon the matter. In concrete term, the relevant elements are chromatics, dissonance, modulation, and the four-voice prolongation, typical of Coste.

Fétis also gives expression to his interest to 'old' music in a tangible way. The *Concert historique* he organizes in April 1840 is an example. The announcement lists the program which includes a *Vilhanccio* [sic] for six female voices and six guitars, a piece which is already played with Aguado on April 14, 1835. Now the names of the guitarists are given: the MM. Carcassi, Coste, Roehder, Vimeux, Losset and Charpentier. The names Carcassi and Coste are known, and those of the other unknown four have now been rescued from oblivion. Between the two parts of the concert Huerta is in the program with an *air de danse* from the 17th century by Espinel.[401] But the concert is cancelled, the musicians from the Opéra don't get permission to sing.[402] These include Julie Dorus-Gras, soprano, whose maiden name is van Steenkiste, originally from Valenciennes, and just the same age as Coste, and Mme Labarre, the spouse of the harpist.[403] Mme Widemann, of whom nothing is known apart from her participation in three of Coste's concerts in 1840, is also mentioned here. The *Villancico* remains popular with the public, the piece is in Fétis's program until 1855. at which time it becomes apparent that it was composed by Soto de Puebla, at the time of Philip II. *La France musicale* writes: 'Alard played *La Romanesca*, accompanied by violins, bass violins, batarde violin and guitar. What an admirable melancholy is in this poetic *Romanesca!*'[404] The *Concert historique* of April 1840 is the only one in which Coste would have played.

---

[399] Fétis, François Joseph: 'Esquisse de l'histoire de l'harmonie', in: *Revue et Gazette musicale de Paris*, 1840, English translation Mary I. Arlin, Harmonologia series No. 7, Pendragon Press, Stuyvesant NY, 1994, p. xxxv-xxxvi.
[400] Fétis, François Joseph: 'Esquisse de l'histoire de l'harmonie', in: *Revue et Gazette musicale de Paris*, 1840, English translation Mary I. Arlin, Harmonologia series No. 7, Pendragon Press, Stuyvesant NY, 1994, p. xxxvi-xxxvii.
[401] *Le Ménestrel*, vol. VII, no. 21, 19 IV 1840, p. [4]: '[...] concert historique [...] Concerto di Camera [...] Jean Strobach (1602) [...] Coste, théorbe [...] *Vilhancico espagnol* [...] Carcassi, Coste, Roehder, Vimeux, Losset et Charpentier, guitare.'
[402] *Le Ménestrel*, vol. VII, no. 22, 26 IV 1840, p. [3]: 'Duprez et plusieurs autres artistes de l'Opéra n'ayant pu obtenir l'autorisation de chanter au *Concert historique* annoncé par M. Fétis, ce concert n'a pu avoir lieu.'
[403] Colas, D.: 'Dorus-Gras, Julie'; Fauquet, J.-M.: 'Labarre, Théodore', in: Fauquet, Joël-Marie: *Dictionnaire de la Musique en France au XIXe siècle*, Paris, Fayard, 2003, p. 398, 651.
[404] *La France musicale*, vol. XIX, no. 16, 22 IV 1855, p. 122: 'Alard a joué la *Romanesca* avec accompagnement de violes, basses de violes, viole batarde et guitare. Quelle adorable mélancolie il y a dans cette poétique *Romanesca!*'

V — Souvenirs

Concerts 1840

In 1840 there are more concerts with guitar. Despite the fact that the guitar does not seem to be such an established instrument. it still has its place on the concert stage. After Coste's concert on March 29 in salle Herz, another concert with the guitar is given there on April 11, this time by Huerta. After Spain, England and Ireland this travelling virtuoso is in Paris again in 1840 and takes part in nine concerts there, including the one on April 11 in salle Herz is announced as a 'great musical matinée, serious and comical, given by M. Levasseur.'[405] This bass singer sings a program in which the important and principal artists, MM Haumann and Huerta perform. The Polish guitarist Scizepanowski [sic] can also be heard in this period, he plays in a concert around April 12, 1840, as well as on March 1 and April 18, 1841 in the salle Herz. 'Again a concert in the salle of M. Herz. Again and again, the salle of M. Herz!'[406] as *La France musicale* describes the rush in this concert hall, twice. And it remains busy with Herz, also with the guitar, because this musical newspaper mentions another concert with Coste on July 26:

In the research of our review of the concerts, we found an important omission: M. Coste, an important guitarist, could be heard with success in a concert that he organized with much care, in the salle of M.. Herz. We hope to be excused for this unintentional error. After all, this concert, in which M. Coste and Mme Wideman [sic] gave a brilliant performance, made a great impact in the musical world.[407]

It is remarkable that this is an as yet undiscovered concert date for Coste. If other guitarists regularly play in Paris and there is an omission with regards to Coste, there could be more concerts by him in Paris. Still, Coste was not a travelling virtuoso like Huerta and Szczepanowski, whose name is spelled inconsistently in the press of the time, just like Liszt sometimes misspelt as Lizst, and perhaps Coste, as a local artist. was less interesting for frequent performances An infant prodigy on the guitar is of greater interest to the public, like Regondi, seven years of age, who performs on April 28, 1830, and now Mlle Lovrins, ten years of age, in a show combining musical and literary elements on June 4, 1840 in the Société d'Émulation.[408]

The year 1840 is also the probable date of two of Coste's compositions, the *Rondeau de Concert* opus 12 and *Caprice sur l'air espagnol Cachucha* opus 13; the arrangement of the chanson *La Petite Savoyarde* finds its way to the press. The numbers of Coste's early editions with Richault,

3699.R. opus 7 'Strauss' in 1838 (reviewed in chapter IV)

4431.R. opus 13 *La Cachucha* in 1840

4513.R. opus 12 *Rondeau de Concert* in 1840

4782.R. opus 10 *Scherzo & Pastorale* in 1841

would give cause to discuss these works here, apart from what could be presumed by the opus numbers, but Anik Devriès warns that these editorial numbers should be treated with great distrust. They are not exceedingly chronological, some numbers are reserved for certain authors.[409] It is plausible that these works are composed in this period, and better data are not available. The historical perspective

---

[405] *La France musicale*, vol. III, no. 14, 5 IV 1840, p. 147: '[...] grande matinée musicale, sérieuse ett comique [...] Huerta.'; Huerta, Trinitario in: Coldwell, Robert & Javier Suàrez-Pajares: *A.T. Huerta, Life and Works*, DGA Editions, Sevilla, 2006, p. 22-23; Colas, D. 'Levasseur, Nicolas', in: Fauquet, Joël-Marie: *Dictionnaire de la Musique en France au XIXe siècle*, Paris, Fayard, 2003, p. 693.

[406] *La France musicale*, vol. III, no. 15, 12 IV 1840, p. 155: 'Szizepanowski [sic]'; Huerta; vol. IV, no. 7, 14 II 1841, p. 55: 'Szczepanowski'; no. 10, 7 III 1841, p. 78: Éncore, et toujours, la salle de M. Herz! [...] Encore une soirée musicale dans la salle de M. Herz!'

[407] *La France musicale*, vol. III, no. 30, 26 VII 1840, p. 279: 'En examinant notre revue sur les concerts, nous apercevons une omission importante: M. Coste, guitariste distingué, s'est fait entendre avec succès dans le concert qu'il avait monté avec beaucoup de soin dans la salle de H. Herz. Nous désirons que cette omission bien involontaire ne nous soit pas imputé à blâme. D'ailleurs, ce concert dans lequel M. Coste et Mme Wideman [sic] se sont montrés avec éclat, a eu du retentisssement dans le monde musical.'

[408] *Revue musicale de Paris*, tome VII, vol. II, 8 V 1830, p. 17: 'petit artiste [Regondi]'; *Revue et Gazette musicale de Paris*, vol. VII, no. 39, 7 VI 1840, p. 331: 'petite guitariste [Lovrins]'; vol. XIV, no. 19, 9 V 1847, p. 157-158: ' petite virtuose de huit ans [Séron]'.

[409] Devriès, Anik & François Lesure: *Dictionnaire des éditeurs de musique français*, Genève, Minkoff, 1979-1988, vol. II, p. 367-369.

aside, playing and analyzing the musical works give a clear view on the composer's progression. For the sake of complete, opus 9 *Lucia di Lammermoor* also is discussed, it is certainly published in 1841. This impressive range of compositions show Coste's diversity as a composer.

Opus 12, *Rondeau de Concert* 1840

This work in two parts by Coste is dedicated to his pupil Clarisse Lelorin, who must have had a considerable level of skill to be able to play this piece. It is far beyond didactic in character, including in respect to its musical structure. Despite the fact that it is not certain it should be dated in 1840, based on the Richault's publication number, the pieces fit very well into Coste's development as a composer in this period of his life. The Dane Søffren Degen, who visited Coste in 1855, and who buys or copies many of his works, thinks it is worthwhile to write a second part to it to be able to play it as a duet. This addition to the work does not go beyond some simple chords and many rests.[410] The title page of the copy in the Rischel & Birket-Smith collection carries Coste's dedication and signature in manuscript: 'à Monsieur Degen, Hommage d'amitié.' In this work Coste strays considerably from the rigid rondo structure, gives ample room to his creativity, and even starts with an open question, the diminished seventh chord full of tension. Taking the theme of the rondo as a passing dominant is a nice invention, whereby a new direction is chosen, on a pedal point on A to the fourth and the fifth degree, a progression which also occurs many times with the Classical composers. The piece ends with repeated chords and rocket figures and the dominant-tonic cadence to confirm the key. The open ended beginning is answered with an exclamation mark in this way. Apart from this, the work can be characterized as light Romantic, with its many changes of tempo, prescription of dynamics and articulation, some ornamentation, many chromatics and chords full of tension, as well as some cadenzas. Clarisse Lelorin would certainly have delighted audiences if she played it in a mixed concert for pupils, for instance.

Opus 13, *La Cachucha* 1840

Musical life in Paris is developing, but the ball remains as popular as ever, along with the associated dances. New dances also are introduced in public halls like La Chaumière, Tivoli, Le Jardin Turc, such as the Polka, the Mazurka and the Cachucha. From the dance hall these are brought to the salons by the instrumentalist's fingers, and conquer all of Paris. Dolores Serral introduces the cachucha, originally from Andalusia, in 1836 in Paris. In the very same year Fanny Elssler (1810-1884), the legendary prima ballerina of the Romantic ballet, dances the cachucha in the Opéra in the ballet-pantomime *Le Diable boiteux* by maître de ballet Jean Coralli (1779-1854) to music by Casimir Gide (1804-1868). The dance becomes a rage and is received with so much enthusiasm that she continues to dance it, under a different title, as a separate act throughout the rest of her career.[411] With this the status of this dance is established, a gracious, lively and passionate Spanish dance, traditionally in triple meter and accompanied with castagnettes, suiting the Hispanicism of the period, with the boléro and the habanera dances.[412] Coste dedicates this work to his 16-year-old pupil Mlle Olive Pauilhé, who he marries 31 years later![413] The melody is striking and can instantly be recognized; in form and structure it has the characteristics of a traditional folksong, which Gide probably inserted in the ballet in its original form. Ambroise Thomas (1811-1896), of whose *Le Perruquier de la Régence* Coste made an arrangement

---

[410] Kk Rischel Ms.41 mu7910.0483, Coste, *Rondeau de Concert*.
[411] Fauquet, J.-M.: 'cachucha'; Jacq-Mioche, S. & N. Lécomte: 'Coralli, Jean'; Lecomte, N.: 'Diable boiteaux, Le'; Lecomte, N.: 'Elssler, Fanny'; Kocevar, É.: 'Gide, Casimir', in: Fauquet, Joël-Marie: *Dictionnaire de la Musique en France au XIXe siècle*, Paris, Fayard, 2003, p. 193, 317, 380, 425, 514.
[412] Pistone, Danièle: *La musique en France de la Révolution à 1900*, Paris, Honoré Champion, 1979, p.21; Haan, De: see: Robijns, J. & Miep Zijlstra: *Algemene Muziek Encyclopedie*, De Haan, Weesp, 1983, vol. 2 p.90 cachucha; Prat, Domingo: *Diccionario biografico, bibliografico, critico, de Guitarras, Guitarristas y Guitarreros*, Buenos Aires, 1934 (reprint 1986), p.427; Walter, Horst: 'Fanny Elssler' in: Sadie, Stanley ed.: *The New Grove Dictionary of Music and Musicians*, London, Macmillan, 1980. vol. 6, p.146; id. in: Sadie, Stanley, ed.: *The New Grove Dictionary of Music and Musicians*, second edition, London, Macmillan, 2001, vol. 8, p. 170-171.
[413] Archives de Paris, *Acte de mariage Napoléon Coste & Louise Olive Pauilhé*, 11 I 1871, série V2E 5Mi 3/210; Archives de Paris, *Acte de déces Napoléon Coste*, 15 I 1883, série V2E 5Mi 3/1256.

70 Cachucha danced by Fanny Elssler

already in 1838, does the same in the ballet *La Gipsy* in 1839, again with Fanny Elssler.[414] In this way not only opera selections like *La Famille Suisse* and folk melodies like *La Romanesca* are chosen as a theme for a composition, but also dance forms like the cachucha. Czerny does exactly the same thing in a piano piece in 1838, Huerta in a guitar piece in 1841, as does Legnani,[415] and Coste does this in his *Capriche sur l'Air Espagnol La Cachucha* opus 13, all with the same melody.[416] The date of this work, according to Baillie around 1835,[417] must be somewhere between the aforementioned introduction of the dance in 1836 and the date on which publisher Richault moves from the address indicated on the edition, boulevard Poissonnière no.16 au 1er, to number 26, on November 14, 1841. The number of the edition 4331.R. might indicate it is published in 1840, but the numbers of Richault's catalogue are not very reliable, as already noted.[418] With two cadenzas as a passage to a subsequent episode and the developments in harmony, the Romantic characteristics are quite restricted, but this can hardly be otherwise in such a folk-oriented dance structure. It is the introduction that shows the most Romantic

---

[414] Lecomte, N.: 'Gipsy, La'; Fauser, A.: 'Thomas, Ambroise', in: Fauquet, Joël-Marie: *Dictionnaire de la Musique en France au XIXe siècle*, Paris, Fayard, 2003, p. 516, 1216-1217.

[415] Kk Rischel 494 mu 6703.1289 U48: Legnani: *La Gitana e la Cachucha*.

[416] *La France Musicale*, vol. I, no. 9, 22 II 1838, p. 6: la Cachucha, par M. Czerny; *Bibliographie de la France*, vol. XXX, no. 10, 6 III 1841, p. 120: la Cachucha, Huerta; Coldwell, Robert & Javier Suàrez-Pajares: *A. T. Huerta, Life and Works*, DGA Editions, 2006, p. 106-109.

[417] Baillie, Laureen: *The Catalogue of Printed Music in the British Library to 1980*, London, Saur, 1982, p. 58.

[418] Devriès, Anik & François Lesure: *Dictionnaire des éditeurs de musique français*, vol. II, De 1820, Geneva, 1979, p. 365, 369.

character, in this regard. This four page work is not very difficult to play, despite the application of many possibilities involving register and pitch, but to call this piece didactic, goes too far, it is certainly a mature composition.

CHANSON, *LA PETITE SAVOYARDE* - BARROILHET [ARR. COSTE] 1840

In 1840 *La Petite Savoyarde* with words from Lacoste Dubouig and music by Paul Baroilhet [sic] from the Académie Royale de Musique is also published by the Bureaux de la France Musicale, 6, rue Neuve St-Marc, with an accompaniment for guitar by Nap. Coste. Above the page of music itself the name of Barroilhet is spelled correctly, while at that time mistakes in spelling are made quite often in various publications. It is dedicated to Mademoiselle Marguerite d'Anjou. According to the British Library this chanson has been dated to around 1840.[419] On the last page of this edition of *La France musicale* eleven separate numbers from *Le Lac des Fées* by Auber are advertised, in an arrangement for voice and guitar by Carcassi; this guitarist still is active in Paris. This opera by Auber is performed in 1839, thus the date of the chanson probably is correct.[420] In 1841 the chanson is mentioned as published in the *Bibliographie de la France*, without any mention of Coste, however.[421] The chanson has been added to the Thematic Catalogue. The title page shows a young beggar-girl

71 La petite Savoyarde

in traditional garb, from the Savoie, of course, with a skirt and bare feet, who sings her chansons, to a number of rich youngsters amusing themselves under a large tree. The girl accompanies herself with a hurdy-gurdy, attached to a belt hanging over her shoulder. She calls upon the Virgin Mary, she sings and prays, and believes in happiness. She is from the Savoie, from where the good god sent her, she sings about her misery: this morning her good mother died of starvation. This chanson is in the popular tradition. Paul Barroilhet (1810-1871) is a baritone singer in the choir of the Opéra in Paris and he is a teacher at the Conservatoire as a talented baritone who sang in Rossini's *Othello*, Donizetti's *Lucia di Lammermoor* and Rossini's *Guillaume Tell*.[422] While his personality as a baritone singer might have been an inspiration to many composers,[423] his qualities as a composer do not compare to that. In the music nothing can be heard of the overwhelming Romantic sadness of a chanson. Coste's intentions can only be regarded as commercial. The number of such chansons is countless in this period. There is

---

[419] Baillie, Laureen: *The Catalogue of Printed Music in the British Library to 1980*, London, 1982, p. 58.
[420] Longyear, R.M.: 'Auber' in *The New Grove Dictionary of Music and Musicians*, ed. Stanley Sadie, London, Macmillan, 1980, vol. 1, p. 681; Schneider, Herbert: 'Auber', in: *The New Grove Dictionary of Music and Musicians*, second edition, London, Macmillan, 2001, vol. 2, p. 157.
[421] *Bibliographie de la France*, vol. XXX, no. 30, 24 VII 1841, p. 372: '*La petite Savoyarde*, paroles de M. Lacoste-Dubouig, musique de Paul Barroilhet. - A Paris, rue Neuve-Saint-Marc, n. 6.'
[422] Dandelot, A.: *La Société des Concerts du Conservatoire de 1828 à 1897*, Paris, 1923, p. 8.
[423] Colas, D.: 'Barroilhet, Paul', in: Fauquet, Joël-Marie: *Dictionnaire de la Musique en France au XIXe siècle*, Paris, Fayard, 2003, p. 103.

V — Souvenirs 95

even one with the same title with words, music and guitar accompaniment by a certain Briqueville.[424] In the same manner Scribe and Auber's opera *Zanetta, ou Jouer avec le Feu* has its opening night on May 18, 1840 in the Opéra and on the following July 19 publisher Troupenas advertises 14 separate numbers from it with both piano and guitar accompaniment.[425] It doesn't say who arranged them for guitar.[426] Carcassi also publishes a *Mélange sur Zanetta*, Vimeux even a *Fantaisie sur Zanetta* for guitar and flute or guitar and violin, with Troupenas, as witnessed by the advertisement *La France musicale* on November 8, 1840.[427] Composers and arrangers immediately set out to profit from this opera's reputation, further contributing to its popularity. The guitar, as well as the piano, functions as an accompanying instrument for chansons and opera selections. The guitar is cheaper and therefore gains a greater foothold in the lower classes, who have less money and more interest in popular music. To reach this public, opera selections are published soon after their premiere in an arrangement both for voice and piano and for voice and guitar.

Opus 9, *Lucia di Lamermoor* [i.e. Lammermoor] 1841

This work of Coste's is published by Bernart Latte with the number B.L. 1845. According to the catalogue, this work can be dated to the years 1838-1839. The later editions of Mayaud and Grus are identical to Latte's edition in regard to the print and page size, the first even copies the B.L.- number.[428] The *Bibliographie de la France* mentions the edition in 1841 as 'Divertissement pour guitare par Nap. Coste. prix 4-50' under the section 'Lucia di Lamermoor' [sic, Italian] under which many editions of parts and arrangements from this opera are listed, making certain it was written before this time.[429]

72 Donizetti, Naples

---

[424] *Bibliographie de la France*, vol. XXXI, no. 42, 15 X 1842, p. 587: '*La Savoiarde*, romance, paroles, musique et accompganement de guiitare de H. Briqueville. - Imp. -lith. de Brulat à Avignon.'
[425] Schneider, H.: 'Zanetta, ou Joueur avec feu', in: Fauquet, Joël-Marie: *Dictionnaire de la Musique en France au XIXe siècle*, Paris, Fayard, 2003, p. 1324.
[426] *La France musicale*, vol. III, no. 19, 19 VII 1840: 'Zanetta, opéra d'Auber.'
[427] *La France musicale*, vol. III, no. 45, 8 XI 1840: 'Math. Carcassi. Mélange sur *Zanetta*'.
[428] Devriès, Anik & François Lesure: *Dictionnaire des éditeurs de musique français*, Genève, Minkoff, 1979-1988, vol. II, p. 203, 307-309.
[429] *Bibliographie de la France*, vol. XXX, no. 44, 30 X 1841, p. 540: 'Divertissement pour guitare, par Nap. Coste. Prix 4-50'.

The opera by Donizetti is based on Walter Scott's novel *The Bride of Lammermoor*. This historical novel, on the subject of a real occurrence in a real place, tells the intrigues around the succession and possession of the title and the estate of Ravenswood at the end of the 17th century. It was published in 1819. The story is set in 1669 in the Lammermuir Hills in Scotland, East of Edinburgh, where Lucy Ashton, daughter of the master of the estate Ravenswood, falls in love with Edgar Ravenswood, the attractive son of the former owner. Everything goes wrong: Lucy is driven into insanity by the manipulation and paternalism of her mother, who forces her to marry someone else, despite her engagement with Edgar. In insanity Lucy stabs the groom on the day of their wedding, after which she is overwhelmed by emotion and dies. After her funeral, Edgar is challenged to a duel by Lucy's brother, but going to the place of the duel, he disappears without a trace into the mist.[430] It is a kind of Romeo and Juliet in reverse, a novel in which Donizetti found enough drama to base an opera on. In 1835 Donizetti is in Paris at the invitation of Rossini and sees the Grand Opéra of Meyerbeer and Halévy. Back in Naples he writes *Lucia di Lamermoor*. In 1839 the opera is staged in Paris in translation, and in a revision by Donizetti.[431] In his divertissement Napoleon Coste uses several fragments from the opera, divided into four segments after the introduction. Regarding the dates, the piece may well have been composed around 1839-1840, following the practice of 'domestication' of opera, although this is not merely an arrangement of opera parts for domestic use, but has a decidedly higher level of sophistication, structure and pretention. This is the picture that emerges in the sketch of the opera's content in the descriptive analysis. As it appears, Coste was not only inspired by the music of the opera, but also by the drama. There is much variation and unrest in the work, it is constantly in motion, and in this way it is a reflection of the state of mind of the main character of the opera, Lucy. The diminished seventh chord, which is repeated five times, is unique in this work, resulting in a great deal of tension, allowing it to represent Lucy's fatal attack on her groom, after which a release follows in the music. This is Coste's own invention, and bears no relation with Donizetti's 'Spargi d'amaro' in question. He dedicates the work to Madame Deshaulles, of whom nothing is known, apart from this. Neither is known she was Coste's pupil or admirer or if she was captivated by the subject matter. Coste elaborates the themes of this composition further than in the traditional variation form, from which he deviates to a great degree to make a real divertimento out of it, an entertaining musical piece, in which the subject is approached from different contrasting angles, and which shows a certain virtuosity as well.

COULEUR LOCALE 1840

Meanwhile the guitar demonstrates itself as a colorful instrument in a different way in the musical world of Paris in this period. In 1834 *Le Ménestrel* already published the short story *Jack, le Guitariste*, about a guitar-playing monkey in Ceylon, as mentioned in chapter IV. Now, in 1840, Cordelier Delanoue publishes, in *La France musicale*, a serial in four parts *Le Joueur de Guitare*, in which a more literary Romantic image of the guitar is presented. It is a sad story about a young hunch-backed man Lucien, a guitar teacher, who tries to earn some money on the Champs Élysées by playing the guitar, dressed in black, which accentuates his paleness even more. When he was young, his father died in a duel, and his mother's love turned into hatred. Now he lives alone in his shabby little room with no company other than his grief and his guitar. Then he meets his mother, now remarried, in a scene where she faints as he approaches her for some money, playing the guitar with his eyes full of tears. This is witnessed on the Champs Élysées by her husband, M. d'Espéramont, his own daughter Céline, and Alfred de Valrans, a friend of her father, who has his eye on the daughter. Then he is visited by his mother's husband and his friend with the proposition to leave Paris in exchange for a large sum of money. He refuses. Thereupon his mother is forced by her husband and his friend to legally renounce her son. But just when she is about to sign the document, she hears a voice through the open window, singing a chanson

---

[430] Scott, Walter: *The Bride of Lammermoor*, Introduction Fiona Robertson, Oxford, Oxford University Press, 2008, p. viii, 338-339, 348.
[431] Ashbrook, William: 'Donizetti, Gaetano', in: Sadie, Stanley, ed.: *The New Grove Dictionary of Music and Musicians*, London, Macmillan, 1980, vol. 5, p. 555; Smart, Mary Ann: 'Donizetti', in: Sadie, Stanley, ed.: *The New Grove Dictionary of Music and Musicians*, second edition, London, Macmillan, 2001, vol. 6, p. 471-475.

accompanied by a guitar, the last lines of which are: 'From my guitar, a string breaks, just like my voice.' She turns towards the solicitor with the words: 'My son! I will not renounce my son! Sir, I will not sign!' It is indeed her son who is singing at that moment, and in a dramatic reunion she gives him his father's farewell letter, in which he is told not to take revenge on his killer, who turns out to be Valrans. Lucien is in love with Céline, who prefers Valrans, nevertheless. This is too sad for Lucien, who leaves Paris with a broken heart and broken strings. Later, after some embezzlements and great losses at the stock market, d'Espéramont commits suicide. Céline and Valrans get married. Still, when he strolls along the Tuileries, the writer thinks he recognizes Madame d'Espéramont in the crowd, holding the strong arm of a less pale-looking young man.[432] In this serial, much is made of matters such as poverty and richness, misfortune, death, sadness and desperate love are widely exposed. Plenty of tears are shed. It is well written by an author who is a contemplative story-teller, with dialogues, cliff hangers, and plot twists in every episode. Remarkably, the choice is explicitly made for feelings above cool and objective calculation, which eventually prove to be deceptive. Emotions play an important role, and the readers of the story, above all the female ones, can enjoy wiping away their tears over so much distress. These Romantic images from 1840 are connected to the guitar, as the instrument becomes a symbol of poverty, sorrow and above all, emotions. This Romantic image is even confirmed, but more diverse, in the opera *El Guitarrero* by Scribe and Halévy, which has its opening night in 1841. In this opera the young guitarist Riccardo wails out love songs in Santaren, Portugal, under Zarah's balcony. He wants to marry her or die. A passing nobleman, Villareal, has an idea and offers to present himself as his son. With this mistaken identity he marries Zarah and he saves the country at the same time, because Villareal's real son cannot be abducted now. He is even given the title of nobility as a reward for this. It is a love story with a happy ending, double roles, disguises and some political intrigues, just the makings for an exciting opera. It is interesting to read what *La France musicale*, writes on the music, apart from what has just been said:

73 Halévy

M. Halévy has written a complete overture for Le Guitarrero. The introduction is a lovely piece. It has very good, and at the same time very new, combination of instruments in it. The tuning of the guitar mi la re sol si mi is introduced in an original way, first it appears in the basses and the violins with pizzicato and then it appears in the wind instruments in a sweet harmony. M. Halévy evidently meant to show some local color and he succeeded in this; one might think one is hearing a piece of old Spanish music in ternary meter. All this is very well composed.[433]

After this the story of the opera in three acts is told and it is explained how the composer has expressed this in the music and the instrumentation. The literary image of the guitar is not the only thing connected to a Romantic character: the tuning of the guitar is also reflected in the music. And folk music also plays a role, as local color. In this connection it is interesting to note what Coste wrote in a letter to Schult in 1867:

---

[432] *La France musicale*, vol. III, no. 18, 3 V 1840, p. 177-180, no. 19, 10 V 1840, p. 189-191, no. 20, 17 V 1840, p. 197-199, no. 21, 24 V 1840, p. 206-208: 'Le Joueur de Guitare.'

[433] *La France musicale*, vol. IV, no. 4, 24 I 1841, p. 26: 'M. Halévy a fait pour le *Guitarrero*, une ouverture complète. L'introduction est une morceau délicieux, il y a une combinaison instrumentale des plus heureuses et des plus neuves en même temps. L'accord de la guitare *mi la re sol si mi* y est introduit d'une manière très originale; il est d'abord dit par les basses et les violons en *pizzicato* et repris ensuite par les instruments à vent qui font entendre une harmonie suave. H. Halévy a voulu évidemment faire de la couleur locale, et il y a réussi; on croirait entendre un morceau de vieille musique espagnole à trois temps; tout cela est très habilement traité.'

Halévy told me one day: 'It is unfortunate that you are so attached to an instrument that does not reward you for the work and care it has cost you.' What do you want?, I replied. I love it with all its imperfections. It is a child who is ill and to which I have become attached due to its weakness, and then it charms you and speaks to your soul.[434]

Halévy criticizes the instrument, but Coste defends it in a Romantic way: the guitar may be weak, but it speaks to the soul. With the same title as this piece Gustave Courbet produces a presumed self-portrait in 1844. First it was called 'Jeune homme dans un paysage' and was it was accepted by the Salon with this name in 1845. Originally it was believed to be a self-portrait, until *Le Sculpteur* from 1845, with the same size, was seen as its counterpart. This was believed to be a self-portrait, with Courbet in a dramatic pose, sculpting tools at hand, set in a landscape in clair-obscure. The first painting appears to be the violinist Promayet, his friend, with a guitar but without clair obscure. In that case *Le Guitarrero* might appeal to the collective memory as the image of the troubadour. It seems Courbet painted it over a period of two weeks. The bearded head alludes to Spanish art.[435] But couldn't it be that this painting also is the reflection on Halévy's opera? The image fits the story and the music perfectly. In any case, the image certainly fits the idea of the singing Romantic person who expresses his feelings accompanied by the guitar, sitting under a

74 Le Guitarrero, Courbet 1844

tree in an imaginary landscape with a vista full of clouds. Courbet himself says in his exhibition in 1855: 'Historical art is in essence contemporary. Even allegory and metaphor form the realism.'[436] The Romantic image of the guitar is just as multifaceted, but still very different from Coste's real activities as a concert guitarist, composer, editor, arranger and teacher.

Société 1841

In 1841 the *Revue et Gazette musicale de Paris* briefly reports:

M. Ferdinand Carulli, to whom the musical art owes more than 500 works, has died. He was 71 years old.[437]

Carulli dies on February 17, or according to Torta, who wrote his biography as a PhD dissertation, on February 14, and his oeuvre encompasses 366 opus numbers.[438] The number of his works is inversely proportional to the number of words devoted to him. Apparently he did not play such an important artistic role in Paris; Sor's obituary was more extensive. Now only Carcassi and Molino remain from this generation of Classical guitarists. Coste remains quite active and seeks to enlarge his world. In 1841 he joins the *Société académique des Enfants d'Apollon*. This society is founded in 1741 and reorganized in 1806. It is one of the organizations that survived the revolutions. It is a great honor to be part of its

---

[434] Coste-Schult, 7 X 1867: 'Halévy me disait un jour: "il est facheux que vous vous soyez ainsi attaché à un instrument qui ne vous récompense pas du travail et des soins qu'il vous a coûté". Que voulez-vous, lui répondis-je, je l'aime avec ses imperfections. C'est un enfant malade auquel je me suis attaché en raison de sa faiblesse et puis, il vous charme et parle à l'ame.'
[435] Bajou, Valérie: *Courbet*, Paris, Biro, 2003, p. 46-47.
[436] Bajou, Valérie: *Courbet*, Paris, Biro, 2003, p. 167.
[437] *Revue et Gazette musicale de Paris*, vol. VIII, no. 15, 21 II 1841, p.120: 'M. Ferdinand Carulli, a qui l'art musical doit plus de 500 ouvrages pour la *guitare*, vient de mourir. Il était agé de soixante-onze ans.'
[438] Torta, Mario: *Catalogo tematico delle opere di Ferdinando Carulli*, Lucca, Libreria Musicale Italiana, 1993, p. XII, XXXV.

V — Souvenirs

music department, with members like Dancla, Habeneck, Hummel, Liszt, Panseron and Thomas, as well as violinist Tilmant.[439] Coste may have been admitted thanks to the advocacy of members with whom he has played in concerts earlier, such as pianist Chaulieu, oboist Delacour, double bass-player Gouffé, organist Pollet, violinist Tilmant or violinist Vandenberghe. Oboist Charles Triébert, with whom Coste became friends, possibly in 1843, has been member of this select company since 1833.[440] And just like Tilmant and Triébert before him, Coste demonstrates his abilities with his entry in 1841 in one of the monthly meetings this society organizes for and by its members. The description of the program for the month of December 1841, as published in 1881 by the chairman of 1865 Maurice Decourcelle, himself a pianist and composer, says: 'Fantaisie et variations for guitar, composed and performed by M. Coste.'[441] The most recent Fantaisie with variations Coste composed, *Fantaisie de Concert* [Meyerbeer] opus 6, is from 1837 and is published by Coste himself. In his summary of the monthly sessions Decourcelle mainly mentions works composed by his confrères, and those are played by the members of the society without preliminary rehearsals, for a select group, because these performances are not open to the public.[442] By then Coste's piece is four years old, and *Fantaisie Norma* opus 16, a fantasy without real variations, has been performed and published three years before. If it is the case that it is tradition to play a new work in the monthly concerts, he is more likely to have played *Divertissement Lucia di Lamermoor* opus 9, which was published in October. It is not really a fantasy with variations as is suggested by the title, but it may pass for one. There is no certainty in this, one can only speak of probability. The entry on the reissue of *Norma* opus 16 is a help: it says it piece has been performed at the Conservatoire de Musique, and this is just cause, just as it is with *Le Tournoi* opus 15, to place it in December 1841 at the last monthly meeting of the year of the Apollo society, which organizes the annual concerts there, and perhaps also the monthly ones. The relatively closed nature of these monthly meetings of the *Société académique des Enfants d'Apollon* means that few reviews are published. Critic Henri Blanchard, who has been a member since 1825, sometimes writes on the subject, but more often on the annual concert, whose program mainly exists of works played in the monthly meetings. From 1831 up to 1850 these yearly concerts take place in the hall of the Conservatoire on Ascension Day.[443] Coste performs there in 1843. With his entry into the *Société académique des Enfants d'Apollon* Coste now belongs to the musical élite of Paris.

Then the sad, but inevitable news arrives about his mother, Anne Pierrette Dénéria, who dies in Valenciennes on February 11, 1842.[444] Apart from her death certificate, no information has been found, such as whether she was bed stricken, whether Coste visited her and arranged the funeral, or attended it. And unlike Coste's father she is not mentioned in the local newspaper. Coste himself is mentioned, but that is in connection to a concert; the newspaper follows his development.

---

[439] Cooper, Jeffrey: *The rise of instrumental music and concert series in Paris, 1828-1871*, Ann Arbor, UMi Press, 1983, p. 258; Fauquet, Joël-Marie: 'Société académique des enfants d'Apollon', in: Fauquet, Joël-Marie: *Dictionnaire de la Musique en France au XIXe siècle*, Paris, Fayard, 2003, p. 1152.

[440] Decourcelle, Maurice: *La Société des Enfants d'Apollon (1741-1880): programmes des concerts annuels...*, Paris, Durand, 1881, p. 17 Tilmant, vl, concert 15 I 1838; Chaulieu, pf, concert 21 II 1835; Triébert, ob; p. 18 Gouffé, cb, concert 15 I 1838; p. 24 Delacour, ob, concert 21 II 1835; p. 28, Pollet, org, concert 21 II 1835; p. 29, Vandenberg [sic], vl, concert 21 II 1835; Triébert, ob.

[441] Decourcelle, Maurice: *La Société des Enfants d'Apollon (1741-1880): programmes des concerts annuels...*, Paris, Durand, 1881, p. 157: 'Fantaisie et variations pour la guitare, composées et exécutees pas M. Coste.'

[442] Decourcelle, Maurice: *La Société des Enfants d'Apollon (1741-1880): programmes des concerts annuels...*, Paris, Durand, 1881, p. 4: '[...] séances mensuelles, dans lequel, j'ai surtout mentionné lers oeuvres composées par nos confrères [...]'; p. 6: 'On exécutait dans l'intimité (car le public n'était pas admis), sans répétitions préalables, [...]'.

[443] Decourcelle, Maurice: *La Société des Enfants d'Apollon (1741-1880): programmes des concerts annuels...*, Paris, Durand, 1881, p. 23: 'Blanchard, 1825'; p. 67-85: 'Salle du Conservatoire'; p. 78: 'M. Coste *Le Tournoi*'; Fauquet, Joël-Marie: 'Société académique des enfants d'Apollon', in: Fauquet, Joël-Marie: *Dictionnaire de la Musique en France au XIXe siècle*, Paris, Fayard, 2003, p. 1152; *Revue et Gazette musicale de Paris*, vol. XIX, no. 49, 5 XII 1852, p. 451: 'Auditions musicales. La Société académique des Enfants d'Apollon [...]'.

[444] Valenciennes, Bibliothèque Municipale, *Acte de décès Anne Pierrette Dénéria*, 11 II 1842, fonds modernes, série E: Etat civil, E1, R56.

Heptacorde 1842

Coste plays his seven-stringed guitar in a concert that probably takes place in the week before April 3, 1842:

> *M. Coste, a guitarist of great merit, who plays a guitar with seven strings, is giving a concert in the salons of Duport, in which he earned great successes.*[445]

In the following week, on April 8, Coste gives a concert with others, which for that period is extensively reported in the news, three papers write about it. To give a good picture of the musical reality of Coste's concerts, and because not very much is written about him, later, it is useful to let the press speak for itself. On April 5, 1842 the *Echo de la Frontière* of Valenciennes announces the concert:

> *M. Coste, young guitarist from Valenciennes, whose reputation among the real lovers of music in Paris is very great, is giving a concert there on Sunday 8 April, in which the young Lecointe, who has a talent that is already famous now, can be heard in the instrumental part.*[446]

The violinist Lecointe, pupil of Baillot, also is originally from Valenciennes, and now he plays together with Coste. In the *Revue et Gazette musicale de Paris* Henri Blanchard writes a review of the concert on April 17 under the head:

> *M. Coste*
>
> *Defying the discredit into which the guitar has fallen, this instrument of melancholy, which made Edelmone say in the Othello of Ducis: 'It is the faithful friend of desolate distress' M. Coste, Sor's heir, successor of the Sors, the Aguados, the Carcassis, has given his concert too, and played piano works by Hummel to a surprised audience. This commitment to this Iberian instrument is just as special as the talent Coste shows on his instrument.*[447]

Despite Blanchard's belonging to the musical élite of the *Société académique des Enfants d'Apollon*, together with Coste, he persists in his negative opinion of the guitar, drawn in the literary Romantic image, and he does not go further than mentioning Coste's the talent in transcribing Hummel's works. There is no trace to be found of these transcriptions. *La France musicale* is more positive on the concert, either Léon or Marie Escudier, one of the brothers, writes on April 17, 1842:

> *What can be said about the concert given by M. Napoléon Coste. Despite the decline into which the guitar has fallen, this intrepid guitarist persists in the study of this instrument with a laudable perseverance. He performed twice and was listened to with the greatest attention. If there aren't a great number of guitar amateurs, there is, nevertheless, a large audience to applaud this skillful guitarist, as a compensation. M. Coste is first class; he plays with unbelievable rapidity and a perfect purity. In a duet with one of his pupils he sent the audience into ecstasy.*[448]

---

[445] *Le Ménestrel*, vol. IX, no. 18, 3 IV 1842, p. [2]: 'M. Coste, guitariste d'un grand mérite, qui se sert d'une guitare à sept cordes, a donné une soirée dans les salons de Duport où il a obtenu de beaux succès.'

[446] *L'Echo de la Frontière*, Valenciennes, 21ᵉ Année, mar. 5 IV 1842, no. 2623, p. 164: 'M. *Coste*, jeune guitariste de Valenciennes, dont la réputation s'est fort étendue à Paris parmi les vrai *dilettanti*, y donne dimanche 8 avril un concert auquel on entendra, dans la partie instrumentale, le jeune *Lecointe*, qui possède aujourd'hui un talent déà`en renom.'

[447] *Revue et Gazette musicale de Paris*, vol. IX, no. 16, 17 IV 1842, p.168: 'M. Coste. Bravant le discrédit dans lequel est tombée la guitare, cet instrument de mélancolie qui fait dire à Edelmone, dans l'*Othello* de Ducis: C'est le fidèle ami du chagrin solitaire, M. Coste, l'héritier, le continuateur des Sor, des Aguado, des Carcassi, a donné aussi son concert, et a fait entendre à son public surpris des morceaux de piano de Hummel. Ce dévouement à l'instrument ibérien a quelque chose d'aussi extraordinaire que le talent de M. Coste montre sur cet instrument.'

[448] *La France musicale*, vol. V, no. 15, 17 IV 1842, p. 153: 'Que vous dire du concert donné par M. Napoléon Coste. Ce guitariste intrépide, malgré le dépérissement où est tombée la guitare, poursuit avec une louable persévérance l'étude de cet instrument. Deux fois il s'est fait entendre et il a été écouté avec le plus grand intérêt. S'il n'y a pas un grand nombre d'amateurs de guitare, il y a au moins un public nombreux pour applaudir l'habile guitariste, c'est là une compensation. M. Coste est de première force; il joue avec une incroyable agilité et une pureté parfaite. Dans un duo avec une de ses élèves, il a transporté son auditoire.'

V — Souvenirs

This last criticism clearly shows the excellent reception that Coste's playing the guitar enjoys with the public, in spite of the critic's own opinion of the guitar. Playing together with a female pupil in a duet suits the traditional musical practice of the period, which is gradually changing, and it also suits the practice of playing one's own compositions. His first duet for two guitars is published by Richault, perhaps one year earlier.[449] It is dedicated to Mlle Caroline Montigny, his pupil. It is therefore likely she played this piece in this concert together with Coste. Also *Étude* 19 opus 38 is dedicated to her, a piece of a high technical and musical level, which might be indicative of her playing. She might be the daughter of Paul de Montigny, director of the hospital, to whom Coste dedicated his *Fantaisie Armide* opus 4 and *Grand Caprice* opus 11. All this is a testament of a good relationship.

Opus 10, *Scherzo et Pastorale* - duet 1841?

On the title page of Richault's edition the order of the two parts is reversed, the piece starts with the pastorale and ends with the scherzo, The reason why should be obvious: in a performance of these two waltzes it is more effective, as a rule, to put the most 'spectacular' piece at the end. But these works are not so spectacular. With this composition, it is difficult to imagine that the audience was moved to enthusiasm for the performance by Coste and his pupil. Perhaps other aesthetic considerations were involved. The hall could have been filled with family and acquaintances, or else Caroline might have been a very beautiful girl, a matter that would not have gone unnoticed by the press at the time. The date of Richault's edition could very well correspond with the date of the concert, around 1840. These are two 'valses brillantes' indeed, in which a clear distinction is made between the parts of 'maître' and 'élève', unless, which is also a possibility, the master was subservient to the solo part in the accompaniment. The piece is divided into a simple accompanying part with some chords, and a melodic solo part, which is not very hard to play. Both options remain open. Coste composed more difficult solo pieces earlier. It suits him that he does not go so far in this composition. Rather, he chooses simplicity. It is a work with a didactic purpose, which would suit Carulli very well. The analysis of the content can therefore be brief. It is a duet written in a rather Classical style, with a folk-like character. While it is certainly no masterpiece, this composition bears the marks of an adept guitar composer, who shows great skill in employing the few possibilities that he uses in it.

Bad press 1842

The success Coste has with is concerts contrasts strikingly with a certain critic's opinion of the guitar. Henri Blanchard (1791-1848), a violinist, composer and music critic, known for by his erudition, the finesse in his judgement and the quality of his style, makes a sketch of the guitar that is not very favorable.[450] In the *Revue et Gazette musicale*, to which he contributed since it was founded in 1835, he publishes on October 2, 1842 a short article entitled *Les Guitaristes*. In it, he regards those who play the guitar as a dwindling species, like the dog-wolves.

> *What now is a guitarist in the infinite population of instrumentalists? [...] a wagon's fifth wheel [...] The guitar is and will always be the national instrument of Spain, the mysterious interpreter of love [...] and also was the favorite instrument in France for a long time, [...] The guitar was fashionable in the last thirty years at all levels of society.*[451]

He mentions many guitar methods, Sor, Aguado, Carcassi and Castellacci as the interpreters of difficult music, and Huerta, who, according to him, does such special and funny things with his guitar as well, being a bad musician. After listing many composers he continues:

---

[449] Devriès, Anik & François Lesure: *Dictionnaire des éditeurs de musique français*, Vol. II, De 1820, Geneva, 1979, p. 365, 369.
[450] Bailbé, J.M.: 'Henri-Louis Blanchard', in: Fauquet, Joël-Marie: *Dictionnaire de la Musique en France au XIXe siècle*, Paris, Fayard, 2003, p. 150.
[451] *Revue et Gazette musicale de Paris*, vol. IX, no. 40, 2 X 1842, p. 395: 'Qu'est-ce qu'un guitariste dans la population incessamment croissante des instrumentalistes? [...] une cinquième roue à une carosse, [...] La guitare, qui est et sera toujours l'instrument national de l'Espagne, l'interprète mystérieux de l'amour, [...] La guitare devint l'instrument à la mode dans toutes les classes de la sociéte', il y a trente ans.'

Despite its few pretensions, despite the softness of its harmony, despite its thousand intimate charms, [...] this instrument can only be found in the hands of Figaro, [...] in the Théâtre-Français, or still in the hands of the many virtuosos in the open air, The guitar has decayed to the category of Bolivar's hats [...] and of the many ditties, which are, so to speak, made for the vaudeville.[452]

After using many other metaphors to reinforce his statement, he draws his conclusion:

At this place we must quote the opinion of the great musician Beck concerning the instrument [...] 'what a waste of time!' This exclamation best expresses the judgement one has to pass on the guitar and those who are seriously and pretentiously occupied with this forgotten instrument.[453]

After this, to conclude his article on the guitarists, he sings a hymn of praise for the violin, the Dona Maria and the Victoria of the musical kingdom. The guitar has disappeared from his discussion. These words cannot be misunderstood: in his opinion the guitar has fallen into the wrong hands. He does not take the instrument seriously, but instead favors the violin, his own instrument. Remarkably, he does not mention Coste, who is performing at a high level as a composer and a guitarist. He is either deliberately neglecting him, Coste is clearly an active figure in Paris musical life, or he is unabashedly exposing his prejudice. Indeed, both men are a members of the *Société académique des Enfants d'Apollon*, indeed. In any case, this is the sort of criticism levelled at the guitar, but thankfully there are other critics who are more favorable.

After Castil Blaze's humiliation of the instrument in 1834 already in *Le Ménestrel*[454] and Henri Blanchard's mortification in 1842 in the *Revue et Gazette musicale de Paris*, the guitar finds a 'warm defender' of the guitar in relation with other instruments in Léon Gozlan's essay, which is published in the *Démocratie pacifique*. A summary can be found in *La France musicale* in 1843:

The guitar has been banished from society by the piano. Yet there is no other instrument with which a young man can paint his love for a woman, without looking like a hunchback, as those do who play the violin; without spitting in a hollow piece of wood with a monkey face, as those do who play the flute; without turning one's back to the person to whom one is said to be yearning, as do those who play the piano. It is only with the guitar that one can show the love one feels for someone with one's face, without grimace, without convulsion. And still this instrument is hounded with anathema, it is banned, it is demolished. I want to rehabilitate it![455]

This appeal goes head-on against the negativism to which the guitar was subjected in those days, not based on a sketch of the successes of the instrument in concerts, but rather on the old-fashioned example of the guitar as an accompaniment to a romance, an expression of one's love. The essay is deemed important enough that a summary of it is published for the readers of this musical magazine, one of the three which appear in Paris for years.

The position of the guitar in Paris in this period can be deduced from the concerts in which the instrument is featured, as can be seen in the announcements and reviews of which many have

---

[452] *Revue et Gazette musicale de Paris*, vol. IX, no. 40, 2 X 1842, p. 395: 'Malgré son peu de prétention, malgré la douceur de son harmonie, malgré ses mille charmes intimes, [...] cet instrument ne figure plus que dans les mains de Figaro, [...] au Théâtre-Français, ou bien dans celles de quelques virtuoses en plein vent, [...] La guitare est donc tombée dans la catégorie des chapeaux à la Bolivar, [...] et du couplet dit de facture dans les vaudevilles.'

[453] *Revue et Gazette musicale de Paris*, vol. IX, no. 40, 2 X 1842, p. 395-396: 'nous croyons devoir citer [...] l'opinion [...] de Beck, musicien d'une haute portée [...] que de temps perdu! Cette exclamation formulait on ne peut mieux le jugement qu'on doit porter sur la guitare et ceux qui s'occupent sérieusement et prétentieusement de cet instrument oublié.'

[454] *Le Ménestrel*, vol. II, no. 42, 14 IX 1834, p. [1]: 'La guitare n'est point à dédaigner.'

[455] *La France musicale*, vol. VI, no. 32, 6 VIII 1843, p. 238: "'La guitare a été bannie de notre société par le piano. Pourtant il n'existe qu'un seul instrument avec lequel un jeune homme puisse peindre son amour à une femme sans paraître bossu, comme ceux qui jouent du violon; sans cracher avec les mines de singe dans un trou fait dans un morceau de bois creux, comme font ceux qui jouent de la flûte; sans montrer le dos à celle pour qui l'on dit soupirer, ainsi qu'il arrive à ceux gui touchent du piano; il n'existe en effet que la guitare avec laquelle on puisse exprimer de face à une personne, et sans grimace, sans contorsion, l'amour dont on est saisi en la voyant. Et l'on poursuit d'anathème, ou exile, on brise cet instrument. Moi je le réhabilite!'"

already been discussed, and the publications of original works and arrangements of opera selections by guitarists, as is shown in advertisements that have already been discussed from a historical and analytical perspective. Developments in guitar construction can also be significant, as is apparent from the exhibition of musical instruments in 1844. In *La France musicale* of May 12 of that year there is a map of the part of the exhibition in the Palais de l'Industrie with products by the makers of musical instruments. The reader is able to take this supplementary sheet with him when he visits the exhibition. Many manufacturers have a stand at this exhibition, such as Érard, Pape, Herz, Pleyel and Souffleto, of course, known for their own concert halls and who have a major stand here, but also oboe manufacturer Frédéric Triébert, the younger brother of Charles, and luthier Lacôte, who is possibly already showing his seven-string guitar at a much smaller stand. The exhibition is quite capacious, with larger and smaller stands in a row and in 'islands' between the corridors. The many names on the map give an overall picture of the big and little fish in the manufacture of instruments.[456] But here again the guitar comes out short-changed. In the same edition of the musical magazine, Adolphe, Vicomte de Pontécoulant gives a review of the guitar and the harp, in a series of articles on musical instruments on the occasion of the exhibition:

> *Of all stringed instruments the guitar is the ugliest. [...] After being very fashionable for a long time it is now forgotten. [...] At present it can only be found in the hands of poor singers in the street. It has been completely forgotten by the upper class of society. [...] Five manufacturers have made the effort to make guitars, have spent time and money to revive an instrument which is dead, despite all the talent and the likes of Huerta and Coste. [...] But these manufacturers wished to pay the last tribute of respect to the guitar: they are flowers on a grave. Requiescat in pace.*[457]

These critics are not very favorable to the guitar. François Fétis in the *Revue musicale de Paris*, Castil Blaze in *Le Ménestrel*, Henri Blanchard in the *Revue et Gazette musicale de Paris* and Adolphe, Vicomte de Pontécoulant of *La France musicale*.[458] With such bad press the instrument has slim chances of succeeding.

Concerts 1843

Nevertheless, the guitar can be heard in concerts. In 1843 even five concerts can be found in the music bulletins in which Coste is mentioned. *Le Ménestrel* writes on April 9, 1843:

> *M. Coste, a guitarist of great merit, announces a concert which will take place on Tuesday 18 April at Soufletot. [sic]*[459]

This concert may have been postponed to April 25, because *La France musicale* announces on Sunday, April 23, 1843:

> *Concert of M. Coste, Tuesday 25, at 8 o'clock in the evening, in the salons of M. Soufleto, 171 [sic], rue Montmartre.*[460]

---

[456] *La France musicale*, vol. VII, no. 19, 12 V 1844, loose leaflet in front: 'Plan'.
[457] *La France musicale*, vol. VII, no. 19, 12 V 1844, p. 147: 'De tous les instrumens [sic[à cordes le plus ingrat c'est la guitare; [...] Après avoir été longtemps fort à la mode, la guitare a été abandonnée. On ne la voit plus aujourd'hui que dans les mains de pauvres chanteurs des rues, et elle serait serait tout à fait oubliée de la haute classe de la société, [...] Cinq facteurs se sont donné la peine de fabriquer des guitares; ils ont dépensé du temps et de lo'argent pour ranimer un instrument mort, malgré tout le talent et des Huerta, des Coste. [...] Mais ces facteurs ont voulu rendre à la guitare un dernier hommage: ce sont les fleurs semées sur sa tombe. *Requiescat in pace*.'
[458] *Revue musicale de Paris*, 1828, tome III, p. 303-304: 'mauvais son'; 1829, tome V, p. 181: 'petit instrument'; 1830, vol. VII, tome I, p. 267: 'instrument ingrat'; *Le Ménestrel*, vol. II, no. 42, 14 IX 1834, p. [1]: 'La guitare n'est point à dédaigner.'; *Revue et Gazette musicale de Paris*, vol. IX, no. 40, 2 X 1842, p.395: 'instrument oublié'; vol. XVI, no. 41,14 X 1849, p. 325: 'pauvre guitare'; vol. XIX, no. 16,18 IV 1852, p. 123: 'la guitare est morte'.
[459] *Le Ménestrel*, vol. X, no. 19, 9 IV 1843, p. [3]: 'M. Coste. , guitariste d'un grand mérite, annonce un concert pour mardi 18 avril, chez M. Soufletot [sic].'
[460] *La France musicale*, vol. VI, no. 17, 23 IV 1843, p. 143: 'Concert de M. N. Coste, mardi 25, à 8 heures du soir, dans les salons de M. Soufleto, 171 [sic], rue Montmartre.'

Nothing more is said here, Tuesday 25 must be in April 1843 of course, and Souffleto's hall is located at rue Montmartre 71, not that far away from Coste's home address at rue de l'Échiquier no. 23. The concert of April 25 in Souffleto's salle is also announced in the *Revue et Gazette musicale de Paris* of April 23.[461] As far as this date is concerned, there is a peculiar circumstance in that, according to *Le Ménestrel* of Sunday, April 23, 1843, Coste also plays on April 25, 1843, but then on Wednesday at 2 o'clock in the afternoon in the salle of piano manufacturer Bernard. The announcement has an interesting text:

> *M. Coste, the distinguished guitarist, definitive announces his concert on Wednesday 25 April in the salle of Bernard, at two o'clock in the afternoon. The gentlemen Verroust, Coken, Coche, Dancla, Masone, Soler, and the ladies Masone, Vavasseur, and Nordet will be heard. The beneficiary will perform three as yet unpublished compositions.*[462]

The date is probably mistaken, in a way that the intended day was Wednesday 26 April, the day after the concert at Souffleto's. Apart from that, it would have been very demanding for Coste to play in two concerts in one day. Playing three unpublished works means that Coste, as the organizer of this matinee, has given himself a prominent place in the large company giving this mixed concert. Stanislas Verroust plays the oboe again, just as in the concert with Coste on April 29, 1840; François Coken [i.e. Cokken; Kocken] plays the bassoon, just as in the concert with Coste on April 10, 1840; Victor Coche (1806-1881) is a flautist as well as a violoncellist and introduces the Boehm flute in Paris in 1832, when he is a teacher at the Conservatoire; Charles Dancla (1817-1907) is a violinist and a composer, and already a celebrity in the musical world, if that is indeed the person referred to, because his brothers Philippe (1819-1862), a violoncellist and Jean-Pierre (1822-1895), a violinist and a composer, are also working in Paris.[463] No information can be found on the other participants, except for Soler, who plays the oboe, but a great deal of chamber music must have been played in this concert, and there must have been singing as well, as would have been considered appropriate. Coste has surrounded himself with a company of prominent musicians. The three unpublished works he composed which are concerned here, may be the *Introduction and Variations Le Pirate* WoO 9 from circa 1837, which is not published even later, the *Caprice* opus 8 from 1840?, but more likely the *Grand Caprice* opus 11 from 1842? and the *Deuxième Polonaise* opus 14, also circa 1842. The first work and the last two are the most solid, and from opus 8, as already known, the first part is included in opus 11 and the second part in opus 14. He might also have played *Le Tournoi* opus 15 even before his presentation of the piece at the Conservatoire, as is stated on the title page; in 1843 it still is unpublished. So there is no dearth of choices for the now 39-year-old guitarist/composer. Together, these works make a serious program and show his talents as a guitarist and composer in an exemplary way. For the purpose of rehearsal it is likely that the program – or parts of it – is played the day before, in the evening, in another hall, to another audience.

In 1843 Coste gets a favorable press. On May 28 J. Lovy, who follows Panseron as the editor of *Le Ménestrel*, the four-page magazine usually carrying a *Romance* for voice and piano, writes a short review of a concert in which Coste performs:

> *Last Tuesday [sic i.e. Thursday] the Société des Enfans [sic] d'Apollon gave its 102nd annual public concert in the hall of the Conservatoire. There was no lack of interest for this matinee. Several of our well-known*

---

[461] *Revue et Gazette musicale d Paris*, vol. X no. 17, 23 IV 1843, p. 145: 'Concerts Annoncés. 25 avril à 8 heures M. Coste. Salons Soufleto.'
[462] *Le Ménestrel*, vol. X, no. 21, 23 IV 1843, p. [3]: 'M. Coste, guitariste distingué, annonce définitivement son concert pour le mercredi, 25 avril, salle Bernard, à 2 heures de l'après midi. On y entendra MM. Verroust, Coken, Coche, Dancla, Masone, Soler, et Mmes Masone, Vavasseur et Nordet. Le bénéficiaure y fera entendre trois morceaux inédits de sa composition.'; Miteran, Alain: *Histoire de la Guitare*, Bourg-la-Reine, Zurfluh, 1976, 2e ed. 1997, p. 184.
[463] Hondré, E.: 'Coche, Victor'; Jeltsch, J.: 'Cokken (Kocken), Jean'; Penesco, A. & J.-M. Fauquet: 'Dancla, Charles, & Philippe & Jean-Pierre'; Badol-Bertrand, F & J.-M. Fauquet: 'Verroust, Stanislas', in: Fauquet, Joël-Marie: *Dictionnaire de la Musique en France au XIXe siècle*, Paris, Fayard, 2003, p. 289, 290, 346-348, 1269.

V — Souvenirs

75 Salle du Conservatoire

artists, Mme Rossi-Gaccia, Mme Potier, Antoine Kontski, Alexis Dupont, Coste the guitarist, could be heard and were applauded.[464]

Then more names are mentioned along with what they have played, including oboist Triébert, Coste's friend, and Soler again, also an oboist. It is remarkable that in the list of renowned artists only Coste is named by instrument. Nothing is written on his performance, either. Alexis Dupont (1796-1874) is the tenor singer who left the stage of the Opéra-Comique in 1840 to sing in the salons, and Mme Potier (1817-1870) is the wife of composer Henri Potier. She is a soprano singer and pianist and also sings at the Opéra-Comique.[465]

Coste has found a circle of well-known – and less-known – musicians in this *Société académique des Enfants d'Apollon*, as the society is correctly called. As already mentioned, in 1841 he joins this illustrious company of which the aforementioned people are members. He probably plays his opus 16 *Norma* in December and plays an own composition in the program on Ascension Day May 25, 1843. (*Le Ménestrel* gives a wrong day.) The program is published by Decourcelle, which is as yet the only program found that includes Coste.[466] As usual the annual concert of the society opens and concludes with an orchestral work, often by Beethoven, but in this case by Haydn, and a contemporary composer or colleague. It consists of two parts, separated by a 'discours' by one of the members of the board, this time M. Coubard D'Aulnay, chancellor, on a musical or artistic subject; the society has different

---

[464] *Le Ménestrel*, vol. X, no. 26, 28 V 1843, p. [3-4]: 'La *Société des Enfans [sic] d'Apollon* a tenu mardi [sic] dernier sa 102ᵉ séance annuelle et publique, dans la salle du Conservatoire. Cette matinée ne manquait pas d'intérêt. Plusieurs de nos artistes de renom, Mme Rossi-Garcia, Mme Potier, Antoine Kontski, Alexis Dupont, Coste le guitariste, se sont fait entendre et applaudir.'

[465] Gann, A.G.: ; Dupont, dit Alexis'; Kocevar, É.: 'Potier, Henri & Marie de Cussy', in: Fauquet, Joël-Marie: *Dictionnaire de la Musique en France au XIXe siècle*, Paris, Fayard, 2003, p. 411, 991.

[466] Decourcelle, Maurice: *La Société des Enfants d'Apollon (1741-1880): programmes des concerts annuels...*, Paris, Durand, 1881, p. 78: Ascension 25 mai 1843, Salle du Conservatoire, M. Coste *Le Tournoi*, fantaisie pour la guitare, Coste.'

sections.[467] Other parts of the program may have already been played at the monthly meetings, such as no. 4 Morceau de chant by Dupond and no. 6 Romances by and with Thys in the first half, and no. 3 Solo de violon by and with Aumont and no. 5 Ouverture for orchestra by Ermel in the second half.[468] Coste plays his piece of bravura *Le Tournoi* opus 15 as a 'fantaisie pour la guitare', allowing this composition to be dated to 1843. Decourcelle's book is quite accurate and is full of names and composition titles, making it an important source of information on Coste.

— 78 —

ASCENSION 25 MAI 1843
SALLE DU CONSERVATOIRE

M. PRUMIER, *Président*.

Première partie :

EXÉCUTANTS		COMPOSITEURS
		MM.
ORCHESTRE ..	1. Symphonie....................	HAYDN.
Mme Rossi-Caccia	2. Air........................	...
MM. Triébert, Soler et Roméréne.......	3. Trio pour 2 hautbois et cor anglais.	BEETHOVEN.
M. A. Dupond..	4. Morceau de chant............	...
M. Coste.......	5. *Le tournoi*, fantaisie pour la guitare...................	COSTE.
M. Thys......	6. Romances...................	A. THYS.

Discours par M. COUBARD D'AULNAY, chancelier.

Deuxième partie :

M. A. de Kontski........	1. Concerto de piano..........	A. de Kontski.
Mme Potier.....	2. Air........................	...
M. Aumont....	3. Solo de violon.............	Aumont.
Mme Potier.....	4. Romances..................	...
ORCHESTRE...	5. Ouverture..................	Ermel.

Chef d'orchestre : M. MANÉRA
Accompagnateur : M. H. POTIER

76 Concert May 25, 1843

---

[467] Decourcelle, Maurice: *La Société des Enfants d'Apollon (1741-1880): programmes des concerts annuels...*, Paris, Durand, 1881, p. 3: '[...] la section musicale [...]'.

[468] Decourcelle, Maurice: *La Société des Enfants d'Apollon (1741-1880): programmes des concerts annuels...*, Paris, Durand, 1881, p. 157: 'Ermel, Coste, décembre 1841'; p. 158: Dupont, septembre 1842; p. 159: Thys, janvier 1843; p. 160: Amant, mai 1843.

He is mentioned sixteen times, among which ten new found dates when he plays, but whereas the monthly meetings are not open to the public, the annual are. In the review in *Le Ménestrel* also M. Thys emerges, who sings two romances of his own composition; these romances are advertised on the same page of the magazine: they are already published. Nothing further is known about Thys, but apart from being a member of the Apollo-society, he is a member of the freemasons loge *Les Frères Unis Inséparables* in 1851, together with Triébert and Coste.[469]

Opus 15, *Le Tournoi* 1843

An indication on the title page of the edition of *Le Tournoi, Fantaisie Chevaleresque* opus 15 says that the work is performed by the author at the Conservatoire of music. This appears to be the hall where the 102nd annual concert of the *Société académique des Enfants d'Apollon* takes place on Ascension Day in 1843. The edition of *Fantaisie 'Norma'* opus 16 has the same indication, but it is not certain whether this piece is played in the same setting. The opus number could indicate that it is written around the same time. However, *Norma* can be pinned down to 1838, because it is played in a concert then, while *Le Tournoi* can be dated to 1843 in the concert of the Apollo society. Both of the works are published by Challiot: *Norma* in 1843 according to the *Bibliographie de la France*, and *Le Tournoi* in 1844 according to the number of the Challiot edition. Apparently the publication of *Norma* had to wait until 1843, and perhaps the opus number was assigned to it then. The two works are close to each other in style characteristics.

According to Brian Jeffery *Le Tournoi* is the start of a period with more original compositions. He considers this a long, complex work, full of imagination, which deserves the attention of guitarists.[470] Joerg Sommermeyer's opinion is that the work should be classified with the programmatic music in Coste's oeuvre; clearly the Waverley novels of Scott are descriptively involved, a manner he could also have taken from Berlioz.[471] Mario Dell'Ara makes the remark that Coste starts a distinguishable series of programmatic music in his works here, which stands out from all other works. Opus 15 plays with horn and brass effects, but the style still is Classic (if not 18th-century).[472] Finally Monica Burzik characterizes *Le Tournoi* as a virtuoso piece with theatrical effects like depicting tournaments of chivalry, following the historic novels of Scott, such as *Ivanhoe* from 1820.[473] Strikingly, only four authors have devoted some words to *Le Tournoi*, and then only between 1983 and 2000.

Coste's source of inspiration now lies not in an opera, but in a knightly tournament, which cannot be anything but *Ivanhoe*, the very popular romance of chivalry by Walter Scott from 1819, in which Prince John of England leads a two-day tournament. A mysterious masked knight named Desdichado is victorious on the first day, giving his credit to Lady Rowena. On the second day fights in groups take place, Desdichado is victorious again and has to unmask himself. He turns out to be Wilfred van Ivanhoe, who has returned from the crusades. Prince John now also fears the return of King Richard. Coste dedicates his work to 'M. H. Berlioz', who earlier, in 1831 already found inspiration for his overtures *Waverley* and *Rob Roy McGregor* in the novels of the same name by Walter Scott, *Waverley* from 1814 and *Rob Roy* from 1818. The influence of the Scottish novelist is also noticeable in Coste's *Le Tournoi*. The descriptive analysis shows how he concretely worked out his inspiration in this composition. In a musical descriptive way Coste depicts the story of the tournament. In the introduction of 22 measures much variation in rest and movement can be found, along with quite some surprising dissonances and harmonic contrasts. Together with musical allusions to the trumpet, which are evident because Coste himself explains this on p. 14 of his *Méthode*, this part incorporates many Romantic style elements.

---

[469] Cotte, Roger: *La musique maçonnique et ses musiciens*, Paris, Editions du Borrégo, 1987, p. 141.
[470] Jeffery, Brian: 'Napoléon Coste' in: *Cahiers de la Guitare*, Boissy-St-Léger, Association Guitares et Luths, vol. 6, 1983, p. 10.
[471] Sommermeyer, Joerg: 'Noten, The Guitar Works of Napoleon Coste...', in: *Nova Giulianiad*, 1984 Nr. 3, p. 168. [auszug website 2002]
[472] Dell'Ara, Mario: *Manuale di storia della chitarra*, Ancona, Bèrben, 1988, p. 136.
[473] Burzik, Monika: 'Coste, Napoléon', in: *Die Musik in Geschichte und Gegenwart*, ed. Blume, Finscher, Kassel, Bärenreiter, 2000, vol. 4, Kol. 1716.

77 Le Tournoi op. 15, manuscript Coste

For the second part, which encompasses 217 measures in seven pages, it will suffice to mention the most important, or most striking, characteristics that Coste is developing in his composition. The signs of musical elements, which are worked out further in later pieces, are already audible in this piece. Many formal characteristics and style elements that can be interpreted as Romantic can be discerned in this composition, such as the way he deviates from the Classical phrase structure, a cadenza, idée fixe, intensive ornamentation, striking arpeggios and rhythms. The music of *Le Tournoi* opus 15 recognizably tells the story of a tournament, of chivalry from a novel, set against the background of freemasonry. It contains musical allusions and many changes in slow and fast passages. The work presents many harmonic surprises, many chromatics and indications of articulation and dynamics. Coste clearly develops himself to be a composer of high standard.

V — Souvenirs

FREEMASONRY 1843

Another, less literary source of inspiration for *Le Tournoi* opus 15 could have been Coste's membership in the freemasons lodge *Les Frères Unis Inséparables* in Paris. He becomes a member in 1843, but his sympathies could have been of an earlier date. In freemasonry chivalry is held in high esteem, especially in the Scottish rite.[474] This lodge is founded in 1775 and is occupied mainly with cultural and philanthropic activities. During the July Monarchy the lodge only has some twenty members, but after 1840 that number rises to 75. Most of these are musicians, teachers at the Conservatoire, such as Barroilhet and Panseron, and composers like Thomas and Berlioz, a company that suits Coste perfectly.[475] The lodge still exists today and their website has information on Coste.

78 Grades Coste in Loge maçonnique

He appears to have already been initiated in 1843. He is registered as a pupil on June 27, 1843, which is his birthday. Later, on November 14, 1843 he is elevated to the rank of fellow, and then on December 12, 1843 he becomes a master. He has a tempestuous career in the lodge. The website shows photographs from the registry to prove the dates.[476] Remarkably, Coste enters his birth date in the registry as June 28, 1806, while this actually has to be June 27, 1805, according to his birth certificate. Maybe he himself made an error in calculating the Revolutionary calendar, and this is very likely how the wrong date entered the tradition. The handwriting in the entry bears a strong resemblance to that of Coste.

79 Registration Coste Loge maçonnique

This second registration must have been after 1871, as he enters '50, rue du Faubourg St-Martin' as his address. The Freemasons' lodge is the keeper of the annual 'Concert de Loge', in which Coste may have performed regularly as a member, but only one concert can be found, in 1852.[477] In this way Coste is a member of two highly principled companies in 1843: the *Société académique des Enfants d'Apollon* and the Freemasons' lodge *Les Frères Unis Inséparables*. He is not the only one who is a member of both organizations – Amant, Panseron, Prumier, Thys and Triébert are too – but in the lodge only since 1851, Coste is ahead of them in this matter.[478] In the tradition of the freemasons music, the ritual of *La colonne d'harmonie* is introduced in 1848, with two clarinets, two horn, two bassoons, a trombone, a small flute and two drummers, in which Triébert and Thys can play along.[479]

---

[474] Cotte, Roger: *La musique maçonnique et ses musiciens*, Paris, Editions du Borrégo, 1987, p. 141, 151.
[475] http://www.vrijmetselaarsgilde.eu/Maconnieke%20Encyclopedie/Franc-M/fra-f-03.htm.
[476] http://www.mvmm.org/m/docs/coste.html.
[477] *Revue et Gazette musicale de Paris*, vol. XIX, no.8, 22 II 1852, p. 58-59: 'La salle de concert [...]'.
[478] Cotte, Roger: *La musique maçonnique et ses musiciens*, Paris, Editions du Borrégo, 1987, p. 140-143, 167, 187-188, 193.
[479] Cotte, Roger: *La musique maçonnique et ses musiciens*, Paris, Editions du Borrégo, 1987, p. 137.

Concert 1843

Then comes the fifth concert with Coste in the year 1843, which is given on November 5. It is a concert with pupils of Bodin, about whom, just as Laurelli before, nothing is known, other than this:

> *M. Bodin's piano lessons continue to be successful. Every month the pupils of this excellent teacher prove their indisputable progress, and become accustomed to making good music in the company of good artists. Among the latter last Sunday was M. Coste, the accomplished guitarist, and Mme Bulté, the young and charming singer, who performs better every day in the salons.*[480]

What he plays is not told. Nine years will now pass before another of Coste's concerts can be found in the press. Meanwhile some of Coste's new compositions come to light, because in this same year, 1843, the *Fantaisie 'Norma'* opus 16 is published with Challiot and *Le Tournoi* opus 15 goes to press in 1844.[481] By this point Coste has published eight of his works with Richault and three with other publishers, Romagnesi, Lacôte and Grus. Now he goes to Challiot, later to Schonenberger, and Richault does not publish Coste's compositions until 1856. Until the archives of these publishers can be examined, if any remain, the reason for this transfer will remain a guess.

Hispanicism 1843

The Hispanicism in the exotic Romantic image of the guitar as an instrument becomes manifest in real life, the public gets what it wants. Gradually more guitarists from Spain appear on the Parisian musical scene. Huerta already had a large following in the thirties, but now Caceres, Viñas, Ciebra and Bosch play in the halls as well. In 1843 this development is complained about in *Le Journal des Théâtres*, edited by Victor Herbin:

> *While it is clear that the eternal crunching of the guitar may charm the ears of the Spaniards, on the other side of the Pyrenees this appears to be profoundly annoying.*[482]

In February 1845 Caceres plays in a concert in which all the musicians are Spanish. He accompanies a sérénade espagnole which is sung by Mme Lozano in a local color that reminds the Spaniards in the audience of old Iberia.[483] The word 'guitar' is not mentioned in the review, but Caceres plays again five years later, and then he plays the guitar, for sure.[484] José Vignas [Viñas], an 'Espagnol pur sang' gives a concert in October 1849. He sings chansons from Andalusia and plays the *Jota Aragonese* and various boléros and cachuchas even better. After a jab at the poor and neglected guitar, critic Henri Blanchard from the *Revue et Gazette musicale de Paris* cites Ducis's verse again, 'It is the faithful friend of desolate distress.' Viñas plays extraordinary well, but even now it remains: 'What a waste of time.'[485] Blanchard thus repeats his same old tune from seven years earlier, in precisely the same words, and is not capable of putting his prejudice aside. He quotes himself another time at the concert of the gentlemen Ciebra and Caceres in the edition of April 18, 1852 and reinforces his opinion by citing the words of Bossuet: 'The guitar is dying, the guitar is dead.'[486] Blanchard says that apart from this Ciebra took this instrument, of such a little sound, and made it speak, made it sing in an air from *Robert le Diable*, with which he, along with other pieces in duet, elicited as much surprise as applause with the public.

---

[480] *Le Ménestrel*, vol. X, no. 50, 12 XI 1843, p. [3]: 'Les cours de piano de M. Bodin poursuivent leur vogue. Chaque mois les élèves de cet excellent professeur prouvent des progrès incontestables, et acquièrent l'habitude de faire de bonne musique en compagnie de nos bons artistes. Au nombre de ces derniers figuraient dimanche dernier, M. Coste l'habile guitariste, et Mlle Bulté, jeune et charmante cantatrice, qui se pose chaque jour de mieux en mieux dans nos salons.'

[481] *Bibliographie de la France*, vol. XXXII, no. 35, 2I X 1843, p. 452: '*Fantaisie Norma*, Nap. Coste, [op. 16] prix 5-0; Chez Challiot, rue Saint-Honoré, n. 336.'

[482] *Le Journal des Théâtres*, vol. I, no. 57, dim. 29 X 1843, p. 1: '[...] il est évident que l'éternel grincement de guitare qui charme les oreilles espagnoles paraîtra profondément ennuyeux de l'autre côté des Pyrénées, [...]'.

[483] *Revue et Gazette musicale de Paris*, vol. XII, no. 7, 16 II 1845, p. 52: '[...] une sérénade espagnole [...] avec M. Caceres [...]'.

[484] *Revue et Gazette musicale de Paris*, vol. XIX, no. 16, 18 IV 1852, p. 123: '[...] la guitare [...] qui la font revivre, MM. Cibra et Caceres; [...]'.

[485] *Revue et Gazette musicale de Paris*, vol. XVI, no. 41, 14 X 1849, p. 325: '[...] C'est le fidèle ami du chagrin solitaire. [...]joue excessivement bien [...] que de temps perdu!'

[486] *Revue et Gazette musicale de Paris*, vol. XIX, no. 16, 18 IV 1852, p. 123: 'la guitare se meurt, la guitare est morte!'

V — Souvenirs

Around this year the Spanish guitarist Jaime Bosch settles in Paris. In his biography of Tárrega, Emilio Pujol writes of him and Coste:

Despite the higher value of his French contemporary Napoléon Coste, his success as a guitarist led him to be regarded as "the king of the guitar" in the capital of France.[487]

In this period Coste is still active as a guitarist and a composer and his fame later even extends to Spain. The way of considering the guitar as an Iberic instrument still exists in 1850, as the next review shows:

The black Malibran, or if you prefer, the singing Ourika, who has been spoken about for some time now, performed for a small audience in the salon of the director of the Opéra. [...] Mme Martinez (because that is her real name) [...] sings, accompanying herself with much talent, even elegance on the guitar, and she performs her chansons as an excellent actress [...] Her voice [...] is not very strong in this, but on the other hand it does lend itself to the suppleness of the most fast-moving parts, of the variation in merry of grievous accents, mocking or melancholy. [...] We think her majesty the Queen of Spain has had very good reasons to admit her to the ranks of the artists of her court.[488]

Apparently the guitar is appreciated as an accompaniment to emotional Spanish singing. In this way a new generation of Spaniards can be discerned to champion the guitar, even as the old generation of Italians disappears, including Niccolo Paganini, also a guitarist, who dies in 1840, Ferdinando Carulli in 1841, Luigi Castellacci in 1845, François Molino in 1847, and Matteo Carcassi in 1853.[489] Only Luigi Legnani and two artists from Coste's generation, Marco Aurelio Zani de Ferranti and Giulio Regondi, are still active around 1860. The Italians were strongly represented in Paris in the first half of the 19th century. This is going to change half-way the century. Many traditional Spanish works can be heard in the concerts, albeit presented as 'local color'. Pujol, one of Tárrega's pupils in the so-called 'Spanish school', mentions that Tárrega himself travelled to Paris through Lyon in 1881, and played there in Odéon on the occasion of a festival to the 200th anniversary of Calderón's death, with Victor Hugo as chairman.[490] The literary Romantic view of the guitar lives on, in the theatre, for instance. Victor Herbin writes in his *Journal des Théâtres* in 1847 about the early death of the young actor Lepeintre:

The grace of his person enamored him; he played the Léanders and the Almavivas of vaudeville, picked his guitar, climbed balconies and rushed to conquer widows and pupils; then suddenly his face grew dark, his temper wild. He who resided in ruins of castles, the obscure caves, the mysterious archs [...][491]

The guitar still is a Romantic cliché.

Méthode Coste-Sor 1851

In 1844 Coste composes another series of *Quadrilles* WoO 5, which is partly the same as the first series from opus 3. These are also obligatory works, which show few Romanticism or originality, apart from some virtuosity, which was also present in the first series. Coste may have taken up this work again at the request of a pupil. It is not published, The anonymous transcript is dated May 21, 1844,

---

[487] Pujol. Emilio: *Tárrega, Ensayo biográfico*, Lisboa, Ramos, 1960, p. 88: 'Sus exítos como guitarista, a pesar del valor superior de su coetáneo francés Napoléon Coste, le valerion ser considerado en la capital de Francia como "el rey de la guitarra"'.
[488] *Revue et Gazette musicale de Paris*, vol. XXIII, no. 17, 9 VI 1850, p. 195: 'La *Malibran* noire, ou si vous aimez mieux, l'*Ourika* chantante dont on parle depuis quelque temps, s'est fait entendre d'un petit nombre de personnes dans le salon du directeur de l'Opéra. [...] Mme Martinez (car tel est son vrai nom) [...] chante , en s'accompagnant de la guitare avec beaucoup de talent, élégance même, et elle mime ses chansons en comédienne excellente. Sa voix [...] n'en est pas tres-fort, en revanche elle se prête à la volubilité des mouvements les plus rapides, à la variété des accents joyeux ou douloureux, mocqeurs ou mélancoliques. [...] Nous rrouvons donc que Sa Majesté la reine d'Espagne a eu grandement raison de l'admetter parmi les artistes de sa chambre royale.'
[489] *Revue et Gazette musicale de Paris*, vol. XX, no. 4, 23 I 1853, p. 31: 'M. Mateo [sic] Carcassi [...] vient de mourir'.
[490] Pujol. Emilio: *Tárrega, Ensayo biográfico*, Lisboa, Ramos, 1960, p. 90.
[491] *Le Journal des Théâtres*, vol. V, no. 398, mer. 3 V 1847, p. 1: 'Les graces de sa personne en firent d'abord un amoureux; il joua les Léandre et les Almaviva de vaudeville, pinça de la guitare, escalada les balcons et courut à la conquête des veuves et des pupilles; puis tout à coup son regard devient sombre, son humeur féroce; le voici qui habite les châteaux en ruines, les noirs caveaux, les voûtes mystérieuses, [...].'

meaning that it must have been composed, and opus 3 revised, before that date.[492] Nevertheless, Coste remains the only French guitarist who demonstrates himself at a high artistic level in concerts and compositions. His skills as a guitar teacher not only come forward in his playing in ensemble with a pupil in Sor's *Souvenir de Russie* on March 29, 1840 and his duet *Scherzo et Pastorale* opus 10 with his pupil Caroline Montigny in the concert on April 8, 1842, but mostly in the revised edition of Sor's method in 1851, published with the title *Méthode de Guitare par Fernando Sor Rédigée et Augmentée par N. Coste*, in short the *Méthode* Coste-Sor. To Coste the *Méthode* of Sor himself from 1830 is the starting point. Fétis discusses this comprehensively and favorably in his *Revue musicale*.[493] At that time playing the guitar is very much in vogue; between 1826, when Sor comes to Paris, and 1830, 23 different methods for guitar appear, including those of Aguado, Carulli, Ledhuy, Molino, Meissonnier and Salomon,[494] quite an array, and written by the most renowned guitarists as well. The reason why Sor decided to publish his method, is apparent from its structure and its content. In his introduction he explains that he, who is regarded as a phenomenon by the guitarists, has no more tools available than anyone else:

> *The Music, the reasoning, and the preference I have in general for results above displays of difficulty, that simply is my only secret. Their [guitarists] surprise only arises from the way they look at the guitar: while they say that the guitar is primarily meant for accompaniment, and is accordingly classified as a harmony-instrument, they begin to treat it as a melody instrument; because their first exercises are scales [..] with which great difficulties arise in adding suitable bass-notes, unless they are open strings, and even greater problems when adding one or two voices in between them.*[495]

Sor is right in this: looking at the methods of Molino (1823), Carulli (1825), Carcassi (1825) and Aguado (1826), these are indeed the premises, with all the problems that ensue as a result. Ironically, Sor adds the following in a footnote:

> *They thought they could overcome this imperfection by adding a number of strings to the guitar, but isn't it easier to learn to use six, first?*[496]

Here he criticizes the phenomenon in this period of supplementing the guitar with additional strings. This criticism may also be aimed at Coste himself, who has plans for a seven-string guitar. However, Sor himself regularly prescribes tuning the sixth string to D, so he may not have had many objections to Coste's plans. Somewhat further, he writes:

> *I love music, I feel it. Through the study of harmony and counterpoint, which familiarized me with the natural progress and nature of chords and their inversions, with the way of moving from a melody to the bass or to one of the intermediate voices, to augment the number of notes by one or two voices, while others continue their slower movement, I have made demands on the instrument of this sort and have learned that it is more suitable for this than for the continuous rumbling of sixteenth and thirty-second notes in diatonic and chromatic scales.*[497]

---

[492] Kk Rischel Ms. 46 mu 7908.1085, Coste: *Deux Quadrilles*.
[493] *Revue musicale de Paris*, vol. V, no. 2, 12 II 1831, p. 12-13: '*Méthode pour la guitare, par Ferdinand Sor.*'
[494] Stenstadvold, Erik: *An Annotated Bibliography of Guitar Methods, 1760-1860*, Organologia: Musical Instruments and Performance Practice No. 4, London, Pendragon Press, 2010, p. 5-6.
[495] Sor, Fernando: *Méthode pour La Guitare*, L'Auteur, Parijs, 1830, repr. Minkoff, Genève, 1981, p. 2: 'La Musique, le raisonnement, et la préférence que je donne en général aux résultats sur l'étalage de la difficulté, voilà tout mon secret. Leur étonnement ne vient que de la manière dont ils envisagent la guitare: tout en disant que cet instrument est principalement destiné à l'accompagnement, et, par là, le classant parmi les instruments d'harmonie, ils commencent toujours par le traiter comme instrument de mélodie; car leurs premières leçons sont toujours des gammes [...] fait éprouver de grandes difficultés lorsqu'il s'agit d'y ajouter une basse correcte, si elle ne se trouve dans les cordes à vide, et bien plus grande s'il faut y ajouter encore une ou deux parties intermédiaires.'
[496] Sor, Fernando: *Méthode pour La Guitare*, L'Auteur, Parijs, 1830, repr. Minkoff, Genève, 1981, p. 2n: 'On a cru remédier à cet inconvénient en ajoutant à la guitare un nombre de cordes filées; mais ne serait-il pas plus simple d'apprendre à se servir des six?'
[497] Sor, Fernando: *Méthode pour La Guitare*, L'Auteur, Parijs, 1830, repr. Minkoff, Genève, 1981, p. 3: 'J'aime la musique, je la sens; l'étude de l'harmonie et du contre-point m'ayant familiarisé avec la marche et la nature des accords et leurs renversements, avec la manière de passer de la mélodie à la basse ou à quelqu'une des parties intermédiaires, d'augmenter le nombre des figures d'une ou de deux parties, tandis que les autres conservant leur marche plus lente, j'ai exigé de l'instrument des choses dans ce genre, et j'ai trouvé qu'il s'y prête mieux qu'au fatras continuel des doubles et des triples croches en gammes diatoniques ou chromatiques.'

V — Souvenirs 113

Sor's *Méthode* has great influence on guitar playing in general and on Coste in particular. The method is discussed many times.[498] Sor's approach differs from what is usual at the time and this gives his composition for the guitar a different result. By applying his musical principles, his music reaches a higher level than the mere accompaniment of a melody; there are more intermediate voices and counter-voices. His music is fuller and richer, more polyphonic and harmonic than that of other composers around him in Paris. He himself mentions the great importance of mastering two aspects of music, counterpoint and harmony, and then it is worth mentioning again that Coste, as his pupil and friend, was taught in these subjects by Sor, in theory and practice. Apart from the historical indications in this *Méthode* there are also clues in the content of the *Méthode* Coste-Sor. Sor intends his method to be for the amateur music-lovers. He does not want to instruct teachers, because the door of the royal library is open and the Encyclopedic Dictionary is available for everyone who wishes to consult it. Teachers can always take this step out of their own self-esteem, with which they can truly benefit in the future.[499] With this recommendation Sor ends his introduction, in which he makes a sketch of his musical premises. He works this out in text, about the technique of playing the guitar in all aspects, in three parts: first the instrument, the hands and the stroke, the neck and the fingering; then the intervals, melody, harmonics, accompaniments and finally an analysis. His conclusion is in twelve points, of which the last one is:

Consider reasoning to be of great value and routine to be nothing.[500]

After this, images of good and bad hand and body positions follow, which are discussed in the first part. The exercises that begin with chords and intervals indeed, and not with scales, do not have any explanatory text, except for the titles in French and in German (the *Méthode* is published both in Paris, Bonn and London). Sor gives a clear explanation of his approach that expounds upon his premises in his 88 pages of essay. Intended for the amateur or the professional guitarist, he emphasizes the importance of active, independent study for those who want to follow him in approaching the guitar music in a sensible way, above all, to avoid bad habits. This is unique, and it is probably for this reason that he entrusted the method to Coste, who, simply added the didactic aspect, put the exercises in a certain order, inserted explanations and fleshed out Sor's ideas in a substantial number of his own exercises. In this way the line from Sor to Coste is continued.

The *Méthode de guitare par Fernando Sor Rédigée et Augmentée par N. Coste* is published by Schonenberger, and the edition number S. No. 1726 points to the year 1851,[501] despite the fact that the years 1845 and 1860 are also mentioned in the literature, without a demonstrable source, however.[502] The copy of this edition in the British Library, identical to the second one in Det Kongelige Bibliotek in Copenhagen, has a title page with an engraving of a female guitar player, sitting aslant to a sturdy

---

[498] Rossi, Adriano: 'Sor und seine Gitarrenschule', in: *Die Gitarre*, IV, Berlin, 1923, no. 3-4, p. 16-19; V, 1924, no. 5-6, p. 29-35; Schwarz-Reiflingen, Erwin: 'Zur Neuausgabe der Gitarreschule von Fernando Sor', in: *Die Gitarre*, Berlin, 1922, Jahrgang III, Heft 11, p. 98-10; Sor, Fernando: 'Über Gitarreschulen', in: *Der Gitarrefreund*, München, 1926, Heft 27, p. 79-82; Jeffery, Brian: *Fernando Sor, Composer and Guitarist*, London, Tecla, 1977; second edition 1994, p. 93-96; Moser, Wolf: 'Fernando Sor und seine "Methode pour la guitare"', in: *Gitarre und Laute*, Köln, vol. I, 1979, no. 1, p. 26-32; Ribouillault, Danielle: *La technique de guitare en France dans la première moitié du XIXe siècle*, thèse musicologie, Paris, Sorbonne, 1980; Roberts, John: 'Sor's method for the Spanish guitar', in: *Guitar*, 1980, jan., no. 30, p. 22-24; Moser, Wolf: *Ich, Fernando Sor, Versuch einer Autobiographie und gitarristische Schriften*, Lyon, Saint-Georges, 2nd ed., 2005, p. 141-165.

[499] Sor, Fernando: *Méthode pour La Guitare*, L'Auteur, Parijs, 1830, repr. Minkoff, Genève, 1981, p. 5-6: 'Quant aux professeurs, je ne prétends point donner de leçons; [...] car la Bibliothèque royale ayant ses portes ouvertes, et le Dictionnaire encyclopédique étant à la disposition de ceux qui veut le consulter, [...] ils feraient toujours une démarche qui intéresserait leur amour-propre, et dont ils retireraient un profit réel pour l'avenir.'

[500] Sor, Fernando: *Méthode pour La Guitare*, L'Auteur, Parijs, 1830, repr. Minkoff, Genève, 1981, p. 88: '12e et dernière. De tenir le raisonnement pour beaucoup, et la routine pour rien.'

[501] Devriès, Anik & François Lesure: *Dictionnaire des éditeurs de musique français*, Genève, Minkoff, 1979-1988, vol. II, p. 395-396.

[502] Baillie, Laureen: *The Catalogue of Printed Music in the British Library to 1980*, London, Saur, 1982, p. 58, c. 1845; Stenstadvold, Erik 'Napoleon Costes Beitrag zu den 20 Etüden von Fernando Sor', in: *Gitarre und Laute*, Köln, vol. VI, 1984, no. 3, p. 14-17, c. 1845; Turnbull, Harvey: *The Guitar from the Renaissance to the Present Day*, London, Batsford, 1974, repr. 1976, p. 60, c. 1845; Ribouillault, Danielle: *La technique de guitare en France dans la première moitié du XIXe siècle*, Ph.D. Paris, Sorbonne, 1980, p. 22, 1860?

80 Title page Méthode Coste-Sor

music stand, in a dress with beautiful pleats, the left leg raised a bit, playing the seven-string guitar, which must be a Lacôte, the Coste guitar. In spite of the incorrect proportions it is a suitable image, and drawings of positions of the left and right hands are grouped around it, coming from Sor's method. The title page makes clear that this must be a guitar method of high standard. In contrast with Sor, after a short introduction on the history of the guitar and Sor's contribution to it, Coste begins immediately with a technical discussion of the art of playing. It is remarkable that the explanatory text is in French as well as in Spanish. Sor's original edition is in French (and German). Coste may have used Sor's manuscript for this edition.

In the first part he continues with very easy exercises, which gradually become musically more interesting. Some of these fit Sor's style so well, that the question arises as to whether they aren't actually Sor's. In the second part he begins with a reference to Sor's explanation of how other musical instruments, the horn, the trumpet, the oboe and the harp can be imitated, with exactly the same musical examples as Sor. This idea of onomatopoeia can be regularly found in several methods of the preceding period, Aguado writes about imitating the bassoon and harmonica, while Carcassi discusses the tambourine, for instance.[503] These are internal musical references, a feature that can be called Romantic and which have therefore been listed in the style characteristics in chapter IV 'Style' of the thematic catalogue.

Because Coste, just like Sor, thinks it is important to have a good knowledge of the guitar neck, he copies these musical examples. Two technical details must be discussed here, that have far-reaching consequences for opinions on playing the guitar. In his method Sor first explains that he uses the fingers thumb *P*, index finger *i*, and middle finger *m*, because of the position of the right hand over the strings.

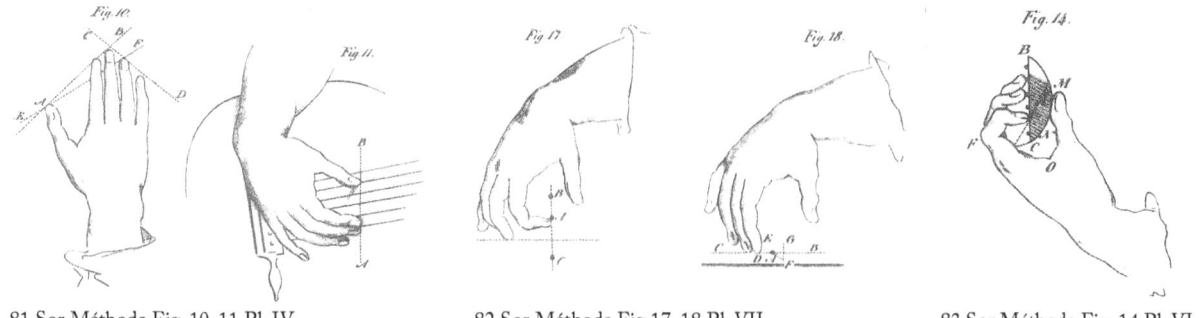

81 Sor Méthode Fig. 10, 11 Pl. IV   82 Sor Méthode Fig.17, 18 Pl. VII   83 Sor Méthode Fig. 14 Pl. VI

These fingers can form a straight line and are able to strike the strings quickly and nimbly. The thumb *P* then moves in the opposite direction, as can be seen in Sor's illustration 35 Fig. 10, 11 and Coste-Sor's illustration 34 Fig. 4, 5. The use of the ring finger *a* puts the hand in an uncomfortable position, and therefore it is only used for chords and arpeggios multiple parts.[504]

84 Sor Étude no. 11 Méthode Coste-Sor   85 Coste Les Bords du Rhin opus 18 m. 122

This conception has consequences for the musical interpretation, as can be deduced from the study of Sor's *Étude* 24 opus 35, which is embodied in the *Méthode* Coste-Sor as *Étude* no. 11, apart from that, with the same chord-progressions as *Étude* 11 opus 6. Here the fingering with *P, i* and *m* gives a completely different musical result, in which the polyphony is more audible and the piece is technically easier to play, more sensible than with *P, i, m* and *a*. In the middle voices a kind of tremolando emerges with *P* and *i*, instead of *i* and *m*.

Coste indicates that the little finger of the right hand can be placed on the soundboard. He also thinks that the ring finger is too weak to be used, other than for complete chords and certain arpeggios, in which its use is absolutely necessary.[505] *Étude* no. 11 from the *Méthode* Coste-Sor can be played as an arpeggio as well, but with a different musical result in that case. With respect to striking the strings with the fingers of the right hand, Sor writes that the direction of the stroke must be parallel to the soundboard, in the direction of the adjacent string, the finger bent as little as possible, resulting in a vibration of the string parallel to the neck as a result, thus producing a good sound.[506] He specifically explains this, with illustrations, as can be seen in Sor's illustration 37 Fig. 18 and Coste-Sor's illustration 34 Fig. 7. It really is a necessary precondition for good guitar technique. Applying this technique is not possible without placing the tip of the finger on the string before the stroke, but Sor is not explicit

---

[503] Ribouillault, Danielle: *La technique de guitare en France dans la première moitié du XIXe siècle*, thèse musicologie, Paris, Sorbonne, 1980, p. 332.

[504] Sor, Ferdinand: *Méthode pour La Guitare*, Paris, L'Auteur, 1830, repr. Minkoff, Genève, 1981, p. 14, Pl. IV Fig. 10, p. 18, 28.

[505] Sor, Ferdinand & N. Coste: *Méthode complète pour la Guitare...*, Paris, Schonenberger, 1851, p. 3: '[...] petit doigt puisse se poser sur la table [...] Le petit doigt ne se pose guère [...] en l'attaquant avec la partie du doigt qui se rapproche le plus de l'ongle, [...] L'Annulaire étant très faible il faut éviter de s'en servir autrement que pour le complément des accords et certains arpèges où son usage est d'une nécessité absolue.'

[506] Sor, Ferdinand: *Méthode pour La Guitare*, Paris, L'Auteur, 1830, repr. Minkoff, Genève, 1981, p. 14, Pl. IV Fig. 11; p. 18, Pl. VII Fig. 17, Fig. 18.

in this. Coste is more clear on this point: in the *Méthode* Coste-Sor he concludes that while playing arpeggios every finger that follows must be placed on the string beforehand, a step which is called preparation.[507]

This premise is thought through consistently and applied in the practice of playing Coste's works, especially where he prescribes arpeggios where the bass string must be muted, as in *Les Bords du Rhin* opus 18 measure 122, for instance. Applying this technique, the sound production is under perfect control, just as descriptions of his playing indicate. This opens up more possibilities for playing rapid arpeggios, which can be executed with a plain and clear articulation. As far as the matter of playing with or without one's fingernails is concerned, Sor has already spoken clearly on this matter in 1830: when he speaks about imitating the oboe, he uses as little fingernail as possible. He adds that he has never heard a guitarist playing with nails who had a bearable sound. He makes an exception for Aguado, whose use of fingernails he forgives because of his excellent qualities.[508] Coste is not very clear in his description of playing with nails: the stroke must be executed with the part of the finger that is the very closest as possible to the nail.[509] If the fingernail is not short, this may mean playing with one's nails.

Sor is also very clear in his *Méthode* in 1830 about the playing position and the use of the left hand. He writes that the thumb of the left hand must be held at the back of the guitar's neck to optimize the use of the fingers. Coste follows him in this in the *Méthode* Coste-Sor. This was the breaking point with Molino and Carulli, who sometimes placed the left thumb over the neck, even pressing bass notes with it, but this issue is no longer relevant in 1851.

In the third part as well, Coste mainly continues with a mixture of Sor's exercises and examples, with some of his own, for the intervals third and sixth, which are especially used in guitar music because of their splendid effectiveness for achieving a full consonance.

The fourth part is almost completely lifted from Sor's method, apart from the *Rêverie Nocturne*, with its many flageolets, and the appendix about the seventh string where Coste sketches his contribution to the development of the seven-string guitar by Lacôte:

> *Some years ago I had a guitar made in Lacôte's workshop in Paris which had a fuller sound and especially a more beautiful sound. [...] with this I obtained a sound which was practically double [...] the quality is incomparably more beautiful. The addition of a seventh string completed the instrument's system [...].*[510]

What's more, he declares that this instrument, which he calls the 'heptacorde', earned the appreciation of the jury in the last industrial fair. The following examples and studies are composed by Coste himself. These are followed by the much discussed and much praised transcriptions of Visée from 1686 follow, from baroque guitar tablature to Classic guitar mensural notation. Coste came in contact with this 'old' music in Fétis's 'concerts historiques' and the monthly 'séances' of the *Société académique des Enfants d'Apollon*, and probably became interested this way. He is the first guitar composer to do this. Moreover, in the 19th-century programs of the 'Concerts du Conservatoire' with Bach and Haendel, a revival of 'old' music is perceptible. Coste transcribed the pieces from a book from Visée's time, as he writes to Schult on December 8, 1874:

---

[507] Sor, Ferdinand & N. Coste: *Méthode complète pour la Guitare...*, Paris, Schonenberger, 1851, p. 19: '[...] préparer ceux de la main droite contre les cordes avant d'attaquer et leur prendre l'ordre suivant: pouce, index, medium et annulaire lorsque l'emploi de ce dernier devient indispensable.'

[508] Sor, Ferdinand: *Méthode pour La Guitare*, Paris, L'Auteur, 1830, repr. Minkoff, Genève, 1981, p. 21-22: 'j'emploie le peu d'ongle que j'ai [...] Je n'ai entendu de ma vie un guitariste dont le jeu fût supportable s'il jouait avec les ongles. [...] leur jeu est au mien ce que le clavecin était au piano-forté [...] M. Aguado ait autant d'excellentes qualités qu'il en a pour lui faire pardonner l'emploi des ongles [...]'.

[509] Sor, Ferdinand & N. Coste: *Méthode complète pour la Guitare...*, Paris, Schonenberger, 1851, p. 3: 'l'attaquant avec la partie du doigt qui se rapproche le plus de l'ongle, [...]'.

[510] Sor, Ferdinand & N. Coste: *Méthode complète pour la Guitare...*, Paris, Schonenberger, 1851, p. 45: 'Il y a quelques années, je fis confectionner dans les ateliers de M. Lacôte luthier à Paris, une Guitare dont la construction fut étudié de manière à fournir un plus grand volume et surtout une plus belle qualité de son. [...] j'obtiens un son presque double [...] la qualité en est incomparablement plus belle. L'addition d'une septième corde complettait le système de l'instrument [...]'.

V — Souvenirs 117

> [...] towards the end, some small pieces by Robert de Visée, guitarist of Louis XIV, that I transcribed from a book of that time, to the guitar.[511]

The last part of the *Méthode* consists of his own selection of Sor's etudes, they come from opus 6, 29, 31 and 35, with the most difficult étude from opus 29 at the end, making a progressive didactic structure is evident. The number of mistakes is reduced to a minimum, sometimes a correction is made to the original is in question, sometimes even an improvement.[512] The simple études from opus 6 are not included. The page numbering starts anew here. This selection of études is later published separately, and this is the starting point of the famous standard selection of Segovia.[513]

Coste has arranged Sor's method thoroughly, and his influence is clearly visible. Especially because of the concordances, similarities and consequences that emerge from the exercises in the method and from the selection of Sor's études included, the *Méthode* could be regarded as the key work for the musical relation between Coste and Sor, apart from the importance Sor attached to counterpoint and harmony and the fact that Coste studied these subjects, as already discussed. The concordances consist of Sor's exercises and études Coste used without changes. The similarities are Coste's original exercises, which are strongly related to Sor's work in intention and style. The consequences are the conclusions Coste draws from Sor's intentions, elaborated in exercises in this method, as well as the musical ideas Coste exploits in other compositions. The latter are important for following Coste's development in musical style. For this reason these are explained in relation to the content in the descriptive analysis, which are restricted to those études that show Coste's musical notions most clearly. Examples, technical exercises and studies concerning the keys, intervals and scales show these to a lesser degree and are therefore not very relevant in this context, except for the purpose of evaluating their didactic aspect, which is why these are not discussed here. However, two of Sor's studies in Coste's selection are discussed because of the correlation that can be found with the two men's compositions, in which Sor's influence on Coste can be established.

Just as for the *Études* opus 38, 26 instances can be found in the literature after 1883 in which the *Méthode* Coste-Sor is cited. Apart from citations in the handbooks, it is usually just a matter of a brief mention.[514] Sometimes the work is discussed more in relation to the content. In 1927 Erwin Schwarz-Reiflingen writes that the *Méthode*, which Coste arranged and expanded with own compositions, shows just how much Sor and Coste were kindred spirits.[515] He points out that Sor himself had difficulties in

---

[511] Coste-Schult, 8 XII 1874: '[...] vers la fin, quelques petites pièces de Robert de Visée, guittariste de Louis XIV, que j'ai transcrites d'après un ouvrage du temps, à la guitare.'

[512] Sor, Ferdinand & N. Coste: *Méthode complète pour la Guitare...*, Paris, Schonenberger, 1851, dl. II, p. 7 no. 7 m. 3, m. 14, cf. op. 6 no. 2; p. 9 no. 9 m. 25, cf. op.35 no. 22; p. 14 no. 13 m. 15, cf. op. 31 no. 19; p. 16 no. 14 m. 20, cf. op. 31 no. 20.

[513] Jeffery, Brian: 'Andrés Segovia's edition (1945) of Sor's "Twenty Studies"', in: *Soundboard*, vol. VIII/4, 1981, p. 253-255; Stenstadvold, Erik: 'Coste's contribution to the "20 Studies" by Sor', *Soundboard*, vol. XI, no. 2, 1984, p. 136-140; Schwarz-Reiflingen, Erwin: 'Costes Bearbeitung der Sor-Schule', in: *Die Gitarre*, Berlin, 1927, Jahrgang VIII, Heft 7/8, [Coste-Heft] p. 51-52.

[514] Stockmann-Kursk, J.: 'Napoléon Coste', in: *Der Guitarrefreund, Mitteilungen des Internationalen Guitarristen-Verbandes*, München, 3. Jahrgang, 1902, Heft 5, p. 56; Zuth, Josef: 'Coste, Napoléon', in: *Handbuch der Laute und Gitarre*, Wien, Doblinger, 1926-28, repr. Hildesheim, Olms, 1978, p. 73; Sharpe, A.P.: *The Story of the Spanish Guitar*, London, Clifford Essex, 1954, 4th ed. 1968, p. 27; Radke, Hans: 'Coste, Napoléon', in: *Die Musik in Geschichte und Gegenwart*, ed. Blume, Kassel, Bärenreiter, 1956, ed. 1973, vol. XV (Supplement 1) Kol. 1617; Carfagna, Carlo & A. Caprani: *Profilo Storico della Chitarra*, Ancona-Milano, Bèrben, 1966, p. 54; Sasser, William Gray: *The guitar works of Fernando Sor*, Ph.D. University of North Carolina, 1960, Ann Arbor, Michigan, 1975, p. 63; Turnbull, Harvey: *The Guitar from the Renaissance to the Present Day*, London, Batsford, 1974, repr. 1976, p. 60; Cooper, Jeffrey: 'Coste, Napoléon', in: Sadie, Stanley ed: *The New Grove Dictionary of Music and Musicians*, London, Macmillan, 1980, vol. 4, p. 824; Wynberg, Simon: '...zur Rettung Napoleon Costes', in: *Gitarre und Laute*, Köln, vol. III, 1981, no. 5, p. 31; Jeffery, Brian & Erik Marchélie: 'Napoléon Coste" in: *Cahiers de la Guitare*, Boissy-St-Léger, Association Guitares et Luths, vol. 6, 1983, p. 11; Dell'Ara, Mario: *Manuale di storia della chitarra*, Ancona, Bèrben, 1988, p. 26, 93, 105; Piris, Bernard: *Fernando Sor, Une guitare à l'orée du Romantisme*, Arles, Aubier, 1989, p. 86-87; Jaworski, Roman: 'Napoleon Coste 1805-1883, une histoire perdue', in: *Valentiana*, Valenciennes, Association Valentiana, 1992, no. 10, p. 78; Burzik, Monika: 'Coste, Napoléon', in: *Die Musik in Geschichte und Gegenwart*, ed. Blume, Finscher, Kassel, Bärenreiter, 2000, vol. 4, Kol. 1714; Stenstadvold, Erik: 'Coste, Napoléon', in: Sadie, Stanley ed: *The New Grove Dictionary of Music and Musicians*, Second edition, London, Macmillan, 2001, p. 534; Moser, Wolf: *Ich, Fernando Sor, Versuch einer Autobiographie und gitarristische Schriften*, Lyon, Saint-Georges, 2nd ed., 2005, p. 129-130; Roncet, Noël: *Napoléon Coste, Compositeur, 1805-1883*, Amondans, 2005, p. 39.

[515] Schwarz-Reiflingen, Erwin: 'Napoleon Coste', in: *Die Gitarre*, Berlin, 1927, Jahrgang VIII, Heft 7/8, [Coste-Heft] p. 45.

writing pieces for beginners, but that Coste suffers from the same shortcoming: the pieces increase too quickly in difficulty. In this connection it is interesting to see how close Sor and Coste are, musically speaking. Yet, Coste does not give up his individuality. His light and fluent style make his compositions recognizable, the easy and informal way Coste shows in his mastery of the fingerboard is surprising. There are no large stretching positions and the voicing is always logical. The first 29 exercises are Coste's, making his share by no means small. While Sor, in a modern way, makes the pupil discover the rules himself through examples, forcing him to learn in that way, Coste omits these elaborations to allow the pupil to proceed in a quick and skillful fashion, as he writes in the foreword. A very useful and necessary addition is Sor's études opus 6 and opus 29 in progressive order and provided with Coste's fingering, according to Schwarz-Reiflingen.[516] Mario Giordano follows in 1934 with the remark that in the *Méthode* one can clearly see how the complete technique of the left hand is based on the movement in changing positions, and how this contrasts with Sor's 26 études, which concern left-hand spreading positions, culminating in extreme spreading in étude in E-flat (24) and the other, very important one in C (25). Because of the special character of Coste's music, even the most complicated études are accessible for all guitarists.[517] So far, we only encounter favorable reviews. But in his biography of Sor in 1977, Brian Jeffery opines that after Sor's death, Napoléon Coste rendered a disservice to his friend's remembrance by publishing a mutilation of the original. He warns the reader that there are few resemblances with the original version. However, he fails to state his reasons for this view.[518] In 1980 Danielle Ribouillault has a totally different notion when she speaks about the guitar technique. Coste carries Sor's premises through and refines these even more precisely; he polishes this left-hand technique and carries the master's innovations through to it most extreme consequences, at the same time creating a modern guitar technique, which has not changed much ever since.[519] Johannes Klier joins Jeffery 1980, also without stating any reasons, and thinks Coste did Sor a disservice by publishing this edition. He omits the original text and adds a number of Sor's études instead.[520] After giving a technical example, Jan Anton van Hoek again has the view that a better and more sound dexterity in guitar technique is achieved for the first time in this method.[521] Erik Stenstadvold compares Coste's versions of a number of studies with those of Sor in 1984, also discussing Segovia's version.[522] This comparison is apparently from the angle of musical technique. This is why this is mentioned in the thematic catalogue for the études in question. Mario Dell'Ara is brief in mentioning the *Méthode*. His view is that Coste developed a theoretical and hypothetical work into a practical method in the reworking of Sor's *Méthode*.[523] There are no important differences in the opinions on the method over the years, only Jeffery and Klier are somewhat critical. Others are favorable on Coste's approach. The origin of the modern guitar technique is attributed to Coste. Apart from this, he is the first person to show an interest in 'old' music, in the transcriptions of Robert de Visée's works.

The references with Sor's studies in this method are about étude 24 on p. 28-29 [i.e. étude 22 opus 29] and étude 25 on p. 30-31 [i.e. étude 17 opus 29]. None of the exercises are very special as far as the formal characteristics of phrase, ornamentation, key, meter and tempo are concerned. Nevertheless, there are many prescriptions of dynamics and articulation. Just as in almost all guitar music, many ascending and descending legatos can be found in scale passages, but not more than usual in this case. Primarily striking are the melodic chromatics, the interesting harmonic progressions, a single modulation, two

---

[516] Schwarz-Reiflingen, Erwin: 'Costes Bearbeitung der Sor-Schule', in: *Die Gitarre*, Berlin, 1927, Jahrgang VIII, Heft 7/8, [Coste-Heft] p. 51-52.
[517] Giordano, Mario: 'Napoléon Coste e le sue opere', in: *Il plettro*, febbraio 1934, no. 2, p. 7.
[518] Jeffery, Brian: *Fernando Sor, Composer and Guitarist*, London, Tecla, 1977; second edition 1994, p. 96.
[519] Ribouillault, Danielle: *La technique de guitare en France dans la première moitié du XIXe siècle*, PhD, Paris, Sorbonne, 1980, p. 159.
[520] Klier, Johannes & Ingrid Hacker: *Die Gitarre, Ein Instrument und seine Geschichte*, Bad Schussenried, Biblioteca de la Guitarra, 1980, p. 154.
[521] Hoek, Jan Anton van: *Die Gitarrenmusik im 19. Jahrhundert*, Wilhelmshaven, Heinrichshofen Verlag, 1983, p. 59, 70.
[522] Stenstadvold, Erik: 'Coste's contribution to the "20 Studies" by Sor', *Soundboard*, vol. XI, no. 2, 1984, p. 136-140; Stenstadvold, Erik 'Napoleon Costes Beitrag zu den 20 Etüden von Fernando Sor', in: *Gitarre und Laute*, Köln, vol. VI, 1984, no. 3, p. 14-17.
[523] Dell'Ara, Mario: 'Metodi e Trattati', in: Ruggiero Chiesa, ed.: *La Chitarra*, Torino, Edizioni di Torino, 1990, p. 256.

cadenzas, campanella effects and the explanation of the onomatopoeia in some études. The Romantic style characteristics are unequally distributed among this selection of the études, most of these are not very notable, some, in contrast, are almost performance pieces. A comparison of Coste's and Sor's works in this method and elsewhere, shows, apart from the historical connection, the existence of the musical link between the two. Could Sor's music be Romantic already? To a certain extent it is, but Coste takes Sor's notions further, in a way the Romanticism in his works flourishes.

MAKAROFF 1851

Coste's relation to Sor is confirmed once more by the Russian nobleman Makaroff (1810-1890), who travels through Europe. This enthusiastic amateur guitarist has given up a military career to devote himself to the guitar.[524] After mastering the guitar through self-instruction in his home town Tula, practicing twelve hours a day with a metronome to be able to play as fast as possible, he has lessons in harmony in Moscow and starts writing compositions which, he himself claims, are very successful and favorable. In Tula he takes part in his first concert, and in St. Petersburg he meets the German pianist Damcke. He collects guitars, which he orders in writing from Stauffer in Vienna. He also wants to inform himself about the situation in Europe concerning guitar soloists, guitar composers and luthiers. That is why he travels with his first wife to the musical capitols of Europe, such as Brussels, London, Paris, Naples and Vienna, as he discusses in great detail in his memoirs. In Brussels he meets the famous Zani de Ferranti, guitarist to the king, whom he describes as brilliant and having good manners. He also thinks him to be old-fashioned, because he resists adding more strings to the guitar, which is a common practice in Russia.[525] Then, in 1851, he goes to London, not to visit the world exhibition, held there from May 1 through October 15, but for the guitar music, to meet the famous Schultz. In his hotel they play each other's repertoire for one another and Schultz is so impressed by Makaroff's playing he embraces him with the words: 'In Paris or Vienna you would be called the greatest guitarist in the world!'[526] The nobleman is not known for his modesty. He is so impressed by Schultz that he does not make the effort to visit the guitarists Ciebra and Regondi, but instead rushes on to Paris, where he probably arrives in the autumn. There he meets Carcassi, who, as he says, is also known in Russia by guitar lovers for his 'thin' musical compositions, and then he writes:

> *I also met a pupil of famous Sor, Napoléon Coste, who was the publisher of Sor's music at the same time. We became good friends. He was an intelligent and charming Frenchman, modest, and a very passionate admirer of the guitar. He often visited me, and then we played several of Sor's compositions in duet. He played with great clarity, softness and purity of tone, but, for some reason, his playing did not throw the listener into a rapture, did not arouse enthusiasm in the way Schultz or even Ferranti did with their performance.*[527]

In January 1852 he leaves for Naples and then goes to Vienna, where he is thrilled by the women there, but also meets Scherzer, the luthier, becomes deeply acquainted to Mertz, and is very impressed. He believes him to be the best guitarist of Germany. He describes his performance as full of power, energy, feeling, clearness and expression. Nevertheless he suffers from the shortcomings of the German school – the buzzing of the basses, the way the rapid passages are sometimes stifled. He does buy five of Mertz's unpublished compositions and brings them along to St. Petersburg, a journey leading past Prague, Dresden, Leipzig, Frankfurt and finally Berlin. As a reason for not publishing his work, Mertz

---

[524] Makaroff, Nikolai Petrovich de: 'The memoirs of Makaroff', in: *the Guitar Review*, New York, The Society of the Classic Guitar, 1946-48, (vol. I reprint 1974/1975) no. 1, p. 10.
[525] Makaroff, Nikolai Petrovich de: 'The memoirs of Makaroff', in: *the Guitar Review*, New York, The Society of the Classic Guitar, 1946-48, (vol. I reprint 1974/1975) no. 2, p. 33.
[526] Makaroff, Nikolai Petrovich de: 'The memoirs of Makaroff', in: *the Guitar Review*, New York, The Society of the Classic Guitar, 1946-48, (vol. I reprint 1974/1975) no. 2, 1947, p. 34.
[527] Makaroff, Nikolai Petrovich de: 'The memoirs of Makaroff', in: *the Guitar Review*, New York, The Society of the Classic Guitar, 1946-48, (vol. I reprint 1974/1975) no. 3, 1947, p. 56.

indicates that in this way they remain new for his concerts again and again.[528] Were he to publish them, in six months they would be old. As Makaroff explicitly recounts he buys Mertz's compositions at a modest price. This might lead to the presumption that he could have done the same with Coste's compositions, which may have been the reason for Coste's dedications to him. Back in Russia, Makaroff later has the idea to save the guitar from its demise by setting up a competition for guitar composition and guitar construction. He has a straight-forward opinion on how the guitar should be played, and he wants to disseminate his vision in a concrete form. All this has an influence on Coste's development and also makes it clear that Coste has some international fame.

CONCERT LODGE 1852

Being a member of the Freemasons 'music-lodge' in Paris, *Les Frères Unis Inséparables*, Coste has good contacts with renowned musicians. Freemasonry in general is surrounded by secrets, but the musical activities still shed some light on Coste's relation with many of the members of these united, inseparable brethren. They are mentioned by name in Roger Cotte's monograph on the music and its musicians of masonry, including Coste. He is mentioned as 'Professeur de guitare' in 1851 in the company of Charles Triébert, 'Professeur de Hautbois au Conservatoire'. He is even a prominent member, because Coste is mentioned again in 1864-1865, and from 1870 until 1872 he even rose in the ranks to become secretary. This illustrious company includes famous musicians as well, such as singer Auguste Panseron, singer Charles Duvernoy, composer Giacomo Meyerbeer, flautist Louis Dorus, hailing from Valenciennes, and clarinet player Hyacinthe Klosé.[529] This freemasons' lodge, familiar to Coste, organizes the annual concerts, in which he possibly plays, in any case in 1852 for certain. After the glorious times in the beginning of the 19th century, the concerts have now transformed into simple concerts for charity. The audience consists of secular sympathizers, the artists often included.[530] The musical activities of this lodge remain relative modest. And sometimes the tradition of *La colonne d'harmonie* with woodwinds and brass and drummers is deviated from, for instance when Triébert plays a solo for oboe accompanied by Édouard Batiste on the harmonium, a recently invented musical instrument, which is called an organ on this occasion.[531] Why wouldn't Coste, as an established guitarist, play in one or more of these concerts? Furthermore, there is a strong relationship with the Conservatoire. Many of the teachers are involved in this lodge, in the Apollo society, and are in this way connected to Coste as well. They are violinist Henri Aumont, organist Antoine Batiste, singer Enrico Delle-Sedie, bassoonist Louis Jancourt, harpists Antoine Prumier (junior and senior), pianist Henri Ravina and singer Gustave Roger, with the exception of Meyerbeer, a dozen musicians from the Conservatoire, enough to give a concert together.[532] And they do give a concert on Sunday, February 15, 1852, the lodge's only concert of which a review could be found mentioning Coste. This critique is published *Revue et Gazette musicale de Paris* a week later, and it describes a somewhat peculiar atmosphere:

> *The concert hall of the artists musicians in the boulevart [sic] Bonne-Nouvelle (formerly Diorama) offered a picturesque image. A musical and somewhat theatrical performance was given. The artists and some of the listeners were decorated, embellished with blue, red ribbons of knights, commanders, who for a moment had us thinking that we had landed in a European congress by mistake. Luckily this was not the case. The dignitaries, adorned with ribbons, merely represented high Rosicrucians, brethren orators and sentinels of the order of freemasons, who asked their virtuoso brethren to perform duets, trios, cavatines, romances, soli,*

---

[528] Makaroff, Nikolai Petrovich de: 'The memoirs of Makaroff', in: *the Guitar Review*, New York, The Society of the Classic Guitar, 1946-48, (vol. I reprint 1974/1975) no. 3, 1947, p. 58-59.
[529] Cotte, Roger: *La musique maçonnique et ses musiciens*, Paris, Editions du Borrégo, 1987, p. 140-143.
[530] Cotte, Roger: *La musique maçonnique et ses musiciens*, Paris, Editions du Borrégo, 1987, p. 138.
[531] Cotte, Roger: *La musique maçonnique et ses musiciens*, Paris, Editions du Borrégo, 1987, p. 144; Dieterlen, M, 'Harmonium', in: Fauquet, Joël-Marie: *Dictionnaire de la Musique en France au XIXe siècle*, Paris, Fayard, 2003, p. 575-576.
[532] Cotte, Roger: *La musique maçonnique et ses musiciens*, Paris, Editions du Borrégo, 1987, p. 167, 173-175, 179-180, 184, 187-189, 193.

chansonnettes, before the altar of their charity and for their unfortunate brethren, and together they made a charming program with a fruitful and varied concert.[533]

One can't fault the critic for a lack of irony. He provides a colorful sketch of what was enacted, but he is obviously not one of the brethren. The red and blue ribbons probably represent different ranks in the Scottish Rite, two of which are knight and commander.[534] The concert is given for a good cause (not described) concerning the less fortunate brethren. Among the performing musicians are some ladies, the lodge apparently is open-minded, but after all it is a concert for the world in Paris, already worldly at that time. The critic continues:

To dedicate a madrigal to each of the artists who performed in the concert would take too long. Therefore we limit ourselves to merely saying that in this abundant and full musical exhibition we took note of a perfect trio by M. Bellon for flute, oboe and English horn, played by MM Petiton, Blainville and Triébert; chansonnettes villageoises, delightfully sung by Mme Charles Ponchard, and not less delightfully accompanied on the oboe by the same Triébert; the Sentinelle, this martial and knightly song by Choron from the time of the empire, embellished by variations on the piano, the violin and the guitar, by Hummel, and performed by MM Ponchard, Franck, Léopold Dancla and Coste. MM Panseron, as a composer and accompanist, Wartel, Bussine and Mlle Tillemont, first-prize-winners of the Conservatoire, were united, as singers and benefactors, in this beautiful piece. So, honor to these artists and the freemason's lodge of the Frères-unis-inséparables![535]

The concert is attended by a mixed company of ladies and gentlemen, both members of the lodge, such as M. Petiton, Triébert, Panseron and Coste, who belong to the lodge's brethren, and nonmembers, such as Mme Ponchard and Mme Tillemont and MM Blainville, Ponchard, Franck, Dancla, Wartel and Bussine.[536] The connection to the Conservatoire is clear from the review, as teachers participate as well as students. Coste does not present his own work here, but he joins an ensemble in an accompaniment. His participation in the annual concerts on behalf of the orphan children is limited to this only one in 1852. His practical participation in freemasonry does not go any further. The influence on his works is hardly perceptible, other than some interest in knighthood in opus 15 *Le Tournoi*, of which the inspiration can be attributed to Walter Scott's novel *Ivanhoe*. Moreover, knighthood is not an idea that is strictly restricted to the lodge: it is one of the many phenomena visible in Romanticism.

Souvenirs 1852

It is not only literary historical subjects, opera motifs or political events are Coste's source of inspiration for composing: he also shapes personal memories into music, after his *Souvenirs de Flandres* opus 5 in 1835 now in his *Souvenirs, Sept Morceaux Episodiques* opus 17-23 in 1852, as well. The collection is a sort of musical voyage through his past, to Ornans, the place where he grew up, the

---

[533] *Revue et Gazette musicale de Paris*, vol. XIX, no. 8, 22 II 1852, p. 58-59: 'La salle de concerts des artistes-musiciens, sise au boulevart Bonne-Nouvelle (ancien Diorama), offrait un coup d'oeil assez pittoresque dimanche passé. On y donnait une séance musicale et quelque peu dramatique. Les artistes et plusieurs auditeurs étaient ornés. décorés de cordons bleus, rouges, de chevaliers, de commandeurs, qui nous ont fait penser un moment que le hasard nous avait poussé au sein de quelque congrès européen. Il n'en était heureusement rien. Ces dignitaires enrubanés représentaient seulement des grands roses-croix, des frères orateurs, tuileurs, de l'ordre maçonnique, qui avaient prié leurs frères virtuoses de venir déposer sur l'autel de la bienfaisance et pour des frères malheureux, des duos, des trios, cavatines, romances, *soli*, chansonnettes, qui ont formé un charmant programme dont il est résulté un concert varié et productif.'
[534] Cotte, Roger: *La musique maçonnique et ses musiciens*, Paris, Editions du Borrégo, 1987, p. 195-198.
[535] *Revue et Gazette musicale de Paris*, vol. XIX, no. 8, 22 II 1852, p. 59: 'Lancer un madrigal à chaqun des artistes qui ont figuré dans ce concert serait un peu long. Nous nous bornerons donc à dire qu'on a remarqué dans cette abondante et riche exhibition musicale un excellent trio de M. Bellon pour flûte, hautbois et cor anglais, fort bien dit par MM. Petiton, Blainville et Triébert; des chansonnettes villageoises, chantées délicieusement par Mme Charles Ponchard, et non moins délicieusement accampagnées sur le hautbois par ce même Triebert; la *Sentinelle*, ce chant guerrier et chevaleresque de Choron, du temps de l'empire, orné de variations de piano, violon et guitare, par Hummel, et dit par MM. Ponchard, Franck, Léopold Dancla et Coste. MM. Panseron, comme compositeur et accompagnateur, Wartel, Bussine et Mlle Tillemont, premiers prix du Conservatoire, se sont associés, comme chanteurs et philanthropes, à cette bonne oeuvre. Honneur donc à ces artistes et à la loge maçonnique des Frères-unis-inséparables!'
[536] Cotte, Roger: *La musique maçonnique et ses musiciens*, Paris, Editions du Borrégo, 1987, p. 140-143, 166-194.

Rhine, which he crossed on his way to the North, to Delfzijl, where he stayed with his father, along the Zuiderzee, which he passed again on his march to the South, back to France. These first four places are historically demonstrable. The last three are not, but even so, *Les Cloches* Coste may contain memories of carillons, such as could have chimed in and around Valenciennes. Meulan and Auteuil are small villages in the vicinity of Paris, of which Coste might have happy memories from the early period when he was there, perhaps, and why not, dancing a waltz with his sweetheart, as a Romantic young lover. Apart from the mostly lyrical introductions, there are no fewer than five waltzes of note, of which two, being scherzos, have a merry character. Aside from the past, which appears here with extra-musical references, several musical characteristics of the Romanticism can be recognized in these works , as is pointed out in the analysis of them; the explanation is therefore a mixture of both.

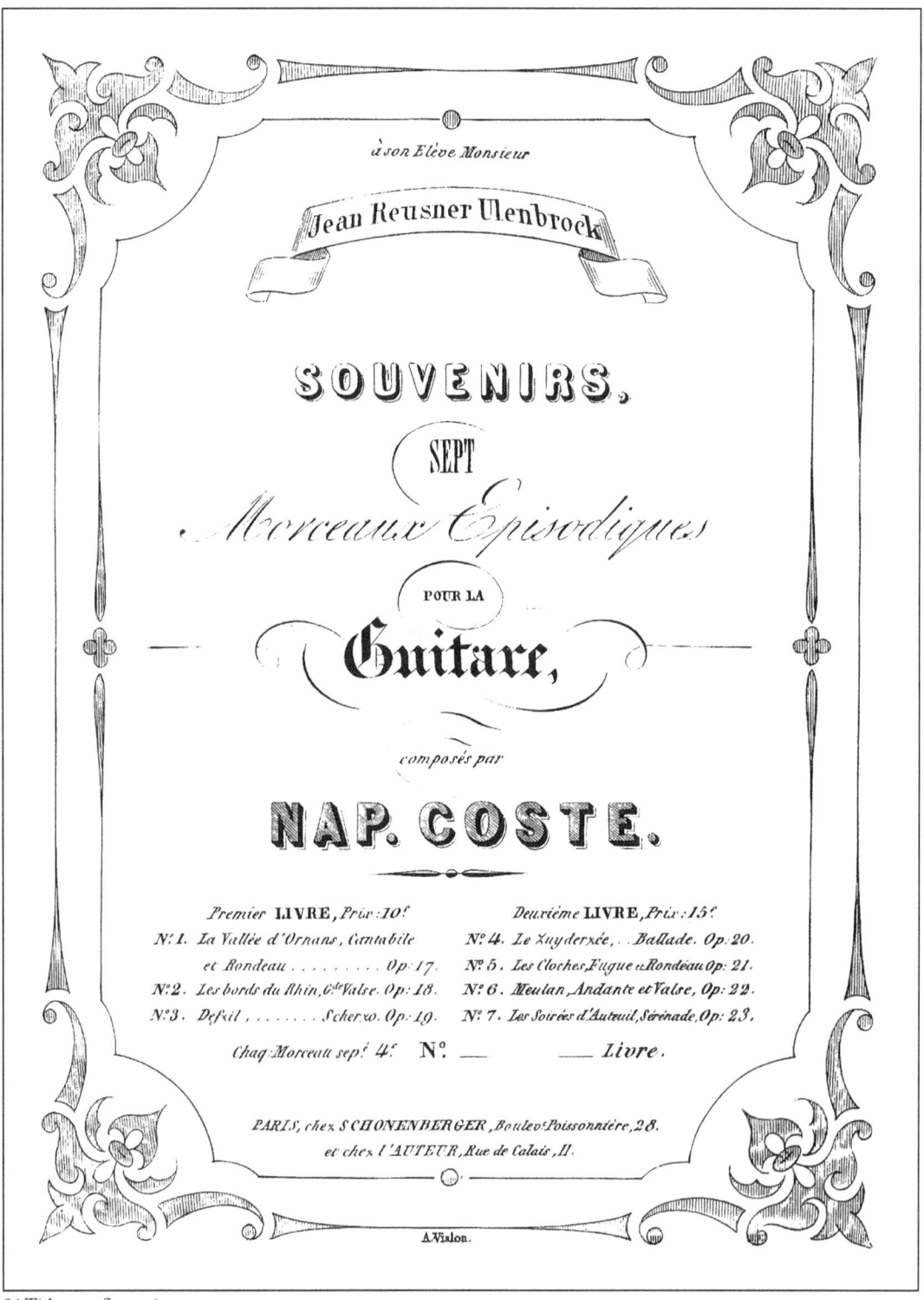

86 Title page Souvenirs

V — Souvenirs

The seven episodic musical compositions for guitar are published by Schonenberger, boulevard Poissonnière, 28 and by the author himself, rue de Calais, 11. Coste has found, with the *Méthode*, his sixth editor for these works in Schonenberger, after the publication of earlier work by Romagnesi, Richault, Lacôte, Challiot and Latte. It remains a guess as to the reason for this dispersal, as long as the letters in which Coste possibly expresses his opinion on this matter cannot be found. Apart from an artistic frame engraved by A. Vialon, the title page of the edition shows Coste's new address, his fourth in Paris. After rue Bleue no. 28, 1829, rue du [Vieux] Colombier no. 25, 1832 and rue de L'Échiquier no. 23, 1837, it is now rue de Calais no. 11, where Berlioz came to live at no. 4 in 1856, across the street. Coste makes quite a trek around the city, but the reason why remains a guess. From the right bank of the Seine to the left bank, and back again. Rue de L'Échiquier really was closer to the boulevard Poissonnière – with its publishers Richault and Schonenberger between place de Clichy and place Pigalle – than the rue de Calais. The *Bibliographie de la France* reports the edition twice, first as a collection, second with *Meulan* opus 22 mentioned separately, which makes the determining the date of these souvenirs easy.[537] He dedicates the work to his pupil, M. Jean Reussner Ulenbrock, who comes from Riga, according to the dedication of *Étude* 16 opus 38. Coste's new idea is to

87 Rue de Calais no. 11, 2007

write a whole series of works referring to place names, says Brian Jeffery. These works are often long and interesting, and the harmonic style in the middle and at the end of his works is developing in a completely new way for the world of the guitar.[538] Referring to the *Souvenirs* Joerg Sommermeyer finds this music so essentially programmatic that Coste might as well be called the Berlioz of the guitar. The numerous sketches of landscapes, concerning Coste's juvenile memories, are often written in a very pastoral way, evoking associations.[539] With Mario Dell'Ara the titles of the seven episodic works recall to memories of landscapes. This 'symphonic poem' for the guitar has some valuable fascinating moments, but lacks real melodic originality, many harmonic inventions remain a very important element in the whole work, along with a good taste in color and an intelligent use of instrumental means.[540] Only three authors have had something to say about these special guitar works. Therefore the descriptive analysis can tell more about the character of this music. This results of this study into Coste's Romantic style have been applied in performance practice in the interpretation, which, supplementing the descriptive analysis, can be heard on the compact disc included with this volume, with *Souvenirs, Sept Morceaux Épisodiques* opus 17-23, performed by the author.

Opus 17, *La Vallée d'Ornans* 1852

The first work in this series must be the realization in sound of Coste's memories of his early childhood in the quiet place of Ornans in the department of Doubs on the river Loue. He lived there from his second to his eighth year. In 1852 this is some forty years earlier, a remote past for Coste, the memory of which he wants to revive will be Romanticised without any doubt. Gustave Courbet made

---

[537] *Bibliographie de la France*, 17 VII 1852, p. 432: 'Nap. Coste. Souvenirs. Sept morceaux épisodiques pour la guitare. Prix de chaque morceau 4-00'; 31 VII 1852, p. 466: 'Nap. Coste. (Souvenirs, sept morceaux épisodiques pour la guitare.) No. 6. Meulan, andante et valse, op. 22 4-00 A Paris chez Schonenberger.'
[538] Jeffery, Brian: 'Napoléon Coste" in: *Cahiers de la Guitare*, Boissy-St-Léger, Association Guitares et Luths, vol. 6, 1983, p. 10.
[539] Sommermeyer, Joerg: 'Noten, The Guitar Works of Napoleon Coste...', in: *Nova Giulianiad*, 1984 Nr. 3, p. 168. [auszug website 2002]
[540] Dell'Ara, Mario: *Manuale di storia della chitarra*, Ancona, Bèrben, 1988, p. 136.

88 La Vallée d'Ornans - Vernier, c. 1850

an engraving with the same title, which can be found in the Bibliothèque municipal of Besançon, an image also used by Brian Jeffery as a cover for his edition of the piece. First the composer creates a quiet, calm atmosphere, and then a walking movement and a great deal of change by the modulation from e to C, chromatic colors and tense chords on a pedal point. Apart from the concordance with Sor's *Étude* 17 opus 29 there are elements reminiscent of his *Les Adieux* opus 21: an opening with the same chords, an ongoing movement in eighths on a pedal point to which other voices move in contrast. Coste prescribes many dynamic changes, applies motifs like the 'spark', the 'rocket' and the 'parachute' in a free lyricism, but nevertheless he knows how to preserve the unity in this work. The characteristics found in his music so far return in his later works. They show aspects of the musical structure of his music.

This is also the case in the second part of opus 17, *Les Montagnards*. Coste uses the same title in the singular for *Le Montagnard* opus 34[a] for oboe and piano in 1861, which is also a rondo, but apart from some stylistic elements, there is no resemblance. However, the titles, such as *La Vallée d'Ornans*, are the expression of the Romantic predilection for to landscapes and mountains, with the mountain dweller.

It is a rondo with an almost continuous movement in eighths and sixteenths, in arpeggio or in a rhythmic melody and accompaniment. The straightforward modulation to the third degree is striking and, with its lack of middle voices, can be characterized as rather 'square'. In this second part several style elements can be found as well, folklore, prolongations, chromatic colored passages, a dissonant chord, and expolitio, which is an immediate repeat of a part of a phrase. The best to do is to listen to the music, or better yet to play it and the discussion about this piece in the descriptive analysis includes a number of characteristics which are typical for Coste's Romantic style as a result, which can lead to a better understanding and greater enjoyment of the music.

Opus 18, *Les Bords du Rhin* 1852

The second composition which depicts, as it were, Coste's voyage through time and space takes us along the Rhine, the longest river in Western-Europe, floating not too far from Ornans, in such a way

V — Souvenirs

89 Les Bords du Rhin op.18, manuscript Coste

that it may well be possible that Coste once took a trip up there. If we take the title of the collection literally, he actually did so, or else he crossed the Rhine in Holland, on his trip to or from Delfzil. But it is not so spectacular there, a broad and slowly flowing stream. The upper stream is the border between France and Germany, a fact that offers interesting possibilities to interpretation, a gracious French waltz on the one side, a playful German waltz on the other side. Even then the French were not so fond of Germans. Such an interpretation may seem forced, but the form and the content of the music provide performing guitarist with an opportunity to give this piece a programmatic meaning. It is an enraptured waltz of which the form can be distinguished into two parts, as far as themes and key are concerned, the first part in A, the second in D, after which the A part is resumed. Both parts have aspects of a mixed song-rondo form, *A-B-A' C-D-C' A"*. Coste does not give any indication for tempo. In this way the performer is free to adept the performance to his own feeling. The 'French' part opens with a trumpet motif, followed by an ascending prolongation, after which a 'parachute' motif and an ascending octave passage in chromatics bring the movement to a sudden standstill, 'abruptio'. The next bourdon motif alludes to folklore. The second, 'German' part has a lengthened phrase which deviates from the periodicity in the part where the music is in III-major, a chromatic-third relation. Then passing dominants and dissonant chords follow in a harmonic acceleration. The application of rests, different from the notation of rhythm, is striking, especially when it occurs in an arpeggio where the thumb must mute the bass and the other fingers have to play the broken chord that way. This special style characteristic of Coste contrasts with the tendency of guitarists in his time to sustain the sound as long as possible, to play legato. Opus 18 in A is an excellent continuation of opus 17 in E, as a work in dominant-tonic relation, and being in a 3/4 time, after the 6/8 and 2/4 time, it is surprisingly also totally different in character, in such a way that the two pieces can very well be played consecutively.

Opus 19, Delfzil 1852

Now come Coste's two 'Dutch' compositions, after *Ornans* in e and E, *Le Rhin* in A, D and A, in key subsequently in d and D and again in d and D. This descending fifth relation is the reason why these compositions can be performed one after another and go well together in a program. Holland made an indelible impression on the young boy who would later become a composer.

The question is to what degree this is perceptible in the two compositions *Delfzil* and *Le Zuyderzée*. The descriptive analysis of the two works may give the answer. The musical form *A B C B A* of opus 19 can be regarded as an irregular rondo form. The melodic aspect is subject of change after change and it is not very elaborated, but it is strongly rhythmic by tone repetition. Sometimes chromatics is applied, as well as harmonic acceleration or deceleration of shortened or lengthened phrases. The harmony is mostly a traditional Classic II-V-I, with regularly occurring #II and #IV. In one place the work modulates with a faster harmonic rhythm. As is required in a scherzo the work is cheerful in character due to the waltz rhythm, the tone repetitions, the clearly articulated staccato, the two 'sparks' as portamento glissando with a very comical character, directly followed by playful non-stroke left hand legatos. This work is programmatic in this sense of making the connection with simple folk waltzes with continuously renewing melodics. It is cheerful, amusing to play, pleasant to listen to, certainly

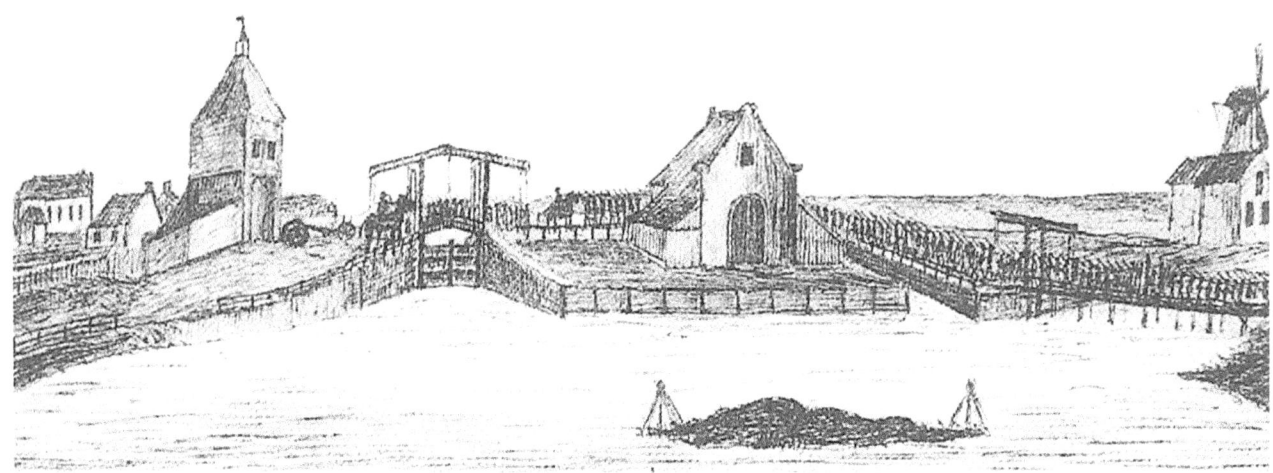

90 Delfzjil 1814

entertaining with surprising guitar effects, such as legatos, scale passages, staccatos, flageolets, and nice diminished chords as appoggiatura. With its succession of melodic themes the composition can be regarded as episodic, almost rhapsodic, a composition worthy of Delfzijl, that small walled fortress. A short study appears on the page after the end of the work, probably to fill the half-empty page, as it bears no musical relation to the actual composition.

Opus 20, *Le Zuyderzée*

On the way from Delfzijl to the south, Napoléon Coste and his father certainly passed or even crossed the Zuiderzee. This at the time beautiful, but dangerous inland sea that brought the local people prosperity as well as sorrow, has inspired Coste to compose a strong programmatic work. It is appropriately called 'Ballade' (there is a Dutch song by Louis Davids with this title in 1932...) and it has a prescribed scordatura from the sixth string to D. This makes the guitar sound deeper, a feature strongly advocated by the composer, on Lacôte's 'heptacorde' in particular. This work also is episodic, as mentioned on the title page. Instead of elaborating upon the theme in variations, rhythm and harmony, this composition finds its strength in very rich melodics. New and fresh tunes are continually introduced that entertain both the listener and the performer. The guitarist can enjoy the versatility of his instrument which emerges from these compositions.

91 Zuiderzee

The listener can be absorbed by the depictive effect of the many melodic themes that pass in succession. Here the rhythms of his themes and motifs, the rather Classical tonal harmony with an occasional modulating passage are characteristic of Coste as a composer. The cheerful mood of his waltzing melodies and rhythms remain typical. The loaded word programmatic comes immediately to mind. However, often the conversion of a story or an image or a memory into music is utterly arbitrary and subject to free interpretation. What is the meaning of a melody, a rhythm, a motif, a harmony? As far as these two works are concerned, the titles can be given a free interpretation and the performer and listener can apply their own fantasy to the Delfzijl and Zuiderzee of the 19th century. The references are not so explicit as to fit in one particular way. There is room for imagination, but the scope and direction of this are given.

OPUS 21, *LES CLOCHES*

The next work in this collection of seven episodic pieces consists two parts: the first is a *Fugue*, the second is a *Rondeau*. The fugue is in the key of a, while the rondo which follows is in the parallel major, perfectly suitable in the course of this series of works. The title alludes to bells, and the imitated sound of chimes is set to music in a motif that consists of a third, octave and sixth interval in high position with campanella, literally clocks here, in a harmony where only the first five tones of the scale are played. It is not clear which chime provided Coste with his inspiration: Paris does not have a strong tradition in this, Flanders does have such a tradition. In the north of France carillons are well known, also in St-Amand, close to Valenciennes where even is a factory 'Fonderie de Cloches'. But beyond there that is hardly the case: there clocks play a so called musical warning before the hour is struck at most.[541] After his birth country Ornans, his travel past the Rhine, his stay in Delfzijl and his voyage past the Zuiderzee, in this composition Coste now arrives in the town where he lived in his youth.

92 Cloches 'Les Trois Soeurs' St-Amand

The symbolism of this can be taken even further in the fugue, as a fantasy of his development as a young composer, where many elements coincide in a harmonic movement, guided by a theme. The fugue has a short theme in a, which is repeated in imitation, continued in contrapuntal voices in a modulating harmony, but there is no real exposition in a formal way, the texture is more like fugato. However, the theme does return in other keys, the subdominant and the dominant, and there is a lot of chromatic elaboration. The rondo is rich in contrasts, with a pivot tone modulation, harmonic differences and passages. The final effect is caused by dissonant chords and complex arpeggio, before Coste diminishes the sound at the end with the chime motif in double harmonics and ends the rondo with a V-I cadence. From the descriptive analysis many depictive elements emerge which make this work a quite varied, fascinating whole. The chime element here, which might just as well be the transcription of the tuning of *Les Trois Soeurs* in St-Amand, is very effective.

OPUS 22, *MEULAN*

In the music one can hear Coste must have had pleasant, possibly Romantic memories of the small village, northwest of Paris. Just like many other Parisians, he will have taken a rest on the Seine in the summer to get away from the rush and heat of the city. The quiet movement of the beginning of this composition may depict this and, continuing this Romantic fantasy, the sudden change with a fierce chord to a much higher tempo might be the young man's falling in love, transitioning later into a merry

---

[541] Coeuroy, André: *La musique et le peuple en France*, Paris, Stock, 1941, p. 44-45; http://www.clocherobecourt.com/Robecourt/Monde07-59Valenciennes.php.

93 Meulan op. 22, manuscript Coste

waltz, where he dances with his sweetheart. Dancing the waltz is a favorite pastime for many French people, especially when a figured melody on a folk bourdon is concerned. The *Bibliographie de la France* mentions the andante as well as the waltz. Though lacking enrapturing inventions, the music also has a gripping lyricism and a gallant movement, the waltz making up the larger part of this 'souvenir'. The first part has a lyrical melody with a rippling accompaniment in 6/8 time, broken by joint motifs in free lyricism. This ends in a harmonic chord in the key of E, before a fierce E chord, directly followed by an octave motif which returns as an idée fixe and leads into the second part, in a contrasting chromatic lowered VI. This part shows many style elements which are becoming typical for Coste , a three-voice prolongation, a cadenza, arpeggios in complementary rhythm, a folk music passage, a modulation in pulsating chords, and many different passages. The Romantic spirit is evident in this music. It is an amusing work with many interesting musical aspects, but which nonetheless forms a coherent whole.

OPUS 23, *LES SOIRÉES D'AUTEUIL*

At the end of this journey through Coste's memories there is an appropriate serenade, which breathes an atmosphere that is almost still, before the series is completed with a festive scherzo. In it a notable peculiar theme is present which returns as a rondo part, with a great deal of dazzling passagework that makes clear that the seven episodic works are really coming to an end. Auteuil is an even smaller village than Meulan, west of Paris, a place where Coste's family, relatives, acquaintances or pupils may have lived, and where he, taking the title literally, may have spent pleasant and cheerful evenings. His real memories remain obscure; there are no biographical indications of his connection to this village, other than this composition. But spending quiet soirées in small villages in France is, to this day, a favorite pastime for many French people, and every self-respecting town organizes a street fair around the bandstand on the village square on a summer night, with music, eating and drinking together, conversation, and spins on the dance floor. The scherzo is a waltz again. Coste really likes this genre of music. From the descriptive analysis, as can be expected by now, a considerable number of musical building blocks emerge which can be distinguished as Romantic, perfectly suiting the first six compositions of this set, but the final part of this work is quite flamboyant. The lyrical melody gives the Andantino a calm movement with a harmonic excursion to the submediant and coloring with dissonant chords. These are resumed with an arpeggio accompaniment, ending in chromatic passages in thirds and sixths and a quiet ending chord on the tonic. The scherzo is very original in its themes, contrasts and diction, providing a convincing closure to the souvenirs. The theme in triplets leads strikingly towards #4 and has a comical character, despite the minor key. Here intensive harmonic passages can be noticed as well, as well as a contrasting part in the corresponding major key. The arpeggio passage is very well written with a contrapuntal inner voicing in the part where the repeat is elaborated. A joint motif with free lyricism leads to an expolitio, followed by a complete descending chromatic scale, ending in a confirming cadence in the corresponding major key. When this journey has come to an end, the multifaceted nature of the seven works and great changes in them can be noticed, which do justice to the episodic title. It would go too far to call them rhapsodic; the works have too much internal cohesion for that. They are varied, but the parts are certainly musically coherent.

V — Souvenirs

In these solid compositions Coste shows his great talent as a composer. An applause is the eventual goal of the seven repetitions of the final chord, with which the consecutive very guitar-like keys of this collection e-E-A-d-D-d-D-a-A-E-A-a-A find their closure. The harmonic relation of the first three works *La Vallée d'Ornans*, *Les Bords du Rhin* and *Delfzil* is one of dominant-tonic, after which the key of d-minor and D-major which is reached is continued in *Le Zuyderzée*. The last three works – *Les Cloches*, *Meulan* and *Soirées d'Auteuil* – form a tonic-dominant-tonic cycle, a closed entity. In this way, regarding A-major as the final key, the tonal gravity lies in the subdominant, in a plagal relation, which relativizes the Classical dominant-tonic relation. Looking at the many Romantic formal characteristics and style elements which unfold themselves in these works, an evident development of the composer in the Romantic style can be seen.

Oboe 1855

Coste has met the oboe in several concerts already. On March 29, 1840 and April 26, 1843 he plays in a concert with oboist Stanislas Verroust. Soler, an unknown musician, also plays the oboe in this last concert, and again on May 28, 1843, that time together with Charles Triébert, Coste's friend. Coste's road to the oboe seems to go through the *Société académique des Enfants d'Apollon* and the *Frères Unis Inséparables* as well, the Freemasons' 'musical lodge' in Paris. He is going to be occupied with composing for this instrument, for his friend Triébert, and clarinet, for his colleague Klosé, both belonging to these circles. In December 1852 a *Sérénade* for oboe, clarinet and guitar, composed by M. Coste is played during the monthly, informal meeting of the society, performed by Triébert, Klosé and Coste.[542] The *Fantaisie de Concert* opus 35 for two oboes and piano and the *Caprice* WoO 3 for two oboes without accompaniment aside, no other work for two wind instruments by Coste is known of. He did write two more serenades, *Soirées d'Auteuil* opus 23 and *Grande Sérénade* opus 30, but these are for guitar solo, which is why this must be an unknown work. For this reason the piece will be called *Sérénade* WoO 13 and we have to wait for the piece to be discovered in one of the libraries or archives where his works are found.

In these years Coste is very active in composing, because in February 1855 a *Romance sans parole* by his hand is performed by M. Triébert on the English horn during one of the monthly concerts of the *Société académique des Enfants d'Apollon*, where Coste can often be heard.[543] Decourcelle's publication is a rich source of information about Coste and his music, but it does not mention whether he himself played, which surely must have been the case, because the work, better known with the title *Consolazione, Romance sans paroles* opus 25 is written for oboe and guitar, a very simple little work that can be played easily on the English horn by its low position, adding more color to the sound than the oboe does. One way or another, this information puts opus 25 in the year 1855, rather than 1856, which can be deduced from the edition, because on August 16, 1856 the announcement is made in the *Bibliographie de la France* that *Consolazione* opus 25 for oboe or violin and guitar is published by Colombier and it is entered on '19 VI 1856' in the register.[544] The work is dedicated to Charles de Bériot, so it must have been intended for violin and guitar in the first place. The 'romance sans paroles' with it's quiet lyrical melody could not have been a challenge to Bériot, with an easy arpeggio accompaniment moreover, very guitaristic, but not pianistic. In the second edition later by Frédéric Triébert, brother of the oboist Charles Triébert, who died in 1867, the work is dedicated to the latter, and another work is added to it, by which it gets the collective title *Regrets et Consolations* opus 25 & 36. Apart from the dedication the instrumentation is changed as well, now being for oboe or violin, violoncello or flute, with piano

---

[542] Decourcelle, Maurice: *La Société des Enfants d'Apollon (1741-1880): programmes des concerts annuels...*, Paris, Durand, 1881, p. 178: 'Sérénade pour hautbois, clarinette et guitarre [sic], composée par M. Coste, exécuté par MM. Triebert [sic], Klosé et Coste.'

[543] Decourcelle, Maurice: *La Société des Enfants d'Apollon (1741-1880): programmes des concerts annuels...*, Paris, Durand, 1881, p. 183: 'Romance sans parole, composée par M. Coste, exécuté sur le cor anglais par M. Triébert.'

[544] *Bibliographie de la France*, vol. XLV, no. 33, 16 VIII 1856, p. 862: 'N. Coste. Consolazione, romance sans paroles, composée pour hautbois ou violon, avec accompagnement de piano, op. 25.; 6-00 A Paris, chez Colombier.'; Paris, Archives nationales, Registres de Dépôt légal de musique, Musique, *Op.25 Consolazione*, F18* VIII 1 à 157, No. 20 1856, 3 janvier - 11 novembre, p.35 No.: 1641. 19 VI 1856.

accompaniment. However, there is no score in key of F and the position in the key of G is rather high for the cello. On Coste's manuscript of *Les Regrets*, currently in the Kongelige Bibliotek in Copenhagen, the instrumentation is once again different, now for oboe and guitar or piano and in tiny letters harp, too. Here Coste writes that the piece is an excerpt from the *Fantaisie* for the same instruments. He refers to his *Fantaisie Sonate* opus 34[b], of which only one page remained in manuscript, also in the Kongelige Bibliotek in Copenhagen. On the title page of the first autograph a sketch in pencil can be found of the first measures of the second, which shows the connection between the two once more. Opus 36 is complete. Without any doubt Coste himself has accompanied his *Romance sans parole* in Triébert's performance in February 1855.

Soirée 1855

In this period between 1840 and 1855, Coste has composed at least a number of ten larger works of which the *Souvenirs* as a set of seven works are enough to fill half a recital. There is no indication he really performed these in this way. Up to this point he has only participated in mixed concerts in which he sometimes played a solo of his own composition. Nothing is known about solo concerts for guitar in this time, Those were only given by great pianists, and then only rarely. In this period this is not something that the performance practice is focused on. Yet there is an indication that Coste may have played his *Souvenirs* in a concert. On April 22, 1855 the *Revue et Gazette musicale de Paris* makes the following announcement:

> *The able guitarist, Nap. Coste, announces a soirée musicale one can hear M. Paulin, the former first tenor of the Académie impériale de musique, Mme Numa Blanc de Labarte, and the MM. Lebouc, Guerreau, Casimir Ney, Triébert and Klosé. The beneficiary will perform several of his compositions, as well.*[545]

As usual, this is a mixed concert, in which Coste, as the beneficiary, has secured the company of tenor Louis-Joseph Paulin (1814-1867), who made his debut in *Les Huguenots* and interpreted great roles in the Opéra, until he gives performances in 1855 with cellist Lebouc with Classical and historical music. In 1860 he becomes a singing instructor at the Conservatoire.[546] He is a top-notch singer, and he also is an ambitious advocate of 'old' music', probably inspired by Fétis, together with the somewhat younger cellist Charles Lebouc (1822-1893), who plays in the orchestra of the Opéra after his graduating from the Conservatoire, and is very active in ensemble music. Lebouc also belongs to the circles of the *Société académique des Enfants d'Apollon*. He is elected chairman in 1863.[547] He organizes matinée concerts on a regular basis at his home, in his salons at rue Vivienne no. 12, twelve a year, together with Adolphe Blanc, who is possibly the husband of Mme Blanc de Labarte, who also takes part in the concert, probably as a singer.[548] If so, the location where the soirée is held is obvious. It is not mentioned in the announcement, but is probably assumed to be understood by the fact Lebouc is performing. Guerreau (1823-1882) is known to have earned a second prize for violin in 1839 at the Conservatoire, he plays in the orchestra of the Opéra-Comique from 1844 on.[549] Casimir Ney plays the violin in Coste's next known concert, later in August that year and of course does the same in this one. Charles Triébert is known by now, the oboist who becomes Coste's friend in this time. He already played with him in the earlier 'Apollon' concert on May 23, 1843. Coste composes works for him and his pupils. Then there is Hyacinthe Klosé (1808-1880), the clarinet-player whose solo Coste transcribes for oboe, piano and string quartet. He was also at the Conservatoire and he often plays chamber music, apart from

---

[545] *Revue et Gazette musicale de Paris,* vol. XXII, no. 16, 22 IV 1855, p. 127: 'L'habile guitarriste [sic], Nap. Coste, annonce une soirée musicale dans laquelle on entendra M. Paulin, ex-premier ténor de l'Académie impériale de musique, Mme Numa Blanc de Labarte, et MM. Lebouc, Guerreau, Casimir Ney, Triébert et Klosé. Le bénéficiaire exécutera aussi plusieurs de ses compositions.'

[546] Kocevar, É.: 'Paulin, Louis-Joseph' in: Fauquet, Joël-Marie: *Dictionnaire de la Musique en France au XIXe siècle*, Paris, Fayard, 2003, p. 946.

[547] Fauquet, J.-M.: 'Lebouc, Charles', in: Fauquet, Joël-Marie: *Dictionnaire de la Musique en France au XIXe siècle*, Paris, Fayard, 2003, p. 672.

[548] Fauquet, J.-M.: 'Blanc, Adolphe', in: Fauquet, Joël-Marie: *Dictionnaire de la Musique en France au XIXe siècle*, Paris, Fayard, 2003, p. 149-150.

[549] Pierre, Constant: *Le Conservatoire national de musique et de déclamation: documents historiques et administratifs*, Paris, Imprimerie nationale, 1900, p. 769.

V — Souvenirs

his career in military music. In 1839 he becomes a teacher at the Conservatoire. In 1861 he joins the Freemasons' lodge, where Coste and Triébert are already members.[550] Together with Lebouc and Coste, Guerreau, Ney and Triébert are also 'children of Apollo', and with singing, violin, violoncello, clarinet, oboe and guitar the program will have been very multifaceted. The remark that Coste will play several of his own compositions may justify the assumption that he played his *Souvenirs*, which are published in 1852. When the concert takes place is not mentioned either. Around this time there also is a yearly concert organized by M. Gouffé in the salle Pleyel, with a review in *La France musicale* on May 6, 1855, where five of the above-mentioned musicians play, with the particularity that Vuillaume's octobasse is played, but Coste is not mentioned here, making it unlikely that this is the same concert.[551]

Employ 1855

Nevertheless, while he seems to be making good progress in his career in this period, there are sources indicating that he took on an administrative job at the Caisse Municipale of Paris starting on April 1, 1855, earning him 1,200 francs a month.[552] While the sources describe this amount as his monthly salary, it must actually be his annual salary, because as a librarian at the conservatory Berlioz earns 1,500 francs a year in a better paying job.[553] In comparison, it is interesting to know that a 'maître valet' in agriculture earns around 400 or 600 francs a year in this period.[554] In the early literature on Coste no mention is made of this administrative job at the municipality, as with Läpke in 1884 and Shtokman [Stockmann] in 1902. The first indication is made by Gelas in 1927, who only says that the famous guitarist is working as a simple employee at the financial department of Paris, but he does not give any reference.[555] Many other 'old' literary sources, such as Buek, Schwarz-Reiflingen and Rischel, make no mention either, and Simon Wynberg, who edited the modern edition of Coste's works only indicates that Coste was a civil servant in Paris during his later years. Roman Jaworski, who authored a study on this matter, gives evidence that Coste held such a position, in 1992, with reference to Coste's file at the Préfecture de la Seine in Paris.[556] Coste did not have a happy time there. In a letter of 15 June 1858 to the Danish guitarist Søffren Degen, who visited him in this period, he makes his complaint:

You know I had a little job at the Préfecture de la Seine. While this position had its drawbacks, paralyzing my weak spirit as a composer and as an artist, I could make a modest living out of it. It didn't amount to much, but when I did not have any lessons to give, a thing that often occurs, I would not lack any necessities. But well, my dear friend, I don't have this job anymore, it was eliminated a long time ago, that is to say that three or four months ago I was vaguely forewarned. Yet I did not really believe this, and I was convinced that, if this came to pass, they would give me a compensation. And finally, the moment has come. They didn't say 'leave!', but the job was gone.[557]

---

[550] Jeltsch, J.: 'Klosé, Hyacinthe', in: Fauquet, Joël-Marie: *Dictionnaire de la Musique en France au XIXe siècle*, Paris, Fayard, 2003, p. 648; Cotte, Roger: *La musique maçonnique et ses musiciens*, Paris, Editions du Borrégo, 1987, p. 180.

[551] *La France musicale*, vol. XIX, no. 18, 6 V 1855, p. 140: 'Concert annuel de M. Gouffé.'

[552] Roncet, Noël: *Napoléon Coste, Compositeur, 1805-1883*, Amondans, 2005, p. 23; Jaworski, Roman: 'Napoleon Coste 1805-1883, une histoire perdue', in: *Valentiana*, Valenciennes, Association Valentiana, 1992, no. 10, p. 76, 77.

[553] Pierre, Constant: *Le Conservatoire national de musique et de déclamation: documents historiques et administratifs*, Paris, Imprimerie nationale, 1900, p. 425.

[554] Chevallier, Émile: *Les salaires au XIXe siècle*, Paris, Hachette, 1887, p. 33.

[555] Läpke, Richard: 'Biographie Napoleon Coste' in: *Internationale Gitarre-Zeitung*, Jahrgang I, Nr. 4 (Jan.1884), und Nr.5 (Febr.1884), Leipzig, transcr. Eduard Fack, 'Die Meister', unp. p. 118-119; Stockmann-Kursk, J.: 'Napoléon Coste', in: *Der Guitarrefreund, Mitteilungen des Internationalen Guitarristen-Verbandes*, München, 3. Jahrgang, 1902, Heft 5, p. 55-56. [French translation in IV, 2, 1903, p. 17-19, HT1]; Gelas, Lucien: 'Biographische Notizen über Napoleon Coste', in: *Die Gitarre*, Berlin, Jahrgang VIII, 1927, Heft 11/12, p. 82.

[556] Wynberg, Simon: '...zur Rettung Napoleon Costes', in: *Gitarre und Laute*, Köln, vol. III, 1981, no. 5, p. 29; Jaworski, Roman: 'Napoleon Coste 1805-1883, une histoire perdue', in: *Valentiana*, Valenciennes, 1992, no. 10, p. 76-77.

[557] Coste-Degen, 15 VI 1858, Århus, Statsbiblioteket, Søffren Degens Papirer, Manuscript no.27b, p. 1-2: 'Vous savez que j'avais à la préfecture de la Seine un petit emploi. Cet emploi avait certes bien des inconvénients et paralysant bien mon faible génie de compositeur et d'artiste, mais il me fesait vivre modestement. C'était peu de chose, mais si je n'avais pas de leçons, ce qui m'arrive souvent, j'étais assuré de ne pas manque du nécessaire. eh bien, mon cher ami, cet emploi je ne l'ai plus. il a été supprimé depuis longtemps, c'est à dire depuis trois, ou quatre mois j'avais été prévenu vaguement; Cependant je ne croyais pas la chose sérieuse et j'étais fondé de croire que si elle avais lieu on m'accorderait au moins un dédommagement. enfin le moment est arrivé, on ne m'a pas dit: allez-vous en! Mais l'emploi n'existait plus.'

That little job was not problem-free. As he writes in this first letter to be found, Coste only worked at this job for three years to make a living, out of sheer necessity, because he had an insufficient number of pupils. But if this job is eliminated, he will be without income, so he asks for another job:

That is why I asked to be transferred to another department. They told me the rules prohibit appointing a man of my age, a matter in which they are very strict. This really appalled me, I turned my back on the person who gave me this answer and made my way out of there, regretting having made such a humiliating misstep. You understand, my dear Degen, that I had to suffer, impressionable and sensitive as I am.[558]

Here for the first time, from Coste's own words, something can be said upon his Romantic personality. He indicates that he is very sensible, having a modest impression of his talent, but does not accept any injustice done to him. And this job troubles him, but to his great regret he cannot quit it, as appears later. This lowly bureaucratic post stands in stark contrast to Coste's fame, which is of international proportions. The Russian nobleman Nicolai de Makaroff went to Paris to meet Coste as early as 1851, and now he is visited by Søffren Degen from Denmark too. Both are of great importance to Coste's music.

DEGEN 1855

Søffren Degen (1816-1885) comes from Copenhagen and is specialized in the new technique of daguerreotypes. He is performing as an actor in theatre groups and as a cellist in a group of musicians, and he is becoming Denmark's most important guitarist halfway through the 19th century.[559] He is so interested in the instrument that he is looking for a guitar with a deeper sound, despite the fact that the instrument was on the decline in Copenhagen, losing ground to the new symbol of status for the bourgeoisie, the piano. He finds this deeper sound in his 'invention' of the heptacorde guitar, for which he applies for a patent in 1845, with the intent to have it made by luthier Knudsen.[560] He is probably already informed about the Napoléon Coste's Lacôte guitar at this point, and he wants to put it on the market in Denmark under his own name, as the patent is based on his own blueprints.[561]

94 Søffren Degen

In his capacity as a photographer he asks for a grant in 1855 to travel to Paris and study the latest techniques. According to Erling Møldrup it is there that he meets Napoléon Coste and becomes his friend.[562] This must have given him the opportunity to make the first photograph of Coste currently known, an image discovered by Møldrup in the Kongelige Bibliotek in Copenhagen. In this picture he has Degen's heptacorde guitar in his hand.[563] On his journey back, as an admirer, Degen brings along all Coste's works printed by that time, as well as some transcripts of unpublished manuscripts.[564] These

---

[558] Coste-Degen, 15 VI 1858, Århus, Statsbiblioteket, Søffren Degens Papirer, Manuscript no.27b, p. 2-3: '[…] alors j'ai demandé à être emploié dans une autre partie du service. on m'a dit que les réglements s'opposent à l'admission d'un homme de mon âge on est bien sévère la-dessus. cela m'a révolté, j'ai tourné le dos à celui qui m'a fait cette réponse et je me suis sauvé en emportant le regret d'avoir fait une démarche humilliante. Vous comprendrez, mon cher Degen, ce que j'ai dû souffrir impressionnable et sensible comme je le suis.'

[559] Rischel, Thorvald: 'Bibliographische Notizen zu den Gitarrenwerken von Napoleon Coste', in: *Die Gitarre*, Berlijn, 1927, Jahrgang VIII, Heft 7/8, [Coste-Heft] p. 47.

[560] Møldrup, Erling: *Guitaren, et eksotisk instrument i den danske musik*, Copenhagen, Kontrapunkt, 1997, p. 125.

[561] Århus, Statsbiblioteket, drawing: *Degen Heptachord Guitar*, Søffren Degens Papirer, Manuscript no. 27b.

[562] Møldrup, Erling: *Guitaren, et eksotisk instrument i den danske musik*, Copenhagen, Kontrapunkt, 1997, p. 131.

[563] Kopenhavn, Kongelige Bibliotek, Portraetsamlingen, *Coste, Napoleon*,1806 [sic]-1883, guitarspiller, by Degen, 184295 (1939 nr.138). [see p. 135 and elaborated version on p. 251]

[564] Rischel, Thorvald: 'Bibliographische Notizen zu den Gitarrenwerken von Napoleon Coste', in: *Die Gitarre*, Berlin, 1927, Jahrgang VIII, Heft 7/8, [Coste-Heft] p. 47.

V — Souvenirs   133

are later found again in the Rischel & Birket-Smith collection. They are now part of the Kongelige Bibliotek in Copenhagen, digitized and accessible for all. Two letters are known from Coste to Degen, from the first in 1858 a personal image of Coste emerges. The Dane seems to be a valuable friend to Coste and his music. He writes second guitar parts for his *Rondeau de Concert* opus 12, *Le Passage des Alpes* opus 27, 28[a] & 40 and *La Source du Lyson* opus 47. These second guitar parts to Coste's works do not exhibit any convincing virtuosity. Coste dedicates his *Étude* 9 opus 38 and *Feuilles d'Automne* opus 41 to him. Neither of these works are particularly difficult, but they do display a certain virtuosity in rapid passages and a cadenza in high positions, and Coste, as a skillful and experienced teacher, knows his friend's capabilities very well.

Duet 1855

The next concert with Coste that can be found in the reviews up to this point takes place on Sunday, August 12, 1855. As only 32 concerts are traceable in his concert career running from 1829 through 1879 – one of which did not take place, another of which went unmentioned and many others of which took place in an intimate circle – it is important to pay attention to all of them. Apparent small details can nevertheless tell something about Coste's position in the Parisian musical world and the position of the guitar on the concert stage, where, according to the review of the 'Expositions Universelles' of 1855 the guitar is played in a very restricted musical circle.[565] This concert, newly discovered, is again one of the monthly meetings of the *Société académique des Enfants d'Apollon*. On August 26, 1855 an extensive review of this concert can be found in La France musicale. After mentioning the performances of Mme Farrenc in her Trio for piano, violin and cello, with MM Cuvillon and Lebouc, after which M. Casimir Ney joins the party as a violinist for a Mozart quartet, it is time for the guitar:

> *They also gave a great applause for a duet for two guitars, composed by M. Coste, performed by this capable artist and another artist whose name slips my memory, after which the former of these virtuosos performed a fantasy of his own composition which contained some charming elements, a stimulating and distinguishing harmony. This very difficult work, though performed by the composer with ease and suppleness, was much liked and received a lively applause.*[566]

Then come the other participants of the concert, along with other compositions by Mme Farrenc, the writer remarking that she is a female composer, which is extraordinary for those days. She is highly praised in this review. Coste s unnamed duet could be the *Scherzo et Pastorale* opus 10 of course, but that piece was already composed in 1841 and was possibly played in the concert of April 8, 1842 with his pupil Caroline Montigny.[567] It has not yet been possible to date Coste's two other duets, *Duetto* WoO 6 and the *Grand Duo* WoO 8, only one of which could have been performed in this concert. Bearing the word 'virtuosos' in mind, *Grand Duo* is much more likely because that work shows this characteristic much more than the *Duetto*. This conclusion seems to be justified, since according to the summary of these concerts in Decourcelle's publication, a *Concertino, andante, barcarolle* for two guitars by Coste is performed, exactly the parts that make up the *Grand Duo*![568] This allows us to date the work to 1855. Based on the description given in the review, the guitarist with whom Coste played remains a guess. Assuming that a virtuoso piece is played, it is not very likely that this guitarist is a pupil. Huerta is not in Paris that year. Zani de Ferranti and Legnani are, but they are so well known in the concert world that their name could not have be forgotten by the critic. It must be some unknown guitarist, apparently one

---

[565] *Revue et Gazette musicale de Paris*, vol. XXII, no. 32, 12 VIII 1855, p. 251: '[...] la guitare, instrument pincé dont le cercle musical est fort borrné [...]'.
[566] *La France musicale*, vol. XIX, no. 34, 26 VIII 1855, p. 267: 'On a aussi fort applaudi un duo pour deux guitares, de la composition de M. Coste, exécuté par cet habile professeur et un autre artiste, dont le nom m'échappe; puis le premier de ces virtuoses a fait entendre une fantaisie de sa composition qui renferme des choses charmantes, d'une harmonie piquante et distinguée. Ce morceau, fort difficile, mais que l'auteur exécute avec beaucoup d'aisance et de grace, a été fort goûté et vivement applaudi.'
[567] *La France musicale*, vol. V, no. 15, 17 IV 1842, p. 153: 'Dans un duo avec une de ses élèves [...]'.
[568] Decourcelle, Maurice: *La Société des Enfants d'Apollon (1741-1880): programmes des concerts annuels...*, Paris, Durand, 1881, p. 184: 'Concertino, andante, barcarolle pour deux guitares, composés par M. Coste, exécutés par MM. Coste et De la Richardière.'

with a name too difficult for a Frenchman to remember. If this is so, the Dane Søffren Degen comes to mind, who visits Paris in precisely this period and becomes friends with Coste. It is tempting to put Degen and Coste in this concert together, but this idea is disproven by the facts. Decourcelle mentions MM Coste and de la Richardière as performers, making the name of the second guitarist known. M. Bourgeois de la Richardière joins the society in 1852 and takes part in the monthly concert of April 1853 with a guitar solo. He might not be a professional guitarist, as amateurs also are admitted, and Coste dedicates his *Étude* no. 2 opus 38 to him later. Here he plays Coste's *Grand Duo* together with the composer. And then Coste himself plays, performing a difficult piece with great ease, which is both charming and stimulating, with interesting harmonies as well. The most recent composition with this title, which also meets these characteristics, is the *Fantaisie symphonique* opus 28[b], dedicated to Søffren Degen. For a composer of Coste's status it goes without saying that the program must include the performance of a new work. Nothing more can be said with certainty here.

In this chapter, many actual facts on Coste have come to light, many reflections on his works have led to a greater understanding of his compositions, a sketch has been drawn of the position of the guitar in the Parisian musical world. Coste appears to be developing into a capable guitarist and a prolific composer of high standard, as confirmed by the words written in his own time. His fame has grown internationally, and, above all, his work is going to be awarded.

V — *Souvenirs*

95 Napoléon Coste -Degen, c. 1855

VI
Grande Sérénade

In 1856 Monsieur de Makaroff, a Russian nobleman, opened a competition in Brussels in which all European guitarists were invited [...] J. Mertz from Vienna, who died after entering his works, had four votes for first prize, against three that were given to Nap. Coste from Paris for the second prize. Due to Mertz's death, Napoléon Coste is left as the only remaining prize-winner of this European competition.[569]

MEMOIRS

After Nicolai de Makaroff makes the acquaintance of Napoléon Coste in 1851 in Paris, he continues his travel through Europe, searching for guitarists, luthiers and composers who are also guitarists at the time. He gives account of this in his memoirs, which were published between 1859 and 1882 in different editions in the Russian language. They are a very subjective source of information on the world of the guitar halfway through the 19th century. Parts of these memoirs, which are important for the guitar, are published for the first time in 1910 in *Der Gitarrefreund*,[570] in a translation in German, with summaries and citations, and later in 1946 in *The Guitar Review* in a direct translation into English.[571] Matanya Ophee gives his opinion on these memoirs in 1982, with the addition of parts that were not translated until then, and he sheds a different light upon certain things.[572] From these sources an image can be given of the events that were of great importance to Coste, in particular his way of composing.

In his travel record Makaroff devotes a short paragraph to Coste, in contrast with the many long ones dedicated to Mertz, and he draws the conclusion that he had met many guitarists on his trip, of which just a few made a profound impression on him: Zani de Ferranti, Schulz, Ciebra and Mertz. Nevertheless, somewhat earlier he wrote that he had left London without making the acquaintance of Regondi and Ciebra, impressed as he was by Schulz. His memoirs have more inconsistencies, such as Stauffer living in Prague.[573] He somehow ordered guitars from Scherzer and Fischer, which he happily unpacks back in Russia. He does not like Fischer's guitar, but he finds Scherzer's ten-string guitar to be excellent. He is in continuous correspondence with Mertz. He has bought five of his compositions, which he takes along and studies. In his reflections on the journey it saddens him that he must draw the conclusion, despite his keen interest in the guitar, that the instrument has come to the end of its existence. He realizes that the pianoforte is being improved and developed, just as other, less important instruments. But no one seems to have any serious interest in improving the guitar, he complains, and he wonders if the guitar has really been lost forever. He thinks a competition can provide an important source of motivation, bringing progress in all sectors of human enterprise. In this way he gets the idea of holding a competition. With a sort of painful hope he embarks on this endeavor.

---

[569] Coste, Napoléon: 'Sérénade opus 30', in: Wynberg, Simon: *The Guitar Works of Napoleon Coste*, facsimile edition, Monaco, 1981, vol. IV, p. 51: 'En 1856 a été ouvert à Bruxelles par Mr. de Makaroff, noble Seigneur Russe, un concours auquel ont été conviés tous les guitaristes de l'Europe [...] J. Mertz de Vienne, mort depuis l'envoi de ses oeuvres, a obtenu 4 voix pour le premier prix contre 3 qui ont été données à Nap. Coste de Paris et lui ont valu le second prix. Par le fait du décès de Mertz, Napoléon Coste est donc resté l'unique lauréat de ce concours Européen.'

[570] Makarow (Stockmann) (Stockhausen?) 'Aus den Lebenserinnerungen des russischen Gitarrevirtuosen N. P. Makarow', in: *Der Gitarrefreund, Mitteilungen der Gitarristischen Vereinigung*, 11. Jahrgang 1910, Heft 6 p. 43-45; 12. Jahrgang, 1911 Heft 1 p. 1-3; Heft 2 p. 11-13; Heft 3 p. 23-25; Heft 4 p. 35-37; Heft 5 p. 45-47;.... [H. 6 fehlt im Bestand].

[571] Makaroff, Nikolai Petrovich de: 'The Memoirs of Makaroff', in: *The Guitar Review*, New York, The Society of the Classic Guitar, 1946-48, (vol. I reprint 1974/1975) no. 1, 1946, p. 10-12, no. 2, 1947, p. 32-34, no. 3, 1947, p. 56-59, no. 5, 1948, p. 109-113.

[572] Ophee, Matanya: 'The Memoirs of Makaroff, A Second Look', in: *Soundboard*, the journal of the Guitar Foundation of America, vol. IX, no. 3, 1982, p. 226-233.

[573] Makaroff, N. de: 'The Memoirs of Makaroff', in: *The Guitar Review*, no. 1, 1946, p. 10-12, no. 2 p. 56-59; Ophee, M.: 'The Memoirs of Makaroff, A Second Look', in: *Soundboard*, vol.IX, no. 3, 1982, p. 232.

COMPETITION

In March 1856 Makaroff writes the program for this competition: there are four prizes in two categories, for the two best compositions and for the two best guitars, preferably ten-stringed.[574] This would make it a real guitar competition, but without any audience or concerts. Out of the five criteria that the guitar composition must meet, which Makaroff includes in his memoirs, the first two are interesting enough to be mentioned here:

1. Guitar compositions must be original, or fantasies on known melodies. Their most important qualities must be originality and gracefulness of musical thought, above all the correct development and perfection of the musical idea. They also must show new ideas of style, taste and brilliant effects, in such a way that the composition in its entirety remains within the scope and means of the instrument. They also should reflect all musical possibilities and qualities possessed by the guitar.

2. Compositions must be written as a solo for the six- or ten-string guitar, or with the addition of an accompaniment by piano or string-quartet.[575]

The other three criteria concern the availability of the composer to perform his work, that a single composition can win two prizes, that preference will be given to works played during the competition and that it should also be possible for them to be played by the best artists.

Makaroff pays the prizes out of his own pocket, but he obtains ownership of the winning compositions, as he promises to take it upon himself in getting them published. He decides that the competition should take place in Brussels and sets a deadline of before October 1856 for entering both the compositions and the guitars. Now, half a year is quite a short period for such a thing, therefore the deadline is extended to December. Makaroff may have already shared his idea with others on his first trip through Europe in 1851, in spite of what he writes in his memoirs; in that case the composers and the luthiers have had ample opportunity to prepare themselves. The choice to make Brussels the venue can probably be attributed to the Crimean war, which was fought between Russia and Turkey from 1853 until 1856, and in which France, England and Austria were involved. Russia invades the Turkish territory around the Danube to liberate Istanbul, which, under the name Constantinople, is the cradle of the Russian orthodoxy. England and France do not accept a Russian domination of the Bosporus, and the Crimean war ensues.[576] Russia and France are in a state of war with each other, making the Belgian capital a neutral place for an international competition organized by a Russian nobleman.[577] Still, Coste does not intend to remain impartial in the case of the Crimean war. He writes a composition *Le Départ* opus 31, with as a second part 'Le Retour, Marche triomphale', but the work is too late to submit to the competition. The Russian nobleman would not have appreciated such an entry; as a retired soldier he must have been loyal to his country, the Russian fleet was destroyed, the country was humiliated internationally, and in Coste's composition the French troops make a glorious return on '29 Décembre 1855!...' as, significantly, is mentioned on *Le Retour*. The question arises why Coste sent the Russian a such politically sensitive piece. Or, perhaps the secretary of the jury, Schott, the editor, protected Coste by not giving the piece to Makaroff before it was too late. These hypotheses cannot be proven.

The Russian nobleman translates his regulations for the competition, and they are published in several French and German newspapers, or at least that is what he writes. He does not say which newspapers he means, and neither does he say why no English, Austrian and Belgian newspapers are included. On his journey through Europe he visits London, Vienna and Brussels, and he meets guitarists there, who have been deprived of this news. There is no mention whatsoever of this competition in

---

[574] Makaroff, N. de: 'The Memoirs of Makaroff', in: *The Guitar Review*, no. 5, 1948, p. 109-110.
[575] Makaroff, N. de: 'The Memoirs of Makaroff', in: *The Guitar Review*, no. 5, 1948, p. 110.
[576] Funekotter, Bart: 'Orlando Figes: De Krimoorlog', in: *NRC Handelsblad*, 17 XII 2010, Boeken, p. 3.
[577] Ophee, M.: 'The Memoirs of Makaroff, A Second Look', in: *Soundboard*, vol.IX, no. 3, 1982, p. 230.

VI — *Grande Sérénade* 139

96 Nicolai de Makaroff

music magazines in these months, apart from the *Revue et Gazette musicale de Paris*, which briefly announces the contest on June 29, 1856. There Makaroff is not mentioned by name. The news can be found in the 'Étranger' column and reads as follows:

> *Saint Petersburg. –A passionate lover of the guitar promises two prizes in the competition: one of 200 and one of 125 roubles, which will be given to the writer of the two best compositions for this instrument; separately from that, he promises two prizes of 200 and 125 roubles for two guitars, which, just like the compositions, must be delivered to the Russian delegation in Brussels before the 1st of November 1856.*[578]

This is a message so scant and late that Coste really had to have heard of the competition from another source to be able to participate in it. The *Observateur Belge* does not publish the information on this competition until October 28, 1856. *La Presse Belge* follows suit on the 29th, and by then Makaroff has already arrived in Brussels.[579] The assumption can be justified that Makaroff himself has informed the guitar composers and luthiers he had in mind beforehand in a letter on the competition and the regulations. He corresponds intensively with Mertz and Scherzer, for instance.

---

[578] *Revue et Gazette musicale de Paris*, vol. XXIII no. 26, 29 VI 1856, p. 210: 'Saint-Petersbourg. - Un amateur passionné de la guitare vient de mettre au concours deux prix: l'un de 200 et l'autre de 125 roubles d'argent, qui seront décernés à l'auteur des deux meilleurs compositions pour cet instrument; en outre, il a consacré deux autres prix, de 200 et 125 roubles pour deux guitares lesquelles devront être adressées, ainsi que les manuscrits, à la légation russe, à Bruxelles, avant le 1er novembre 1856.'

[579] *L' Observateur Belge*, Bruxelles, Coché-Mommens, 21e Année, no. 301, 28 X 1856: 'Concours ouvert par M. de Makaroff. [...]'; *La Presse Belge*, Journal politique, commercial et industriel, Bruxelles; 1e année, no. 221, merc. 29 X 1856: 'Concours ouvert [...].'

Brussels

On his journey to Brussels that year, Makaroff makes use of the opportunity to visit several guitarists in Aken, Fuldt, Wurzburg and Munich, before he settles into a 'very cozy apartment' in the Belgian capital. There he announces himself to Fétis, director of the conservatory, with the intention of giving the competition a platform at the highest musical standard. But Fétis has already voiced a rather low opinion of the guitar in the past. He turns Makaroff out, apart from being completely occupied with celebrating his 50th wedding anniversary, which involves major musical festivities.[580] The Russian nobleman's pride is hurt, so much so that he gives his opinion on Fétis in his memoirs in terms that cannot be misunderstood.[581] So he turns to the lesser gods, such as Damcke, whom he still knows from Saint Petersburg and who cordially invites him and introduces him to other teachers from the conservatory, including Servais, Léonard, Blaes, Bender, Kufferath, musicians who are going to take part in the jury of the competition. Strikingly, there is no luthier in this group to judge the instruments submitted.

Makaroff must have arrived in Brussels in September 1856, because according to the memoirs Damcke advised him to give a concert to introduce himself to the public. As he says himself, he does this on Sunday, September 23 at 1 o'clock in the afternoon in the Société Philharmonique in Brussels. Makaroff employs the Julian calendar, which is in use in Russia and is twelve days behind the Gregorian calendar used in Western Europe. So, all the dates he mentions in his memoirs must be converted for that period. To avoid any confusion with these two calendars, from now on in this book all dates are given in the Gregorian calendar. The concert takes place on October 5, and both of the above-mentioned Brussels newspapers announce it on October 3.[582] According to Makaroff it is attended by all music-lovers in Brussels. There are at least 400 people in the audience. Makaroff plays solo, without accompaniment – making it a real recital – on his ten-stringed Scherzer guitar, and he proudly reports that his guitar sounded so good that the people in the lobby, entering the hall, could not believe it was a guitar; instead, they thought what they heard was a piano. Then Makaroff writes that the audience became very enthusiastic when he played his *Mazurka* and *Carnaval de Venise*.[583] In these pieces he uses a special technique, which he developed himself and was unknown to all other guitarists, with the theme played on the bass strings and a fast trill played on the gut strings with four fingers. He is an enormous success, still on his own account, because when he finished he was surrounded by a number of people who cheered for him and shook his hand. At many people's request he repeats his Mazurka, and plays an encore, an unpublished work by Mertz, *Fantaisie Liebestrank*, which he regards as one of the most beautiful pieces ever written for guitar.[584] He has a great admiration for Mertz, but Makaroff also respects Coste and dedicates his *Étude Pensez à moi* opus 6 to him, probably written after his visit to Paris.[585]

He himself is showered in accolades in Brussels too, not only according to his memoirs, but also in the reviews. These appear in the Brussels newspapers *Le Guide musical* and *L'Écho de Bruxelles* and *Le Télégraphe* on October 9 and 14, respectively, with precisely the same wording in both publications:

---

[580] Ophee, M.: 'The Memoirs of Makaroff, A Second Look', in: *Soundboard*, vol.IX, no. 3, 1982, p. 232; Ophee, Matanya: 'Seltenes & Curioses für Guitarre' in: *Gitarre und Laute*, Köln, 1982, vol. III, no.5, p. 286.

[581] Makarow (Stockmann) 'Aus den Lebenserinnerungen des russischen Gitarrevirtuosen N. P. Makarow', in: *Der Gitarrefreund, Mitteilungen der Gitarristischen Vereinigung*, 11. Jahrgang 1910, 12. Jahrgang, 1911 Heft 5 p. 45; Ophee, M.: 'The Memoirs of Makaroff, A Second Look', in: *Soundboard*, vol.IX, no. 3, 1982, p. 227-228.

[582] Makaroff, N. de: 'The Memoirs of Makaroff', in: *The Guitar Review*, no. 5, 1948, p. 111 [wrong month]; Makarow: 'Aus den Lebenserinnerungen...', in: *Der Gitarrefreund*, 12. Jahrgang 1911, Heft 5 p. 45; *L'Observateur Belge*, Bruxelles, Coché-Mommens, 21ᵉ Année, no. 276, 3 X 1856: 'M. de Makaroff donnera, dimanche prochain, 5 octobre, à une heure de relevée, dans la salle de la Société Philharmonique, une matinée musicale.'; *La Presse Belge*, Journal politique, commercial et industriel, Bruxelles; 1ᵉ année, no. 195, 3 X 1856; no. 221: 'M. de Makaroff donnera [...].'

[583] Kk Rischel 511 mu 6703.1982 U48 Makaroff, *Carnaval de Venise* op. 4.

[584] Makaroff, N. de: 'The Memoirs of Makaroff', in: *The Guitar Review*, no. 5, 1948, p. 111; Makarow: 'Aus den Lebenserinnerungen...', in: *Der Gitarrefreund*, 12. Jahrgang 1911 Heft 5 p. 46.

[585] Kk Rischel Ms. 138 mu 6710.1189 Makaroff, *Pensez à moi...* op. 6.

The guitar is such a deserted, forgotten instrument, one speaks of it as an imaginary thing, or even as a childhood memory; [...] When one has seen the instrument M. de Makaroff uses, and without knowing that it was really a guitar, one wouldn't have guessed so. From the very first notes one could see the surprise on the faces of the audience, but this surprise soon changed into the enchantment of listening to sounds so soft, so velvety, so pure, that M. de Makaroff produces on his instrument. [...] M. de Makaroff shines not only in his admirable performance, but also in his compositions, the results of an excellent education. His Mazurka is admirable in its melody and enthusiasm, and his Carnaval can compete in originality with the best pieces written in the genre.[586]

Then the competition is mentioned in the last two newspapers. After they mention the prizes, Makaroff is praised for his great generosity as a patron of the arts. The review comes from *Le Guide musical*, a magazine also published in Paris by Schott-frères, from the great German publisher's office in Brussels, guided by Peter Schott, who also is the secretary of the competition. The question arises to what extent this review is colored by this fact. This aside, the competition is not mentioned in this magazine as it is in the other two.

One of the members of the audience is M. Adan, a guitar music enthusiast, according to Makaroff, and an associate of the Belgian minister of finance. He is the person to whom Coste dedicates his opus 31 *Le Départ*, the dedication to which says that this gentleman is general director of the estate of the Kingdom of Belgium, and also *Étude* no. 23 opus 38. Coste must have made his acquaintance during his visit to Brussels on the occasion of the competition. And should it be the case that Coste has had a sense of humor here, he has used the very same technique in this *Étude* Makaroff claimed to have invented, from the beginning to the very end, a technique that might allude to counting money, which employs the same finger movement. If so, this is a nod to Adan as well as to Makaroff, but this aside, it is by no means certain. Makaroff's *Carnaval de Venise*, with the above-mentioned passage, is published by Matanya Ophee, along with his article, together with an explanation and more news on the concert.[587] The piece also can be found digitally in the Rischel & Birket-Smith collection in the Kongelige Bibliotek in Copenhagen.[588]

97 Henri Adan

---

[586] *Le Guide musical*, 2ᵉ Année, 9 Octobre 1856, no. 32: 'La guitare est tellement délaissée, oubliée, que l'on n'en parle que comme d'un objet imaginaire, ou bien comme d'un souvenir d'enfance; [...] Si l'on n'avait vu l'instrument dont se sert M. de Makaroff, si l'on n'eût su que c'était bien une guitare, certes on ne l'aurait pas deviné. Aux premières notes, on a vu l'étonnement se peindre sur toutes les figures; mais cet étonnement a bien vite fait place au charme d'entendre des sons aussi moëlleux, aussi veloutés, aussi purs que ceux que M. de Makaroff tire de son instrument. [...] M. de Makaroff ne brille pas seulement par une exécution merveilleuse mais encore par ses compositions, fruits d'excellentes études. Sa *Mazurka* est admirable de mélodie et de verve, et son *Carnaval* peut rivaliser d'originalité avec ce que l'on a composé de mieux dans ce genre.'; *L'Echo de Bruxelles*, Bruxelles, XVe Année, 14 X 1856, no. 288: 'On lit dans le *Guide musical* de Paris:[sic]'; *Le Télégraphe*, Bruxelles, 3ᵉ Année, 14 X 1856 no. 288: 'On lit dans le *Guide musical* de Paris: [sic]'.

[587] Ophee, Matanya: 'Seltenes & Curioses für Guitarre' in: *Gitarre und Laute*, Köln, 1982, vol. III, no.5, p. 286-293.

[588] https://rex.kb.dk/primo-explore/fulldisplay?vid=NUI&search_scope=KGL&docid=MUS01000069167

Jury

Soon after Makaroff's concert the competition begins. The members of the jury are:

98 Valentin Bender

Valentin Bender (1801-1873); he studies the clarinet in Worms before becoming the solo clarinet player in the Dutch army in 1819. Then he goes to Paris in 1823, ends up in the war against Spain and goes to Belgium after the revolution of 1830 to become the conductor of the *Partikuliere Muziekkapel* of King Leopold I, as well as director of the *Société Philharmonique*.[589]

99 Joseph Blaes

Joseph Blaes (1814-1892), a virtuoso clarinet player, studies at the conservatoire of Brussels before travelling through Europe. As a soloist he visits London, St. Petersburg and Moscow. He earns an honorary medal at the Société des Concerts in Paris in 1839. He performs with Liszt and Rubinstein and is appointed as a teacher at the conservatoire of Brussels in 1844.[590]

---

[589] Fétis, François Joseph: *Biographie universelle des musiciens et bibliographie générale de la musique*, Paris, Firmin-Didot, 2me éd. 1860-1881, tome 1, p. 338; http://nl.wikipedia.org/wiki/Jean-Valentin_Bender.

[590] Fétis, François Joseph: *Biographie universelle des musiciens et bibliographie générale de la musique*, Paris, Firmin-Didot, 2me éd. 1860-1881, tome 1, p. 431; Weston, Pamela: 'Blaes, Arnold Joseph' in: Sadie, Stanley, ed.: *The New Grove Dictionary of Music and Musicians*, London, Macmillan, 1980, vol. 2, p. 772; id. in: Sadie, Stanley, ed.:*The New Grove Dictionary of Music and Musicians*, second edition, London, Macmillan, 2001, vol. 2, p. 670.

VI — *Grande Sérénade* 143

Bertold Damcke (1812-1875); organ player, conductor and composer. In 1845 he is in St. Petersburg at the performance of Berlioz's *Symphonie fantastique,* and he may have met Makaroff on this occasion. In 1853 he resides in Brussels, marries Servais's sister and in 1859 he finally settles in Paris, where he organizes musical performances at his home, with Kreutzer, Liszt and Berlioz. He publishes articles in the *Revue et Gazette musicale de Paris* on a regular basis.[591]

100 Bertold Damcke

Hubert Kufferath (1818-1896), violinist, pianist, conductor and composer, comes from a family of musicians. He studies piano and composition with Mendelssohn and after a life as a travelling virtuoso he settles in Brussels in 1844 as a piano teacher and composer. There he starts a series of chamber music concerts, together with Léonard and Servais and his home becomes a meeting point for Wieniawski, Bériot and Clara Schumann. In 1872 he becomes a teacher in counterpoint and fugue at the conservatoire in Brussels.[592]

101 Hubert Kufferath

---

[591] Kocevar, É. & J.-M. Fauquet: 'Damcke, Bertold' in: Fauquet, Joël-Marie: *Dictionnaire de la Musique en France au XIXe siècle*, Paris, Fayard, 2003, p. 343

[592] Fétis, François Joseph: *Biographie universelle des musiciens et bibliographie générale de la musique*, Paris, Firmin-Didot, 2me éd. 1860-1881, tome 5, p. 125-126; Riessauw, Anne-Marie: 'Hubert-Ferdinand Kufferath' in : Sadie, Stanley, ed.: *The New Grove Dictionary of Music and Musicians*, London, Macmillan, 1980, vol. 10, p. 292; id. in: Sadie, Stanley, ed.:*The New Grove Dictionary of Music and Musicians*, second edition, London, Macmillan, 2001, vol. 14, p. 1-2.

102 Hubert Léonard

Hubert Léonard (1819-1890); violinist and composer. In the 1830s he studies with Habeneck in Paris. He plays in the orchestra of the Opéra and the Opéra-Comique, before going to Brussels in 1849. There he becomes the successor of Charles de Bériot in 1853 as a teacher at the conservatoire of Brussels. In 1866 he finally goes to Paris, where he is active as a teacher, a soloist and a chamber musician.[593]

103 Adrien Servais

Adrien François Servais (1807-1866); he is the famous violoncellist who plays the Stradivarius that is still known as the 'Servais'-cello. His first great success in 1834 in Paris is followed by concerts in London. Then he travels through Europe to Russia, where he often plays his own compositions. In 1848 he becomes a teacher at the conservatoire of Brussels.[594]

Peter Schott, the secretary of the jury, is the director of the branch of the German publishing-house Schott, first in Antwerp, then from 1843 on, in Brussels. Since 1740 the company is based in Mainz, but there are also branches in Paris (1826), London (1835) and Leipzig (c.1840).[595]

---

[593] Penesco, A.: 'Léonard, Hubert' in: Fauquet, Joël-Marie: *Dictionnaire de la Musique en France au XIXe siècle*, Paris, Fayard, 2003, p. 688.

[594] Peire, Patrick: 'Adrien François Servais' in: Sadie, Stanley, ed.: *The New Grove Dictionary of Music and Musicians*, London, Macmillan, 1980, vol. 17, p. 188; Mailly, Edouard: *Les origines du conservatoire royal de musique de Bruxelles*, Bruxelles, Hayez, 1879, p. 3-11.

[595] Müller, Hans-Christian: 'Schott', in: Sadie, Stanley, ed.: *The New Grove Dictionary of Music and Musicians*, second edition, London, Macmillan, 2001, vol. 22, p. 633-634; http://www.schott-musik.de/about/profil/index.html.

VI — Grande Sérénade   145

In the beginning of October, after Makaroff's concert, who permits himself an lavish lifestyle, this prominent party is invited for a luxurious twelve-course dinner at the Dubost restaurant, with oysters, accompanied with two bottles of Chablis, turtle soup, lobster, fish, along with twelve bottles of champagne, game with six bottles of Bordeaux, and a dessert served with coffee and liqueurs. Monsieur de Makaroff and the gentlemen musicians enjoy the meal exceedingly, a point which he emphasizes in his memoirs. 'And how much do you think this complete luxury cost me? Only 149 francs!', he says frankly. For comparison, the hall for his concert cost a mere 21 francs to rent, and to make the proportionate cost clear, the first prize for best composition is 800 francs, while the second prize is 500 francs.[596] Makaroff is also very frank in his opinion on guitars and guitarists, as well as on his expenses and his gastronomical pleasures. Not only does this produce an interesting picture of the situation concerning the guitar and guitarists of that time, but also of the circumstances he wanted to be engaged in. Writing about the dinner, he mentions nine people, and assuming that he has not made a mistake and that the translation is correct, couldn't it be that M. Adan is the ninth person? He was already quite visible at the concert, having written a composition entitled *Rondo*, dedicated to Makaroff. Anyhow, the Brussels musicians must have been in favor of being a member of the jury for the contest, after having enjoyed the copious initial dinner to which they were invited.

The first session of the jury meeting takes place on October 16, where Makaroff is chosen to be chairman. Compositions and guitars arrive on a daily basis at secretary Schott's address at his publishing house, a total of around sixty compositions by thirty competitors. Makaroff has brought four of Mertz's compositions from St. Petersburg, which were sent to him there. In accordance with the regulations of the competition, the closing date is set to December 1, but the date is later extended to December 10.[597] The matter of this date leads one to surmise that at least Mertz was informed before about the coming competition. Makaroff writes the regulations in March and leaves St. Petersburg in July, with the four compositions by Mertz. That leaves him with just a few weeks to write 23 pages of music, being in bad health, on top of that. Apart from this, the composers must have been informed about the criteria the compositions needed to meet with regards to content, and these rules are not published anywhere. Makaroff must have approached them personally, despite of what he says in his memoirs.

In the meantime, Makaroff stays occupied receiving visitors, including guitarist Szczepanowski, who according to Makaroff plays to empty halls and is now boasting about himself. He shows Szczepanowski the door with the remark that there 'are only two guitarists, Zani de Ferranti and Schulz, who far surpass all other guitarists alive, including you and me.'[598] Makaroff corresponds with Mertz, until he receives a card from his widow informing him that the composer has deceased, which grieves him very much, because of his friendship and esteem. He organizes a musical evening with Damcke and Servais in his apartment, where he is very successful with the ladies in attendance, playing his *Carnaval de Venise* on his guitar. Composer Yradier also comes to visit him, for whom he plays Mertz's *Montecchi* fantasie, after which this composer gives up working on his own composition on this theme; he cannot compete with such a beautiful work anymore.[599] Ciebra and Coste also come to Brussels on the occasion of the contest; the regulations say the jury will prefer works that are played for them by a guitarist, who can be the composer himself.[600] In this connection, Makaroff writes that Coste had brought four compositions, but he does not mention the date Coste arrived. This must have been before the closing date for entering compositions in the competition, and in this way the question arises as to why Coste did not submit the fifth composition, *Le Départ* opus 31, at the time. Had he not finished it yet, then, or was it politically incorrect to do so due to the Crimean war? Makaroff does speak a lot about Ciebra, coming from Sevilla, who has already been working in Paris and London for

---

[596] Makaroff, N. de : 'The Memoirs of Makaroff', in: *The Guitar Review*, no. 5, 1948, p. 110-111.
[597] Makarow: 'Aus den Lebenserinnerungen...', in: *Der Gitarrefreund*, 12. Jahrgang, 1911 Heft 5 p. 46.
[598] Makarow: 'Aus den Lebenserinnerungen...', in: *Der Gitarrefreund*, 12. Jahrgang, 1911 Heft 5 p. 47; Ophee, M.: 'The Memoirs of Makaroff, A Second Look', in: *Soundboard*, vol.IX, no. 3, 1982, p. 228.
[599] Makaroff, N. de: 'The Memoirs of Makaroff', in: *The Guitar Review*, no. 5, 1948, p. 111-112.
[600] Makaroff, N. de: 'The Memoirs of Makaroff', in: *The Guitar Review*, no. 5, 1948, p. 110.

years. Makaroff considers him to be a mediocre composer, but also a remarkable player, who holds his right hand in an oblique position and who does not strike the strings with his very long nails, but rather pushes against them, resulting in a deep, tuneful sound. He also has a 'celestial vibrato'. But this way of playing has its downside, says Makaroff: in fast passages the sound becomes unpleasantly harsh. This style of playing is clearly in conformity with the flamenco style today; the oblique position of the right hand confirms this.[601] Makaroff is very specific in the report of his experience in Brussels.

Deliberations

And then the competition is held, on Wednesday, December 10, 1856. Makaroff writes how the great day of allocating the prizes finally came. At 8 o'clock in the evening the members of the jury all come to his apartment. He opens the meeting. After deliberations a decision is made to vote. Only 40 of the 64 compositions are regarded as worthy of being admitted to the competition. Out of these 40, the following compositions are considered prize-worthy:

Four compositions by Mertz.
Four compositions by Coste.
Two compositions by Komarny.
One composition by Kühnel.

104 J. K. Mertz?

This comes to a total of eleven compositions. Before the contest began, the Russian had said he would not regard Mertz's death as an obstacle for admitting his compositions to the competition, and in case one of those won, the prize awarded would be sent to his widow.[602] This proposal leads one to believe that Makaroff had originally written in the regulations that the jury's preference should be given to works played by the composer. In his memoirs he later added that a work could also be played by someone else, otherwise he would not have been obliged to discuss this unforeseen circumstance with the members of the jury. Coste and Ciebra make a point of rushing to Brussels to present their own works. A different matter in the regulations goes unmentioned: Coste's compositions are intended to be played on the heptacorde, the seven-string Lacôte instrument, and in some cases this special type of guitar is the only instrument on which they can be played. These works can also be played on the ten-string guitar that Makaroff specifically mentions in the regulations, of course, but strictly speaking, the jury must have turned a blind eye on this matter. This may have also been an argument for awarding the first prize to Mertz.

After this, Makaroff describes in his memoirs a development he calls the 'intrigue', and the fact that he avoids mentioning the intriguer's name draws all the more attention to this person's identity, leading to a little detective story. Matanya Ophee and Astrid Stempnik discuss both this matter and Makaroff's relation to Fétis.[603] Makaroff first takes the reader back to the dinner with the members of the jury. At the end of the meal, Fétis's name was mentioned, upon which the Russian nobleman reacted with some strong expressions, as if he had been bitten by a viper. Servais and Blaes were not disturbed at all. Makaroff, who took part in the chamber concert at his home, already knew Damcke's serious disdain for the director. Bender and Kufferath aren't teachers at the conservatory, so they don't have a relation

---

[601] Bone, Philip J.: 'Ciebra, Jose Marie de', in: *The Guitar and the Mandolin*, London, Schott, 2nd ed, 1954, reprint 1972, p. 79; Makaroff, N. de: 'The Memoirs of Makaroff', in: *The Guitar Review*, no. 5, 1948, p. 112.
[602] Makaroff, N. de: 'The Memoirs of Makaroff', in: *The Guitar Review*, no. 5, 1948, p. 112-113.
[603] Ophee, M.: 'The Memoirs of Makaroff, A Second Look', in: *Soundboard*, vol.IX, no. 3, 1982, p. 232; Ophee, Matanya: 'Seltenes & Curioses für Guitarre' in: *Gitarre und Laute*, Köln, 1982, vol. III, no.5, p. 286; Stempnik, Astrid: *Caspar Joseph Mertz, Leben und Werk...*, Frankfurt am Main, Lang, 1990, p. 375-376.

VI — Grande Sérénade

of dependence on Fétis. In this way, Léonard, the youngest member of the group, is the only left who could have played the role of intriguer, if there really is one at all, to make objections to Makaroff's opinion and the result of the competition twice, to Makaroff's great displeasure. Makaroff writes that, in considering the selection of compositions that were worthy for consideration, he proposed awarding the first prize to Mertz's *Concertino*, and the second prize to Coste's *Sérénade* opus 30.[604]

Makaroff's mind is already made up before the works are taken into consideration, and he influences the jury in his direction. But then the intriguer raises an objection: while Mertz's compositions may be clearly superior to all the others as far as inspiration and transparency are concerned, they contain mistakes, such as an incorrect resolution of the seventh, in the Maestoso of the *Concertino* measure 35,

105 Concertino Mertz m. 35

where a diminished seventh chord on the seventh degree of the key of C is notated with a g-sharp instead of an a-flat.[605] In defense, Makaroff says this has no influence on the sound, and that moreover it occurs many times in guitar music. But then the intriguer tries again. He poses the question whether Makaroff would object if Mertz took second prize. Now Makaroff cannot defend his opinion and reluctantly says he would accept this. Then they vote. Schott provides seven slips of paper on which the members of the jury, including Makaroff, will jot down two names, one for first prize and one for second prize. Makaroff sketches his relief on the result: for first prize there are four votes for Mertz, three for Coste, and for the second prize there are four votes for Coste, two for Kühnel and one for Komarny.[606] Makaroff can be satisfied, as the result conforms to his proposal. He immediately sends a messenger to Coste, asking him to come with his guitar, because the jury wanted to hear his compositions to decide which one was best to receive the prize. Coste comes immediately, his face beaming with joy. He begins to kiss Makaroff, to embrace him and says he thinks he is receiving the greatest honor in be awarded second prize after Mertz, the greatest guitar composer of that time. The Russian introduces him to the members of the jury, and after many congratulations he plays his compositions. His *Sérénade* is recognized as the best.[607] So, Makaroff has already met Coste in Brussels and knows where he is staying. The messenger in question could have been Adan, of course, who had met both Makaroff and Coste. Coste's reaction seems very exaggerated in this description. His personal letters show a very distinguished man who behaved very correctly in social settings. Kissing and embracing do not fit this picture, but Makaroff has the tendency to lose all sense of proportion. In 1867 Coste writes to Schult about the results:

> *When after the decision of the jury I was summoned to him to play my compositions, Servais shook my hand and told me this: 'You deserved first prize, and I voted for you.' Kuffrat and Léonard told me the same thing. Of the four or five pieces submitted by Mertz only one remained in the running. The others were*

---

[604] Ophee, M.: 'The Memoirs of Makaroff, A Second Look', in: *Soundboard*, vol.IX, no. 3, 1982, p. 229.
[605] Ophee, M.: 'The Memoirs of Makaroff, A Second Look', in: *Soundboard*, vol.IX, no. 3, 1982, p. 231; Mertz, Johann Kaspar: *Guitar Works, Concertino*, ed. Simon Wynberg, Monaco, Chanterelle, 1982, vol. I, p. 3.
[606] Makaroff, N. de: 'The Memoirs of Makaroff', in: *The Guitar Review*, no. 5, 1948, p. 113; Ophee, M.: 'The Memoirs of Makaroff, A Second Look', in: *Soundboard*, vol.IX, no. 3, 1982, p. 229.
[607] Makaroff, N. de: 'The Memoirs of Makaroff', in: *The Guitar Review*, no. 5, 1948, p. 113.

eliminated for being too weak. I had four of them that remained in the running and were judged by the three main members of the jury to be superior. But there were seven of them.[608]

It is certain that Coste played *Grande Sérénade* opus 30 on this occasion, but the second work remains a guess. Also he writes that only one of Mertz's compositions remained in the running for a prize. When Coste finishes playing, the jury turns its attention to the seven guitars entered in the contest, and Makaroff plays some easy chords on them. The guitars from Scherzer and Argusen [Arhusen?] emerge as the best, without debate, so first and second prize are awarded to them. Makaroff buys both instruments with a bonus and rewards the jury with two pounds of tea each, following the Russian tradition. The next morning he sends 800 fr. to Mertz's widow and a comparable amount to Scherzer. On his way back to Russia he brings along the manuscripts of the compositions, according to Ophee.[609] He has to, as he already indicated in point three of the regulations that he will publish them.[610] Coste returns to Paris with his guitar, probably by train, according to the timetable, from the Brussels station des Bogards.[611]

Press

On Saturday, December 20, 1856 *L'Observateur Belge* reports the results of the competition, including some specific details:

> *The competition for guitars and compositions for this instrument, which was set up by M. Makaroff in our city, took place on the 10th of this month. The jury [...] assembled last night [...] to give its verdict [...]. The first prize has been awarded to the composition entitled Concertino in la by J. K. Mertz, from Vienna. Second prize goes to the piece named Grande Sérénade, op. 30, composed by Nap. Coste, from Paris. [...] Thereupon M. Coste, one of the prize winners who came from Paris, performed some of the competitors' compositions, including the winning Sérénade. M. Makaroff also played some of Mertz's works. This performance completely justified the jury's excellent approval.*[612]

Now it appears that there has been another session with Makaroff, the jury and Coste, apart from December 10, in which Coste and Makaroff both played, unless the critic was making a correction to the date when publishing it in the newspaper. Exactly the same notice appears in *La Presse Belge* on December 21.[613] On January 4, 1857 this report also emerges in the *Revue et Gazette musicale de Paris*, in addition to a letter sent to the magazine by Makaroff. There he writes Mertz's obituary, praises his music highly, even more highly than Giuliani's: a noble, great style, full of originality, with new brilliant effects, the expression of a thorough knowledge of music, accompanied by extraordinary taste, an indefatigable enthusiasm and finally all the things that charm and enthrall the listener, without ever being boring. As an owner of some of his manuscripts he says he will publish those to support his widow, though he never actually does.[614] And not a word about Coste. This is different from *Le*

---

[608] Coste-Schult, 7 X 1867: 'Lorsque, après la décision du jury, je fus appelé devant lui pour faire entendre mes compositions, Servais me tendit la main et me dit ceci: "vous avez mérité le premier prix et je vous ai donné ma voix". Kuffrat et Léonard m'en dirent autant. En effet des 4 ou 5 morceaux présentés par Mertz un seul est resté au concours, les autres furent écartés comme trop faibles, J'en avais 4 qui sont restés et jugés supérieurs par les trois principaux membres du jury. Mais ils étaient sept.'

[609] Ophee, M.: 'The Memoirs of Makaroff, A Second Look', in: *Soundboard*, vol.IX, no. 3, 1982, p. 231.

[610] *L'Observateur Belge*, 21ᵉ Année, no. 301, 28 X 1856: '3. M. de Makaroff fera publier, immédiatement après le concours, les manuscrits qui auront été couronnés.'

[611] *L'Observateur Belge*, Bruxelles, Coché-Mommens, 21ᵉ Année, no. 340, 4 XII 1856: 'Chemins de fer - Départs. Station des Bogards. Pour Paris 8-15 m. x. 1ᵉ et 2ᵉ cl. 2 h. x. 1ᵉ cl. 7 soir, 1ᵉ et 2ᵉ cl.'

[612] *L'Observateur Belge*, Bruxelles, Coché-Mommens, 21ᵉ Année, no. 355, 20 XII 1856: 'Le concours de guitares et de compositions pour cet instrument, institué dans notre ville par M. de Makaroff, a eu lieu le 10 de ce mois. Le jury [...] s'est réuni hier soir pour se prononcer [...] Le premier prix a été décerné à la composition intitulée: *Concertino en la*, de J.K. Mertz, de Vienne. Le second prix à celle intitulée: *Grande sérénade*, op. 30, composée par Nap. Coste, de Paris. [...] M. Coste, l'un des lauréats dus concours, qui était venu de Paris, a fait entendre ensuite quelques-unes des compositions des concurrents, et entre autres la *Sérénade* couronnée. M. de Makaroff a également joué quelques-unes des oeuvres de M. Mertz. Cette audition a pleinement justifié l'excellente appréciation du jury.'

[613] *La Presse Belge*, Bruxelles; 1ᵉ année, no. 274, 21 XII 1856: 'Le concours [...] appréciation du jury.'

[614] *Revue et Gazette musicale de Paris*, vol. XXIV, no. 1, 4 I 1857, p. 6-7: 'Guitare et Guitaristes. Concours Makaroff à Bruxelles.'

Ménestrel that same Sunday, in which J. Lovy joins in the choir of critics singing of the demise of the guitar:

> *The guitar has been dead, for a long time, alas! And yet the poor thing takes a fancy to resurrecting itself from time to time – as in a tragedy – to surprise the people. As in tragedy, the guitar has its kings, its confidants and its three unities of action, unity of sound, unity of grating the ears.*[615]

He continues with this metaphor for some time, disapproving of Makaroff's initiative, and he makes a rather morbid comparison:

It appears that the famous Austrian artist did not want to survive the guitar competition. Facing the opinion of the masses he preferred to die, rather than subjecting himself to applause. Sublime false shame![616]

M. Lovy does not have a high opinion of the instrument. Still, he makes an effort to produce a factual account of Coste winning second prize with his serenade, and in doing so, he casually calls him 'one of our distinguished musicians and composers'. 'Let us talk about the heroes of the Crimea now', he adds to this, concerning Makaroff playing the guitar. Apparently this war, in which Russia is involved, is still fresh in memory.[617] Not very elevating, in any case, and a sad end of the information that comes forward from contemporary sources, too.

Compositions

Coste's works for the competition are published by Girod, but not all of them. In the edition of opus 29 and opus 30, Coste and his editor take advantage of the honor bestowed on the composer, not only in mentioning this on the title page, but in a preface as well, with a short report on the competition. Due to Mertz's death, it proudly states that the conclusion can be made that Napoléon Coste is now the only laureate still alive in this European contest. Then the four compositions entered in the competition are listed, which are *Les Feuilles d'Automne* opus 27, *Fantaisie symphonique* opus 28[b], *La Chasse des Sylphes* opus 29 and *Grande Sérénade* opus 30, which took second prize. The report also says *Le Départ* opus 31 was submitted too late. In small type the promise is made to subsequently publish the works with Girod, but that did not happen with the *Fantaisie symphonique*.[618] In this way, using a source other than Makaroff's memoirs it can be deduced which works are concerned here, but this is not so easy. There is a work called *Feuilles d'Automne* by Coste, opus 41, dedicated to Søffren Degen and published in 1876, which consists of twelve easy waltzes and which in no way could have been seriously considered for entry in this competition, despite the fact that the title page says so. As if the matter weren't already confusing enough, it is also noted that most of the work is included in the trilogy entitled *Le Passage des Alpes* opus 27, 28 and 40. But this is the first key to unravelling the puzzle. Not a single note in opus 41 has even the slightest resemblance to those in the trilogy, as Simon Wynberg rightly remarks.[619] According to him, the publication of *Le Passage des Alpes* can be dated between 1862 and 1866, so it is plausible to assume Coste renamed *Les Feuilles d'Automne* later, after the competition. But were there three parts at that time? The second key to the riddle can be found in the music itself. The first part, *Maestoso*, is almost identical to the first part of *Deuxième Polonaise* opus 14. Coste may have used this piece on this occasion. It wasn't published yet, but on its own it has a total

---

[615] *Le Ménestrel*, vol. XIV, no. 5, 4 I 1857, p. [3]: 'Il y a longtemps que la guitare est morte, hélas! Et pourtant la pauvrette s'amuse à ressusciter de temps en temps, - comme la Tragédie, - pour ébahir les populations. Comme la tragédie, la guitare a ses rois, ses confidents et ses trois unités, - unité d'action, unité de son, unité de grincement.'

[616] *Le Ménestrel*, vol. XIV, no. 5, 4 I 1857, p. [3]: 'Il paraît que le célèbre artiste autrichien n'a pas voulu survivre à la réalisation d'un concours de guitare. En présence de l'attitude des masses, il a mieux aimé se laisser mourir que de subir son ovation. Sublime fausse-honte!'

[617] *Le Ménestrel*, vol. XIV, no. 5, 4 I 1857, p. [3]: '[...] l'un de nos musiciens et compositeurs distingués. [...] Que l'on vienne après cela nous parler des héros de Crimée!'

[618] Wynberg, Simon: *The Guitar Works of Napoleon Coste*, facsimile edition, Monaco, 1981, vol. IV, p. 33, *La Chasse des Sylphes*; p. 35, 'En 1856 a été ouvert [...] concours'; p. 49, *Sérénade*; p. 51 'En 1856 a été ouvert [...] concours'.

[619] Wynberg, Simon: *The Guitar Works of Napoleon Coste*, facsimile edition, Monaco, 1981, vol. IV, Introduction.

of 61 measures, which is a bit short compared to the other compositions he entered, which have 150 (opus 31) up to 567 (opus 29) measures. It is most likely that he added the 33 measures from *Le Passage des Alpes*, which end in an open closure on the dominant D7 of the key of G, in which the *Marche* opus 28 begins, which suits it perfectly. This part again is almost identical to the unpublished *Marche triumphale* opus 26, which was waiting, so to speak, to be added to *Les Feuilles d'Automne* in question, to make a total of 193 measures, sufficient to be entered in the competition in terms of both quantity and quality. If all this is correct, it may be that the *Rondo* opus 40 has been added to the composition, which is published with a new name. The higher opus number also points in this direction. All other titles of the works that were entered in the contest are published with their original titles by Girod, 16 Boulevard Montmartre, established there since 1853.

As has been said, out of a total of 64 works by 31 composers the jury selected eleven compositions by four composers to be judged for prizes. This means that 53 pieces by 27 creative artists were not selected. Now the question arises who they were. First of all the guitarists Makaroff met on his first journey through the world of the guitar in 1851 can be examined. These are:[620]

Kamberger, who is famous on the banks of the Rhine. Makaroff thinks he plays powerfully, enthusiastically and with a good technique, but, like all German guitarists, without sensitivity, sufficient clarity and perfection;

Zani de Ferranti in Brussels, who he thinks plays tastefully, with a rich sound and full of expression, the likes of which Makaroff has never heard. He holds him in high esteem;

Schulz in London, who, according to Makaroff's description, plays with extraordinary speed and clearness, powerfully, with sweet plucking, brilliance and expression. He buys fifteen of his compositions;

Carcassi in Paris, who is known in Russia for his easy, 'scanty' musical compositions;

Coste in Paris, the intelligent and friendly Frenchman, who plays with great clarity and sensitivity, sublime clarity of tone, but who is not able to captivate the listener. Like Mertz, Coste made it onto the shortlist of composers to be considered for a prize;

Mertz in Vienna, whom Makaroff regards as the best guitarist in Germany. He plays with power, energy, feeling, clarity and expression, but with the shortcomings of the German school, with buzzing basses and smothered rapid passages.

Makaroff is even more impressed by his compositions, a number of which he buys in manuscript form and which stand in contrast to modern composers lacking talent, such as, according to him, Padovetz, Carcassi, Bobrovich, Bayer, Soussman, Küffner, Pettol (Pettoletti?), etc. whom he mentions in his memoirs. On his second journey in 1856 there are some more guitarists:[621]

Jansen and Fischer, whom he meets in Aachen, the latter of whom exhibits all the characteristics of German guitar technique, fast and powerful indeed, but without clarity, articulation or softness;

Rilling in Fulda, Brand in Wurzburg and Franz in München, three German guitarists whom he just mentions and does not reflect on;

Szczepanowski, whom he meets in Brussels and who is so boastful of himself that Makaroff shows him the door before he has even played anything;

Ciebra, whom he also meets in Brussels. This guitarist plays his own compositions, which are not so good, in a Spanish way, with a very sensible, deep melodic tone and a beautiful vibrato, but sometimes with an unpleasantly metal-like timbre as well.

---

[620] Makaroff, N. de: 'The Memoirs of Makaroff', in: *The Guitar Review*, no. 2, 1947, p. 32-34; no. 3, p. 56-59; Makarow: 'Aus den Lebenserinnerungen...', in: *Der Gitarrefreund*, 12. Jahrgang, 1911 Heft 1, p. 1-2; Heft 2, p. 11; Heft 3, p. 24; Heft 4, p. 36-37.

[621] Makaroff, N. de: 'The Memoirs of Makaroff', in: *The Guitar Review*, no. 5, 1948, p. 110, 112; Makarow: 'Aus den Lebenserinnerungen...', in: *Der Gitarrefreund*, 12. Jahrgang, 1911 Heft 5, p. 46-47; Ophee, M.: 'The Memoirs of Makaroff, A Second Look', in: *Soundboard*, vol. IX, no. 3, 1982, p. 228, 232.

Considering the way that Makaroff wished to manipulate the jury's decision, many composers can be dropped from this list, regardless of whether they actually submitted a composition to the contest. Only Zani de Ferranti and Schulz remain, which restricts the question of participation to them. Makaroff bought Schulz's published compositions, and maybe some manuscripts too, which he possibly handed over to the jury, as he did with Mertz's works. But somehow they failed to pass the selection. But the more crucial question is why Zani de Ferranti did not enter this competition, which took place right in his own city of Brussels. Carcassi died in 1853, but Legnani and Diabelli also are renowned composers for the guitar. Did they not find the competition interesting enough, or did they perhaps not hear of it at all? Diabelli's attention is probably focused solely on his publishing house, and, being 75 years of age, he is also getting on in years. The same can be said of Legnani, who was also born in the 18th century and is now 66 years of age. A competition is of little importance so late in one's career. Regondi is still very active in London, playing the guitar as well as the concertina. It is a genuine possibility that he entered the competition, but if he did, his works did not pass the selection. Then, finally, the Spanish guitarists Makaroff did not visit may have had a shot at being honored with a prize in the contest: Huerta, Bosch and Arcas. There is no source saying they did. The question of whether Zani de Ferranti entered the competition is answered in the negative by his biographer, Marc Van de Cruys. As a reason, he notes, Zani de Ferranti resigned from his position at the conservatory in Brussels to go to Italy, where he marries the young singer Euphémie Wittmann on May 5, 1855 in Bologna. In July 1856 he travels with her to Austria to give concerts, despite the ongoing Crimean war, and returns to Italy, where she died in the autumn, tragically, not even 24 years of age.[622] Zani de Ferranti really had better things to do than thinking about the competition in Brussels, apart from the possibility that he wasn't even informed. According to Marc Van de Cruys, the importance of the publicity for the contest is merely exaggerated by guitarists. He is right, of course, but still, Makaroff could have told Zani de Ferranti about his plan on his journey in 1851. After all, Makaroff held him in high esteem. In his biography of Zani de Ferranti, Simon Wynberg also describes the circumstances around the competition, and he thinks the musical-political intrigue is the reason for Zani de Ferranti's failure to participate, apart from his good relation to Fétis, who is very occupied with his golden wedding anniversary.[623] But to go as far as Marc van de Cruys in asserting that Makaroff set up the whole competition merely to benefit Mertz and Scherzer, who both won prizes in the competition, is beyond reason.[624] Makaroff is in good relations with both and already owns several of Mertz's compositions and a Scherzer, and such a venture is a decidedly complicated way to support them. The best approach is to assume that the Russian nobleman's intentions are sincere. One way or another, the competition is of great importance to Napoléon Coste, who writes his most important works for it. The 53 works of the 27 other composers that did not win an award are in deposit with Schott frères, in accordance with the regulations, where they had to be collected before March 1, 1857, after which date they would be destroyed.[625] If perchance some uncollected compositions did not get destroyed, the Schott archives may contain a large pile of compositions, possibly unknown and possibly interesting to the world of the guitar. They must have been moved elsewhere, because Schott no longer has a branch in Brussels. A query into this matter revealed that no copies of any of compositions in the competition are to be found in Schott's archives.[626]

---

[622] Cruys, Marcus G.S. Van de: *The King's guitarist: The life and times of Marco Aurelio Zani de Ferranti*, Wijnegem, Homunculus, 2005, p. 100-102.
[623] Wynberg, Simon: *Marco Aurelio Zani de Ferranti*, a biography, Heidelberg, Chanterelle, 1989, p. 43-44.
[624] Cruys, Marcus G.S. Van de: *The King's guitarist: The life and times of Marco Aurelio Zani de Ferranti*, Wijnegem, Homunculus, 2005, p. 103.
[625] *L'Observateur Belge*, Bruxelles, Coché-Mommens, 21ᵉ Année, no. 301, 28 X 1856: 'Celles qui n'auront pas été retirées avant le 1ᵉʳ mars 1857 seront anéanties.'
[626] judith.kadel@schott-music.com: mail 15 XI 2012, info@schott-music.com.

Opus 27, *Les Feuilles d'Automne* [i.e. *Le Passage des Alpes* - Maestoso m. 1-59 i.e. opus 14 *Deuxième Polonaise* - Introduction]

This work is later published as a part of *Le Passage des Alpes* opus 27, 28 and 40 by Richault, sometime between 1862 and 1866 according to Wynberg, but the correct date cannot be established because the edition number is missing. As has been concluded before, the work may have consisted of two parts at the time of the competition: the *Maestoso*, which is essentially the same as the introduction of opus 14 *Deuxième Polonaise*, to which a number of transition measures have been added to connect it to the second part, the *Marche*, which is in turn identical to the *Marche triumphale* opus 26. In this way in *Feuilles d'Automne* consists of two reused works. Changing the opus number from 26 to 28 can be explained by the order of the pieces: if opus 27 is the first part, it is strange for the second part to be called opus 26. Opus 28 now is rather full, with the Marche, the *Fantaisie symphonique* and the *Divertissement*, so Wynberg feels obliged to make a division by adding [b] and [c] for the last two pieces.[627] Unlike the two other published works opus 29 and opus 30, the title page of *Le Passage des Alpes* does not say it was entered in the competition. With the new title the work is dedicated to Madame La Comtesse Nadaillac Delessert, in a way that now the third part opus 40 is added. Aside from Baron d'Outhoorn of opus 50 she is the only French nobility to be included in Coste's dedications. There is also Lord Ashburnham from opus 3, but he must have been English. It is possible that it was the countess who suggested to Coste that he give the work this title, one that refers to the glorious expedition of Napoléon Bonaparte and his army to Italy in 1800.[628] That could mean that she belonged to the new nobility established by Napoléon Bonaparte, given that the old nobility was not so fond of the revolutionary commander. Joerg Sommermeyer criticizes the composition in 1984. He thinks it is one of Coste's less convincing programmatic compositions,

106 Nadaillac Delessert

because it lacks unity in musical thought and because the piece consists of elements thrown together in an unorganized fashion.[629] Mario Dell'Ara, on the contrary, is of the opinion that in this trilogy Coste developed his Romantic descriptive style to perfection, but not yet had reached a sublime unity of thought.[630]

In opus 27 a theme is taken up again, figured, diminuated, a theme that returns in opus 28. The tight musical form of the march, in which musical themes are elaborated, varied and repeated, firmly contradicts the opinion stated in the two citations above. In this programmatic interpretation the music sketches in atmosphere and even in tempo the expedition of Napoléon Bonaparte, admired by Coste, who even bears his name. The many hardships the famous traveler had to endure are presented in this programmatic work, in many gradations of musical passages, rhythms, atmospheres, sudden changes and gripping melodies. In this the renewed programmatic meaning should emerge. he work is reused, after all. The music of the *Maestoso* shows many of the style elements described in the Thematic Catalogue in Chapter IV, and in their application these characteristics contribute greatly to the possible understanding of the piece as narrative, program music, that nevertheless has no unambiguous relation of music and story. The narrative lyricism, the ever-changing rhythms and the often interrupted

---

[627] Wynberg, Simon: *The Guitar Works of Napoleon Coste*, facsimile edition, Monaco, 1981, vol. IV, IX, Introduction.
[628] http://www.vallee-du-ciron.com/Documents/Ouvrages/Michelant/1800.Alpes.htm
[629] Sommermeyer, Joerg: 'Noten, The Guitar Works of Napoleon Coste...', in: *Nova Giulianiad*, 1984 Nr. 3, p. 167-169. [auszug website 2002]
[630] Dell'Ara, Mario: *Manuale di storia della chitarra*, Ancona, Bèrben, 1988, p. 136.

movement are aspects of the dynamic character of this music, catching the attention of the listener as well as of the performer. Knowledge of the musical content can contribute, by way of the descriptive analysis, to the interpretation of the guitarist.

Opus 28, *Marche*

The second part, the *Marche*, later part of *Le Passage des Alpes* as opus 28, is a sustained march, with no indication of tempo, but with a trio. The intensive passing dominant cadences add to the harmonic motion of the piece. It has movement, but still in a continuous tempo, without any indications. Invariably, the time remains four-four. The rhythm is punctuated most of the time, with many applications of rests, in alternation with movement in eights and triplets. There are some indications for dynamics and articulation. The story is implicit: the marching movement, the military trumpets, the heroic punctuated rhythm, enhanced by the application of rests. Along with the element of folklore, the music of this piece contains at least twelve characteristics that can be called Romantic. The third part, the Rondo, may not have started out as part of the piece. The two parts of *Les Feuilles d'Automne* give enough cause to conclude Coste has found his style in Romanticism. This work is certainly one of his most important compositions.

Opus 28[b], *Fantaisie symphonique*

Despite Makaroff's and Girod's intention, this work did not get published until 1983, when Simon Wynberg included it in volume IX of his complete edition.[631] A transcript survives in the Rischel & Birket-Smith collection of the Kongelige Bibliotek in Copenhagen, as is the case with most of Coste's works. There, in measure 6 of the first part, what is presumed to be a correction is made, where the b♭ should be replaced by an a, something which is by all means incorrect. Nevertheless, Wynberg adopts this, which has led this error to slip into the modern edition. It still needs to be corrected. The b♭ is musically logical as a repeat of the preceding motif in a lower octave. The title may allude to Berlioz's *Symphonie fantastique*, 36 years earlier. Coste was an admirer of the composer, as witnessed by his dedication of opus 15 *Le Tournoi*. The choice to give this piece a non-programmatic title means that the extra-musical references are not obvious. The five parts are episodic as a compilation and in structure. The mood changes many times from strong rhythmic motifs to lyrical melodies, always with a rich harmony and polyphonic passages.

107 Fantaisie symphonique op. 28[b], transcript

The beautiful Andante, with its very Romantic and lyrical melody, is included in a shortened form in the *Études* as no. 14, dedicated to his spouse. As a finale, the Scherzo shows interesting musical and guitaristic findings, with humor, in the sustained movement of a waltz, Coste's favorite genre. The five parts of this *Fantaisie symphonique* together form a varied whole as far as tempo, time and rhythm are concerned. Thematic similarity, the reappearance of similar passages, the closure and the idée fixe

---

[631] Wynberg, Simon: *The Guitar Works of Napoleon Coste*, facsimile edition, Monaco, 1981, vol. IX, p. 27, *Fantaisie symphonique*.

create a musical unity, which is further enhanced by the structure of form and the tonalities. With the cadenzas, often preceded by an abruptio, the harmonic contrasts of the major mediant, the relative major, for instance, and the melodic chromatics, there are many style characteristics of his composition to be found in this work. The different modulations, the attention to the subdominant, the plagal Moll-Dur cadence, the Neapolitan sixth-chord and the deceptive closure, reinforce this image in sound. In this way the work meets 12 of the 21 criteria for formal characteristics and style elements present in Coste's guitar music.

Opus 29, *La Chasse des Sylphes*

In the interpretation of the extra-musical reference of *La Chasse des Sylphes* the air-ghosts, sylphes, in Celtic and German mythology, creatures which move between heaven and earth, can cause thunderstorms, and to whom, for that reason, Charlemagne wanted to organize a great hunt, which he later abandoned.[632] The composition itself does not lead one to interpret the music in this way. The sylphes are described by the alchemist Paracelsus (1493-1541) as elementary ghosts from medieval magic, who exist somewhere between immortality and mortality. Oberon, the king of the elves, is himself a sylphe.[633] His lady is Titania, and these two characters are brought to the stage by Shakespeare in his *A Midsummer-Night's Dream*. This play from 1595-1596 is a drama which was an inspiration to composers. For example, in 1826 Mendelssohn writes his overture opus 21 for orchestra with this title alluding to Shakespeare's play, and this is performed in the 'Concert du Conservatoire' in 1851. Apart from this, Carl Maria von Weber writes his opera *Oberon* in 1825-1826, based on the epic of Wieland from 1760. Parts of this work are also in the program of the 'Concerts du Conservatoire', in 1855, as is *La Damnation de Faust* in 1849, the *Légende dramatique* for choir by Hector Berlioz from 1845-1846, of which a 'Choeur de Gnomes et Sylphes' and then a 'Ballet des Sylphes' are part of, part two, scene 7.[634] Coste may have heard these works in a performance, as this literary theme plays a role in music of that time. The sylphes are a source of inspiration, not only for Romantic composers, but also later in 1909 for choreographer Fokine in *Les Sylphides*.

In spite of the occurrence of a rhythmic joint-motif in the form of a repeated eights triplet followed by a quarter note in the *Ballet des Sylphes* van Berlioz, which in a certain way bears some likeness to the opening motif in the fourth part of Coste's work, and some chord elaborations in part I measures 17, 21 and 23 and in part II measures 163 and 165, which bear a faint likeness to the last motif of Weber's Oberon. There is no thematic relation to be found between Coste's composition and the works of the other three composers. The composition is quite original. But what intentions Coste had in this composition may come to light in the descriptive analysis of the work in the chapter concerning this matter. The conclusion drawn there is as follows. The four parts of *La Chasse des Sylphes* opus 29 are very diverse in character, due to the many intensive harmonic movements, of which the augmented dominant cadences are particularly noteworthy. The work is multi-faceted with respect to thematic transformation, where several themes are elaborated and combined, while others can even be regarded as idées fixes. Melodic chromatics does not occur frequently. This phenomenon is mostly applied in a harmonic way, where the continuous modulating character, especially in the first and the third parts, drive the tonic into the background, almost making it floating, hovering. Coste firmly applies this. Sometimes internal musical references can also be found in this work, like a trumpet, a horn and bourdons, which can have a narrative function in themselves, pointing to Shakespeare's *A Midsummer-Night's Dream*. At least four references are plausible: the singing fairies in the folk musical passage in the first part, the hunt with the horns in the flageolet and signal motifs in the second part, the braying of the donkey in the beginning of the third part with the unusual large interval in the melody, and the trumpets, which Shakespeare also mentions in his fourth act and which reappear repeatedly in the fourth part.

---

[632] http://rr0.org/Sylphes.html [Charlemagne 742?-814]
[633] 'Paracelsus' in: *Grote Winkler Prins*, Elsevier, Amsterdam, 1974, vol. 15, p. 89; 'Sylfe' in: vol. 18, p. 191.
[634] Dandelot, A.: *La Société des Concerts du Conservatoire de 1828 à 1897*, Paris, Delagrave, 1923, p. 40-41.

VI — *Grande Sérénade* 155

108 La Chasse des Sylphes - Coste op. 29 III m. 1-6

This aside, there are still other folk music-like and dissonant passages that may have a narrative intention, but cannot be brought into direct relation with extra-musical phenomena and merely perpetuate the atmosphere. In this way, Coste achieves a structural unity in this sense by repeating the theme in this composition. With the structural characteristics and style elements – such as deviation from the periodic phrase structure, use of a cadenza, the many figurations of various kinds, the ornamentation, the already mentioned intensive harmonic movement, style figures such as rocket and spark, time and tempo changes, and prescription of dynamics and articulation – and the way this part of the play is set to music, the piece meets at least 15 of the 21 criteria defined for Romanticism. For these reasons this work is one of the best compositions Coste wrote.

Opus 30, *Grande Sérénade*

The prize-winning work *Grande Sérénade* is understandably dedicated by Coste to Monsieur N. de Makaroff in Girod's edition. No contemporary manuscript or transcript has been found, but Frederik Birket-Smith (1880-1952) made a copy dated June 5, 1924, which is in the Kongelige Bibliotek in Copenhagen. Girod's edition is from 1857, because it is registered by the printer Moucelot on June 8 of that year in the register of music editions, which is maintained without interruption from 1841 on.[635] The 64 enormous folio volumes of this register until the year 1883 in the Archives nationales in Paris are a reliable source of dates for those compositions of Coste's that cannot be deduced otherwise. Not all of the volumes are accessible, however, and not all of Coste's works have been entered. So far, only those of opus 25, 30 and 31 could be found, while Monsieur Moucelot could easily have walked over to the registry for opus 29. His name and address are mentioned on the last page of that edition as well as on the first of opus 30. So, the register is incomplete, as far as Coste is concerned.[636] Joerg Sommermeyer's opinion on this composition is that it contains theatrical elements, and in that way seems operatic, while at the same time being completely original, without allusions to other works. Coste has written it in such a way that he can effectively show his instrumental skills and creativity as a composer.[637] In 1999 Umberto Realino describes some musical aspects of the *Grande Sérénade*. According to him the style of the first part is improvisational, and it shows directly the whole diapason of the instrument in a virtuosic way. He makes a formal analogy with the first parts of Carulli's *Trois Solos* opus 76. This similarity may be there, but Carulli elaborates one musical motif or theme in every part, while Coste shows a much greater and more intensive variation. Realino also notices the chromatic modulation to the second part, but fails to make the connection to folk music there. Neither does he point to Berlioz in the *Marche et Choeur de Pèlerins* [sic], while this connection is obvious. But he does think a beautiful play between the sopranos and the basses can be heard. The characteristic rhythm of the bolero resumes the energy of the beginning, while evoking an exotic atmosphere.[638]

---
[635] Paris, Archives nationales, F18* VIII 1 à 157, No. 21, p. 35 No.: 1641, 8 VI 1857, Coste: *Sérénade*.
[636] Coste, Napoléon: 'La Chasse des Sylphes', 'Grande Sérénade' in: Wynberg, Simon: *The Guitar Works of Napoleon Coste*, facsimile edition, Monaco, 1981, Vol. IV, p. 47, 'Moucelot'; p. 52, 'Moucelot'.
[637] Sommermeyer, Joerg: 'Noten, The Guitar Works of Napoleon Coste...', in: *Nova Giulianiad*, 1984 Nr. 3, p. 168 [auszug website 2002].
[638] Realino, Umberto: *Un siècle de guitare en France 1750-1850*, unp. thèse Sorbonne, repr. Atelier national, Lille, 1999, p. 383-385.

The work consists of four parts, of which the first two and the last must be played without interruption. The title *Marche et Choeur de Pélerins* refers to Berlioz's *Marche de pèlerins*, part II of *Harold en Italie* from 1834. The ever-returning 'prière du soir' in this piece is characterized by an intensive reharmonization of a varied melody, sometimes modulating and sometimes not, in several inversions and voices. Its rhythm bears a certain resemblance to Coste's chorale, were it not for the fact that the latter has an anacrusis. Just like Berlioz, Coste varies the melody and elaborates the phrases harmonically. The *Bolero* of the third part is the only one of Spanish genre ever written by Coste. Sor wrote several of them, mostly for voice accompanied by guitar or piano. Castellacci and Huerta both composed one, so Coste may have become acquainted genre through them. The bolero is related to the cachucha – Coste wrote one in opus 13 – and the rhythm of the bolero is somewhat similar to that of the polonaise, of which Coste wrote two, opus 14 and opus 44, making this work a good fit in this composer's oeuvre. The title of the last part, *Final*, sounds like Spanish, and combined with Spain, pilgrims and choirs it makes one think of Santiago de Compostela, a destination to which several pilgrimage routes passed through France. But whether pilgrims also dance and sing the bolero is questionable, although in Santiago there is the old tradition of 'La Tuna', where groups of students are allowed to earn some money by playing and singing a repertoire that included the jota, the malagueña, the serenata and perhaps also the bolero. Those groups seem to have been playing in Paris too, as early as the 15th century.[639] Whether Coste knew of this tradition is by no means certain. The way the themes and motifs are elaborated, and even enhanced by the return of phrases in an altered or unaltered way, give the *Grande Sérénade* opus 30 a solid structure. Often Coste deviates from the periodic phrase structure, but rigidly maintains it in folk music passages. A very intense harmonic development is alternated with harmonic rest, sometimes even standstill, and there Coste prescribes a powerful rhythm. Many stylistic figures noted in his music up to this point are applied in a more varied and intense way. Chromatic figurations of melodies, alteration of chords and modulation play an important role in this piece. Coste gradually employs less melodic chromatics, in favor of harmonic chromatics, with a modulating effect. Along with several time changes, the guitaristic effects of glissando, legato, arpeggio and staccato are striking. The principles of the Spanish phrygian cadence and rasgueado, quite exotic to a Frenchman and here applied in a modest way, clearly come forward in the Bolero and the Final. In this way it is a powerful piece, meeting the demands of the competition in several ways. The work is original, expresses a coherent musical thought and exhibits many new ideas of style, taste and brilliance in its effects. It is a virtuosic piece, but nonetheless quite playable. It employs the instrument's many musical resources.

Mertz

Having analyzed and described the four works Coste entered in the competition and drawn conclusions about them in this chapter, the question now arises as to why the last work was awarded a prize. There is no jury report, and no justification can be found in Makaroff's concerning how the criteria were applied, which means that the only way to answer the question is by taking the position of the members of the jury to bring to light what their considerations may have been. Astrid Stempnik has done just this in her biography of Mertz, taking both his works and those of Coste into consideration. Her conclusion is that the two winning compositions – Mertz's *Concertino* and Coste's *Grande Sérénade* – are similar as far as brilliance and thematic structure are concerned. The main keys of both are a-minor and A-major, whereas the *Sérénade* also has C-major. Both composers largely refrain from elaborating their themes, though Coste displays more elaboration than Mertz, due to the intensive way that he uses the thematic material. He relates both main themes in the development of the *Finale*, for instance, while Mertz uses new material there, except for a motif from the first theme. The parallels between the two works must have played a part in these works both being awarded a prize.[640]

---

[639] Ramos, Javier Iglesias & Domingo Rojas Cantera: *Canta La Tuna!*, Santiago de Compostela, Detritus, 2000, p. 3-11.
[640] Stempnik, Astrid: *Caspar Joseph Mertz, Leben und Werk...*, Frankfurt am Main, Lang, 1990, p. 379-382, 413.

In 1996 Andrew Dancescu also took the effort to look at the *Concertino* and analyze it. He published his findings in *The Guitar Review* and his conclusion, which in short is as follows. The musical drama in this work can be called heroic, due to the stormy sphere, full of energy. It is centered around the harmonic relation between A and C. It is the melody itself that eventually gives the work its harmonic coloring, rhythmic motion, action and cadence. Breaking through tonality is not Mertz's first concern, according to Dancescu. The composer primarily aims to develop the musical means for achieving metaphor and foreshadowing. It has the highest level of technique, and the communicative possibilities are extraordinary. Finally, he thinks the aesthetics are comparable to that of Chopin or Liszt.[641] This last claim really goes too far. The piece obviously does show several characteristics of the Romantics, just as determined in the chapter on 'Style' in the Thematic Catalogue – tremolando, chromatic passage work and scales, rocket and parachute motifs, leaping figurations, tremolo, cadenza and some diminished and double diminished seventh chords – but the harmonic structure and thematics are not at all innovative or spectacular. The dramatic impression it gives mainly emerges from the technical acrobatics, the rush of the arpeggio and the figurations with many, many notes, and rather than in the harmonic or thematic development.

The four compositions Coste entered in the contest can be regarded as the principal works of his oeuvre. The first two parts of *Le Passage des Alpes* opus 27 & 28, entered as *Les Feuilles d'Automne*, do not form a coherent whole in this sense there is returning thematic material. Only a theme connects the two. Both are musical works of a high standard, which can also be played as a single work. Together with the *Rondo*, which was not added at the time, they form a very diverse trilogy, in the literal sense of the title word. The fact that Coste made a synthesis of earlier work lays the foundation for this. The *Fantaisie symphonique* opus 28[b] is different in the following way: it is a new composition written especially for this competition, composed of no fewer than five parts in two halves, which have a far more thematic relationship. These two halves are very diverse, full of surprises, but written in a very effective way, using a limited number of means, making it transparent and clear. In that way it may not have met expectations on how the musical resources of the instrument should be used. In that sense, the *La Chasse des Sylphes* opus 29 is far more Romantic; it has an intensive harmonic development, great changes in mood and contrasts in motion, but in the last part the work becomes discursive compared to opus 30. The *Grande Sérénade* opus 30 is more compact, more intense in its harmony, and it has a very strong rhythm, different from the previous three works. It meets at least eighteen of the criteria mapped out in the analysis chart for identifying Romantic aspects of his music.

Opus 31, *Le Départ*

For one reason or another, this work was entered in the competition too late, but it was meant for it, nevertheless. Also, the date of this work also makes it appropriate for discussion in this chapter. It is published by Girod in the series works that were entered in the contest, and it is listed on 5 September 1857 in the register of publications in the Archives nationales by printer Moucelot.[642] The piece is dedicated to M. Adan, Directeur Général des Domines du Royaume de Belgique. Later, Coste also dedicates his *Étude* 23 opus 38 to him, with its nimble-fingered arpeggio and staccato bass theme, the standard for which was set by Llobet around 1925. Coste may have met Adan during his visit to Brussels for the competition, Adan himself is mentioned by Makaroff, and he probably took part in the jury's buffet, and he was a dedicated lover of the guitar and player. This is how Coste came to make the dedication to him then, or later. The explanation of the works in Girod's edition of *La Chasse des Sylphes* opus 29 and *Grande Sérénade* opus 30 does not say *Le Départ* was received after the closing date of the contest, so it also is probable that Coste brought it along to Brussels himself.

---

[641] Dancescu, Andrew: 'Johann Kaspar Mertz' Concertino - An Analysis', in: *Guitar Review*, New York, The Society of the Classic Guitar, no. 105, 1996, p. 18-22.
[642] Paris, Archives nationales, F18* VIII 1 à 157, No. 22, p. 234 No.: 2686, 5 IX 1857, Coste: *Le Départ*.

The first part, *Le Départ*, depicts the departure of the soldiers to the Crimean War. There are many arpeggio movements, with fierce arpeggiato interruptions. The chromatics are mostly used in a harmonic way, no longer so much in melodic coloration. Some trumpet imitations enhance the military idea, and the great harmonic unrest, supported by the broken chromatic octave series and the time and rhythm changes, interrupted by joint motifs and ending in figuration work, make the battle on the front audible in the Andante and Agitato at the end of this part. After the victory follows the return, the second part, the triumphant entry in Paris. Coste significantly gives the date, '29 Décembre 1855!...', but the victory is tempered by the minor key. Perhaps here the Florence Nightingale phenomenon emerges, when the opposite of the military heroism resounds in the music. Her selfless works were in the newspapers of the time, making her name a household word throughout the world.

109 Crimean War

The march does not come up to heroic expectations, in the way that Coste's opus 5, opus 15 and opus 28 do. Coste is strictly periodic in this part, he reuses thematic and motivic material, with a great sense of unity as a result. Trumpet motifs and a folk music passage give a special color to this part, but the interesting harmonic motion in particular is very intense, especially in the passage between *A* and *B*, where the tonic almost vanishes. No victory here; are these the disabled passing by in this march in Paris? Together with the deviation from the periodic structure of the phrase, the cadenza, the figurations, ornaments, tempo changes, dynamics and articulation, a many-sided story of the Crimean War is told. In this way, this work shows 14 characteristics which can be called Romantic according to the list. But as far as external musical references are concerned, the narrative of the music, many questions arise. The work is eclipsed by the last two works. It consists of two parts and is much shorter, and fewer musical ideas have been used. Nevertheless, it can be included in the list of Coste's main compositions, just as the other works that were submitted on time. Coste does not make use of the seventh string here, so the work can be played on a six-string guitar without problems.

With this departure and, not so very triumphal, return, it is, in a certain sense, saying goodbye to Coste's most important compositions. The *Marche funèbre* opus 43, *Souvenir(s) du Jura* opus 44, *Divagation* opus 45, *La Source du Lyson* opus 47 and the *Études de Genre* opus 38 still have to come, but the most interesting things about Coste's art may have been said now. The other works, which are eclipsed by his abilities, will be discussed nonetheless, but they will not add too much to the understanding of his way of composing. Now the situation of the musical world in Paris around 1856 will be sketched first, guided by the issues that were discussed in the first intermezzo, to clarify the changing circumstances concerning the guitar. The next chapters will bring to light the opportunities Coste had to use his success this competition to further his career.

110 Royal Library, Brussels, 2007

Intermezzo II

The instrument was even a sort of favorite in France and Italy; but for some time now it has started to become neglected everywhere, or completely abandoned for some time in favor of the piano, whose perfection and well-earned popularity grows by the day.[643]

Economy

In the same way that in the first intermezzo the year 1828, when Coste arrived in Paris, was taken as the point of reference for examining the musical world and the world outside it, the year 1856 will be the point of departure for this second intermezzo. This is the year in which Coste participates in the Makaroff competition, travelling to Brussels to submit his compositions. His entries prove to be among his very best compositions, he wins a prize in the competition and returns with this honor to the splendid city where he has resided for the past 28 years. There he has proved his worth on the concert scene and belongs to a musical network of musicians, composers and publishers, as well as Freemasons, either in an organized fashion or informally. He gives private lesson, but also has a job at the Caisse Municipale in Paris as an administrator. In Paris after 1848, the day-to-day circumstances have changed, as have circumstances in the musical world, at times gradually, sometimes abruptly. And unlike the period before 1828, considering that Coste now belongs to that world, the situation can be related directly to him.

In 1845, a mediocre grain harvest in France leads to depleted stocks, while at the same time continuing rains aggravate the outbreak potato blight. The following year an exceptional drought causes a poor grain harvest, leading to rising prices, including that of bread. The agricultural crisis is reflected in the cost of living, which for a laborer between 1845 and 1847 rises 13%, which is followed by an industrial and political crisis. In 1848, grain harvest and wine production are good and prices are low, but the economic crisis continues, profits from agriculture are minimal and drop even further as the industrial crisis continues and unemployment remains high. These problems are exacerbated by that year's cholera epidemic, which claims thousands of lives, but which spares Coste. This situation contributes to the creation of the revolution of 1848, which brings the Deuxième République to power, and the coup of 1851, in spite of the fact that food prices have dropped 21% thanks to good harvests. In 1852, the Second Empire allows the economy to quickly pick up again. Various measures encourage taking out credit and undertaking large projects, especially the construction of new railways and urban development.[644] But the salaries of staff and instructors at the conservatory have hardly changed since 1830. In 1830 Cherubini earns 8,000 fr. a year as a director. Similarly, Auber, a voice instructor, earns 2,000 fr. in both 1830 and 1855, while the violin instructor Baillot earns 2,000 fr. in 1830 and Alard earns 1,200 fr. in 1855.[645] The Crimean War has a greater impact than just disrupting the planned Makaroff competition and grain imports, causing severe food shortages in 1856; the cost of living for the man in the street rises 33% since 1851. The situation bounces back and forth between prosperity and adversity, and there are large fluctuations in the economy. A good harvest and the end of the Crimean War, after which grain imports resume, lead to a sharp decline in food prices, but then comes a financial crisis. This new crisis does not last long: in 1859 the economy is back on the road to recovery.

---

[643] Soullier, Charles: *Nouveau dictionnaire de musique illustré...*, Paris, Bazault, 1855, p. 140: 'Cet instrument avait même joui de quelque faveur en France et en Italie; mais il commence depuis quelque temps à être partout un peu négligé ou délaissé entièrement pour le piano, dont le perfectionnement et la popularité méritée redoublent de jour en jour.'
[644] Singer-Kerel, J.: *Le coût de la vie à Paris de 1840 à 1954*, Paris, A.Colin, 1961, p. 98.
[645] Pierre, Constant: *Le Conservatoire national de musique et de déclamation: documents historiques et administratifs*, Paris, Imprimerie nationale, 1900, p. 420, 425.

Until the end of the Second Empire in 1870, there are no more spectacular slumps and the situation is relatively prosperous.[646] From around 1865, the period of uncertainty in the lives of Parisians, with economic, social and political unrest, is followed by a time of greater stability. Coste should be in a position to profit from this by cashing in on his great success in the competition, but it appears that to secure his financial situation he had no choice but to take an administrative position alongside his artistic career.

Infrastructure

At the same time, Paris itself is undergoing drastic changes due to the plans of Baron Haussmann, on which work begins in 1852 under the Second Empire. As a response to the enormous population growth and the failure of the revolution of 1848, the boulevards are widened, so that the streets no longer belong to 'the revolution' and so uprisings can be put down more easily with charges. Cafés and high-end shops are installed on the major boulevards, and the dangerous intersections, where barricades were erected in 1851, are neutralized. This part of Paris is practically lost to industry, the common people and the revolution. The victorious parades now pass through these beautiful new districts, but the middle classes no longer feel at home here. For every three native Parisians there are now two inhabitants from the provinces. The Second Empire does not seek urban power only through electoral support; it also wants to win the heart of the capital which has just risen up against the coup d'état, but which refuses to applaud for the regime. Not only is the new situation criticized, it is accepted with mixed feelings.[647] The feelings for the revolution remain deeply engrained in the hearts of the Parisians.

Haussmann and Napoleon III are responsible for giving Paris the layout it still has today. Coste has lived at 11 rue de Calais since 1851, and, with rue de Clichy around the corner and boulevard Haussmann further up, he has been able to observe the construction work for several years.[648] The city has now been divided into twenty 'arrondissements'. Coste lives in the 9th. But Paris is also being stripped of its origins. Large, compact constructions are going up in the Cité, and in one of them Coste has found his miserable job.[649] In 1856 les Halles are built, the famous covered market whose memory today is preserved only by a few remaining cornerstones. In 1855 the Exposition universelle is held, whose primary participants are Parisian businesses and in which a small space is set aside for guitar-makers. It is also the year of the army's glorious return from the Crimea, followed by the beginning of peace negotiations, also in Paris. It is to this event that Coste dedicated his opus 31, which is probably wisely held back by Schott in the competition. The city has had its Gare du Nord since 1846, which is in all probability the station from which Coste departs for Brussels in 1856. The annexation of 1860 also brings Auteuil within the city limits, Auteuil of which Coste has fond memories, according to opus 23. Between 1851 and 1866, the city's population grows from 1 million to 1.8 million inhabitants, and Paris continues to grow, reaching 2.3 million residents in 1886, Traffic is still a problem, but more streets are outfitted with pavements, totaling 1,000 km in 1869. A horse-drawn tram is introduced in 1856, but only between place de la Concorde and Boulogne-sur-Seine. It is considered too dangerous to drive over the major boulevards. Paris also has its hospitals, of course, 28 of them to be exact. Coste may have needed to go to one in 1863 and 1874 after he injured his left shoulder. Considering his intensive correspondence, Coste is a keen user of the postal service and has got an large circle of people with whom he corresponds, although only a few of his letters have been preserved. The city has many postboxes, which during the Second Empire are emptied as many as eight times per day.[650] In this period, Paris experiences great prosperity and industrial growth, enabling the appearance of the large Parisian department stores: the Bon Marché in 1852, the Louvre in 1865 and La Samaritaine in 1869.

---

[646] Singer-Kerel, J.: *Le coût de la vie à Paris de 1840 à 1954*, Paris, A.Colin, 1961, p. 99-100.
[647] Gaillard, Jeanne: *Paris, la ville, 1852-1870, l'urbanisme Parisien à l'heure d'Haussman...*[sic], Paris, Honoré Champion, 1977, p. 559-565.
[648] Leconte, André, ed.: *Plan de Paris par Arrondissement*, Paris, 1977, p.21, Arr. 9.
[649] Hillairet, Jacques: *Dictionnaire historique des rues de Paris*, Paris, Les Éditions de Minuit, 1963-1972, p. 11.
[650] Hillairet, Jacques: *Dictionnaire historique des rues de Paris*, Paris, Les Éditions de Minuit, 1963-1972, p. 17, 30, 31, 33, 36, 37, 39, 45.

Musical life

The citizen's monarchy of Louis-Philippe, which fell due to economic problems, was followed by the Second Republic in 1848. Freedoms were curtailed, and the café-concerts, for example, must now have a license, but unlike in 1830 no major changes occur in the way musical life is structured. While it is true that songs that were banned during the monarchy can be heard again, the repertoire in the theatres goes largely unchanged, with Meyerbeer's *Le Prophète* in 1849, Adam's *Le Toreador* in 1850 and Gounod's *Sapho* in 1851. The Second Empire of 1852, which is at first rather authoritarian, but later becomes more liberal, brings little change. However, the decree of 1864 even promises freedom of theatre activities. This allows the new genre of the operetta to blossom, which is institutionalized by the permission Offenbach obtains to open the Boofes-Parisiens theatre in 1855. The cosmopolitan character of the city also brings with it more German influence, with Wagner concerts in the Théâtre-Italien in 1860 and the production of *Tannhäuser* in 1861, which is poorly received. A counter-movement arises to protect French music, as seen by developments such as the creation of the Société des Auteurs, Compositeurs et Éditeurs de Musique in 1850.[652] The café-concerts blossom, the city is filled with 'bals publiques' and the Eldorado of fame opens in 1858. Paris is becoming sophisticated. The socialist tendencies of the previous period can still be found in Courbet's realism in his private exhibition 'Le Réalisme' in 1855 and later in Zola's first book in 1864, after which naturalism emerges as a literary school. Paris also reconciles itself with sacred art and church music. Organs built by Cavaillé-Coll are consecrated in the Saint-Sulpice church in 1862 and in Notre-Dame in 1868, forming the basis for France's great organ culture.[653] The bourgeoisie does not play an important role in the arts during the Restoration of 1815 and at the beginning of the July Monarchy in 1830, except for a few individuals at the top of the hierarchy. That changes after 1848, when the material prosperity helps this group advance and they start playing an increasingly normative role, serving as a standard all deviations from which are rejected. For that reason, Romanticism as excessive art barely survives the revolution of 1848.

Institutions

The conservatoire remains an institution that is very influential on musical life. It determines standards for students uses standardizing methods. Auber is now the director of this school. Berlioz is still the librarian as Fétis's successor, and renowned musicians teach there, such as Cokken for the bassoon, Mme Farrenc and Henri Herz for piano, Klosé for clarinet, Panseron for voice and Verroust for oboe, instructors who have already appeared with Coste in concerts.[654] As the dominant class, the bourgeoisie determines the artistic tastes during the Second Empire. Here and there a democratic wind blows that particularly manifests itself in changes in the places where concerts are given and in the construction of a few new performance halls: the Châtelet theatre, the Théâtre-Lyrique, the Palais Garnier, larger halls for a larger audience and a lower admission fee. That means competition for the Théâtre-Italien and the Opéra-Comique. However, Habeneck's successor at the 'Concerts du Conservatoire', the violinist Tilmant, who becomes vice-president and concertmaster in 1859 maintains his devotion to the elite. It is Pasdeloup (1819-1887) who democratizes the symphony orchestra, when starting in 1861 he organizes the famous Concerts Populaire de Musique Classique in the Cirque

---

[651] Pistone, Danièle: *La musique en France de la Révolution à 1900*, Paris, Honoré Champion, 1979, p. 24; Wennekes, Emmanuel Gerhardus Johannes: *Het Paleis voor Volksvlijt...*, Den Haag, SDU, 1999, p. 16-20.
[652] Guillo, Laurent: 'Legal Aspects', in: Rasch, Rudolf, ed.: *Music Publishing in Europe 1600-1900*, Berlin, Berliner Wissenschafts-Verlag, 2005, p. 137.
[653] Pistone, Danièle: *La musique en France de la Révolution à 1900*, Paris, Honoré Champion, 1979, p. 23-26.
[654] Soullier, Charles: *Annuaire musical 1855*, Paris, Saint-Étienne, 1854, p. 20-21.

Napoléon, with 5,000 seats and a very low admission charge. He takes a big risk in doing so, but the concerts are attended by over 4,000 people.[655]

Chamber music concerts are still given in the well-known Pleyel and Érard halls and the number of professional ensembles grows, leading to the disappearance of amateur theatre as well as to an expansion of the repertoire. It is here that virtuosi like Joachim, Moschelès and Anton Rubinstein establish their reputations. In addition to Beethoven, now Schubert, Mendelssohn and Schumann are played, as well as Saint-Saëns and Lalo. The Lamoureux quartet begins, as did Pasdeloup, with 'séances populaires de musique classique' which one could attend for a moderate admission fee, with a repertoire that had not altered much. These concerts have a societal purpose: to make music accessible for as large an audience as possible.[656] Musical life in the salons becomes increasingly restricted to insiders, and the programming is conservative. To find the Romantic movement one must turn to the artists' circles. Pauline Viardot's salon, whose shining star is Saint-Saëns, plays a prominent role in this respect.[657] But various halls have closed down, such as the Gymnase musical and the salle Chantereine in 1854.[658]

And then there are also the orphéons, the choir, fanfare and harmony associations that succeeded in surviving beyond 1830, but that really start blossoming now. Associations, with members from workers' circles and the middle class can be found in villages, provincial towns and in the capital. They organize competitions, festivals, performances and give a great boost to the sense of local identity as an expression of nationalism. The quadrille remains a popular choice at dance events, but Lasalle's gibe at this dance is yet to come.[659] In around 1855 Coste writes two sets in WoO 5, when the café-concert becomes popular with the working and middle classes.[660] And in 1853 Napoleon III restores the concerts in the imperial court and appoints Auber maître de chapelle. In addition to this post, Auber also serves as director of the conservatory and chairman of the Concerts du Conservatoire, making him a key figure. But even this arena will become competitive, with the Seghers's Société de Sainte-Cécile and Berlioz's Grande Société Philharmonique, although both of these were short-lived. While the concert becomes popularized, at the same time it undergoes professionalization. The benefit concert disappears around 1860. The solo concert, the recital, has come onto the scene, and composers start writing for them. The programming changes. Now a concert consists of the complete works of a single canonized composer, and recitals start being given of the 24 preludes written by Chopin, who had died in 1849, leaving behind a large body of work, or of Bach's 24 preludes and fugues.[661] But this left the guitar without a venue: there were no solo concerts for the plucked instrument.

Concert world

Musicologist William Weber points out that there is a watershed moment in European music in 1848. The major growth in both the audience and the variety of tastes causes the various types of concerts to start differentiating themselves. A hierarchical order also comes into being, linked to the institutions, at least with the musical idealists. Concerts with chamber music, orchestras and the recital constitute the high culture of musical life. Concerts described as commercial entertainment for a general audience take on new forms, such as opera selections and popular chansons in particular. After 1850, this development entails the hegemony of classical music, but that authority is limited.

---

[655] Dandelot, A.: *La Société des Concerts du Conservatoire de 1828 à 1897*, Paris, Delagrave, 1923, p. 47.
[656] Fauquet, Joël-Marie: 'Les sociétés de musique de chambre' in: Bailbé [et al]: *La musique en France à l'epoque romantique (1830-1870)*, Paris, Flammarion, 1991, p. 181.
[657] Eigeldinger, Jean-Jacques: 'Introduction'; in: Bailbé [et al]: *La musique en France à l'epoque romantique (1830-1870)*, Paris, Flammarion, 1991, p. 19.
[658] Fauquet, J.-M.: 'salle de concert', in: Fauquet, Joël-Marie: *Dictionnaire de la Musique en France au XIXe siècle*, Paris, Fayard, 2003, p. 1113.
[659] Lasalle, Albert: *Dictionnaire de la musique appliquée à l'amour*, Paris, Librairie internationale, 1868, p. 225.
[660] Eigeldinger, Jean-Jacques: 'Introduction'; in: Bailbé [et al]: *La musique en France à l'epoque romantique (1830-1870)*, Paris, Flammarion, 1991, p. 16-19.
[661] Bernard, Elisabeth: 'Musique et communication' in: Bailbé [et al]: *La musique en France à l'epoque romantique (1830-1870)*, Paris, Flammarion, 1991, p. 95; Almanach musical pour 1854..., Paris, Houssiaux ed., 1854, p. 94-95, 81.

Intermezzo II 163

Around 1870, music education, sacred music and the most important formal concerts are dominated by advocates of serious music. Classical music is also considered to be a source of bourgeois and national pride. Italian opera is displaced by French opera and the operetta. This watershed is accurately sketched by the Viennese critic Selmar Bagge in 1860 in terms of reactionaries who are wary of new music, progressives who dogmatically follow Wagner and liberals who use classical models to judge new works. Similar processes are taking place outside of Paris, as well. And the *Revue et Gazette musicale de Paris* even describes the action taken by Pasdeloup in 1861 as the defense of equality for all Frenchmen in the court of music. The culture has changed. The basic principle becomes one of 'educating the public' in high culture. Programs are supplemented with explanatory text, and the intelligentsia of the music world, including George Grove, claim authority. Classical music becomes canonized, while at the same time being popularized. Around 1860 practically the only works being played in orchestral concerts are those of dead composers. Conservatism is at its highpoint. One even speaks of the 'Louvre of music'. Musical tastes are defined by a repertoire of classical works, supported by a systematic knowledge of music. In the years 1850-1860 the café-concert enjoys tremendous growth. There opera selections and chansons are sung for a middle-class audience who eat, drink and comment on what is happening on stage. The idea of popular music is no longer as new as that of classical music was in 1810, and it is becoming increasingly professional in nature. A strong tradition is created, for many of the social classes, separated from the classical world, independent of elitist institutions, but still linked to general cultural movements. Only opera escapes from being identified with either classical or popular, allowing it to play a role for the entire world of music.[662]

Public convention

In the concert halls, the convention that the audience should remain silent, introduced in the 1830s, is having increasing impact. Criticism and suppression of spontaneous behavior does not remain limited to the upper class; audience behavior changes in character elsewhere as well. Up and down the social spectrum, the audience's attitude during concerts and performances becomes detached. This behavior succeeds in becoming the standard due to a coalescence that occurs in the tastes and manners of the working and the lower merchant classes. With opera-goers a similar development is underway: people are listening more and more seriously. In chamber music, the performance practice shifts from the mixed concert to the solo concert. The distinction grows stronger between the professional musician and the amateur, who gradually disappears from the stage. The attitude of the audience changes in the sense that what was once an interested connoisseur who is keen on showing off his knowledge in comments and consideration for the performers has now turned into a passive listener, who listens attentively at an appropriate distance, in silence, with respect for the venerable soloist, later with the house lights extinguished. This development is partially inspired by the increased complexity of the musical works. The position of the musician becomes respectable due to the great efforts that he (female musicians are almost exclusively singers) demands of himself while making it all seem effortless. The ideal of performing the most difficult of works with a casual air is still a part of the convention. The ecstatic way of performing, already introduced by Paganini in the 1830s and continued by Liszt, who is still in Paris in 1853 and 1861, quickly devolves into a gimmick that is taken less and less seriously. Both ways of performing persist in the concerts, while in the popular cafés-concerts the old-fashioned custom of eating, drinking and talking during the performance lives on. A distinction can also be observed in the attitude towards listening between classical and popular music.[663]

---

[662] Weber, William: *The Great Transformation of Musical Taste*, Cambridge, Cambridge University Press, 2008, p. 235-236, 238, 240, 252, 259, 293, 299-240.
[663] Johnson, James H.: *Listening in Paris: a cultural history*, Berkeley, University of Berkeley Press, 1995, p. 199-203, 228-229, 270-271; Weber, William: *The Great Transformation of Musical Taste*, Cambridge, Cambridge University Press, 2008, p. 235-236, 272, 293-294, 299-300.

Publishers

Until 1856, Coste was in contact with eight different publishers, large and small, who have published nineteen of his works: Romagnesi, Richault, Lacôte, Challiot, Latte, Schonenberger, Colombier and Girod, often located in the same part of town as the conservatoire.[664] Two of his compositions are self-published, while his remaining pieces remained unpublished. Even after 1856, publishers continue to publish his works, until 1876, when Coste starts publishing his last works himself. The *Méthode* Coste-Sor, which is published Schonenberger in 1851, is practically the last guitar method to appear until 1860, the only exception being Buttigni whose method appears in 1857. This marks the end of the great influx of guitar methods that came into swing in the 1820s.[665] That is both characteristic of interest in the guitar as an instrument and a reflection of the situation in public chamber music concerts, in which Coste can hardly be found anymore. The music publishing world itself is under pressure. There are many bankruptcies, and publishers are more wary of taking on new works. The Romagnesi publishing house, together with the magazine *L'Abeille musical* is sold to Aulagnier in 1850, Challiot transfers rights to his catalogue to Coudray in 1866, Richault remains in business until 1898, publishing three more of Coste's works, Latte closes shop in 1854, and Schonenberger remains active until 1875, when the firm is sold to Lemoine, but it publishes just another work by Coste after the *Souvenirs*. It is publishers like Hirsch, Lemoine, Chatot, Triébert, Richault and Katto who publish Coste's work after 1856. In the world of the publishers as well, people are seeking a certain level of organization, with the Cercle de la Librairie in 1866, and they start focusing more on marketing to a large audience, by making the repertoire of professional and semi-professional theatres accessible to amateurs. Romances and chansonnettes are published with covers that do not project an image of artistic ambition. As the concert world becomes popularized, publishing houses do not lag behind and selects the repertoire for the concert-going audience.[666]

Dedications

Dedications say something about a composer's personal and possibly also about financial relations, as well as his position in his social-cultural environment. In his memoirs, Nicolai de Makaroff writes that on his visit to Vienna he purchased a number of unpublished works from Mertz for a small sum of money.[667] This might indicate a financial motivation behind some of the dedications. However, in this connection a brief overview will suffice of the dedications made by the three great Classicists Sor, Giuliani and Carulli and the three Romanticists Coste, Mertz and Zani de Ferranti. Now the question arises concerning the circumstances around these and other dedications. Until now no research has been conducted on the sociology of dedications. In the 19th century dedications are often made by the publisher, making it unclear whether Coste made the dedications all by himself.[668] This phenomenon is liable to change in this period. From the sequential works of Napoléon Coste a long list of names emerges of those to whom they are dedicated. Are these more than with 'classical' composers and the other 'Romantic' composers? A short survey of the 'classics' – Sor, Giuliani and Carulli – and the 'Romantics' – Mertz, Zani de Ferranti and Coste – can give some insight. Sor dedicates many of his works to friends, pupils, nobility, musicians, studies to disciples in general, works to Aguado, Regondi, Coste – opus 63, the duet *Souvenir de Russie* – and dedications with a wink, such as *à qui les voudra, à celui qui a moins de patience* and *à ceux qui ayant appris à jouer de cet instrument, voyant de grandes*

---

[664] Devriès, Anik & François Lesure: *Dictionnaire des éditeurs de musique français*, Genève, Minkoff, 1979-1988, vol. II, p. 17.

[665] Stenstadvold, Erik: *An Annotated Bibliography of Guitar Methods, 1760-1860*, Organologia: Musical Instruments and Performance Practice No. 4, London, Pendragon Press, 2010, p. 3-6.

[666] Devriès, Anik & François Lesure: *Dictionnaire des éditeurs de musique français*, Genève, Minkoff, 1979-1988, vol. II, p. 8, 11-12, 98-99, 191, 246, 276, 365, 372, 395, 415; Soullier, Charles: *Annuaire musical 1855*, Paris, Saint-Étienne, 1854, p. 35-36.

[667] Makaroff, N.: 'The memoirs of Makaroff', in: *The Guitar Review*, no. 3, p. 59.

[668] Jones, David Wyn: 'What Do Surviving Copies of Early Printed Music Tell Us?', in: Rasch, Rudolf, ed.: *Music Publishing in Europe 1600-1900*, Berlin, Berliner Wissenschafts-Verlag, 2005, p. 147.

difficultés où on n'y a que de la correction opus 53. 48 dedications all together in his 72 works for guitar.[669] Giuliani wrote 194 works of which 62, sometimes by the editor, were dedicated to counts, countesses, dukes, duchesses, barons, baronesses, princes and princesses, and only some to ordinary civilians, pupils, and a fellow composer, Moretti, opus 112.[670] With Carulli this number is much smaller. He has 56 dedications to 52 different people among them fellow composers Carcassi, Coste, – opus 328 *Duo Concertant* – Fossa and Lemoine, in a total of 366 opus numbers, 398 works.[671] Coste might have played duets not only with Sor, but with Carulli too. With Mertz the list is not so long, it includes 14 names of dedication in his 207 compositions.[672] Zani de Ferranti dedicates 13 works to individuals, including king Leopold I of Belgium, one to Legnani and one to Carulli, as well as two to general classes of people like 'amateurs' and 'élèves', which makes 15 dedications on 89 works.[673] This attitude towards dedication may point to a change in this phenomenon in practice, as a reflection of concert practice and new public conventions. The following table shows Sor coming out ahead, numerically speaking, with Coste and Giuliani lagging far behind in second and third place.

Dedications numerically

composer	dedications	works	percentage
Sor	48	72	67%
Giuliani	62	194	32%
Carulli	56	398	14%
Mertz	14	207	7%
Zani	15	89	17%
Coste	45	122	37%

Numerically the Classics have many dedications, except for Carulli. Among the Romantics Coste has many of them, while Zani and Mertz dedicate much less. A shift in the dedications can also be seen away from nobility and towards the bourgeoisie in the transition from the Classics to the Romantics. Could dedications have something to do with the composer's position? By the 19th century, the time that the license for an edition could be obtained by dedicating a work to a ruler already belongs to the past. Composers are no longer in the employ of the nobility, either. The bourgeoisie also refrains from employing musicians; it is too expensive and out of fashion. There are other, cheaper ways to enjoy music. Guitar composers give public concerts, play in salons, teach and publish their compositions and arrangements. If this is still not enough to make a living, they take on another job, as Coste himself was forced to do. If the person to whom the work has been dedicated has also contributed to the publication costs, that could have been necessary due to the composer's poor financial position and/or him unknown or insufficiently popular. But Sor is very well known and well-off due to his score for the very successful ballet *Cendrillon*, which was performed about 104 times between 1823 and 1830 in Paris's Opéra.[674] A perceptible change is going on in composers' attitudes with respect to dedications and the social position of the people to whom works are dedicated.

Dedications feature prominently in Coste's work. A total of 45 names grace his 122 various works, by which is meant that each opus number consists of various works, such as the 25 *Études* that make up his opus 38. This comes to 22 dedications just up to his *Études* in opus 38, while 21 of his 25 *Études* in

---

[669] Jeffery, Brian: *Fernando Sor, Composer and Guitarist*, London, 1977; second edition 1994, p. 149-173.
[670] Heck, Thomas Fitzsimmons: *Mauro Giuliani: Virtuoso Guitarist and Composer*, Columbus, 1995, p. 196-225.
[671] Torta, Mario: *Catalogo tematico delle opere di Ferdinando Carulli*, Lucca, 1993, p. 764-765.
[672] Stempnik, Astrid: *Caspar Joseph Mertz, Leben und Werk...*, Lang, Frankfurt am Main, 1990, vol. II p. X.
[673] Wynberg, Simon: *Marco Aurelio Zani de Ferranti*, a biography, Chanterelle, Heidelberg, 1989, p. 65-70.
[674] Lajarte, Théodore de: *Bibliothèque Musicale du Théâtre de l'Opéra*, Vol. 2, Paris, 1878, p. 104.

opus 38 are dedicated to various individuals, some of whom had already received dedications in earlier works. These people include 10 pupils, 8 friends, 1 family member, 1 composer and 1 publisher. After that come another 13 dedications up through opus 53, as well as 5 of the works without an opus number. Out of this list of names a few individuals emerge whose identities can be ascertained, and sometimes even a portrait of them can be found. M. Adan of opus 31 and opus 38, no. 23 has a financial position at the Belgian royal court. Coste runs into him during his participation in the Makaroff competition. Hector Berlioz is given opus 15, *Le Tournoi*. Søffren Degen can be satisfied with having opus 28[b], opus 41 and *Étude* 9 opus 38 dedicated to him. This is Coste's friend from Copenhagen who visited him in 1855 in Paris, when he probably took the second photograph discovered of him – which is from an earlier date – in which he is wearing a top hat and poses with Degen's guitar. Opus 5, *Souvenirs de Flandres*, which is linked to Valenciennes in northern France, is dedicated to his mother Anne Pierrette Dénéria. *Grande Sérénade*, opus 30, is dedicated to Nicolas de Makaroff, as is *Étude* 25 opus 38. *Grande Sérénade* is the work that took second prize in the Russian's competition in Brussels in 1856. Opus 27, 28 and 40 are dedicated to the noblewoman Madame la Comtesse Nadaillac Delessert. We know that Coste dedicated his opus 13, *La Cachucha* to his pupil Louise Olive Pauilhé in around 1840. He did not marry her until 1871, and he then writes opus 43 for her, nothing less than a *Marche funèbre...*, an extract of which can be found in *Étude* 14, which is dedicated to her, in opus 38.

Dedications can easily become subject to change: three of his *Études* in opus 38 are given a different dedication in the second edition of the work. There is a known photograph of M. J. Schult(z), a merchant from Stockholm, in which he poses in the same way as in the most well-known photograph of Coste taken by Disdéri, with a number of guitars in front of him. So, he must have been familiar with the photo of Coste. *Divagation* opus 45 is dedicated to Schult as well as *Étude* no. 24, opus 38. Finally, Coste writes three pieces for his friend the oboist Charles Triébert, *Regretz et Consolations* opus 25 + 36 and *Le Montagnard* opus 34[a], both for oboe and piano, as well as a *Concertino* WoO 4 that had apparently been lost, but which has since been found in the Biblioteket in Copenhagen. And then there are a few dedications of a more general nature, including *Aux Parisiens* WoO 2, *Le Livre d'Or* opus 52 for the Club des Guitaristes de Leipzig and the song *Le Petit Ange rose* WoO 11 for young mothers. That means that only 13 of the works with or without opus number bear no dedication at all, and that the overwhelming majority of Coste's compositions are dedicated either to individuals or entire categories of people.

Because the *Études* include 25 works and many dedications, more than half of them (24) of the total number of dedications that Coste ever made (47), many of these names are covered here. These include a number of names that will have since become familiar to the reader: Richardière (no. 2), Holm (no. 7), Degen (no. 9), his wife Olive Pauilhé (no. 14), Caroline Montigny (no. 19), Adan (no. 23) and Makaroff (no. 25), figures who have been mentioned in this biography in discussions of different stages in Coste's life. That is also a reason to assume that opus 38 is a collection of works that were composed over a long span of time and which only now have been assembled, arranged in order and published. The many other names in the dedication up to the études are unknown, but Coste has built up an extensive circle of acquaintances in the guitar world, including internationally. Holm (no. 7) comes from Copenhagen, just like Degen (no. 9), Ulenbrock (no. 16) comes from Riga, Adan (no. 23) from Brussels, Schult(z) (no. 24) from Stockholm and Makaroff (no. 25) from St. Petersburg, as is known. The names of Mlle Harris (no. 17), M. Gozzoli (no. 20) and Lord Asburnham [sic] (no. 21) also have an international flair, but these men might also just have lived in Paris, because the last person is a pupil, just as emerges from the dedication of opus 3 from 1830, where he is named as Ashburnham. He is very loyal to his teacher when he is still taking lessons from Coste in 1872. Ten of the names are mentioned as being pupils, including Ulenbrock, who must have been living in Paris. Nine of the individuals mentioned appear exclusively in the études. The others have some other works dedicated to them, an additional indication that the études were composed over the course of several years, as well as of the loyalty of Coste's pupils. There are just seven women among the 24 individuals who received dedications, whereas the assumption is that at this time the guitar was principally played by female amateurs. But this turns out not to be expressed in the number of his pupils. Coste corresponded with quite a few international contacts, in Genoa, Livorno, Marseille and particularly with Degen, opus 28[b], opus 41 and opus 38, no. 9, and Holm, opus 39, opus 38, no. 7 in Copenhagen, Hallberg opus 53, *Duetto* WoO 6, and Schult, opus 45, opus 38, no. 24.[675] Coste has tailored the music of the *Études* to the people to whom he dedicated it. The table in the appendices presents the names and the works used in the dedications.

Press

In the 1830s eleven new music periodicals were started, a few of which were only short-lived, while others survived for much longer. In 1856 *Le Ménestrel* still appears on a weekly basis, but the chanson, which for years graced the two centerfold pages, has disappeared. Up through 1883 only five articles about the guitar can be found in this publication.[676]

1856 is also the last year in which the *Bibliographie de la France* appears, which each week provided the Parisian public with the titles of new literary and musical publications. The last mention of a work by Coste concerns his *Consolazione* opus 25 for oboe and piano.[677] The *Revue et Gazette musicale* has acquired an important status. It is in this journal that the most traces of guitar-related activities can been found, fourteen of them, to be exact. *La France musicale*, associated with the Escudier publishing house, continues to appear weekly and yields the same picture as the previous journal: only three guitar-related items. Of the nine other periodicals established since 1830, only *L'Univers musical* still exists in 1856, which does not carry any news about Coste. One can use these journals dedicated to music to form an image of the musical world of Paris at the time, but they devote little space to the guitar and music written for it. *Le Journal des débats* gives no attention at all to the instrument. This situation means that the sketch of developments in musical criticism regarding the guitar and music written for it has to limit itself to 22 articles, most of which are nothing but announcements of commercial information. The picture that emerges is simple: the guitar appears to have literally disappeared from both the stage and the press. No trace can be found of Coste's public concerts. He still plays in the séances of the Société académique des Enfants d'Apollon, but those monthly performances are not open to the public.[678]

Instruments

The industrialization of instrument-making, which has been under way since 1830, comes to a halt during the economic crisis of 1847. The crisis hits small craftsmen in Paris the hardest, including the guitar-makers, who were not all that fond of mechanization, the violin and the guitar having the most traditional means of production in the sector. In addition to the 41% decrease in the number of craftsman, the crisis also hits piano- and organ-makers, with the number of workers in this trade decreasing by 68% and 74%, respectively. Ten of the stringed instrument makers work alone, eight employ staff and three even have more than ten employees, but of these instrument-makers only a few build guitars.[679] But Paris remains the center of the instrument-making world, nevertheless. The piano plays the dominant role. The instrument literally grows from five octaves at the start of the century to six, six and a half and even seven octaves after 1860. The number of organ-builders is half the number of piano-builders. The aforementioned Cavaillé-Coll is the most prominent, but Debain's harmonium from 1841 is very popular, and there are many experimental compositions and performances. The families of wind instruments by the Belgian maker Adolphe Sax, with saxhorns and saxophones,

---

[675] Coste-Schult 2 IX 1874; Coste-Hallberg 25 VI 1877, 29 IV 1881.
[676] *Le Ménestrel*, vol. XIV, no. 5, 4 I 1857, p. [3].
[677] *Bibliographie de la France*, vol. XLV, no. 33, 16 VIII 1856, p. 862: 'N. Coste. Consolazione, romance sans paroles, composée pour hautbois ou violon, avec accompagnement de piano. 6-00 A Paris, chez Colombier.'
[678] Decourcelle, Maurice: *La Société académique des Enfants d'Apollon, programmes des concerts annuels...*, Paris, Durand, 1881, p. 18, 24, 78, 108, 156-157, 177-179, 183-184, 188, 192, 197, 203-204, 208-210, 214, 217, 222, 231, 236, 240.
[679] Haine, Malou: *Les facteurs d'instruments de musique à Paris au 19ᵉ siècle des artisans face à l'industrialisation*, Bruxelles, Université de Bruxelles, 1984, p. 65, 79, 108, 145.

continue to dominate the market, in spite of the many inventions made by others. The harp is an instrument that disappears in the Romantic period. At this point, it is only made to order by piano-builders like Pleyel and Érard.[680]

In 1856, guitar-maker René Lacôte (1785-1868), nicknamed the 'Stradivarius of the guitar,' has his workshop at rue de Louvois no. 10, where his pupils Huel and possibly also Valance and Eulry also practice this art. The brothers François and George Chanot, and Jean-Joseph Coffé-Goguette do the same; they make guitars of the Molino type. And finally, Laprévotte, Gérard and Grobert are also active as guitar-makers in Paris. Different experimental shapes of the guitar's body and sound hole appear, but there is an overall tendency to build guitars with a larger body and a bigger sound,[681] sometimes with more than six strings, as in the case of Napoléon Coste's own Lacôte guitar from around 1850.[682] In this way, the guitar's demise can also been seen in the field of instrument-making, in addition to concerts, publishing and the press. Guitar-makers have not completely disappeared, but it is doubtful whether production was on a large scale. nevertheless, there seems to be a revival of the instrument, as Soullier writes in 1855:

The instrument was even a sort of favorite in France and Italy; but for some time now it has started to become neglected everywhere, or completely abandoned for some time in favor of the piano, whose perfection and well-earned popularity grows by the day.[683]

LOCATIONS

During his lifetime in Paris, Coste lived at seven different addresses, was in contact with many editors and played in concerts in salons, salles and theatres. As might be expected given the great diversity and high quality of culture in the metropolis, all his activities took place in an area comprising no more than sixteen square kilometers, in the center of Paris. This is illustrated in a map on page 261 in the appendices, along with the addresses where he lived and those of his editors and the salons and theatres. Unfortunately, the addresses of his many pupils could not be found, only their names survived in his dedications. But as can be concluded from one of his last letters, in which he writes that he now is receiving his pupils at his home, he must have given them guitar lessons at their home:

I stopped giving lessons in town. My pupils all come to my home to take their lessons.[684]

The center of Paris is the venue for a great number cultural events organized by the elite Coste was part of. In real life he could have walked with his guitar and manuscripts from his home to the several addresses where his artistic life was made manifest.

ROMANTICISM

François Fétis refined his music theory in 1835 and set the development of the history of harmony on the phase of the 'omnitony.' He proceeds from the premise of tonality as an absolute concept, formulated by intellect. In this theory, relations between pitches are not determined by nature. They are logical, necessary ideas through which concepts of relativity and quantity inherent in these relations

---

[680] Haine, Malou: 'Les facteurs d'instruments de musique à l'époque romantique' in: Bailbé [et al]: *La musique en France à l'epoque romantique (1830-1870)*, Paris, Flammarion, 1991, p. 102, 104-105, 108,

[681] Sinier, Daniel & Françoise de Ridder: *La Guitare, Paris 1650-1950*, Cremona, Il Salabue, 2007, p. 40, 52-66; Pierre, Constant: *Les Facteurs d'instruments de musique*, Paris, Sagot, 1893, p. 270-275; Vannes, René: *Dictionaire Universel des Luthiers*, Paris, 1951, 3ᵉ ed. Bruxelles, 1988, p. 58, 64, 98, 125, 138, 169, 198, 202, 372.

[682] Dugot, Joël: 'Napoléon Coste et René Lacôte', in: *Les Cahiers de la Guitare*, Boissy-St-Léger, Association Guitares et Luths, no. 70, avril 1999, p. 32-34.

[683] Soullier, Charles: *Nouveau dictionnaire de musique illustré...*, Paris, Bazault, 1855, p. 140: 'Cet instrument, [...] très en vogue chez les Espagnols, [...] avait même joui de quelque faveur en France et en Italie; mais il commence depuis quelque temps à être partout un peu négligé ou délaissé entièrement pour le piano, dont le perfectionnement et la popularité méritée redoublent de jour en jour.'

[684] Coste-Hallberg, 8 I 1882: 'J'ai renoncé à donner des leçons en ville. Mes élèves viennent tous prendre leurs leçons chez moi.'

Intermezzo II 169

are merely forms of our understanding of them. Art does not undergo progress; it merely changes.[685] In this way he in a way already foresees the logical outcome of the saturation of the dissonance that results in atonality, while at the same time abandoning the notion of progress. This occurs in around 1848, when Romantic music comes under attack. In the short period of the revolution, critics characterize Romantic music for the first time as philosophical and political. Hegel considers music to be the most Romantic of the arts, liberated from text and the expression of meaning. Music's inward orientation, as well as its emancipation from external reference, come to be viewed as a lack of mental content, and thus empty, so that, strictly speaking, music is no longer art. Music becomes so Romantic that it proves that art is no longer the bearer of the spirit, and this means the end of art. Krüger objects: feelings are an important aspect of the spirit, music is not devoid of thoughts, and he proposes the idea of logocentrism, in which word and thought coincide. The critics' anti-Romantic tendency in these years is followed by neo-Romanticism. The metaphysical premise of Hegel's notion of idea above pure musical meaning is denied by Hanslick. Listening to music is above all a thought process; without mental activity no aesthetic pleasure can even take place. Music is natural, passive and emotional, making it feminine in nature. This is a view that in 1851 leads Wagner to write in his theoretical work *Opera und Drama* that music is a woman, bringing the character of music to a figurative extreme. However, the revolt in criticism proves to have as little effect on Romantic music as the revolution itself.[686]

Around 1856, the drama of opposing sentiments, expressed in contrast and opposition, has become old-fashioned and has been largely replaced by increased intensity. There was a great variety of means to achieve this: the tension can be heightened using rhythm, harmony, pitch, dynamics, dissonance, texture, which could be combined, or even statically repeated, indicating the presence of motion. In the second half of the 19th century, contrasting basic material in music has largely disappeared. Opening themes with astonishing contrasts in intensity become rare. Most composers are primarily concerned with creating material that both commands a reasonable level of attention and maintains excitement. An effective increase in importance of a theme's development can be noticed, but seldom does one come across the original sudden, dramatic and even exaggerated waves of intensity of the sort one finds in composers from the 1830s and 40s. There is a change in the tonal system, which, due to a rich, complex chromatics, becomes less precise and more diffuse. This leads to the tonality crisis at the end of the 19th century, in which timbre grows more important. The richer mediant relations that dominate the 19th century make a new scale of expression of feeling possible, but reduce the simple precision of harmonic meaning which had previously been easier for the audience to hear. Dissatisfaction with the old-fashioned harmonic system leads the importance of pitch to be replaced with the importance of timbre.[687]

The descriptive analysis in this book based on 21 criteria make clear that, in his guitar music, Napoléon Coste manifests many of the typical Romantic style features. In that sense, in his compositions he reflects the stream of innovations that have been made in the first half of the 19th century, primarily in music for solo instruments such as the piano, but also in orchestral works. He applies these in a way that is markedly tailored to the guitar, consistent with Berlioz's remark in his *Traité d'instrumentation et d'orchestration* that without playing the instrument, one cannot write multi-voiced pieces for guitar that are full of melodic lines, in which all of the instrument's possibilities come to the fore.[688]

---

[685] Christensen, Thomas: 'Fétis and emerging tonal consciousness', in: Bent, Ian, ed.: *Music theory in the age of Romanticism*, Cambridge, Cambridge University Press, 1996, p. 44-45.
[686] Pedersen, Sanna: 'Romantic music under siege', in: Bent, Ian, ed.: *Music theory in the age of Romanticism*, Cambridge, Cambridge University Press, 1996, p. 59-63, 72-73.
[687] Rosen, Charles: *Music and Sentiment*, New Haven, London, Yale University Press, 2010, p. 114, 116, 212-122, 127.
[688] Berlioz, Hector: *Grand traité d'instrumentation et d'orchestration modernes*, Paris, Lemoine, 1843, p. 86: On ne peut, je le répète, sans en jouer, écrire pour la Guitare des morceaux à plusieurs parties, chargés de traits, et dans lesquels toutes les ressources de l'instrument sont mises en oeuvre.'

Coste went down the road of Romanticism, which led to the composition of his most prominent works. In that sense his guitar compositions are on par with those written for other solo instruments. Now that in the middle of the 19th century this same Romanticism comes under attack, it seems obvious that in what follows this study will reveal whether this can be perceived in his way of composing. The distinction between classical and popular music becomes more and more pronounced, and it may be that this aspect also plays a role in Coste's life and that one may be able to hear and see it. The following chapters discuss substantive musical aspects, as well as social-cultural aspects. The altered situation in 1856 is significant for Coste and his music. If he follows it, he will be sovereign in his choice; if he situates himself outside of it, he will succeed in escaping it.

111 Olry & Lacôte, heptacordes at auction, 1995

VII
Études de Genre

How much I now regret returning to my post after the contest. I should have left that miserable job and travelled. The success I had just obtained would have been an excellent passport. Anyway, such was God's will.[689]

RETURN 1856

Napoléon Coste is 51 years old when he returns to Paris with his laurels from the Makaroff competition in December 1856. There he resumes his activities again: as a private guitar instructor; as a composer, writing and publishing his works; as a guitarist, participating in concerts; but also as an administrator at the Préfecture de la Seine, fulfilling tasks that were anything but artistic. He describes his regrets about this in his letter of June 15, 1858 to Søffren Degen. Coste should have capitalized on his award by travelling across the music world of Europe as a virtuoso guitarist as others had before him – Huerta, Zani de Ferranti, Szczepanowski – and he now sees that as a missed opportunity. There are various factors that may have led him to this decision. Coste has established himself in the artistic circles of the *Société académique des Enfants d'Apollon* and the *Frères Unis Inséparables*, in which he is surrounded by other composers and musicians. He plays music with them and gives concerts with them, at least this is recorded one time at the Masonic lodge, in 1852. He also has pupils who afford him a certain amount of income security, pupils with a high standard of musical ability, as evidenced by the études that he writes for them and that he dedicates to them. Paris is also the best city for publishing his prize-winning works, as must have been obvious to him. But Coste shows his humility when he writes of his 'feeble genius as a composer and artist.'[690] And that may partially underlie his decision to remain in Paris. Moreover, he is not a traveler, as he says himself.[691] And then there is Louise Olive Pauilhé, a pupil who plays an important role in his life, and whom he finally marries in 1871.[692] She is already mentioned in 1840 as being his pupil, when Coste dedicates his Caprice *La Cachucha* opus 13 to her. The publication of *La Chasse des Sylphes* opus 29, of the winning *Sérénade* opus 30 and of *Le Départ* opus 31 was all handled by Girod, the latter two of which, in any case, appeared in 1857. Coste worked with great accuracy: the editions turn up very few printing errors, as Simon Wynberg indicates in the photographic reprinting of them in 1981.[693] Girod has his office at boulevard Montmartre no. 16, while Coste lives not far away at rue de Calais no. 11, in the same arrondissement, Opéra, which is now intersected by the new boulevard Haussmann, or where major construction work on the intersection is underway, in any case, extending the boulevard Montmartre diagonally through that district.

CONCERTS 1856-1858

A short time before the review of June 6, 1858, Ciebra plays in the Salle de Beethoven:

M. José de Ciebra, a Spanish nobleman and guitarist, plays a very nice fantasy on Donizetti's Lucrezia Borgia.[694]

---

[689] Coste-Degen, 15 VI 1858, Århus, Statsbiblioteket, Søffren Degens Papirer, Manuscript no. 27b, p. 3: 'Combien je regrette maintenant d'être revenu à mon poste après le concours! j'aurais dû quitter ce misérable emploi à cette époque et me mettre à voyager. Le succès que je venais d'obtenir était pour moi un excellent passeport. enfin, Dieu l'a voulu.'

[690] Coste-Degen, 15 VI 1858, Århus, Statsbiblioteket, Søffren Degens Papirer, Manuscript no. 27b, p. 1: '[...] mon faible génie de compositeur et d'artiste.'

[691] Coste-Degen, 17 VI 1863, Århus, Statsbiblioteket, Søffren Degens Papirer, Manuscript no. 27b, p. 4: '[...] vous. savez que je ne suis pas voyageur, [...]'.

[692] Paris, Archives de Paris, *Acte de mariage Napoléon Coste & Louise Olive Pauilhé*, 11 I 1871, Série V2E 5Mi 3/210.

[693] Wynberg, Simon: *The Guitar Works of Napoléon Coste*, facsimile edition, Monaco, 1981, vol. IV, commentary.

[694] *Revue et Gazette musicale de Paris*, vol. XIV, no. 23, 6 I 1858, p. 190: 'M. José de Ciebra, noble espagnol et guitariste, jouant une fort jolie fantaisie sur la romance de la Lucrezia Borgia, de Donizetti.'

On Tuesday, March 29, 1859, Jaime Bosch (1829-1895) describes Coste as a 'remarkable guitarist' in Paris at a *soirée* hosted by M. and Mme Herwyn and reports that he received enthusiastic cheers of applause. In May of that year it is Zani de Ferranti's moment of fame at the

> *[...] studio of a famous painter [...] as first guitarist of the King of Belgium, doubtless also of the whole world, [...] with distinguished compositions, a rich tone and style. He shows great variety in sound, expressive power, sensitive and indescribably poetic accents of that pitiful guitar, what has fallen victim to the piano.*[695]

In February 1860 he again needs to do take on the exhausted capabilities of his instrument.[696] And Bosch is still doing well in the French capital, where 'people know that the guitar has fallen into disuse practically everywhere, but that it is still used in Spain.'[697] Coste heard both them and Sokolowski play, and he shares his thoughts on them with Schult in 1875:

> *For a number of years now hardly anyone worthy of note has come on the scene. The last ones include Huerta, Ciebra, Sokolowski and one named Bosch. Huerta plays brilliantly and has been blessed with nimble fingers. Unschooled in everything a good artist musician needs to know, he plays the most informal rhapsodies with an unparalleled energy (he plays with his nails). Ciebra is more serious, and, more importantly, more of a musician. He also plays with his nails. Both have been dubbed the 'Paganini of the guitar'. I have hardly heard the Russian Sokolowski at all. They say he's got talent. Bosch or Bosche is not as good, but is pleasant to listen to [...].*[698]

In giving his opinion, Coste draws on his knowledge as a guitarist. It is remarkable that he twice mentions that they use their nails. That could mean that he didn't take use of the nails for granted and found it noteworthy. Otherwise he would not have mentioned it. So, he himself must play without using his nails. In the official musical press, Coste's name appears once more, but in the programs of the monthly members-only musical meetings of the *Société académique des Enfants d'Apollon*, which Maurice Decourcelle publishes in 1881, Coste can be found many times starting from 1857.[699] In October 1857, at the Apollo Society's 'séance mensuel', he plays *Le Départ, fantaisie pour la guitare* opus 31, the work that was not entered for consideration in the Makaroff competition and was therefore not played in it. Thus, Coste does play it a year later, in an entirely different circle, and it is well received, because Decourcelle mentions works composed by fellow artists or enthusiasts, as well as performances by artists who have obtained some level of notoriety.[700] Other musicians who play during this meeting are the already familiar Casimir Ney, violist, who plays in an *Andante varié et finale* by A. Blanc, which must refer to his quintet with two cellos, opus 53.[701] *Le Départ* opus 31 has just recently been published, in September. It may have earned him quite some attention: the piece requires a virtuoso performer and is engaging, all the more so due to its chauvinistic subject matter.

---

[695] *Revue et Gazette musicale de Paris*, vol. XIV, no. 14, 3 I 1859, p. 115: 'Herwyn [...] soirée musicale [...] mardi [...] Bosch, le guitariste si remarcable'; no. 18, 1 V 1859, p. 142: "[...] atelier d'un peintre célèbre. [...] Zani de Ferranti, qui, s'il est le premier guitariste de S.M. le roi des Belges, il l'est aussi, sans contredit, du monde entier. [...] la variété d'effets, la force de l'expression, l'accent pathétique, poétique et indescriptible de cette infortunée guitare, victime du piano.'

[696] *Revue et Gazette musicale de Paris*, vol. XXVIII no. 6, 5 II 1860, p. 44: '[...] lutter contre les ressources exiguës de son instrument [...].'

[697] *Revue et Gazette musicale de Paris*, vol. XXVIII no. 19, 12 V 1861, p. 148: On sait que la guitare, aujourd'hui presque partout tombée en desuétude, a encore conservé en Espagne, [...].'

[698] Coste-Schult, 17 IV 1875: 'Depuis un certain nombre d'années il n'en est guère venu de remarquables. Les derniers sont: Huerta, Ciebra, Sokolowski et un nommé Bosch. Huerta a un jeu brillant et il est doué d'une belle organisation. Ignorant de tout ce qui constitue de savoir d'un artiste musicien et jouant les plus informes rapsodies avec un àplomb sans pareil (il se sert des ongles). Ciebra est plus sérieux et surtout plus musicien. Il joue aussi avec les ongles. [...] Tous les deux s'intitulent de Paganini de la guitare. Je n'ai point entendu le Russe Sokolowski; on dit qu'il a du talent. Bosche ou Bosch n'est pas fort mais joue agréablement [...].'

[699] Decourcelle, Maurice: *La Société des Enfants d'Apollon (1741-1880): programmes des concerts annuels...*, Paris, Durand, 1881, pp. 188, 197, 226, 231, 236, 240; Cooper, Jeffrey: *The Rise of Instrumental Music and Concert Series in Paris, 1828-1871*, Ann Arbor, UMi Press, 1983, pp. 257-258.

[700] Decourcelle, Maurice: *La Société des Enfants d'Apollon (1741-1880): programmes des concerts annuels...*, Paris, Durand, 1881, p. 188: *Le Départ*, fantaisie pour la guitare, composée et exécutée par M. Coste.'

[701] Fauquet, J.-M.: Blanc, Adolphe', in: Fauquet, Joël-Marie: *Dictionnaire de la Musique en France au XIXe siècle*, Paris, Fayard, 2003, p. 150.

VII — Études de Genre

Letters 1858

In 1858 Coste seems to have moved from the narrow rue de Calais no. 11 to the much wider rue Blanche no. 100, near the place Blanche, both in the 9th arrondissement, the new address being around the corner from the old one. This address was unearthed by Noël Roncet in a letter that Coste writes on May 15, 1858 to the Ministry of War concerning the state of the military service of his father, Jean François Coste. Roncet doesn't mention the reason, and neither does he say why Coste is still interested in this matter after so many years.[702] The reason for moving to a new residence so nearby could have to do with Haussmann's ongoing construction work, as well as with financial matters if the new apartment was less expensive. Coste continues to have financial difficulties, as shown by the way he is obliged to stay at his unrewarding job at the Caisse Municipale. Then, on June 15, 1858, Coste writes his first known letter to Søffren Degen in Copenhagen. The other part of the correspondence has not been found, but still much can be deduced from the way Coste replies the Degen's letter. Coste complains about the job he holds and talks about his personal circumstances:

112 Rue Blanche no. 100, 2007

> *You know that I had a minor job at the Seine prefecture. This job had certain unpleasant aspects due to the way it paralyzed my feeble genius as a composer and artist, but it afforded me a humble existence. So that gave me something, but if I didn't have any lessons, something that occurs often, I could be sure that I wouldn't lack anything necessary, but anyway, my dear friend, I no longer have that job. It was eliminated quite a while ago, that is, three or four months ago I was vaguely informed. However, I didn't believe the matter was serious, and I was justified in thinking that if it ever happened they would at least give me compensation, In any case, the time came. They didn't say "now leave!", but the job had ceased to exist.[703]*

The job has its problems. Coste was obliged to accept it so he could earn a living during periods when he had no pupils. But when the job is eliminated, he is suddenly without a source of income and asks for another job:

> *So I asked to be given a job in another part of the agency. They told me that the rules didn't allow hiring a man of my age. They are quite strict about that. That simply appalled me. I turned my back to the person who had given me this response and ran away, regretting that I had taken such a humiliating step. You wouldn't believe how much I suffered from that, Degen, considering how impressionable and sensitive I am.[704]*

---

[702] Roncet, Noël: *Napoléon Coste, Compositeur 1805-1883*, Amondans, 2005, pp. 25-26.

[703] Coste-Degen, 15 VI 1858, Århus, Statsbiblioteket, Søffren Degens Papirer, Manuscript no. 1-2: 'Vous savez que j'avais à la préfecture de la Seine un petit emploi. Cet emploi avait certes bien des inconvénients et paralysant bien mon faible génie de compositeur et d'artiste, mais il me fesait vivre modestement. C'était peu de chose, mais si je n'avais pas de leçons, ce qui m'arrive souvent, j'étais assuré de ne pas manquer du nécessaire. eh bien, mon cher ami, cet emploi je ne l'ai plus. il a été supprimé depuis longtemps, c'est à dire depuis trois, ou quatre mois j'avais été prévenu vaguement; Cependant je ne croyais pas la chose sérieuse et j'étais fondé de croire que si elle avais lieu on m'accorderait au moins un dédommagement. enfin le moment est arrivé, on ne m'a pas dit: allez-vous en! Mais l 'emploi n'existait plus.'

[704] Coste-Étegen, 15 VI 1858, Århus, Statsbiblioteket, Søffren Degens Papirer, Manuscript no. 2-3: '[...] alors j'ai demandé à être employé dans une autre partie du service. on m'a dit que les réglements s'opposent à l'admission d'un homme de mon âge on est bien sévère ladessus. cela m'a révolté, j'ai tourné le dos à celui qui m'a fait cette réponse et je me suis sauvé en emportant le regret d'avoir fait une démarche humilliante. Vous comprendrez, mon cher Degen, ce que j'ai dû souffrir impressionnable et sensible comme je le suis.' [fc. see appendix]

This is the first time that we can discern something about Coste's personality using his own words. He indicates that he is quite sensitive, that he has a modest impression of his own talent, but also that he does not take well to wrongs done to him. He has problems with the job, but cannot give it up. He is financially dependent on this position, takes a humiliating and unwise step and expresses his regret that he missed the opportunity to go on a concert tour. In his own words he expresses himself as a sensitive person, with respect for human relationships and the status quo. After that Coste writes that he has sent him the *Méthode* and that he was shocked at the price of the postage, which was now 10 fr. instead of the 7 fr. he had mentioned earlier. He included two copies of *La Consolazione* for oboe, violin or cello and piano. That work must be opus 25 which was played by Triébert, perhaps together with Coste at the Apollo society, in February 1855,[705] before Degen's visit Coste in Paris, and published by Colombier in 1856, meaning that Degen had not been able to acquire a copy at that time.[706] Coste concludes the letter by saying:

> *The engraving of the Fantaisie symphonique that is dedicated to you, has been delayed by all my Troubles, but I hope to take it up again very shortly. Farewell, dear friend. Give my respectful regards to your dear, kind sister and rest assured of the steadfast devotion of your loving friend N. Coste.*[707]

In this section, with the extensive formalities Coste uses to conclude the latter, it will be noted that their relationship was affectionate, that Coste was quite cordial and that Degen had perhaps been accompanied by his sister on his visit to Coste in 1855. Coste indicates that he is working on the publication of the *Fantaisie symphonique* opus 28[b], but apparently those plans did not go through, because no copy of it has been found, and also because part of that work appears as *Étude* 14 opus 38 with an addition between brackets 'Inédite', thus not published in 1872 when this opus appears. There this Andante is dedicated to his wife.[708] Here he dedicates the work to Degen, who, differently from with the *Rondeau de Concert* opus 12, *Le Passage des Alpes* opus 27, 28 & 40 and *La Source du Lyson* opus 47, he cannot write a second guitar part because he has not received this music.[709] Degen has collected many of Coste's editions and copies, which were even sent to him by the composer himself. Their relationship is of great significance for the guitar in Denmark. One of the few faithful pupils who Degen still had in his later years, Thorvald Rischel, inherited the large collection of sheet music that Degen left behind, including many published and unpublished guitar works by Napoléon Coste. Rischel expanded the collection by travelling to Paris in 1883, after Coste's death. There he purchased various unpublished works from Coste's widow. In 1893, after the death of the composer's widow, he travelled again to the town of Thiais near Choisy-le-Roi to search her estate for Coste's *Grand Duo* WoO 8.[710] This is how the Rischel & Birket-Smith Collection in the Royal Library in Copenhagen came into being.[711]

---

[705] Decourcelle, Maurice: *La Société des Enfants d'Apollon (1741-1880): programmes des concerts annuels...*, Paris, Durand, 1881, p. 183: Romance sans parole, composée par M. Coste, exécutée sur le cor anglais par M. Triebert.

[706] *Bibliographie de la France*, vol. XLV, no. 33, 16 VIII 1856, p. 862: N. Coste. Consolazione, romance sans paroles, composée pour hautbois ou violon, avec accompagnement de piano. 25. 6-00 A Paris, chez Colombier.

[707] Coste-Degen, 15 VI 1858, Århus, Statsbiblioteket, Søffren Degens Papirer, Manuscript no. 27b, p. 4: 'La gravure de la Fantaisie symphonique qui vous est dédiée, a été un peu retardé par toutes mes Misères mais j'espère la reprendre incessamment. Adieu, cher ami, présentez à votre aimable et chère soeur l'hommage de ma respectueuse amitié et croyez à l'attachement et au dévouement inaltérable de Votre affectionné N. Coste.'

[708] Wynberg, Simon: *The Guitar Works of Napoléon Coste*, facsimile edition, Monaco, 1981, vol. I, commentary, p. 15.

[709] Wynberg, Simon: *The Guitar Works of Napoléon Coste*, facsimile edition, Monaco, 1981, vol. VII, Introduction, Guitar II. p. 17-26.

[710] Møldrup, Erling: *Guitaren, et eksotisk instrument i den danske musik*, Copenhagen, Kontrapunkt, 1997, p. 132; Rischel, Thorvald: Bibliographische Notizen zu den Gitarrenwerken von Napoléon Coste', in: *Die Gitarre*, Berlin, 1927, Jahrgang VIII, Heft 7/8, [Coste-Heft] p. 48.

[711] Torpp Larsson, Jytte: *Catalogue of the Rischel and Birket-Smith Collection*, Columbus, Orphée, 1989, p. i-iii.

VII — *Études de Genre*

Opus 33[a], *Mazurka* 1860

This library includes the only copy of this piece that can be found, which has since been digitized and made available to the public,[712] of the *Mazurka* opus 33[a] that was published around 1860 by a certain I. Hirsch, at rue Nôtre Dame de Nazareth no. 27 in Paris, according to the signature on this single-page work.[713] Bearing the opus numbering in mind, opus 32 seem to be missing. According to Thorvald Rischel it does not exist.[714] It is remarkable that there are so many works with opus number 28, which Wynberg rightly distinguishes as three separate works using the letters a, b and c. The same is done with opus 33 and 34, each of which include two works. It may be that the work simply has yet to be found, in which case a good candidate would be the title *Sérénade* for oboe, clarinet and guitar, which was discovered in the annals of the *Société académique des Enfants d'Apollon* and has been assigned the provisional number WoO 13. But the date of this work, 1852, contradicts this possibility. While all this discussion of an unfound work may seem excessive, it does make it easier to search, with the title *Sérénade* WoO 13, the instrumentation oboe, clarinet and guitar, date 1852 and possible numbering opus 32 at hand.

The *Mazurka* opus 33[a] proves to be a simple little piece of 48 measures, with many repetitions, using the requisite *A-B-A* form, which is apparent from the number of measures, fulfilling the customary characteristics of the mazurka. Chopin wrote some fifty of these as extensive, inventive pieces,[715] whereas Coste only composed this simple one, but he did fill it with very elegant and stylish motifs, successful campanellas, gracious glissandos and legatos, albeit with few Romantic style elements other than some key-confirming chromatic melodic coloring. It is a very nice little piece, of which an audio recording has yet to appear. Although one can recognize Coste's style in this piece, it is provisionally the last work that Coste writes for guitar solo until the *Études de Genre* opus 38, which appear around 1872. The latter were doubtless written earlier, probably for pupils and tailored for pedagogical purposes.

Holm 1863

That is not the case for other circumstances in Coste's life, including during this period. The second letter found to Søffren Degen, dated October 17, 1863, contains information on this.[716] After a few short pleasantries about the letter previously received from Degen, Coste turns to the issue of letters from that other Dane, M. Holm, whom he finds very pleasant, helped by the fact that he has received a photograph from him. The gentleman in question is Johan G. Holm from Copenhagen, to whom Coste dedicates his *Étude 7* opus 38 and who must be a fierce guitar player, because this étude has both speed and a bit of virtuosity and moves over many positions with three-voice chord prolongations, broken chords and scale passages. The *Andante et Menuet* opus 39 is also dedicated to J. G. Holm, another indication of the friendly nature of their relationship. That piece is mature and of a level of difficulty comparable to that of the étude. Erling Møldrup publishes a photograph of Holm in his essay about the guitar in Danish music, listing as his source the Kongelige Bibliotek, but the image cannot be found in the digital catalogue of that library, making it impossible to date. Holm plays on a 'theorboed' guitar, as is customary in Denmark, with a body that has a specially shaped girth. His left foot rests on the floor, without a foot support, so that the neck and strings are in a very low position. But it may be that this position is a pose and that he actually positions himself differently when he plays. If this is the photo of Holm referred to in the letter, he may have sent Coste a copy of it.[717] Holm also makes

---

[712] Kk Rischel 156 mu 6701.0683 (eks. 1) U 48, Coste: *Mazurka pour la guitare* op. 33, https://rex.kb.dk/primo-explore/fulldisplay?vid=NUI&search_scope=KGL&docid=MUS01000081231, 16 XI 2014.
[713] Wynberg, Simon: *The Guitar Works of Napoléon Coste*, facsimile edition, Monaco, 1981, vol. IV, Introduction, p. 69.
[714] Rischel, Thorvald: Bibliographische Notizen zu den Gitarrenwerken von Napoléon Coste', in: *Die Gitarre*, Berlin, 1927, Jahrgang VIII, Heft 7/8, [Coste-Heft] p. 50.
[715] Brown, Maurice J.E., & Czeslaw R. Halski: Mazurka', in: Sadie, Stanley ed.: *The New Grove Dictionary of Music and Musicians*, Vol.1-20, Macmillan, London, 1980. Vol.11, p. 865-866.
[716] Coste-Degen, 17 X 1863, Århus, Statsbiblioteket Søffren Degens Papirer, Manuscript no. 27. [fc. see appendix]
[717] Møldrup, Erling: *Guitaren, et eksotisk instrument i den danske musik*, Copenhagen, Kontrapunkt, 1997, p. 198.

113 Johan G. Holm

copies of various works by Coste, such as the *Scherzo et Pastorale* opus 10, *Duetto* WoO 6, two works for guitar duet, and of *Caprice La Cachucha* opus 13, *Le Pirate* WoO 9, copies that can also be found in the Rischel & Birket-Smith collections. Holm must have been a great admirer of Coste, having made such an effort, and Thorvald Rischel must have been a good collector. Coste also corresponds with Holm. He further writes in his letter to Degen:

> *He [Holm] has informed you of the disastrous accident, which has deprived me of the use of my left arm for almost six months now. For a long time I had given up the hope of ever being able to use it again, and I am happy to be able to report that I am beginning to try placing my fingers on the neck of my guitar, which must have grown quite bored of the long silence to which it had been condemned. But it is so weak, and I would need to overcome such obstacles in order to regain the playing ability I once had!*[718]

Accident 1863

The message he writes, in both extremely distinguished and very correct language, is that in February 1863, thus after his November 1862 concert at the monthly musical gatherings of the musicians of the Apollo society, he had the fall which is described by so many people, in which he suffers such a bad fracture to his left arm that he can no longer play. That was thus also the reason that he did not

---

[718] Coste-Degen, 17 VI 1863, Århus, Statsbiblioteket, Søffren Degens Papirer, Manuscript no. 27, pp. 1-2: 'Il vous a fait part de l'accident funeste qui depuis six mois bientôt, m'a privé de l'usage du bras gauche; j'ai désespéré longtemps de pouvoir m'en servir jamais, et je suis heureux de vous annoncer que je commence à essayer de poser les doigts sur le manche de ma guitare qui a du bien s'ennuye [sic] du long silence auquel elle a été condamné. Mais quelle faiblesse et que d'obstacles j'aurais à vaincre pour recouvrer l'exécution d'autrefois, hélas!'

VII — Études de Genre

177

return to the stage again until November 1874. In his letter he does not tell about the circumstances under which the fateful accident occurred, but it is likely that, when this happened in the Salle du Conservatoire, where the monthly meetings of the Apollo society take place, he could have fallen on the stairs there, as most other salles don't have a stage, and thus no stairs. There are at least twenty-one biographical publications about Coste's life in which this unfortunate incident is mentioned, and four authors write that he tripped on the stairs up to the podium, which is, of course, possible. Twelve authors in 13 publications indicate that it was his right arm, which is obviously incorrect, even though they are frequently consulted reference works, and sometimes even of relatively recent date.[719] In six of the publications, the authors refrain from going into detail and simply speak of an accident involving one of his arms that kept him from moving forward with his career.[720] And all these authors speak of the year 1863 or around that time, while none of them names the left arm, as would be correct. Two recent biographies, those of Noël Roncet and Roman Jaworski, do correctly identify the left arm, but they do so based on their research information for the year 1874, in which Coste applies for leave from his position at the Préfecture de la Seine due to a fracture.[721] Coste appears to be seriously hindered twice by this fracture to his left arm, in both 1863 and in 1874. At the end of this letter, he does write in a postscript that his shoulder is gradually improving. He also writes numerous times how much he regrets not being able to play duets, which would have also encouraged him to write more. There are now only three duets for guitar by Coste: the *Scherzo et Pastorale* opus 10, the *Duetto* WoO 6 and the *Grand Duo* WoO 8. He gives indications that he indeed knows Degen's sister personally, writing that she seems to him to be a friendly, outstanding individual.

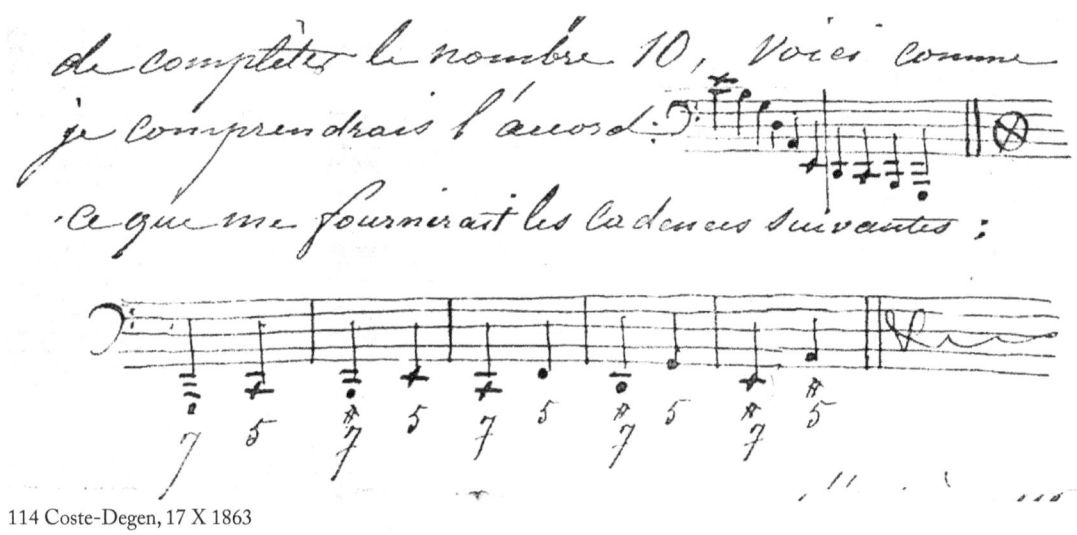

114 Coste-Degen, 17 X 1863

---

[719] Bellow, Alexander: *The Illustrated History of the Guitar*, New York, Colombo, 1970, p. 174; Bone, Philip J.: Coste, Napoléon', in: *The Guitar and the Mandolin*, London, Schott, 2nd ed., 1954, reprint 1972, p. 84; Buek, Fritz: *Die Gitarre und ihre Meister*, Berlin, Robert Lienau, 1926, 2nd ed. 1935, p. 107; Burzik, Monika: Coste, Napoléon', in: *Die Musik in Geschichte und Gegenwart*, ed. Blume, Finscher, Kassel, Bärenreiter, 2000, vol. 4, Kol. 1714; Carfagna, Carlo & A. Caprani: *Profilo Storico della Chitarra*, Ancona-Milano, Bèrben, 1966, p. 56; Radke, Hans: Coste, Napoléon', in: *Die Musik in Geschichte und Gegenwart*, ed. Blume, Kassel, Bärenreiter, 1956, ed. 1973, vol. XV (Supplement 1) Kol. 1616; Schwarz-Reiflingen, Erwin: Napoléon Coste', in: *Die Gitarre*, Berlin, 1927, Jahrgang VIII, Heft 7/8, [Coste-Heft] p. Shtokman [Stockmann], J.: Napoléon Coste', in: Der Guitarrefreund: Mitteilungen des Internationalen Guitarristen-Verbandes, München, 3. Jahrgang, 1902, Heft 5, p. 56; Summerfield, Maurice J.: *The Classical Guitar: Its Evolution, Players & Personalities since 1800*, Newcastle-upon-Tyne, Ashley Mark, 4th ed. 1996, p. 79; Wade, Graham: *Traditions of the Classical Guitar*, London, Calder, 1980, pp. 98, 113, 129; Wade, Graham: *A Concise History of the Classic Guitar*, Pacific, Mel Bay, 2001, p. Wynberg, Simon: *The Guitar Works of Napoléon Coste*, facsimile edition, Monaco, 1981, vol. III, Introduction; Zuth, Josef: Coste, Napoléon', in: *Handbuch der Laute und Gitarre*, Wien, Doblinger, 1926-28, repr. Hildesheim, Olms, 1978, p. 73.

[720] Cooper, Jeffrey: Coste, Napoléon', in: Sadie, Stanley ed.: *The New Grove Dictionary of Music and Musicians*, second edition, London, Macmillan, 1980, vol. 4, p. 824; Läpke, Richard: 'Biographie Napoléon Coste' in: *Internationale Gitarre-Zeitung*, Jahrgang I, Nr. 4 (Jan.1884), und Nr. 5 (Febr. 1884), Leipzig, transcr. Eduard Fack, 'Die Meister', unp. p. 119; Powroïniak, Józef: Coste, Napoléon', in: *Gitarrenlexikon*, Berlin, Verlag Neue Musik, 1979, p. 36; Radole, Giuseppe: *Liuto, chitarra e vihuela, storia e letteratura*, Milano, Suvini Zerboni, 1979, 3rd ed. 1997, p. 154; Viglietti, Cedar: *Origen e historia de la guitarra*, Buenos Aires, Albatros, 1976, p. 59, 77, 84; Wynberg, Simon: '...zur Rettung Napoléon Costes', in: *Gitarre und Laute*, Köln, vol. III, 1981, no. 5, p. 30.

[721] Jaworski, Roman: 'Napoléon Coste 1805-1883, une histoire perdue', in: *Valentiana*, Valenciennes, 1992, no. 10, p. 77; Roncet, Noël: *Napoléon Coste, Compositeur, 1805-1883*, Amondans, 2005, p. 26.

After giving Degen some words of encouragement about dealing with his personal problems, he turns to the subject of the ten-stringed guitar that Holm has had built. Coste limits himself to adding a seventh string, as is known, and that is enough for him, but if additional strings must still be added to the guitar, he is of the opinion that the bass strings should be tuned descending diatonically – i.e. with D - C - B - and then G, in order to make good cadences possible. He accompanies both remarks with handwritten musical notation, but notably not in the customary transposed notation used for the guitar, but in the correct octave using the F clef, as he himself remarks for completeness' sake, but that is intended for the guitar-maker, naturally. But why he omits the A between B and G, remains obscure, why not make it an eleven-stringed guitar? In the photograph of Holm, one can indeed see that he is playing a ten-stringed guitar. Coste continues with the remark that *Le Montagnard* opus 34[a] should really be played on an oboe, that he doesn't think he is much of a traveler and thus will not go visit Degen, that he has become much older and that Degen is one of the dearest and most esteemed people he knows. He ends with a somewhat less elaborate signature than in the letter from 1858. He also adds a postscript to the effect that he had written the letter much earlier, but that he lost Degen's letter and had found it again only a few days earlier. He also wishes him well, and those are Coste's last known words to Degen.[722] No letters other than these two are available, and this is the reason for considering them so carefully. Coste conducts documented correspondence with Degen, Holm and Hallberg. These two letters to Degen have been found, but no letters to Holm have turned up. Of the 36 letters to Hallberg, only one is available in photocopy, the others are transcripts in an unknown handwriting.[723] And then there are the six notes to Gruel recently purchased by Norbert Fischer in Halen, which have been used here in connection with Coste's final years in chapter VIII.

WoO 7, *L'Enfant au Berceau* 1864

Coste begins his career in Paris with a concert in the Gymnase musical in 1829 and with the composition and publishing of *Aux Parisiens* WoO 2 for voice and piano in 1830, the revolutionary chanson in which he articulates the heroism of the people in melody and accompaniment. The only chansons to be found after this one are by other composers and arranged by Coste for voice and guitar, many of them by Schubert, one by Thomas and another by Concone, both in 1838, and one by Barroilhet, in 1840. With these pieces Coste is following the fashion to arrange chansons or opera pieces for his instrument, to be played in private homes by amateurs and enthusiasts. After that it would take 24 more years before he finally dabbles in this genre again, with *L'Enfant au Berceau* WoO 7, which appears in 1864 in Paris published by Chatot. The only copy found to date is in the Bibliothèque nationale in Paris. It was never published again after that.[724] According to the lyricist Jules Adenis, the sylphs in the chanson need to use their wings to gently rock the sleeping child to prevent him from crying. After *La Chasse des Sylphes* opus 29 these air creatures are again set to music here by Coste, who in this chanson demonstrates his now fully developed mastery of musical Romanticism. The text is set to music in a programmatic way. It modulates continually, has an open ending, uses extratonal chords and deviates from periodicity. Coste also gives instructions for dynamics and execution, for heightened expression. It is a truly Romantic song. Remarkably, this chanson features many more Romantic features than do his works with oboe. It is dedicated to Mme Amica Petiteau, possibly a pupil who has been recently blessed with a child. Actually, there are four known original chansons known by Coste, the last two of which, *Lolla* WoO 10 and *Le Petit Ange rose* WoO 11 from 1878, will be discussed in chapter VIII. The chanson in question capitalizes on the popularity of a general topic, and it is commercial in intent.

---

[722] Coste-Degen, 17 VI 1863, Århus, Statsbiblioteket, Søffren Degens Papirer, Manuscript no. 27, p. 4.
[723] Napoléon Coste - späte Briefe 1867-1882, aus dem Nachlass von Georg Meier/Willy Meier-Pauselius", I. und W. Holzschuh, Hamburg; acquisition by mediation of Andreas Stevens, Hilden; transcripts from the originals in an unkown handwriting and translations in German.
[724] Pn Vm7 44.834, Coste: *L'Enfant au Berceau* [WoO 7].

VII — *Études de Genre* 179

Photograph of instruments 1867

For the sake of people he corresponds with abroad, such as Holm and Degen in Copenhagen and Hallberg and Schult in Stockholm, Coste has a portrait of himself made by the photographer Disdéri in 1867:

115 Napoléon Coste - Disdéri c. 1867

I have just had a photograph taken, not only of my guitar, but of my big arch-lute guitar, the theorbo, the cystre and myself. Unfortunately, during the procedure a ray of sunlight came and hit the arrangement and myself, in such a way that the top of the instruments and one side of my face got overexposed. But by using a magnifying glass you can see things as they actually are. As for my face, you already have it, and that shows how I look perfectly.[725]

He explains what instruments are concerned, as well as remarking that the photograph did not turn out well. But Schult appears to already have his portrait, which is doubtless the photograph Degen took of Coste in 1855.

Disdéri (1819-1889) became famous by photographing Napoléon Bonaparte and his army, and became rich by making cheap calling cards with a double lens. Thousands of these can be seen in

---

[725] Coste-Schult, 7 X 1867: 'Je viens de faire photographier non seulement ma guitare, mais ma grande guitare archluth, le Théorbe, le Cystre et moi-même. Malheureusement un rayon de soleil est venu pendant l'opération frapper le groupe et moi-même, de sorte que le haut des instruments et un côté de ma figure ont été brûlés. Mais à l'aide d'une loupe vous pourrez voir les choses telles qu'elles sont. Quant à ma figure vous l'avez déjà et celle-là est parfaite de ressemblance.'

the database of the Musée d'Orsay, but no photograph of Coste can be found among them, though others can be found that use the same props.[726] This copy comes from the Kongelige Bibliotek in Copenhagen.[727] The heptacorde guitar in the photo is certainly Coste's own instrument, as described in the letter. The way the tailpiece is cut away is a 'croix pattée alésée arrondi', possibly originating from the symbolism of the Knights Templar.[728] Considering that this symbol was also used as the 'iron cross' by the Prussians, who occupied Paris in 1871, Coste may have had it replaced at a later date.[729] The heptacorde, was purchased by the Musée de la Musique in Paris as Coste's own instrument and which was restored there, has a heart-shaped recess.[730] When Coste sends the photograph to Hallberg ten years later, Coste appears to be rather unsatisfied with it:

> *I am sending you a photograph in which you will find the bridge mounted on my model of guitar, a large guitar that belonged to Louis XIV, who played it; a theorbo (I) and a cystre, both converted into guitars. This photograph got overexposed by sunlight, giving me a black fringe of a beard, which makes my face look odd and makes me look eighty years old. Being 70 is good enough.*[731]

Coste writes that the arch-lute guitar is originally from Louis XIV's collection. He purchased it from a merchant in 1848 for the *Concerts historiques*, which organized a committee under the chairmanship of Fétis, but which, again, ultimately did not take place due to a disagreement with the Commission Impériale. Coste had the instrument customized so that he could play it like a guitar, as he also did with the cystre and the theorbo, and he did some research in the library of the Conservatoire to make transcriptions of old tablatures. The instrument was described in 1983 by Abondance, and again in 1988 by Dugot.[732] Coste was obliged to sell his theorbo, which he considered to be a splendid instrument, to make ends meet. He mentions the instrument in 1877 in his letter to Hallberg, so it must be the very same guitar.[733]

Concerts 1865-1872

Due to the 'disastrous accident', as Coste himself describes it in his letter of October 17, 1863, the guitarist can no longer use his left arm to play the guitar. That is why it is not until 1874 that he appears again in the Paris musical press and the annals of the *Société académique des Enfants d'Apollon*, where the guitar is played again in the monthly performances. It appears that the instrument does not disappear from the stage there, for 'Monsieur Bosc' (i.e. Bosch) plays his own composition *La Retraite fantaisie* there in June 1865.[734] Bosch returns to Paris in 1861 after a tour through Germany. In 1872 and later he gives various concerts, in which his performance and technique is highly praised, but:

---

[726] http://www.cndp.fr/themadoc/niepce/disderi.htm, 30 X 2007; http://www.musee-orsay.fr/fr/outils-transversaux/recherche/tout-le-site.html, November 17, 2014.
[727] Kopenhavn, Kongelige Bibliotek, Portraetsamlingen, *Coste, Napoléon*, 1806 [sic]-1883, guitarspiller, Disdéri.
[728] Sinier, Daniel & Françoise de Ridder: *La Guitare, Paris 1650-1950*, Cremona, Il Salabue, 2007, pp. 56-57.
[729] https://fr.wikipedia.org/wiki/Croix_pattée, 17 XI 2014.
[730] http://collectionsdumusee.philharmoniedeparis.fr/0158354-guitare-a-sept-cordes-lacote-coste.aspx, 17 XI 2014; Abondance, Pierre: 'Guitare de Napoléon Coste', in: *Les Cahiers de la Guitare*, Paris, 1983, No. 6, p. 11; Dugot, Joël: 'Napoléon Coste et René Lacôte', in: *Les Cahiers de la Guitare*, Boissy-St-Léger, Association Guitares et Luths, no. 70, avril 1999, pp. 32-34; Ribouillault, Danielle: 'La "Guitaromanie": du salon à la salle de concert', in: *Instrumentistes et Luthiers Parisiens*, Florence Gétreau, ed., Paris, La Ville de Paris, 1988, p. 192.
[731] Coste-Hallberg, 7 III 1877: 'Je vous envoie une photographie où vous trouverez le chevalet appliqué sur une guitare de mon modèle, une grande guitare ayant appartenue à Louis XIV qui en jouait; un theorb (l) et un cystre, tous deux convertis en guitare. Cette photographie à été brûlée par un coup de soleil qui m'a fait un collier de barbe noire et m'a drôlement arrangé la figure que j'ai l'air d'avoir 80 ans. C'est bien aussi d'en avoir 70.'
[732] Abondance, Pierre: 'Guitare de Napoléon Coste', in: *Les Cahiers de la guitare*, Paris, 1983, no. 6, p. 11; Dugot, Joël: *Guitare basse, auteur inconnu, fin du XVIIIe siècle (?)*, in: *Instrumentistes et Luthiers Parisiens*, Florence Gétreau, ed., Paris, La Ville de Paris, 1988, p. 172.
[733] Coste-Schult, 7 X 1867; Coste-Gruel, 16 VI 1879; Coste-Hallberg, 7 III 1877.
[734] Decourcelle, Maurice: *La Société des Enfants d'Apollon (1741-1880): programmes des concerts annuels...*, Paris, Durand, 1881, p. 203: '*La retraite*, fantaisie pour la guitare, composée et exécutée par M. Bosc.'

VII — Études de Genre 181

[...] never before has this unrewarding instrument, as has been demonstrated by the Huertas and the Paganinis, proved itself to us to lend itself to such beautiful things.[735]

Also in 1872, Giulio Regondi (1822-1872) dies in London, where he resides from 1831 after his performances as a travelling child prodigy, giving a concert twice a year, in which he plays the concertino in addition to the guitar. However, not much more of his life work has survived than four études and five recital pieces.[736] At Schult's request, Coste examined two of Regondi's works and gives his opinion in a letter dated November 2, 1876:

The first two that I examined, the Fête villageoise and an air varié, made a very bad impression on me. I find these compositions completely lacking in ideas and charm. The former is tortured and is often harmonically defective. Op. 23 is much better. It is the work of a composer with thorough knowledge of the instrument and who possesses solid means of execution, but who lacks a knowledge of counterpoint, without which one cannot produce anything perfectly regular in composition. At times the harmony is too loaded, and at others of a deplorable paucity. All of this is poorly written for the guitar. You will undoubtedly think that I am a bit severe, dear sir. It just appears to me that you are putting Regondi on par with Sor in your opinion, if not above him. That's like comparing a pygmy with a giant, and it certainly isn't Regondi who's the giant.[737]

Huerta is also active as a guitarist in Paris venues in the 1860s, despite the fact that he was declared dead for a short while in 1855.[738] He is quite alive again in 1861, including in the salle Pleyel,[739] where Sokolowski also performs in 1865.[740] This Polish guitarist made a great impression at his debut in Paris in January of 1864, in which the critic felt called to revise his negative prejudices over what he had found to be a dull-sounding and unrewarding instrument.[741] The blind man Jean Vailati, who is also a virtuoso mandolin player, performs in the Théâtre international 1867.[742] The guitar certainly has not yet disappeared from the concert stage in Paris, but the piano is dominant, as emerges in the review of the pianist Marmontel's soirée in *Le Ménestrel*:

[...] in the midst of the triumphant vibrations of the piano, suddenly the guitar appears, like an apparition! The guitar, forgotten, neglected, sweet victim of man's injustice! A true artist, M. de Folly has undertaken to rehabilitate the pleasant instrument that once supported the voices of our grandmothers. M. de Folly has taken it upon himself discover some unknown qualities in the guitar, which have long remained hidden to the layman's fingernails. He makes it sing like a violin. It is no longer the thin, languid sound for which it is often criticized, the thin and frail pizzicato; it's a little orchestra with its chords, from which the

---

[735] *Revue et Gazette musicale de Paris*, vol. XXVIII no. 9, 3 III 1861, p. 70: 'M. Bosch, le célèbre guitariste est de retour à Paris.'; vol. XXXIX, no. 8, 25 II 1872, p. 63: '[...] jamais cet ingrat instrument, qu'illustrèrent pourtant les Huerta et les Paganini, ne nous avait paru capable de se prêter à de si jolie choses.'

[736] Regondi, Giulio in: Wynberg, Simon: *Giulio Regondi, Complete Works for Guitar*, Monaco, 1981, Essay.

[737] Coste-Schult, 2 XI 1876: 'Les deux premiers que j'ai examiné, la fête villageoise et un air varié, m'avaient fort mal disposé. J'ai trouvé ces compositions absolument dépourvues d'idées et de charme. Cela est tourmenté et souvent d'une harmonie défectueuse. L'op. 23 est de beaucoup meilleur. C'est l'oeuvre d'un artiste ayant une profonde connaissance de l'instrument et qui possède de solides moyens d'exécution mais à qui il manque la science du contrepoint sans laquelle on ne peut rien produire de parfaitement régulier en composition. Tantôt l'harmonie est trop chargée et tantôt d'une pauvreté déplorable. Tout cela est mal écrit pour la guitare. Vous me trouverez sans doute un peu sévère, cher Monsieur, c'est qu'il m'a semblé que vous placez dans votre opinion Regondi à coté de Sor, si non au dessus. C'est comparer un pygmée à un géant et certes ce n'est pas Regondi qui est le géant.'

[738] *Revue et Gazette musicale de Paris*, vol. XXII, no. 44, 4 XI 1855, p. 348: 'Huerta. [...] le Paganini de la guitare, vient de se suicider à Nice'; vol. XXIII no. 10, 9 III 1856, p. 79: '*M. Huerta, le célèbre guitariste [...] se trouve en bonne santé.*'; La France musicale, vol. XX, no. 6, 10 II 1856, p. 47: 'Le célèbre guittariste Huerta [...] annoncé mort [...] est à Madrid.'

[739] *Le Ménestrel*, vol. XXVII, no. 42 (740), 16 IX 1860, p. 336: 'Huerta à Paris.'; vol. XXVIII, no. 16 (757), 17 III 1861, p. 127: Le beau concert du guitariste Huerta, merc. '20 mars'; vol. XXXII, no. 19 (967), 9 IV 1865, p. 152: '27 avril Salle Pleyel, M. Huerta, guitariste de S. M. la reine d'Espagne.'

[740] *La France musicale*, vol. XXIX, no. 11, 12 III 1865, p. 83: 'Mardi 14 à 8 h. du soir, M. Sokolowski, guitariste. [...] salle Pleyel.'

[741] *Revue et Gazette musicale de Paris*, vol. XXXI, no. 4, 24 I 1864, p. 26: 'Sokolowski [...] instrument sourd et ingrat [...] rebattre nos préjuges.'

[742] *Revue et Gazette musicale de Paris*, vol. XXX, no. 15, 12 I 1863, p. 118: '[...] Nadar [...] atelier [...] Vailati, l'aveugle [...] clairvoyant, [...] mandoline [...] Carnaval de Venise sur une seule corde'; no. 18, 3 V 1863, p. 141: 'Un aveugle, M. Jean Vailati [...] salle Herz [...] la pauvre mandoline.'; vol. XXXIV, no. 29, 21 VII 1867, p. 231: '[...] guitariste Vailati [...] matinée musicale Théâtre International'.

melody springs with clarity. M. de Folly has performed some variations on La Carnaval de Venise with a dexterity rarely seen and received the applause he deserved.[743]

One of the things than can be learnt from this is that the guitar is played with the fingernails. Just as in 1843, when Léon Gozlan felt obliged to defend the guitar, in 1864 too, the predominant opinion is that the guitar is old-fashioned, an instrument whose capabilities have been exhausted, wholly unworthy of an artist's time and effort. Performances by first-class performers like Bosch, Zani de Ferranti, Huerta and De Folly come as a surprise.[744] In the few reviews of guitar concerts that appear in this period, the musical press shows a certain disdain for the instrument.[745] To the extent that such criticism in the press wields any influence on the sort of audience that attends concerts of this high standard, it certainly does not help improve the guitar's position in the élite musical world. The guitar is still used for popular music, as shown by the description of:

a poorly attired Italian women, with a pleasant and cultured appearance, who in front of café Riche tries to drum up the establishment's generosity by singing airs from Italian operas, accompanying herself with the guitar.[746]

The guitar continues to turn up in the monthly concerts of the *Société académique des Enfants d'Apollon*, because in August 1865 a duet by Leduc is performed there, with Decourcelle, known from his publication about this society, at the piano, and de la Richardière on the guitar. Bourgeois de la Richardière is an old acquaintance, who already in April 1853 gives a performance on these occasions and who joins Coste in performing the latter's *Grand Duo* WoO 8 as *Concertino* for two guitars in August 1855. De la Richardière performs there on other occasions as well, playing a duet called *Capuletti* by Neuland in July 1867, a *Sérénade* by Küffner and a *Nocturne* by Molino in August 1869 together with Decourcelle with the same line-up in 1869, a *Valse espagnole* and, just like Bosch in June 1865, *La Retraite*, which this time proves to be an arrangement, in July 1871. That is the society's first concert after the capitulation of Paris to the Prussians. The musicians convene in spite of this serious event, but without playing and listening to music. De la Richardière plays once more at the society in August 1873, this time a *Sérénade* for piano and guitar by Call and a *Mélange* written by Carulli on an air by Rossini, which was already 'old' music at the time.[747] Coste then dedicated his *Étude 2* opus 38 to him, and de la Richardière joins the company of guitarists who perform in Paris in this period: Bosch, Zani de Ferranti, Huerta, Sokolowski, Vailati and de Folly.

---

[743] *Le Ménestrel*, vol. XXXI, no. 13 (909), 28 II 1864, p. 102: '[...] au milieu des vibrations triomphantes du piano, s'est tout à coup montrée, comme une apparition, la guitare! La guitare, oubliée, délaissée, douce victime de l'injustice des hommes! Un artiste, M. de Folly a entrepris la réhabilitation de l'instrument aimable qui soutenait les voix de nos grand'mères. M. de Folly s'est avisé de découvrir à la guitare des qualités inconnues, longtemps cachés aux ongles profanes; il fait chanter comme le violon: ce n'est plus le son maigre et languissant qu'on lui reproche, le pizzicato fluet et sec, c'est un petit orchestre avec ses accords, sur lesquels se délache nettement la mélodie. M. de Folly a exécuté, avec une rare dextérité, des variations sur la Carnaval de Venise, et a été applaudi comme il méritait.'

[744] *La France musicale*, vol. VI, no. 32, 6 VIII 1843, p. 238: 'La guitare vient de trouver un chaud défenseur [...] Gozlan [...] novelle.'

[745] *Revue et Gazette musicale de Paris*, vol. XIV, no. 18, 1 V 1859, p. 142: '[...] Ferranti [...] infortunée guitare, victime du piano'; vol. XXVII, no. 6, 5 II 1860, pp. 43-44: '[...] Ferranti [...] ressources exiguës'; vol. XXXI, no. 4, 24 I 1864, p. 26: '[...] début Sokolowski [...] instrument sourd et ingrat'; no. 5, 31 I 1864, p. 35: '[...] Sokolowski [...] bravos les plus vifs.'; no. 14, 3 I 1864, p. 106: '[...] Sokolowski [...] autre but à ses efforts.'; vol. XXXII, no. 12, 19 III 1865, p. 89: '[...] Sokolowski [...] instrument ingrat [...]'; vol. XXXIX, no. 8, 25 II 1872, p. 63: '[...] Bosch [...] instrument ingrat.'; vol. XLV, no. 14, 5 I 1874, p. 110: '[...] Bosch [...] instrument aux ressources assez restreintes.'

[746] *Revue et Gazette musicale de Paris*, vol. XXXIII, no. 34, 26 VIII 1866, p. 271: '[...] une Italienne, pauvrement vêtue, mais d'une physique agréable et décent, arrêtée devant le café Riche, cherchait à exciter la générosité des consommateurs en chantant avec une superbe voix de contralto, qu'elle accompagnait de la guitare, [...] des airs d'opéra Italien.'

[747] Decourcelle, Maurice: La Société des Enfants d'*Apollon (1741-1880): programmes des concerts annuels...*, Paris, Durand, 1881, p. 204: Duo pour piano et guitare, composé par A. Leduc, exécuté par MM. Decourcelle et De la Richardière.'; p. 209: Duo pour piano et guitare sur *I Capuletti*, composé par Neuland, exécuté par MM. Decourcelle et De la Richardière.'; p. 214: 'Sérénade composé par Kufner; premier nocturne par Molino, pour piano et guitare, exécutés par MM. Decourcelle et De la Richardière.'; p. 217: 'Les graves événements [...]'; 'Valse espagnole; La retraite espagnole, arrangées pour la guitare et exécutées par M. De la Richardière.'; p. 222: Sérénade pour piano et guitare, composée par De Call; mélange sur des airs de Rossini, pour piano et guitare, composé par Carulli, exécutés par MM. Delille et De la Richardière.

VII — Études de Genre

Oboe 1861-1869

In this period Coste mainly begins writing works for other instruments, ten such works, of which seven can be dated and the other three cannot, for ensembles with oboe, violin, voice, piano and/or guitar. The missing *Sérénade* WoO 13 [opus 32?] and the *Consolazione* opus 25 originate from an earlier period, 1856 and 1855 to be precise, which brings the total number of compositions for ensemble with oboe to twelve. These compositions are renamed later on. The circumstances surrounding that have been explained, but they are not discussed with respect to the analysis of their style. They lie outside the framework that has been set, one of the reasons being that few elements of Romantic style can be identified in them. These works are from a standard different from that of pieces for solo guitar, as can quickly be deduced by perusing the sheets of music, some of them printed and others handwritten. Three of these are in Coste's own handwriting. There is also an arrangement of the Klosé's *10ᵉ Solo* for oboe and piano or string quartet dating from 1867. The compositions with oboe were written between 1861 and 1868 at rue Blanche no. 100. Seven of them were never published. Coste finds it increasingly difficult to get his works published.

116 Charles Triébert

First comes *Le Montagnard* opus 34[a] in 1861, the second work by Coste bearing this title. The second part of *La Vallée d'Ormans* opus 17 from the *Sept souvenirs* is also called *Les Montagnards*, a composition for guitar solo in which the mountain folk are depicted as a melodious people. Opus 34[a] is written for oboe or violin with piano or guitar and dedicated to Charles Triébert, the oboist from the Théâtre-Italien orchestra, as indicated on the title page, as well as from the Opéra-Comique. Together with Coste he is a member of the Freemasons' lodge *Les Frères Unis Inséparables* and becomes an instructor at the conservatory in 1863. Coste first makes Triébert's acquaintance in 1843, when they are both billed on the program of the annual public concert of the *Société académique des Enfants d'Apollon* on Ascension day, in which Coste played *Le Tournoi* opus 15, while Triébert played in a trio by Beethoven.[748] In 1855, he probably plays *Consolazione* together with him, which was still dedicated to violinist Bériot as *Romance sans parole* opus 25 in one of the monthly meetings of the Apollo musicians. Other than the title, there are few if any musical similarities between the two 'montagnards', at most the rhythm in the bass in the rondo of both compositions, creating a folk atmosphere, especially when that is used with a pedal point as in the duet. Referring to this work in his letter to Degen dated October 17, 1863, Coste writes that it absolutely must be played with the oboe, wondering whether the same sort of oboes that can be had in Denmark that one finds in France, by which he probably means the instruments of Frédéric Triébert, Charles's younger brother. Coste has heard the German instruments with a big sound that are similar to the clarinet and are good for use in

---

[748] Decourcelle, Maurice: *La Société des Enfants d'Apollon (1741-1880): programmes des concerts annuels...*, Paris, Durand, 1881, p. 78: Triébert, Soler et Romedène. 3. Trio pour 2 hautbois et cor anglais. Beethoven. M. Coste. 5. *Le Tournoi*, fantaisie pour la guitare. Coste.

an orchestra, but which lack the finesse necessary for this particular piece.'[749] With these words he is revising his original indication that the piece is for violin, preferring the (French) oboe.

The *Concertino* without an opus number, and therefore assigned the number WoO 4, for oboe and piano, is also dedicated to Charles Triébert. Only a handwritten manuscript of it is known to exist, which is in the Kongelige Bibliotek in Copenhagen, possibly in Coste's own hand, and it is in any case signed by him on the first page with the dedication and the partially illegible date of 30 Xbre 186?,[750] that is, December 30, somewhere in the 1860s. It is a rather long piece in three parts, in which the piano merely plays an accompanying role with repeated and broken chords, interrupted from time to time by joint motifs and light passagework. In this work as well, a character akin to folk music can be heard in the regularly appearing bourdon, which, aside from the melodic chromatics used here and there, is the only Romantic element that can be found in this piece.

Additional compositions for oboe and piano have resurfaced that were never published and have only be found in manuscript form, such as *Marche et Scherzo* opus 33[b] written in 1862 and the undated *Fantaisie Sonate* opus 34[b], giving us two doubly-assigned opus numbers. The composer has given these opus numbers to published works and apparently left the same numbers unaltered on unpublished compositions. In his own edition of these works for oboe, Simon Wynberg makes a distinction between [a] and [b] and refrains from publishing the *Fantaisie Sonate* opus 34[b] in 1983.[751] The manuscript is not complete and only contains a single page, preceded by three manuscript pages of the *Rondeau* WoO 12, distinguished as Ms 35b and Ms 35a in the Kongelige Bibliotek in Copenhagen.[752] The rondeau is also for oboe and piano. In his overview of what pieces are played at the monthly meetings of the *Société académique des Enfants d'Apollon*, Decourcelle mentions that in November 1862 Triébert and Coste played the *Romance sans parole* opus 25, just as they did in February 1855, as well as a *Sonate pour guitare et cor [anglais]*, both of them by Coste.[753] Because the *Fantaisie Sonate* opus 34[b] in Coste's handwriting is incomplete, a better candidate for this work might be *Sonate* WoO 14, allowing to date this work with that year, except for the fact that it is written for oboe or violin and piano and that no guitar part has been found. The piano part is not much more complex than those for the earlier works with piano written by Coste, such as *Aux Parisiens* WoO 2, *Le Montagnard* opus 34[a] and the *Concertino* WoO 4 described above, making it quite possible that he himself was the accompanist, given that the meetings were closed to non-members. However, the *Fantaisie Sonate* opus 34[b] and the *Rondeau* WoO 12 remain undated.

Opus 35, *Fantaisie de Concert* 1866

Another work that Coste wrote for the oboe, either solo or together with other instruments, is the *Fantaisie de Concert* opus 35 for two oboes and piano, published by Triébert in 1866 in Paris. Between 1866 and 1878, the instrument-maker and publisher Frédéric Triébert (1813-1878) is living at rue de Tracy no. 6, so the dating of Coste's *Fantaisie de Concert* could well be correct.[754] This *Fantaisie* may have been written for charity, because it is dedicated to M. Delaby and M. Larrieux from the Institute Impérial des Jeunes Aveugles, Lauréat du Conservatoire (Classe de M. Triébert). Both gentlemen have been admitted to the imperial institute for blind youth and must play everything by ear, or have been learning the piece by Braille-writing. Louis Braille (1809-1852), who himself became blind at a young

---

[749] Coste-Degen, 17 VI 1863, Århus, Statsbiblioteket, Søffren Degens Papirer, Manuscript no. 27b, p. 4: '[...] les hautbois allemands que j'ai entendus ont un gros son qui rapproche de la clarinette. Ils sont bons à l'orchestre, mais ils manquent de finesse, qualité essentielle et nécessaire pour le morceau en question.'; Jeltsch, J.: 'hautbois', in: Fauquet, Joël-Marie: *Dictionnaire de la Musique en France au XIXe siècle*, Paris, Fayard, 2003, p. 581.

[750] Kk Rischel Ms. 37 mu 7908.0990, Coste: *Concertino pour hautbois* [WoO 4].

[751] Wynberg, Simon: *The Guitar Works of Napoléon Coste*, facsimile edition, Monaco, 1983, vol. VIII, Introduction.

[752] Kk Rischel Ms. 35 a mu 7908.1782, Coste: *Rondeau* [WoO 12]; Kk Rischel Ms. 35 b mu 7908.1783, Coste: *Fantaisie Sonate* op. 34[b].

[753] Decourcelle, Maurice: *La Société des Enfants d'Apollon (1741-1880): programmes des concerts annuels...*, Paris, Durand, 1881, p. 183: 'Romance sans parole, composée par M. Coste, exécutée sur le cor anglais par M. Triebert;' p. 197: Sonate pour guitare et cor, composée par M. Coste, exécutée par M. Triebert et Coste.

[754] Devriès, Anik & François Lesure: *Dictionnaire des éditeurs de musique français*, Genève, Minkoff, 1979-1988, vol. II, p. 415.

VII — Études de Genre

age and was admitted to the very same institute, had already devised the writing bearing his name in 1829, not only for text, but also for music, which lead its adoption at this Parisian institute for the blind.[755] They study at the conservatory under the direction of Charles Triébert, who evidently did an excellent job, since both pupils were practically virtuosos. The work is a theme with variations, a form that by 1866 is no longer in fashion. There is no trace of a performance. Despite its technical virtuosity, this music is archaic in character, containing few Romantic aspects, but Coste is an accomplished musician, and the composition has a solid structure and is skillfully written.

DIXIÈME SOLO - HYACINTHE KLOSÉ [ARR. COSTE] 1867

In 1867 Hyacinthe Klosé's (1808-1880) *Dixième Solo* is performed for a competition organized by the conservatory, where the clarinettist started teaching in 1839, in an arrangement by Coste for oboe and piano or string quartet 'ad libitum.'[756] Just like Coste, Klosé has joined the Freemasons' lodge *Les Frères Unis Inséparables* and played the lost *Sérénade* for oboe, clarinet and guitar together with Triébert and Coste in 1852.[757] He appears with the same musicians in the concert organized by Coste in April 1855. Klosé is an acquaintance of Coste, but his name is not listed as a member of the *Société académique des Enfants d'Apollon*, in spite of the fact that this arrangement of his work is played on May 22, 1873 as part of the society's annual concert, but with the title *Solo de hautbois*.[758] The copy in Paris that is dated 1868 by the Bibliothèque nationale has the same number in the parts for string quartet, but both the oboe part and the title page are missing.[759] Richault's edition for oboe and piano, which can be found in the Kongelige Bibliotek in Copenhagen, shows this work as being dedicated to 'M. Colin, professeur de Hautbois au Conservatoire Impérial de musique.'[760] Charles Colin (1832-1881) does in fact teach the oboe there, but only starting in 1868. So he could have entered the work into the competition in 1867 to obtain this position, as a successor to Charles Triébert, who had just passed away.[761] Richault's publication number matches this dating.

TRIÉBERT 1867

Charles Triébert dies on July 18, 1867, at the age of 57.[762] Not only was he a personal friend of Napoléon Coste; he was also a highly valued member of the *Société académique des Enfants d'Apollon*, who in November 1867 put a *Prière, hommage à la mémoire de Triébert* by d'Aubigny for oboe and woodwinds on the program for the monthly meeting. He is the only member to be given such an honor.[763] He often played there himself, including with Coste,[764] who write the following to Schult in October:

It is above all the loss of a very dear friend, a noble artist, our first oboist (Triébert), who has passed on after a long illness. He took me into his family. Try to imagine my grief.[765]

---

[755] Grote Winkler Prins Encyclopedie, Amsterdam, Elsevier, 1967, vol. IV, p. 457.
[756] Jeltsch, J.: Klosé, Hyacinthe-Éléonor', in: Fauquet, Joël-Marie: *Dictionnaire de la Musique en France au XIXe siècle*, Paris, Fayard, 2003, p. 648.
[757] Cotte, Roger: *La musique maçonnique et ses musiciens*, Paris, Editions du Borrégo, 1987, pp. 141, 143.
[758] Decourcelle, Maurice: *La Société des Enfants d'Apollon (1741-1880): programmes des concerts annuels...*, Paris, Durand, 1881, p. 108: '[...] Solo de hautbois (arrangé par M. Coste. Klosé.'
[759] Pn [Vm 19.23, Klosé: *10ᵉ Solo*, Arrangé pour le Hautbois. par Nap. Coste. (No oboe part.)
[760] Kk Rischel 178 mu 6701.1082 (eks. 1) U72, Klosé, H.: *10ᵉ Solo*, transcrit pour le hautbois. avec accompt. de piano ou quatuor ad libitum par Nap. Coste. (No string quartet parts.)
[761] Kocevar, É.: Colin, Charles-Joseph', in: Fauquet, Joël-Marie: *Dictionnaire de la Musique en France au XIXe siècle*, Paris, Fayard, 2003, p. 291.
[762] Triébert, Charles-Louis', in: Fauquet, Joël-Marie: *Dictionnaire de la Musique en France au XIXe siècle*, Paris, Fayard, 2003, pp. 1233-1234.
[763] Decourcelle, Maurice: La Société des Enfants d'*Apollon (1741-1880): programmes des concerts annuels...*, Paris, Durand, 1881, p. 78: 'Hommage à la mémoire de Triébert [...] composé par M. d'Aubigny, exécuté par MM. [...] Blanc, Adam, [...] Dupont, Jancourt [...]'.
[764] Decourcelle, Maurice: La Société des Enfants d'*Apollon (1741-1880): programmes des concerts annuels...*, Paris, Durand, 1881, pp. 78, 138-9, 166, 170, 174, 176, 178, 183, 193, 197, 199, 210.
[765] Coste-Schult, 7 X 1867: 'D'abord la perte d'un ami bien chèr, un noble artiste, notre premier hautboist (Triébert), qui a succombé après une longue maladie. Il me tenait lieu de famille. Jugez de ma douleur.'

He was of great significance for Coste's compositions with oboe. In 1868 he dedicates his *Regrets et Consolations* opus 36 to his memory. In this edition of Frédéric Triébert the two works *Consolazione* opus 25, which in the 1856 edition was still dedicated to violinist Charles de Bériot, and *Les Regrets*, brought together under opus 36. There is no mention of either opus 25 or Bériot.

OPUS 37, *CAVATINE* 1869

The *Cavatine* for oboe or viola or flute and piano opus 37, which appeared in 1869, is the third and last work by Coste to be published by Frédéric Triébert. It is dedicated to a certain Sigisbert Molard, about whom no further information can be located. He was undoubtedly an oboist, a friend, according to the dedication, bringing Coste's circle of oboist friends to a total of five: Triébert, Delaby, Larrieux, Colin and Molard. This work also deviates in few aspects from those already described for the previous works. Its content is archaic, and it is not very Romantic, except for the fact that the piano part is somewhat more interesting, that there is more melody in the accompanying chords and that it has more chromatic passages in octaves. The piece consists of a single section with a total of 103 measures, making it somewhat short. A copy of the first edition is available in both the Kongelige Bibliotek in Copenhagen and the Bibliothèque nationale in Paris.[766] And to end with, there is the undated *Caprice* WoO 3 for two oboes, a duet without accompaniment in chords, of which only Coste's own manuscript has been preserved in the Rischel & Birket-Smith collection in Copenhagen. It may be a sketch for a composition, complete but with cross-outs. The piece is not intended to have any accompaniment, according to the title Coste gives it, and there is also no dedication.

In this period, Coste is composing numerous works for the oboe, but in them he does not attain the same high standard as in his guitar compositions, including those for oboe and guitar. That said, they are beautiful, graceful melodies, completely in his style, with simple chord accompaniment in repeated or arpeggiated chords, joint motifs as interludes, a bit of chromatics here and there, but not modulating or with contrastive harmony. One comes up empty-handed in the search for ornamentation, interesting figuration, dissonance, prolongation, dynamics and articulation, while there are a few allusions to folk music with pedal points and bourdons. Four of these works have appeared in modern editions by Chanterelle, in the edition and adaptation of Simon Wynberg, opus 25 & 36, opus 33[b], opus 34[a]. The other compositions still await publication: the *Caprice* WoO 3, the *Concertino* WoO 4, the *Rondeau* WoO 12, the *Sonate* WoO 14, all complete works in manuscript form that are publicly accessible in the Rischel & Birket-Smith collection at the Kongelige Bibliotek in Copenhagen. The works for oboe that appeared during Coste's time – the *Fantaisie de Concert* opus 35 and the *Cavatine* opus 37 – can be found there too, as well as in Paris at the Bibliothèque nationale. The *Sérénade* WoO 13 still remains to be found. This brings our discussion of the works for oboe in the 17-year period of Coste's life to a close. With the passing of Charles Triébert, the oboe disappears from Coste's works after the publication of *Cavatine* opus 37 in 1869.

MASONIC LODGE 1870

After Coste's participation in the annual concert of the Freemasons' lodge *Les Frères Unis Inséparable* on 15 February 1852, which were also written up each year between 1861 and 1869 in the *Revue et Gazette musicale de Paris*, no further mention is made of Coste and his guitar. He is not mentioned a single time after that concert where the critic was so exuberant about the colorful ribbons at the 'European conference.'[767] An overview of lodge concerts between 1852 and 1874 is included in the appendices. Other than Triébert and pianist Delle-Sedie, who play regularly at these concerts, Coste has no musical results from his membership, where new rising stars continue to appear, such as the young blond Swedish singer Mlle Christine Nilsson (1843-1921), who makes a good impression on

---

[766] Kk Rischel 159 mu 6701.0883 U72, Nap. Coste: *Cavatine pour hautbois ou violon ou flûte et piano* Op. 37; Pn [K 1012, Nap. Coste: *Cavatine pour Hautbois ou Violon ou Flûte et Piano* Op. 37.
[767] *Revue et Gazette musicale de Paris*, vol. XIX, no. 8, 22 II 1852, p. 58-59: '[…].congrès européen.'

VII — *Études de Genre* 187

the Freemasons.⁷⁶⁸ In 1870 Coste has the honor of becoming secretary of the lodge.⁷⁶⁹ In this capacity he may have been involved in the organization of the lodge concert that takes place on April 30, 1870, a few months before the war with Prussia. The review of this concert, which does not refer to Coste, mentions the annual character of the concert, the charitable cause for which 1,200 fr. have been raised, the vocal part, in which Christine Nilsson sings a *Chanson suédoise*, matched in excellence by the instrumental accompaniment and finally the honor bestowed by the dignitaries on the event with their usual grace.⁷⁷⁰ Whatever it was Coste was seeking at the Freemasons' lodge, it had no apparent influence on his career as a musician, apart from possibly arranging the *Chanson suédoise* for guitar in his *Livre d'Or* opus 52 as the first of the *Airs Suédois* no. 17. Their predilection was obviously not the guitar, but, for example, the Colonne d'Harmonie, directed by Panseron, and the young singing blond, who made the charitable collection of funds a success. The concerts are organized for a charitable cause: to assist the shelter for the orphans entrusted to the lodge.⁷⁷¹

Marriage 1871

In August 1870 the musical life of the *Société académique des Enfants d'Apollon* comes to a standstill, and they are not alone; the 'serious events' have also had a disastrous effect on everyday life in Paris.⁷⁷² On July 19, 1870, the Prussians' rise in power starting in 1864 and the opposition of the French republicans to the Napoléon III's Deuxième République lead to a declaration of war against Germany, prompted by the complications surrounding the succession to the throne in Spain. The Franco-German war, 1870-1871, was of short duration. Napoleon is deposed, after his debacle at Sedan on September 1, 1870, where he is obliged to surrender with 86,000 troops. The Troisième République is declared on September 4. In the winter the Prussians lay siege to Paris. The city is bombarded and is in ruins, including the rue du Faubourg St-Martin, and it is forced to capitulate. Paris is symbolically occupied, and Prussian troops with their iron crosses on pointed helmets march down the Champs Élysées. In the bloody week of May 21-28, 1871, the 'Commune' is declared, resulting in acts of arson, destruction and bloodbaths. The political chaos is great, and the Freemasons are considered subversive. After a ceasefire, a humiliating peace treaty is signed that includes costly reparations.⁷⁷³ The first effect of these events is to distract Coste from his projects:

*The disastrous circumstances and painful events of 1870 and 71 made me lose sight of this project, as well as many others.*⁷⁷⁴

The project he mentions in this letter is the arrangement of Swedish melodies into a Fantaisie. Then, right in the middle of this dangerous turmoil, Napoléon Coste and Louise Olive Pauilhé decide to tie the knot:

The eleventh of February of the year one thousand eight hundred seventy-one, in the afternoon, in the tenth mairie of Paris, Mister Edouard Degouve Dominique, registrar, performed the marriage of Claude Antoine Jean Georges Napoléon Coste, employed at the Seine Préfecture, born in Amondans (Doubs) the twenty-seventh of June of the year one thousand eight hundred five, residing in Paris, boulevard

---

⁷⁶⁸ *Revue et Gazette musicale de Paris*, vol. XXXIV, no. 10, 10 III 1867, p. 77; vol. XXXV, no. 12, 22 III 1868, pp. 90-91; vol. XXXVI, no. 14, 4 IV 1869, pp. 116-117; vol. XXXVII, no. ??, 6 III 1870, p. 77; Kocevar, É: 'Nilsson, Christine', in: Fauquet, Joël-Marie: *Dictionnaire de la Musique en France au XIXe siècle*, Paris, Fayard, 2003, p. 866.

⁷⁶⁹ Cotte, Roger: *La musique maçonnique et ses musiciens*, Paris, Editions du Borrégo, 1987, p. 140-141.

⁷⁷⁰ *Revue et Gazette musicale de Paris*, vol. XXXVI, no. 10, 6 III 1870, p. 77: '[...] chaque année [...] partie vocale [...] offrande de 1.200 francs [...] bienfaisance [...] Mlle Nilsson chantait l'*Ave maria* de Gounod, [...] *Chanson suédoise* [...] La partie instrumentale ne cédait en rien à la vocale. [...] les dignitaires de la loge faisaient les honneurs avec leur bonne grâce accoutumée.'; Cotte, Roger: *La musique maçonnique et ses musiciens*, Paris, Editions du Borrégo, 1987, p. 144-145.

⁷⁷¹ *Revue et Gazette musicale de Paris*, 27 XII 1857, p. 422.

⁷⁷² Decourcelle, Maurice: *La Société des Enfants d'Apollon (1741-1880): programmes des concerts annuels...*, Paris, Durand, 1881, p. 217.

⁷⁷³ 'Frans-Duitse oorlog', in: Wiggers, A. J. red.: *Grote Winkler Prins*, Amsterdam, 1963, vol. VII, p. 699; 'Le Troisième République', in: *Paris, guide de tourisme*, Paris, Michelin, 1997-1998, p. 13.

⁷⁷⁴ Coste-Hallberg, 23 II 1877: 'Les circonstances néfastes et les événements douloureux de 1870 et 71 m'ont fait perdre de vue ce projet ainsi que beaucoup d'autres.'

Rochechouard 84, oldest son of #[cross-out] Jean François Coste and Anne Pierrette Dénéria, his wife, both of them deceased, on the one hand. And of Louise Olive Pauilhé, without a profession, born in Paris on the fifteenth of September of the year one thousand eight hundred forty-four, residing in Paris, rue du Faubourg Saint-Martin, 50, oldest daughter of Alexandre Olive Pauilhé and of Marie Anne Françoise Vanrycke, his wife, both of them deceased, on the other hand. [...].[775]

The only time that Coste says anything about the reason for this comes years later in 1881, when in a letter to Hallberg he writes that Louise saved his life in 1871.[776] The marriage certificate shows that Coste has moved house again, from rue Blanche no. 100, where he had been living since 1858, to the broad and busy boulevard Rochechouard no. 84, which is also in the 9th arrondissement. This is Coste's sixth address in Paris. He moves fairly often.

His last address would be rue du Faubourg St-Martin no. 50 in the 10th arrondissement, when he moves in with his wife and pupil Louise. That is just two blocks away from rue de l'Échiquier no. 23, where he lived between 1837 and 1852, so this part of the city is familiar territory for him. It is noteworthy that Coste's date of birth indicated on the marriage certificate is the correct one, unlike the one he uses when joining the Freemasons in 1843. Even more remarkable is his wife's date of birth. The certificate lists it as September 7, 1844, whereas she was actually born in 1825. That year can be deduced from Napoléon Coste's death certificate, which indicates that widow attains 58 years of age on January 15, 1883.[777] Furthermore, she is already his pupil in 1840, when Coste dedicates his Caprice *La Cachucha* opus 13 to Mlle Olive Pauilhé. It is quite remarkable that such a substantial error has crept into an official marriage certificate, but there are also four cross-outs and corrections on the certificate, attesting to a certain degree of sloppiness. These are corrected in the margins, signed after being read and approved by the newly-weds, leading their signatures to appear five times on the documents, in addition to those of the four witnesses. The document sheds some light on the life of Coste, who is not known as a guitarist or composer, but rather as an employee of the Préfecture de la Seine. Going by this document, he has been working there for sixteen years now, and currently has a higher salary of 1,800 fr.[778] Louise Olive Pauilhé was born in 1825, and she is 15 years old at the time of the dedication of opus 13 in 1840. That is a bit young for a marriage, but thirty years is quite a long time to wait.[779] Various explanations can be found for this. They may have had a romantic relationship without being married, but economic circumstances could have played a role. As a musician, Coste does not have much income security, as shown by the fact that he is obliged to take an unattractive office job in 1855. Or they may have lost track of one another and have met again at a much later date.

---

[775] *Acte de Mariage* 58 Coste et Pauilhé, Pap Série V2E 5 Mi 3/210, 11 II 1871: 'L'An mil huit cent soixante onze le onze Février, midi, en la dixième Mairie de Paris et par Monsieur Édouard Degouve Dominique Officier de l'État Civil a été célébré publiquement le mariage de Claude Antoine Jean Georges Napoléon Coste, employé à la Préfecture de la Seine né à Amondans (Doubs) le vingt sept juin mil huit cent cinq, demeurant à Paris, Boulevard Rochechouard 84, fils majeur de # [cross-out] Jean François Coste et de Anne Pierrette Denéria, son épouse, décédés, d'une part. Et de Louise Olive Pauilhé, sans profession, née à Paris le quinze septembre mil huit cent quarante quatre, demeurant à Paris, rue du Faubourg Saint-Martin, 50, fille majeure de Alexandre Olive Pauilhé et de Marie Anne Françoise Vanrycke, son épouse, décédés, d'autre part.' [complete text]: 'Les actes annexés sont ceux des publications faites à cette Mairie, et à la dix huitième les démarches ## vingt neuf janvier dernier [crossed-out text] affichés sans opposition [crossed-out text] ceux de naissance ### et ceux de décès des père et mère de la contractante, par eux et par nous paraphés desquels nous avons donné lecture ainsi que du Chapitre adm. du Code Civil titre du mariage. Les contractants présents nous ont déclaré séparément prendre pour épouse, l'un Louise Olive Pauilhé, l'autre Claude Antoine Jean Georges Napoléon Coste, et en outre qu'il n'a pas été fait de contrat de mariage et de suite nous avons prononcé au nom de la loi l'union en mariage En personne de 1ᵉ Jacques François Hippolyte Marie, Ansier caissier central du Ministère de l'Intérieur, âgé de soixante dix huit ans, Faubourg Poissonnière 123; 2ᵉ Félix Lagare, chef de section à la Préfecture de la Seine, Chevalier de la Légion d'Honneur, âgé de cinquante cinq ans, Boulevard du Temple, 10; 3ᵉ Ernest Miliotti Attaché au Ministère de l'Intérieur âgé de cinquante trois ans, [crossed out: Quai Bourbon 15] Quai Bourbon 15; 4ᵉ Pierre Charles Édouard Minaux, retiré âgé de soixante deux ans, demeurant Boulevard Bourbon 15, qui ont signé avec nous et les épouses après lecture.'

[776] Coste-Hallberg, 8 II 1881. 'En 1871 elle m'avait déjà sauvé la vie.'

[777] *Acte de Décès* de Napoléon Coste, Pap Série V2E 5Mi 3/1256, 15 I 1883: '[...] époux de Louise Olive Pauilhé, agée de cinquante-huit ans, sans profession; [...]'.

[778] Jaworski, Roman: 'Napoléon Coste 1805-1883, une histoire perdue', in: *Valentiana*, Valenciennes, 1992, no. 10, p. 77.

[779] *Acte de Décès* de Napoléon Coste, Pap Série V2E 5Mi 3/1256, 15 I 1883.

VII — Études de Genre

Yet another possibility is that they lived together for a time and only got married later, not an unusual practice for artists, as Chopin and Sand did. or that they had only had a church wedding and were now following that up with a civil marriage, which had now become the norm. That also makes one wonder whether the couple had any children, a question that arises from a message from the French guitar-makers Daniel Sinier and Françoise de Ridder in 2011. They mention Coste's Lacôte guitar at 1995 auction in Paris [Illustration 111]. This heptacorde was then purchased by the Cité de la Musique museum. According to Sinier, it came from a collection of the heirs of M. E. Petetin, as he writes, Coste's son-in-law, to whom he dedicated *Étude 1* from opus 38. Petetin's name also appears in a Lacôte guitar that Coste had converted into a seven-stringed instrument. Sinier mentions that Coste had one or two daughters.[780] The title of the piece *L'Enfant au Berceau* WoO 7 from 1864 may have alluded to some desire on Coste's part to have children, a wish that may or may not have been fulfilled. In 1878 Coste also uses this topic in *Le Petit Ange rose* WoO 11, which is

117 Rue du Faubourg St-Martin, 1871

dedicated to young mothers in general. Both Napoléon Coste and Louise Olive Pauilhé play the guitar and are musical, and any children of theirs may well have followed in their footsteps and taken classes at the conservatory. Constant Pierre, who publishes a reference work about the conservatory in 1900, lists three names under 'Coste', which are possible candidates:

> Coste (Marie-Octavie-Eugénie Carante, called Julie), born in Paris on 28 October 1851, solfeggio 1867, piano 1869 and 1870;
> Coste (Marie-Augustine-Berthe Carante), born in Paris on 2 February 1857, solfeggio 1869, piano 1872 and 1873;
> Coste (Antoine-Jean-Nicolas-Henri), born in Paris on 24 January 1870, acting 1891, 1894, 1895, Odéon 1900.[781]

The years indicated suggest that they may be the couple's children, bearing Napoléon's surname, whether or not they were legitimate. The name Julie is one of the names of Coste's sister, and Antoine Jean is part of the guitarist's own name. But there are no other indications of parenthood, and any claims to that effect seem to be contradicted by the 1871 marriage certificate and Coste's death certificate, in which no mention is made of any children, using the same name twice aside. There is no proof, and the composer Napoléon Coste is certainly not the only person in a metropolis like Paris who bears that family name, such as Madame Coste, for instance, who is the fourth person listed by Constant under this surname. She may be the same Madame Coste who sings a *Mélodie* by Wekerlin in March 1867 at a monthly meeting of the *Société académique des Enfants d'Apollon*.[782] The database of the Archives de Paris does not provide an answer. The archive of birth certificates from before 1860 was lost in the fires that raged in the city in 1871 during the Prussian invasion. There are only cards with names and dates, and the first two names are not there. As for the last of the three names, this child must have been born in the 10th arrondissement, but no trace of him can be found. Moreover, he would have been born at

---

[780] Sinier, Daniel & Françoise de Ridder: *La Guitare, Paris 1650-1950*, Cremona, Il Salabue, 2007, pp. 56-57; email correspondence Sinier de Ridder-Ari van Vliet, 15 XI 2011.
[781] Pierre, Constant: *Le Conservatoire national de musique et de déclamation: documents historiques et administratifs*, Paris, Imprimerie nationale, 1900, p. 726.
[782] Decourcelle, Maurice: *La Société des Enfants d'Apollon (1741-1880): programmes des concerts annuels...*, Paris, Durand, 1881, p. 208: '*La bouquetière des fiancés*, mélodie de Wekerlin, chantée par Mme Coste.'

his mother's unlikely age of 45.[783] That said, the surname Coste does not appear all that often in the sources consulted, in which the composer is generally referred to as Nap. Coste. Further research would require identifying possibilities to be confirmed or even impossibilities to be eliminated. In any case, in none of Coste's fifty letters is there even a hint about the existence of children, while Coste does send his wife's greetings regularly. They also play duets together:

> *I have the good fortune of having in my wife the most perfect partner that one can imagine. She is, I believe, the most remarkable amateur who exists as a woman, and I don't know of an artist capable of replacing her.*[784]

Going by the works Coste dedicated to Louise Pauilhé, *Étude* 14 from opus 38 circa 1872, and *Marche funèbre et Rondeau* opus 43 in 1876, she is most certainly an accomplished guitarist if she is able to play these pieces. Coste also writes three duets for guitars, and there are also four adaptations of Sor's duets, making plenty of works available to play together. At rue du Faubourg St-Martin no. 50, Coste self-publishes twelve of his last compositions, but first his *25 Études de Genre* were published by Richault in around 1872, the next to the last work to appear with there.

OPUS 38, *25 ÉTUDES DE GENRE* 1872

So, in approximately 1872 the *25 Études de Genre* opus 38, or just *Études* for short, were published by Richault. Besides the fact that these studies are among the most well-known and widely circulating works of Coste, the exact date of publication remains uncertain. While Richault's publication number of 14030.R. may refer to 1872, a new 15000 series begins in that year, and 14131 appears in 1875. Richault's numbering is not consistent; some composers have their own personal series and new series are begun without completing the previous one, so the numbering must be approached with a certain amount of caution.[785] It is certain is that the publication appeared after 1871, as *Étude* 14 is dedicated 'à ma Femme'. In his letter to Schult of September 2, 1874 Coste writes:

> *I have had the pleasure of finally sending you a collection of 25 Études, which I have just published. I have taken the liberty, thinking that you would not take displeasure in it, of putting your name at the top of one of these little compositions. [...] and I think, if I am not deluding myself, that in this publication I have set new boundaries for musical science as applied to the guitar.*[786]

In that case, Coste published the *Études* opus 38 in 1874, placing a dedication to Schult on no. 24. He indicates that he has extended the boundaries of musical knowledge for the guitar. On the other hand, the dedication in Coste's handwriting to M. Petetin may just as well have led to the note on the title page which includes the year 1873, that is probably made by the dedicatee himself, of which the last words are illegible:

> *Given by M. Coste in 1873 before my departure to [...?]*[787]

Nearly all of Coste's works are forgotten after his death in 1883, but not these études. They are published in Breviers, in collections, separately, and as selections with publishers and in periodicals. Examples of them can be found in many European libraries, from Utrecht to Siena, from Cambridge to St. Petersburg. But the original manuscripts are nowhere to be found, except for the copy by Egasse de C., the copyist who copied many of Coste's works, such as *La Ronde de Mai* now, which is *Étude* 20,

---

[783] http://archives.paris.fr/s/7/tables-decennales/?
[784] Coste-Schult, 20 VII 1876: 'J'ai l'avantage de posséder dans ma femme le partner le plus parfait que l'on puisse imaginer. Elle est je crois l'amateur la plus remarquable qui existe comme femme et je ne connais pas d'artiste capable de la remplacer.'
[785] Devriès, Anik & François Lesure: *Dictionnaire des éditeurs de musique français*, Genève, Minkoff, 1979-1988, vol. II, p. 368-369.
[786] Coste-Schult, 2 IX 1874: 'J'ai eu le plaisir de vous adresser dernièrement un cahier de 25 Études que je viens de publier. Je me suis permis, pensant que cela ne pouvait vous être désagréable, de mettre vôtre nom en tête de l'une de ces petites compositions. Vous voyez, chèr Monsieur, que malgré les cruels désastres qui sont venus fondre sur ma chère patrie, je n'ai point abandonné notre instrument, et je crois, si je me fais pas illusion, avoir encore dans cette publication étendu les bornes de la science musicale appliquée à la guitare.'
[787] *25 Études de Genre* op. 38 Lam Spencer Collection XX(159224.1): 'Donné par M. Coste en 1873 avant mon départ pour [...?].'

VII — *Études de Genre* 191

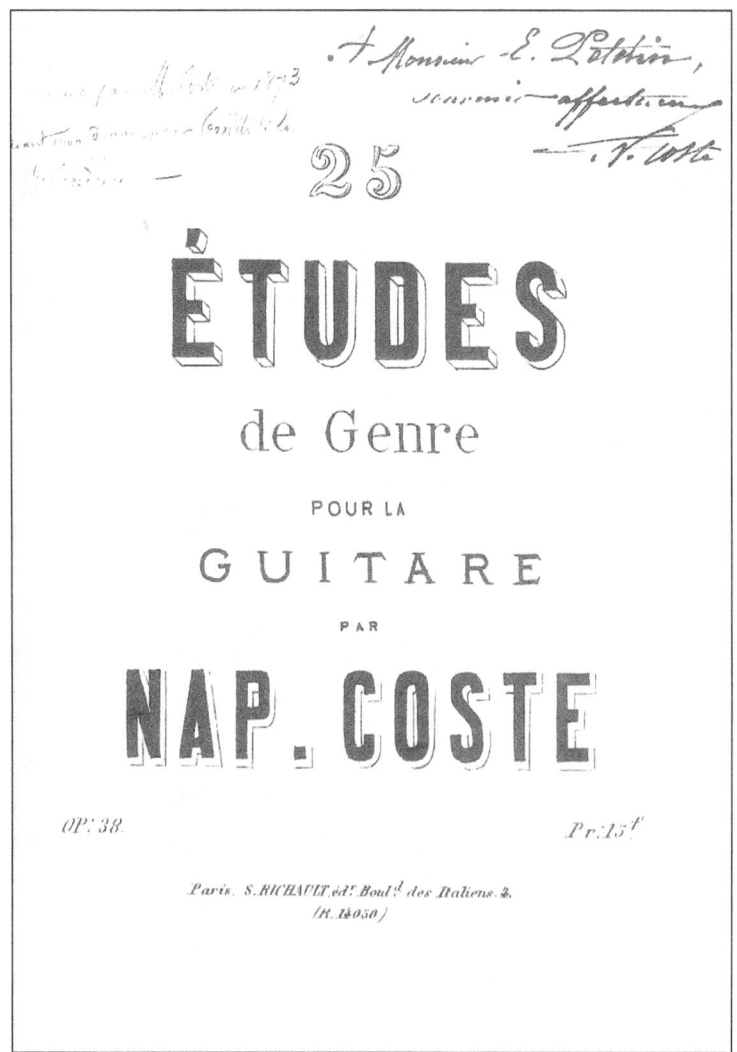

118 25 Études opus 38 Title page

not to be confused with opus 42, with the same title that appears in 1876.[788] From a great number of references in literature about guitar music also can be deduced that opus 38 was widely disseminated and was not something a guitar specialist could ignore. The situation is similar with recordings. Famous guitarists like Segovia played a few of these études,[789] and Llobet set the standard with his very fast tempo for *Étude 23*,[790] but we must wait till the year 2000 to hear recordings of the entire work by Jeffrey McFadden[791] and Marco Riboni.[792] This information is given in the Thematic Catalogue, with references to the literature in which more details about the history of the *Études* opus 38 can be found, as it unfolded after 1883. This is one of the threads along which Coste's name as a composer can be followed in a short historiography, aside from that of the *Méthode* Coste-Sor. Other compositions such as the *Souvenirs* opus 17-23 and *Le Tournoi* opus 15 are not discussed very often, and, notably, those written before the Makaroff competition are only seldom mentioned.

There do exist publications about Coste after 1883, such as that of Richard Läpke in 1884 and Shtokman [Stockmann] in 1902, but they do not mention the études.[793] The first publication in which the *Études* opus 38 are mentioned is by Fritz Buek, who in 1926 writes that each of the 25 études

---

[788] Kk Rischel Ms. 50 mu 6612.2781 [La Ronde de Mai]
[789] Andrés Segovia, no. 1, 2, 1972, MCA Records, MCD 42073, 1990.
[790] Miguel Llobet, no. 23, c. 1929, Chanterelle CHR 001, 1993.
[791] Jeffrey McFadden, no. 1-25, Naxos 8.554354 2000.
[792] Marco Riboni, no. 1-25, Nuova Era Records, 7350, 2000.
[793] Läpke, Richard: 'Biographie Napoléon Coste' in: *Internationale Gitarre-Zeitung*, Jahrgang I, no. 4 (Jan.1884), no. 5 (Febr.1884), Leipzig, transcr. Eduard Fack, 'Die Meister', unp. pp. 118-119; Shtokman [Stockmann], J.: Napoléon Coste', in: *Der Guitarrefreund: Mitteilungen des Internationalen Guitarristen-Verbandes*, München, 3. Jahrgang, 1902, Heft 5, pp. 55-56.

represent an important step in mastery of guitar technique and that many of them could also serve as performance pieces.[794] In 1927 Erwin Schwarz-Reiflingen remarks that opus 38 is Coste's greatest masterpiece, which approaches guitar problems by example and is a player's best preparation for the études of Sor. He places them in the same league as those of Sor, while at the same time they surpass Sor's in their use of natural finger positions and new, hitherto unfamiliar effects.[795] The interest taken in Coste by German writers, some 42 years after his passing, may be the result of his good contacts with the Club des Guitaristes de Leipzig, to which he dedicates his *Le Livre d'Or du Guitariste* opus 52 in 1880; Germany has a lively guitar culture in around 1900. It is harder to account for the attention he receives in Italy, where Mario Giordano sings words of praise in *Il Plettro*, in which he mentions no. 7, 15, 17 and 19 of opus 38. According to him, a theoretician who, beginning with the beauty of the melodic concept, attempts a cold analytic study of particular compositions by Coste, cannot fail to have surprising admiration for the perfect implementation of the voices, the pulsating polyphony that is attractive and moving, always remaining within the strict boundaries of the style.[796] That is easy to imagine with the last four of the études mentioned, but not with no. 7, where arpeggios and figuration make it easier to characterize in terms of melody with accompaniment. In 1954 A. P. Sharpe, editor of *B.M.G.*, the monthly magazine for 'all players of instruments with frets', is of the opinion that the 25 études were far from being easy to perform, but will always be part of the treasury of literature for the guitar.[797] Konrad Ragossnig takes a more technical approach to the études in 1978. He considers opus 38 to be indispensable practice material for obtaining a high standard of playing chords, legatos and in high positions.[798] In contrast, Giuseppe Radole again stresses the polyphony, which in his words represents every ideal.[799] In an article in *Il Fronimo*, Matanya Ophee notes in 1981 that Sor wrote not a single work that can be compared with Coste's *Étude* no. 19 with respect to harmonic structure and consistency, or with his *Études* no. 17, 20 and 22, which clearly show Coste's musical superiority.[800] *Études* 17 and 19 both have sustained three-part harmony, while no. 20, which is dedicated to Adan, has a pulsating bass with a continuously repeated arpeggio. As for no. 22, that is the Tarantella, which is also characterized by a consistent and well thought-out musical idea. In his 1983 book about guitar music in the 19th century, Jan Anton van Hoek discusses various technical aspects of guitar playing, such as flageolets, ornaments, rhythm, rests and matters pertaining to composition such as polyphony, complete with examples from works that include Coste's études. More generally, he notes that these études are very mature, interesting and significant and that they include some very beautiful concert works, point out the last one in the series in particular.[801] In 1988, after discussing a few of Coste's other works, such as the *Sept Souvenirs* and *La Source du Lyson*, Mario Dell'Ara writes that nowhere is the composer's masterful hand more evident than in his 25 études. Originating from source material by Sor, Coste's études are skillfully composed and endowed with characteristic Romantically inspired melodies. A tight and strict harmonic/polyphonic way of writing make these works the most original and distinctive in history.[802] This historiographical work has nothing but admiration for the opus 38 études, both generally for the entire series and singling out a few études in particular, as well as specifically with regards to certain technical and compositional aspects. The articles published by Marco Riboni in 2000 are discussed in the analytical treatment of these works. He not only played them, but also analyzed

---

[794] Buek, Fritz: *Die Gitarre und ihre Meister*, Berlin, Robert Lienau, 1926, 2nd ed. 1935, p. 108.
[795] Schwarz-Reiflingen, Erwin: Besprechungen. Napoléon Coste. op. 38...., in: *Die Gitarre*, Berlin, 1927, Jahrgang VIII, Heft 7/8, [Coste-Heft] pp. 52-53.
[796] Giordano, Mario: 'Napoléon Coste e le sue opere' in: *Il plettro*, febbraio 1934, no. 2, p. 7.
[797] Sharpe, A. P.: *The Story of the Spanish Guitar*, London, Clifford Essex, 1954, 4th ed. 1968, p. 27.
[798] Ragossnig, Konrad: *Handbuch der Gitarre und Laute*, Schott, Mainz, 1978, p. 81.
[799] Radole, Giuseppe: *Liuto, chitarra e vihuela, storia e letteratura*, Milano, Suvini Zerboni, 1979, 3rd ed. 1997, p. 155.
[800] Ophee, Matanya: 'In difesa dei "due amici"' in: *Il Fronimo*, Milano, Suvini Zerboni, vol. IX, no. 36, 1981, p. 10.
[801] Hoek, Jan Anton van: *Die Gitarrenmusik im 19. Jahrhundert*, Wilhelmshaven, Heinrichshofen Verlag, 1983, pp. 20, 21, 40, 60, 62, 78, 83.
[802] Dell'Ara, Mario: *Manuale di storia della chitarra*, Ancona, Bèrben, 1988, p. 137.

VII — Études de Genre 193

them; for him, practice and theory go hand in hand.[803] In many other guides and articles that have appeared about Coste since 1929, his *Études* are merely mentioned, without any further information.[804] It is clear that Coste wrote the études in the context of being a private guitar instructor, to be played by his pupils and tailored to their individual musical abilities and limitations. They are intended for use as instructional material for teaching pupils musical genres. It was only later that Coste published these works as a collection. He did not write the *Études* from a primarily technical perspective, as Giuliani, Carcassi and Carulli often did, but more from a musical point of view, similar to Sor. Here too a concurrent opinion emerges concerning guitar music. In this way, they have become mainly minor but sometimes major performance pieces, arranged in order according to level of difficulty. Except for *Études* 4, 5, 10 and 22, they have all been given a dedication. In the second edition, the dedications for *Études* 6, 12 and 13 have been changed to designate a different person. According to Simon Wynberg, the second edition appears some seven years later, using the same plates, but a number of amendments have been made.[805] Part of the foreword to opus 38 reads as follows:

> *The Études, which we submit to you in appreciation of the artists and studious amateurs who have remained loyal to the guitar, are the result of a labor based on a profound knowledge and great love for the instrument and of the art of music. The author has persevered in his work to justify the success bestowed upon him in 1856 in the competition in Brussels. [...] These modest creations are dedicated to some talented amateurs and of whom the author has fond memories.*[806]

The phrase 'who have remained loyal to the guitar' confirms Coste's awareness that the guitar is no longer played as much as before in Paris, at either the professional or amateur level. One can trace an artistic line from the Makaroff competition to these études. After that in the foreword, the seventh string and its use are explained. The title 'modest works', which is in keeping with his character, point to Coste's own words; he has written this text himself, but hasn't literally signed it.

In addition to the historiography of the literature concerning the *Études*, and as a transition to the conclusions of the descriptive analysis of it, the introduction given by Marco Riboni to his analyses provides important insights. He first describes the place occupied by Coste and the guitar in Paris, a situation that can now be assumed to be familiar to the reader, but in which he partially attributes the guitar's fall from favor to major developments in the sound of the piano. He then turns his attention to the Romanticism of the time:

> *Setting aside strictly personal questions of aesthetics and taste, we are convinced that this successful collection of études represents the most significant work in the catalogue of this French musician. There are certainly other compositions that enjoy greater popularity today on the concert stage (if you think of Le [sic] Source*

---

[803] Riboni, Marco: 25 études op. 38 di Napoléon Coste', in: *Il Fronimo*, Milano, Suvini Zerboni, vol. XXVIII no. 109, 2000, pp. 1423; no. 110, pp. 43-49; no. 111, pp. 38-44.

[804] Zuth, Josef: Coste, Napoléon', in: *Handbuch der Laute und Gitarre*, Wien, Doblinger, 1926-28, repr. Hildesheim, Olms, 1978, p. 73; Radke, Hans: Coste, Napoléon', in: *Die Musik in Geschichte und Gegenwart*, ed. Blume, Kassel, Bärenreiter, 1956, ed. 1973, vol. XV (Supplement 1) Kol. 1616; Cooper, Jeffrey: Coste, Napoléon', in: Sadie, Stanley ed.: *The New Grove Dictionary of Music and Musicians*, second edition, London, Macmillan, 1980, vol. 4, p. 824; Wynberg, Simon: '...zur Rettung Napoléon Costes', in: *Gitarre und Laute*, Köln, vol. III, 1981, no. 5, p. 30; McCready, Sue: *Classical Guitar Companion*, Bimport, Musical New Services, 1982, p. 22-23; Jeffery, Brian & Erik Marchélie: 'Napoléon Coste', in: *Cahiers de la Guitare*, Boissy-St-Léger, Association Guitares et Luths, vol. 6, 1983, p. 9; Heck, Thomas Fitzsimmons: *Mauro Giuliani: Virtuoso Guitarist and Composer*, Columbus, Orphée, 1995, p. 147 [Tarantella]; Moser, Wolf: *Francisco Tárrega, Werden und Wirkung*, Lyon, Saint-Georges, 1996, p. 340; Møldrup, Erling: *Guitaren, et eksotisk instrument i den danske musik*, Kopenhagen, Kontrapunkt, 1997, p. 132; Realino, Umberto: *Un siècle de guitare en France 1750-1850*, unpublished thesis, Sorbonne, repr. Atelier National, Lille, 1999, p. 389; Burzik, Monika: Coste, Napoléon', in: *Die Musik in Geschichte und Gegenwart*, ed. Blume, Finscher, Kassel, Bärenreiter, 2000, vol. 4, Kol. 1715-1716; Roncet, Noël: *Napoléon Coste, Compositeur, 1805-1883*, Amondans, 2005, p. 39.

[805] Wynberg, Simon: *Napoléon Coste, 25 Études de Genre*, Reprint of the 2nd Richault edition c. 1880, Heidelberg, Chanterelle, 2006, Introduction.

[806] Wynberg, Simon: *The Guitar Works of Napoléon Coste*, facsimile edition, Monaco, 1981, vol. I, p. 1; *Napoléon Coste, 25 Études de Genre*, Reprint of the 2nd Richault edition c. 1880, Heidelberg, Chanterelle, 2006, p. 1: 'Les Etudes que nous soumettons à l'appréciation des artistes et des amateurs studieux restés fidèles à la guitare, sont le résultat d'un travail basé sur une profonde connaissance et un grand amour de l'instrument et de l'art musical. L'Auteur a persévéré dans son oeuvre afin de justifier le succès qu'il obtint en 1856 au concours de Bruxelles. [...] Ces modestes productions sont dédiées à des amateurs de talent et à des élèves dont le souvenir est cher à l'auteur.'

du Lyson op. 47, for instance) but we are of the opinion that in his Études, Coste succeeds in attaining his highest results, achieving a remarkable synthesis of artistic inspiration, good taste, a sense of form, knowledge of harmony and melodic freshness. Furthermore, precisely due to the fact that he was forced to remain within the set formal constraints and aesthetics of such a well-defined structure as a collection of études, he succeeds in limiting the error that so often occurs in his production, which is an at times excessively salon-like taste and a certain discursiveness and academic rigidity. And not only that: opus 38 is suffused with that Romantic atmosphere, which, according to traditional handbooks, supposedly link Coste to Regondi and Mertz. It seems appropriate to make a remark on this point. Coste's Romanticism – as we have confirmed and will show in the rest of this article in the formal and harmonic analysis – is unambiguously present in the Études. However, it can be established that these studies were published in 1873 (naturally, we cannot know when he composed them), or more than forty years after Hector Berlioz, practically his contemporary, had his Symphonie fantastique performed in Paris, the French Romantic manifesto, so to speak. Other than Berlioz, in decades prior to that, people like Schumann, Chopin, Liszt and other representatives of Romantic music had spread Romanticism throughout Europe. The comparison with these great individuals is naturally not intended to be qualitative, but it is meaningful from a purely chronological point of view: the question is not whether Coste was a more or less Romantic musician (he was), but rather the fact that he considered himself as a contemporary of an artistic movement which in fact already at that time had existed for at least four decades (and concerning musical aesthetics in the second half of the 1800s, years weigh as heavily as grinding stones). Perhaps it would be more logical to call him late-Romantic. But it is not merely a question of terminology: the important thing is to bear in mind just how extremely separated the guitar world had become from the wider musical world in the second half of the 19th century Something also needs to be made clear concerning musical language. On more than one occasion it has been established that Coste's chromaticism is a clear phenomenon of the Romantic tendencies, so to speak, a connotation of the modernity and of the development of the language in comparison with predecessors from the Classical period (such as Giuliani, Carulli, etc.). Coste's chromaticism is without doubt more developed than that of his illustrious colleagues, but in this case as well, it was rather slow in coming if we compare it with developments in the musical world at the time.[807]

---

[807] Riboni, Marco: 25 études op. 38 di Napoléon Coste', in: *Il Fronimo*, Milano, Suvini Zerboni, vol. XXVIII no. 109, 2000, p. 1415; 'A prescindere da questioni estetiche e di gusto strettamente personali, abbiamo la convinzione che questa riuscita raccolta di studi rappresenti l'opera più significativa del catalogo del musicista francese. Certo vi sono altre composizioni che oggi in ambito concertistico godono di maggiore popolarità (si pensi ad esempio a Le [sic] Source du Lyson op. 47), ma siamo dell'opinione che negli Études Coste riesca a cogliere i suoi più alti risultati realizzando una mirabile sintesi fra ispirazione artistica, buon gusto, senso della forma, sapienza armonica e freschezza melodica. Inoltre, proprio perchè costretto a rimanere entro i precisi vincoli formali ed estetica determinati da una struttura ben definita quale appunto una raccolta di studi, egli riesce felicemente a mitigare i difetti che sovente connotano la sua produzione, ossia il gusto a volte eccessivamente salottiero, una certa prolissità e qualque irrigidimento accademico. Non solo: nell'op. 38 assai frequentemente si respira quell'aura romantica che, secondo la manuelistica tradizionale, accomunerebbe Coste a Regondi e Mertz. Proprio a questo proposiito, ci sembra opportuno aprire una parentesi. Il romanticismo di Coste – come appunto abbiamo affermato e come dimostreremo nel prosieguo di questo articolo nell'analisi formale e armonica – è indubbiamente presente negli Études; tuttavia è bene precisare que egli pubblicò questi studi circa nel 1873 (ovviamente non possiamo sapere quando effettivamente li compose), ossia più di quarant'anni dopo che i quasi coetaneo Hector Berlioz aveva fatte eseguire a Parigi nel 1830 le Symphonie fantastique, vale a dire il manifesto romanticismo francese. Oltre a Berlioz, anche i vari Schumann, Chopin, Liszt e gli altri alfieri della musica romantica ormai da diversi decenni avevano diffuso il Romanticismo in Eurpoa. Il confronto con questi grandi personaggi non vuole ovviamente essere qualitativo, bensì significativo dal punto di vista strettamente cronologico: la questione non è se Coste fosse o meno un musicista romantico (e comunche lo era), ma il fatto che lo si consideri contemporaneo a una tendenza artistica che in realtà era ormai già in essere da almeno quattro decenni (e, per quando riguarda lestetica musicale, nelle seconda metà dellOttocento gli anni pesano come macigni). Forse sarebbe più logico definirlo tarde-romantico. Comunque, non si tratta semplicemente di un problema di terminologia: l'importante è rendersi conto quanto il chitarismo della seconda metà dell'Ottocento fosse sempre più vistosamente scollato dall'ambiente musicale generale. Anche in merito al linguaggio musicale vi è qualcosa da puntualizzare. Più volte si è affermato come il cromatismo di Coste fosse un chiaro sintomo di appartenenza alle tendenze romantiche, quasi una connotazione di modernità e di evoluzione del linguaggio rispetto ai suo predecessori del periodo classico (i vari Giuliani, Carulli, ecc.). Indubbiamente il cromatismo di Coste è più sviluppato di quello di suoi illustri colleghi ma, anche in questo caso, assai in ritardo se paragonato a cuantoallora stava accadendo nel mondo musicale. [English translation based on a translation into Dutch by Gerrit Berveling].

Riboni thus establishes a relation between guitar music and the Romanticism of the time, noting that the former lags behind the latter. What he says about the études themselves is considered in the analytical discussion related to this chapter, and in this connection it should be stressed that his analysis is based on comparable but different assumptions than those used in the present study. He indicates that he analyses the études formally and harmonically, mentioning chromaticism in particular. In the analyses that follow, the features of Romantic guitar music defined are central against the background of the formal and harmonic analysis, a difference in nuance, which nevertheless had influence on its goal-oriented nature and in that way also on the results. While at times that yields certain differences, the opinions generally concur. Furthermore, in this study the identification of the Romantic characteristics is concerned, and not a merely structural harmonic analysis. The picture that emerges from this is briefly sketched in what follows, in chronological order and with a final conclusion. The conclusion might be that the *Études* constitute the key to Coste's compositions.

Analysis

Étude 1 is a simple, but charming étude in which only a few chromatics and a lengthened phrase are visible as a Romantic feature. The character becomes predominantly determined by the descending bass motif and the after-picked chords. Considering this étude, M. Petetin, to whom the small piece is dedicated, must not have been a particularly capable player.

In *Étude* 2 the ostinato bass motif and the pedal point are decisive for the character of this piece. The many legatos, some of them on the bias, in which the periodicity is also interrupted, some melodic chromatics, the accents, all represent the slightly Romantic character of this étude. That is further reinforced by the contrast between the tonic and major-mediant, as well as the absence of the relative. Played quickly, the étude can give the impression that it is a virtuoso piece, but it is not really difficult. It is perfectly suitable for a guitarist who is good at accompaniment, as shown by the duet WoO 8, which Coste performs together with M. de la Richardière, to whom this étude is dedicated, at the monthly meeting of the Apollo musicians on August 12, 1855.

Étude 3 is characterized by the campanella arpeggio, which determines not only the guitar-specific character of this piece that, but also its Romantic character. But it is the ascending chromatic chord progressions that are particularly decisive. This piece can also be characterized as slightly Romantic. M. Janicot, to whom the piece is dedicated, must have also been charmed by the beautiful descending chromatic passage, which also has hints of Baroque.

With respect to form and content, *Étude* 4 is very stable, almost Classical. The piece's melodic chromatics consists of a few pivot tones, while the harmonic chromatics consists of three diminished seventh chords. Only a small excursion from the dominant to the dominant indicates a bit of interesting harmonic movement, which moreover is based on the plagal IV-I progression, and the end more with Classical V-I cadences. With its 28 measures this piece is a beautiful musical miniature, which does not bear a dedication.

Étude 5 has a great deal of harmonic and metrical movement. It is also an étude with a lot of harmonically developed chromatics, with melodic chromatic pivot tones, as well. From a technical perspective, this is not really an easy piece, with its many passing dominants and changes of position. A few campanellas and glissandos color the articulation, which, along some dynamic indications, contribute to the Romantic feeling, which is created chiefly by the unrest in the harmony. This creates tension with the sustained movement in 16th notes. A few similarities with Coste's *Étude* 9, *Étude* 15 and *Ornans* opus 17 place this étude within his style.

What is so Romantic about *Étude* 6 is predominantly the cadenza, in which a great deal of chromatic design can be heard. It is intended to be performed with free lyricism, including the fermatas. The only thing of harmonic interest here is in the casual passing dominants and the movement between relative and dominant, with the Neapolitan sixth chord occurring as a surprise. The cadenza and the da capo give the piece an *ABA* form. The similarities to *Le Tournoi* opus 15, *Les Bords du Rhin* opus 18 and *Fantaisie symphonique* opus 28[b] make it recognizably his style. The identities of M. C. Panco and Mme Hitz, to whom the étude is dedicated in the first and second printings, remain unknown.

Especially due to the intensive metrical movement, the melodic figurations of the chords, sometimes in three voices, but overwhelmingly in two, with the movement in the bass creating unrest in the chord position, can be called *Étude* 7 Romantic. Two phrases of deviant length and a bit of harmonic and melodic chromatics contribute to this characterization, as do the passing dominants, which occur regularly. The *Andante et Menuet* opus 39 has the same texture, and both works, which are dedicated to M. Holm from Copenhagen, have a restless character. Riboni's words give an apt characterization of this *Étude*: 'Coste seems to be inspired with a holy fire to make a harmonically full and rich "pasta".'[808]

Étude 8 has a playful character that is sketched in predominantly short motifs. The longer phrases are often written with joint motifs in which chromatics is sometimes used. The question and answer pairs in the passage in thirds of the ascending prolongation is further developed in the second part and shows similarities to other works by Coste: opus 18, 28 and 28[b]. This work, which is somewhat longer work than the preceding one, is fresh and multifaceted in its musical ideas. It clearly has a few identifiable Romantic characteristics. Riboni goes so far as to call this piece a Classic minuet, which even has a trio.[809] There is something to be said for that, but generally speaking a minuet is not meant to be playful, as is the case here. The piece is dedicated to Mme Marsoudet, just like *Souvenir(s) du Jura* opus 44.

The Andantino and the 2/4 time give *Étude* 9 a peaceful character, just like that of *Étude* 4. The continuing movement in 8th notes with folk-music-like Alberti basses is interrupted twice with diatonic passagework in 32nd notes atop a pedal point, with a great deal of melodic chromatics appearing, modulating in both cases. The campanella legatos, a Neapolitan sixth chord, a few sparks and two three-voice chord prolongations with harmonic intensity signal a bit of Romanticism, showing some similarity to opus 38 no. 5 and 15, as well as opus 27. Like opus 41 *Feuilles d'Automne*, which was also dedicated to Degen, from a technical standpoint this étude is not so difficult, quite unlike the *Fantaisie symphonique* opus 28[b], which is also dedicated to the same man. Riboni compares the *Étude* with a second part of a sonatina, whose passages he believes bear witness to Romantic virtuosity in a Classical structural form.[810]

Étude 10 consists of three parts of divergent character, a broken chord triplet in 8th notes with an 8th-note rest and quarter note movement, a high pedal point figured with bass motifs and an ascending glissando motif as an anacrusis in contrast with staccato chords. The piece begins with a prolongation of type 9.1, after which we go through a few passing dominants to finally reach the dominant. This dominant is sustained in the pedal point part, after which the key of D returns with a traditional I-IV-II-V-I cadence in the glissando section. The 3/4 time and the pulsating rhythms give the piece a dancing character. Here Coste develops a preference for a sharp composition style. The piece is written in a playful way. The great deal of dynamics and the passing dominants together give the piece a touch of Romanticism.

Rhythmically, *Étude* 11 is entirely pulsating in character. The harmony moves between tonics, with passing dominants in the first part and submediant (relative) in the second part, also with little excursions, this time with diminished chords in measures 25-26, a half-diminished chord in measure 38 and passing dominants to the dominant of the relative. There is a great deal of harmonic movement in this part. Many campanella chords occur, due to the high position. The continuous chord movement in different positions, accompanied by the triplet legatos, make this étude technically difficult. The form and the phrasing remaining rather Classical, it is the chord positions and the chromatic coloring

---

[808] Riboni, Marco: '25 études op. 38 di Napoléon Coste', in: *Il Fronimo*, Milano, Suvini Zerboni, vol. XXVIII no. 109, 2000, p. 22.
[809] Riboni, Marco: '25 études op. 38 di Napoléon Coste', in: *Il Fronimo*, Milano, Suvini Zerboni, vol. XXVIII no. 109, 2000, p. 22.
[810] Riboni, Marco: '25 études op. 38 di Napoléon Coste', in: *Il Fronimo*, Milano, Suvini Zerboni, vol. XXVIII no. 109, 2000, p. 23.

that constitute the Romantic aspects of this work. This étude is dedicated to Mlle Cornélie Fallon, about whom no information has been found. The technique and the style are completely consistent with the first and fourth variations of Sor's Mozart variations opus 9.

As a prélude *Étude* 12 is an example of intensive melodic movement within the harmony, which is first conceived in whole-note chords in arpeggio, and thereafter with an intensive harmonic movement of one chord per beat in this 4/4 time in the key of C. The second phrase has a lot of 'Sturm und Drang'. With an leaping melodic passage, Coste reaches the highest note on the neck of his Lacôte guitar. On a guitar without this high range this étude can only be played with a modification in flageolets. For that reason, M. Cerclier from the dedication must have played a heptacorde. A four-voice prolongation with diminished seventh chords as a series of passing dominants and a conventional dominant-tonic cadence conclude this piece, in which only the intensive melodic effect, the chord intensity and the prolongation can be labelled as Romantic. The level of difficulty of this prélude for Cerclier, to whom it is dedicated, is moderate. Riboni calls the étude a sort of short caprice and has also found an allusion in measures 5-8 of this étude with measures 22-23 of Diabelli's Sonate III, part I, allegro moderato, giving that very 'Sturm und Drang' passage a corresponding reference in a Classical work.[811]

Étude 13, Allegretto, consists mainly of immediately repeated, sometimes figured, phrases structured in either four or two measures. With three indications for a different tempo, the étude stays in quarter notes with fixed chords and moves in the second part with suspended 8th notes, until the beginning is resumed. The harmonic movement is fairly calm, with many suspensions and figurations in the broken chords, and it is primarily the tonic, dominant and submediant that are in play, with a fleeting Neapolitan sixth chord and a deceptive ending occurring in the last submediant. The chromatics is expressed almost exclusively in the passing dominants, which have a modulating function. This étude also is of a moderate technical standard for Garancelle, to whom it is dedicated. Riboni is of the opinion that this piece is a minuet just like *Étude* no. 8, but generally speaking a minuet has a two-bar structure in the phrase, while this piece alternates between four and two-bar phrases, as well as two shortened three-bar phrases.[812]

Étude 14 consists of a portion from the lyrical fourth section of the *Fantaisie symphonique* opus 28[b]. The restful melody is supported with a gently flowing, but contrasting accompaniment in a 16th-note arpeggio. A harmonically interesting moment is the modulation to V-minor and Moll-Dur, which moves to the relative with a few dissonant chords. After a more intensive bass come a double-diminished chord, a diminished chord and a cadenza, where the motion is brought to a stop. After a four-voice prolongation the piece is resumed and ended, after a Moll-Dur chord, with a concluding cadence. The title shows that the *Fantaisie symphonique* was not published. The piece is dedicated to his wife Louise Olive Pauilhé, making it clear that the *Études* opus 38 were published after 1871, when Coste got married. Riboni characterizes the piece as a 'romance sans paroles', with a great deal of 'Sehnsucht' and calls it a symphonic-choral composition due to the four-voice progressions.[813]

With its various allusions to *Études* 5, 9, 17 and 19 from opus 38, as well as to *Ornans* opus 17, part II, *Étude* 15 is closely related to other works by Coste. The periodicity is interrupted regularly in the phrasing. The harmonic movement on the pedal point is plagal, and the elaboration in the melody and harmony of the acciacatura chromatics is modulating and predominated by passing dominants. Rhythmically there is a continuous movement in 16th notes, interrupted only by 32nd notes in passages in thirds and joint motif passages. A striking element is the sequence that Coste uses very seldom elsewhere. The final, four-voice prolongation is an example of this piece's harmonic intensity. Nothing is known about Mme Page, to whom this piece is dedicated, other than her name listed here.

---

[811] Riboni, Marco: '25 études op. 38 di Napoléon Coste', in: *Il Fronimo*, Milano, Suvini Zerboni, vol. XXVIII no. 110, 2000, p. 44.
[812] Riboni, Marco: '25 études op. 38 di Napoléon Coste', in: *Il Fronimo*, Milano, Suvini Zerboni, vol. XXVIII no. 110, 2000, p. 44.
[813] Riboni, Marco: '25 études op. 38 di Napoléon Coste', in: *Il Fronimo*, Milano, Suvini Zerboni, vol. XXVIII no. 110, 2000, p. 44-45.

Étude 16 has 66 measures; the *Études* comprising opus 38 become gradually longer. The piece has a typical rhythm, the same one as the beginning of number 10. The long harmonic movement on the pedal point on the dominant of this key of g-minor, so seldom used by Coste, can involve folk references. The periodicity in the phrasing is interrupted twice, precisely where important transitions occur in the structure and the harmony. A cadenza, various dissonant chords and melodic passage work give the piece a bit 'Sturm und Drang' for M. Ulenbrock from Riga, to whom it is dedicated, just like the *Sept Souvenirs* opus 17-23. In connection with this étude Riboni discusses the mazurka that Chopin made famous in Paris and explains Coste's use as a reflex of his interest in the old genre.[814] However, he does not include the same remark when discussing *Étude* 10, which has exactly the same rhythm and thus must also be a mazurka. Furthermore, the passage in triplets that is structurally part of both études occurs sporadically in Chopin's mazurkas, only in opus 6 no. 1, opus 7, no. 4, opus 30, no. 2, so it was not Coste's intent to write a mazurka. And Coste only wrote one mazurka, opus 33[a], which does not resemble these études in any way.

Étude 17, dedicated to Mlle Harris, is written predominantly in three voices, but sometimes in four. This étude is similar to *Étude* 19. In an intensive harmonic movement with many passing dominants and excursions to the relative, some melodic chromatics can also be heard the melodic figurations. The shortened phrases, which are used several times, reinforce the intensity of the chord progression. At times Coste repeats a new invention, expolitio, or alternatively uses a sequence of chords, but with decreasing tension. With two four-voice prolongations, a few dissonant chords such as diminished, half-diminished and augmented, and even Moll-Dur, the movement does not stand still for a single moment until the final cadence is reached. In his analytical description of this étude, Marco Riboni argues that here Coste, as an expression of his interest in the Baroque music of Robert de Visée, of which he made transcriptions, is making an allusion to the practice of basso continuo, which is particularly apparent in measures 24 and 32.[815] However, while dissonant harmonies do occur in Baroque guitar music, chromatic pivot tones are rare and passing dominants are used sparingly.[816]

Étude 18 has a pulsating character that is mainly established by the movement in fixed chords, followed by triplets and the immediately repeated chord inventions, reinforced by the echo dynamics. The chromatics is used entirely to harmonic ends in passages that are sometimes modulating in passing dominants. Coste expands his sequence-based cadence technique further, with a nice 'Spanish cadence', for instance, in measures 3-6. The few dissonant chords nevertheless contribute to the intensive harmonic movement: in each measure there are many chords that are continuously figured, which gives this étude great movement. With two rocket figures on a pedal point, a lot of dynamics and a striking three-voice passage where the countervoices are stopped, this *Étude* is a good example of Coste's intensively elaborated harmonic style. Just like opus 2, 'Weigl', the étude is dedicated to Mme Pascal, about whom nothing else is known. Considering this *Étude*, Riboni is reminded of Baroque music and even names Scarlatti, but at the same time he thinks the sustained tension gives the étude impressive dynamic energy, making it one of the most Romantic pieces of opus 38.[817]

Étude 19 was written for Mlle Caroline Montigny, as was the duet *Scherzo et Pastorale* opus 10, but this work has an unparalleled harmonic intensity and is written entirely in three voices, as noted earlier, but is sometimes also executed in four voices, similarly to *Étude* 17. Everywhere here Coste writes in as many as four chords per measure, in 8th notes in 2/4 time. The penetrating harmonic movement has a strong modulating character, despite the fact that the most striking contrast in keys is that from A to F. Melodic chromatics is almost entirely lacking. Everything is worked out harmonically in series of passing dominants, chord progressions and prolongations, with many, sometimes striking,

---

[814] Riboni, Marco: '25 études op. 38 di Napoléon Coste', in: *Il Fronimo*, Milano, Suvini Zerboni, vol. XXVIII no. 110, 2000, p. 45-46.
[815] Riboni, Marco: '25 études op. 38 di Napoléon Coste', in: *Il Fronimo*, Milano, Suvini Zerboni, vol. XXVIII no. 110, 2000, p. 46.
[816] Vliet, Ari van: 'Gitaarmuziek in de tweede helft van de zeventiende eeuw', in: *De Tabulatuur*, Driebergen, Nederlandse Luitvereniging, vol. XIV, no. 51, 1 V 1997, p. 15-21.
[817] Riboni, Marco: '25 études op. 38 di Napoléon Coste', in: *Il Fronimo*, Milano, Suvini Zerboni, vol. XXVIII no. 110, 2000, p. 47.

dissonant chords including not only many diminished seventh chords, but also hard-diminished, double-diminished and augmented chords. With its few similarities to other works, this étude can be considered as having a central position in Coste's work.

Étude 20. This étude has a folk music character, that is mainly due to the sustained pulsating rhythm, which marks the piece as 'dansant'. The many pedal points with a stopped bass are thematically figured in alternate inversions and motifs in thirds, which strongly unify the piece. The modulation to the parallel minor is the only remarkable feature. Dissonant chords appear but sparingly, but a certain harmonic tension can be detected in the melodic chromatics and contrast with the pedal point, which is something reinforced by the diminished seventh, Moll-Dur and double-diminished seventh chords. All of that in combination and a few shortened phrases, which speed up the motion, the many campanella legatos, which give a jingling effect, but especially the sheer virtuosity of the work, make this étude typical for the Romantic aspect of Coste style. This work is dedicated to M. Gozzoli, who is also lucky enough to have the *Valse favorite* opus 46 dedicated to him.

The character of *Étude* 21 is entirely determined by the pulsating chord rhythm and the joint motifs in melodic triplets. In the latter Coste here uses a great deal of melodic chromatics in contrast with the previous études. Dissonant chords such as diminished, half-diminished and double-diminished occur in places with a modulating effect, each time on a pedal point. The technique of immediately repeating a musical invention, expolitio, can also be found in this work. Moll-Dur chords at the end of the first part and the plagal cadence with them at the end also give this étude a folk music atmosphere. For Riboni it is a characteristic opera melody accompanied with chords, and he emphasizes the vocal aspect of it, something that is contradicted by the practically isorhythmic repetitions of the melody.[818] Just like the *Quadrilles* opus 3, the work is dedicated to Lord Asburnham and is one of Coste's lesser-known études. It is an interesting work, not least due to its alternating combination of chords and melody, but especially in the techniques that go along with this style but which are not often found in guitar music. There are many changes in position, but the musical expressive power dominates the guitar technique in it.

Étude 22. This famous tarantella étude consists almost entirely of broken passages in thirds. That makes this étude so characteristic, in addition to the practical absence of basses in the middle section, which contributes to its floating character. However, the periodicity in the continuous movement in octaves in 6/8 time is interrupted a few times. In the succession of two measures at measure 32 Coste uses the compositional technique of immediately repeating of a musical element, the expolitio, while the following 7-bar phrase speeds up the harmonic motion in measure 45. Harmonically, the piece is a striking, but pleasant cross between harmonic minor, modal and chromatic progressions, which are mostly in passing dominants. The Romantic content is reinforced by a few of the by now familiar chord prolongations of both the descending and mixed ascending-descending type, in addition to the decidedly characteristic dissonant chords – diminished seventh on raised IV – of which there are only a few. The lowered seventh degree of the scale makes the work modal, while the modulation to the dominant make it tonal and the switching between I minor and I major are harmonically surprising. The folk music aspect is reinforced by the pedal point passage in measures 49-57, in addition to the Moll-Dur progressions that occur earlier in measures 25 and 31, after which a modulation to the dominant takes place. The piece ends in a traditional fashion in V-I progressions, but there is a nice parachute arpeggio before the end. The relatively numerous dynamic indications are certainly used for expressive effect. The character of *Étude* 22 affords this short étude a unique position in Coste's oeuvre.

Étude 23. The stopped ostinato bass and the continuous arpeggio in thirds and sixths determine overwhelmingly determine the character of this work. This continuous movement is reminiscent of folk music, but the periodicity of the phrasing is regularly interrupted, and there are also some notable harmonic events. These include the passing dominants and half-diminished and diminished seventh

---

[818] Riboni, Marco: '25 études op. 38 di Napoléon Coste', in: *Il Fronimo*, Milano, Suvini Zerboni, vol. XXVIII no. 110, 2000, p. 48.

chords, but especially the minor-key variants of the I, V and IV degrees of the scales, having a folk music effect as well as a Moll-Dur effect. In addition to chord prolongations, the development section has a floating harmony, due to the absence of a confirming cadence. The reprise is periodic and does not provide many more surprises other than a V-minor, passing dominants and a V/I chord, after which the theme is imitated in the bass in measure 60 and a harmonic acceleration occurs in a prolongation. Then the rhythm shifts to anacrusis, and confirming cadences come in a six-bar phrase. This étude is one of Coste's best-known pieces, alongside *Études* 20 and 22. Remarkably, all three of these *Études* are characterized by a continuous ostinato movement, major-minor contrasts, interruption of the periodicity, passing dominants and dissonant chords. According to the dedication of *Le Départ* opus 31, M. Adan, 'de Bruxelles', to whom this *Étude* from opus 38 is dedicated, occupies a finance-related position the Kingdom of Belgium.

Étude 24 is the most thematically developed piece in this collection. The theme bears similarities to other works by Coste, and various other passages also correspond to those in other works, making this a key piece in his style. Overwhelmingly written in three voices, with many figurations, there are nevertheless a few four-voice progressions to be found in it, as well as some recognizable prolongations. The periodicity in this simple *ABA* form is interrupted a few times, there are many dissonant chords and passing dominants, and the piece modulates not only to the supertonic and the dominant, but also to the chromatic submediant, by means of a pivot tone. The rhythm vacillates between movement in 8th notes and in 16th notes, but there is some virtuosity to be found in the tremolando and the diatonic passagework. The chromatics is mainly used in a harmonic way. This well-balanced work deserves attention just as much as some of Coste's better-known pieces. It is dedicated to 'M. Schult(z), de Stokolm', just like *Divagation* opus 45.

Save the exceptional key and time, *Étude* 25 is a rather traditional with its *ABA* form, its phrasing and its harmony. The latter stands in great contrast with the strong dissonance of a major seventh chord and half-diminished lowered ninth chord in the intermediary phrase before the reprise. Now diminished and double-diminished seventh chords and passing dominants appear, with figurations in free lyricism, and abruptio. Immediate repetition, expolitio, of a motif can also be recognized here. A few pedal points with contrasting dissonance and series of passing dominants account for the harmonic movement of this piece, which proceeds in a rather traditional fashion, going through I, V, IV and VI. Smaller note values are used here in broken chords, largely for rhythmic effect. At times the piece practically stands still, and sometimes there are strong progressions in prolongations, so that there is still quite some variety. Just like *Grande Sérénade* opus 30, this *Étude* is dedicated to the Russian nobleman Makaroff, composed with many broken chords and barré chords.

With respect to formal characteristics, the Romantic in the music of the *Études* opus 38 is expressed not in the structural form, which is usually a simple or composite song form, but rather in the regularly occurring interruption of the periodicity in the phrasing. One remarkable thing here is the increasingly frequent 'expolitio' style element, borrowed from rhetoric, in which a musical idea is immediately repeated, sometimes verbatim and sometimes modified. It is also remarkable that Coste prescribes a cadenza on various occasions, including a quite long one in *Étude* 6, making this style element an unmistakable feature of his style of composition, and he even has his pupils practice it. Musical material, both melodic and harmonic, is reworked in many ways: in smaller note values, passagework, rocket and parachute motifs. Ornamentation is used sporadically by Coste in these *Études*, and considering the short length of the pieces in this collection, looking for an idée fixe is futile. Coste uses gradually less melodic chromatics in the development that can be noted in his works, including in this collection; he increasingly opts to use harmonic alternations. There is an abundance of these, with many diminished seventh chords, double-diminished seventh chords and passing dominants appearing, a few times hard-diminished and, quite strikingly, major seventh and diminished lowered ninth in measures of 24, 25 and 44 of *Étude* 25, with a high degree of harmonic dissonance, which can compete with Wagner's Tristan chord, which, in contrast, is worked out polyphonically.[819] Notable modulations include chromatic pivot tone modulation, major-minor contrast, IV minor and lowered VI, and particularly also V minor and 'major in minor'. Three-voice chord progressions are more the rule than the exception, a few times entire études are written in three voices, and the four-voice progressions so typical of Coste can be found in various places. He composes melodically in his style but with a very intensive harmonic arrangement, which often also includes an intensive harmonic movement. Here he does not use chord progressions of various types unabridged; they are often written with variation. Besides series of passing dominants, such special harmonic progressions can be heard as Neapolitan sixths, Trugschluss and Moll-Dur, as well as a Picardy third on one occasion. A few unusual key and time signatures are used in the études. Arpeggios are used often, naturally, with *Études* 23, 24 and 25 being notable examples. The pulsating rhythm in *Études* 10, 11, 16, 18, 20 and 21 drives the movement forward and is extremely expressive, and the stopped rhythm of the well-known *Études* 18, 20 and 23 is legendary. In addition to the practically ubiquitous legatos, Coste gives few indications for articulation. In this collection he works more with dynamic contrasts, sometimes as an echo effect, as in measures 64-67 of *Étude* 24. And finally, a few elements of folk music can be recognized, in a bourdon or a figured pedal point, which brings the number of formal features and stylistic elements that can be considered Romantic to 15 of the total 21 defined, as listed in chapter IV 'Style' of the thematic catalogue. The places where the stylistic elements in the études occur can be found in the corresponding appendices. Not only do the character and quality of these style elements provide a good overview of the style Coste develops; in *25 Études de Genre* opus 38 they also constitute a key to his life work.

The appearance of this work has been set to the year 1872, but alternatively it might have been 1873, as is indicated in the note on the title page of the first edition,[820] giving sufficient reason to discuss this collection at the end of this chapter, making 1873 the beginning of the last chapter in the biographical sketch of Coste's life, before the conclusion in chapter IX. In the life of this composer and guitarist the main activities are giving concerts, teaching pupils and writing and publishing works. All the activities for which information is available in the sources consulted are taken up once again in order to shed light on the life and works of this composer, of whom the picture is growing increasingly clear, using the words of the time to the greatest extent possible.

119 Rue du Fauborg St- Martin

---

[819] Borgdorff, Henk: Ernst Kurth, *Romantische Harmonik*, 1920, in: Grijp, Louis Peter & Paul Scheepers, ed.: *Van Aristoxenos tot Stockhausen*, Wolters-Noordhoff, Groningen, 1990, pp. 436-439.
[820] 25 *Études de Genre* op. 38 Lam Spencer Collection XX(159224.1): 'Donné par M. Coste en 1873 avant mon départ pour [...?].'

VIII
Divagation

We are also sorry to announce the death of M. Napoléon Coste, the excellent guitarist-composer: he was 78 years of age. Up to the end of his career he kept his passion for his art, and, not too long ago, he published the Livre d'Or des Guitaristes, an important work, worthy of the musicians attention.[821]

Concerts 1873-1876

In this period of Coste's final years, the life in Paris of the composer and guitarist can be followed closely, in every year events emerge from the sources, worth-while mentioning, such as concerts, publications and letters. From these, an image of his life can be sketched, even better when he models his memories in his programmatic works. In the period between 1857 and 1872, 20 concerts with guitar were found, apart from the 2 in which Coste participated, but now there are only 3 concerts found in the literature, with Jaime Bosch and Francisco Tárrega, apart from the 7 with Coste. Bosch, the Spanish guitarist, who settled in Paris in 1861, is still active in giving concerts, such as on April 6, 1873 and April 5, 1874.[822] In this period, these are all the concerts with guitar that could be found in the musical press, which is represented principally by the *Revue et Gazette musicale de Paris*, until 1880, and *Le Ménestrel*, with 8 pages now, but without the initial chanson. The issues of *La Presse musicale*, *L'art musical* and *Le Monde Artiste* could not be found. The last volume of *La France musicale* appeared in 1870. According to this information, presuming that the reviews represent the real number of concerts, the guitar appears to have been vanished from the concert stage in Paris. On top of this, Trinidad Huerta died in Paris on June 19, 1874, the Spanish guitarist who always was very active in concerts during his presence there, with whom an important representative has gone.[823] Coste complains about the popularity of the piano:

> *I do not deny that the piano is a tremendously powerful instrument on which some admirable music is played. The power pianists have is mighty. They play thousands of notes at a dizzying speed. [...] It's a horrible epidemic. Since one doesn't need a musical organization to play the piano, anyone can do so, either well or poorly, leading to this endless craze. In every house you hear this atrocious instrument being clanked on from the basement to the attic. In the building we live in there are only three of them, and we are quite fortunate that they are seldom played, but one hears a lot of them in the distance in the neighborhood.[824]*

The 'guitar mania' is superseded by the 'piano mania'. But Coste gives concerts as well. According to reports and his own letters, in 1874 he suffers a heavy fall from a stairway and dislocates his left shoulder blade, making him feel the need to ask his superiors at the Préfecture de la Seine for a 25-day leave of absence on July 30 so he can undergo hydrotherapy to alleviate the pain.[825] However, that does not keep him from participating in the monthly, members-only concert of the *Société académique*

---

[821] *Le Ménestrel*, vol. 49, no. 9, 28 I 1883, p. [8]: 'Nous avons le regret d'annoncer aussi la mort de M. Napoléon Coste, éminent guitariste-compositeur: il était âgé de 78 ans. Jusqu'à la fin de sa carrière, il avait gardé la passion de son art et, il y a peu de temps encore, il publiait le Livre d'or des Guitaristes, ouvrage important et digne de l'attention des musiciens.'

[822] *Revue et Gazette musicale de Paris*, vol. XXVIII, no. 9, 3 III 1861, p. 70: 'M. Bosch, le célèbre guitariste est de retour à Paris'; vol. XL, no. 14, 6 IV 1873, p. 110: '[...] concert guitariste Bosch'; vol. XLI, no. 14, 5 IV 1874, p. 110: '[...] guitariste Espagnol J. Bosch'.

[823] Coldwell, Robert: *A.T. Huerta, Life and Works*, DGA Editions, 2006, p. 51.

[824] Coste-Schult, 20 VII 1876: 'Je ne nie pas que le piano ne soit un instrument d'une puissance formidable et sur lequel on joue d'admirable musique. La force des pianistes est prodigieuse. Ils font des myriades de notes avec une rapidité que vous donne le vertige. [...] C'est une affreuse épidémie. Comme il n'est pas nécessaire pour jouer du piano d'avoir une organisation musicale, chacun peut en jouer bien et mal. De là une manie sans fin. Dans toutes les maisons de la cave au grenier on entend tapoter cet affreux instrument. Dans la maison que nous habitons il n'y en a que trois et fort heureusement on les joue peu, mais on entend beaucoup au loin dans le voisinage.'

[825] Jaworski, Roman: 'Napoléon Coste 1805-1883, une histoire perdue', in: *Valentiana*, Valenciennes, 1992, no. 10, p. 77; Roncet, Noël: *Napoléon Coste, Compositeur, 1805-1883*, Amondans, 2005, p. 26.

des Enfants d'Apollon, where he plays an *Introduction et Polonaise* and three *Études*.[826] One also reads: 'composed and performed by M. Coste', so the hydrotherapy must have helped him considerably. On December 8 he writes the following words to Schult in the context of the *Études* opus 38:

> *I have most recently had a real success at the Société Académique des Enfants d'Apollon, performing a few of this little pieces. There were some first-class composers and artists who played masterpieces by Beethoven and Mozart, etc. Anyway, my friend, in spite of this formidable company, I was praised, complimented and warmly applauded. And yet I have not played in public for quite a long time, and, as an aggravating factor, my left shoulder blade is still dislocated, making me a sort of oddity for the doctors, and worst of all I'm 68 years old! So these little pieces must be of some value?*[827]

The concerts of the society usually take place on the second Sunday of each month, so this can even be dated to November 8, 1874. Decourcelle's descriptions are generally accurate, as shown by that of the November 1876 concert, of which a review can also be found in the *Revue et Gazette musicale de Paris*, in which the names of the composers and performers, as well as the titles of the works, largely match.[828] Contrary to all literature about Coste, in which it is claimed that he can no longer perform after his injury, he turns out to have continued participating in concerts. As for the first work in this 'séance', it may have been the *Deuxième Polonaise* opus 14 which was played, or more likely the *Souvenir(s) du Jura* opus 44, a work that appears in 1876 and consists of an Andante and a Polonaise, of which Coste wrote three. As for the third étude, played in addition to the two specified by Decourcelle, Coste can take his pick out of the 25 *Études de Genre* opus 38, which had just been published. Other études, such as the *Étude* from opus 19 based on *Delfzil* and opus 53 no. 5, which appears in 1881, are unlikely candidates. And then there are the *Études* in the 1851 *Méthode*, but that only contains two that can be considered performance pieces: the *Introduction et Allegretto* on pp. 31-33 and the *Rêverie Nocturne* on pp. 43-44. A selection from opus 38 is thus an obvious possibility, containing as it does many works suitable for performance. The only personal connection between the études and the society resides in the person of de la Richardière, who performs regularly in this circle, but that concerns *Étude* 3 again, which is dedicated to him, one of the simpler études and not really a performance piece (although this is one of the few to have been recorded by Segovia). Which three Coste played remains shrouded in mystery, but his technique must have been back up to standard to be able to play this repertoire.

In this period there are short notes by Coste from 1874 and 1875 addressed to Léon Gruel and which were discovered by Norbert Fischer. Gruel is one of Coste's pupils according to the dedication of *La Ronde de Mai* opus 42 from 1876. These notes concern appointments for lessons, such as:

> *I am completely at your disposal starting from 8 o'clock.*

and social calls like:

> *It may be that you are intending to come see us this evening with your ladies. I hasten to warn you that we are going to the Beaulieu concert. Therefore we will not be at home.*[829]

His relationship with Gruel is personal, yet businesslike, and Coste himself also goes to concerts.

---

[826] Decourcelle, Maurice: *La Société académique des Enfants d'Apollon*, programmes des concerts annuels..., Paris, Durand, 1881, p. 226: 'Introduction et polonaise; trois études pour la guitare, composées et exécutées par M. Coste.'

[827] Coste-Schult, 8 XII 1874: 'J'ai eu dernièrement un véritable succès à la Société académique des Enfants d'Apollon, en y exécutant quelques unes de ces petites pièces. Il y avait là des compositeurs et des artistes de 1ᵉʳ ordre qui avaient fait entendre des chefs d'oeuvre de Beethoven, de Mozart etc. Et bien Monsieur, malgré ce voisinage redoutable, j'ai été fêté, complimenté et chaleureusement applaudi. Et pourtant depuis bien longtemps je ne m'étais faire entendre, et, circonstance aggravante, j'ai toujours l'omoplate gauche décrochée, ce qui fait de moi une espèce de phénomène au dire des médecins, et ce qu'il y a de pis, j'ai 68 ans! Il faut donc que ces petits morceaux aient une certaine valeur?'

[828] Decourcelle, Maurice: *La Société académique des Enfants d'Apollon*, programmes des concerts annuels..., Paris, Durand, 1881, p. 232; *Revue et Gazette musicale de Paris*, vol. XLIII, no. 47, 19 XI 1876, p. 374, 'séance mensuelle des Enfants d'Apollon.'

[829] Coste-Gruel, 12 XII 1874: 'Je serai tout à votre disposition mardi soir à partir de 8 heures'; Coste-Gruel, 22 IV 1875: 'Il se pourrait que vous eussiez l'intention de nous venir voir le soir avec vos Dames. Je me hâte de vous prévoir que nous allons au concert Beaulieu. Par conséquence nous serons absents de chez nous'; Archiv Norbert Fischer, Halen.

VIII — Divagation 205

Retirement 1875

Napoléon Coste may have perceived it as a great liberation to retire from his administrative post at the Caisse Municipale on April 1, 1875. Remarkably, his income increases significantly. He now makes 2,100 fr. a month.[830] In his letter to Degen from 1858 he complains about that miserable little job, which he should never have returned to after receiving his laurels in 1856.[831] Now his hands were completely free for playing the guitar, composing, teaching and giving concerts. The guitar-playing must have gone well because in these final years he gives concerts at the *Société académique des Enfants d'Apollon*, while the fact that he writes and publishes 16 additional works for solo guitar and for voice with guitar attest to the success of his composition endeavors. He began teaching from the time he first arrived in Paris. Certain of his pupils have now become familiar, some from the dedications of the *Études* opus 38, including that to M. Gruel, to whom Coste writes the notes quoted above. He was married to his pupil Louise Olive Pauilhé, with whom he plays duets, of which there are plenty, whether by Coste himself or by others. After the recovering from his two unfortunate falls in 1863 and 1874 and his retirement from his administrative post, he now enjoys a creative and productive time.

Société 1874-1879

Coste has entered into the musical upper class, as a composer and as a guitarist. Nothing is known in this period about Coste's possible participation as guitarist and composer in the *Loge maçonnique des Frères Unis Inséparables*. No overview exists of the Freemasons lodge, and examining the lodge's annual concerts between 1852 and 1872 Coste's name ceases to appear after 1852. The monthly musical meeting of the *Société académique des Enfants d'Apollon* continue to be held, in addition to the annual public concerts, until June 30, 1880. In the overview of this society, Coste's names appears several times, beginning on November 8, 1874, probably with his *Souvenir(s) du Jura* opus 44 and three *Études*, as described above. On July 9, 1876 he plays an *Andante et Scherzo*.[832]

Considering that Decourcelle is not always good at indicating the correct titles of the works performed, and because no work with this title appears in Coste's oeuvre, it is also inviting to attempt to trace this reference back to a known work. Coste wrote various scherzos, of which the first *Pastorale et Scherzo* opus 10 from 1841(?) for two guitars. *Delfzil* opus 19 is also a scherzo, but that piece consists of a single part, but *Soirées d'Auteuil* opus 23, also from the *Souvenirs, Sept Morceaux Épisodiques* from 1852, does have two parts, but it was published 24 years earlier. The second part of the *Fantaisie symphonique* opus 28[b] includes an Andante and a Scherzo, but that was written in 1856 and is thus also not new. Assuming that it is a commonplace occurrence to play a fairly new or unpublished work at the musical meetings of the Apollo Society, something that, as far as Coste is concerned, has already been shown, it could be *Andante & Menuet* opus 39, a composition that according to the copy in the Bibliothèque nationale in 1876 was published by Richault.[833] This is the first of seven menuets written by Coste, so that there are no overriding concerns against thinking that this work was played in a concert in July 1876, except for the fact that *Souvenir(s) du Jura, Andante et Polonaise* opus 44 also consists of two parts, of which the polonaise could just as easily be considered to be a scherzo, given its lively, cheerful character. Due to the sequence of the opus numbers the choice remains the first of these. Decourcelle apparently does not mention all the works and composers that are performed in the monthly meetings of the society. Coste himself describes a concert that is still unknown:

> *In the last monthly concert of the Enfants d'Apollon I played my new fantaisie (Divagation) with a success that took me aback. I was called back to the stage and applauded like a prima Donna. At first I thought they*

---

[830] Jaworski, Roman: 'Napoléon Coste 1805-1883, une histoire perdue', in: *Valentiana*, Valenciennes, 1992, no. 10, p. 78.
[831] Coste-Degen, 15 VI 1858, p. 3: 'j'aurais dû quitter ce misérable emploi [...]'.
[832] Decourcelle, Maurice: *La Société académique des Enfants d'Apollon*, programmes des concerts annuels..., Paris, Durand, 1881, p. 231: 'Andante et scherzo pour la guitare, composés et exécutés par M. Coste.'
[833] Pn [Vm9 3544. Coste, *Andante et menuet* opus 39.

were making fun of me, but the composers I know and others were in attendance were so kind as to explain to me the great impression I had made.[834]

Considering the fact, as mentioned earlier, that the monthly meetings take place faithfully on the second Sunday of the month, the new concert date of August 12, 1877 emerges, where Coste played his *Divagation* opus 45.

OPUS 39, *ANDANTE & MENUET* 1876

This work's year of publication by Richault agrees with Richault's address: between 1862 and 1898 the publishing house is located at boulevard des Italiens no. 4. After the previous publication with Richault of opus 38, that publisher stopped including the works in the running series numbering, preferring to list them separately. In the case of opus 39 that is N.C., which are naturally the composer's initials. With the subsequent, and final, publication with Richault of *Le Passage des Alpes* opus 27, 28 & 40 the numbering is N.C. 2, so that the assumption is justifiable that opus 39 was published earlier. Why Coste opts for the old and perhaps even archaic minuet genre – this is the first one he writes with this title – may be due to his interest in the music of Robert de Visée, three of whose minuets he transcribes in the 1851 *Méthode*. He transcribes an additional one later in 1880 in his *Livre d'Or* opus 52, in which he also transcribes one by Exaudet, two by Beethoven and one by Haydn. But at the same time, in his *Méthode* and *Le Livre d'Or du guitariste* he does not write an allemande, a gavotte, sarabande, bourrée, gigue, passacaille, all of which, like the minuet, are included in Baroque suites. The reason is obvious: of all these genres, the minuet is the only one still used by Classical composers. The others fall into disuse, and Coste simply follows this practice. The composition is dedicated to M. J. G. Holm, and Coste may have sent hem a copy signed 'hommage de l'auteur N. Coste' in the composer's own hand, a copy now in the Kongelige Bibliotek in Copenhagen.[835]

The Romantic content in the *Andante et Menuet* is to be found chiefly in the Andante, where Coste has opted for a free musical form. The *Menuet* is obbligato, and meets the requirements of the genre, but no more than that. It is marred once more by the structural false relation, Querstand, between g against g#. By contrast, the Andante has many Romantic features. It is an interesting work with various surprising progressions, many dissonant chords, passing dominants and modulation. Rhythmically the piece offers many surprises, with a great variation in arpeggios, repeated chords and free lyricism. It has plagal Moll-Dur progressions, prolongations, rocket figures and campanella chords, an interplay of elements that mark this first part as Romantic.

OPUS 40, *RONDO* [I.E. PART III *LE PASSAGE DES ALPES* OPUS 27, 28 & 40] 1876

With the publication of the complete work *Le Passage des Alpes*, not only has the title been completely replaced of the original composition called *Les Feuilles d'Automne* as entered in the Makaroff competition in 1856; the third section, has been added to it, the *Rondo*, a successful completion to the piece, which now consists of three parts, balancing it out quite nicely. Coste clearly opts for the Italian term instead of the French equivalent 'rondeau'. After all, the trek through the Alps leads to Italy. The work is dedicated to Mme La Comtesse de Nadaillac Delessert, who is in close contact with Coste in this period. The handwritten dedication graces the edition of *Marche funèbre et Rondeau* opus 43 in the Spencer Collection in London, where manuscripts and publications such as this work, which according to Robert Spencer probably originate from this woman's collection.[836] If this noblewoman

---

[834] Coste-Hallberg, 23 VIII 1877: 'J'ai fait entendre au dernier concert mensuel des Enfants d'Apollon ma nouvelle fantaisie (Divagation) avec un succès qui m'a bien étonné. J'ai été rappelé et applaudi comme une prima Donna. J'ai cru d'abord que l'on se moquait de moi, mais les compositeurs de ma connaissance et autres qui se trouvaient là ont bien voulu me donner l'explication de l'effet que j'avais produit.'

[835] Coste-Degen, 17 X 1863: 'M. Holm a la boulé de m'écrire de loin en loin [...]'; Kk Rischel 161 mu 6701.1183 U48, Coste, *Andante et Menuet* opus 39.

[836] Lam XX(159262.1) Spencer Collection, Coste, *Le Passage des Alpes* opus 27, 28 & 40, previously owned by the Comtesse de Nadaillac Delessert.

VIII — Divagation

was able to play this piece, she must have been a guitarist of the highest standard. Artistically and from the perspective of the guitar technique it requires, this trilogy is one of the composer's best works. Richault's publication of this work is the second one, going by the new N.C. 2 numbering, so the dating should logically come after opus 39, but nothing can be certain with Richault's numbering. Holding to that year for the publication date seems the most obvious choice. It is the last work of Coste's to appear with that publisher. The change in the title has already been discussed at length in chapter VI. Coste may have found inspiration in his namesake's Bonaparte journey over the Alps in 1800. In this way, the possibility is also created to name opus 41 *Feuilles d'Automne*, the next work to be discussed. But first it must be seen in how the Rondo fits musically with the first two parts of the work, which are older, and to what extent the personal Romantic style developed by Coste is recognizable in it.

There are nice contrasts in the rhythms between the constituent parts of the *Rondo*. This is reinforced by a single chromatic modulation, and the lengthened and shortened phrases conspire to produce a strong harmonic rhythm, which is accompanied by dissonant chords. Furthermore, the free lyricism in the melodic passages is striking, as are the short cadenza and the descending chromatic joint motif, which appears quite characteristically in the first part and in the reprise. A folk music passage on a pedal point in the middle section contrasts colorfully against the two parts that flank it. Coste gives many instructions for articulation, tempo and dynamics, which clearly add to the Romantic caliber of the work. Due to its continuous movement in melodic figuration and arpeggios, the stretto has a convincingly finalizing effect.

Opus 41, *Feuilles d'Automne* 1876

The reason this collection of twelve waltzes can be given this name is that the same title became available when the trilogy opus 27, 28 & 40 was renamed *Le Passage des Alpes*. To make things clear, this is also indicated on the title page of this collection, as is the fact that the earlier piece 'Autumn Leaves' was entered in the Makaroff competition in 1856 and has largely been incorporated into the trilogy. This shows clearly that the rondo was indeed added to it at a later date. Opus 41 is one of the four works that Coste self-published in 1876, continuing the numbering initiated by Richault with N.C. 3.[837] The title *Feuilles d'Automne* is the same as that in Victor Hugo's collection of poems published in 1831, which inspired Liszt to compose the symphonic poem *Ce qu'on entend sur la montagne* in 1848. But no details other than the title coincide with this collection. Hugo's poetry inspired works by many other composers as well, including Berlioz, Lalo, Massenet, Saint-Saëns and Vierne. At this point Coste is publishing practically all his works himself. He did that earlier with his first chanson *Aux Parisiens* WoO 2 in 1830, *Fantaisie Armide* opus 4 in 1832 and *Fantaisie 'Meyerbeer'* opus 6 in 1837, but that is in the distant past. Up until this opus 41, Coste's works either appear with various publishers or remain unpublished. The situation in the field of music publishing has apparently changed with respect to Coste and guitar music. Popular chansons still find ready buyers, but there is practically no market for compositions of high artistic merit. He writes about this inscription and the following opus number in a letter to Schult on July 20, 1876, so the dating of both of them is correct.[838] Coste dedicates the collection to Søffren Degen, just as earlier with *Étude* 9 opus 38, none of them technically difficult pieces. If Coste tailored these works to suit him, he must have been a second-rate player, as also shown by the simple accompanying second guitar parts that Degen wrote for opus 12, 27, 28, 40 and 47. In his 1934 article about Napoléon Coste and his works, Mario Giordano calls opus 41 a suggestive collection of waltzes, in which one does not know what to admire more: the discriminating melodic workmanship, the treasures of harmonization or the most intelligent use of guitar effects. According to him, the greatest value of this work nevertheless lies in its unity, with the twelve waltzes being very closely connected by a single musical idea, with various expressions of rhythm and melody give the

---

[837] Pn [Vm9 3552, Coste, *Feuilles d'Automne* opus 41.
[838] Coste-Schult, 20 VII 1876: 'Mon op. 41 (Les feuilles d'automne 12 valses) est à la gravure et l'op. 42 suivra de près.'

Feuilles d'Automne a melancholy character that is characteristic of all of Coste's works.[839] According to Joerg Sommermeyer the twelve waltzes should be classed with Coste's miniature works, in which without a mandatory constructive idea he lets natural, undetermined harmony and spontaneous, natural ornamentation run free.[840] The twelve waltzes in this collection of autumn leaves certainly may bear this Romantic title, not much Romanticism can be found in the music itself, the opinions just discussed notwithstanding. Aside from the greater length of these waltzes, they are comparable to the transcriptions Coste made of Strauss's waltzes, opus 7, in around 1838.

All of the works are periodic. All but one of the waltzes alternate with a trio, nine of them in the subdominant, one in the parallel and one in the relative. One can thus discern a preconceived musical form. Coste gives a great many instructions for dynamics and articulation, which help make the music lively. Waltz no. 6 has a cadenza, waltz no. 7 has a 5-bar phrase and waltz no. 10 has a flageolet passage and a trumpet imitation. What little harmonic movement there is consists of passing dominants, a few diminished seventh chords on raised II and IV, and there are two Neapolitan sixth chords and two double-diminished seventh chords. A Moll-Dur chord can also be spotted in measure 29 of no. 8. With a single rocket figure, a parachute figure, and some sparks that can be found again in no. 8, a few instances of chord prolongation and expolitio, the immediate repetition of a musical idea, the number of Romantic features is so small that this work will certainly not be thought of by posterity as particularly Romantic, regardless of the Romantic character Giordano seems to find in it. The stylistic features he lists can be found much more frequently in other works by Coste than in this one. Coste's gallant melodic style can still be recognized, but that can be found in practically all of his works; the character of these pieces is generally happy and cheerful, just like most of Coste's works. The work may have been intended as a didactic piece, or was perhaps adapted to suit Degen's tastes and playing ability. But Coste also dedicated his *Fantaisie symphonique* opus 28[b] to him, which is a musical masterpiece. The 'raison d'être' for this piece may have been commercial, as it is not very in keeping with Coste's developments as a composer up to this point.

Opus 42, *La Ronde de Mai* 1876

Exactly when Coste self-published his *La Ronde de Mai* is not known, but the edition in the Bibliothèque nationale in Paris indicates the year 1876, and the publication number N.C. 4 also points in that direction.[841] Coste's letter to Schult of July 20, 1876 confirms this.[842] He dedicates the work to his pupil Léon Gruel, who, if he was capable of playing this piece, must have been an accomplished guitarist. If one may believe a few of Coste's letters to Gruel, the two met in 1874 and are on good terms with each other. A hand-written homage on an edition in the Kongelige Bibliotek in Copenhagen is practically illegible, making it impossible to make out either the name or the date. The *Ronde* in the title refers to the second section, the Scherzo, while the remainder of the extended title indicates that he piece is preceded by a Larghetto that does begin until measure 5, after the Andante maestoso. According to the subtitle the work is a divertissement.

The piece reveals many Romantic features: the alternation between the chord rhythm and passagework in free lyricism, the three cadenzas and the dissonant chords in part I, the melodic chromatics, the intensive harmonic movement and the striking cadences in part II. The sustained movement and the theme of the Scherzo shows a thematic and rhythmic relationship with *Étude* 20 from opus 38, but here the piece is much shorter and it is actually ended prematurely with a plagal Moll-Dur cadence and a final cadence that is unexpectedly interrupted by a melodic passage. Remarkably, in this work Coste resumes his Romantic composition style, making *La Ronde de Mai* one of the more interesting pieces in his oeuvre.

---

[839] Giordano, Mario: 'Napoléon Coste e le sue opere', in: *Il plettro*, febbraio 1934, no. 2, p. 7.
[840] Sommermeyer, Joerg: 'Noten, The Guitar Works of Napoléon Coste...', in: *Nova Giulianiad*, 1984 Nr. 3, p. 169, http://home.tonline.de/home/Rechtsanwalt.Joerg.Sommermeyer/ng3.htm, July 10, 2002.
[841] Pn [Vm9 3558, Coste, *La Ronde de Mai* opus 42.
[842] Coste-Schult, 20 VII 1876: 'Mon op. 41 (Les feuilles d'automne 12 valses) est à la gravure et l'op. 42 suivra de près.'

OPUS 43, MARCHE FUNÈBRE ET RONDEAU 1876

The series of editions of new works by Coste is followed up with the publication of *Marche funèbre et Rondeau* opus 43, which is again a Coste publication using number N.C. 5. So, it can by dated as 1876, the same year indicated on the copy in the Bibliothèque nationale in Paris.[843] The combination of these two parts is quite remarkable: a funeral march followed by a cheerful rondo, but a certain consolation can emanate from the latter after so much sorrow in the first part. But even the first part has a transition to the parallel major that contrasts considerably with the ongoing stately marching movement. Sor also does this in 1836 in his *Fantaisie élégiaque* opus 59, but the sorrowful atmosphere doesn't change there. Furthermore, besides the title, there is also a relationship between the two works in terms of content. Coste even inserts a few quotations from measures 3-4 and 52-55 of Sor's march in measures 4 and 22 of his own piece.

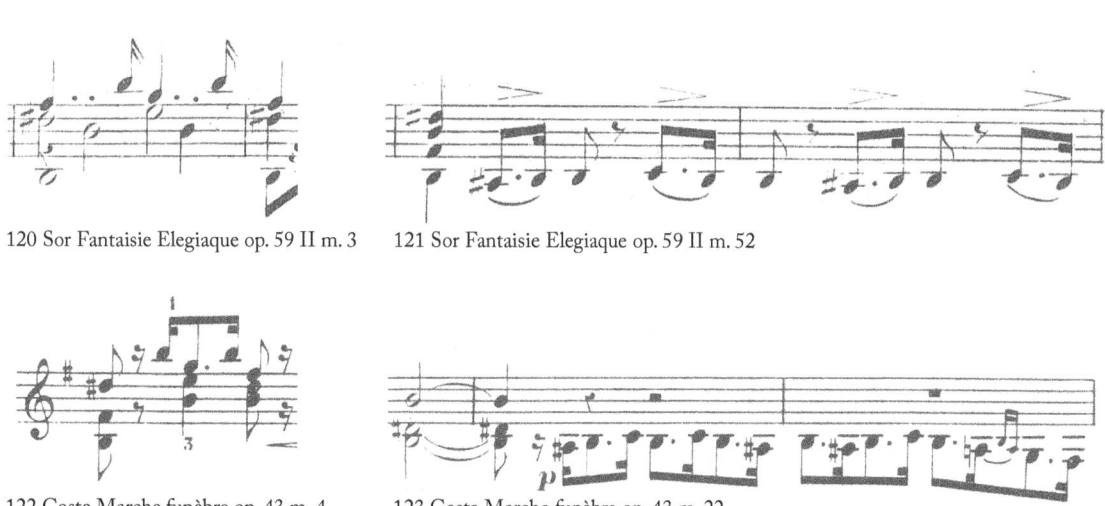

120 Sor Fantaisie Elegiaque op. 59 II m. 3   121 Sor Fantaisie Elegiaque op. 59 II m. 52

122 Coste Marche funèbre op. 43 m. 4   123 Coste Marche funèbre op. 43 m. 22

Coste knew the work by Sor, and moreover there are no other works with this title to be found in the guitar literature of this period. Chopin's *Marche funèbre* and that of Beethoven are very well known, but Coste clearly isn't taking his cue from them. Rather he is following Sor's lead, making this yet another example of Sor's influence on Coste. Where Sor uses a few Romantic elements in his composition, these are much more prevalent in Coste's piece. He dedicates the piece to Mme Coste, his pupil and wife, but just why it has to be a *Marche funèbre* now is unclear. Sor's work is of the same level of difficulty as Coste's, so that is not the reason, she was able to play both. Did some event take place that made Coste feel the need to console her musically, or did she simply find it an attractive genre? It is a traditional Romantic theme. These questions will have to remain unanswered if no additional personal details emerge of the two people's lives in this period. For this reason it must suffice here to simply repeat the conclusion that was given in the descriptive analysis that the piece should be classified together with Coste's more Romantic pieces.

For the first time in his works, in this piece Coste applies a certain amount of development and synthesis of the thematic material in his work, as well as alternating three types of rhythms. Despite the fact that the main keys are traditional, the piece exhibits many dissonant chords, especially augmented seventh chords, alongside the diminished seventh and double-diminished seventh chords that are customary for him. Plagal progressions can also be found, as well as Moll-Dur, Neapolitan sixths and a modal modulation to the relative. Several times the use of expolitio leads to inserted measures, lengthening the phrase. The passagework also has melodic chromatics, more so in this work than in previous works. The rhythm is not free, but rather metric. The contrast between the sections and the many recognizable stylistic features make this a Romantic work.

---

[843] Pn [Vm 3554?, Coste, *Marche funèbre et Rondeau* opus 43.

Opus 44, *Souvenir(s) du Jura, Andante et Polonaise* 1876

Coste's next work, the very successful and Romantic composition *Souvenir(s) du Jura* opus 44, which has *Andante et Polonaise* as its main title, was published in 1876, as suggested by the opus number. On November 2, 1876 Coste writes to Schult:

I recently sent you two newly engraved works; I hope you received them. The plates are ready for opus 44. I am correcting the proofs. Others will be published in due course, but I have to determine the exact figure for the sum to be allocated to this endeavor.[844]

And one month later, the piece is published, as he writes to Hallberg on December 21, 1876, that he will send a copy to him:

I am sending you, sir, some pieces I composed. The last of which, Andante et Polonaise op. 44 [...][845]

Just like *Étude* no. 8 from opus 38, this work is dedicated to the otherwise unknown Mme Marsoudet, whose maiden name was Victorine Oudet. Coste may have mentioned her maiden name because it was the name she had when he first took her on as a pupil. In his forward to the edition of *La Source du Lyson* opus 47, Brian Jeffery traces another one of Coste's 'memories' to the area: the dedication to Mme Marsoudet de Salins is deduced to be the widow of the poet Jean-Baptiste Marsoudet, who lived in the area and died in 1843.[846]

Furthermore, his 'souvenirs' only concern the *Souvenirs de Flandres* opus 5 from 1835, which can be considered 'early memories', and the *Sept Souvenirs* opus 17-23 from 1852, a kaleidoscope of episodic works of diverse character. While these 'souvenirs' in opus 44 are later memories, they are from an earlier period than those of opus 5 because they concern his early youth in the *département* of Doubs, which can be considered part of the Jura, geographically speaking. Now he recounts his memories of the Jura, the area along the border with Switzerland, with its many oblong lakes and jagged landscape, where he lives until he is seven. But he also visited the region with his wife in 1875, which supports the programmatic interpretation of the music:

During our journey to the Jura in de Franche-Comté in 1875 we visited some delightful places, and notably we stopped in the valley of Nans near Besançon.[847]

It appears that he and his wife visited the region in 1875, which explains the program of the music. The situation is a bit different with *La Source du Lyson* opus 47, which was already finished and was only later given this title. Opus 44 was thus composed between 1875 and 1876 when it was published.

The Andante is the introduction to the theme, representing Coste's memories, with a flageolet passage resembling a music box, which also serves as a motif for the theme of the polonaise. Many of Coste's characteristic stylistic features can be found in it: passagework, this time also constructed as a sequence, cadenzas and harmonic chord progressions with a great number of diminished sevenths, half-diminished sevenths, double-diminished sevenths, Neapolitan sixths and Moll-Dur chords. The campanella theme of the polonaise has its characteristic rhythm, and it is not only repeated, but also figured and developed. Here Coste takes a more structural approach to the thematic material, but he continues to introduce new material as the piece proceeds. The chromatics is predominantly used harmonically in the many dissonant chord progressions, a few of which have quite intense movement. In addition to repeating passages in diminution, smaller note values, expolitio, rocket and parachute

---

[844] Coste-Schult, 2 XI 1876: 'Je vous ai adressé dernièrement deux ouvrages nouvellement gravés. L'op. 44 est gravé, j'en corrige les épreuves. D'autres paraîtront encore à la longue, mais je dois arrêter ici le chiffre de la somme affectée à cette entreprise.'

[845] Coste-Hallberg, 21 XII 1876: 'Je vous adresse, Monsieur, quelques morceaux de ma composition. Le dernier part, Andante et Polonaise op. 44 [...]'

[846] Jeffery, Brian: Napoléon Coste: *La Source du Lyson* opus 47, London, Tecla, 1982, http://www.tecla.com/extras/0001/0021/0021pref.htm, December 17, 2014.

[847] Coste-Hallberg, 18 X 1878: 'Dans notre voyage 1875 dans le Jura en Franche-Comté nous visitâmes des sites ravissants et notamment nous nous arrêtâmes dans la vallée de Nans près de Besançon.'

124 Jura, le Miroir d'Ornans, Courbet

figures, Coste gives many indications for tempo, dynamics and articulation, include the seldom-used staccato and vibrato. It is the third polonaise that Coste writes, joining the earlier opus 8 and opus 14, and it also has a completely unique character. The two parts to his memories of the Jura form a closely-knit musical whole, with a decidedly cheerful character and recognizably written in Coste's Romantic style.

Guitarists 1877-1878

In 1877 a performance takes place with someone called Coste that is both unexplained and improbably. On March 25, in its 'Courrier du Théâtres' section *Le Figaro* announces: 'In the Variétés, at a quarter past one, an exceptional performance for the benefit of M. Coste.[848] This announcement comes between others titled 'Aux Italiens' and 'Au Gymnase'. After the war of 1870 the 'Théâtre des Variétés' at 7, boulevard Montmartre puts on opera-bouffes and operettas by Offenbach, Hervé and Lecocq, which begs the question as to what Coste was doing there, if the announcement indeed refers to Napoléon Coste, the composer-guitarist.[849] The name appears correctly if it does refer to him, but it is doubtful whether such an exceptional show would be organized for him in a large theatre.

Another piece of information, one of a completely different nature but certain, is the death of Luigi Legnani on August 5, 1877 in Ravenna at the age of 87.[850] He leaves behind an extensive body of work, in which, considering the long period of time over which he composed, one must certainly be able to find a certain amount of Romanticism.[851] Only once does he visit Paris, in October 1835, where he gives a concert, but then he breaks his arm, and the subsequent concert is taken over by Sor and Aguado,

---

[848] *Le Figaro*, vol. XXIII, série 3, no. 84, 25 III 1877, p. 3, Courrier des Théâtres: 'Aux Variétés, à une heure et quart, représentation extraordinaire au bénéfice de M. Coste.'
[849] Wild, N.: 'Théâtre des Variétés', in: Fauquet, Joël-Marie: *Dictionnaire de la Musique en France au XIXe siècle*, Paris, Fayard, 2003, p. 1257.
[850] Bone, Philip J.: Legnani,. Luigi', in: *The Guitar and the Mandolin*, London, Schott, 2nd ed, 1954, reprint 1972, p. 104.
[851] Rossato, Daniela: 'Luigi Rinaldo Legnani' in: *Il Fronimo*, Milano, Suvini Zerboni, vol. VII, no. 27, 1979, p. 5-15.

but on Legnani's behalf.[852] A year later, on November 28, 1878, Marco Aurelio Zani de Ferranti dies in Pisa.[853] For the most part of his life he was a travelling virtuoso who visited Paris various times. He also held a position in Brussels as guitarist to the king of Belgium. His works for guitar solo can be called Romantic. He is considered one of the three great Romantics in guitar music, alongside Mertz, who died in 1856, and Coste. The classical and Romantic generation of guitarists doesn't just disappear from the concert stage; it literally dies out. But Coste continues to compose, writing various works of a high standard that emerge in this period. This can be seen from an overview of 'new works' that appear on the back side of the title page of *Divagation* opus 45, in which the incorrect spelling *Paysage [sic] des Alpes* [i.e. *Passage*] opus 27, 28 & 40, results in a curious play on words.

Opus 45, *Divagation* 1877

The chronology can be deduced from the successive catalogues of new works by Coste as given in his editions, except for the fact that the title of *Le Passage des Alpes* has been corrected. Each time one or more new works are added. But the dating is made clear in Coste's letter of August 23, 1877 to Hallberg, in which he writes that he played the work at the meeting of the *Société académique des Enfants d'Apollon* and that the work would be ready at the engraver on the 20th of next month.[854] Coste has since made the acquaintance of M. J. Schult from Stockholm, either in person or through correspondence. It is to this gentleman that *Divagation* opus 45 is dedicated, and the dedication indicates that he is Coste's friend. He must have been a good guitar-player to take on this piece, as it is decidedly not easy to play. This M. J. Schult is thus the same person as F. Schultz from Stockholm to whom *Étude* 24 opus 38 from 1872 is dedicated. At least that is what Thorvald Rischel writes in his bibliographical notes in 1927: a merchant whose acquaintance Søffren Degen made while on a trip to Sweden and became his pupil, as is also the case with Adolph Hallberg. F. Schult owns a large collection of guitar music. The two men correspond with Coste and obtain all that remains of Coste's music. Schult also has copies made of works by Coste that have not been printed, and the composer corrects them himself.[855] Schult and Hallberg probably know each other as well. On the copy of the unpublished *Duetto* WoO 6 Hallberg writes that this is a 'token of his friendship.'[856] It is possible that there is only one gentleman named (A.) F. Schult(z) in Stockholm with whom Coste

125 F. Schult

---

[852] *Le Ménestrel*, vol. II, no. 47, 18 X 1835, p. [4]: 'Le célèbre guitariste. M. Legnani, [...] s'est fait entendre dimanche dernier;' *Gazette musicale de Paris*, vol. II, no. 42, 18 X 1835, p. 336: 'Le guitariste Legnani [...] revenu parmi nous.'; no.48, 29 XI 1835; p. 395: '[...] M. Lagnani [sic] [...] casser le bras [...] Aguado et Sor [...]; no. 49, 6 XII 1835, p. 403 .[...] au bénéfice de M. Lagnani [sic] [...] Sor [...]'; Prefumo, Danilo: 'L'attività concertistica di Luigi Legnani...' in: *Il Fronimo*, Milano, Suvini Zerboni, vol. X, no. 41, 1982, p. 22.

[853] *Revue et Gazette musicale de Paris*, vol. XLV, no. 50, 15 XII 1878, p. 407: 'A Pise est mort, le 28 novembre, Marco Aurelio Zani de Ferranti, né à Bologne, le 6 juillet 1800, (et non 1802 comme dit Fétis, *Biogr. univ. des mus.* t. III, p. 210), virtuose sur la guitare, littérateur et ancien professeur de langue italienne au Conservatoire de Bruxelles. De puis 1827, fixé en Belgique, il y avait obtenu l'indigénat.'

[854] Coste-Hallberg, 23 VIII 1877: 'J'ai donné au graveur le manuscrit de ma dernière composition, la Divagation, qu'il m'a promis pour e 20 du mois prochain.'

[855] Rischel, Thorvald: 'Bibliographische Notizen zu den Gitarrenwerken von Napoléon Coste', in: *Die Gitarre*, Berlin, 1927, Jahrgang VIII, Heft 7/8, [Coste-Heft] p. 48.

[856] Kk Rischel Ms. 59 mu 6701.1082, Coste, *Duetto* WoO 6.

has come into contact and that the composer simply made a mistake when he wrote the dedication of *Divagation* opus 45, but this difference remains. That is also the only 'diversion' (*divagation*) that can be found in the work. The other interpretations of *divagation*, such as 'mindless banter' or 'useless excursion', do not seem applicable here, while the meaning 'displacement of a river bed', interpreted as a meander, seems at least plausible. The four parts that one should distinguish in this work can be called quite varied, both separately and between them. Many musical ideas are conceived in them, but with a certain sense of musical unity, as argued in the conclusion of the descriptive analysis.

The introduction includes allusions to his own works, such as *Le Passage des Alpes* opus 27, but here it is followed by a cadenza as rocket figure, a flageolet passage in harmonies and again a cadenza, now as a parachute figure. In this way various recognizable stylistic elements follow in sequence with joint motifs, arpeggio figurations, passagework with chromatics, again a cadenza and a passage in thirds with chromatic coloring. The harmony has various dissonant chords, a tonic in major (parallel) and passing dominants, which lead to the dominant of the key of d-minor. Various fermatas indicate abruptio, passages in free lyricism. The second part, Andante is just as varied as the first, but here there is a stronger rhythm, nevertheless interrupted by free lyricism in the passagework with a lot of chromatics and abruptio with a cadenza. The motif in measure 10 is strongly reminiscent of that in measure 22 of opus 27. Campanella chords here foreshadow their use in the following parts. Furthermore, after the flageolet passage, the figuration of the final measure is the same motif as in opus 28[b] II, measure 99 and III, measure 83, in a higher octave, representing additional allusions to his own works. The third part again stands in contrast with the second part with the strong harmonic movement that is immediately introduced on the mediant. Rhythmically Coste opts for a dotted-16th-32nd-8th-8th rest chord motif, and strikingly the arpeggio in measure 4 needs to be played entirely with the thumb. Various chord figurations alternate with melodic passages with chromatics. The descending chromatic scale, which is even preceded by a double spark, is supposed to be played entirely staccato, which is very atypical of Coste. The prolongation, which is going to the dominant as closure, can be explained as a very varied version of the well-known prolongation.

The final section actually consists of an introduction and a waltz, in d-minor and D-major. It begins with a chromatic figuration in the bass of the chord in arpeggio, comparable to the opening of *Norma* opus 16 and *Le Zuyderzée* opus 20. The series of passing dominants that follows again has dissonant chords, before it ends on a bass theme in figuration that is later harmonized and which is related to measure 22 of the *Marche funèbre* opus 43, which resembles measures 4 and 52 of Sor's opus 59. With a cadenza, a descending chromatic scale in octaves and a tremolando figured cadence, this section ends in a flageolet passage, which leads into the following waltz in 3/8 time. The waltz has a strong rhythm, and has many spark glissandos and campanella legatos. The harmony does not get interesting until the intermediate section *B*, with its figurations in succession. Then Coste introduces new musical ideas in measure 85, a new rhythm in motifs, a series of passing dominants, Moll-Dur again, after which the theme resumes. The finalizing ending begins with an arpeggio that again must be executed with the right thumb, which is also something new for Coste. It seems that he is still looking for new forms of expression, here in an articulation technique that is new for him. He ends with a plagal Moll-Dur cadence, which is written on the F clef. The work is a kaleidoscope of musical ideas that nevertheless can be reduced to stylistic elements that Coste employs in other works of his. This creates a certain musical unity in the music that seems to contradict the meaning of the name of this piece. In this work too, Coste expresses himself using means such as tempo changes, articulation and dynamics. The phrasing is regularly interrupted and the harmony has passages with intensive changes and urgency: 'Sturm und Drang'. One may not be inclined to call it a masterpiece, but is one of Coste's more important works. It is engaging and quite varied and has many stylistic features that can be labelled as Romantic. All the Romantic elements conspire to make this work an amusing diversion, a real 'divagation'.

Opus 46, *Valse favorite* 1877

This virtuoso piece, bravura as the subtitle calls it, is dedicated to M. V. Gozzoli, one of the many pupils and friends appearing in the list of dedications who remain unknown. It was published 'chez l'auteur' in 1878.[857] The copy in the Kongelige Bibliotek in Copenhagen has a personally signed 'hommage de l'auteur', but the name is illegible. Coste composed this work in 1877. He writes to Hallberg about it:

But I am settling [your payment] with Hummel's Duet (piano and guitar), with Sor's op. 13 and offer you my op. 46, the plates of which are currently being prepared.[858]

In composing this piece, Coste leaned heavily on the waltzes from *Souvenirs de Flandres* opus 5, no. 4 and 5, better than that, he puts them both unabridged in the work. Possibly, the waltzes from opus 5 were M. Gozzoli's favorites, and this could be the reason why Coste took the effort to revisit them to make a new, larger work. In 1934, Mario Giordano writes in his review that the music expresses an almost unfulfilled desire, in which waltzes, such as in opus 46, are being treated with great formal freedom.[859] In 1984, Joerg Sommermeyer describes the work as a kaleidoscope of fireworks in scales and arpeggios, using the most remote corners of the fingerboard.[860] But only few Romantic characteristics emerge from the descriptive analysis.

The two waltzes, both joined in opus 5 already, now are preceded by and introduction with other material from opus 5, along with new musical ideas, such as an elaborated theme, and a kind of coda as a finale with more new material, with some harmonic surprises, such as the chromatic submediant. In this way a sort of 'medley' emerges, with gallant old and new melodies, albeit true to Coste's musical style. The variations Coste writes are intelligent and add to the boisterous character he wants to give to the music. It is notable that the cadenza in measure 25 of opus 5, no. 5, is written in a completely metrical way in measure 165 of opus 46, part III, and has a completely different appearance, not as a cadenza anymore. In the introduction some prolongations can be found. The coda has a striking contrasting chromatic modulation to the lowered sixth degree F of the tonic A, but apart from this little more emerges from the music than a small number of diminished seventh chords, a single Neapolitan sixth chord, a Trugschluss and a Moll-Dur chord, making for few harmonic inventions. As might be expected, when old material is used, much melodic chromatics show up in this piece. Apart from this, just few Romantic style elements can be found in the music. The few variations Coste applies are well chosen and clearly add to the bravura character of the piece.

Concerts 1878-1880

In this period of his life, Coste is very active in composing and publishing works. The latter of these two activities is not without its problems:

After many complications, I will finally be in possession of my last work, opus 45. The engraver and the printer behaved very badly towards me. I gave the latter the plates of my works, 39, 40, 41, 42, 43, 44 and 45. Being unsatisfied about his way of handling things, I asked to have the plates back, and after almost one month, I have not received them, in spite of my insistence. Yet, I visited him, and he promised me to send them tomorrow morning, as well as the printed copies. (If he does not keep his promise, despite my patience,

---

[857] Pn [Vm9 3563, Coste, *Valse favorite* opus 46.
[858] Coste-Hallberg 7 XII 1877: 'Mais je vous donne quittance du Duo de Hummel (piano et guitare), de l'op 13 de Sor et vous permettrez de vous offrir mon op. 46 que l'on grave en ce moment.'
[859] Giordano, Mario: 'Napoléon Coste e le sue opere', in: *Il plettro*, febbraio 1934, no. 2, p. 7.
[860] Sommermeyer, Joerg: 'Noten, The Guitar Works of Napoléon Coste...', in: *Nova Giulianiad*, 1984 Nr. 3, p. 168, http://home.tonline.de/home/Rechtsanwalt.Joerg.Sommermeyer/ng3.htm, 10 VII 2002.

VIII — Divagation

I will be forced to take legal steps, which would be disappointing and would cause even more delay in the delivery of what I have been awaiting for so long).[861]

But he realizes that he does not have much time anymore, an observation for which he makes apologies, because he actually does feel happy:

But I am arriving at the time in my career where the future is rather short, have I not lived long enough? Nevertheless, I continue with my work, as long as it pleases God to let me keep a spark of intelligence, and without any hope to leave my name to those hereafter, who will consign me to oblivion. [...] As I reread this rather sad paragraph, I realize I have unlatched my melancholic sentiment, in a way that might make you think that I am not happy. The truth is that my everyday life is going on smoothly in the bosom of domestic bliss, and that I don't have any worries about the future.[862]

After these prudent effusions of his state of mind, it is the year 1878 which first brings a number of concerts, some of which he takes part in, apart from the successive compositions that emerged in this final period of Coste's life. The composer/guitarist is certainly not involved In the first of these concerts. It takes place on January 20 at the Théâtre de la Porte-Saint-Martin, normally a venue for opera and drama performances, an unusual place for the guitarist.[863] M. Coste is mentioned as a participant in the 'modern part of the program', in the waltz from Reber's opera *La Nuit de Noël* from 1848.[864] This probably is a misspelling of Mme Coste, the female singer of whom nothing further is known, apart from her one-time participation in the monthly meeting of the *Société académique des Enfants d'Apollon* in March 1867.[865] Moreover, if the guitar was played in an opera, its role would have been modest, so the name of the guitarist would not have been mentioned separately in a review, while the name of a vocal soloist most certainly would be. Speaking of the Apollo Society, now the two monthly meetings can be mentioned, in which Coste does take part in 1878. The first is in April, presumably the 14th, as these concerts take place on the second Sunday every month, which is apparently why Decourcelle does not mention the date. In this concert *Le Petit Ange rose* WoO 11, a melody by M. Coste, is sung by Mme Germance. It is composed for voice and piano, but the pianist is not mentioned. The piano part is quite easy, and perhaps Coste played the accompaniment himself.[866] By now Coste must have been fully recovered from his injury in 1874, making him able to play at his previous standard, as he performs *La Chasse des Sylphes* opus 29, dating from 1856, in a 'séance' of the *Société académique des Enfants d'Apollon* in June 1878. Decourcelle erroneously writes *Le chant des Sylphes*, which results in a nice pun, if one thinks of the sylphs who sing a song in Shakespeare's *A Midsummer Night's Dream*, to which the music refers. This work is one of the composer's most artistic masterpieces, and it is of

---

[861] Coste-Hallberg, 15 X 1877: 'Après bien des péripéties je vais enfin entrer en possession de mon dernier morceau op. 45. Le graveur et l'imprimeur se sont fort mal conduits à mon égard. J'avais laissé chez le dernier les planches de mes ouvrages 39, 40, 41, 42, 43, 44 et 45. N'ayant pas été satisfait de sa manière d'agir, je lui ai réclamé les planches et depuis près d'un mois, malgré mes instances, je n'ai pu encore obtenir satisfaction. Cependant je viens le voir et il m'a promis de me les envoyer demain matin ainsi que les exemplaires. (Si contre mon attente il manquerait à sa promesse, je serais forcé l'employer des notes juridiques, ce qui serait bien regrettable et apporterait encore un nouveau retard à la livraison que j'attends depuis si longtemps.)'

[862] Coste-Hallberg, 25 I 1878: 'Mais j'arrive au temps de ma carrière, mon avenir sera bien court, n'ai-je pas déjà assez vécu? Néanmoins je continuerai à travailler, tant qu'il plaira à Dieu de me conserver une lueur d'intelligence et sans avoir l'espérance de leguer mon nom à la postérité qui me laissera dans l'oubli. [...] En relisant ce paragraphe un peu triste je m'aperçois que je me suis laissé aller à mon sentiment mélancolique qui pourrait faire supposer que je ne suis pas heureux. La vérité est que mon existence s'écoule doucement au sein du bonheur domestique et que je n'ai aucun souci de l' avenir.'

[863] Wild, N.: 'Théâtre de la Porte-Saint-Martin', in: Fauquet, Joël-Marie: *Dictionnaire de la Musique en France au XIXe siècle*, Paris, Fayard, 2003, p. 989.

[864] *Revue et Gazette musicale de Paris*, vol. XLV, no. 3, 20 I 1878, p. 22: 'Le concert Cressonnois [...] partie moderne [...] la valse de la Nuit de Noël de Reber (avec M. Coste) [...]'.

[865] Decourcelle, Maurice: *La Société académique des Enfants d'Apollon*, programmes des concerts annuels..., Paris, Durand, 1881, p. 208: '[...] chantée par Mme Coste.'

[866] Decourcelle, Maurice: *La Société académique des Enfants d'Apollon*, programmes des concerts annuels..., Paris, Durand, 1881, p. 236: '[...] L'ange rose, mélodie de M. Coste, chantées par Mme Germance.'

a high technical standard. The program says it is composed and performed by M. Coste.[867] However, Decourcelle, whose book is rather reliable until now, makes another mistake, apart from the spelling of the title. In his letter to Hallberg, Coste mentions this concert and he tells what he is going to play:

> *I just finished a grand solo, which I am going to play in the monthly concert of the société des Enfants d'Apollon in a week.*[868]

The newly finished work is *La Source du Lyson* opus 47, from 1878, Decourcelle's mistake in the title is an easy one to make, as the 'grand solo' can certainly be called a 'fantaisie', and it is performed by Coste on June 9, 1878, for aforesaid reasons. It is the second Sunday of the month in the Apollo tradition, after all. But Coste didn't play in the annual concert of the society, on Ascension Day of that year, of which an extensive review can be found in the *Revue et Gazette musicale de Paris*, Coste only takes part in such a concert in 1843 with *Le Tournoi*.[869] But Coste does play many times in the Théâtre-Français, in 1879-1880, in the foyer, a guitar solo on January 1, 1880, in spite of the severe cold of -24°C. that afflicts Paris that winter, the lowest temperature ever recorded there, causing Coste chilblained hands, damaging his fingertips:[870]

> *What's more, the severe cold that has prevailed here for so long has almost paralyzed my hands, causing my fingertips to soften in a peculiar way.. [...] In this situation, I have to accompany a song, a romance by Cherubini, in the théâtre Français, every time they play le mariage de Figaro, which has totaled 32 times since the beginning of November last year. [...] It happened several times that the artists of this theatre, of which you know for sure it is the best of the world, asked me to perform, especially on the first day of the year. There was a great reception in the foyer, a large gathering of the elite, which included senators, delegates, generals. I had a great success with playing my valse favorite (op. 46), one of my easiest works, which is very demanding to perform, nevertheless. I really do not know how I was able to play so well with those hands so bad.*[871]

Indeed, *Le Mariage de Figaro* is being performed in the theatre.[872] Before the performance or during the interval, Coste accompanies the only chanson by Cherubini for voice and guitar, *Romance d'Essex à Élisabeth*, from 1790.[873] The work he plays on New Year's day is *Valse favorite* opus 46 from 1878, a composition which has already been discussed. It appears that Coste plays in public in his old age, even when this is in a New Year's reception. But this is the last mention of Coste's concerts.

WoO 11, *Le Petit Ange Rose* 1878

Coste's chanson is a berceuse and it is dedicated 'aux jeunes mères'. It is published by Katto in Paris in 1878, so there is no doubt about the date.[874] M. Pélan d'Angers lyrics for this piece are not very lofty, and are rather conventional: 'sleep my little rose-colored angel, my heart is praying for you, not

---

[867] Decourcelle, Maurice: *La Société académique des Enfants d'Apollon*, programmes des concerts annuels..., Paris, Durand, 1881, p. 236: '*Le chant des Sylphes*, fantaisie pour la guitare, composé et exécuté par M. Coste.'

[868] Coste-Hallberg, 28 V 1878: 'Je viens de terminer un grand solo [i.e. op. 47 Source Lyson 1878], que je jouerai dans huit jours au concert mensuel de la société des Enfants d'Apollon.' [i.e. concert 2ᵉ Sunday = 9 June 1878, op. 29 Chasse des Sylphes?].

[869] Decourcelle, Maurice: *La Société académique des Enfants d'Apollon*, programmes des concerts annuels..., Paris, Durand, 1881, p. 78, 113; *Revue et Gazette musicale de Paris*, vol. XLV, no. 23, 9 VI 1878, p. 182, La Société des Enfants d'Apollon

[870] http://gemiddeldgezien.nl/meer-gemiddelden/90-gemiddelde-temperatuur-parijs, December 12, 2014.

[871] Coste-Hallberg, 19 II 1880: 'De plus le froid cruel qui a régné ici pendant si longtemps m'a presque paralysé les mains en me causant un ramolissement singulier de l'extrémité des doigts. [...] Ainsi, je dois accompagner un air, la romance de Cherubini, au théâtre Français, toutes les fois que l'on joue le mariage de Figaro, et celà est arrivé 32 fois depuis le commencement de novembre dernier.[...] il est arrivé plusieurs fois que les artistes de ce théâtre qui est, comme vous le savez sans doute, le premier du monde, m'ont demandé de me faire entendre, notamment au premier jour de l'année. Il y avait grande réception au foyer, une assemblée nombreuse d'élite dans laquelle se trouvait des Sénateurs, des Députés, des Généraux. J'ai obtenu un grand succès en jouant ma valse favorite (op. 46) qui est un de mes ouvrages les plus faciles, mais que exige pourtant beaucoup d'exécution. Je ne sais vraiment comment j'ai pu m'en tirer aussi heureusement avec d'aussi mauvaises mains' [lowest temperature ever recorded in Paris -23.9 degrees, probably December 1879].

[872] *Le Ménestrel*, vol. XXXV, no. 52 (2535), 23 XI 1879, p. 411, Mariage de Figaro, Théâtre-Français.

[873] Deane, Basil: 'Cherubini, Luigi, works', in: Sadie, Stanley, ed.: *The New Grove Dictionary of Music and Musicians*, London, Macmillan, 1980, vol. 4, p. 212.

[874] Pn [Vm7 44.836, Coste, *Le Petit Ange rose* WoO 11.

VIII — Divagation 217

awakening you, how beautiful he is when he slumbers, his golden lips are like a flower in the morning's sunbeams.' The melody has a diapason of a sixth, which is very folk-music like, and the accompaniment also has much folklore in it, in addition to the parallel in minor that sometimes appears, that being a Romantic feature. Coste really tries to make this chanson a Romantic one. Although the name of Mme Germance appears only once in Coste's life, it can be added to the list of his acquaintances, just as that of Pélan d'Angers, who's lyrics were Coste's starting point for composing this song, as well as the chanson *Lolla*, a chanson that also appears in 1878.

WoO 10, *Lolla* 1878

Coste's last found song is *Lolla*, it has the subtitle 'mélodie', with lyrics by M. Pélan d'Angers once again. It is also published by Katto in 1878 and it is dedicated to M. Jules Lefort, of whom no other connection with Coste can be found.[875] It is a love song with few artistic pretensions. 'When my trusty gondola sails the gentle waves, Lolla! Lolla! Caressing the water, the breath of wind says to me, Lolla! Lolla!' Should Lolla be an Italian girl, the gondola could be floating in Venice. One way or another, the sense of nature is in connection with the love for Lolla. The few Romantic style elements can be found in the expression of the words, the bass motif as an idée fixe, to the extent that this is possible in such a short piece, and the open beginning.

Chansons play a minor role in Coste's works, and they can even be compared to his arrangements for voice and guitar, easy pieces with little Romanticism. In editions of them that appear, they do not have an opus number, which is typical for his opinion of them, as he writes to Hallberg:

Against my will, I have published two melodies for voice and piano. I will send them to you. But I must warn you, they are very mediocre, this genre of composition does not attract me at all. It is my wife who wanted them to be published. I wash my hands (like Pilate).[876]

But Coste does know how to get them published by Katto, chansons for voice and piano probably still are very popular, even in this period. This is different from the next work that is published by Katto in 1878.

Opus 47, *La Source du Lyson (Fête villageoise)* 1878

The Lison is a small river near Ornans, the place where Coste lived in his early childhood, as is discussed earlier. Apparently, he has fond memories of the place, and now he visits the region where his family still may be living, according to Noël Roncet.[877] The first is confirmed by Coste's letter to Hallberg, dated 18 October 1878:

Dear Sir, you ask me about the meaning of the words that appear at the top of my new work: La Source du Lyson? This is how I came to give the work this title. First, it was going to be called Fête villageoise, but I realized (after it was engraved) that other works by different authors already had this name. I stopped the production of my work and started looking. On our trip to the Jura in 1875 in the Franche-Comté, we visited some marvelous sites, and we stayed in the valley of Nans, near Besançon, in particular. This valley is one of the most beautiful and most remarkable things one could admire. It is to the memory of these enchanting places that I gave a new name to this particular piece.[878]

---

[875] Pn [Vm7 44.835, Coste, *Lolla* WoO 10.
[876] Coste-Hallberg, 3 III 1878: 'J'ai bien malgré moi fait paraître 2 mélodies pour chant et piano. Je vous les enverrai. Seulement je vous préviens qu'elles sont d'une grande médiocrité, ce genre de composition n'a aucun attrait pour moi. C'est ma femme qui a voulu qu'elles soient publiées. Je m'en lave mes mains (comme Pilate).'
[877] Roncet, Noël: *Napoléon Coste, Compositeur, 1805-1883*, Amondans, 2005, p. 36-37.
[878] Coste-Hallberg, 18 X 1878: 'Vous me demandez, cher Monsieur, ce que signifie la lettre de mon dernier ouvrage: La Source du Lyson? Voici comment j'ai été amené à donner ce titre à ce morceau. Il devait d'abord s'appeler Fête villageoise, mais je me suis aperçu (après que celui-ci fut gravé) que d'autres ouvrages de différents auteurs portaient déjà cette qualification. J'arrêtai le tirage de mon oeuvre et je cherchai. Dans notre voyage 1875 dans le Jura en Franche-Comté nous visitâmes des sites ravissants et notamment nous nous arrêtâmes dans la vallée de Nans près de Besançon. Cette vallée est une des choses les plus belles et les plus curieuses que l'on puisse admirer. C'est en souvenir de ces lieux enchanteurs, que j'ai fait subir un nouveau baptême au morceau en question.'

Indeed, Coste and his wife visited the region and certainly had a look at *La Source du Lyson*, which remains a tourist attraction to this day. However, the programmatic meaning of the music is undermined by the fact that the piece was already written, with *Fête villageoise* as a title. Coste renames the piece, impressed by the natural wonders of this place. The original title now becomes the subtitle, so its inspiration was not of this kind at all. After the series of self-published works, from opus 41 on, this work is published by Katto, who is located at rue de Sts-Pères no. 17. This publisher comes from Brussels. He has a branch-office at this address in Paris since 1864 and takes care of the last work Coste succeeded in having published by a publisher, after *Lolla* and *Le Petit Ange rose*.[879] The initials N.C. don't reveal a date, but the copy in the Bibliothèque nationale indicates the year 1878.[880] Remarkably, the identical example in the Kongelige Bibliotek in Copenhagen mentions 'Chez l'Auteur. 50. Rue du Faub.g St-Martin' as the publisher, with the title *Fête villageoise* opus 47, making clear Coste also published this work himself.[881] But, according to the letter to Hallberg it must have been composed before Coste's journey to the Jura in 1875. Thorvald Rischel thinks this edition is a proof.[882] The other copy in this library is Katto's edition. Coste signed it himself with 'hommage de l'auteur' for M. Schult.[883] Both versions are dedicated to his pupil Mlle Marie Daly, of whom nothing further is known. Søffren Degen wrote an easy second guitar part for it, which has been published in a modern edition by Simon Wynberg, just as the ones for opus 12 and 27, 28 & 40.[884] But, Coste does not really like this second part. He says Degen's effort is a waste of time and that he had better start studying, in order to be able to play it well:

> *I want to thank you, dear friend, for having sent me the experiment of our brave Degen, who has taken so many pains to perform a useless task. I say useless, because the work to which he adopted a second guitar part, cannot endure such an arrangement. This work (op. 47, Source du Lyson) is written in such a serious counterpoint, that one cannot adapt it with an accompaniment. Still, I have played it with my wife, and we were not satisfied with the result. He would better off playing it and studying it to be able to perform it in a bearable way.*[885]

This work, opus 47, is reviewed a few times in later literature, for the first time in 1927 by Thorvald Rischel. In the first part, he recognizes the babbling water of the source, in the second part the pastoral idyll, and in the third part the rural dance and party. Possibly, he says, the composition came into existence, influenced by Berlioz's program music and Beethoven's pastorale.[886] The first possibility is rather feasible, the second might be the atmosphere that emanates from the music. In 1979, Giuseppe Radole thinks that opus 47 occupies a central position among his works, along with opus 45, 12 and 30. It is in *La Source du Lyson* that Coste parts with the bombastic character of his style and returns to the essence.[887] Brian Jeffery thinks it is one of the most attractive of Coste's pieces and publishes it separately in 1982 in his own edition, which includes an extensive preface. He says its harmonies are rich, its rhythms strong, its relation to the French landscape solid. This appears to be the source of the river Lyson, a well-known attraction in France, only five miles away from Coste's place of birth. Coste's music sketches this area and, even more importantly, the rural life in the countryside he

---

[879] Devriès, Anik & François Lesure: *Dictionnaire des éditeurs de musique français*, Genève, Minkoff, 1979-1988, vol. II, p. 246.

[880] Pn [Vm9 3560 Coste, *La Source du Lyson* opus 47.

[881] Kk Rischel 169 mu 6701.0787 U48 Coste, *Fête villageoise* [i.e. *La Source du Lyson*] opus 47.

[882] Rischel, Thorvald: 'Bibliographische Notizen zu den Gitarrenwerken von Napoléon Coste', in: *Die Gitarre*, Berlin, 1927, Jahrgang VIII, Heft 7/8, [Coste-Heft] p. 51.

[883] Kk Rischel 168 mu 7310.1281 (ekx. 1) U48 Coste, *La Source du Lyson* opus 47.

[884] Wynberg, Simon: *The Guitar Works of Napoléon Coste*, facsimile edition, Monaco, Chanterelle, 1981, 1983, vol. VII; reprint 2006-7.

[885] Coste-Hallberg, 16 XII 1881: 'Je vous remercie, cher ami, de m'avoir envoyé l'essai de notre brave Degen, qui s'est donné bien de la peine pour faire un travail inutile. Je dis inutile, parceque le morceau auquel il a adapté une 2me guitare ne comporte pas un semblable arrangement. Cet ouvrage (op. 47, Source du Lyson) est traité trop sérieusement comme contrepoint pour que l'on puisse y adapter une accompagnement. Je l'ai pourtant essayé avec ma femme et l'effet ne nous a pas satisfait. Il aurait bien mieux fait de le jouer et l'étudier pour se mettre en état de le faire entendre.'

[886] Rischel, Thorvald: 'Bibliographische Notizen zu den Gitarrenwerken von Napoléon Coste', in: *Die Gitarre*, Berlin, 1927, Jahrgang VIII, Heft 7/8, [Coste-Heft] p. 51.

[887] Radole, Giuseppe: *Liuto, chitarra e vihuela, storia e letteratura*, Milano, Suvini Zerboni, 1979, 3ᵉ ed. 1997, p. 154-155.

VIII — Divagation   219

126 La Source du Lyson

dearly loved, apparently.⁸⁸⁸ In the framework of Brian Jeffery's article in 1983, Erik Marchélie gives an analysis of the work. In his opinion, it is one of his most original works. Inspired by a landscape dear to the author, it unmistakably makes us think of Beethoven's pastoral symphony, or Berlioz's symphonies. He also mentions the very same associations. Without any doubt, according to him, descriptive and programmatic elements have been imparted in all of his works, but nature, being the soul of Romanticism, appeals above all to the imagination. He compares the beginning of part I with Giuliani's *Variations concertantes* opus 130, in which effects such as tremolo and arpeggio are connected to happiness. One may object that these techniques are present in almost every work for guitar, and Giuliani is not known for his programmatic music. Marchélie correctly describes several elements of the work, gives musical examples, he notes chromatic modulations, elaborations, chromatics, and intensive harmony. By way of his harmonic inventions, his melodic inspiration and his intelligence in musical form, Coste blows a new, fresh breeze over guitar music in the 19th century.⁸⁸⁹ This last observation may seem a bit exaggerated, as far as this work is concerned, shadowed as it is by Coste's other, greater works, but there is some truth in this remark. Mario Dell'Ara has an even more pronounced opinion in 1988. He thinks *La Source du Lyson* is, without any doubt, the masterpiece in Coste's programmatic

---

[888] Jeffery, Brian: 'Napoléon Coste - renewed acquaintance', in: *Guitar & Lute*, 1982, no. 20, p. 8; Jeffery, Brian: Napoléon Coste: *La Source du Lyson* opus 47, London, Tecla, 1982, http://www.tecla.com/extras/0001/0021/0021pref.htm, 17 XI 2014.

[889] Marchélie, Erik: 'Analyse de la Source du Lyson', in: 'Napoléon Coste" in: *Cahiers de la Guitare*, Boissy-St-Léger, Association Guitares et Luths, vol. 6, 1983, p. 12-13.

work. He knows how to escape from the confusing schemes of earlier works, and returns to his initial simplicity, in which he knows how to express his experience with more gentleness, resulting in a fluent suppleness and ongoing emotional tension.[890] In 1999, Umberto Realino also sees the reflection of the source of the river in the introduction, even a waterfall in the dominant section. The melody of the second part is typically French, he says; the supporting harmonies are very rich, being the essence of Romanticism. In his opinion, the flow of the water is expressed in the 16ths and 32nds of the rhythm. The bourdon points to the village dances, typical for the countryside. He too notices the second theme in the keys of C and F, which are chromatically related to the key of A. A brilliant elaboration gives way first to a chromatic ascending bass line, then to a descending one. The composition is the recapitulation of Coste's stylistic and aesthetic maturity. His contemporaries alike, he discovers the new horizons of modulation in his music, rich in harmony, without neglecting his own feeling for musical beauty, by way of a modest, pleasant expression, in the very French tradition.[891] In his discussion, Realino gives some musical examples and makes the connection to his explanation by analysis, but he goes too far in making connections between natural phenomena and musical characteristics of this opus 47.

In the historiography of this work, in the year 2000, Monica Burzik creates a misunderstanding by confusing the melody in the first two measures of the second part with Beethoven's *Ode an die Freude*. There might be some casual resemblance in the structure of the intervals, but this work really has different accents with its 3/4 time, and the rhythm also is different. Along with other authors, she thinks part III has references to Berlioz.[892] But this is only a superficial resemblance.

The introduction of opus 47 immediately starts with a bass motif in figuration of repeated 16ths, referring to the source and the small river Lison, as it is currently spelled, where the sparkling water comes out of the cave. The harmonic structure goes from I to IV and to V, after which a cadenza leads to the second part, by way of a joint motif. The second part is in the parallel major and it has a gentle melody in 3/4-metre, which is figured with rocket figures and joint motifs, again with some melodic chromatics and melodic figurations. The character of the melody and the accompaniment leads to the composition of three and four-voice prolongations in measure 23 and 29. The harmonic motion here is more intense than in part I, due to its series of passing dominants, Moll-Dur chords and prolongations. There is a higher degree of dissonance too, with diminished seventh chords on raised degrees of the scale, and an augmented seventh chord. Style elements, such as rocket, parachute and diminution add to the Romantic character of this part, which also ends in the dominant, with a rhythmic 16th-dotted 8th chord prolongation. Then a cadenza constitutes the joint motif leading to the third part again. Part III, the *Rondeau villageois*, starts with a slow bourdon in A, and is figured with a simple, but dissonant, melody now and again. This alludes to the folk music one may expect from the title. Coste uses this style element on other occasions, with the same reference: in *Souvenirs de Flandres* opus 5, *Meulan* opus 22, *Fantaisie symphonique* opus 28[b] *La Chasse des Sylphes* opus 29 and *Le Passage des Alpes* opus 27, 28 & 40, which gives enough evidence to contradict Erik Marchélie in his opinion that Coste refers to part III of Berlioz's *Harold en Italie*, because there the bourdon has a different character due to its rhythm and because the melody also does not have any resemblance to this piece.[893] This *A* section is repeated without change, along with the subsequent *B*-section, which has the character of a dance, with its chord rhythm and its motion in 16ths. The harmony is quite simple, but suddenly Coste introduces a new theme in the contrasting key of C, lowered III. Now, more harmonic motion can be noticed, and also a series of passing dominants, a four-voice prolongation and intensive passage work. A rare spark figure in inversion, descending, can be found in measure 64. After the repeat of the *B*-section in the original key of A, Coste once more introduces a new theme, in another contrasting key, this

---

[890] Dell'Ara, Mario: *Manuale di storia della chitarra*, Ancona, Bèrben, 1988, p. 136.
[891] Realino, Umberto: *Un siècle de guitare en France 1750-1850*, unp. thèse Sorbonne, repr. Atelier national, Lille, 1999, p. 386-388.
[892] Burzik, Monika: 'Coste, Napoléon', in: *Die Musik in Geschichte und Gegenwart*, ed. Blume, Finscher, Kassel, Bärenreiter, 2000, vol. 4, Kol. 1716.
[893] Marchélie, Erik: 'Analyse de la Source du Lyson', in: 'Napoléon Coste" in: *Cahiers de la Guitare*, Boissy-St-Léger, Association Guitares et Luths, vol. 6, 1983, p. 12-13.

time of F, lowered VI. This theme is elaborated in the same way as the previous one, with an intensive harmony, one of the few times Coste composes in this way, in passages with melodic chromatics and a campanella chord passage with the sixths on the 2nd and the 4th strings in arpeggio with the 1st and 6th strings open, in a sequence, which also is rare. After a flageolet-tone passage, a reprise follows with the repeat of the *A*-section and the *B*-section , which are elaborated here in a longer phrase with passing dominants. The finalizing end starts very early in measure 127 with parachute figures in expolitio and a remarkable series of augmented dominants. The passage work in 16ths is varied with arpeggios, rocket and parachute figures, supported by unbroken chords, with a harmonic acceleration at times, in measure 152, with one chord for every 8th note, the place where the many alterations refer to the preceding contrasting keys of C and F. A risoluto section confirms the tonic with repeated V-I cadences, ending on the final chord A. The characteristics of this work give just cause for the conclusion to qualify this as a Romantic piece, comparable to *Divagation* opus 45.

OPUS 48 & 49, *QUATRE MARCHES ET SIX PRÉLUDES* 1878

1879 also is the year of the edition of this work, as indicated on the copy in the Bibliothèque nationale.[894] Coste is publishing all of his works by himself, now. The example in the Kongelige

Bibliotek in Copenhagen has Coste's signature on it, with a dedication: *À Monsieur J.G. Holm, son ami, N. Coste*.[895] In one of his letters to Hallberg from this period, he writes about the engraving of the work, which will say, it must have been composed before that, in 1878:

At this moment op. 48 & 49 are being engraved; I hope you'd like to accept a free copy.[896]

He dedicates the work to Pedro Segura, about whom he writes that he is a Spanish general:

At this moment I even give lessons to a young Spanish general, I mean, he looks like having no more that 35 years.[897]

He does not mention the man's name, but the dedication and the date of opus 48 & 49 point in Segura's direction. The example in the Spencer Collection was the starting point for Simon Wynberg's edition in 1981.[898] In his review of the work in 1983, Brian Jeffery refers to Chopin and Liszt on the matter of writing in the genre of prelude. In 1843, Aguado writes a series of 24 preludes in his method, Carulli does the same in a series of 4. And now, Coste writes 6 of them, it is a genre that never received much attention from guitarists, but is worth-while for everyone who wants to play in an authentic way.[899] Jeffery is the only one among the authors who gives his opinion about the musical content of the work, others just mention its title.

Of the four marches, the first two include a trio, the last one has a sort of coda and the third is a rondoletto. It seems Coste has kept himself to the Classical standards: he escapes from the tight harmonic scheme just a few times. In this way, not much Romanticism can be found in these four pieces. In no. 2, there is some harmonic motion, after a lengthened phrase, with a series of passing dominants. The second section of the initial theme is elaborated later on, a technique Coste rarely uses. This part has some chromatics. The rondoletto has a remarkable modulation to the chromatic mediant, but this is used as a dominant going to the relative. In the reprise Coste varies the first section with series of descending chromatics. No. 4 has some harmonic motion in diminished seventh chords, and a chord sequence also is present, which is also rare in his music. The passage in triplets at the end still

---

[894] Pn [Vm9 3556 Coste, *Quatre Marches et Six Préludes* opus 48 & 49.
[895] Kk Rischel 170 mu 6701.0685 (eks. 1) U48 Coste, *Quatre Marches et Six Préludes* opus 48 & 49.
[896] Coste-Hallberg 9 I 1879: 'On grave en ce moment les op. 48 & 49 en un seul livre; vous voudriez hein j'èspère les agréer gratuitement.'
[897] Coste-Hallberg, 18 X 1878: 'Je donne même sur ce moment des leçons à un jeune général espagnol, c'est-à-dire qu'il ne paraît pas avoir 35 ans.'
[898] Lam XX (159235.1) Coste, *Quatre Marches et Six Préludes* opus 48 & 49; Wynberg, Simon: *The Guitar Works of Napoléon Coste*, facsimile edition, vol. I-IX, Monaco, Chanterelle, 1981, 1983; reprint 2006-7.
[899] Jeffery, Brian: 'Napoléon Coste' in: *Cahiers de la Guitare*, Boissy-St-Léger, Association Guitares et Luths, vol. 6, 1983, p. 10.

gives some motion to the piece. The end is classical with its repeated chords on the tonic. These works are not very important, as far as the Romantic specter of Coste's work is concerned.

The six preludes opus 49 are very short, two of them are only 8 measures long, and four of them are just 10 measures long. They are written according to the 'old' sense of the prelude, being a musical foreplay, not in the sense of the great Romantic prelude. The music is very simple, but Coste knows how to realize some Romantic style elements in almost every prelude. There are four-voice and three-voice prolongations, there is a notable arpeggio, some preludes are almost entirely in arpeggio, and some are adorned with campanella legatos. Figurations are present in some passage work in shifting thirds, and in parachute and rocket figures. The harmony shows many passing dominants, a V minor, a Moll-Dur chord and a Trugschluss. In this way many aspects of the Romantic style are present in these musical miniatures.

THEORBO 1879

In spite of his pension, Coste is short of cash again in 1879, perhaps due to the costs of the engravings and the publications, or a lack of pupils. On June 16, 1879 he writes to Léon Gruel:

> *I have seen the merchant in question, and agreed to sell the theorbo for 50 fr. I have nothing left to reduce expenses anymore. If this suits you, let him come and get it tomorrow.*[900]

Apparently, he wants to sell the theorbo for a good price. Although the heptacorde also is theorboed, here it is probably the arch-lute that is in question, the instrument Coste himself gave this name, the theorboed lute-guitar that is on the small pillar on Disderi's photograph of Coste with four instruments, probably taken before 1867.[901] But, three years before the theorbo, he was selling instruments from his collection, as emerges from his letter to Schult on November 2, 1876:

> *I had a beautiful collection of guitars. Since last year I sold 5 or 6 for a very good price, reluctantly, on the contrary, when I see these instruments leave, I feel the pity of a collector, who is attached to the valuable things, he managed to acquire for his own pleasure. But, on the other hand, I am pleased to see that this is the revival of an instrument, which almost appeared to be left behind.*[902]

He specifies the good price he gets for his guitars in his letter to Hallberg on December 21, 1876:

> *The guitar is gaining prestige again. I have pupils. I have a beautiful collection of guitars. Well, reluctantly (because I love my instruments), I have sold three in one month (to my recollection, it's been twenty years since a thing like this happened), the last one, some days ago, was sold for almost 300 francs, and these were not the best of my collection, they are the less good.*[903]

From this collection, a fine guitar was rediscovered in Paris in 2009 by luthier, restorer and expert Erik Pierre Hofmann. It was in a bad condition and during the restoration, it appeared that it was once owned by Coste. The instrument originally was a baroque guitar by Renault & Chatelain, built in 1780, but transformed into a six-string guitar by Lacôte in the 1830s. But this guitar was not transformed in the usual way. A new and much more fashionable bridge was made, a new head was manufactured, together with a new, notably wide neck. The intricate inlay around the soundboard also borders the

---

[900] Coste-Gruel, 16 VI 1879, Archiv Norbert Fischer, Halen: 'J'ai vu le marchand en question, et consent à céder le théorbe pour 50 fr. Je n'ai rien pour obtenir en fait de diminution plus grande. Si cela vous convient, chèr Monsieur, faites le prendre demain matin avant midi. Passé cette heure le dit M.d sera libre d'accepter d'autres propositions.'

[901] Coste-Schult, 7 X 1867: […] 'ma guitare, ma gr 901 ande guitare archluth, le theorbe, le cystre et moi-même.'

[902] Coste-Schult, 2 XI 1876: 'J'avais une belle collection de guitares. Depuis l'année précédente inclusivement j'en ai vendu 5 ou 6 à un prix très élevé, et cela sans le chercher, bien au contraire, car je vois partir ces instruments avec le regret d'un collectionneur qui s'attache aux objets précieux qu'il a réussi à se procurer pour sa jouissance personnelle. Mais d'un autre côté, je vois avec bonheur cet indice de la reprise d'un instrument qui pendant bien des années paraîtrait presque abandonné.'

[903] Coste-Hallberg, 21 XII 1876: 'La guitare reprend faveurs. J'ai des élèves. J'ai une assez belle collection de guitares. Eh bien, sans le chercher (car je tiens à mes instruments), j'en ai trois en quelques mois. (il y a plus de vingt ans que pareil ne s'était produit à ma connaissance), la dernière il y a quelques jours, n'a été payée 300 francs, et ce ne sont pas les meilleurs de ma collection, ce sont les moins bonnes.'

VIII — Divagation

127 Renault & Chatelain

129 Renault & Chatelain

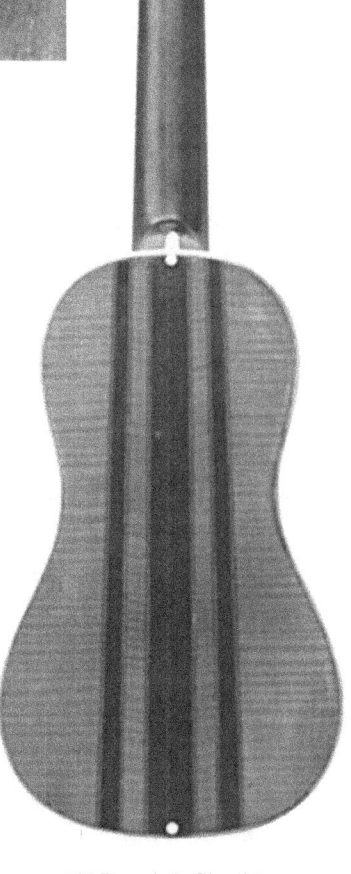

128 Renault & Chatelain

fretboard. This work carries the handprint of the French maker René Lacôte. It is most interesting to note that Lacôte went so far as to re-use the original inlay to border the new fretboard. This work must have been commissioned by Coste, who put his drypoint signature on both sides of the new head, as well as on the heel of the new solid mahogany neck. Another feature that the converted guitar by Renault & Chatelain has in common with most of the heptacordes by Lacôte, is an unusually wide neck for the period. This seems to prove that it was Coste's firm intention to play this guitar, although he was not in desperate need for one more instrument to play. In 2016 the author visited Hofmann and could examine the instrument in its present excellent condition. The extensive report of the restoration process with this information and pictures are used by courtesy of Hofmann.[904]

Coste was a composer, a guitarist, a teacher, and a collector as well. He is proud of his collection, he is attached to the instruments, and he appears to be quite reluctant to sell them. Apart from this, he still is writing arrangements, now of a piece by Sor.

L'ENCOURAGEMENT - FERNANDO SOR OPUS 34 [ARR. COSTE] 1879

In the list of Coste's works, this arrangement emerges for the first time in opus 50, on the back of the title page. Apparently, he arranged Sor's duet before, or in 1879, for '2 Guitares concertantes' and published it by himself in this period with the number NC51.[905] The initial work by Sor was published in 1828.[906] The parts of Sor's duet are conceived in teacher-pupil format, meaning that the first part, the melody, is a solo part for the pupil, and the second part, the chords, is an accompaniment for the

---

[904] Hofmann, Erik Pierre: *Presentation and Expert Report on a Historic Guitar Formerly Owned by Napoléon Coste (1805-1883)*, Germolles-sur-Grosne, Les Robins, 2016, p. 2, 26-28.
[905] Kk Rischel 732 mu 6705.0981 U74 Sor-Coste, *L'Encouragement* opus 34.
[906] Jeffery, Brian: *Fernando Sor, Composer and Guitarist*, London, Tecla, 1977; second edition 1994, p. 161.

teacher, subordinate to the pupil. It is written in the 'theme and variations' genre, with an introduction and a waltz as a finale. In the many repeats, Coste finds a reason to alternate the two parts on a regular basis, in such a way that two equal parts emerge, in accordance with the subtitle. Coste is quite satisfied with the result of his arrangement:

> *I have a Duo by Sor, with the title L'Encouragement, which is written for one guitar singing the whole time, while the other only plays the accompaniment. It is a charming composition, but really absurd. I arranged it for two equal concert guitar parts, so I could play it with my wife. The result is just marvelous. If I can find 25 subscribers at 5 fr. each, I have it engraved.*[907]

This also gives additional evidence that Coste played together with his spouse. In 1927, Erwin Schwarz-Reiflingen has the opinion that this sufficiently shows that Coste writes in Sor's spirit, just as in his own works.[908] Brian Jeffery writes an article about the work in 1981, and he emphasizes the pedagogical aspect of Sor's edition, who dedicated it 'à une de mes élèves', an aspect Coste has changed in such a way, that one cannot present this as Sor's work anymore.[909] This is not the only one of Sor's duets that Coste arranges in this way. According to Jeffery, he does the same with *Divertissement* opus 38, *Le premier pas vers moi* opus 53, and *Souvenir de Russie* opus 63.[910] However, no example of Sor's opus 53 has been found. Examples of his opus 38 and opus 63 are in the Spencer Collection of the library of the Royal Academy of Music in London.[911] And one more duet, which Jeffery does not mention, is the arrangement of Sor's *Fantaisie* opus 54(bis). This work is not published, but the transcript is in the Kongelige Bibliotek in Copenhagen.[912] Coste also arranged and published some of Sor's works for guitar solo, such as *Mes Ennuis* opus 43, *Voyons c'est ça* opus 45 and several 'oeuvres choisies' in successive volumes.[913]

So, Coste was intensively occupied with Sor's works for guitar solo and duet. In his letter to Hallberg, he explains his intentions to publish his own works and those of Sor:

> *I have received 20 fr. you sent for the music (15 fr.) and I think 5 fr. for the subscription of Sor's Duo (Encouragement), which I intend to publish. I only forgot to tell you, my dear friend, that I am just looking for support and not for having money sent to me in advance, because, if I do not find enough subscribers, I won't have the work engraved; I already have more than enough expenses in the publication of my poor works, without attempting other projects.*[914]

As he has started to publish works by himself now and have them engraved, he asks people who are interested to subscribe for the edition. When there are not enough subscribers, plans to publish the edition are cancelled.

Opus 50, *Adagio et Divertissements* 1879

Just as in the year before, Coste plays one of his own compositions again, in one of the monthly meetings of the *Société académique des Enfants d'Apollon*, on September 14, 1879, the second Sunday of

---

[907] Coste-Hallberg, 22 III 1879: *'J'ai un Duo de Sor intitulé L'Encouragement qui à été écrit pour une guitare chantant toujours, tandis que l'autre ne fait qu'accompagner. C'est une composition charmante mais vraiment absurde. Je l'ai arrangé pour 2 guitares égales et concertantes pour le jouer avec ma femme. L'effet en est ravissant. Si je puis trouver 25 souscripteurs à 5 fr. chaque, je le ferai graver.'*
[908] Schwarz-Reiflingen, Erwin: 'Napoléon Coste', in: *Die Gitarre*, Berlin, 1927, Jahrgang VIII, Heft 7/8, [Coste-Heft] p. 45-46.
[909] Jeffery, Brian: 'Il vero testo de l'Encouragement di Fernando Sor' in: *Il Fronimo*, Milano, Suvini Zerboni, vol. IX, no. 34, 1981, p. 34-35.
[910] Jeffery, Brian: *Fernando Sor, Composer and Guitarist*, London, Tecla, 1977; second edition 1994, p. 163, 165, 168.
[911] Lam XX (143921.1) Sor-Coste, *Divertissement* opus 38; Lam XX (144014.1) Sor-Coste, *Souvenir de Russie* opus 63.
[912] Kk Rischel Ms. 217 mu 7910.0285 Sor-Coste, *Fantaisie* opus 54 (bis).
[913] Lam XX (143950.1) Sor-Coste, *Mes Ennuis* opus 43; Lam XX (158396.1) Sor-Coste, *Voyons c'est ça* opus 45; Lam XX (158396.1) Sor-Coste, *Oeuvres Choisies* 1-4.
[914] Coste-Hallberg, 4 IV 1879: *'J'ai reçu votre envoi de 20 fr. pour la musique (15 fr) et je suppose 5 fr. comme souscription au Sors Duo (Encouragement) que mon intention est de publier. Seulement j'ai oublié de vous dire, mon cher ami, que je cherche des adhésions mais qu'il ne faut pas m'envoyer d'argent d'avance parceque si je ne trouvais pas le nombre voulu de souscripteurs, je ne ferais pas graver cet ouvrage; j'ai déjà bien assez des dépenses que je fais pour la publication de mes pauvres oeuvres sans m'embarquer dans d'autres entreprises.'*

VIII — Divagation 225

the month, as usual. Now he performs an *Adagio, scherzo, menuet en mazurka*.[915] He writes to Hallberg about this on September 17, 1879:

> *I played my last composition op. 50 Adagio, Scherzo, Menuet et Mazurka, the 2nd Sunday of this month at the société des Enfants d'Apollon. They were received well and a poet gave me a very flattering impromptu.*[916]

The work had a good reception, and there is no doubt that the work in question here is *Adagio et Divertissements* opus 50, the parts of the piece are the same, although the fourth part, Andantino, is not mentioned by Decourcelle, and the last part Minuetto alla Mazourka, is abbreviated. The work is dedicated to M. Le Baron d'Outhoorn, a nobleman of whom nothing further is known. Coste publishes it himself, according to the catalogue of the Bibliothèque nationale, in 1879.[917] The copies in the Kongelige Bibliotek in Copenhagen and in the Spencer Collection of the Royal Academy of Music in London are identical, out of which the last one served as the basis for the Chanterelle facsimile edition of Simon Wynberg, who forgot to mention the omission of the third sharp of the key of A on the second page of the Minuetto alla Mazourka.[918] For the first time, Coste uses metronome indications for tempo, which he does again, for the last time, in opus 51.

Just as in many of his other works, Coste's way of composing is outstanding in the first, slow part. The melody is gripping from the outset, with its four-voice harmony, modulating to the dominant in the answering phrase. The repeat of this part is figured in diminution, with a harmony of passing dominants and a single diminished seventh chord. This subsequently leads to III-major, with a lyrical melody and chord repetitions, as well as more free lyricism in the melody, now on top of an accompaniment. The harmony is more intensive here, with diminished seventh chords and a Moll-Dur chord, in a modulation to the sixth degree of the scale. In the following reprise, the theme is elaborated upon, modulating through a raised IV with abruptio, going to the dominant in a transition with a cadenza to a chromatic figuration and two series of four-voice chords, ending on the tonic. Part II, the Scherzo, has fewer Romantic elements in it. There are some prolongations, some passing dominants, a diminished seventh chord and two Moll-Dur cadences. The trio is written entirely in a single arpeggio-pattern. The return of the use of chromatics in the melody is another striking feature. Until now Coste preferred to use chromatics harmonically in his works. Part III, the Menuet, is written in a Classical form. The Romantic characteristics in this part are some diminished seventh chords, figurations with chromatics, a rocket figure and very remarkable campanella legatos. The trio of this part is elaborated, a V-minor emerges and there is a Moll-Dur chord again. Ornaments are rare: Coste tries to find expression in the articulation and in the dynamics instead, here in a number of chords with arpeggiato. With its 16 measures, part IV, Andantino, is very short. The only notable thing is the horn-harmony in the first eight measures. Some passing dominants and a modulation to the dominant can be mentioned as being the few Romantic elements. The last part, Minuetto, is in the key of a minor at first, then in the key of A major. This is the only time Coste gives the indication to 'soffocare', suffocate. A few passing dominants show harmonic motion, while double legatos and glissandos with campanella legatos set the atmosphere of this part. The reprise is not elaborated, but it does have a final closure. Coste's style can easily be recognized in the lyrical melodies of the final parts, the first part excels in its many Romantic characteristics.

---

[915] Decourcelle, Maurice: *La Société académique des Enfants d'Apollon*, programmes des concerts annuels..., Paris, Durand, 1881, p. 240: 'Adagio, scherzo, menuet et mazurka pour la guitare, composés et exécutés par M. Coste.'
[916] Coste-Hallberg, 17 IX 1879: 'J'ai joué ma dernière publication op. 50 Adagio, Scherzo, Menuet et Mazurka le 2me Dimanche de ce mois à la société des Enfants d'Apollon. Les compositions ont été bien accueillis et un poète m'a adressé un impromptu très flatteur.'
[917] Pn [Vm9 3543, Coste *Adagio et Divertissements* opus 50.
[918] Kk Rischel 172 mu 6701.1682 U48, Coste *Adagio et Divertissements* opus 50; Lam XX(159235.1) Spencer Collection Coste *Adagio et Divertissements* opus 50; Wynberg, Simon: *The Guitar Works of Napoléon Coste*, facsimile edition, Monaco, Chanterelle, 1981, 1983, vol. VI, p. 7.

Opus 51, *Récréation du Guitariste* 1880

From opus 45 on, Coste lists his works in his own editions on the reverse of the title page. Opus 50 and 51 are mentioned in the editions of both 50 and 51, allowing one to presume that they appeared around the same time.[919] Since the Bibliothèque nationale gives 1880 as a date, they probably appeared early that year.[920] Coste dedicates the work to M. Jules Audéoude. The copy of this edition in the Kongelige Bibliotek in Copenhagen has the same handwritten dedication to M. Schult as opus 41, 44 and 47, so he may as well have ordered all these works from Coste.[921] The title reveals that this opus 51 consists of 14 easy pieces of work, which are easy to listen to, and in this way, are attractive to the amateur guitarist. As a result, it is also quite conceivable that five of these pieces were published in the magazine of the *Freie Vereinigung zur Förderung guter Guitarremusik* in Augsburg, in the early 20th century.[922] Joerg Sommermeyer is the only person to make a short remark upon this collection in 1984. He thinks the pieces are very inventive, as far as melody is concerned.[923] Other authors just mention the title in their list. In this collection, Coste gives metronome indications for the second, and last time.

Each of the 14 pieces has a different character. They are entertaining most of the time, and it is a pleasure to play them and to hear them. Not many Romantic characteristics can be found, but Coste's gallant melodic style can certainly be recognized. The Barcarolle of no. 1 is so similar to *Santa Lucia*, that an Italian singer used it as an accompaniment.[924] Overall, Romantic features are rare in this collection. The most intensive harmonic motion can be found in passing dominants. Apart from that, I-minor and V-minor emerge, caused by the predominant modal harmony, which is evident in transitions to the relative, at times. Three prolongations are used incidentally. From no. 6 on, some diminished seventh chords, Moll-Dur chords and one Trugschluss occur. Harmonic acceleration is used in no. 7, with passing dominants. In Chasse no. 9, the so-called imitation of the horn is striking, as are the flageolet tones, along with a I-minor again, sounding like folk music. The Moll-Dur cadence at the end of the last part is significant for the modal tendencies in this collection. The work has didactic intentions, and possibly commercial ones as well, as no 'Sturm und Drang', which Coste uses so often, can be found in it. Nevertheless, his creative line of work can be recognized, inserting new material again and again, instead of elaborating themes and varying existing motifs already introduced.

Opus 52, *Le Livre d'Or du Guitariste* 1880

In this period of his final years, Coste turns increasingly to writing pedagogical pieces, hardly composing solo works for his own performance anymore. The pieces in *Le Livre d'Or* opus 52, fit in this development. They are meant for the amateur, but in this work is dealing with transcriptions and arrangements of pieces and fragments of works by the great masters, as the subtitle says: 'suite de pièces et fragments extraits d'oeuvres des grands maîtres et appliqués à la guitare.' The collection consists almost completely of 'old music': only Donizetti (1779-1848) could pass for a contemporary composer. The entry the Bibliothèque nationale indicates the year 1880.[925] Like the *Méthode*, Coste includes transcriptions of compositions by Robert de Visée in this album, nine pieces, to be precise. Their source could be the *Livre de Pièces pour la Guitarre*, of which Coste might have had a copy of his own, or may have seen one in the Royal library.[926] The public's interest in 'classical music' has risen because of the *Concerts du Conservatoire* and Fétis's *Concerts historiques*, some years earlier, but the main source of

---

[919] Wynberg, Simon: *The Guitar Works of Napoléon Coste*, facsimile edition, Monaco, Chanterelle, 1981, 1983, vol. VI, p. 14, 25.

[920] Pn [Vm9 3557 Coste, *Récréation du Guitariste* opus 51.

[921] Kk Rischel 173 mu 6701.0482 U48.

[922] No. 1 Barcarolle ed. 1907 in Skma Boije 1037; No.3 Rondoletto ed. 1924 in Skma Boije 1037; No. 10 Mélancolie ed. 1907 in Skma Boije 1034; No. 12 Andante Menuet ed. 1906 in Skma Boije 1032; No. 14 Barcarolle ed. 1906 in Skma Boije 1032.

[923] Sommermeyer, Joerg: 'Noten, The Guitar Works of Napoléon Coste...', in: *Nova Giulianiad*, in: *Nova Giulianiad*, 1984 nr. 3, p. 167-169, http://home.t-online.de/home/Rechtsanwalt.Joerg.Sommermeyer/ng3.htm, 10 VII 2002.

[924] Albarello, Stefano: *Eco del Vesuvio*, Napoléon Coste: Barcarole op.51 no.1, Tactus TC 790001, 2004. Liner notes Stefano Albarello. Guitar: Pasquale Vinaccia 1889, Naples.

[925] Pn [Vm9 3543 Coste, *Le Livre d'Or du Guitariste* opus 52.

[926] Coste-Schult, 8 XII 1874: '[...] pièces de Robert de Visée, [...] transcrites d'après un ouvrage du temps.'

VIII — Divagation

this collection may have been the monthly meetings and the annual concerts of the *Société académique des Enfants d'Apollon*. Between 1841 and 1866 a total of twelve compositions were performed that probably are included in Coste's collection in transcription for guitar solo. This has been established with certainty for six pieces, while for the other six pieces this could not be done, such as *Airs Suédois*, but one of these two is certain, nevertheless, as Coste mentions this melody with notation, in his letter to Schult, on December 8, 1874:

> *I have already received the Swedish airs, you had the kindness of sending me. They include some charming ones, especially this one:*[927]

130 Air Suédois

The first of these *Airs Suédois* may be the *Chanson suédoise* that Christine Nilsson sang in the Freemasons concert on April 30, 1870, where Coste might have heard it. But it is more likely that he received the melodies from M. Schult:

> *M. Schult already was so kind to send me some Swedish melodies, among which several are very remarkable. I have transcribed them for guitar with the intention to create a fantaisie from these.*[928]

The accurate references can be found in the thematic catalogue. In his edition 'chez l'auteur' NC 52, the title is not mentioned in the list on the backside of the title page. In this work, Coste again omits the metronome indications. He dedicates the work to the Club des Guitaristes de Leipzig, with which he has been in contact since 1880, according to Läpke.[929] He made the acquaintance of this society by Holm:

> *M. Holm has introduced me to the club of Leipzig. This society is very interesting, its secretary, M. Läpke, has written to me several times. He told me about the beginnings and the organization of this very rare artistic assembly, which may have influence on the future of the guitar.*[930]

Furthermore, Thorvald Rischel knows that Coste is a honorary member of this society, a fact established by Otto Schick.[931] The club's archives have not been found yet. The works in this collection are easy to play, higher positions are almost entirely lacking, with only the Beethoven arrangements having a higher level. They do not contain anything technically impossible, which attests Coste's perfect understanding of his art. He self-publishes this work, just as he did with earlier editions, following the same procedure with *Livre d'Or du Guitariste* opus 52:

> *I received your subscription for the livre d'or du guitariste and I thank you for it. [...] the goal of sending the catalogue is to gather subscriptions to help me a bit with the publication expenses.*[932]

---

[927] Coste-Schult, 8 XII 1874: 'J'ai reçu dans le temps les airs suédois que vous avez eu la bonté de m'envoyer. Il y en a de charmants, un surtout' [i.e. opus 52 no. 17 second one].

[928] Coste-Hallberg, 23 II 1877: 'M. Schult avait déjà eu l'obligeance de m'envoyer une suite de mélodies suédoises dont plusieurs sont très remarquables. Je les ai transcrites pour la guitare avec l'intention d'en faire une fantaisie.'

[929] Läpke, Richard: 'Biographie Napoléon Coste' in: *Internationale Gitarre-Zeitung*, Jahrgang I, no. 4 (Jan.1884), no. 5 (Febr.1884), Leipzig, transcr. Eduard Fack, 'Die Meister', unp. p. 119.

[930] Coste-Hallberg, 5 X 1880: 'Mr. Holm m'a mis en relation avec le club de Leipzig. Cette société est très intéressante; son secrétaire Mr. Läpke m'a écrit plusieurs fois. Il m'a fait connaître les débuts et l'organisation de cette réunion artistique très originale, qui pourra avoir de l'influence sur l'avenir de la guitare.'

[931] Rischel, Thorvald: 'Bibliographische Notizen zu den Gitarrenwerken von Napoléon Coste', in: *Die Gitarre*, Berlin, 1927, Jahrgang VIII, Heft 7/8, [Coste-Heft] p. 47.

[932] Coste-Hallberg, 22 IX 1880: 'J'ai reçu votre souscription au livre d'or du guitariste et je vous en remercie. [...] le but de l'envoi de ce catalogue est de recueillir des adhésions afin de m'aider un peu dans les frais de publication.'

And in his next letter to Hallberg, Coste seems to have found enough subscribers, as he writes that he has had the work engraved:

I am waiting for the proofs of the Livre d'or. There will be another proof, the corrections will take 8 or 10 days. The work will appear around the 25th.[933]

The Bibliothèque nationale appears to be right about the year of this publication: 1880.

Opus 53, Six Pièces originales 1881

This volume is also the last work Coste publishes on his own at his address, rue du Faubourg St-Martin no. 50. The number of the edition, N.C., does not reveal anything about the date, but according to Simon Wynberg, it must be 1881, which is, of course, quite likely in the chronology of his works.[934] Just like *Duetto* WoO 6, this work is dedicated to his friend M. Adolph Hallberg, with whom he corresponds intensively. The example in the Kongelige Bibliotek in Copenhagen has Coste's signature on it, with the dedication: 'A. Monsieur Schult, hommage d'amitié, N. Coste.'[935] The work is published in 1881 indeed, as emerges from his letter to Hallberg on November 8, 1881:

I am charmed that you like the dedication of my last work op. 53. It is a token of my friendship which I am happy to be able to give you, and which you have deserved for your love of your dear instrument.[936]

Wynberg's edition is the facsimile of the copy in the Spencer Collection.[937]

In his last work, Coste also succeeds in attaining a sublime Romanticism. The first piece of this collection, Rêverie, does justice to its title with its associative ongoing harmonic development, the varying rhythm, the arpeggios and the passage work. In spite of his exclusive use of passing dominants, the tonic becomes unclear and is hard to define, even more so due to the emerging Neapolitan sixth chord, and a number of diminished seventh chords. The phrases are shortened or lengthened now. This passage is similar to *Étude* 23 opus 38, measure 21, *La Chasse des Sylphes* opus 29, part I, measure 13, part III, measure 31 and to *Le Départ* opus 31, part II, measure 59, where the floating harmony is a part of the Romantic style. In measure 26 the atmosphere is different due to its parallel minor, the sustained motion in 32nds, the ascending parallel octaves and the repeated chords as an accompaniment of the lyrical melody. After some passage work comes an extensive cadenza, which is the transition to the elaborated reprise. This section is written in arpeggio chords. Back in the key of E, this section could have the function of a finale. It moves along in a 32nd notes motion and has some passing dominant chords, a diminished seventh chord, when it ends with passagework and a Moll-Dur cadence as final closure. The other parts do not offer much Romanticism. The second piece, Rondeau, has a modulation to III major, with a series of passing dominants. No. 3, Menuet, shows some melodic chromatics and is in a rigid musical form, but it does have a lengthened 6-bar phrase, a chord prolongation and passagework in thirds. In no. 4, Scherzo, a few dissonant chords can be found, such as diminished and double diminished, a series of passing dominants, a V-minor as the beginning of a sequence in chords and a cadenza. In the Trio, passing dominants are present again, along with a chord prolongation and an expolitio, lengthening the phrase. No. 5 is an *Étude*, the second one, alongside the one after *Delfzil* opus 19, which is not part of the *Méthode* or the *Etudes* opus 38. It has the same type of arpeggios as *Etude* 22, opus 38, the Tarantella, with similar harmonic progressions. The last piece, No. 6, a Menuet again, is short, but does have some dissonant harmony in its diminished and augmented chords. The piece consists merely of chord cadences with figurations. The first piece of this collection is the only one in which Coste expresses his genius once more, and it shows many elements of his Romantic style.

---

[933] Coste-Hallberg, 5 X 1880: 'J'attends les épreuves du Livre d'or. Il y aura une contrepreuve, les corrections prendront 8 ou 10 jours. L'ouvrage paraîtra vers le 25.'
[934] Wynberg, Simon: *The Guitar Works of Napoléon Coste*, facsimile edition, Monaco, Chanterelle, 1981, 1983, vol. VI, Introduction.
[935] Kk Rischel 175 mu 6701.0581 (eks. 1) U48 Coste, *Six Pièces originales* opus 53.
[936] Coste-Hallberg, 8 XI 1881: 'Je suis charmé que la dédicace de mon dernier oeuvre op. 53 vous soit agréable. C'est une marque d'amitié que je suis heureux d'avoir pu vous donner et que vous avez mérité par votre amour pour votre cher instrument.'
[937] Lam XX((159235.1) Coste, *Six Pièces originales* opus 53.

ILLNESS 1880-1881

In Paris, hardly any concerts with guitar take place in these years, and in them Spanish guitarists are predominant. On May 25, 1881, young Francisco Tárrega (1852-1909) plays in the Odeon, in a festival, organized by the Spanish ambassador, on the occasion of the 200 year memorial of Calderón, where Victor Hugo presides. This rising star from Spain, who will found a school later, is invited by Jaime Bosch, among others.[938] Spain is going to be the country where the most important developments of the guitar take place, now. Coste gradually retires from artistic cultural life, at first due to his wife's illness:

For a long time, my wife has been ill, and this made her suffer from serious weakness.[939]

But two weeks later she seems to be better:

[...] My wife has recovered and I don't have any worries about her health anymore. She just has remained very weak. She can't go out without my accompaniment and support. When she goes down the stairs, she is taken with vertigo, I have to stand before her to hide the void for her.[940]

Also, Coste continues to be liable to fits of cold on his hands:

But, while my body still is healthy enough, I have a serious illness of my hands, which are captured by the cold of these last days. I have chilblained hands, and the joints of my finger are swollen.[941]

Then he is struck by a cerebral congestion at the end of 1881, forcing him to live in isolation from his work and from the musical world:

And then, what you don't know yet, dear friend, is that I have been indisposed very seriously, in such a way that I had to fear for my life. I have had a cerebral congestion. Since then, I am forbidden to do anything. Three times a day I take bromide of potassium to eliminate the congestion. I am living completely like an oyster, no more music, and above all, no more composition. The talent of this poor artist has gone. He hardly has any memories of what he has done. I can't go out without the company of my excellent wife, who continues to give me signs of affection and devotion. That I did not succumb to this terrible attack it is thanks to the good care she lavishes on me with.[942]

Coste is seriously ill now. He can't play in concerts anymore, nor can he compose. A few months later, he feels better, but he laments:

[...] after the serious illness that has struck me, I am happy to be in a reasonable condition. I still have a weak brain. I have made plans for compositions, but it is likely that these plans will never be realized. [...] I have stopped giving lessons in town. My pupils come with me to take their lessons at my home. I have been forced to reject new ones.[943]

---

[938] Pujol. Emilio: *Tárrega, Ensayo biográfico*, Lisboa, Ramos, 1960, p. 89-90.
[939] Coste-Hallberg, 22 IX 1880: 'Ma femme a été longtemps malade et il fait souffrir d'une grande faiblesse.'
[940] Coste-Hallberg, 5 X 1880: 'Ma femme est rétablie et je n'ai plus aucun souci pour sa santé. Seulement il lui est resté une grande faiblesse. Elle ne peut sortir sans que [je] l'accompagne et la soutienne. Lorsqu'elle descend des escaliers elle est prise de vertiges; il faut que je me mette devant elle pour lui cacher le vide.'
[941] Coste-Hallberg, 7 II 1881: 'Seulement si le corps est encore assez solide, mes mains, saisies par le froid de ces dernier temps, sont bien malades. J'ai des engelures et les articulations des doigts sont engorgées.'
[942] Coste-Hallberg, 8 XI 1881: 'Et puis, ce que vous ignorez encore, cher ami, c'est que j'ai été assez gravement indisposé pour que l'on ait eu à vaincre pour mon existence. J'ai eu une congestion cerebrale. Depuis ce jour il m'est défendu de rien faire. Je prends trois fois par jour du bromure de potassium pour éloigner la congestion. Je vis absolument comme une huitre, plus de musique et surtout plus de composition. L'intelligence du pauvre artiste est morte. A peine a-t-il le plus mince souvenir de ce qu'il a produit. Je ne puis plus sortir sans être accompagné par mon excellente femme qui continue à me donner des preuves d'affection et de dévouements. Si je n'ai pas succombé à cette terrible attaque, c'est grâce aux soins intelligents dont elle m'a entouré.'
[943] Coste-Hallberg, 8 I 1882: '[...] après la grave indisposition qui m'a frappé je suis heureux d'être dans un état de santé passable. J'ai toujours la tête un peu faible et écris assez péniblement. Cela me fatigue. Je fais des projets de compositions nouvelles mais il est probable que ces projets ne se réaliseront jamais. [...] J'ai renoncé à donner des leçons en ville. Mes élèves viennent tous prendre leurs leçons chez moi. J'ai été forcé d'en refuser de nouveaux.'

In spite of his old age and his bad health, he still appears to be giving lessons, not at the pupils' homes anymore, but at his own place. Apart from his correspondence with Hallberg, he writes letters to Léon Gruel, even when, for reasons concerning his wife's health, he resides in Thiais, near Choisy-le-Roi where he stays with friends, a painter of ceramics and his family. On July 11 he writes:

Since we left Paris, I was tormented by the fear of not having informed you of our absence and that you could have made the effort of visiting Sunday, as usual. But, on the other hand, I thought I could remember that you said that you would also be away for some time. Everything would be in order, then.[944]

Apparently, Coste does not have a diary for his appointments, every week pupils come at the same time. Coste's last letter to Gruel, with the date 1 September 1882, seems to confirm this:

We will return to Paris next Thursday. I am sorry to move the pleasure of seeing you to Sunday at eight. Our stay in the country has done my wife some good. I hope to see you in good health. [...] Please be so kind as to accept the expression of my kind regards, dear Sir, Your devoted friend, N. Coste.[945]

Nothing more emerges from these short notices than appointments and superficial conversation, but, as always, they are brought to a close with his best regards in very polite words. Coste is very courteous in his correspondence. His final letter to Hallberg on December 5, 1882 is very distressing:

I was a warning to alert me that my career was over and that my end was nearing. Still, my health, being shaken by this attack, has recovered quickly, provided that I could not do anything and that I renounce any thinking work [...] But my wife [...] has fallen ill with a pleuro pneumonia that has endangered her days. [...] Also, the poor guitar has been abandoned, I can't do anything anymore.[946]

He is foreseeing the end of his career as a guitarist and a composer, and sees that his death is coming near.

OBITUARY 1883

Not much later, on January 28, 1883, Napoléon Coste's obituary appears. After that of Gustave Doré, the famous engraver, who died the very same day, J.L. Heugel writes in *Le Ménestrel*:

We are also sorry to announce the death of M. Napoléon Coste, the eminent guitarist-composer: he was 78 years old. Up to the end of his career he kept his passion for his art, and, not too long ago, he published the Livre d'Or des Guitaristes, an important work, worthy of the musicians' attention. M. Coste has made some successful improvements in the construction of his favorite instrument, and succeeded in building up a collection of very expensive guitars. We have heard that he has donated the one presumed to have been owned by Louis XIV to the museum of the Conservatoire, and we wish to inform the amateurs about the other models this excellent teacher has had the pleasure to collect: these are really remarkable instruments, from every point of view.[947]

---

[944] Coste-Gruel, 11 VII 1882, Archiv Norbert Fischer, Halen: 'Depuis que nous avons quitté Paris, je suis tourmenté de la crainte de ne pas vous avoir annoncé notre absence et que vous avez pu vous donner la peine de voir Dimanche comme d'habitude. Mais d'un autre coté je crois me souvenir que vous m'avez annoncé que vous devrez aussi vous absenter pour quelque temps. Tout serait alors pour le mieux.'

[945] Coste-Gruel, 1 IX 1882, Archiv Norbert Fischer, Halen: 'Nous reviendrons à Paris jeudi prochain. J'ai le regret de remettre à Dimanche en huit le plaisir de vous voir. Notre séjour à la campagne a fait quelque bien à ma femme. J'espère vous revoir bien portant. [...] Veuillez, chèr Monsieur, [...] agréer pour vous l'expression de mes sentimens affectueux. Votre tout dévoué N. Coste.'

[946] Coste-Hallberg, 5 XII 1882: 'C'était un avertissement pour me prévenir que ma carrière était terminée et que ma fin approchait. Cependant ma santé, un peu ébranlée par ce coup, a été bientôt rétablie, à condition que je ne ferais plus rien et que je m'abtiendrais de tout travail de tête. [...] Mais ma femme [...] est tombée malade d'une fluxion de poitrine que a mis ses jours en danger. [...] Aussi la pauvre guitare est abandonnée, je ne fais plus rien.'

[947] *Le Ménestrel*, vol. 49, no. 9, 28 I 1883, p. [8], J.L. Heugel, *directeur-gérant:* 'Nous avons le regret d'annoncer aussi la mort de M. Napoléon Coste, éminent guitariste-compositeur: il était âgé de 78 ans. Jusqu'à la fin de sa carrière, il avait gardé la passion de son art et, il y a peu de temps encore, il publiait le Livre d'or des Guitaristes, ouvrage important et digne de l'attention des musiciens. M. Coste avait imaginé quelques heureuses modifications dans la construction de son instrument favori, et il s'étaitplu à former une collection de guitares du plus grand prix. Nous apprenons qu'il a donné au musée du Conservatoire celle qui passait pour avoir appartenu à Louis XIV, et nous signalons aux amateurs les autres modèles que cet excellent professeur avait pris plaisir à rassembler: ce sont là des pièces vraiment remarquables à tous les points de vue.'

VIII — Divagation   231

Now it seems that Coste is a luthier, or even a collector, or else just a good teacher, who also published an edition with transcriptions of well-known popular works by great composers, not the composer who produced the greatest works for guitar of the French Romantic period. It is the last notice the contemporary press produces on Coste. The instrument mentioned, which he has donated to the museum, is the so-called bass guitar, on the far right in Disdéri's photograph. Coste has made adjustments to the head and the tailpiece. According to Dugot, the instrument comes from the 18th century, but Coste thinks Louis XIV has owned it and played it.[948] The musical function that Coste may have had in mind for this instrument, remains obscure. He never composed for the instrument, but it is possible he may have used it in one of Fétis's *Concerts historiques*.

The death certificate says that Coste has died on January 14, 1883.

In the year eighteen hundred eighty-three, the fifteenth of January, at three in the afternoon, the death certificate of Claude Antoine Jean Georges Napoléon Coste, age seventy-eight years, music composer, born in Amondans (Doubs), died at rue du Faubourg Saint-Martin 50, marital home, yesterday evening at nine o'clock, son of Jean François Coste and Anne Pierrette Dénéria, deceased spouses; husband of Louise Olive Pauilhé, age fifty-eight years, without profession.[949]

The full certificate can be read in the appendices. It is remarkable that here, once again, the correct year of birth is mentioned, although he hasn't attained his 78th birthday yet and that his spouse Louise Olive Pauilhé really was born in 1825. Roman Jaworski writes that Coste's death is preceded by an illness, and that he dies in the presence of his friends.[950] These people might as well have been the ones mentioned on the death certificate, Armand Candillon, twenty-seven years of age, merchant, and Gustave Boisson, forty years of age, employee, living at rue du Faubourg Saint-Martin 69, which is opposite the Costes' apartment and thus are not friends, but neighbors.[951] Noël Roncet writes that Coste is buried in cimetière de Montmartre on January 15, not far from Fernando Sor. His grave was removed in 1986 and his remains taken to the ossuary in cimetière Père Lachaise in Paris.[952] Coste leaves his possessions to his spouse.[953] Thorvald Rischel, who travels to France in 1893, in search of the *Grand Duo* WoO 8, and possibly other unknown works by Coste as well, learns that Coste's widow has died in the village of Thiais, near Choisy-le-Roi. The owner of the house, de Rivière, a pigment trader from Paris, shows him a pile of sheet music and tells him that other guitarists have repeatedly searched for Coste's music, and that everything useful has already been taken away. However, Rischel gets the remaining fragments, and, back home, he succeeds in compiling the duet, for which he had searched so long, together with the Swedish guitarist Hallberg.[954] When she died, Coste's widow may have been living in the very same house where they resided some years earlier, in Thiais, near Choisyle-Roi, and possibly the ceramics painter or pigment trader was De Rivière. Napoléon Coste's widow Louise Olive Pauilhé survived the composer for some ten years. Almost all of his works have been preserved, but only his *Études* opus 38 became part of the canon of guitar works during the decennia following his death.

---

[948] Chouquet, Gustave: *Le Musée du Conservatoire National de Musique*. 946 *Catalogue raisonnée des instruments de cette collection*, Paris, 1875, 2/1884, 3 suppls. 1894-1903, 1884, No. 280, p. 68; *Le Musée du Conservatoire de Musique, avec les Ier, IIe et IIIe suppléments*, Genève, Minkoff. 1993, p. 16, 17, 68; Dugot, Joël: *Guitare basse, auteur inconnu, fin du XVIIIe siècle (?)*, in: *Instrumentistes et Luthiers Parisiens*, Florence Gétreau, ed., Paris, 1988, p. 172; http://mediatheque.citedelamusique.fr/masc/?url=/clientbookline/CIMU/toolkit/p_requests/default-instruments.htm, 17 XI 2014.

[949] Paris, Archives de Paris, *Acte de déces Napoléon Coste*, 15 I 1883, Série V2E 5Mi 3/1256: 'L'an mil-huit-cent-quatre-vingt-trois, le quinze-janvier à trois heures du soir, acte de décès de Claude Antoine Jean Georges Napoléon Coste, agé de soixante-dix-huit ans, compositeur de musique, né à Amondans (Doubs), décédé rue du Faubourg Saint-Martin 50. domicile conjugal hier soir à neuf heures; fils de Jean François Coste et de Anne Pierrette Déneria, épouses décédés; époux de Louise Olive Pauilhé, agée de cinquante-huit ans, sans profession.'

[950] Jaworski, Roman: 'Napoléon Coste 1805-1883, une histoire perdue', in: *Valentiana*, Valenciennes, Association Valentiana, 1992, no. 10, p. 78.

[951] Paris, Archives de Paris, *Acte de déces Napoléon Coste*, 15 I 1883, Série V2E 5Mi 3/1256. [see appendix]

[952] Roncet, Noël: *Napoléon Coste, Compositeur, 1805-1883*, Amondans, 2005, p. 28-30.

[953] Paris, Archives de Paris, *Déclarations de succession*, Napoléon Coste, mai 1879 - mai 1883, DQ_2009, I71, p.179, No. 53.

[954] Rischel, Thorvald: 'Bibliographische Notizen zu den Gitarrenwerken von Napoléon Coste', in: *Die Gitarre*, Berlin, 1927, Jahrgang VIII, Heft 7/8, [Coste-Heft] p. 48.

131 Rue du Faubourg St-Martin no. 50, 2007

IX
Finale

Here it is no longer merely a matter of a description, but a secret, indescribable connection between the melody and the sheer immensity of the mountain, and everything this immensity touches in the deepest recesses of our soul. [...] One should hardly endeavor to dissect its phrases or to claim that an analysis of a melody or a chord progression led one to discover the hidden cause that makes this art such a marvelous interpreter of our feelings, an art that evokes both a spectacle and the soul it embodies.[955]

Reception 1884-1992

In the years 1884 through 1992, ten authors of manuals, guitar histories and articles, have written a shorter or longer review of Napoléon Coste's works. In 1884 Richard Läpke writes that the person who made the connection between the old era and the new era has gone with Coste, the man who was personally in contact with people whom we now only can admire through their works.[956] After the turn of the century, Shtokman writes an article on Coste in *Der Guitarrefreund* in 1902, in which he makes a plea to save the works of the greatest French guitarist from oblivion. He also gives an explanation for the lamentable turn in public opinion in a way that disfavors the guitar. Certain individuals appeared who, using their self-appointed authority, took pains to discredit the noble instrument in their words and writings. This prevented Coste's compositions from reaching a wide audience.[957] Shtokman is followed by Fritz Buek, who in 1926 draws the conclusion that the guitar's heyday in France ends with Coste's departure.[958] One year later, Erwin Schwarz-Reiflingen writes extensively about Coste's musical influence, and he is very creative and admiring in his description. The line of guitarists from the instrument's zenith in the previous century comes to an end with Napoléon Coste. As an artist and a musician he matured quite late. A variety of different styles are audible in his compositions, in which French elements alternate with Italian, German and Spanish influences. Coste is truly an exponent of his era. His works are mainly Romantic in their themes and the expression of the sentiment they represent, they are Romantic in his pursuit of the program and his dramatic instrumentation, influenced by Berlioz, and they are 'Coste-like' due to his working method, in which the various style elements are brought together. They are not graced with Sor's clarity of expression, and yet they are full of admirable qualities, which often are of the same artistic standard as Sor's.[959] According to Mario Giordano, who in 1934 has a very lyrical way of writing, the special quality in Coste's music comes about from the perfect balance between idea and technique, a characteristic that is also present in Chopin's and Wieniawski's music. In this way, if Chopin can be called 'pianistic', and Wieniawski 'violinistic', Coste appears to us as being completely 'guitaristic'. His art is grounded in a tremendous enthusiasm, connected to a profound musical culture possessed only by Sor among the guitarists. Giordano thinks that all this makes Coste one of the best representative personalities in the history of the guitar and one of the most interesting musicians of the past century.[960] José de Azpiazu writes briefly about Coste in 1959, saying

---

[955] Koechlin, Ch.: 'Les tendances de la musique moderne Française', in: Lavignac, Albert: *Encyclopédie de la musique...*, Paris, Delagrave, 1925, p. 63: 'Il ne s'agit plus ici d'une simple description, mais d'une secrète, indéfinissable correspondance entre la mélodie, et l'immensité de la montagne, et tout ce que cette immensité remue au plus profond de nous. [...] Il ne faudrait point s'aviser d'en vouloir disséquer les phrases; ni de prétendre, par l'analyse, d'une mélodie ou d'une suite d'accords, découvrir les raisons cachées qui font de cet art l'interprète merveilleux de nos sentiments, l'évocateur à la fois d'un spectacle et de ce qu'il contient d'âme.' [concerning Berlioz's Scène aux champs].

[956] Läpke, Richard: 'Biographie Napoléon Coste' in: *Internationale Gitarre-Zeitung*, Jahrgang I, no. 4 (Jan.1884), no. 5 (Febr.1884), Leipzig, transcr. Eduard Fack, 'Die Meister', unp. p. 119.

[957] Stockmann, J. [Shtokman]: 'Napoléon Coste', in: *Der Guitarrefreund, Mitteilungen des Internationalen Guitarristen-Verbandes*, München, 3. Jahrgang, 1902, Heft 5, p. 56.

[958] Buek, Fritz: *Die Gitarre und ihre Meister*, Berlin, Robert Lienau, 1926, 2e ed. 1935, p. 109.

[959] Schwarz-Reiflingen, Erwin: 'Napoléon Coste', in: *Die Gitarre*, Berlin, 1927, Jahrgang VIII, Heft 7/8, [Coste-Heft] p. 46.

[960] Giordano, Mario: 'Napoléon Coste e le sue opere', in: *Il plettro*, febbraio 959 1934, no. 2, p. 7.

that he is the composer who deserves the most attention and that his études are very worthwhile.[961] In 1970, Alexander Bellow is of the opinion that Coste's most important contribution to the guitar is his revival of interest in baroque music.[962] Józef Powroźniak writes just one paragraph on Coste in his 1979 manual: he devoted himself to composition and wrote more than 50 works, which can be distinguished by a style that is both original and individual.[963] In Brian Jeffery's words from 1982, Napoléon Coste holds a place of honor in the ongoing history of the guitar.[964] Roman Jaworski characterizes Coste's works in 1992 as being imbued with a personal and very original style. He concludes that Coste's works are quite advanced, as compared to those of his contemporaries. Many of his works are technically very demanding, but can be regarded, as pearls in the 19th-century guitar literature, according to Jaworski.[965] All these authors give Coste good reviews, and some make the connection with the Romantic style of the era. These opinions can be complemented with the results of this research. This is the essence of the conclusion of this biography.

Principles

The reception and concept of Romantic music at the beginning of the 20th century is explained in a more general way by French musicologist Charles Koechlin (1867-1950) from a very aesthetical point of view, rather than an analytical approach of the matter, as cited earlier. For him, music is the expression of things that words fail to express. In this way, musicology, being the verbal description of music, is a contradiction in terms. While this approach may satisfy the intuitive or naive listener, the musician and the musicologist want to go a step further. The instruments used by the musicologist also embody sentiment as the motivation for his work, but above all they comprise a technical toolbox enabling him to gain a deeper understanding and better grasp of the music, and to reveal unexpected matters. Form, melody, harmony, meter, expression and Romanticism, all these well-defined formal characteristics and style elements play a prominent role in the descriptive analysis of Coste's works undertaken here: they are concrete tools that make the works of art comprehensible. To give a comparison, the construction workers who built Notre Dame in Paris may have found the inspiration for their years-long work in their spirituality, but one needs more than that to build the cathedral. Knowledge, know-how and craftsmanship are needed, materials and tools, hands and heads, to carry out a grand design. While the building blocks may be the same, it is the artist who decides whether to build the cathedral in a Romanesque or a Gothic style. This is also true for the restorers, who in this metaphor are the performers and the scholars who recreate the music. Extending this comparison to musical craftsmanship, creating an interpretation and a way of understanding music requires sentiment, but knowledge, know-how and analysis are essential. With respect to the matters described in the *Prélude*, the author is an historical-objective academic writer, an interpretative-analytic narrator and a musical-empathic guitarist, making the dissertation to become a chronological artistically pictorial analytic biography of Napoléon Coste.

Taking chronology as a starting point in connection to the (found or not found) biographical details, the social-cultural context, the musical works and the 'objets trouvés', this biography has taken the shape of Coste's works themselves, episodic, quasi-rhapsodic, with themes emerging in succession, in an additive way. This form is identifiable in the *Souvenirs, Sept Morceaux Épisodiques* opus 17-23, in which the many lines of approach result in a musical mosaic, multifaceted, colorful and varied, yet forming coherent whole. This structure is not only expressed in the titles of the chapters, but also in the subjects discussed in them. In this way, this Romantic form is different from the Classical form, in which the musical elements serve a higher purpose, are inserted into a larger structure, in submission to a hierarchical scheme. This Romantic form presents a sequence of musical events, allowing for the

---

[961] Azpiazu, José de: *La Guitare et les Guitaristes*, Basel, Symphonia, 1959, p. 25.
[962] Bellow, Alexander: *The Illustrated History of the Guitar*, New York, Colombo, 1970, p. 174.
[963] Powroźniak, Józef: 'Coste, Napoléon', in: *Gitarrenlexikon*, Berlin, Verlag Neue Musik,1979, p. 36.
[964] Jeffery, Brian: 'Napoléon Coste - renewed acquaintance', in: *Guitar & Lute*, 1982, no. 20, p. 8.
[965] Jaworski, Roman: 'Napoléon Coste 1805-1883, une histoire perdue', in: *Valentiana*, Valenciennes, Association Valentiana,1992, no. 10, p. 78.

IX — Finale 235

development of ideas, being intuitive in all its varieties, and yet resulting in a coherent work, in which both analytic and synthetic aspects are an integral part of the reflections upon the life and the works of the main character, Napoléon Coste.

Aspects

In order to provide an answer to the main question posed at the beginning of this study, which is in how the relation between the guitar and its music, on the one hand, and music and musical life in Paris in the Romantic era on the other hand, manifests itself in the life and works of Napoléon Coste, conclusions must be made concerning the various aspects of the life and the work of the composer, in the same way that the sub-questions posed in the introduction, are answered in the biography.

Social-cultural context

Cultural-artistic circles. Being a guitarist, composer and teacher, Coste enters upper class musical society in Paris, the city that is becoming the musical capital of Europe in this period of time, the city where new developments take place, the cradle of the Romantic music of Chopin, Liszt and Berlioz, to mention just three representative composers. He first comes into contact with musicians who came from Valenciennes, as well as the guitarists of the Classical generation who had settled there, such as Carulli, Carcassi, Aguado and above all Sor, who is of great importance to him, as he probably studies harmony and counterpoint with him, becoming his friend, performing with him in concerts. Coste extends the musical circles that he is part of in joining the *Société académique des Enfants d'Apollon*, with its members Panseron, Prumier and Triébert, who are involved in the *Conservatoire*. He also enters the musical Freemasons lodge *Les Frères Unis Inséparables* and plays in its annual concert in 1852. Coste's dedications show a great variety of famous musicians, such as Berlioz, Bériot and Triébert, of admirers from abroad, such as Degen, Hallberg and Schult, and of nobility, such as Lord Ashburnham, Baron d'Outhoorn and comtesse de Nadaillac Delessert. Other dedications concern members of his family, such as his spouse Louise Olive Pauilhé and his mother Anne Pierrette Dénéria. Remarkably, the composer makes no dedication to his father, Jean-Francois Coste. Coste is the guitar teacher of many pupils, whose names are mentioned in printed and in handwritten dedications, above all in his *Études* opus 38. Coste succeeds in carving out a position for himself in the upper-class of the social-cultural circles of Paris.

Social-political developments. The military career of his father takes Coste to Holland as a child of eight. He depicts his memories of this journey in his compositions *Les Bords du Rhin* opus 18, *Delfzil* opus 19 and *Le Zuyderzée* opus 20. The political riots in Paris in 1830 are reflected in his first edition, a chanson for voice and piano, *Aux Parisiens* WoO 2, in which he sides with the revolutionaries. He also composes a piece on the subject of the Crimean War in 1855, *Le Départ* opus 31, in which the French troops march through Paris after their victory. No trace of the revolution of 1848 can be found in Coste's music. No references to the Prussian invasion of Paris in 1871 appear in any of his compositions either, but the event does have an influence on his personal life in his decision to marry his pupil Louise Olive Pauilhé and move into her apartment at rue du Faubourg St-Martin no. 50, a street that is almost completely in ruins at that time. The decreasing number of concerts and pupils oblige him to accept a clerical post at the Caisse Municipale in 1855, where he remains until his retirement in 1875. In general, Coste does not give evidence of serious social-political commitment, but these events do have some influence upon his life and his works.

Status. In 19th-century Paris, Napoléon Coste achieves high status as a composer and a guitarist, in spite of the guitar's modest role in musical life. The instrument is fiercely attacked by some critics, which certainly does not help to improve its status. The artist enjoys high status, but his guitar is held in low esteem, the instrument is considered to be merely suited to be played by amateurs. Fétis divides the musical worlds into classes of performers, composers and teachers, of whom the teachers constitute the lowest class. He thinks there is also a fourth, highest class, the musical critic. In Fétis's view, Coste should belong to the first three classes, which is ambiguous, but quite realistic from a modern point of view. As a consequence of the widening gap between the Classical, serious music, and the popular, superficial music, Coste and his guitar belong to the middle-class of the musical society. In a series of articles, Liszt describes the social-cultural situation of the artist in society, and Coste fits in well. He may not be a travelling virtuoso like Paganini, he is an accepted and integrated artist, as reflected in his status.

Musical life

Coste's role. 'Great' music, orchestral works, opera and ballet, has assumed enormous proportions in Paris, and music for ensemble and solo instruments, such as piano and violin, can be heard frequently in the salons and salles of the piano manufacturers Érard, Herz and Pleyel. Coste plays in the smaller salons of Dietz, Duport and Petzold. The great flourishing of the benefit mixed-concert tradition in these salles and salons from around 1803 comes to an end after 1848, and the guitar's presence is ever diminishing. Coste joins in concerts in the salons; solo concerts for guitar do not exist at the time. From 1828 until 1839 in the musical magazines there was mention of some 78 concerts with guitar and Coste played in six of them. Between 1840 and 1855 they number 42, and Coste played in 17 of them. From 1857 to 1883 on, 32 concerts were mentioned, and Coste played in only nine of them. Of Coste's 33 concerts mentioned, 11 were private. The guitar is disappearing from the concert stage. The reception the music gets in the musical press describes Coste's performance style as being excellent, pure, gracious and crisp. His compositions are praised for their originality and for their exploring of unknown resources of the guitar. He receives these positive reviews throughout the course of his career.

After 1830 many of Coste's compositions are published by different publishers, such as Challiot, Richault and Schonenberger, showing that he also has good contacts in these circles. Up to 1878 a total of 35 of his works are published by publishers, from 1878 on 12 of his works are self-published, just like the two works with which he started in 1830, and ten of his works remain unpublished. These proportions are not unusual in this period.

Initially, the guitar was very popular for playing in domestic settings by amateurs, but eventually this also declines. Coste writes for this sort of amateur playing with editions of chansons and arrangements of Schubert's Lieder for voice and guitar, around 1838, and also with trivial works like quadrilles and Strauss's waltzes. He contributes little to the domestication of opera.

The low esteem in which music teacher are held does not prevent Coste to have a teaching practice, first at the pupils home, later at his own. The names of numerous pupils emerge from his dedications, many of whom are well-to-do members of the bourgeoisie, but in his final years he has fewer pupils, forcing him to accept an administrative job at the Caisse Municipale.

There are not many guitar makers in Paris, most luthiers are working in Mirecourt. The wave of mechanization brought about by the Industrial Revolution passes both groups by. The luthiers are conservative, the sales are on a small scale. But guitar maker Lacôte does not avoid innovation: he makes Coste's seven-string guitar, the heptacorde. Coste rejects the use of even more strings, as proposed to him by his Danish friend Degen, he thinks the guitar is perfect with seven strings. Nevertheless, he owns a multi-stringed theorbo, and a bass-guitar from the Louis XIV-era, as can be seen on his photograph, taken by Disdéri in 1867.

Position of the guitar. As the guitar is not part of the orchestra and also is not taught at the conservatoire, the instrument does not enjoy a high status. Methods for the instrument are not being authorized by the conservatoire, like those of Baillot, Kreutzer and Rode for the violin are, and those of Adam, Burgmüller and Czerny for the piano. The guitar belongs to the salles, the smaller halls. The general desire for louder instruments in the large halls contributed to this phenomenon. In this way, Coste restricts himself almost entirely to writing music for guitar solo, and chamber music to a certain extent. He also gives way to the eventually changing aesthetics of the guitar as an exotic Iberian instrument through the Hispanicism that emerges in his repertoire. While the guitar is certainly popular for domestic use for the accompaniment of chansons and opera selections, Coste's music of high artistic standard gets played less and less over the course of his lifetime. For this reason, Coste devotes some of his efforts to editions with a didactic and a commercial purpose. Another factor that contributed to the disappearance of the guitar from public musical life of the artistic classes is the literary image that emerges in serial novels, stories and opera. These images relegates the instrument's status to that of an ornament or a stage property. Finally, the supremacy of the piano is said to be the cause of the decline of the guitar. The aforesaid arguments may offer a more carefully balanced appraisal of this matter, the negative reviews in the musical press, the popularity in the lower classes, the Romantic literary image and finally the Hispanicism also share in the guilt here.

TRADITIONS

Classics. The influence of the Classical guitar composer's tradition on Coste emerges from his contacts with members of the Classical generation, especially Sor, and from his study of Carulli's Giuliani's and Sor's works. With respect to musical content, the social-cultural context has substantial implications for Coste's artistic works. He knows how to produce Romanticism in his music coming from the Classical musical tradition. The discussion of Coste's compositions for guitar solo shows how he develops himself into a Romantic guitar composer. He leaves the Classical principles behind in favor of a freer, more additive musical form. The formal characteristics and style elements that are already visible in the Classical guitarists generation, he uses with a greater intensity and freedom of melody and harmony, especially in the remarkable progressions and prolongations.

Musical theory. Coste lives and works in the era of the Romantics and the Romantic sentiment in way of life plays an important role in this, in addition to the music itself, being called Romantic. The tradition of musical theory influences on Coste's Romantic style. Fétis publishes his sketches of the history of harmony, in which the 'polytony' phase, as he calls it, has arrived in this era, with modulation as a central starting point, developing towards omnitony, in which the structure of sound is determined by intellect, rather than by tonal relations. Coste does not go that far in his works, but his music does fit in with the idea of polytony. In his own words, his study of counterpoint and harmony with Sor has led to high-quality compositions.

STYLE

Relations. From literature on musicological analysis of works by Chopin, Liszt, Berlioz and Schubert, a number of characteristics emerge that have served as the starting point for comparing this music with the way the Romantic style manifests itself in Coste's works. These characteristics have been defined in general terms, as far as the abovementioned composers are concerned, and made more specific where Coste's works are concerned. In the general elaboration of musical theory, many similarities have been discovered, many differences have emerged from the possibilities the guitar has to offer, especially in the way Coste has intensified the polyphony and the harmony in his approach to composition.

Characteristics. Coste's music shows a wide spectrum of characteristics of the Romantic style. These can be distinguished as 21 formal characteristics and style elements, which here have been developed into descriptions with examples, by way of the analysis of 45 of his works for guitar solo that could be dated. In doing so, it became clear that with and after the theme-and-variations genre, Coste does not work with the elaboration or continuation of themes, but prefers to compose using subsequential new musical ideas and sometimes using a varied repetition of musical sections, which tends to give his works an episodic or even rhapsodic formal structure, deviating from the Classical formal structures. Only a few sequences and imitating structures have been found in his music. The more Coste develops himself as a composer, the more Romantic characteristics emerge. But this development does not proceed linearly, there are successive waves of periods with very Romantic works and light Romantic works. The latter mostly have a didactic or commercial intention. The conclusion of the results of the analysis, with respect to formal characteristics and style elements, will be discussed in the following paragraphs.

FORM

1. *Phrase.* The phenomenon of the deviation from periodicity clearly emerges from Coste's works, few of his works are entirely periodic. The numerous occurrences of this feature which appears in 30 of his compositions give it a significant role as an aspect of Romanticism. This can also be recognized in his *25 Études de Genre* opus 38, which were conceived more on a musical basis than a merely technical one. Phrases of three, five, six and seven measures occur on a regular basis, sometimes due to the use of expolitio, the immediate repetition of a musical idea, such as in *Feuilles d'Automne* opus 41.

132 Style 1 phrase 4 expolitio

The shortened phrase accelerates the expectation of regularity, while conversely the lengthened phrase delays it, but the many occurrences of both obscure the regularity, giving the composer more freedom to shape his phrases in a musical form, independently of periodicity. With respect to this phenomenon, no development can be found whatsoever: many works show this deviation from periodicity, while many others do not. It contributes to the complexity of the musical form. In *Norma* opus 16, for instance, just one lengthened phrase is present in the introduction, and since the theme comes from Bellini, there is no argument to do otherwise. In the first part of *Grande Sérénade* opus 30, the phrasing is not determined by any particular scheme at all, the musical elements themselves determine the structure, reinforced by the long and slow 12/8 meter. The *Fantaisie symphonique* opus 28[b] and *La Chasse des Sylphes* opus 29 also have many deviations from periodicity. Coste uses the Classical, periodic Trio in eight of his works. The irregular phrase structure is important in all of his programmatic compositions. The most intensive application can be found in *Grand Caprice* opus 11 [i.e. opus 8], *Souvenir(s) du Jura* opus 44 and *Six Préludes* opus 49.

2. *Cadenza.* Coste inserts a cadenza 91 times in 30 of his compositions, rather frequently, one might say, including his études, surprisingly. This makes it an important phenomenon, suiting the genres he uses. The style element can be distinguished in four different types of manifestations, of which the one with glissandos is the rarest, even more so due to the fact that descending glissandos occur but seldom in Coste's works. The harmonic cadenza, the diatonic cadenza and those with or without chromatics, are distributed throughout his works. In the *Fantaisie symphonique* opus 28[b] all four are present.

133 Style 2 cadenza 2 chromatic with glissando

There are short ones, such as in *Lucia di Lamermoor* opus 9, part IV, measure 19, longer ones, such as in the same work in part I, measure 27, and very long ones, such as in *Étude* 6 opus 38, measure 18, accounting for half of the composition. There is no plausible explanation for the occurrence of one of the four types or another. Sometimes they all are present in a work, so there is no visible development in the use of cadenzas in the whole of his works.

With respect to the aspect of form in the music, instances with deviation from periodicity are far more numerous than the cadenzas, but both are important as far as Romanticism is concerned, in 30 of his works, in which the presence of the cadenza is more obvious than the occurrence of a shortened or lengthened phrase.

MELODY

3. *Figuration.* Diminutions, passages, runs, passages of thirds and octaves, rockets, parachutes, campanellas and tremolos have been distinguished as in 18 different types and described in the way they occur in Coste's music. When diatonic passagework is adorned with more melodic chromatics, the character of the music is qualified as being more Romantic.

134 Style 3 figuration 10 passage chromatic

The number of diatonic passages in Coste's works equals the number of passages with chromatics, while he seems to have some restrictions in the latter. In his later works, he uses more diminution, as well as more passages with melodic chromatics. Remarkable figurations with chromatic adjacent upper and lower seconds do not occur often, appearing in only 11 of his works, contributing to the Romantic character in just 6 cases, such as in *Delfzil* opus 19. Passages of thirds can be found often, the more notable passages of octaves appear less frequent, but the latter occur more often in the most Romantic works he wrote in the period he had achieved true mastery, between 1844 and 1856, in opus 15 to opus 31. Rocket figures, sometimes followed by parachute figures, are quite common in his works, including his main works, and above all in his later works, opus 39 to 53, after 1876. Coste seems to pay more attention to virtuosity in these works. Campanella, with or without legato, is very common in his music. This feature also has a virtuoso character and adds much color to the composition due to its open string sound. Coste only uses tremolo a few times, and it is not of any importance to the Romantic character of his works. Contrary to all expectations, considering the fact that he studied counterpoint, he uses melodic imitation quite rare in his works, appearing in only two works, opus 22 and 23, and in this way this phenomenon cannot be regarded as being a Romantic style element. This is different from the application of pedal point, sometimes with chromatic contrasts, which is a very effective means of expression for his composition style. Coste uses this in five of his most important compositions, with varying interpretations. Apart from this, one particular figuration can have a different meaning. The phenomenon of figuration, in all its different ways, add to the Romantic character in 25 of his works.

4. *Ornament.* Coste often uses ornaments in his works. Some of the ornaments described play an important role in the texture of the melody, while others do not. This aspect is important in 19 of his works. A remarkably large number of ornaments can be found in *Le Pirate* WoO 9, *Deuxième Polonaise* opus 14, and therefore also in *Le Passage des Alpes* opus 27, where opus 14 is reused. No relation to program music can be found. Coste often prescribes remarkable ornaments, such as a turn, a trill or a compact trill, but he uses the mordent only a few times.

135 Style 4 ornaments 1-7   136 Style 4 ornament 9 spark

This is different from the less notable appoggiatura and acciacatura with upper or lower second, which he prescribes quite intensively, 229 times in 35 of the works analyzed. The double turn also appears often, 130 times in 29 of the works analyzed. Moreover it is used in series 16 times. The striking portamento-glissando, called the 'spark', can be found 150 times in 34 works. Coste is obviously quite fond of ornamentation, most notably of the spark with its long-distance glissando. Ornamentation is not used for a goal in itself, by way of diminution in repetitions, or freedom of improvisation. Indicated very precisely, embellishments are usually intended for coloring, and when they occur in series, they add virtuosity to the melodic texture. In this way, ornamentation certainly contributes to the music's Romantic character.

5. *Idée fixe*. The idée fixe, introduced in Romantic music by Berlioz, can be found only four times in Coste's music. In *Deuxième Polonaise* opus 14 [i.e. opus 8] it is a rhythmic motif, preceding a varied continuing section, with small changes only. In *Le Tournoi* opus 15, it is a trumpet motif, returning in several successive parts, sometimes with changes, sometimes without. In *Meulan* opus 22, it is a rhythmic motif, followed by a passage in octaves, appearing in different ways. In *Fantaisie symphonique* opus 28[b] it is a harmonic motif, returning in three varied ways.

137 Style 5 idée fixe 3 harmonic motif

The idée fixe is of very low importance in Coste's works, he uses it only a few times. But when it does appear, it has a significant function.

6. *Chromatics*. Coste's preference for ascending chromatics as opposed to descending chromatics is evident in his works. This kind of chromatics with increasing tension is often used as #1 and #2, very often as #4, and less often as #5 and #6, in which he prefers alternating tones over suspended tones and passing tones. This also emerges in his use of chromatic scales, 49 times ascending as opposed to 36 descending. Remarkably, Coste rarely uses key-disturbing chromatics, such as the third and the seventh, while he does use key confirming chromatics with #2 leading to the third, and #4 leading to the fifth even more. Thus, in this respect, Coste remains quite conservative in his composition style, in deference to the Classical tonality, except that his melodic chromatics can principally be found in his early and less important works, and much less in his later, principal works.

138 Style 6 chromatics 3 augmented 2

139 Style 6 chromatics 4 augmented 4

There, he uses more harmonic chromatics and less melodic chromatics, resulting in a higher degree of dissonance, the alteration becoming more part of the structure. The predominant ascending chromatics has a tension-increasing effect, making his music even more animated in character.

Melody in Coste's works frequently involves chromatics, more so than ornaments. However, less key-disturbing chromatics than key-confirming chromatics can be found, so both are of equal importance, due to the fact that key-disturbing chromatics draws more attention. This is also the case with the many figurations, because there are almost just as many diatonic as chromatic figurations. Idée fixe does not play an important role in Coste's works.

Harmony

7. *Dissonance*. Of the chords with alterations, which are classed in the category dissonance, the diminished seventh chord plays the most important role, all the more so by the eight occurrences of a series of very remarkable diminished seventh chord inversions, such as in *Fantaisie de Concert* opus 6. They are present in almost all of Coste's works, contrary to the double-diminished chord, which has the function of a surprising progression, due to its enharmonic similarity to the dominant seventh chord, which is found a total of 69 times in 28 of the works. Coste uses the so-called V7/I chord 59 times in 20 works, but this is often used in Classical guitar music, in which way it is not determining the Romantic degree of his music. He uses the very notable augmented seventh chord much less, only 22 times in 9 works, and the not very notable half-diminished seventh chord, which does not involve any alterations to the key, he uses 31 times in 11 works. He employs the very dissonant hard-diminished seventh chord and the major seventh chord only two times, in *Etude* 19 and 25 opus 38, and the diminished seventh lowered ninth chord just once in *Etude* 25, probably as an experiment, because they do not occur elsewhere.

140 Style 7 dissonance 2 diminished seventh chord series

Dissonant chords other than these are rare in his works and need not be mentioned here, but it should be mentioned that dissonant chords are very important in 31 of his works, especially in his main works, of which the most are programmatic. The intensive use of chords in several degrees of dissonance shows Coste's desire to express Romanticism in harmony.

8. *Modulation*. The same tendency to express Romanticism can be found in Coste's use of modulation. The modulations described and undescribed here play a role in 28 of the compositions analyzed, sometimes a remarkable role, especially in his masterworks. Among these compositions, the programmatic ones are outstanding, this line of approach leads to intensive harmonic contrasts in these compositions. Remarkable contrasts can be found in *Le Passage des Alpes* opus 27, 28 & 40 *Fantaisie symphonique* opus 28[b], *La Chasse des Sylphes* opus 29, *Grande Sérénade* opus 30 and *Le Départ* opus 31, the five works Coste entered in the composition competition in 1856. Additionally, it should be noted that the *Études* opus 38 are also rich in modulations, occurring in 16 of the 25 pieces, and in *Etude* 19 Coste even explains to the player that a certain modulation is enharmonic.

Most occurrences of modulation are found in those to III major and those to lowered VI, such as in the Rondo of *Le Passage des Alpes* opus 40, along with the I-minor and I-major parallel modulations, which are not described here. The first two of these modulations can be called Romantic due to their chromatic character, the latter two cannot be called particularly Romantic. The modulation to V-minor, being a negation of the dominant, is often used as well. Pivot-tone modulations are found nine times, the typical major-minor modulation seven times, and the chromatic lowered II is found eight times.

But even if a certain modulation does not occur so often, it can still contribute to the harmonic intensity, nevertheless, such as lowered II, IV-minor, lowered V and VI major, which add chromatic coloring of the composition.

141 Style 8 modulation 3 major-minor to lowered VI

9. *Prolongation.* Occurring more than 100 times, the very identifiable chord prolongation, which appears in six different forms, is a very common feature in Coste's music. The descending variant is the most frequent, followed by the ascending and the ascending-descending combination. This style element is therefore of great importance in Coste's compositions. Then there often are the three-voice and four-voice chord progressions, including those on a pedal point, among which *Étude* opus 38 no. 17, 18, 19 almost entirely consists of three and four voices, which Coste even mentions in the subtitle of no. 19. He uses this composition technique deliberately and it can even be considered as a characteristic of his style.

142 Style 9 prolongation 8 three voices

The *Méthode* may have been the determining factor for his familiarity with this feature. Sor already uses it in some études, as does Giuliani in opus 12, and Coste applies this technique as early as opus 2, in 1829, before making Sor's acquaintance. For this reason, and through his full colored use of prolongations, Coste was able to find his own way in this technique, and he does not use them in a stereotype way, every progression is different and only the abstract harmonic reduction is common across instances. Variants of prolongation can be found in 32 of the works analyzed, the three- and four-voice prolongations aside. They give Coste's compositions an intense harmonic texture to. They are most numerous in *Les Bords du Rhin* opus 18, *La Source du Lyson* opus 47 and the *Études* opus 38.

10. *Cadence.* Chord progressions, being cadences, are also style elements of harmony. Coste shows a strong preference for passing dominants, sometimes with inserted tonic chords. In 27 of his works more than 100 of them can be found, giving the music a strong harmonic motion. A particular invention, which Coste uses just three times in *La Chasse des Sylphes* opus 29 and only once in *La Source du Lyson* opus 47, is the augmented dominant cadence, which is quite remarkable when used in an arpeggio form, where the fifth first appears as a resolution and is subsequently augmented as a suspension.

143 Style 10 cadence 1a series augmented dominant chords

IX — Finale

The Neapolitan sixth chord and the 'Trugschluss', deceptive closure regularly occur in his compositions, the first 34 times in 22 works, the latter 24 times in 20 works, but Coste's predilection is for the Moll-Dur chord he uses almost 100 times in 24 of his works. These are cadences that he uses principally in the flourishing time of his talent, after 1852. The open closure sometimes appears, mostly in transition to the following part of the composition. Plagal and modal cadences do not occur frequently in his compositions, only a single Picardy third has been found. Cadences contribute to the Romanticism of his compositions in 19 of his works, which are the most important and programmatic works in this case.

11. *Key.* Coste uses merely those keys that are that are predictable for guitar music, based on its tuning. He rarely uses keys that can be called Romantic due to the way they deviate from this principle, such as B-major, B♭-major, g-minor, c-minor and A♭-major, such as in *Fantaisie Armide* opus 4 already. Change of key is employed only in works of multiple parts and in collections, in such a way that the intent cannot be said to be Romantic.

144 Style 11 key 5 A♭

In pieces where he does use 'strange' keys, it does contribute to the Romantic character, such as in *Fantaisie Armide* opus 4, the *Méthode* IV, no. 13 p. 48, *Le Départ* opus 31, part II, and *Étude* 16 and 25 opus 38.

12. *Arpeggio.* Broken chords are common to all guitar music. Therefore, only the most original and distinctive ones have been identified here to be regarded as giving a Romantic character to Coste's music. Ten different arpeggios have been described as being characteristic, due to their voicing, the rhythm or the complexity. Arpeggios in a triple time and double time are the most frequent, where the melody is accompanied by a bass and is figured with the broken chord. His structural use of the right hand ring finger is evident in these arpeggios, differently from Sor. The more complex arpeggios with alternate strings, complementary rhythm, internal voicing and alternating ascending and descending directions are less frequent, but they have an important coloring effect in compositions.

145 Style 12 arpeggio 5 internal voicing

The arpeggio in the scherzo of *Soirées d'Auteuil* opus 23 should be mentioned in particular. Coste uses the notable tremolando seven times in four works, written out completely each time. Finally, the arpeggios in *Étude* 22, the tarantella, and *Étude* 23, the ostinato from opus 38, are particularly noteworthy, in spite of the fact that he uses them just in those works. Arpeggio plays a role as a style element in 17 of the works analyzed here.

The most important Romantic feature in Coste's works is his approach to harmony. Almost all of his works show different aspects of this element, and many of them do so in multiple ways, usually involving dissonance, followed in number by passing dominants and cadences. Modulation and prolongation also have a Romantic character, while arpeggio and key are less important.

METER

13. *Rhythm*. Of the rhythms described in the taxonomy, the three martial rhythms are the most remarkable. Despite the fact that Coste does not use all of them that often, they remain an important characteristic feature in his works. This is not the case with chord repetition: when this occurs, it is very notable, but he does not employ this device frequently. This is different from his use of free lyricism, of which many examples can be found in his *Souvenirs* opus 17-23 and *Le Passage des Alpes* opus 27, 28 & 40, for instance, but very few in the works he wrote for the competition in 1856, and then many again later in his works after 1872.

146 Style 13 rhythm 4 free lyricism

Coste uses genuine antimetry, i.e. other than triplets, in just one single case, in *La Chasse des Sylphes* opus 29. But there it also contrasts the use of pulsating rhythm of chords, sometimes in arpeggio, which he uses many times, just a few times in *Souvenirs*, and many times in his works for the competition where he employs them to impress the listener. In his works for guitar solo, Coste shows a strong preference for powerful rhythms, more so than for antimetry and free lyricism. This aspect plays a role in 15 of the works analyzed.

14. *Time*. Despite the fact that Coste writes many waltzes, the major part of his works is in double time, most of them in common time, 4/4. Yet, many double time measures with a triple time division occur regularly, with 6/8 appearing 24 times 6/8 and 12/8 appearing 4 times. In the triple time measures, the 3/4 time is the most frequent one, occurring more than 60 times, just as many as the 4/4 time, while the 3/8 time occurs 25 times, just like the 6/8 time.

147 Style 14 time 5 metrical shift

The 9/8 time is seen just once, in *Étude* 25 opus 38, and once there is a metrical shift, in *Caprice* opus 8. Taken into consideration if it occurs more than twice in a work, Change of time contributes to the musical unrest and is found in seven works, the most of them in *La Chasse des Sylphes* opus 29, *Grande Sérénade* opus 30 and *Le Départ* opus 31, three of his works for the competition in 1856.

15. *Tempo*. Coste uses many indications for tempo with almost 800 instances in the 45 works analyzed. Of the five main tempos, Coste uses andante and the allegro the most. Together with other indications for tempo, such as allegretto and andantino, he does not venture beyond the conventional boundaries. Only very few times does he opt for very slow and very fast tempos. He prefers to use decelerating interferences, such as standstill, disruption in the form of abruptio and fermata, such as in *Le Tournoi* opus 15, and rallentando, ritardando and plus lent, rather than accelerating ones, such as con fuoco, stretto, accelerando, plus vite, piu mosso and pressez. He makes use of 32 different Italian and French words, in various spellings. He also applies many indications for character that can have an influence on tempo, but are not defined as such. 'Exciting' musical terms, such as animato and resoluto constitute the majority of the 20 other terms, of which gentle ones, such as cantabile, dolce and grazioso are used the most often, out of a small number.

148 Style 15 tempo 1 Larghetto, 2 abruptio, 3 fermata

In just two cases does Coste prescribe metronome numbers, in *Adagio et Divertissements* opus 50 and in *Récréation du Guitariste* opus 51, although this instrument was available for purchase throughout Paris and was in common use. He prefers to give the performer some freedom for interpretation. The aspect of tempo plays a significant role in 25 works, especially in his masterpieces, but in just two of his *Souvenirs*, opus 17 and 20. Coste uses tempo indications very often to enhance the Romanticism in his musical works, especially in *Grand Caprice* opus 11 and in *Le Passage des Alpes* opus 27.

With respect to the aspect of meter in Coste's works, indications for tempo are applied the most frequently, and they are of great importance for the element of unrest in his music. Remarkable rhythms are less frequent. Changes of time cannot be considered remarkable as they are subsidiary to tempo.

Expression

16. *Dynamics*. The indications for dynamics outnumber those for tempo. There are 14 different ones, and 2800 occurrences have been found in the 45 works under consideration here. The indications piano, forte and mezzoforte are found in decreasing order of frequency in the successive works. Coste is quite conservative in this respect, he avoids the more extreme indications, using *pp* and *ff* but rarely, *ppp* and *fff* not at all. Remarkably, *mp* does not occur either, for a moderate dynamics he only uses *mf*. With respect to crescendo and decrescendo he prefers to use the signals < and > more often than the words themselves, with an increase of volume occurring more often than a decrease. He likes this effect of climax. Other indications, such as sforzato en rinforzando can be mentioned in this context, while they occur less frequently, but often nonetheless. These terms also have a climactic effect.

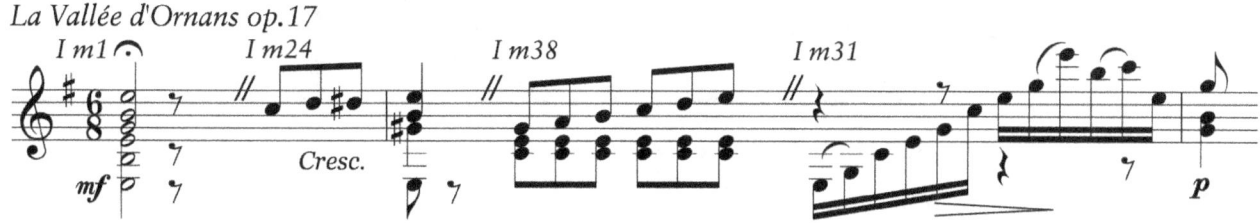

149 Style 16 dynamics 1 mf, 2 cresc., 3 <, 4 >, 5 p

Adhering to the criteria stated, there are 34 works in which dynamics play a role, Coste uses these indications frequently. The greatest intensity, with an average of one indication for dynamics for every two measures, is found in *Deuxième Polonaise* opus 14, *Le Passage des Alpes* opus 27 & 28, *Grande Sérénade* opus 30, *Le Départ* opus 31, *Andante & Menuet* opus 39, *La Ronde de Mai* opus 42, *Marche funèbre et Rondeau* opus 43 and *Quatre Valses* opus 48, thus mostly in his masterpieces, but not exclusively. Dynamics is an important means of expression in Coste's works.

17. *Articulation*. With respect to the formal characteristic of articulation, the legato is omnipresent. There are no works without this means of expression. For this reason the aspect of legato can only be considered to be Romantic when it surpasses the average number of one legato for every two measures. Double legatos have a lower number of occurrences, 46 times in 14 works, but they are very colorful in the music. Of the other seven indications Coste uses, occurring a total of 1,500 times in 45 works, the accent and the glissando are the most significant, the latter mainly due to its long-distance movement on the fingerboard, which is very characteristic for this music. The descending glissando is found only

once, in all other cases Coste uses this feature in its ascending form, increasing the tension. Coste does not prescribe staccato very often, but when he does, there is a series of notes that really have to be played with a short duration, such as in *Norma* opus 16.

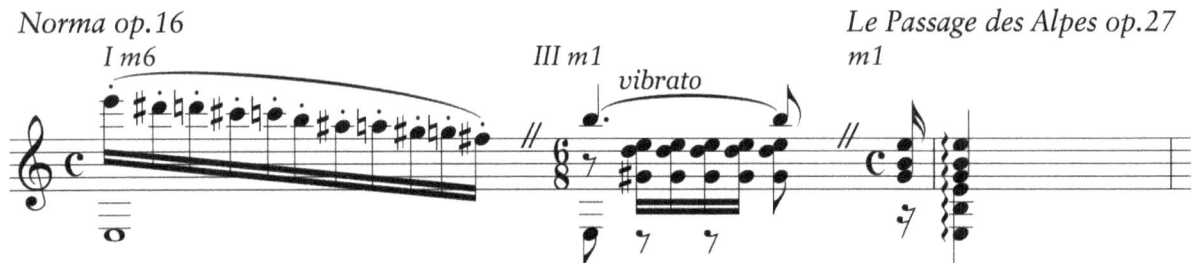

150 Style 17 articulation 6 portato, 7 vibrato, 8 arpeggiato

Portato does not occur many times and vibrato even less, but the latter is very notable when it is prescribed in the four works in which it is found. In *Le Tournoi* opus 15, Coste uses arpeggiato as a means of expression for the first time, then again in the *Méthode*, strikingly not in the *Souvenirs*, but then again in his works for the competition, such as *Grande Sérénade* opus 30, in which he imitates the Spanish guitar rasgueado in the Bolero. Later, he prescribes arpeggiato in *Divagation* opus 45, in which it has to be played using only the thumb, producing the same effect. The aspect of articulation is important in 13 of Coste's works.

18. *Rests*. In *Le Tournoi* opus 15, in 1843, Coste starts writing special indications for rests in countervoices, contrasting the melody. He continues to do so in his later masterpieces, of which most are programmatic. He uses this feature 18 times in ten works. The style element does not occur in works that are less Romantic. Its less notable form, the one with a stopped bass, has been found the most, 43 times in 13 works. This form is also less difficult from a technical point of view. In *Étude* 23 opus 38, the stopped pulsating bass with rests is remarkably used as an ostinato, but this is the only composition where it is written in this way.

151 Style 18 rests 4 mute accompaniment

Muting the accompaniment on adjacent strings of a melody is a difficult technique, which can be executed most effectively when the melody is played with a light vibrato. Coste uses these kind of rests seven times in five works. This feature appears most of all in *Le Passage des Alpes* opus 28[b]. It is important in 15 of his works. This way of writing rests can be called Romantic, but Coste does not use it so often. When he does, this means of expression is very notable in the composition.

Coste composes with many means of expression, especially with dynamics, to give the music power, and with articulation to give the music a remarkable sound. The aspect of rests does not occur frequently, but its application is striking, nevertheless, due to its surprising effect.

Romanticism

19. *Narration*. Many of Coste's compositions have a programmatic title, but only a few show extramusical references in the music itself. Here, heroics is evident in *Le Tournoi* opus 15, dramatics in *Lucia di Lamermoor* opus 9 and the donkey in *La Chasse des Sylphes* opus 29, all with references to literature.

IX — Finale

152 Style 19 narration 2 dramatics -ascending dim. 7 chords

References to nature have been found in *Le Zuyderzée* opus 20, with storm and lightning, and in *La Source du Lyson* opus 47, with babbling water. In some cases, a walking motion in the music can be connected to the title of the work, such as in *Ornans* opus 17. Coste's life in Paris and its surroundings is expressed in two of his *Souvenirs* in 1852, *Meulan* opus 22 and *Les Soirées d'Auteuil* opus 23. As such, there is no direct relation between the musical phenomenon and the extramusical reference, and finding narration in music is a matter of interpretation. In *Le Tournoi* opus 15, and in *La Source du Lyson* opus 47, this is indicated by the title, in other works this is not. It goes without saying that marches usually have a martial rhythm and tempo, Coste wrote nine of these. Similarly, waltzes naturally have a smooth turning motion, Coste wrote 11 of these, but the first mentioned references are the most evident along the spectrum of doubtfully to convincingly programmatic. Nevertheless, 20 of the 45 works that have been analyzed, can be called programmatic in a narrative way, of which ten have an evident extramusical reference.

20. *Folklore*. Five different ways of bourdon have been found in Coste's works. Clearly, this is an expression of folk music, and despite the fact that bourdon occurs just 34 times in 16 works, the phenomenon is very identifiable in its nature and has a notable influence on the expression of the music. A striking bourdon with an appoggiatura emerges in *Les Bords du Rhin* opus 18. The bourdon with figuration is most frequent, appearing 15 times in nine works. The bourdon with arpeggio and a pulsating rhythm can be found nine times in eight works. Coste writes the abovementioned arpeggiato mostly in folklore passages, making a connection between the two.

153 Style 20 folklore 5 arpeggio with legato

In *Grande Sérénade* opus 30, Coste's most important work, an excellent combination of arpeggio and legato emerges. Along with the style element no. 10 cadence with plagal and modal effect already mentioned, the occurrence of folklore makes a clear contribution to the Romanticism in Coste's music.

21. *Onomatopoeia*. Coste regularly imitates the sound of the trumpet and the horn, a technique already explained by Sor in his method, a total of 32 times in 12 works, but it is not always clear exactly what instrument is being imitated. Sometimes he writes the intended instrument above the notes, as in *Marche triumphale* opus 26, for instance, a piece that returns as *Le Passage des Alpes* opus 28[b]. In *Le Tournoi* opus 15 the sound of trumpets is also a self-evident application of melody and harmony.

154 Style 21 onomatopoeia 5 flageolet

Sor's oboe and harp are not reflected in Coste's music, but he does use the flageolet sound a great number of times, a technique explained by Coste in the *Méthode Coste-Sor*, with an example taken from *Ornans* opus 17. The flageolet has been found 47 times in 19 works. Just once does Coste imitate the sound of chimes, in *Les Cloches* opus 21, in which this sound is a structural part of the work. The phenomenon of onomatopoeia is an important feature in Coste's works, with its 82 instances in 22 works.

With respect to Romanticism in Coste's works, the narrative aspect plays a certain role. The features folklore and onomatopoeia are clearly present, while his use of rests less evident. All three items make an important contribution to the Romantic sentiment, as expressed in the works analyzed.

The importance of Romanticism in Coste's music is mainly determined by its harmonic aspects, in which complexity and intensity are central in his texture. His approach to altered chords and dissonants bears a relation to that of Liszt, his harmonic developments to that of Berlioz, his harmonic freedom to that of Chopin. His chromatic modulations, whether or not with pivot-tones, can be related to those of Schubert. In doing so, Coste is not in an isolated position, but he knows how to make his own mark in his work within this musical framework, nevertheless, and he makes an optimal use of the resources of the guitar. In his writing of melody, figurations are most determining, also in the virtuoso aspect. Without being an imitator, his musical texture has similarities with the figuration and passages of Chopin, his use of chromatics with that of Schubert, his technical demand with the virtuosity of Liszt, all this in connection with his perfect mastering of the instrument, of which he crossed the boundaries of limitation, pursuing Sor's foundations. With respect to the aspect of expression, dynamics and articulation contribute to the sentiment of his Romantic music in particular. In this regard, musical references can be made with Chopin's vocal portamento and Schubert's arioso. Few indications of exoticism have been found, except for the influences of Spanish music, which could be part of this feature. Coste's Romanticism is made of narration and folklore, as well as the use of rests, which contribute to its character. Historicism plays a role here, in his programmatic works in particular, which represent musical dramatics, comparable to Berlioz.

For all these different aspects, Coste can be placed in the center of the musical developments, taking place in the Romantic music in Paris, in the 19th century. He is aware of the musical ideas that live among his contemporaries, and has succeeded in shaping these into his music, in a very original and innovative way, taking his own position in this musical world. Being a modest composer for a modest instrument in his own words, Napoléon Coste has attained the summit of the Romantic guitar music in his masterworks, is the conclusion.

INTERPRETATION

This study into the formal characteristics and the style elements of Coste's music has been accompanied by an implementation of its results in performance practice. On the other hand, this experience has also had an influence on the descriptive analysis of 45 of Coste's works for guitar solo. The 21 different aspects, as described and classified in the taxonomy in the thematic catalogue, have been evaluated to their quality in the reality of practice, performance and recording. In the course of this practical implementation, it became clear that Coste's intentions and musical ideas were represented precisely in the imprint of his music in publications. In this way, the many indications for expression, and particularly in the harmonic intensity, evidently emerge from the performance practice. It goes without saying that no evidence whatsoever can be found for the way the guitarist and the audience in the 19th century may have played or have heard the music. However, historical performance practice is able to evoke a sound image that approaches the aesthetics of the time in a way accessible to the modern musician and audience, based on research into editions, reviews, opinions and principles, as expressed in the historical sources. In this way, this approach can be verified in theory and practice.

Coda

Of the three great composers of Romantic guitar music, with Mertz and Zani de Ferranti, Coste can be considered the most important. The volume of their works is not very different, it is the musical level that sets Coste apart here. Mertz has a preference for extravagance, bravura and virtuosity, without showing much musical content, such as melodic voicing and harmonic development. Zani de Ferranti shows more of these two Romantic criteria, he writes program music, but he fails to escape from the theme-and-variations genre and opera selections, to tackle the great musical form. In comparison, Coste surpasses both of these composers in musical standards, he knows how to create a multifaceted palette of Romantic elements, intensified even more by his complex harmonic texture. His works are diverse and varied and are attractive to the guitarist, the listener and the analyst alike, both in major form and in detail. From his early works on, which already witness some turbulence, he exhibits great development in the midst of the century through his masterpieces, with the compositions for the Makaroff competition playing the greatest role. His tendency towards virtuosity and complexity is of such a subtle and logical kind that his music attains a technical high standard, never at the cost of the ease of playing. Coste's musical expression, to which he devotes a great deal of attention, matures in his compositions. The Romanticism in his music has now been explained in a comprehensible way, by means of the analysis and the classification of the many criteria in this study.

With Coste, passing in 1883, the most important guitar composer vanishes from the Parisian stage. He joined musicians from Valenciennes who attained a high status in Paris, he associated himself with renowned musicians in artistic upper-classes, he had the major part of this works published with successful publishers, he had a private practice giving guitar lessons to pupils from well-to-do classes, and he participated in many mixed concerts in the salons and salles. Due to the decreasing interest in the guitar in art music, in favor of popular music, the guitar gradually vanished from the concert stage, helped along by the incessant negative reviews of the instrument on the part of certain critics. In this, the stereotypical image of the guitar as a Romantic stage property, and the rising phenomenon of Hispanicism, brought about by Spanish guitarists, also contribute to this development. Nevertheless, his works became dispersed throughout Europe, but were seldom played anymore, because of their assumed difficulty, and their use of the heptacorde, which had seven strings and a diapason of two octaves, which were prescribed in many works. Some works can be played with a scordatura, but in *Étude* 12 opus 38, and the *Fantaisie symphonique* opus 28[b] for instance, this instrument cannot be replaced. His compositions found their way into collections that were eventually found again in libraries in Copenhagen, London and Paris. Only his *Études* opus 38 have made their way into the canon of repertoire that came into existence during his time. Almost all attention goes to the school of Tárrega in Spain, the instrument is triumphant with Llobet, Pujol and Segovia, with whom the division between composer and performer became manifest. Some études remain on the guitarist's music stand, but Coste's major works drop out of sight. In 1981, Coste's compositions received renewed attention with Wynberg's complete edition with Chanterelle. His principal works are now included in concert programs and recordings, that can be found in the discography and the Thematic Catalogue. Coste's music is once again reviewed in articles, as emerges from the bibliographies. But no biography had appeared until now. This Biography with a Thematic Catalogue is meant to provide verifiable information, and systematic treatment of the life and works of the French guitar composer Napoléon Coste, in order to give him the place he deserves, along with J. K. Mertz and Marco Aurelio Zani de Ferranti, as one the great three of the Romantic composers in the history of the guitar, if not the greatest.

155 In honor of Napoléon Coste

Appendices

Chronology			
Ch	year	Coste event	social-cultural context
I	1754	Jean François Coste born in Cléron April 23	Louis XV (1715-1774) - École militaire, Panthéon
	1774	J.F. Coste 1st marriage Claudine Pretet November 8	Louis XVI (1774-1792)
	1789	Julie born 1783; Jeanne-Etienne born 1785; Jeanne-Pierrette born ?	French Revolution July 14; Directoire (1789-1799)
	1792		First Republic September 22; *Marseillaise*, Republican calendar: An I, 1 Vendémiaire
	1793		Louis XVI decapitated, Louvre opened
	1795		Conservatoire founded, Gossec, Méhul, Cherubini
	1797		Carulli in Paris
	1799		Consulat & Empire (1799-1814); Napoleon Bonaparte
	1800	Claudine Pretet dies, leaves 3 daughters	
	1801	J.F. Coste 2nd marriage Anne Pierrette Denéria January 18	
	1802	Cathérine-Françoise born in Besançon January 24	
	1803	J.F. Coste chosen mayor of Amondans February 21	
II	1805	Napoléon Coste born in Amondans June 27	Bonaparte - defeated at Trafalgar
	1807	J.F. Coste dismissed as mayor	
	1809	Coste & family in Ornans	Carulli *Méthode*
	1813	J.F. Coste & Napoléon in Langeoog in French army February 27	Bonaparte defeated at Leipzig; Giuliani *Méthode*
	1813	J.F. Coste & Napoléon in Delfzijl in French army November 19	Allies occupy Paris
	1814	J.F. Coste & Napoléon leave Delfzijl in French army May 23; in Lille June 9	Restauration (1814-1824); Louis XVIII; Bonaparte to Elba; escapes; start *Bibliographie de la France*
III	1815	J.F. Coste & Napoléon & family in Valenciennes; Nap. Coste falls ill, age 11	Bonaparte defeated at Waterloo June 18
	1820		Molino in Paris
	1823		Liszt in Paris, concert Théâtre-Italien March 7, 1824; Rossini in Paris
	1825	Nap. Coste teacher in music	Aguado in Paris; Carulli *Méthode* op. 241
	1826	Coste? concert in Valenciennes May 15	Sor returns to Paris
	1827	Coste concert Valenciennes March 24; gives guitar lessons *Méthode* Carulli Coste? concert Condé April 16; in Valenciennes April 17	Fétis starts *Revue musicale*; Gymnase musical; Weigl *Emmeline* in Paris
	1828	Coste & Sagrini concert Valenciennes February 17; Coste concert Valenciennes December 14	Schultz in Paris; Berlioz *Waverley*; Habeneck starts Concerts du Conservatoire
IV	1829	Coste in Paris, rue Bleue, 28; concert in Gymnase musical March 27	Marescot *La Guitaromanie*
	1830	*Aux Parisiens* WoO 2, December 25; *Weigl* op.2; *2 Quadrilles* op. 3	Monarchie de Juillet; Opera Veron; Sor *Méthode*, Huerta, Regondi in Paris
	1831	Coste concert salons Petzold April 17	Carulli op. 328 to Coste; *Armide* in Opera; Chopin, Paganini in Paris
	1832	Coste rue du Vieux Colombier, 25; *Armide* op. 4;	Aguado tripodison; Schmidt in Paris; cholera epidemia; Zani *Niaiserie*
	1833		Heugel starts *Le Ménestrel*; Bellini *Norma* in Paris; *Il Pirata* in Paris
	1834		Schlesinger starts *Gazette musicale*
	1835	Coste concert Grenelle 21 II ; 7th string; *Flandres* op. 5; J.F. Coste dies 12 IV	Gare de l'Ouest; *Revue et Gazette musicale*; Sor & Liszt concert; Legnani in Paris
	1836	*La Romanesca* [op. 19b]	Zani in Paris; *Cachucha* in Opera
	1837	Coste rue de l'Échiquier, 23; *Fantaisie Meyerbeer* op. 8; *Il Pirata* WoO 9	Strauss in Paris; Escudier starts *La France musicale*
	1838	Coste & Sor, concert Hôtel de Ville January 15, salon Duport April 10, salon Pape April 22; *Strauss Walses* op. 7; *Fantaisie Norma* op. 16; *Chansons* Schubert arr.	Aguado leaves for Madrid December 20
	1839	Coste inherits guitar Sor August 11	Sor dies July 10 ; Donizetti *Lucia di Lamermoor* in Opera;
V	1840	Coste concert salon Petzold February 16; salle Herz March 29; salle Herz July .. Caprice op. 8; Rondeau op. 12; Cachucha op. 13 to pupil Louise Olive Pauilhé; Savoyarde arr.	Fétis Esquisse de l'histoire de l'harmonie; Paganini dies in Nice; Szczepanowski in Paris
	1841	Coste concert Société December 12; Lucia Lamermoor op. 9; Scherzo & Pastorale op.10	Carulli dies February 14; Halévy Le Guitarrero in Opera;
	1842	Coste concert Duport April 8; Heptacorde April <3; A.P. Denéria dies February 11 Grand Caprice op. 11; Deuxième Polonaise op.14	
	1843	Coste concert Souffleto April 18; Souffleto April 25; Bernard April 28; Société May 25; Bodin November 5; Le Tournoi op. 15; member Freemasons Lodge June 27	
	1844	Deux Quadrilles WoO 5	Lacôte in Exposition Universelle; Courbet Le Guitarrero
	1845		Castellacci dies, Caceres in Paris

	1846		Paris Gare du Nord
	1847		Molino dies
	1848		Deuxième République; Second Empire (1848-1870)
	1849		Vignas in Paris; Aguado dies in Madrid
V	1851	Méthode Coste-Sor	Makaroff visits Coste
	1852	Coste rue de Calais, 11; Coste concert Freemasons February 15; Société December 14 Sept Souvenirs op. 17-23; Sérénade WoO 13	Haussmann works (1852-1870); Napoleon III (1852-1870); Bosch in Paris;
	1853		Carcassi dies; Crimean war (1853-1856)
	1855	Coste concert Société February 11; Lebouc April >22; Société August 12; works at Caisse municipale; Consolazione op. 25; Gran Duo WoO 8	Degen visits Coste, photograph; Exposition Universelle
VI	1856	Coste in Makaroff competition, Brussels; Passage Alpes op. 27, 28; Fantaisie symphonique op. 28[b]; Chasse Sylphes op. 29; Grande Sérénade op. 30; Le Départ op. 31	Makaroff competition in Brussels December 10
VII	1857	Coste concert Société October 11	Meissonnier dies May 24
	1858	Coste rue Blanche, 100	Ciebra in Paris
	1859		Bosch, Zani in Paris
	1860	Mazurka op. 33[a]	
	1861	Le Montagnard op. 34[a]; Concertino WoO 4?	Huerta in Paris
	1862	Coste concert Société November 9; Marche et Scherzo op. 33[b]; Sonate WoO 14	
	1863	Coste falls, injures left shoulder	
	1864	Chanson L'Enfant au Berceau WoO 7	Sokolowski in Paris
	1866	Fantaisie de Concert op. 35	
	1867	Coste photograph Disdéri; 10me Solo Klosé arr. Coste	Triébert dies; Exposition Universelle
	1868	Regrets et Consolations op. 36	
	1869	Cavatine op. 37	
	1870	Coste boulevard Rochechouard, 84; Coste secretary Freemasons Lodge	Troisième République (1870-1900); Paris under siege by Prussians
	1871	Coste marries Louise Olive Pauilhé February 11; rue du Fbg St-Martin, 50	capitulation Paris, commune
	1872	25 Études op. 38	Regondi dies in London May 6
VIII	1874	Coste concert Société November 8; injures left shoulder July 30	Huerta dies June 19
	1875	Coste & Pauilhé travel to Jura, Ornans, Source du Lyson; Coste pensioned from Caisse municipale	
	1876	Coste concert Société July 9; Andante & Menuet op. 39; Le Passage des Alpes, Rondo op. 40; Feuilles d'Automne op. 41; La Ronde de Mai op. 42; Marche funèbre & Rondeau op. 43; Souvenir(s) du Jura op. 44	
	1877	Coste concert Société August 12; Divagation op. 45; Valse favorite op. 46	Legnani dies in Ravenna August 5
	1878	Coste concert Société April 14, June 9; La Source du Lyson op. 47; 4 Valses & 6 Préludes op. 48 & 49; Lolla WoO 10; Petit Ange rose WoO 11	Zani de Ferranti dies in Pisa November 28
	1879	Coste concert Société September 14; sells theorbo; Adagio et Divertissements op. 50; Sor L'Encouragement arr.	
	1880	Coste 32 concerts Théâtre Français January 1; Récréation du Guitariste op. 51; Livre d'Or op. 52	severe cold in winter '79-'80, -23,9 degrees
	1881	Six Pièces originales op. 53	Tárrega in Paris May 25
	1882	Coste & Pauilhé in Choisy-le-Roi July 11; Coste falls ill November 8	
	1883	Coste dies in Paris January 14, buried January 15	Gustave Doré dies January 14

Concerts, Coste in and around Valenciennes - Chapter III 1815-1828 [6]			
date	artist	location [source]	work
May 15, 1826 Monday	Coste?	concert in St-Amand. 'La musicomanie... jeune guitariste de Valenciennes' Il a manqué six souscripteurs pour complétér....la douzaine' prix 1fr p.p. [PA May 20, 1826, no. 467, p. 165]	
March 24, 1827 Saturday	M. Coste	concert in salon Chinois, Valenciennes, artistes et amateurs Société Philharmonique with ball 'Le talent... Les variations de M. Coste ont fait un très grand plaisir, mais la guitare joue toujours un triste rôle dans un concert' [PA March 14, 1827, no. 552, p. 526; March 28, 1827, no. 556, p. 545]	? Opus 2 *Famille Suisse* Weigl
April 16, 1827 Monday	Coste?	concert in Condé, same Italian female singer as April 17. [MHV April 1827, concert]	
April 17, 1827 Tuesday	Coste?	concert in salon Chinois, Valenciennes, with Italian female singer and artists from Valenciennes, with ball - No. 6. Solo de guitare [PA April 14, 1827, no. 561, p. 568]	
February 27, 1828 Wednesday	Sagrini & Coste	concert in Valenciennes, with ball: 'Coste a dignement rivalisé avec lui' en 'à Valenciennes pas de beau concert sans bal, à Paris pas de bonne fête sans gendarmes' grandes variations concertantes pour deux guitares' [PA February 20, 1828, no. 651, p. 59-60; March 1, 1828, no. 654, p. 70]	Giuliani op.130 [CGu], must be op.35
December 14, 1828 Sunday	Coste	concert in Valenciennes, amateurs et artistes Soc. Phil. in Salon Chinois 'on s'est trouvé dans le ténèbre'. [PA December 6, 1828, no. 734 p. 480; December 10, 1828, no. 735, p. 486; December 17, 1828, no. 737, p. 495]	

Appendices   253

Concerts, Coste in Paris - Chapter IV 1829-1839 [6]			
date	artist	location [source]	work
March 27, 1829, Friday	Coste	Gymnase musical 'On lit dans l'Observateur des beaux-arts... variations exécutées avec une précision parfaite' [EFV April 1, 1829 no. 767] [OBA March 29, 1829 p. 416]	Weigl-variations?
April 17, 1831, Sunday	Coste a.o.	salons de Petzold 'concert, M. Costes, jeune guitariste distigué, à huit heures, plusieurs de nos meilleures artistes [Fig. April 13, 1831 p. 4] [LesF2 p. 166] z	
February 21, 1835, Saturday	Coste a.m.o.	Théâtre de Grenelle, troisième légion, solo de guitare, 'entendu avec un plaisir toujours nouveau...' [LP February 20, 1835, p. 66; March 5, 1835, p. 68] Mme Deligny voc, MM. Fontaine vl. comp, Chaulieu pf. comp, Vandenberghe [vl], Nicole [vla], Benazet vlc, Delacour [cb], Pollet org, Castelli	
January 15?, 1838	Sor & C.	salle Saint-Jean, Hôtel de Ville, concert de Mlle Sardi, Sor & Coste 'duo sur la guitare... n'a pas produit un grand effet.' [LFM January 21, 1838, p. 6]	duo Sor Divertissement opus 62?
April 10, 1838, Tuesday	Coste & Sor a.m.o.	salons Duport 'guitariste très distigué' Duo avec Sor; [MHV April 19, 1838, p. 198] [LFM April 1, 1838, p. 7; April 15, 1838, p. 5.] [RGMP May 6, 1838 p. 190] Mme D'Hennin voc, Bouchers voc, MM. Magliano voc, Schianski voc, Walcknaer voc; Tilmant frères vl vlc, Dauprat, Sor gt, Koken [i.e. Cokken fg], Lecointe vl, Gouffé, Burgmüller pf, Concone pf	Fantaisie Norma op.16, Sor Souvenir de Russie? Deuxième Polonaise op.14 Hummel/Giuliani
April 22, 1838, Sunday	Sor & Coste a.o.	salons Pape Mlle Mazel, 'une des plus intéressantes soirées' [LFM April 29, 1838, p. 7] [JefB5 p. 10] Mlle Mazel voc, D'Hennin voc, Bertuccat, MM. Lafont vl, Sor gt, Pantaleoni, Chaudesaigues	Sor Souvenir de Russie?

Concerts, with guitar in Paris - Chapter IV 1828-1839 [72]			
date	artist	location [information]	source
January 26, 1828	Sor a.o.	salon Dietz, solo de guitare	RM tome 3, 1828 p.40-41; JefB1 p. 85
1828	Schultz a.o.	Schultz & Hummel concerto de Giuliani;	RM tome 3, 1828 p. 142-143
1828	frères Schultz	salons Pape guitare tierce, M. Léonard S. Ajax de la guitare	RM tome 3, 1828 p. 155-157
April .., 1828	Sor a.o.	concert Mme Robert 'morceau guitare'	RM tome 3, 1828 p. 302-303
April 20, 1828	Sor a.o.	salle rue Clery 'Sor a du talent', Liszt	RM tome 3, 1828 p. 303-304
May 7, 1828	Sor a.o.	salons Dietz, Sowinski pf	RM tome 3, 1828 p. 300
May 18, 1828	Sor	concert bénéfice, 'exécution étonnante'	RM tome 3, 1828 p. 402-403
March 11, 1829	Sor a.o.	salons Dietz, Sowinski pf, 'les honneurs', 'grand talent... petit instrument'	RM vol.5,1829 p.115, 181
April 11, 1829	Sor a.o.	hôtel Fesch, Liszt, Panseron	RM vol.5,1829 p.240, 276-7; JefB1 p. 85
April 14, 1829	Ch. Sor a.o.	salon Dietz, Aguado, [Carlos] 'brillante exécution'	RM vol.5,1829, p.304
April 28, 1829	Sor a.o.	salle rue Chantereine, 'Herz pf, Sentinelle'	RM vol.5,1829 p.349-351
March 27, 1830	Sor a.o.	salons Pape, Sowinski pf	RM vol.7,1829-30 p
March 30, 1830	Sor a.o.	salle Taitbout, Panseron voc, 'dommage' Fétis: 'instrument ingrat'	RM vol.7,1830 p.215, 267 JefB5 p9 JefB6p11
April 13, 1830	Regondi	concert Edmond Huillier	DelM1 p. 21 LesF2 p. 141
April 27, 1830	Regondi	salon Dietz, petit artiste haut de trois pieds... guitare;	RM vol.7, 8 V 1830, p.16-18
April 28, 1830	Regondi	salons Chantereine, à 8.30 a.o. Jules Regondi, guitariste age 7 ans	LesF2 p.143
May 1, 1830	Regondi	salons Dietz	DelM1 p. 21 LesF2 p.148
June 20, 1830	Regondi	salle Menus-Plaisirs	DelM1 p.21
July 17, 1830	Sor a.o.	salons Erard, concert Mme Farrenc, Hummel, 'grand plaisir'	RM vol.8, 1830 p. 346, 376 LesF2 p.148
July 30, 1830	Sor	concert-payment Louis-Philippe	JefB1 p. 102
August 26, 1830	Regondi	Athenée musical	DelM1 p. 21
August 31, 1830	Regondi a.o.	salle Cléry	LesF2 p. 149
December 26, 1830	Huerta	salons Petzold, à 8, 10 Fr	LesF2 p.150
December 2, 1830	Schmidt		DelM1 p. 21
January 16, 1831	Huerta	salle Taitbout, 'guitariste espagnol; compositions pas très bonnes'	RM vol.8, January 22, 1831, p.330-332
January 16, 1831	Regondi	salons Stoepel, guitariste de 8 ans se fit entendre	LesF2 p. 154
January 16, 1831	Schmidt	salons Pape	DelM1 p. 21
February 4, 1831	Schmidt a.o.	salons Dietz, Schmidt et Kreipl ont joué la guit.	LesF2 p. 155
February 20, 1831	Regondi	salons Petzold, le jeune Regondi, guit.	LesF2 p. 156
March 13, 1831	Regondi	salle Taitbout, Regondi pièces de guitare, Paganini div. morceaux	LesF2 p. 159
March 24, 1831	Regondi	salons Petzold, Regondi 8 ans soirée	LesF2 p. 161
March 27, 1831	Sor a.o..	salons Dietz, Sor& Aguado, benefice Miró pf, soirée Espagnol, 'faible impression'	RM vol.5, No.9, April 2, 1831, p.71 JefB5 p. 10
April 9, 1831	Regondi	salons Petzold, Regondi	LesF2 p. 165
April 18, 1831	Schmidt	salons Dietz, M. Schmidt, guitariste	RM April 23, 1831 p.96
April 19, 1831	Sor a.o.	salons Dietz, Sor 'nouveau succès'	RM April 23, 1831 p.96 JefB5 p. 10
May 3, 1831	Regondi	Théâtre du Gymnase-Dramatique, Malibran	DelM1 p. 21
May 26, 1831	Huerta	Hôtel-de-Ville, Huerta	LesF2 p.170

date	name	subject	source
July, 23 1831	Huerta	salle Chantereine, Huerta	LesF2 p.171
October 27, 1831	Huerta	Athenée Musical, Huerta	LesF2 p 174, RM November 19 p.329-330
November 27, 1831	Regondi		DelM1 p. 21
December 17, 1831	Huerta	Hôtel Fesch, Huerta	LesF2 p.177
December 25, 1831	Sor	salons Petzold, Sor	JefB1 p.102, LesF2 p 178
December 27, 1831	Huerta	salon de Klepfer, Huerta	LesF2 p.179
January 7, 1832	Huerta	salons Dietz, soirée musicale de M. Wagner 'merveilleuse agilité	RM vol.6, No.49, January 14, 1832 p. 394
February 15, 1832	Sor a.o.	salon Dietz, benefice Miró pf, 'jolies choses'	RM vol.6, No.3, February 18, 1832 p. 22 JefB5 p. 10
February 28, 1832	Sor	annonce concert	RM vol.6, February 25, 1832, p. 31
March 17, 1832	Huerta	salons Petzold, solo de guitare, grand effet	RM March 24, 1832, p. 61-62, ColR p. 18
March 21, 1832	Aguado a.o.	salle Chantereine, Aguado & Sor, tripodison	RM December 1832 p.54, 62?
June 15, 1832	Huerta	salons M. Dietz; triomphe, étrange accompagnement	ColR p. 18
December 14, 1832	Huerta	salle Taitbout, plusieurs morceaux	RM December 8, 1832, p.359; ColR p. 18
December 16, 1832	Huerta a.o.	concert historique Fétis, Aguado, Sor, villancico Soto de la Puebla, huit guitares	ColR p. 19
January 21, 1833	Sor a.o.	Sor & Masini concert	JefB1 p.103, RM 1833, p.412
March 19, 1833	Huerta a.o.	salons Dietz, Huerta, Liszt, Panseron, éxcité l'étonnement'	RM vol.7, No.8, March 25, 1833, p.61, ColR p. 19
March 24, 1833	Sor a.m.o.	concert historique, Sor luth, Castellacci? mandoline, Huerta guitare, Mme Dorus	JefB1 p.103, RM vol.7, No.8, March 25, 1833, p.60
March 25, 1833	Sor	salons Petzold, concert annoncé	RM 1833 p.61
April 2, 1833	Huerta a.m.o.	Berlioz bénéfice Smithson	ColR p. 19
April 23, 1833	Huerta	salons Dietz, applaudi	RM April 25, 1833, p. 103; ColR p. 19
May 2, 1833	Huerta	concert Berlioz	ColR p. 19
June 16, 1833	Sor e.a.	coirée Europe littéraire, Sor a fait plaisir, Berlioz	RM vol.7, No.19, June 18, 1833, p.150
April 29, 1834	Sor a.o.	Hôtel de Ville, Mme Duflot et M. Haumann, Nous regrettons que Sor, le guitariste, n'ait pas fait choix d'un morceau plus brillant	LM vol.2, no. 23, May 4, 1834, p. 4
February 18, 1835	Sor a.o.	salons Duport, 'bien applaudis' M. Dorus	RM vol.9, No.8, February 22, 1835, p.61-62
April 14, 1835	Aguado a.o.	Théâtre Italien, Concert Historique Fétis, Aguado luth, Vilhancico, acc.t de six guitares; La Romanesca Baillot	RM vol.9, No.15, April 12, 1835 p.117, 125-6 LM April 19, 1835 p. 4
May 7, 1835	Sor a.o.	salons Pleyel, Sor, Liszt	LM May 3, 1835 p. 4, May 10, 1835 p. 4
October 11, 1835	Legnani	Legnani, grande finale	LM October 18, 1835 p. 4
November 29, 1835	Sor a.o.	Sor & Aguado e.a. bénéfice Legnani cassé le bras descendant d'une voiture	GM no.48, 1835 p.395, 403 JefB5 p. 10
March 16, 1836	Zani de Ferranti	salle Pleyel, Ferranti a.o.	LM March 13, 1836
April 2, 1836	Zani de Ferranti	Zani de Ferranti & Hertz a.o.	JefB1 p.104, 114; Revue de Paris p.133??
c. April 15, 1836	Sor a.o.	Sor & Aguado	MosW3 p.133
April 24, 1836	Sor a.o.	Sor & Aguado, duo, bénéfice Sor, Aguado piédéstal	RGMP March 1836 p.136 JefB5 p. 10
May .., 1836	Sor a.o.	salons Pape, soirée musicale Mansui	JefB1 p.104, Revue de Paris vol.29 p.136
January 29, 1837	Sor a.o.	Mlle Dupont, rue des Bons-Enfans,	LM January 29, 1837
July 2, 1837	Milliet	guitare à 25 cordes, nous a fait entendre, bureaux Ménestrel	LM July 2, 1837

References - Chapter IV 1829-1839			
year	name	subject	source
1828/29	Coste	rue Bleue no. 28 chez l'auteur	Aux Parisiens, Pn VM7 44.830
1830	Weigl Regondi	La Famille Suisse -Emmeline in Opéra comique salons Petzold, solo de concert, petit Jules	RM, June 5, 1830, p. 150-153 Fig. 28 April 1830, p. 3
1831	Carulli	i Duo op. 328 dédié à Monsieur Coste	TorM p. 636; Kk Ms. 248 mu 7910.2682
1831	Gluck	Armide in Opéra	LesF2, p. 56, 222
c.1832	Zani de Ferranti	Niaiserie op. 21 La Famille Suisse	Br, Fétis 2.917 C7
1832	Coste	rue du [Vieux] Colombier no. 25	Fantaisie Armide op. 4 Kk Ms. 52 mu 7908.0987
1835	J.F. Coste	† April 12, 1835 Valenciennes	VAL, fonds mod., série E: Etat civil, E1, R53
1837	Coste	rue de l'Échiquier no. 23 chez l'auteur Strauss in Paris	Fantaisie de Concert op. 6 Pn [K.7130 De Haan, Weesp, 1983, vol.9, p.274.
1838/9	Aguado	leaves for Madrid	JefB8 p. xviii
1839	Sor Donizetti	† July 10, 1839 Paris Lucia di Lamermoor in Opéra	LFM, July 14, 1839, p. 390 NG, 1980 vol. V, p. 555

Appendices

Concerts, Coste in Paris - Chapter V 1840-1855 [*new date] [17]			
date	*artist*	*location [information]*	*work*
* February 16, 1840 Sunday	Coste a.o.	salons Petzold M. et Mme Laurelli,, matinée, solo de guitare [LM February 16, 1840, p. 4, February 23, 1840, p. 4] Mme Féron voc, Alessi voc, Caudron voc, Laurelli pf, MM. Laurelli cl, La Rivière hrp, Achard	
March 29, 1840 Sunday	Coste a.o.	salle Herz, 'grand solo, intitulé *Rêverie*, allegro martial et final' [EFV March 24, 1840, p.790 Moschelès] [LFM March 1, 1840, p.99; April 5, 1840 p.147; Rêverie, Hummel] [RGMP April 19, 1840, p.277] [LM March 22, 1840, p. 3 grand concert; April 5, 1840, p. [3], Souvenir de Russie, élève] Mme Wideman voc, élève gt MM. Verroust ob, Grard, Dancla jeune JP vl, Concone comp	*Caprice* op.8 Hummel/Giuliani; *Grand Divertissement* voc,vl,gt Moschelès; Sor *Souvenir de Russie*
*April .., 1840 didn't take place	Coste a.m.o.	concert historique, Fétis, salle Herz, musique ancienne [LM April 19, 1840, April 26, 1840, ce concert n'a pas pu avoir lieu] [cf April 14, 1835 Aguado RM April 12, 1835 p. 117, 125-126] MM. Carcassi, Coste, Roehder, Vimeux, Losset, Charpentier, *Air de danse* Huerta	*Vilhancico* 16ᵉ E six voix femmes, six guitares
*July .., 1840	Coste a.o.	salle Herz, 'omission importante: M. Coste, guitariste distingué, s'est fait entendre avec succès...' [LFM July 26, 1840, p. 279] Mme Wideman voc	
* December 12, 1841	Coste a.o.	Société des Enfants d'Apollon, Fantaisie et variations pour la guitare, composées et exécutées par M. Coste [DecM p. 157] Mme Sabatier voc, M. Nicou-Choron voc	op. 16 Norma
*April <3, 1842	Coste	Coste guitariste d'un grand mérite, guitare sept cordes, beaux succès [LM April 3, 1842 p. 2]	
April 8, 1842 Sunday	Coste a.o.	salons Duport, Coste deux fois, continuateur des Sor, des Aguado [EFV April 5, 1842 dimanche 8 avril] [MHV April 1842] [MA p.184] [RGMP IX, No.16, April 17, 1842, p.168 M. Coste, l'héritier] [LFM April 17, 1842 Coste première force, duo élève] Mlle élève gt [i.e. Mlle Caroline Montigny?] M. Lecointe vl	morceau de piano Hummel *Scherzo & Pastorale* op. 10?
* April 18, 1843 Tuesday	Coste	Souffleto, guitariste d'un grand mérite, annonce concert [LM April 9, 1843 p. 3, i.e. April 25, 1843?]	
April 25, 1843 Tuesday	Coste	salons Soufleto, à 8 heures du soir [LFM June 23, 1843, p. 143] [RGMP April 23, 1843]	
*April 26, 1843 Wednesday	Coste a.m.o.	Salle Bernard, guitariste distingué, annonce définitivement, à 2 heures, mercredi 25 avril [sic = April 26] [LM April 23, 1843 p. 4] Mme Masone, Vavasseur, Nordet MM. Verroust ob, Coken fg, Coche fl/vlc, Dancla vl, Masone, Soler ob	
* May 25, 1843 Thursday, ascension	Coste a.m.o.	Salle du Conservatoire, Société des Enfants d'Apollon, [DecM p. 78] [LM May 28, 1843 p. 3-4] Mme Rossi-Caccia voc, Potier, MM. A. de Kontski pf, A. Dupont voc, Triébert ob, Romedienne ca, Thys, Maneira dir, Soler ob, Aumont vl, H. Potier pf	*Le Tournoi*, fantaisie pour la guitare, op. 15
* November 5, 1843 Sunday	Coste a.o.	cours de piano M. Bodin, élèves, l'habile guitariste [LM November 12, 1843] Mlle Bulté voc,	
February 15, 1852 Sunday	Coste a.m.o.	salle des concerts, boulevard Bonne Nouvelle, 'congres européen', loge maçonnique des Frères-unis-inséparables, [RGMP February 22, 1852, p. 58-59] MMe Ponchard voc, Tillemont voc; MM. Petiton fl, Blainville ob, Triébert ca, Ponchard pf, Franck pf, L. Dancla vl, Panseron pf, Wartel voc, Bussine voc	*La Sentinelle* Choron, arr. pfs/vl/gt Hummel
* November 14, 1852	Coste a.o.	Société des Enfants d'Apollon; *Sérénade* pour hautbois, clarinette et guitarre [DecM p 178] MM. Triébert ob, Klosé cl	*Sérénade* WoO 13 new work?
* February 11, 1855	Coste a.o.	Société des Enfants d'Apollon; *Romance sans parole* [DecM p. 183] M. Triébert ca	*Romance* op. 25
April, >22, 1855	Coste a.m.o.	annonce soirée 'L'habile guittariste, plusieurs compositions' salle Lebouc? [WynS1 VIII Intr.] [RGMP April 22, 1855, p. 127] [cf LFM May 6, 1855] Mme Blanc de Labarte; MM. Paulin voc, Lebouc vlc, Guerreau vl, Ney vl, Triébert ob, Klosé cl	
* August 12, 1855 Sunday	Coste a.m.o.	Société des Enfants d'Apollon, petit concert de famille [LFM August 26, 1855, p. 267] [DecM p. 184] Mme Farrenc pf comp, Bianchi voc, MM. Cuvillon vl, Lebouc vl, Ney vl, Lindau voc, Bourgeois de la Richardière gt	*Grand Duo* WoO 8 *Fantaisie symphonique* opus 28[b]?

Concerts, with guitar in Paris - Chapter V 1840-1855 [25]			
date	*artist*	*location [information]*	*source*
January 25, 1840	Huerta	concert?	ColR p. 22
March 23, 1840	Huerta	salons Richter	ColR p.22
April < 12, 1840	Szczepanowski	guitariste polonais	LFM April 12, 1840, p. 155
April 11, 1840	Huerta	concert sérieuse et comique salle Herz dans la partie instrumentale	LFM April 5, 1840, p. 147; April 12, 1840, p. 155
April 13, 1840	Huerta	à une heure, partie instrumentale	LFM April 12, 1840, p. 155
April 4, 1840	Mlle Lovrins	concert société d'Emulation, petite guitariste de dix ans	RGMP June 7, 1840, p. 331
June 11, 1840	Huerta	salons rue Montigny 5	RGMP June 7, 1840; ColR p. 22
June < 27, 1840	Huerta	guitare borné ressources, Jota aragonese, adieu	RGMP June 28, 1840, p. 360; ColR p. 23
July 3, 1840	Huerta	concerts Vivienne, soirée	ColR p. 23
July 8, 1840	Huerta	dernière soirée	ColR p. 23
July 10, 1840	Huerta	salon Pavillon Henri IV	ColR p. 23
March 1, 1841	Szczepanowski	chez M. Herz; Un guitariste en 1841!	LFM February 14, 1841, p. 55; March 7, 1841, p. 78
April 18, 1841	Szczepanowski	chez M. Herz, à deux heures	LFM April 11, 1841, p. 127
April < 9, 1843	Szczepanowski	plusieurs fois cet hiver	LFM April 9, 1843

February < 16, 1845	Caceres	'Spanish' concert sérénade espagnole	RGMP February 16, 1845, p. 52
April 17, 1845	Huerta	salle Pleyel	RGMP April 20, 1845; ColR p. 24
May 27, 1845	Huerta	salons Hesselbein	RGMP June 1, 1845, p. 179
July 2, 1845	Huerta	salons Hesselbein, musicien exceptionnel,	RGMP July 6, 1845, p. 222; ColR p. 25
February .., 1846	Huerta	salons Hesselbein, improvisations ingrat instrument	RGMP February 22, 1846, p. 62; ColR p. 25
March .., 1846	Huerta	salons Hesselbein	RGMP March 22, 1846, p. 92; ColR p. 25
April 12, 1846	Huerta e.a.	concert adieu, avec grands artistes de l'Académie royale de musique	RGMP April 12, 1846, p. 118; ColR p. 26
May < 9, 1847	Séron	soirée, petite virtuose de huit ans, petits doigts roses, instrument dépaysé	RGMP May 9, 1847, p. 158
October < 14, 1849	Vignas	temps perdu, chante chansons, *Jota aragonese*	RGMP October 14, 1849, p. 325
April < 18, 1852	Cibra & Caceres	salons Tivoli, guitare est morte, guitare revive	RGMP April 18, 1852, p. 123
July < 8, 1855	Wiesen	salle Hesselbein, guitariste due roi de Bavière et roi des guitaristes	RGMP July 8, 1855, p. 312

References - Chapter V 1840-1855			
year	name	subject	source
1840	Fétis	Esquisse de l'harmonie	RGMP, 1840, transl. Arlin
1841	Halévy Carulli	*Le Guitarrero* opera † February 14, 1841 Paris	LFM January 24, 1841, p. 25-27 Torta, 1993, p. XII, XXV
1842	Blanchard	*Les guitaristes* article	RGMP October 2, 1842, p. 395-396
1843	Gozlan Coste	*La guitare* article Frères Unis Inséparables freemasons lodge	LFM August 6, 1843, p. 238 http://www.mvmm.org/m/docs/coste.html
1844	Lacôte Courbet	Exposition de l'industrie musicale *Le Guitarrero* portrait	LFM May 12, 1844 inlay Bajou, 2003, p. 46-47
1845	Castellacci	† 1845 Paris	ZutJ2 p. 62
1847	Molino	† 1847 Paris	BonP p. 241;
1848	France	Deuxième République	Michelin, Guide Paris, 1997-1998, p. 12; PD p. 23
1849	Aguado	† December 20, 1849 Madrid	PerP p. 129
1851	Makaroff	visits Coste	Guitar Review no. 3, 1947, p. 56
1852	Coste Bosch Haussmann	rue de Calais no. 11 in Paris 'king of the guitar' start works	*Souvenirs* BdlF, July 17, 1852, p. 466 Pujol, 1960, p. 88 Michelin, Guide Paris, 1997-1998, p. 13
1853	Carcassi	† January 16, 1853 Paris	BonP p. 67; ZutJ2 p. 59
1854	Napoléon III	Crimean war	PD p. 24
1855	Coste Degen	Caisse Municipale Paris visits Coste, makes photograph, play together	Jaworski, 1992, p. 76-77 Møldrup, 1997, p. 131

Concerts, Coste in Paris - Chapter VII 1857-1872 [*new date] [2]			
date	artist	location [information]	work
*October 11, 1857	Coste e.a.	Société des Enfants d'Apollon, *Le Départ*, fantaisie pout la guitare, composée et exécutée par M. Coste [DecM p. 188] Mlle Charles, MM. With, Alday, Ney, Pillet, Gouffé	*Le Départ* opus 31
*November 9, 1862	Coste e.a.	Société des Enfants d'Apollon, *Sonate* pour guitare et cor, composée par M. Coste, exécutée par M. Triebert et Coste [DecM p. 197] MM. Triébert ca, Coste gt	*Sonate* WoO 14 *Fantaisie Sonate* opus 34[b]?

Concerts, with guitar in Paris - Chapter VII 1857-1872 [20]			
date	artist	location [information]	source
June < 6, 1858	Ciebra	salle Beethoven, fort jolie fantaisie, *Carnaval de Venise*	RGMP June 6, 1858, p. 190
March 29, 1859	Bosch	soirée Herwyn, guitariste est remarquable	RGMP April 3, 1859, p. 115
May < 1, 1859	Zani de Ferranti	atelier peintre célèbre, infortunée guitare, victime du piano	RGMP May 1, 1859, p. 142
February < 5, 1860	Zani de Ferranti	salle Beethoven, le plus étonnant guitariste, lutter contre ressources exiguës	RGMP February 5, 1860, p. 43-44
March 20, 1861	Huerta	Théâtre-Italien, le beau concert	LM March 17, 1861, p. 127
January < 21, 1864	Sokolowski	qui n'avait jamais paru devant un publique français, rabattre nos préjuges	RGMP January 21, 1864, p. 26
January < 31, 1864	Sokolowski	Le nouveau guitariste, concert Junck, complètè les plaisirs	RGMP January 31, 1864, p. 35
February < 28, 1864	De Folly	soirées Marmontel, guitare victime de l'injustice, réhabilitation	LM February 28, 1864, p. 102
April < 3, 1864	Sokolowski	société Winnen-Orlowska, guitariste polonais, un autre but à ses efforts	RGMP April 3, 1864, p. 106
January 9, 1865	Huerta a.m.o.	un guitariste à seul	ColR p. 49
March 14, 1865	Sokolowski	guitariste, concours de Lavello, salle Pleyel, un instrument ingrat	LFM March 12, 1865, p. 83; RGMP March 19, 1865, p. 89
April 27, 1865	Huerta	salle Pleyel, concours Pommaraye	LM April 9, 1865, p. 152
June 11, 1865	Bosch	séance mensuel Enfants d'Apollon, *La retraite*	DecM p. 203

Appendices

August 13, 1865	Richardière	séance mensuel Enfants d'Apollon, duo Leduc pf/gt Decourcelle/Richardière	DecM p. 204
January 31, 1867	Huerta a.o.	Cirque artistique	ColR p. 49
February 17, 1867	Huerta a.o.	concert Midoz pf, bolero	ColR p. 49
July < 21, 1867	Vailati	Théâtre International, guitariste [aveugle, mandoline]	RGMP July 21, 1867, p. 231; May 3, 1863, p. 141
August 8, 1869	Richardière	séance mensuel Enfants d'Apollon, duo Molino pf/gt Decourcelle/Richardière	DecM p. 214
July 9, 1871	Richardière	séance mensuel Enfants d'Apollon, *valse espagnole*	DecM p. 217
February 21, 1872	Bosch	jolies choses, instrument ingrat	RGMP February 25, 1872, p. 63

References - Chapter VII 1857-1872			
year	name	subject	source
1857	Meissonnier	† < May 24, 1857 Paris	RGMP May 24, 1857, p. 175
1858	Coste-Degen Coste	lettre Coste-Degen June 15, 1858 r ue Blanche no. 100	Århus Statsbiblioteket Ms 27b RonN p. 25
1861	Coste	Loge Maçonnique des Frères Unis Inséparables 18ᵉ	CotR p. 141
1863	Coste-Degen Coste	lettre Coste-Degen October 17, 1863 injures left shoulder, difficulty in playing	Århus Statsbiblioteket Ms 27b Coste-Degen October 17, 1863
1867	Triébert	Hommage mémoire, séance mensuel Enfants d'Apollon	DecM p. 210
1870 <1871	Napoléon III France Coste Coste	July 19, 1870 Prussian war September 4, 1870 Troisième République Loge Maçonnique des Frères Unis Inséparables 18ᵉ secrétaire boulevard Rochechouard no. 84 > 1858 <- 1871	Winkler Prins, 1963, vol. VII, p. 699 Paris, Michelin, 1997-1998, p. 13. CotR p. 141 RonN p. 26
1871	Prussia Coste	capitulation and invasion Paris, commune, 'semaine sanglante' February 11, 1871 acte de mariage Coste Pauilhé, rue du Faubourg St-Martin no. 50	Winkler Prins, 1963, vol. VII, p. 699 Pap Série V2E 5Mi 3/210.
1872	Regondi	† May 6, 1872 London	RGMP May 26, 1872, p. 167

Concerts, Coste in Paris - Chapter VIII 1873-1883 [*new date] [7]			
date	artist	location [information]	work
* November 8, 1874	Coste a.o..	Société des Enfants d'Apollon, *Introduction et polonaise; trois études* pour la guitare, composés et exécutés par M. Coste. [DecM p. 226] Mme Coedes-Mongin pf, M. Lebouc vlc	*Souvenir(s) du Jura* opus 44 *Deuxième Polonaise* opus 14? *Etude* opus 38
* July 9, 1876	Coste a.o..	Société des Enfants d'Apollon, *Andante et Scherzo* pour la guitare, composés et exécutés par M. Coste [DecM p. 231] MM. Lefort voc, Lebouc vlc	*Andante et Scherzo* opus 39?
* August 12, 1877	Coste a.o..	Société des Enfants d'Apollon, *Divagation* opus 45 [Coste-Hallberg, August 23, 1877]	*Divagation* opus 45
? January 14, 1878	Coste? a.m.o.	Théâtre de la Porte-Saint-Martin, concert M. Cressonnois, (avec M. Coste) [RGMP January 20, 1878 p. 22] Mlle Berthe Thibault voc	*la Nuit de Noël* de Reber
* April 14, 1878	Coste a.o..	Société des Enfants d'Apollon, *L'Ange rose*, mélodie de M. Coste, chantées par Mme Germance [DecM p. 236] Mlle Lebrun pf, Mme Germance voc, M. Thomé pf,	*Le Petit Ange rose* WoO 11
* June 9, 1878	Coste a.o..	Société des Enfants d'Apollon, *Le chant des Sylphes*, fantaisie pour la guitare, composée et exécutée par M. Coste. [DecM p. 236] Mlle Miclos pf, Mlle Crower voc	*La Chasse des Sylphes* opus 29
* September 14, 1879	Coste	Société des Enfants d'Apollon, *Adagio, scherzo, menuet et mazurka* pour la guitare, composés et exécutés par M. Coste. [DecM p. 240]	*Adagio et Divertissements* opus 50
* January 1, 1880	Coste	foyer Théâtre-Français, 32 x accompaniment Cherubini	*Valse favorite* opus 26; Cherubini, *Romance d'Essex à Élisabeth*,

Concerts, with guitar in Paris - Chapter VIII 1873-1883 [3]			
date	artist	location [information]	source
April 3, 1873	Bosch	salle Duprez, effets inattendus, La Retraite	RGMP April 6, 1873, p. 110
March 30, 1874	Bosch	guitariste espagnol, charmantes choses, instrument ressources restraintes	RGMP April 5, 1874, p. 110
May 25, 1881	Tárrega	Odeon, 200 year Calderón	PujE2 p. 89-90

References - Chapter VIII 1873-1883			
year	name	subject	source
1874	Huerta	† June 19, 1874 Paris	ColR p. 51
1875	Coste	Coste & wife travel to Jura, Ornans, Source du Lyson	Coste-Hallberg, October 18, 1878
1877	Legnani	† August 5, 1877 Ravenna	BonP p. 104
1878	Zani de Ferranti	† November 28, 1878 Pisa	RGMP December 15, 1878, p. 407

Concerts, Frères-Unis Inséparables			
date	*artist*	*location [information]*	*source*
February 15, 1852 Sunday	Coste a.m.o.	Salle des concerts, boulevart Bonne Nouvelle, 'congres européen', loge maçonnique des Frères-unis-inséparables, MMe Ponchard voc, Tillemont voc; MM. Petiton fl, Blainville ob, Triébert ca, Ponchard pf, Franck pf, L. Dancla vl, Panseron pf, Wartel voc, Bussine voc	RGMP vol. XIX, no. 8, February 22, 1852, p. 58-59
December 20, 1857 Sunday		charmant concert, Mme Guerra voc, MM Léon Triébert, Méhul, Ravina, Godefroid hrp, Roger. Organisé par Panseron, président de Colonne d'hamonie; 500 Fr pour les orphelins	RGMP vol. XXIV, no. 52, December 27, 1857, p. 422
February 10, 1861 Sunday		matinée, orphelins, quintettes, M. Michot voc, Godefroid hrp, Mlls Hamackers voc, Lapommeraye voc	RGMP vol. XXVIII, no. 7, February 17, 1861, p. 49
March < 30, 1862		matinée, orphelins, Mme Cabel, Delle-Sedie, Seligmann, Ravina, Triébert, Jancourt, Delibes?	RGMP vol. XXIX, no. 13, March 30, 1862, p. 103
March < 29, 1863		matinée annuelle, salle du Grand-Orient, Mme Viardot, MM Naudin, Delle-Sedie, Dorus, Taffanel, Jancourt, Ravina, Triébert, Mlle Whitty, orphelins, Association Artistes musiciens	RGMP vol. XXX, no. 13, March 29, 1863, p. 100-101
March < 6, 1864		grande matinée musicale, orphelins, Triébert, Jancourt pf, Ravina, Mlle Barnard pf, Godefroid hrp, Mme Grisi voc, Mario voc, Delle-Sedie voc,	RGMP vol. XXXI, No. 10, March 6, 1864, p. 75-76
February 26, 1865 Sunday		matinée musicale, salle des fêtes maçonniques au Grand Orient de France, orphelins, MM Naudin, Delle-Sedie, Mmes Charton, Scalese, Frezzolini, Dorus, Triébert, Leroy, Baneux, Jancourt, Sighicelli, Peruzzi pf	RGMP vol. XXXII, no. 10, March 5, 1865, p. 75
February 4, 1866 Sunday		grande matinée musicale, salle du Grand-Orient, orphelins, MM Dorus, Triébert, Leroy, Baneux, Jancourt, Sighicelli, Mlle Grossi, Zeiss, Vitali, MM Baragli, Delle Sedie,	RGMP vol. XXXIII, no. 10, March 11, 1866, p. 75
March 3, 1867 Sunday		concert annuel, salle du Grand-Orient, rue Cadet, orphelins, Mlle Nilsson, Carreno pf, MM Delle Sedie, Pagans, Morini, Sighicelli vl, Loys vlc,	RGMP vol. XXXIV, No. 10, March 10, 1867, p. 77
March 15, 1868 Sunday		matinée musicale au Grand-Orient de France, orphelins, Mme Norman-Neruda, Ophelia-Nilsson, Bloch, Barthe-Banderali, M Lamoury vlc, Morini voc, Rosenhain voc,	RGMP vol. XXXV, No. 12, March 22, 1868, p. 90-91
March 21, 1869	airs suédois	matinée musicale, salle du Grand-Orient, orphelins, Mlle Nilsson, M Delle Sedie, Jaël et femme, Mme Barthe-Banderali voc, Palermi, Dunckler voc, Sighicelli vl, Triébert,	RGMP vol. XXXVI, no. 14, April 4, 1869, p. 116-117
April 30, 1870	chanson suédoise	matinée musicale, salle du Grand-Orient, orphelins, Alboni, Mlle Nilsson, Delle-Sedie, Palermi voc, Sighicelli vl, Loys vlc, Lavignac pf	RGMP vol. XXXVII, no. ??, March 6, 1870, p. 77
March 15, 1874		matinée musicale, chaque année, salle du Grand-Orient, orphelins, MM Gardoni, Delle Sedie, Sighicelli, Wormser, Mlle Belval, Mme Barthe-Banderali	RGMP vol. XLI, no. 12, March 22, 1874, p. 77

Appendices

Dedications				
name	addition	work	work	Etudes
Adan	directeur Bruxelles	op. 31		op. 38 no. 23
As(h)burnham, Lord Charles	élève	op. 3		op. 38 no. 21
Audéoude, Jules		op. 51		
Berlioz, Hector	compositeur	op. 15		
Bériot, Ch. de		op. 25 [Pn]		
Cerclier	ami			op. 38 no. 12
Daly, Mlle Marie	élève	op. 47		
Degen, Søffren	ami	op. 28[b]	op. 41	op. 38 no. 9
Delaby, M.	élève de Triebert	op. 35		
Dénéria, Anne Pierrette	mère	op. 5		
Deshaulles, Mme		op. 9		
Digne, M.				op.38 no.12 2 ede
Douillez, Mlle Albertine	élève	op 6		
Fallon, Mlle Cornélie				op. 38 no. 11
Fernandez de Cordova, M. Sassary	élève	op. 16		
Garancelle, M. de				op. 38 no. 13
Gozzoli, M. V,		op. 46		op. 38 no. 20
Gruel, M. Léon	élève	op. 42		op.38 no.13 2 ede
Hallberg, Adolph	ami	op. 53	duetto	
Hitz, Mme				op.38 no.6 2 ede
Harris, Mlle				op. 38 no. 17
Holm, M. J.G. (de Copenhague)	ami	op. 39		op. 38 no. 7
Janicot	ami			op. 38 no. 3
Larrieux	élève de Triebert	op. 35		
Lefort, M. Jules		Lolla		
Lelorin, Mlle Clarisse	élève	op. 12		
Makaroff, M. Nicolas de	concours	op. 30		op. 38 no. 25
Marsoudet, Mme (de Satins)	née Victorine Oudet	op. 44		op. 38 no. 8
Martin, M. N.	élève	op. 14	op. 29	
Meurphy, Édouard [ms]	[de] son.. maître	op.10		
Molard, Sigisbert	ami	op. 37		
Montigny, Mlle Caroline	élève	op. 10		op. 38 no. 19
Montigny, M. Paul (de)	directeur hôpital	op. 4	op. 11	
Nadaillac Delessert	madame la comtesse	op. 27, 28, 40		
Outhoorn, M. Baron d'	monsieur le baron	op. 50		
Page, Mme				op. 38 no. 15
Panco, M. C.				op. 38 no. 6
Pascal, Mme Ad.	née Valentin	op. 2		op. 38 no. 18
Pauilhé, Mlle Olive	élève / femme	op. 13 / op. 43		op. 38 no. 14
Petetin, M. E.				op. 38 no. 1
Petiteau, Mme Amica		l'Enfant au Berceau		
Richardière, M. de la				op. 38 no. 2
Schult(z), M. J.	de Stokolm	op. 45		op. 38 no. 24
Schult, F.	ami		duetto	
Segura, Pedro		op. 48, 49		
Triébert, Charles-Louis, hautboiste	ami (concertino, op.34[a])	op. 25 + 36	op. 34[a] WoO 4	
Ulenbrock, M. Jean Reussner	élève (de Riga)	op. 17-23		op. 38 no. 16

The table shows the names of those to whom works are dedicated indicated in alphabetical order, along with the works that are concerned. In some cases there are more works, sometimes dedications are changed in a second edition. The dedications can be divided into 32 gentlemen and 15 ladies. Apparently Coste had eleven pupils for sure.

Addresses for Coste in Paris

1	C2	1829 Paris, rue Bleue no. 28, (op. 2, 3?) (Aux Parisiens, Chez l'auteur prix 2f00) [BF December 25, 1830-52, p. 834] exists no more since 1859, Coste, prof. de guit. [LesF2 p. 229] [Planque p. 63] DelM1 p. 22] Arr. 9 Fétis, in 1818. [HilJ p. 202]
2	B4	1832 Paris, rue du [Vieux!] Colombier no. 25, près la rue de Seine, (op.4, 5, 13) (chez l'auteur op. 4 prix. 4f50) [BF August 18, 1832, no. 33, p. 472]
3	D2	1837 Paris, rue de l'Echiquier no. 23, (op. 6, 7, 9, 10, 11, 12, 14? 15, 16) (chez l 'auteur op. 6 prix 5f00) [BF August 26, 1837, no. 34, p. 424] [HilJ p. 457]
4	B1	1852 Paris, rue de Calais no. 11, (op. 17 - 23, 25&36, 27, 28 & 40, 29, 30, 31) [op. 17-23, BF 1852, no. 29, p. 432]
5	B1	1858 Paris, rue Blanche no. 100, [RonN p. 25]
6	C1	1858 <1871 Paris, boulevard Rochechouard no. 84, [RonN p. 26] (op. 33[a] - 33[b] - 34[a]? - 35)
7	D2	1871-1883 Paris, rue du Faubourg St-Martin no. 50, (op. 38, 39, 41 - 53), Sor op. 34 l'Encouragement) [HilJ p.512]

Publishing

a	A2	Challiot (Édouard), rue St.Honoré no. 336, Feb.1839-1845. (op. 15 E.C.138 = 1844; op. 16) [BF 1843, no. 35, p. 452] [HopC p. 24-25] [DevA p. 98-99] [SouC2]
b	C3	Chatot (Émile), rue de la Feuillade no. 2, place des Victoires, 1861-1865. (L'Enfant au Berceau 1864) [HopC p. 25] [DevA p. 102-103]
c	C2	Colombier (Jean F.), rue Vivienne no.6, au coin du passage Vivienne, Nov. 1838-1851. (op. 25+36 ob/vl et pi) [HopC p. 29] [DevA p. 114-116] [SouC2]
d	B2	Costallat et cie., chaussée d'Antin no. 15 et boulevard Haussmann, 40, 1895-1905 (*Ave Maria, La Sérénade* - Schubert) No.17560 = 1912) [DevA p. 120-123] [HopC p. 31]
e	C2	C., Egasse de, copiste, rue Lamartine, (op. 4, 6, 11, *La Ronde de Mai*)
f	C2	La France Musicale, Bureaux de. rue Neuve St. Marc no. 6,(La Petite Savoyarde)
g	C2	Girod (Etienne), Editeur, successeur de Launer, boulevard Montmartre no. 16, 1855-1919. (op. 29, 30, 31) [HopC p. 52] [DevA p. 191-2] [SouC2]
h	D2	Grus, Léon, boulevard Bonne Nouvelle no. 31, en face le gymnase (dramatique), 1863-1884. (op. 9 L.G. 3231 = ? later edition) [HopC p. 54] [DevA p. 202-203]
i	D3	Hirsch, I., rue N.D.de Nazareth no. 27, (op. 33[a]) Harand, see Lemoine [HopC p. 56] [DevA p. 209-210] [SouC2]
j	B4	Katto, J., rue des S.ts Pères no. 17, 1864-1884. (op. 47, Lolla, Le Petit Ange Rose) [HopC p. 66] [DevA p. 246]
k	C2	Lacôte, rue de Louvois no. 10, (op. 5 - Richault) (BF 1835-28, p. 448)
l	B2	Latte (Bernard), boulevart des Italiens no. 2, au coin de la galerie de l'Opéra ou, au coin du passage de l'Opéra, 1838-1850. (BF 1841-44 op. 9 B.L.1845 = ?1838-1839?) [HopC p. 68] [DevA p. 256-8] Launer, see Girod
m	C4	Lemoine (François) ainé Harand success., rue de l'Ancienne Comédie no. 20, 1851-1875. (op. 34[a] - H.1292(2) = 1861) [HopC p. 56, 80-81] [DevA p. 209-210, 274-282] [SouC2]
n	C2	Magnier ainé, Imprimerie, rue Lamartine no. 44, (op. 20) [SouC2]
o	C2	Richault (Charles Simon), boulevard Poissonnière no. 16, au 1ᵉʳ, Paris [Arr. 2 Leconte O8], 1825-1841. (op. 2, 3, 5, 7, 10, 12, 13, 19[b]) [HopC p. 104] [DevA p. 362-9] [SouC2]
p	C2	Richault (Charles Simon), boulevard Poissonnière no. 26, au 1ᵉʳ, Nov.1841-okt. 1862. (Op. 2 later edition) [HopC p. 104] [DevA p. 362-9]
q	B2	Richault (Charles Simon), boulevard des Italiens no. 4, Ockt.1862 - June 1898. (op. 27, 28, 40, 38, 39) [HopC p 104] [DevA p. 362-9]
r	C2	Romagnesi, Henri, rue Vivienne no. 21, 1828-1831 (op. 2) [DevA p. 372] [HopC p. 106]
s	C2	Schonenberger (Georges), boulevard Poissonnière no. 28, Oct. 1843- Jul. 1875. (op.17-23, *Méthode*) (Sor Op. 53, 63) [HopC p. 110] [SouC2]
t	D3	Triébert Frédéric), 6, rue de Tracy, square des Arts et Métiers, 1866-1878, (op.25+36, 35, 37) [DevA p. 415] [SouC2]

Salons and Salles [LF2 p.124]

A	C2	Salle Bernard, 17 rue de Buffault [Coste April 25, 1843]
B	C2	Salle Bonne Nouvelle, 18-20 boulevard Bonne Nouvelle [Coste February 15, 1852]
C	C2	Salle du Conservatoire, Menu-Plaisirs (2 r. du Conservatoire) [Coste December 12, 1841; May 23, 1843; December 14, 1852; February 11, 1855; August 12, 1855; October 11, 1857; November 9, 1862; November 8, 1874; July 9, 1874; August 12, 1877; April 14, 1878; June 9, 1878; September 14, 1879]
D	C3	Salons Duport, 83 rue Neuve-des-Petits-Champs [Coste April 10, 1838; April 8, 1842]
E	B3	Théâtre Français (Comédie-Française, place du Théâtre-Français,rue de Richelieu) [Coste January 1, 1880] Théâtre de Grenelle, 55 rue de la Croix-Nivert, 1829, 1300p [Coste February 21, 1835] [outside map, left of A5]
F	B2	Salle Herz, 48 rue de la Victoire, 1838-1885 [Coste March 29, 1840; July 1840]
G	C2	Salle Saint-Jean de l'Hôtel-de-Ville, Gymnase musical, boulevard Bonne-nouvelle, [Coste March 27, 1829] Athénée musical, 1829-1841 [Coste January 15, 1838]
H	C2	Salle Lebouc, 12 r. Vivienne [Coste April 22, 1855]
J	C3	Salons Pape, 10 rue de Valois, et 19 rue des Bons-Enfants [Coste April 22, 1838]
K	C2	Salle Petzold, rue Grange-Batelière, 4 [Coste April 17, 1831; February 16, 1840]
L	C3	Salons Souffleto, 171 rue Montmartre [Coste April 18, 1843; April 25, 1843]

Appendices

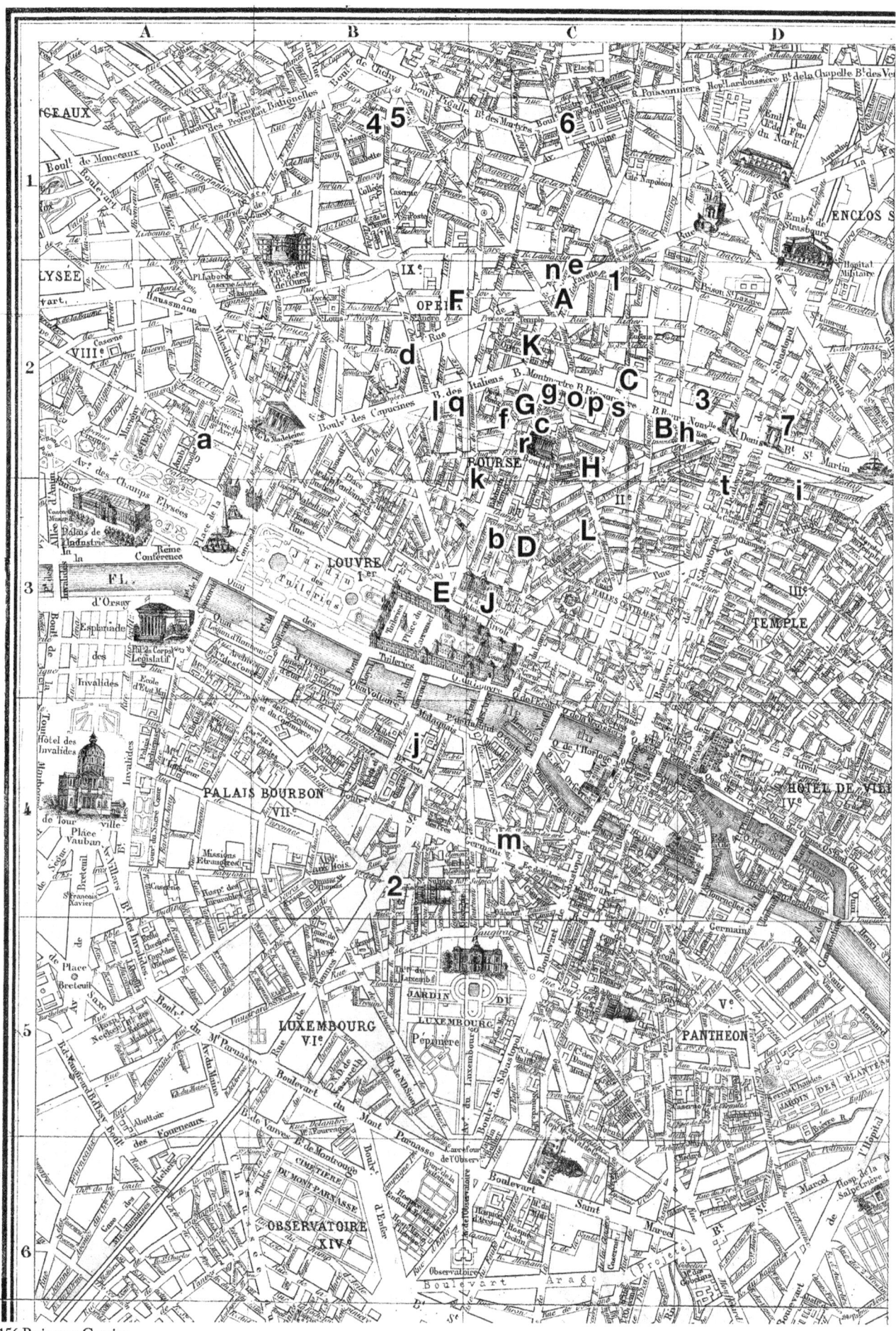

156 Paris map Garnier

List of compositions

Opus numbers

opus 1	[missing]
opus 2	Variations et Finale... sur un motif favori de la Famille Suisse de Weigl
opus 3	2 Quadrilles de Contredanses
opus 4	Fantaisie Composée sur un Motif du ballet d'Armide
opus 5	Souvenirs de Flandres, Marche, Quatre Valses et un Rondeau
opus 6	Fantaisie de Concert [Meyerbeer]
opus 7	16 Walses favorites de Johann Strauss
opus 8	Caprice [i.e. opus 11 & opus 14]
opus 9	Divertissement sur l'Opera Lucia di Lamermoor [sic = Italian] de Donizetti
opus 10	Scherzo et Pastorale (Pastorale et Scherzo) Valses Brillantes
opus 11	Grand Caprice [i.e. opus 8]
opus 12	Rondeau de Concert avec introduction
opus 13	Caprice sur l'air espagnol La Cachucha
opus 14	Deuxième Polonaise [i.e. opus 27, opus 8]
opus 15	Le Tournoi, Fantaisie Chevaleresque
opus 16	Fantaisie sur deux motifs de La Norma
opus 17	La Vallée d'Ornans, Cantabile et Rondeau [Souvenirs no. 1]
opus 18	Les Bords du Rhin, Valse [Souvenirs no. 2]
opus 19	Delfzil, Scherzo [Souvenirs no. 3]
opus [19b]	La Romanesca
opus 20	Le Zuyderzée, Ballade [Souvenirs no. 4]
opus 21	Les Cloches, Fugue et Rondeau [Souvenirs no. 5]
opus 22	Meulan, Andante et Valse [Souvenirs no. 6]
opus 23	Soirées d'Auteuil, Sérénade [Souvenirs no. 7]
opus 24	Grand Solo
opus 25	Consolazione, Romance sans paroles [& op. 36]
opus 26	Marche triumphale
opus 27	Le Passage des Alpes, Trilogie - Maestoso [m.1-59 i.e. 14 I] [& op. 28, 40]
opus 28	Le Passage des Alpes, Trilogie - Marche [i.e. op. 26] [& op. 28, 40]
opus 28[b]	Fantaisie symphonique
opus 28[c]	Divertissement
opus 29	La Chasse des Sylphes
opus 30	Grande Sérénade
opus 31	Le Départ, Fantaisie dramatique
opus 32	[missing] [Sérénade WoO13?]
opus 33[a]	Mazurka
opus 33[b]	Marche et Scherzo
opus 34[a]	Le Montagnard, divertissement pastoral
opus 34[b]	Fantaisie Sonate
opus 35	Fantaisie de Concert
opus 36	Regrets et Consolations [i.e. op. 25 & op. 36]
opus 37	Cavatine
opus 38	25 Études de Genre
opus 39	Andante et Menuet
opus 40	Le Passage des Alpes, Trilogie - Rondo [& op. 27, 28]
opus 41	Feuilles d'Automne, douze Valses
opus 42	La Ronde de Mai
opus 43	Marche funèbre et Rondeau
opus 44	Souvenir(s) du Jura
opus 45	Divagation
opus 46	Valse favorite [cf & i.e. opus 5 no. 4 + 5]
opus 47	La Source du Lyson (Fête villageoise) - Fantaisie
opus 48	Quatre Marches (et Six Préludes) [& op. 49]
opus 49	(Quatre Marches et) Six Préludes [& op. 48]
opus 50	Adagio et Divertissements
opus 51	Récréation du Guitariste, Quatorze Pièces
opus 52	Le Livre d'Or du Guitariste
opus 53	Six Pièces originales

Works without opusnumber [in alphabetical order of title]

WoO 1	Andante et Allegro
WoO 2	Aux Parisiens des 27 28 et 29 Juillet 1830
WoO 3	Caprice Pour Deux Hautbois
WoO 4	Concertino pour Hautbois
WoO 5	Deux Quadrilles
WoO 6	Duetto
WoO 7	L'Enfant au Berceau
WoO 8	Grand Duo
WoO 9	Introduction et Variations sur la Cavatine favorite de l'Opéra Le Pirate [Bellini]
WoO 10	Lolla, Mélodie
WoO 11	Le Petit Ange rose, Berceuse
WoO 12	Rondeau
WoO 13	Sérénade [missing]
WoO 14	Sonate
WoO 15	Valse des Roses [Mètra]
WoO 16	Kleines Tonstück
WoO 17	Valse
WoO 18	Berceuse
WoO 19	Pastorale
WoO 20	Valse

Appendices

Méthode

p. 5	No. 2 1ᵉʳᵉ Leçon
p. 5	No. 3 2ᵉ Leçon
p. 5	No. 4 Gamme
p. 5	No. 5 3ᵉ Leçon
p. 5	No. 6 Gamme
p. 6	Étude
p. 6	No. 7 Ex. A, Ex. B
p. 6	No. 8 Exercice
p. 6	No. 9 Leçon
p. 7	No. 10 Andante
p. 7	No. 11 Exercices
p. 7	No. 12 Leçon
p. 7	No. 13 Leçon
p. 8	No. 14 Exercice sur la gamme
p. 8	No. 15 Gamme
p. 8	No. 16 Exercice sur la gamme
p. 8-9	No. 17 Leçon
p. 9	No. 18 Gamme
p. 10	No. 19 Exercice
p. 10	No. 20 Leçon Andante
p. 11	No. 21 Exercice sur la gamme
p. 11	No. 22 Gamme
p. 11	No. 23 Étude All.o
p. 12	No. 24 Leçon And.te
p. 12	No. 25 Gamme
p. 12-13	No. 26 Leçon Andantino
p. 13	No. 27 Leçon
p. 13	No. 28 Gamme
p. 13	No. 29 Leçon
p. 16	Ex. 10
p. 19	Ex. 15
p. 20	Ex. 16, 17, 18
p. 21	Ex. 20 , 22, 23
p. 22	Ex. 25, 26, 27, 28, 29, 30
p. 25	Ex. 37, 41
p. 26	[Ex. 44]
p. 31-33	Introduction, Allegretto [13A, 13B]
p. 38	Ex. 55
p. 41	Ex. 58bis
p. 42	Ex. 58, 59, 60, 61
p. 43-44	Rêverie Nocturne
p. 45	Ex. [5x]
p. 46	No. 1, 2, 3, 4
p. 47	No. 5, 6, 7, 8
p. 48	No. 9, 10, No. 11 Preludio, No. 12 Preludio
p. 49	No. 13 Étude
p. 49-50	No. 14 Andante
p. 50-51	No. 15 Marche
p. 51	No. 1 Minuetto, No. 2 Bourrée - Visée
p. 52	No. 3 Minuetto, No. 4 Sarabande, No. 5 Gavotte, No. 6 Minuetto - Visée

Arrangements [in alphabetical order by composer]

Adami	Cavatine Italienne
Barroilhet	La Petite Savoyarde
Beethoven	Adelaide
Concone	L'Esquif du Pecheur
Giuliani	Allegro du 2me Concerto opus 36
Hummel	Morceau de piano [missing]
Klosé	10me Solo
Masini	Le Don - Rêverie
[Schubert]	Adieu - Weyrauch
Schubert	Amour et Mystère [Geist de Liebe? Alles um Liebe?] [missing]
	Au bord d'une fontaine [Der Lindenbaum?[missing]
	Ave Maria
	La Barcarolle [Auf dem Wasser zu singen]
	La Berceuse [Schlaflied, Schlummerlied]
	La Colombe [Der Taubenpost] [missing]
	Fais mes Amours [Liebeständelei?] [missing]
	La Fille du Pêcheur [Das Fischermädchen]
	Le jeune Aveugle [Der blinde Knabe?] [missing]
	La jeune Fille et la Mort [Der Tod und das Mädchen]
	La jeune Mère [Wiegenlied]
	La jeune Religieuse [Die junge Nonne] [missing]
	Marguerite [Gretchen am Spinnrade]
	Le meunier voyageur [Das Wandern]
	Les plaintes de la jeune fille [Des Mädchens Klage]
	La Poste [Die Post] [missing]
	Le Ruisseau [?] [missing]
	Salut du matin [[Morgengruss?] [missing]
	La sérénade [Ständchen]
	Sérénade de Shakepeare [Ständchen]
	Sois toujours mes seuls amours [Sei mir gegrüsst]
	Toute ma vie [?] [missing]
Sor	L'Encouragement opus 34
	Divertissement opus 38
	Les deux amis op. 41 [missing]
	Mes Ennuis, Six Bagatelles opus 43
	Six petites pièces [Voyons si c'est ça] opus 45
	Le premier pas vers moi opus 53 [missing]
	Morceau de Concert opus 54
	Fantaisie opus 54bis
	Souvenir de Russie opus 63
Thomas	Le Perruquier de la Régence

Chronology of compositions							
Ch	Year	Op. / WoO / Arr.	Title	Instr	Source of date	Manuscript	Publisher
IV	1829	Opus 2	Variations Famille Suisse	gui	Coste-Hallberg December 21, 1876		Romagnesi
	1830	Opus 3	2 Quadrilles de Contredanses	gui	RM December 18, 1830, p. 191		Richault
		WoO 2	Aux Parisiens	voc/pf	BF December 25, 1830		chez l'Auteur
	1832	Opus 4	Fantaisie Armide	gui	BF August 18, 1832	Egasse de C.	chez l'Auteur
	1835	Opus 5	Souvenirs de Flandres	gui	BF July 11, 1835		Lacôte
	1836 ?	[Opus 19b]	La Romanesca	gui	RisT1 p.49; DevA p. 269		Richault
	1837	Opus 6	Fantaisie de Concert Meyerbeer	gui	BF August 26, 1837	Egasse de C.	chez l'Auteur
	c1837	WoO 9	Intr. & Var. Il Pirata	gui	style > Armide < Norma	Holm	unpublished
	1838 ?	Opus 7	16 Walses Strauss	gui	DevA? p. 369		Richault
	1838	Opus 16	Fantaisie Norma	gui	RGMP May 6, 1838		Challiot
	1838	Arr.	23 Chansons - Schubert	voc/gui	LFM April 8, 1838		Richault
	1838	Arr.	Le Perruqier de la Régence - Thomas	voc/gui	LFM April 29, 1838		Richault
	1838 ?	Arr.	L'Esquif du Pecheur - Concone	voc/gui	Concone		Richault
V	1840 ?	Opus 8	Caprice [Allegro .i.e. opus 11]	gui	RGMP? April 19, 1840	Anon. 1	unpublished
	1840 ?	Opus 12	Rondeau de concert	gui	DevA? p. 365, 369	2nd gui Anon. 1?	Richault
	1840 ?	Opus 13	Caprice La Cachucha	gui	DevA? p.3 69	Holm	Richault
	1840	Arr.	La Petite Savoyarde - Barroilhet	voc/gui	BaiL p. 58		LFM
	1841	Opus 9	Divert.ment Lucia di Lamermoor	gui	BF 30 X 1841		Latte
	1841 ?	Opus 10	Scherzo et Pastorale	2gui	DevA? p. 365, 369	Eggers / Holm	Richault
	1842 ?	Opus 11	Grand Caprice [Allegro i.e. opus 8]	gui	Kk Rischel Ms. 48a	Egasse de C.	unpublished
	>1842	Opus 14	Deuxième Polonaise	gui	Kk Rischel Ms. 27	Anon.1/E. de C.	unpublished
	1843	Opus 15	Le Tournoi, fantaisie chevaleresque	gui	DecM p. 78	Autograph Lam	Challiot
	1844	WoO 5	Deux Quadrilles	gui	Kk Rischel Ms. 46	Anon. 1	unpublished
	1851	Meth.	Méthode Coste-Sor	gui	DevA p. 395-396		Schonenberger
	1852	Opus 17-23	Sept Souvenirs	gui	BF July 17, 1852	Autograph Lam	Schonenberger
		WoO 13	Sérénade [opus 32?]	ob/cl/gui	DecM p. 178	missing	missing
	1855	Opus 25	Consolazione [& opus 36 Les Regrets]	ob/pf	DecM p. 183; BF August 6, 1856	Autograph	Colombier
		WoO 8	Grand duo	2gui	DecM p. 184; LFM p. 267	Anon.	unpublished
VI	1856	Opus 27, 28 (& 40)	Le Passage des Alpes	gui	Makaroff		Richault
		Opus 28 [b]	Fantaisie symphonique	gui	Makaroff	Eggers?	unpublished
		Opus 29	La Chasse des Sylphes	gui	Makaroff		Girod
		Opus 30	Grande Sérénade	gui	Makaroff		Girod
		Opus 31	Le Départ	gui	Makaroff		Girod
VII	1860	Opus 33 [a]	Mazurka	gui	WynS1		Hirsch
	1861	Opus 34 [a]	Le Montagnard	ob/pf	DevA p. 210		Lemoine
	186?	WoO 4	Concertino	ob/pf	Kk Rischel 37	Autograph	unpublished
	1862	Opus 33 [b]	Marche et Scherzo	ob/gui	WynS1	transcript? Lam	unpublished
		WoO 14	Sonate	ob/pf	DecM p. 197	Anon.	unpublished
	1864	WoO 7	L'Enfant au Berceau	voc/pf	Pn Vm7 44.834		Chatot
	1866	Opus 35	Fantaisie de Concert	2ob/pf	Pn L 1167		Triébert
	1867	Arr	Klosé - 10me Solo	ob/pf/sq	Kk Rischel 178		Richault
	1868	Opus 36	Regrets et Consolations [op. 25&36]	ob/pf	Pn [K 1010	Autograph	Triébert
	1869	Opus 37	Cavatine	ob/pf	Pn No. 2317 K 1012		Triébert
	1872?	Opus 38	25 Études	gui	DevA p. 369, HopC p. 104,		Richault
			La Ronde de Mai [cf titel op. 42]	gui	WynS1	Egasse de C.	unpublished
VIII	1876	Opus 39	Andante & Menuet	gui	Pn Vm9 3544		Richault
		Opus (27, 28) & 40	Le Passage des Alpes	gui	Coste-Hallberg October 15, 1876		Richault
		Opus 41	Feuilles d'Automne	gui	Coste-Hallberg October 15, 1876		chez l'Auteur
		Opus 42	La Ronde de Mai	gui	Coste-Hallberg October 15, 1876		chez l'Auteur
		Opus 43	Marche funèbre et Rondeau	gui	Pn Vm 3554?		chez l'Auteur
		Opus 44	Souvenir(s) du Jura	gui	Coste-Hallberg December 21, 1876		chez l'Auteur
	1877	Opus 45	Divagation	gui	Coste-Hallberg September 30, 1877		chez l'Auteur
		Opus 46	Valse favorite	gui	Coste-Hallberg December 7, 1877		chez l'Auteur
	1878	Opus 47	La Source du Lyson	gui	Pn Vm9 3560		Katto
		Opus 48 & 49	Quatre Valses et Six Préludes	gui	Coste-Hallberg 9 I 1979		chez l'Auteur
		WoO 10	Lolla	voc/pf	Pn Vm7 44.835		Katto
		WoO 11	Le Petit Ange rose	voc/pf	Pn Vm7 44.836		Katto
	1879	Opus 50	Adagio et Divertissements	gui	Pn Vm9 3543		chez l'Auteur
		Arr.	Sor - L'Encouragement	2gui	Coste-Hallberg March 22, 1879		
	1880	Opus 51	Récréation du Guitariste	gui	Pn Vm9 3557		chez l'Auteur
		Opus 52	Livre d'Or du Guitariste	gui	Coste-Hallberg September 22, 1880		chez l'Auteur
	1881	Opus 53	Six Pièces originales	gui	WynS1		chez l'Auteur

Appendices

Compositions - without date						
Year	Op. WoO Arr.	Title	Instr	Source of date	Manuscript	Publisher
	Opus 24	Grand Solo	gui		Egasse de C.	unpublished
c. 1855?	Opus 26	Marche triumphale	gui	RisT1 p. 49-50	Anon.	unpublished
	Opus 28[c]	Divertissement	gui		Egasse de C.	unpublished
	Opus 32	missing				
	Opus 34[b]	Fantaisie Sonate [1 p.]	vl-ob/pf-gui	DecM p. 197?	Autograph	unpublished
	WoO 1	Andante et Allegro	gui		Autograph?	unpublished
	WoO 3	Caprice	2ob		Autograph	unpublished
	WoO 5	Deux Quadrilles	gui		Anon. 1	unpublished
	WoO 6	Duetto	2gui		Holm	unpublished
	WoO 12	Rondeau	ob/pf		Autograph	unpublished
	WoO 15	Valse des Roses	gui		Autograph	unpublished
	WoO 16	Kleines Tonstück	gui		Anon.	unpublished
	WoO 17	Valse	gui		Autograph	unpublished
	WoO 18	Berceuse	gui		Autograph	unpublished
	WoO 19	Pastorale	gui		Autograph	unpublished
	WoO 20	valse	gui		Autograph	unpublished

Compositions - with oboe						
Year	Op. WoO Arr.	Title	Instr	Source of date	Manuscript	Publisher
1852	WoO 13	Sérénade	ob/cl/gui	DecM p. 178		
1855	Opus 25	Consolazione [& opus 36 Les Regrets]	ob/pf	DecM p. 183; BF August 6, 1856	Autograph	Colombier
1861 186?	Opus 34 [a] WoO 4	Le Montagnard Concertino	ob/pf ob/pf	DevA p. 210 Kk Rischel 37	Autograph	Lemoine unpublished
1862	Opus 33 [b] WoO 14	Marche et Scherzo Sonate	ob/gui ob/pf	WynS1 DecM p. 197	afschrift? Lam Anon.	unpublished unpublished
1866	Opus 35	Fantaisie de Concert	2ob/pf	Pn L 1167		Triébert
1867	Arr	Klosé - 10me Solo	ob/pf/sq	Kk Rischel 178		Richault
1868	Opus 36	Regrets et Consolations [op. 25&36]	ob/pf	Pn [K 1010	Autograph	Triébert
1869	Opus 37	Cavatine	ob/pf	Pn No. 2317 K 1012		Triébert
?	Opus 34[b]	Fantaisie Sonate [1 p.]	vl-ob/pf-gui	DecM p. 197 ?	Autograph	unpublished
?	WoO 3	Caprice	2ob		Autograph	unpublished
?	WoO 12	Rondeau	ob/pf		Autograph	unpublished

Programmatic compositions						
Nature	Cities	History	Sentiment	Death	Folklore	Opera
Flandres opus 5	Delfzil opus 19	Tournoi opus 15	Regrets opus 25	Marche funèbre opus 43	Ronde Mai opus 42	Famille Suisse opus 2
Vallée Ornans opus 17	Cloches opus 21	Chasse Sylphes opus 29	Consolations opus 36		Rondeau Villageois opus 47	Armide opus 4
Bords du Rhin opus 18	Meulan opus 22	Le Départ opus 31	Divagation opus 45			Meyerbeer opus 6
Zuyderzée opus 20	Auteuil opus 23	Choeur Pèlerins opus 30				Lucia di Lamermoor opus 9
Passage Alpes opus 27, 28 & 40						Norma opus 16
Montagnard opus 17; opus 34a						Le Pirate WoO 9
Feuilles d'Automne opus 41						
Jura opus 44						
Source Lyson opus 47						

Concordance opus 8, 11, 14 and 27			
Caprice opus 8	*Grand Caprice* opus 11	*Deuxième Polonaise* opus 14	Le Passage des Alpes opus 27
	I Introduction		
	II Andante maestoso		
I Allegro	III Allegro		
		I Introduction	I Maestoso
II Polonaise		II Polonaise	

Abbreviations

general abbreviations

acc.	accompaniment
anon.	anonymous
arr.	arrangement
c.	circa
cf	confer
ded.	dedication
dim.	dimanche (Sunday)
ed.	edition
etc	et cetera
ex.	example
f	following page
ff	following pages
facs.	facsimile
fc	photocopy
fl	flute
gui	guitar
Hz	Hertz (frequency)
i.e.	id est (this is)
jeu.	jeudi (Thursday)
Kol.	Kolom (column)
lun.	lundi (Monday)
M.	Monsieur (sir, mister)
mar.	mardi (Tuesday)
mer.	mercredi (Wednesday)
Mlle	Mademoiselle (miss)
MM.	Messieurs (plural)
Mme	Madame (misses)
MS	manuscript
ob	oboe
op. cit.	opere citato
op.	opus
p.	page
pf.	pianoforte
publ.	publication
res.	resembles
sam.	samedi (Saturday)
unp.	unpublished
ven.	vendredi (Friday)
vl.	violin
vlc.	violoncello
voc.	vocal, singing
WoO	without opus number

sigla libraries

A	Århus, Statsbiblioteket
Au	Amsterdam, Universiteitsbibliotheek
B	Besançon, Bibliothèque Municipale
Bad	Besançon, Archives départementales
Bds	Berlin, Deutsche Staatsbibliothek
Br	Koninklijke Bibliothèque Royale Brussels
Dgh	Gemeentehuis Delfzijl
DHk	Den Haag, Koninklijke Bibliotheek
DHnmi	Den Haag, Nederlands Muziek Instituut
Kk	Kopenhagen, Det Kongelige Bibliotek
Kn	National Museum of Denmark
Lam	London, Royal Academy of Music
Lbl	London, The British Library
Mbs	München, Bayrische Staatsbibliothek
Pan	Paris, Archives nationales
Pap	Archives de Paris
Pbh	Bibliothèque Historique de la Ville de Paris
Pcdv	Paris, Château de Vincennes
Pcm	Paris, Cité de la Musique
Pn	Paris, Bibliothèque nationale (Département de la Musique)
Sk	Sweden, Kunglige bibliotheket
Skma	Sweden, Statens musikbibliotek
Uu	Utrecht, Universiteitsbibliotheek
VAL	Valenciennes, Bibliothèque Municipale

bibliographical: magazines, sources, literature

BF	Bibliographie de la France
EdB	Echo de Bruxelles
EFV	Echo's de la Frontière Valenciennes
Fig	Le Figaro
GM	Gazette musicale de Paris
JD	Journal des Débats
LFM	La France musicale
LPB	La Presse Belge
LaM	La Mélodie
LGM	Le Guide Musical
LM	Le Ménestrel
LP	Le Pianiste
LTB	Le Télégraphe, Bruxelles
OB	Observateur Belge
PA	Petites Affiches Valenciennes
RGMP	Revue et Gazette musicale de Paris
RM	Revue musicale
TdP	Tablettes de Polymnie

Appendices

Certificates

Acte de naissance Napoléon Coste, Besançon, Archives départementales, État Civil, Amondans, N, 1793-1872, 5 Mi 177.

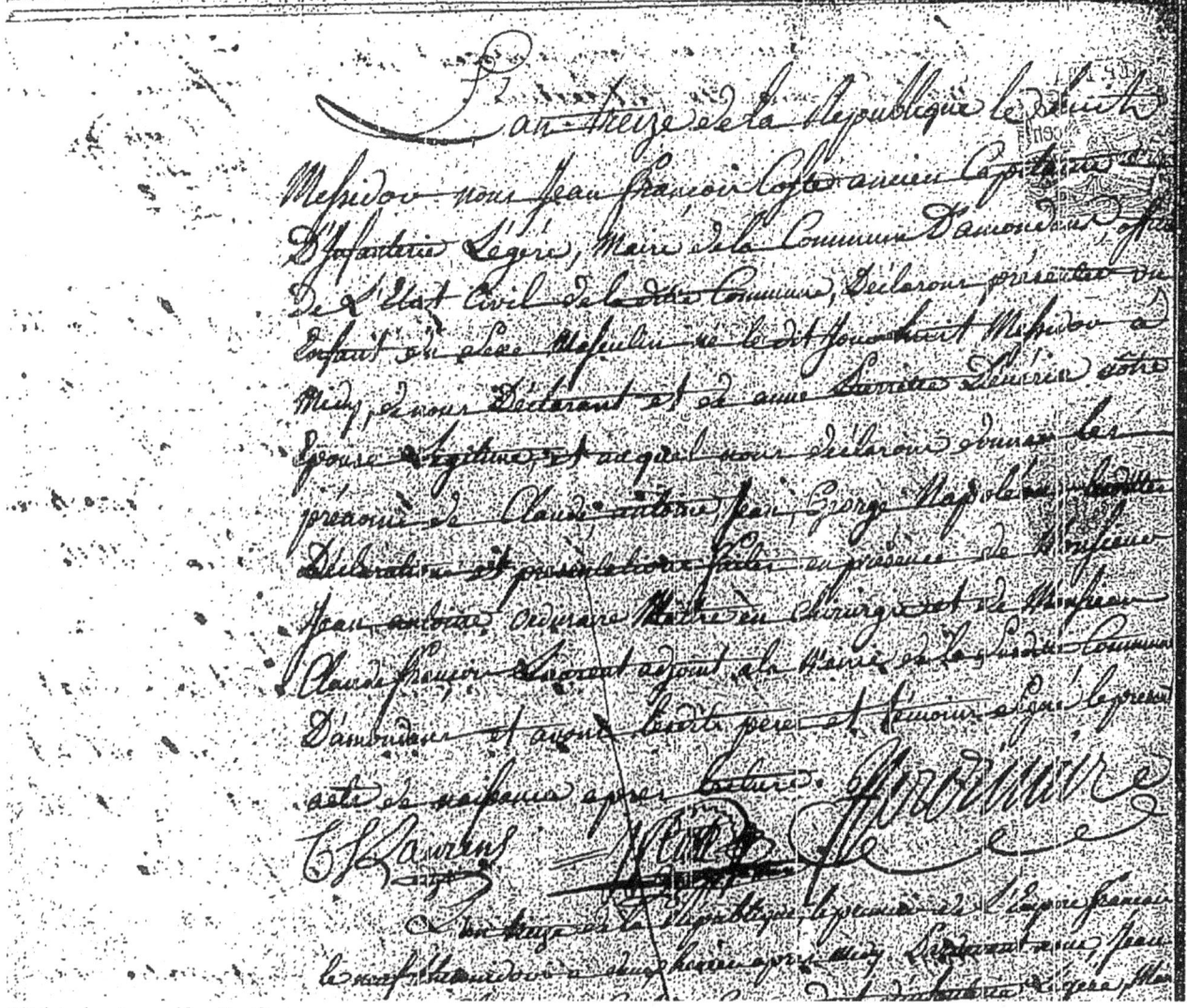

157 Acte de naissance Napoléon Coste

Acte de mariage Napoléon Coste & Louise Olive Pauilhé, Paris, Archives de Paris, February 11, 1871, Série V2E 5Mi 3/210.

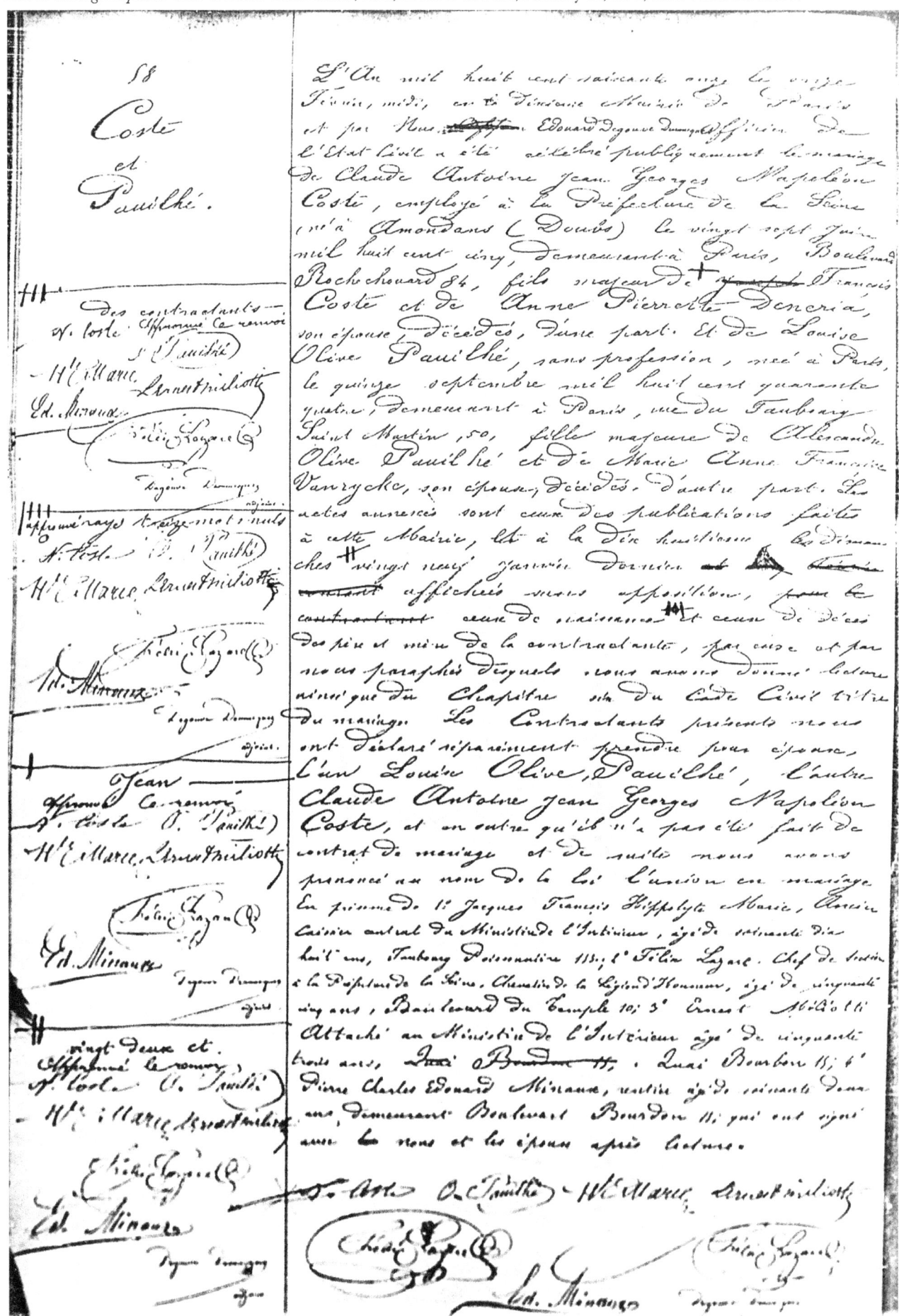

158 Acte de mariage Coste-Pauilhé

Appendices

Acte de décès Napoléon Coste, Paris, Archives de Paris, January 15, 1883, Série V2E 5Mi 3/1256.

159 Acte de décès Napoléon Coste

Op. 30 Sérénade, Registres de Dépôt légal de musique, Paris, Archives nationales, Musique, F18* VIII 1 à 157, No. 21, November 11, 1856 - August 5, 1857, p.122 No.: 1882. June 8, 1857.

160 Enregistrement opus 30

Op.31 Le Départ, Registres de Dépôt légal de musique, Paris, Archives nationales, Musique, F18* VIII 1 à 157, No. 22, August 5, 1857 - September 5, 1858, No.: 2686. September 5, 1857

161 Enregistrement opus 31

Letters

Coste-Degen, June 15, 1858, Århus, Statsbiblioteket, 4p., Søffren Degens Papirer, Manuscript no. 27b. [p. 1]

Paris 15 Juin 1858

Mon cher Degen,

Vous devez me trouver bien négligent de ne pas vous avoir répondu depuis si longtemps. mais ne m'en voulez pas trop, mon ami, j'ai passé par bien des épreuves depuis quelque temps et j'ai eu tant de préoccupations fâcheuses que je suis un peu excusable.

Vous savez que j'avais à la préfecture de la Seine un petit emploi. Cet emploi avait certes bien des inconvénients et paralysait bien mon faible génie de compositeur et d'artiste. mais il me faisait vivre modestement. c'était peu de chose, mais si je n'avais pas de leçons, ce qui m'arrive souvent, j'étais assuré de ne pas

Coste-Degen, October 17, 1863, Århus, Statsbiblioteket, 4 p., Søffren Degens Papirer, Manuscript no. 27b. [p. 1]

Paris 17 8bre 1863.

Mon cher Degen,

J'ai reçu votre bonne et affectueuse lettre avec un bien grand plaisir car il y avait bien longtemps que je n'avais eu de vos nouvelles directement. Mr Holm a la bonté de m'écrire de tems en tems, ce qui m'est extrêmement agréable et il a eu même l'amabillité de me faire parvenir son portrait Photographié. C'est une attention dont je lui suis très reconnaissant. Il vous a fait part de l'accident funeste qui depuis six mois bientôt, m'a privé de l'usage du bras gauche ; j'ai désespéré longtems de pouvoir m'en servir jamais, et je suis heureux de vous annoncer que je commence à essayer de poser les doigts sur le manche de ma Guitare qui a du bien s'ennuyer du long silence auquel elle a été condamnée

Coste-Gruel, June 16, 1879, 1 p., Norbert Fischer, Halen.

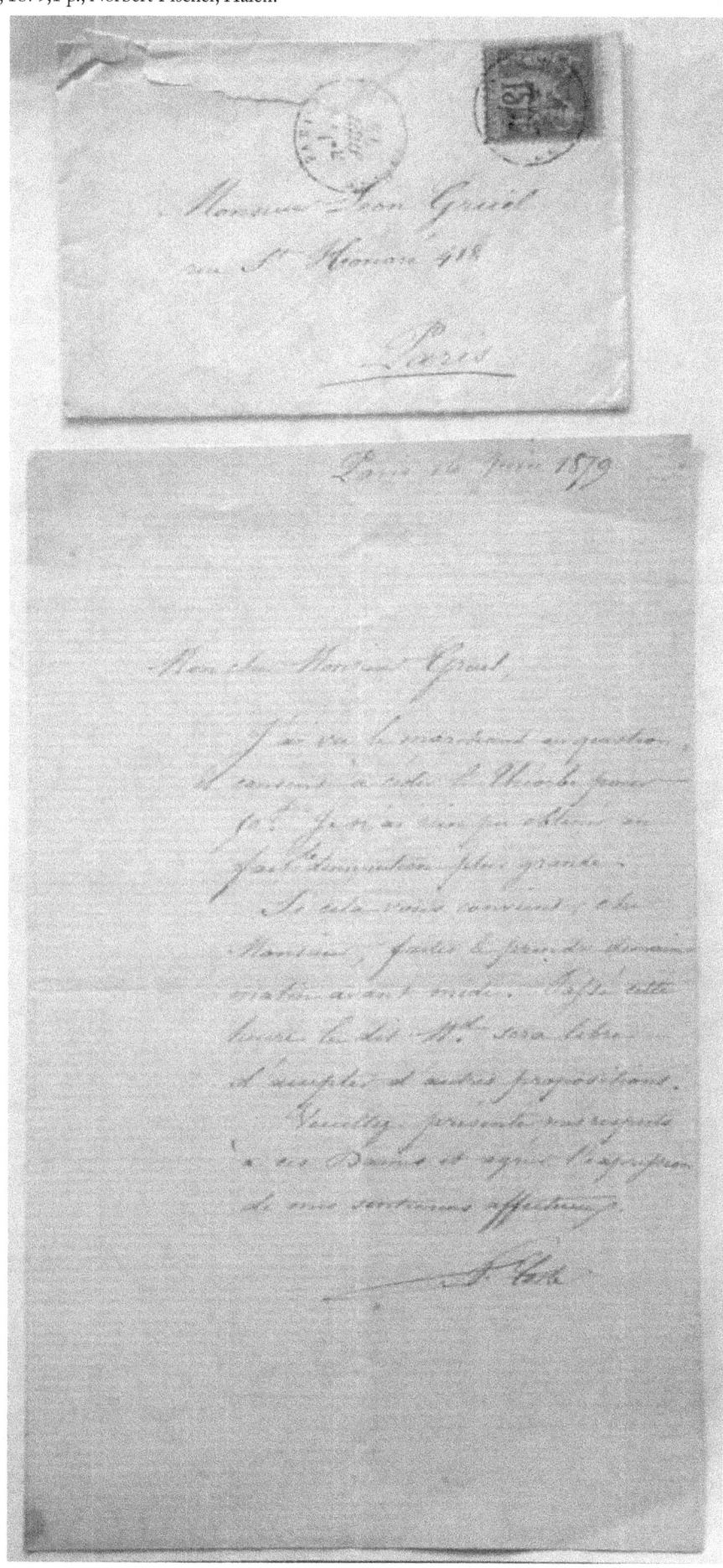

164 Coste-Gruel, June 16, 1879

Coste-Hallberg, September 22, 1880, "Napoléon Coste - späte Briefe 1867-1882", aus dem Nachlass von Georg Meier/Willy Meier-Pauselius, I. und W. Holzschuh, Hamburg.

165 Coste-Hallberg, September 22, 1880

Bibliographies

Literature

The abbreviations only concern the literature to which references are made in the appendices, the bibliography of magazines. They have the first three letters of the surname of the author, the first letter of the first name and a number when there are more publications.

Abondance, Pierre: 'Guitare de Napoléon Coste', in: *Les Cahiers de la Guitare*, Paris, 1983, no. 6, p. 11.
Albert, K.: 'Strauss, Johann', in: Robijns, J. & Miep Zijlstra: *Algemene Muziek Encyclopedie*, vol. 9 Weesp, De Haan, 1983, p. 274.
Allorto, Enrico: 'L'organologia' in: Chiesa, Ruggiero, ed.: *La Chitarra*, Torino, Edizioni di Torino, 1990, p. 3-10.
Almanach musical pour 1854..., Paris, Houssiaux ed., 1854, p. 8-9, 29.
Almanach musical pour 1855..., Paris, Houssiaux ed., 1855, p...
Almanach musical pour 1856 3ᵉ Année..., Paris, Houssiaux ed., 1856, p. 35.
Annala, Hannu & Heiki Mätlik: *Handbook of Guitar and Lute Composers*, Pacific, Mel Bay, 2007, p. 61-62, 66-69.
Ashbrook, William: 'Donizetti, Gaetano', in: Sadie, Stanley, ed.: *The New Grove Dictionary of Music and Musicians*, London, Macmillan, 1980, vol. 5, p. 555.
Azpiazu, José de: *La Guitare et les Guitaristes*, Basel, Symphonia, 1959, p. 25.
Bacon, Tony & Russel Cleveland, a.o.: *The Classical Guitar*, London, 1997, p. 109.
Bailbé, Joseph Marc: 'La critique musicale au *Journal des Débats*' in: Bailbé [et al]: *La musique en France à l'epoque romantique (1830-1870)*, Paris, Flammarion, 1991, p. 11-13.

BaiL Baillie, Laureen: *The Catalogue of Printed Music in the British Library to 1980*, London, Saur, 1982, p. 58.

Bajou, Valérie: *Courbet*, Paris, Biro, 2003, p. 46-47, 160-167.
Ballard, James: 'Fernando Sor' in: *The Guitar Review*, New York, The Society of the Classic Guitar, vol. I, no 1, 1946, (vol. I reprint 1974/1975) p. 6-8.
Baronnet, Jean: *Regard d'un Parisien sur la Commune, Photographies inédites de la Bibliothèque historique de la Ville de Paris*, Paris, Gallimard, 2006, p. 25.
Beard, David & Kenneth Gloag: *Musicology: the key concepts*, London, Routledge, 2005, Introduction, p. 3, 5-6, 10-11.
Becker, Heinz: 'Meyerbeer, Giacomo', in: Sadie, Stanley, ed.: *The New Grove Dictionary of Music and Musicians*, London, Macmillan, 1980, vol.12, p. 247-249, 254.
Bellow, Alexander: *The Illustrated History of the Guitar*, New York, Colombo, 1970, p. 137-146, 165, 166, 172-174.
Bent, Ian, ed.: *Music theory in the age of Romanticism*, Cambridge, Cambridge University Press, 1996; Leslie David Blasius: 'The mechanics of sensation and the construction of the Romantic musical experience', p. 3-24.
Berlioz, Hector: *Grand traité d'instrumentation et d'orchestration modernes*, Paris, Lemoine, 1843, nouvelle edition c. 1860, p. 83-86.
Berlioz, Hector: 'Die Gitarre', (1843) in: *Gitarre und Laute*, Köln, vol. II, 1980, no. 3, p. 22-24 (i.e. p. 1-3), no. 4, p. 24-25 (i.e. p. 4-5).
Berlioz, Hector: *La Critique musicale*, ed. H. Robert Cohen, Yves Gérard, vol. I, Paris, Buchet/Chastel, 1996-..., p. 9-11 Armide - Gluck, 229-231, 443-445; vol. II, p. 253-254, 261-262 Huerta, 313-316 Coste, 637, 641-642.
Berlioz, Hector: *Correspondance générale*, vol. 2, Paris, Flammarion, 1972, p. 252-3, 262-3, 265.
Berlioz, Hector: *Mémoires de Hector Berlioz...*, Paris, Calmann-Lévy, 1919, p. 16, 53, 154, 221, 301, 337, 350.
Bernard, Élisabeth: 'Musique et communication' in: Bailbé [et al]: *La musique en France à l'epoque romantique (1830-1870)*, Paris, Flammarion, 1991. p. 63-69, 72-88.
Beukema, Hans: *Een wandeling door de vesting Delfzijl, anno 1850*, Delfzijl, Tekst & Advies, 1999, p. 16-19.
Blasius, Leslie David: 'The mechanics of sensation and the construction of the Romantic musical experience', in: Bent, Ian, ed.: *Music theory in the age of Romanticism*, Cambridge, Cambridge University Press, 1996, p. 3-24.
Blume, Friedrich: *Classic and Romantic Music, A Comprehensive Survey*, New York - London, Norton, 1970; vertaling *Musik in Geschichte und Gegenwart*, Kassel, Bärenreiter, 1948-1986.
Bödeker, Hans Erich, Patrice Veit et Michael Werner, ed.: *Les sociétés de musique en Europe 1700-1900*, Berlin, Berliner Wissenschafts Verlag, 2007; Laure Schnapper: 'La société des compositeurs de musique ou l'émergence d'une nouvelle corporation', p. 349-370; Philippe Gumplowicz: 'Le rêve et la mission. La Musique et le peuple en France 1789-1848', p. 373-400.
Bödeker, Hans Erich, Patrice Veit et Michael Werner, ed.: *Organisateurs et formes d'organisation du concert en Europe 1700-1920*, Berlin, Berliner Wissenschafts Verlag, 2008; Myriam Chymènes: 'Élites sociales et vie musicale parisienne sous la Troisième République: promotion, diffusion, création', p. 31-46; Bruno Moysan: 'Pratiques lisztiennes du concert', p. 133-156; Laure Schnapper: 'Le rôle des facteurs de piano', p. 237-256.
Bödeker, Hans Erich, Patrice Veit et Michael Werner, ed.: *Espaces et lieux de concert en Europe 1700-1920*, Berlin, Berliner Wissenschafts Verlag, 2008; Constance Himmelfarb: 'La <<Nouvelle Athènes>>: une colonie d'artistes à Paris sous le duc d'Orléans, p. 79-100; Antoine Lilti: 'Le concert au salon: musique et sociabilité à Paris au VIIIe siècle', p. 125-146.
Bötticher, Wolfgang: *Einführung in die musikalische Romantik*, Darmstadt, Wissenschaftliche Buchgesellschaft, 1983, p. 25, 31-33, 38, 113-115, 165-169.

Bonds, Ray, ed.: *The Illustrated Directory of Guitars*, London, 2001. p. 54-55. [heptacorde]

BonP   Bone, Philip J.: 'Coste, Napoléon', in: *The Guitar and the Mandolin*, London, Schott, 2nd ed, 1954, reprint 1972, p. 84-85, 97.

Borgdorff, Henk: 'Ernst Kurth, *Romantische Harmonik*, 1920, in: Grijp, Louis Peter & Paul Scheepers, ed.: *Van Aristoxenos tot Stockhausen*, Wolters-Noordhoff, Groningen, 1990, p. 436-439.

Bottema, Jaap: *Delfzijl, Schetsen uit de Franse Tijd (1795-1814)*, Bedum, Profiel, 2004, cover, p. 9, 31, 36, 39, 49, 51, 58, 80, 117-120.

Boyd, Malcolm: 'Elegy', in: Sadie, Stanley, ed.: *The New Grove Dictionary of Music and Musicians*, London, Macmillan, 1980, vol.6, p.111-112; id. in: Sadie, Stanley, ed.:*The New Grove Dictionary of Music and Musicians*, second edition, London, Macmillan, 2001, vol. 8, p. 111-112.

Brook, Barry S.: *Thematic Catalogues in Music*, New York, Pendragon Press, 1972, p. vii-x, xv-xvi.

Brook, Barry S.: 'Thematic catalogue', in: Sadie, Stanley, ed.: *The New Grove Dictionary of Music and Musicians*, London, Macmillan, 1980, vol. 18, p. 732-736; id. in: Sadie, Stanley, ed.:*The New Grove Dictionary of Music and Musicians*, second edition, London, Macmillan, 2001, vol. 25, p. 348-352.

BroM   Brown, Maurice J.E. & Eric Sams: 'Schubert', in: Sadie, Stanley, ed.: *The New Grove Dictionary of Music and Musicians*, London, Macmillan, 1980, vol.16, p.795, 796, 803-807; id. in: Sadie, Stanley, ed.:*The New Grove Dictionary of Music and Musicians*, second edition, London, Macmillan, 2001, vol. 22, p. 700-721.

Brown, Maurice J.E.: 'Ballade', in: Sadie, Stanley, ed.: *The New Grove Dictionary of Music and Musicians*, London, Macmillan, 1980, vol.2, p.78-79.

Brown, Maurice: 'Ballade', in: *The New Grove Dictionary of Music and Musicians*, second edition, London, Macmillan, 2001, vol. 2, p. 554.

Brown, Maurice J.E.: 'Barcarole', in: Sadie, Stanley, ed.: *The New Grove Dictionary of Music and Musicians*, London, Macmillan, 1980, vol.2, p.145.

Brown, Maurice J.E., & Czeslaw R. Halski: 'Mazurka', in: Sadie, Stanley, ed.: *The New Grove Dictionary of Music and Musicians*, London, Macmillan, 1980, vol.11, p.865-866.

Brown, Maurice J.E., & Jósef W. Reiss: 'Polonaise', vol.15, p.49-52.

Brzoska, Matthias: 'Meyerbeer', in: Sadie, Stanley, ed.:*The New Grove Dictionary of Music and Musicians*, second edition, London, Macmillan, 2001, vol. 16, p. 566-569.

BueF   Buek, Fritz: *Die Gitarre und ihre Meister*, Berlin, Robert Lienau, 1926, 2^e ed. 1935, p. 104-109.

Buek, Fritz, see (Stockmann?) Stockhausen [Shtokman], see Makarow: 'Aus den Lebenserinnerungen des russischen Gitarrevirtuosen N. P. Makarow', in: *Der Gitarrefreund, Mitteilungen der Gitarristischen Vereinigung*, 11. Jahrgang 1910, Heft 6 p. 43-45; 12. Jahrgang, 1911 Heft 1 p. 1-3; Heft 2 p. 11-13; Heft 3 p. 23-25; Heft 4 p. 35-37; Heft 5 p. 45-47; .... [H. 6 fehlt im Bestand]

BurM   Burzik, Monika: 'Coste, Napoléon', in: *Die Musik in Geschichte und Gegenwart*, ed. Blume, Finscher, Kassel, Bärenreiter, 2000, vol. 4, Kol. 1714-1717.

CarC1   Carfagna, Carlo & A. Caprani: *Profilo Storico della Chitarra*, Ancona-Milano, Bèrben, 1966, p. 23, 44, 54, 56, 57, 79.

Carfagna, Carlo & Mario Gangi: *Dizionario chitarristico italiano*, Ancona, Bèrben, 1968, p. 17, 18, 35-36, 47, 52.

Carfagna, Carlo & Michele Greci: *Chitarra, storia e imagini*, Roma, Fratelli Palombi, 2000, p. 147-148.

CarM   Carner, Mosco & Max Schönherr: 'Strauss, (1) Johann', in: Sadie, Stanley, ed.: *The New Grove Dictionary of Music and Musicians*, London, Macmillan, 1980, vol.18, p.207-208.

Chaîné, Jacques: *The Orphée Data-base of Guitar Records*, Columbus, Orphée, 1990, p. 268, 269.

Chaîné, Jacques: *The Orphée Data-base of Guitar Records, 1991 Suppl.*, Columbus, Orphée, 1991, p. 72.

Chapalain, Guy: 'Luigi Sagrini', in: *Les Cahiers de la Guitare*, Boissy-St-Léger, Association Guitares et Luths, no. 68, 1998, p. 36.

Chapman, Richard: *Guitar, Music, History, Players*, London, 2000, p. 17.

Cherpillod, André: *La kalendaro tra la tempo, tra la spaco*, Cournegard, Blanchetière, 2002, p. 151-159, 203.

Chevallier, Émile: *Les salaires au XIXe siècle*, Paris, Hachette, 1887.

Chew, Geoffrey & Owen Jander: 'Pastorale', in: Sadie, Stanley, ed.: *The New Grove Dictionary of Music and Musicians*, London, Macmillan, 1980, vol.14, p.290-296; id. in: Sadie, Stanley, ed.:*The New Grove Dictionary of Music and Musicians*, second edition, London, Macmillan, 2001, vol. 19, p. 217, 224.

Chiesa, Maria Tibaldi: *Paganini, la vita e l'opera*, Milano, Garzanti, 1949, p. 471-476.

Chiesa, Ruggiero: 'La diteggiatura', in: Chiesa, Ruggiero, ed.: *La Chitarra*, Torino, Edizioni di Torino, 1990, p. 169-231.

Chiesa, Ruggero: 'The Guitar Works of Ferdinando Carulli', in: *Guitar Review*, New York, The Society of the Classic Guitar, no. 88, 1992, p. 7-11; no. 89, 1992, p. 28-32.

Chouquet, Gustave: *Le Musée du Conservatoire national de Musique. Catalogue raisonnée des instruments de cette Collection*, Paris, 1875, 2/1884, 3 suppls. 1894-1903, 1884, no. 280, p. 68; *Le Musée du Conservatoire de Musique, avec les Ier, IIe et IIIe suppléments*, Genève, Minkoff, 1993, p. 16, 17, 68.

Chymènes, Myriam: 'Élites sociales et vie musicale parisienne sous la Troisième République: promotion, diffusion, création', in: Bödeker, Hans Erich Patrice Veit et Michael Werner, ed.: *Organisateurs et formes d'organisation du concert en Europe 1700-1920*, Berlin, Berliner Wissenschafts Verlag, 2008; p. 31-46.

Claudon, Francis: *La musique des romantiques*, Paris, Presses Universitaires de France, 1992, p. 11-15, 31-37, 51-55.

Cloutier, Diane: *Revue musicale 1827-1835*, serie: 'Répertoire international de la presse musicale', vol. I-II, Ann Arbor, UMI, 1991.

Coeuroy, André: *La musique et le peuple en France*, Paris, Stock, 1941.

ColR   Coldwell, Robert & Suárez-Pajares, Javier: *A.T. Huerta, Life and Works*, DGA Editions, 2006.

Coldwell, Robert: 'Luigi Sagrini', in: *Soundboard*, the journal of the Guitar Foundation of America, vol. XXXVII, no. 1, 2011, p. 51-52.

Bibliographies

	Cole, Malcolm: 'Rondo', in: Sadie, Stanley, ed.: *The New Grove Dictionary of Music and Musicians*, London, Macmillan, 1980, vol.16, p.170, 172, 176; id. in: Sadie, Stanley, ed.:*The New Grove Dictionary of Music and Musicians*, second edition, London, Macmillan, 2001, vol. 21, p. 654.
CooJ1	Cooper, Jeffrey: 'Coste, Napoléon', in: Sadie, Stanley ed: *The New Grove Dictionary of Music and Musicians*, London, Macmillan, 1980, vol. 4, p. 824.
	Cooper, Jeffrey: *The rise of instrumental music and concert series in Paris, 1828-1871*, Ann Arbor, UMi Press, 1983.
	Cooper, Martin: 'France, §1, 5, 6, 7: Art Music', in: Sadie, Stanley ed: *The New Grove Dictionary of Music and Musicians*, London, Macmillan, 1980, vol. 6, p. 749-752.
CotR	Cotte, Roger: *La musique maçonnique et ses musiciens*, Paris, Editions du Borrégo, 1987, p. 137-156, 161, 165-209, 214, 216, 218, 220, 223-227, 229-240.
	Croll, Gerhard: 'Gluck, Christoph Willibald von', in: Sadie, Stanley, ed.: *The New Grove Dictionary of Music and Musicians*, London, Macmillan, 1980, vol. 7, p. 465, 472.
	Cruys, Marcus G.S. Van de: *The King's guitarist: The life and times of Marco Aurelio Zani de Ferranti*, Wijnegem, Homunculus, 2005, p. 20-21, 30, 35, 41, 52-53, 102, 177.
	Dahlhaus, Carl: 'Die Musik des 19. Jahrhunderts' in: Carl Dahlhaus ed.: *Neues Handbuch der Musikwissenschaft*, vol. VI, Wiesbaden, Athenaion, 1980-1995, p. 13-21, 73-79, 87-92, 110-118, 118-125, 252-261, 261-269, 302-310.
	Dahlhaus, Carl & Norbert Miller: *Europäische Romantik in der Musik*, Bd. 2, Stuttgart, Metzler, 1999/2007, p. 639, 641-643, 924-925, 927-939, 956-972, 983.
	Dancescu, Andrew: 'Johann Kaspar Mertz' Concertino - An Analysis', in: *Guitar Review*, New York, The Society of the Classic Guitar, no. 105, 1996, p. 18-22.
	Dandelot, A.: *La Société des Concerts du Conservatoire de 1828 à 1897*, Paris, Delagrave, 1923, p. 1-9, 40-47.
	Deane, Basil: 'Cherubini, Luigi, works', in: Sadie, Stanley, ed.: *The New Grove Dictionary of Music and Musicians*, London, Macmillan, 1980, vol. 4, p. 212.
DecM	Decourcelle, Maurice: *La Société académique des Enfants d'Apollon*, programmes des concerts annuels..., Paris, Durand, 1881, p. 18, 24, 78,108, 156-157, 177-179, 183-184, 188, 192, 197, 203-204, 208-210, 214, 217, 222, 231, 236, 240.
DelM1	Dell'Ara, Mario: 'La chitarra a Parigi negli anni 1830-1831', in: *Il Fronimo*, Milano, Suvini Zerboni, vol. XVI, no. 63, 1988, p. 19-25.
DelM2	Dell'Ara, Mario: 'Metodi e Trattati', in: Ruggiero Chiesa, ed.: *La Chitarra*, Torino, Edizioni di Torino, 1990, p. 256-257.
DelM3	Dell'Ara, Mario: *Manuale di storia della chitarra*, Ancona, Bèrben, 1988, p. 136-137.
DelM4	Dell'Ara, Mario: 'Ferdinando Carulli' in: *Il Fronimo*, Milano, Suvini Zerboni, 1979, vol. VII, no. 28, p. 5-23.
	Dell'Ara, Mario: 'Luigi, Valentino e Francesco Molino' in: *Il Fronimo*, Milano, Suvini Zerboni, 1985, vol. XIII, no. 50, p. 14-43.
	DeNora, Tia: *"Mozart's spirit from Haydn's hands"? : the social bases and social consequences of Beethoves success and vanguard style during his first decade in Vienna, 1792-1803*, San Diego, University of California, 1989, p. 187, 199, 205, 207, 218.
DevA	Devriès, Anik & François Lesure: *Dictionnaire des éditeurs de musique français*, Genève, Minkoff, 1979-1988, vol. II, p. 7-21, 26, 89, 98-99, 102-103, 114-116, 120-123, 191-193, 202-203, 219-226, 246, 256-259, 274-282, 307-317, 362-369, 372-373, 394-398, 415.
	Dömling, Wolfgang: *Hector Berlioz. Symphonie fantastique*, München, Fink, 1985, p. 18, 56, 66-67.
	Donington, Robert: *The Interpretation of Early Music*, London, Faber and Faber, 1990, p. 195, 198, 220, 225, 231, 255, 266, 275.
	Downes, Stephen: 'Mazurka', in: Sadie, Stanley, ed.:*The New Grove Dictionary of Music and Musicians*, second edition, London, Macmillan, 2001, vol. 16, p. 189-190.
	Downes, Stephen: 'Polonaise', in: Sadie, Stanley, ed.:*The New Grove Dictionary of Music and Musicians*, second edition, London, Macmillan, 2001, vol. 20, p. 45-47.
	Drabkin, William: 'Berceuse', in: Sadie, Stanley, ed.: *The New Grove Dictionary of Music and Musicians*, London, Macmillan, 1980, vol. 2, p. 519.
	Drabkin, William: 'Fantasia', in: Sadie, Stanley, ed.: *The New Grove Dictionary of Music and Musicians*, London, Macmillan, 1980, vol. 6, p.390.
	Dugot, Joël: *Guitare basse, auteur inconnu, fin du XVIIIe siècle (?)*, in: *Instrumentistes et Luthiers Parisiens*, Florence Gétreau, ed., Paris, 1988, p. 172.
	Dugot, Joël: 'Napoléon Coste et René Lacôte', in: *Les Cahiers de la Guitare*, Boissy-St-Léger, Association Guitares et Luths, no. 70, avril 1999, p. 32-34.
	Eigeldinger, Jean-Jacques: 'Introduction', in: Bailbé, Joseph Marc: 'La critique musicale au *Journal des Débats*' in: Bailbé [et al]: *La musique en France à l'epoque romantique (1830-1870)*, Paris, Flammarion, 1991, p 7-20.
	Einstein, Alfred: *Music in the Romantic Era, a history of musical thought in the 19th century*, New York - London, Norton, 1947, repr.1975.
	Ellis, Katharine: *Music criticism in nineteenth-century France: La Revue et Gazette musicale de Paris 1834 -80*, Cambridge, New York, Cambridge University Press, 1995, p. 33-55.
	Erpf, Hermann: *Form und Struktur in der Musik*, Schott, Mainz, 1967, p. 152-154.
	Evans, Tom and Mary Anne: *Guitars From the Renaissance to Rock*, London, Paddington Press, 1977, p. 117, 152-159.
	Fage, Juste Adrien de la: *Histoire générale de la musique et de danse*, Paris, Comptoir des Imprimeurs Unis, 1844, repr. 1978.
	Fauquet, Joël-Marie: *Dictionnaire de la Musique en France au XIXe siècle*, Paris, Fayard, 2003, p. 19, 66, 91, 150, 193, 214, 218, 221, 226, 229, 230, 251, 264-266, 269-273, 292-293, 303-305, 308-312, 323, 333-336, 343, 422-424, 433-435, 448-450, 542, 546, 548-554, 578-592, 603, 626, 648, 655, 667, 670, 686, 688, 741, 747, 766, 811-812, 841-842, 928-929, 933-934, 942, 965, 976-977, 981-982, 995-1002, 1025, 1040, 1061-1062, 1093-1094, 1113-1116, 1133, 1135-1136, 1152, 1154, 1156, 1160-1161, 1172-1173, 1195, 1200-1201.

Fauquet, Joël-Marie: 'Les sociétés de musique de chambre' in: Bailbé [et al]: *La musique en France à l"epoque romantique (1830-1870)*, Paris, Flammarion, 1991, 167-170, 187, 196.

Ferguson, Howard: 'Prelude', in: Sadie, Stanley, ed.: *The New Grove Dictionary of Music and Musicians*, London, Macmillan, 1980, vol.15, p.210-212; id. in: Sadie, Stanley, ed.: *The New Grove Dictionary of Music and Musicians*, second edition, London, Macmillan, 2001, vol. 20, p. 293.

Fétis, François Joseph: *Biographie universelle des musiciens et bibliographie générale de la musique*, Paris, Firmin-Didot, 2me éd. 1860-1881, tome I p. 36, 362-365, 337-338, 430-431; tome II p. 186, 198-199, 207, 418; tome IV p. 316-317, 323, 337; tome V p. 59, 125-126, 240, 246. 254-255, 275-276; tome VII p. 16-17; tome VIII p. 21-22, 66, 257, 439-440; suppl. Arthur Pougin, tome II p. 531.

Fétis, François Joseph: *Biographie universelle des musiciens et bibliographie générale de la musique*, Paris, Fournier, 1835-1844.

Fétis, François Joseph: *Notice biographique sur Nicolo Paganini suivie de l'analyse de ses ouvrages et précédée d'une esquisse de l'histoire du violon*, Paris, Schoneneberger, 1851, p. 85-95.

Fétis, François Joseph: 'Esquisse de l'histoire de l'harmonie', in: *Revue et Gazette musicale de Paris*, 1840, no. 9, 20, 24, 35, 40, 52, 63, 67, 68, 72, 73, 75, 76, 77; English translation Mary I. Arlin, Harmonologia series No.7, Pendragon Press, Stuyvesant NY, 1994.

Fortune, Nigel: 'Air', in: Sadie, Stanley, ed.: *The New Grove Dictionary of Music and Musicians*, London, Macmillan, 1980, vol.1, p.180; id in: Sadie, Stanley, ed.: *The New Grove Dictionary of Music and Musicians*, second edition, London, Macmillan, 2001, vol. 1, p. 252-256.

Fromrich, Yane: *Musique et caricature en France au XIXe siècle*, Iconographe musicale, II, ed. Lesure, Genève, Minkoff, 1973, p. 121.

Gaillard, Jeanne: *Paris, la ville, 1852-1870, l'urbanisme Parisien à l'heure d'Haussman.* [sic], Paris, Honoré Champion, 1977, p. 47-48, 203-206, 376-377, 559-573.

Gardeton, César: *Annales de la musique ou almanach musical pour l'an 1819 et 1820*, Paris, 1819, repr. Genève, Minkoff, 1978, p. 100-101; 1820 p. 52-55.

Gardeton, César: *Bibliographie musicale de la France et de l'étranger*, Paris, 1822, repr. Genève, Minkoff, 1978, p. 164-7, 177-186, 190-206, 214, 517, 526, 531, 543, 547, 560, 563, 572, 580.

Gelas, Lucien: 'Biographische Notizen über Napoléon Coste', in: *Die Gitarre*, Berlin, Jahrgang VIII, 1927, Heft 11/12, p. 82.

Gelbart, Matthew: *The Invention of "Folk Music" and "Art Music"*, Cambridge, Cambridge University Press, 2007, p. 11, 111-120, 138-144.

Gétreau, Florence: *Instrumentistes et luthiers parisiens XVIIe-XIXe siècles*, Paris, 1988, p.172 [i.e. Dugot, J.]

GioM   Giordano, Mario: 'Napoléon Coste e le sue opere', in: *Il plettro*, febbraio 1934, no. 2, p. 7.

Gossett, Philip: 'Rossini, Gioachino', in: Sadie, Stanley, ed.: *The New Grove Dictionary of Music and Musicians*, London, Macmillan, 1980, vol.16, p.229, 238-239, 244; id. in: Sadie, Stanley, ed.: *The New Grove Dictionary of Music and Musicians*, second edition, London, Macmillan, 2001, vol. 21, p. 748-751.

Grout, Donald Jay & Claude Palisca: *A History of Western Music*, London, Dent, 1988.

Grunfeld, Frederic V.: *The Art and Times of the Guitar*, New York, 1969, p. 163-210.

Guitare Napoléon Coste, 'Trois guitares du musée de la Musique' in: *Diapason*, Boulogne, 12/2000, p.57.

Gumplowicz, Philippe: 'Le rêve et la mission. La musique et le peuple en France 1789-1848' in: Bödeker, Hans Erich, Patrice Veit et Michael Werner, ed.: *Les sociétés de musique en Europe 1700-1900*, Berlin, Berliner Wissenschafts Verlag, 2007, p. 373-400.

Gorio, Francesco: 'Note sull'interpretazione della musica per chitarra dell'ottocento', in: *Il Fronimo*, Milano, Suvini Zerboni, vol. XIII, no. 44, 1983, p. 32-42.

Gorio, Francesco: 'Wenzeslaus Thomas Matiegka', in: *Il Fronimo*, Milano, Suvini Zerboni, vol. XV, no. 52, 1985, p. 24-41; no. 53, p. 7-26; vol. XVI, no. 54, 1986, p. 18-45; no. 55, p. 26-40.

Green, Richard D., ed.: *Foundations in Music Bibliography*, New York, London, Norwood (Australia), The Haworth Press, Inc., 1993, p. 21, 40, 200, 215.

Grégoir, Edouard: *Documents historiques relatifs à l'art musical et aux artistes musiciens*, vol. 3, Bruxelles, Schott, 1874-1876, p. 81.

Grijp, Louis Peter & Paul Scheepers, ed.: *Van Aristoxenos tot Stockhausen*, Wolters-Noordhoff, Groningen, 1990, Scheepers, p. 293-334, Borgdorff, p. 436-439.

Grunfeld, Frederic V.: *The Art and Times of the Guitar*, New York, MacMillan, 1969, p. 174-204.

Haan, De: zie: Robijns, J. & Miep Zijlstra: *Algemene Muziek Encyclopedie*, De Haan, Weesp, 1983, vol.2, p. 90 Cachucha.

Haine, Malou: *Les facteurs d'instruments de musique à Paris au 19ᵉ siècle des artisans face à l'industrialisation*, Bruxelles, Université de Bruxelles, 1984, p. 21-24, 47-48, 50-59, 62-65, 68, 71, 74, 78-88, 92, 94, 108, 123, 134-135, 142, 145, 147-153, 156, 161, 166, 182, 200, 298-299, 301, 304, 311-315, 318, 321.

Haine, Malou: 'Les facteurs d'instruments de musique à l'époque romantique' in: Bailbé [et al]: *La musique en France à l'epoque romantique (1830-1870)*, Paris, Flammarion, 1991, p. 101-102, 108-115, 119, 123.

Hanekuyk, Judith & Freek Pliester: *Luit en Gitaar*, Den Haag, Haags Gemeentemuseum, 1984. p. 123-124.

Hamilton, Kenneth: 'Berceuse', in: Sadie, Stanley, ed.: *The New Grove Dictionary of Music and Musicians*, second edition, London, Macmillan, 2001, vol. 2, p. 304.

Harmsen, A.J.E.: syllabus retorica, 16.5, http://www.let.leidenuniv.nl/Dutch/Renaissance/SyllabusRetorica.html, 2013.

HecT1   Heck, Thomas Fitzsimmons: *The Birth of the Classic Guitar and its Cultivation in Vienna, reflected in the Career and Compositions of Mauro Giuliani (d.1829)* (with) vol II: *Thematic Catalogue of the complete works of Mauro Giuliani*, Ph.D. Yale University, 1970, Ann Arbor, University Microfilms International, 1977.

HecT2   Heck, Thomas Fitzsimmons: *Mauro Giuliani: Virtuoso Guitarist and Composer*, Columbus, Orphée, 1995, p. 147.

Hedley, Arthur & Maurice Brown: 'Chopin, Fryderyc Franziszek', in: Sadie, Stanley, ed.: *The New Grove Dictionary of Music and Musicians*, London, Macmillan, 1980, vol.4, p.294.

Henke, Mattias: *Joseph Küffner, Leben und Werk des Würzburger Musikers im Spiegel der Geschichte*, Tutzing, Schneider, 1985.

Hickman, Roger & Jack Sage: 'Romance', in: Sadie, Stanley, ed.: *The New Grove Dictionary of Music and Musicians*, London, Macmillan, 1980, vol.16, p.121-126; id. in: Sadie, Stanley, ed.:*The New Grove Dictionary of Music and Musicians*, second edition, London, Macmillan, 2001, vol. 21, p. 574-575.

Hicks, V.: 'Barbershop', in: *The New Grove Dictionary of Music and Musicians*, second edition, London, Macmillan, 2001, vol. 2, p. 697.

HilJ   Hillairet, Jacques: *Dictionnaire historique des rues de Paris*, Paris, Les Èditions de Minuit, 1963-1972, p. 9-45, plan 1808, 202, 280-283, 375-377, 457-458, 511-514; supplément p. 24, 51, 58, 314-315, 642-643.

HoeJ   Hoek, Jan Anton van: *Die Gitarrenmusik im 19. Jahrhundert*, Wilhelmshaven, Heinrichshofen Verlag, 1983, p. 20, 21, 34, 40, 46, 59, 60, 62, 70, 76-78, 83, 90, 93, 96.

Hofmann, Erik Pierre: *Presentation and Expert Report on a Historic Guitar Formely Owned by Napoleon Coste (1805-1883)*, Germolles-sur-Grosne, Les Robins, unpublished, 2016.

Hofmeester, Theodorus M.: 'Is There a School of Tárrega', in: *The Guitar Review*, New York, The Society of the Classic Guitar, vol. I no. 1, october-november 1946, p. 4-6, (reprint 1974/1975 vol. I).

HopC   Hopkinson, Cecil: *A Dictionary of Parisian Music Publishers 1700-1950*, London, 1954, p. V, 24-25, 29, 31, 52, 54, 56, 58, 66-68, 80, 81, 89-90, 99, 104-106, 110-111, 128.

Hutchings, Arthur: 'Concertino', in: Sadie, Stanley, ed.: *The New Grove Dictionary of Music and Musicians*, London, Macmillan, 1980, vol.4 p.626; id. in: Sadie, Stanley, ed.:*The New Grove Dictionary of Music and Musicians*, second edition, London, Macmillan, 2001, vol. 6, p. 240.

Jacquot, Albert: *Dictionnaire pratique et raisonné des instruments de musique anciens et modernes*, Paris, Fischbacher, 1886, p. 41, 100,-103. [LF2 p. 436].

James, Anthony R.: 'Divertissement', in: Sadie, Stanley, ed.: *The New Grove Dictionary of Music and Musicians*, London, Macmillan, 1980, vol. 5, p.506-507; id. in: Sadie, Stanley, ed.:*The New Grove Dictionary of Music and Musicians*, second edition, London, Macmillan, 2001, vol. 6, p. 394-396.

Jacquot, Albert.: *La Lutherie Lorraine et Française*, Paris, 1912, p. 157-158.

JanJ   Jansen, Johannes: 'Simon Wynberg: The Guitar Works of Napoléon Coste, Bd. VIII u. IX.' in: *Gitarre und Laute*, Köln, vol. V, 1983, no. 5, p. 302.

Janssens, Robert: *Geschiedenis van de luit en de gitaar*, Antwerpen, 1980, p. 81, 151.

JapM   Jape, Mijndert, ed.: *Classical Guitar Music In Print*, vol. 7, Philadelphia, Musicdata,1989, p. 2, 27, 67, 239. Suppl. 1998, p. 29-30, 183.

JawR   Jaworski, Roman: 'Napoléon Coste 1805-1883, une histoire perdue', in: *Valentiana*, Valenciennes, Association Valentiana,1992, no. 10, p. 67-80.

JefB1   Jeffery, Brian: *Fernando Sor, Composer and Guitarist*, London, Tecla, 1977; second edition 1994, p. 86, 93, 96, 104, 114, 161, 165, 168, 174, 187, 190.

JefB2   Jeffery, Brian: 'Napoléon Costes Jugend', in: *Gitarre und Laute*, Köln, vol. IV, 1982, no. 5, p. 253-256.

JefB3   Jeffery, Brian: 'Napoléon Coste - renewed acquaintance', in: *Guitar & Lute*, 1982, no. 20, p. 8.

JefB4   Jeffery, Brian & Erik Marchélie: 'Napoléon Coste" in: *Cahiers de la Guitare*, Boissy-St-Léger, Association Guitares et Luths, vol. 6, 1983, p. 9-14.

JefB5   Jeffery, Brian: 'Fernando Sor, concert performer', in: *Guitar Review*, New York, The Society of the Classic Guitar, no. 39, summer 1974, p. 6-10. [vertaling van JB6].

JefB6   Jeffery, Brian: 'L'attivita' concertistica di Fernando Sor' in: *Il Fronimo*, Milano, Suvini Zerboni, vol. II, no. 6, 1974, p. 6-13.

JefB7   Jeffery, Brian: 'Il vero testo de l'Encouragement di Fernando Sor' in: *Il Fronimo*, Milano, Suvini Zerboni, vol. IX, no. 34, 1981, p. 34-35.

JefB8   Jeffery, Brian: *Dionisio Aguado*, biography and bibliography, Heidelberg, Chanterelle, 1994, p. xv-xvii.

JefB9   Jeffery, Brian: 'I metodi per chitarra di Dionisio Aguado' in: *Il Fronimo*, Milano, Suvini Zerboni, vol. VIII, no. 30, 1980, p. 17-25.

JefB10   Jeffery, Brian: 'Andrés Segovia's edition (1945) of Sor's "Twenty Studies"', in: *Soundboard*, the journal of the Guitar Foundation of America, vol. VIII/4, 1981, p. 253-255.

JefB11   Jeffery, Brian, ed. Schubert, Franz: Schubert Lieder, London, Tecla, 2011.

JefB12   Jeffery, Brian: Napoléon Coste: *La Source du Lyson* opus 47, London, Tecla, 1982, http://www.tecla.com/extras/0001/0021/0021pref.htm, November 17, 2014.

Johnson, James H.: *Listening in Paris: a cultural history*, Berkeley, University of Berkeley Press, 1995, p. 199, 203, 228, 229, 240-246, 270-271.

Kahl, Willi: 'Bolero', in: Sadie, Stanley, ed.: *The New Grove Dictionary of Music and Musicians*, London, Macmillan, 1980, vol.2, p.870; id. in: Sadie, Stanley, ed.:*The New Grove Dictionary of Music and Musicians*, second edition, London, Macmillan, 2001, vol. 2, p. 819-822.

Kantner, Leopold & Irene Holzer, ed.: *Anton Diabelli: thematisch-systematisches Werkverzeignis*, München, Strube, 2006.

Kemp, Peter: 'Strauss', in: Sadie, Stanley, ed.:*The New Grove Dictionary of Music and Musicians*, second edition, London, Macmillan, 2001, vol. 24, p. 475.

KliJ   Klier, Johannes & Ingrid Hacker: *Die Gitarre, Ein Instrument und seine Geschichte*, Bad Schussenried, Biblioteca de la Guitarra, 1980, p. 169.

Kloe, Jan J. de: *Boris Perott, A Life with the Guitar*, Heidelberg, Chanterelle, 2012, p. 12.

Koechlin, Ch.: 'Les tendances de la musique moderne Française', in: Lavignac, Albert: *Encyclopédie de la musique...*, Paris, Delagrave, 1925, p. 63.

Kornel, Michalowski: 'Chopin', in: Sadie, Stanley, ed.: *The New Grove Dictionary of Music and Musicians*, second edition, London, Macmillan, 2001, vol. 5, p. 706-710.

Kroll, Mark: *Johann Nepomuk Hummel, A Musician's Life and World*, Maryland, The Scarecrow Press, 2007, p. 62-63, 122-123, 159.

Kuronen, Darcy: *Dangerous Curves - The Art of the Guitar*, Boston, 2000, p. 43, 220.

Lamb, Andrew: 'Quadrille', in: Sadie, Stanley, ed.: *The New Grove Dictionary of Music and Musicians*, London, Macmillan, 1980, vol.15, p.489-490; id. in: Sadie, Stanley, ed.: *The New Grove Dictionary of Music and Musicians*, second edition, London, Macmillan, 2001, vol. 20, p. 653-654.

Lamb, Andrew: 'Waltz', in: Sadie, Stanley, ed.: *The New Grove Dictionary of Music and Musicians*, London, Macmillan, 1980, vol.20, p.200-206; id. in: Sadie, Stanley, ed.: *The New Grove Dictionary of Music and Musicians*, second edition, London, Macmillan, 2001, vol. 27, p. 76-77.

Läpke, Richard: 'Biographie Napoléon Coste' in: *Internationale Gitarre-Zeitung*, Jahrgang I, no. 4 (Jan.1884), no. 5 (Febr.1884), Leipzig, transcr. Eduard Fack, 'Die Meister', unp. p. 118-119.

Laforêt, Claude (pseud. Flavien Bonnet-Roy): *La Vie musicale au Temps romantique*, Paris, Peyronnet, 1929, p. 130-131 Huerta, 136-137 Berlioz, 150-151 Sowinski/Chopin, 156-157 Chopin, 164-165 Paganini, 170-179 salons/LFM, 196-211.

Larsen, Jens Peter & Georg Feder: 'Joseph Haydn' in: Sadie, Stanley, ed.: *The New Grove Dictionary of Music and Musicians*, London, Macmillan, 1980, vol.8, p.365.

Lajarte, Théodore de: *Bibliothèque musicale du Théatre de l'Opéra*, Paris, Librairie des Bibliophiles, 1878, vol. II, p. 104, 127, 158, 166, 192.

Lasalle, Albert: *Dictionnaire de la musique appliquée à l'amour*, Paris, Librairie internationale, 1868, p. 145-149, 225-226. Guitare, Quadrille.

Lavignac, Albert: *La Musique et les Musiciens*, Paris, Delagrave, 1895, p. 171.

Lavignac, Albert: *Encyclopédie de la musique*, Paris, Delagrave, 1927, deuxième partie, p. 2010-2018.

Leconte, André, ed.: *Plan de Paris par Arrondissement*, Paris, 1977.

Ledhuy, Adolphe & Henri Bertini: *Encyclopédie pittoresque de la musique...*, Paris, Delloye, 1835, tome I, p. 141-152, Sor, Ave Maria, Dernier Cri des Grecs, O Crux, Mazurka, Mont Serrat, Élève, La Candeur, 165-168, étude Ledhuy, Da Moiselle Lemoine, Caprice Ledhuy; tome II, p. 4-5, origine de la guitare, 33, instruments des Hébreux, 40-45, Le Boléro Sor, 49, Seguidilla, 50, All'o vivace, 101 [=99], Panseron, 104, Giuliani, 123-127, Cherubini, Tripodison Aguado; tome III, p. 105-109, Anatomie du cerveau - organe de la musique, 113-116, Panseron, 154-167, Sor.

Lesure, François (préface): *Guitares, Chefs-d'oeuvre des collections de France*, Paris, La Flûte de Pan, 1980, p. 137, 239, 313, 314.

LesF2   Lesure, François: *La musique à Paris en 1830-1831*, Paris, Bibliothèque nationale, 1983, p. 1-11, 17-18, 24, 27-30, 33-35, 52-62, 71, 104, 115-116, 123-125, 129-130, 137-138, 143, 148, 150-151, 154, 162, 166-167, 170-174, 177-179, 184-186, 190, 206, 222, 229, 271-275, 293, 341-343, 351, 354, 362-363, 431, 435, 437-443. [Lacôte]

Liebaars, Herman: *François-Joseph Fétis en het muziekleven van zijn tijd*, Brussel, Koninklijke Bibliotheek, 1972, p. XI-XXVI, 17, 29-30, 33-34, 37, 71, 139, 206-211, 215-218, 254-255, pl. XIII, XVI, XVII, XIX, XX progr. conc. hist., XXI, XXXIV, XLIII.

LipF   Lippmann, Friedrich: 'Vincenzo Bellini' in: Sadie, Stanley, ed.: *The New Grove Dictionary of Music and Musicians*, London, Macmillan, 1980, vol. 2, p.447-448, 452; id. in: Sadie, Stanley, ed.: *The New Grove Dictionary of Music and Musicians*, second edition, London, Macmillan, 2001, vol. 2, p. 208.

Little, Meredith Ellis: 'Minuet', in: Sadie, Stanley, ed.: *The New Grove Dictionary of Music and Musicians*, London, Macmillan, 1980, vol.12, p.353-358; id. in: Sadie, Stanley, ed.: *The New Grove Dictionary of Music and Musicians*, second edition, London, Macmillan, 2001, vol. 16, p. 744.

Lloyd, Llewelyn: 'Pitch', in: Sadie, Stanley, ed.: *The New Grove Dictionary of Music and Musicians*, second edition, London, Macmillan, 2001, vol. 19, p. 799-800.

Loewenberg, Alfred: 'Romani, Pietro', in: Sadie, Stanley, ed.: *The New Grove Dictionary of Music and Musicians*, London, Macmillan, 1980, vol.16, p.127-128.

Longyear, Rey M.: *Nineteenth-century romanticism in music*, Englewood Cliffs, New Jersey, Prentice-Hall, 1969, p. 1-9, 90-94, 98, 104.

Longyear, R.M.: 'Auber' in: Sadie, Stanley, ed.: *The New Grove Dictionary of Music and Musicians*, London, Macmillan, 1980, vol.1, p.681.

Lopez Poveda, Alberto: *Andrés Segovia, Vida y obra*, Jaén, Universidad de Jaén, 2009, p. 109, 114, 117, 119, 167, 183, 875, 1075, 1100, 1103, 1202.

Lyons, David B.: *lute, vihuela, guitar to 1800: a bibliography*, Detroit, Information Coordinators, 1978.

MacDonald, Hugh: 'Hector Berlioz', in: Sadie, Stanley, ed.: *The New Grove Dictionary of Music and Musicians*, London, Macmillan, 1980, vol.2, p.580-585, 602-603; id. in: Sadie, Stanley, ed.: *The New Grove Dictionary of Music and Musicians*, second edition, London, Macmillan, 2001, vol. 2, p. 384-385, 389.

MacDonald, Hugh: 'Scherzo', in: Sadie, Stanley, ed.: *The New Grove Dictionary of Music and Musicians*, London, Macmillan, 1980, vol.16, p.634-635; id. in: Sadie, Stanley, ed.: *The New Grove Dictionary of Music and Musicians*, second edition, London, Macmillan, 2001, vol. 22, p. 488-489.

Mailly, Edouard: *Les origines du conservatoire royal de musique de Bruxelles*, Bruxelles, Hayez, 1879, p. 3-11.

Makaroff, Nikolai Petrovich de: 'Guitare et Guitaristes'; in: *Revue et Gazette musicale de Paris*, vol. XXIV, no. 1, 4 I 1857, no. 1, p. 6-7.

Bibliographies

	Makarow (Stockmann) (Stockhausen?) 'Aus den Lebenserinnerungen des russischen Gitarrevirtuosen N. P. Makarow', in: *Der Gitarrefreund, Mitteilungen der Gitarristischen Vereinigung*, 11. Jahrgang 1910, Heft 6 p. 43-45; 12. Jahrgang, 1911 Heft 1 p. 1-3; Heft 2 p. 11-13; Heft 3 p. 23-25; Heft 4 p. 35-37; Heft 5 p. 45-47; ....
MakN	Makaroff, Nikolai Petrovich de: 'The memoirs of Makaroff', in: *The Guitar Review*, New York, The Society of the Classic Guitar, 1946-48, (vol. I reprint 1974/1975) no. 1, p. 10-12, no. 2, p. 32-34, no. 3, p. 56-59, no. 5, p. 109-113.
MarE	Marchélie, Erik: 'Analyse de la Source du Lyson', in: 'Napoléon Coste" in: *Cahiers de la Guitare*, Boissy-St-Léger, Association Guitares et Luths, vol. 6, 1983, p. 9-14. [heptacorde] [i.e. JefB4]
	Marescot, Charles de: *La Guitaromanie*, Paris, Archivum Musicum, z.j. no. 16, Studio per Edizione scelte. Firenze, 1985, p. 1, 9, 17, 33.
	Mauerhofer, Alois: *Leonard von Call - Musik des Mittelstandes zur Zeit der Wiener Klassik*, Ph. D. Graz, 1974, eBooks on Demand, 2009.
	McCready, Sue: *Classical Guitar Companion*, Bimport, Musical New Services, 1982, p. 22-23.
	McCrum, Blanche & Helen Jones: *Bibliographical procedures and style*, Washington, Library of Congress, 1954, repr. 1960.
	McCutcheon, Meredith Alice: *Guitar and Vihuela, An Annotated Bibliography*, New York, Pendragon Press, 1985.
	Meier, Georg, *Programm Konzert*, Hamburg, 1921, Archiv Andreas Stevens, Hilden.
MeiG2	Meier, Georg, *Handbuch über Guittar-Musik*, Hamburg, 1934, unp. ms., Archiv Andreas Stevens, Hilden.
	Meyer, Leonard: *Style and Music, Theory, History, and Ideology*, Chicago, London, University of Chicago Press, 1989.
	Michelin, *Guide de Tourisme: Paris*, Paris, Pneu Michelin, 1997-1998, p. 12-13.
MitA	Miteran, Alain: *Histoire de la Guitare*, Bourg-la-Reine, Zurfluh, 1976, 2^e ed. 1997, p. 181-188.
MølE	Møldrup, Erling: *Guitaren, et eksotisk instrument i den danske musik*, Kopenhagen, Kontrapunkt, 1997, p. 125-143, 135 foto Coste, 165, 170, 181, 194-203, 231.
	Moser, Wolf: 'Fernando Sor und seine "Methode pour la guitare"', in: *Gitarre und Laute*, Köln, vol. I, 1979, no. 1, p. 26-32.
	Moser, Wolf: 'Die Gitarre im Leben eines romantischen Komponisten', [Berlioz] in: *Gitarre und Laute*, Köln, vol. II, 1980, no. 4, p. 26-34.
MosW3	Moser, Wolf: *Fernando Sor: Versuch einer Autobiografie und gitarristische Schriften*, [vertaling in Duits van Ledhuy], Köln, Saint-Georges, 1984, p. 53-58, 73-110, 127-134, 142, 147-157.
MosW4	Moser, Wolf: *Gitarre-Musik: ein internationaler katalog*, Hamburg, Berlin, Trekel, vol. I, 1974, p. 42, 181, 199, 275-277; vol. II, 1977, p. 19.
MosW5	Moser, Wolf: *Ich, Fernando Sor, Versuch einer Autobiographie und gitarristische Schriften*, Lyon, Saint-Georges, 2^e ed., 2005, p. 9, 128-131, 136-137, 143, 167, 174, 181, 191-192, 202, 208, 212.
	Moser, Wolf: *Francisco Tárrega, Werden und Wirkung*, Lyon, Saint-Georges, 1996, p. 82, 265, 338, 340, 361, 379, 405, 407, 412.
	Müller, Hans-Christian: 'Schott', in: Sadie, Stanley, ed.: *The New Grove Dictionary of Music and Musicians*, second edition, London, Macmillan, 2001, vol. 22, p. 633-634.
	Neill, Edward: 'Paganini', in: Sadie, Stanley, ed.: *The New Grove Dictionary of Music and Musicians*, second edition, London, Macmillan, 2001, vol. 18, p. 890-891.
	Neubauer, John, et al: *New Paths: aspects of music theory and aesthetics in the age of romanticism*, Leuven, Leuven U.P., 2009.
	Ophee, Matanya: 'Romantische Gitarrenmusik, Kritische Anmerkungen', in: *Gitarre und Laute*, Köln, vol. VII, 1985, no. 5, p. 45-49.
	Ophee, Matanya: 'The Memoirs of Makaroff, A Second Look', in: *Soundboard*, the journal of the Guitar Foundation of America, vol. IX, no. 3, 1982, p. 226-233.
	Ophee, Matanya: 'In difesa dei "due amici"' in: *Il Fronimo*, Milano, Suvini Zerboni, vol. IX, no. 36, 1981, p. 10.
	Ophee, Matanya: 'Seltenes & Curioses für Guitarre' in: *Gitarre und Laute*, Köln, 1982, vol. III, no.5, p. 286-293. [Carnaval de Venise op. 4 N. Makaroff]
	Ophee, Matanya: 'The promotion of Francisco Tárrega - a case history', in: *Soundboard*, the journal of the Guitar Foundation of America vol. VIII no.3, august 1981, p. 153-158.
	Pekacz, Jolanta T.: *Musical biography: towards new paradigms*, Aldershot, Ashgate, 2006.
	Penesco, Anne: 'Le violon en France au temps de Baillot et de Paganini', in: Bailbé, Joseph Marc: 'La critique musicale au *Journal des Débats*' in: Bailbé [et al]: *La musique en France à l'epoque romantique (1830-1870)*, Paris, Flammarion, 1991, p. 199-230.
PerP	Pérez-Díaz, Pompeyo: *Dionisio Aguado y la guitarra clásico-romántica*, Madrid, Alpuerto, 2003, p. 110.
	Pierre, Constant: *Les Facteurs d'instruments de musique*, Paris, Sagot, 1893, p. 275.
	Pierre, Constant: *Le Conservatoire national de musique et de déclamation: documents historiques et administratifs*, Paris, Imprimerie nationale, 1900, p. 403-406, 420-431, 875.
	Pintér-Lück, Éva: 'Norma', in: Batta, András: *Opera*, Könemann, Köln, 1999, p. 28.
PirB	Piris, Bernard: *Fernando Sor, Une guitare à l'orée du Romantisme*, Arles, Aubier, 1989, (+ annexes), [geen annotatie en index!], p. 56, 72-75, 80, 86-90, 145, 157, 159.
	Pistone, Danièle: *La musique en France de la Révolution à 1900*, Paris, Honoré Champion, 1979, p. 4-5, 9-29, 100-103, 202-203.
	Planque: *Agenda musical pour l'année1836*, Paris, 1836, repr. Genève, Minkoff, 1981, p. 1, 10-13, 38-49, 62-77, 86-101. *Agenda musical ou indicateur...2e Année 1836*, p. 1, 30-33, 118-135, 146-151, 158, 167-175, 212-223, 266-279. *Agenda musical ou indicateur .....3e Année 1837*, p. 5, 32-48, 99-119, 137-146, 186-200, 279-282.
	Powroźniak, Józef: 'Coste, Napoléon', in: *Gitarrenlexikon*, Berlin, Verlag Neue Musik,1979, p. 36.
	Prat, Domingo: *Diccionario biografico, bibliografico, critico, de Guitarras, Guitarristas y Guitarreros*, Buenos Aires, Fernando Romero, 1934, repr. Columbus, Orphée, 1986, p. 96-98, 427.

	Prefumo, Danilo: 'L'attività concertistica di Luigi Legnani...' in: *Il Fronimo*, Milano, Suvini Zerboni, vol. X, no. 41, 1982, p. 22.
	Prefumo, Danilo: 'Paganini e la chitarra' in: *Il Fronimo*, Milano, Suvini Zerboni, vol. VI, no. 24, 1978, p. 6-15; no. 23, 1978 p. 6-14.
	Prefumo, Danilo: 'Marc'Aurelio Zani de Ferranti' in: *Il Fronimo*, Milano, Suvini Zerboni, vol. XIII, no. 51, 1985, p. 9-37.
	Pujol, Emilio: *Escuela razonada de la guitarra*, vol. I, Paris, 1933, ed. Buenos Aires, 1956, p. 36.
PujE2	Pujol. Emilio: *Tárrega, Ensayo biográfico*, Lisboa, Ramos, 1960, p. 87-90. 121, 132.
	Pujol, Emilio: *El dilema del sonido en la guitarra*, Buenos Aires, Ricordi, 1960, p. 42-47.
	Pyee-Cohen, Doris & Diane Cloutier: *La Gazette musicale de Paris, 1834-1835; La Revue et Gazette musicale de Paris, 1835-1880*, serie: 'Répertoire international de la presse musicale, vol. I-V, Baltimore, NISC, 1999.
RadH	Radke, Hans: 'Coste, Napoléon', in: *Die Musik in Geschichte und Gegenwart*, ed. Blume, Kassel, Bärenreiter, 1956, ed. 1973, vol. XV (Supplement 1) Kol. 1616-1617.
RadG	Radole, Giuseppe: *Liuto, chitarra e vihuela, storia e letteratura*, Milano, Suvini Zerboni, 1979, 3ᵉ ed. 1997, p. 154-155.
	Ragossnig, Konrad: *Handbuch der Gitarre und Laute*, Mainz, Schott, 1978, p. 81, 125.
	Rasch, Rudolf, ed.: *Music Publishing in Europe 1600-1900*, Berlin, Berliner Wissenschafts-Verlag, 2005, p. 4, 137, 147.
ReaU	Realino, Umberto: *Un siècle de guitare en France 1750-1850*, unp. thèse Sorbonne, repr. Lille, Atelier national, 1999, p. 381-392, 398.
	Reese, Donald T., ed.: *Classical Guitar Music In Print*, vol. 7s, supplement 1998, Philadelphia, Musicdata, p. 2, 21, 29-30, 39, 96, 107, 114, 115, 126, 183. see Jape, M., 1989.
	Rezits, Joseph: *The Guitarist's Resource Guide*, San Diego, Pallma Music Co., 1983.
	Rhodes, J.J.K. & W.R. Thomas: 'Pitch class', in: Sadie, Stanley, ed.: *The New Grove Dictionary of Music and Musicians*, London, Macmillan, 1980, vol.14, p .785.
RibM	Riboni, Marco: '25 études op. 38 di Napoléon Coste', in: *Il Fronimo*, Milano, Suvini Zerboni, vol. XXVIII no. 109, 2000, p. 14-23; no. 110, p. 43-49; no. 111, p. 38-44.
	Ribouillault, Danielle: 'Fernando Sor ou "à l'orée du romantisme, une guitare" [Piris], in: *Les Cahiers de la Guitare*, Boissy-St-Léger, Association Guitares et Luths, 1980, no. 3, p. 34-35.
	Ribouillault, Danielle: 'Technique de la guitare: la position de l'instrument à l'epoque romantique', in: *Les Cahiers de la Guitare*, Boissy-St-Léger, Association Guitares et Luths, 1982, no. 2, p. 28-35.
RibD3	Ribouillault, Danielle: 'La "Guitaromanie": du salon à la salle de concert', in: *Instrumentistes et Luthiers Parisiens*, Florence Gétreau, ed., Paris, La Ville de Paris, 1988, p. 171-194 [p. 172 i.e. Dugot].
RibD4	Ribouillault, Danielle: *La technique de guitare en France dans la première moitié du XIXe siècle*, Ph.D. Paris, Sorbonne, 1980, p. 22, 159, 327, 332, 333.
	Riessauw, Anne-Marie: 'Hubert-Ferdinand Kufferath', in: Sadie, Stanley, ed.: *The New Grove Dictionary of Music and Musicians*, London, Macmillan, 1980, vol. 10, p. 292; id. in: Sadie, Stanley, ed.:*The New Grove Dictionary of Music and Musicians*, second edition, London, Macmillan, 2001, vol. 14, p. 1-2.
RisT1	Rischel, Thorvald: 'Bibliographische Notizen zu den Gitarrenwerken von Napoléon Coste', in: *Die Gitarre*, Berlin, 1927, Jahrgang VIII, Heft 7/8, [Coste-Heft] p. 47-51.
RisT2	Rischel, Thorwald [sic]: 'Zur Geschichte der Gitarre in Dänemark', in: *Die Gitarre*, Berlin, 1931, Jahrgang XII, no. 9/10, p. 70-74, no. 11-12, p. 90-91.
	Roberts, John: 'Sor's method for the Spanish guitar', in: *Guitar*, 1980, jan., no. 30, p. 22-24.
	Robijns, J. & Miep Zijlstra: *Algemene Muziek Encyclopedie*, De Haan, Weesp, 1983, vol.9 p. 274 [Strauss]; vol. 2 p. 90 [Cachucha].
	Robinson, Philip: 'Ambroise Thomas', in: Sadie, Stanley, ed.: *The New Grove Dictionary of Music and Musicians*, London, Macmillan, 1980, vol.18, p.776.
	Rogers, Douglas: 'Giulio Regondi, Guitarist, Concertinist or Melophonist? A Reconnaissance', in: *Guitar Review*, New York, The Society of the Classic Guitar, no. 91, 1992, p. 1-9; no. 92, 1993, p. 14-18; no. 97, 1994, p. 11-17.
	Romanillos, José L.: 'The life of Dionisio Aguado' in *Dionisio Aguado, the complete works for guitar*, vol.1, p. viii-x. [cf JefB7]
	Romanillos, José L.: *Antonio de Torres*, Element Books, Longmead, 1990, p.18, 142.
RonN1	Roncet, Noël: *Napoléon Coste, Compositeur, 1805-1883*, Amondans, 2005.
	Roncet, Noël: *Napoléon Coste, Composer, 1805-1883*, Tecla Editions, 2008, [translation in English of 1ˢᵗ ed.].
	Roncet, Noël: *Exposition Napoléon Coste*, Amondans, 21-26 VI 2005.
	Root, Deane L.: 'Barbershop harmony', in: Sadie, Stanley, ed.: *The New Grove Dictionary of Music and Musicians*, London, Macmillan, 1980, vol. 2, p. 137.
	Rosen, Charles: *The Classical Style: Haydn, Mozart, Beethoven*, London, 1971.
	Rosen, Charles: *The Romantic Generation*, Cambridge, Massachusetts, Harvard University Press, 1995, p. 174, 204, 207.
	Rosen, Charles: *Music and Sentiment*, New Haven, London, Yale University Press, 2010.
	Rossato, Daniela: 'Luigi Rinaldo Legnani' in: *Il Fronimo*, Milano, Suvini Zerboni, vol. VII, no. 27, 1979, p. 5-15.
	Rossi, Adriano: 'Sor und seine Gitarrenschule', in: *Die Gitarre*, IV, Berlin, 1923, no. 3-4, p. 16-19; V, 1924, no. 5-6, p. 29-35, [vertaling van artikel in 'Il Plettro' van Oswald Lorenz].
	Salzer, Felix: *Structural Hearing, tonal coherernce in music*, New York, Dover publications, 1952, p. 10-31, 148-160.
	Sanders, Ernest H.: 'Cantilena', in: Sadie, Stanley, ed.: *The New Grove Dictionary of Music and Musicians*, London, Macmillan, 1980, vol.3, p.729-731; id. in: Sadie, Stanley, ed.:*The New Grove Dictionary of Music and Musicians*, second edition, London, Macmillan, 2001, vol. 5, p. 55-57.
SasW1	Sasser, William Gray: *The guitar works of Fernando Sor*, Ph.D. University of North Carolina, 1960, Ann Arbor, Michigan, 1975, p. 34, 63.

Sasser, William: 'In search of Sor', in: *Guitar Review*, New York, The Society of the Classic Guitar, no. 26, june 1962, p. 13-21.

Scheepers, Paul: 'Heinrich Schenker, *Harmonielehre*, 1907', in: Grijp, Louis Peter & Paul Scheepers, ed.: *Van Aristoxenos tot Stockhausen*, Wolters-Noordhoff, Groningen, 1990, p. 293-334.

Schmitz, Alexander: *Das Gitarrenbuch*, Frankfurt am Main, 1982, p. 61.

Schneider, Herbert: 'Auber', in: *The New Grove Dictionary of Music and Musicians*, second edition, London, Macmillan, 2001, vol. 2, p. 157.

Schopenhauer, Arthur: 'Aphorismen zur Lebensweisheit', in: *Parerga und Paralipomena*, Berlin, Hayn, 1851, repr. Leipzig, Insel Verlag, 1917, p. 112; translation Hans Driessen, Amsterdam, Wereldbibliotheek, 1991, p. 114.

Schwandt, Erich: 'Capriccio', in: Sadie, Stanley, ed.: *The New Grove Dictionary of Music and Musicians*, London, Macmillan, 1980, vol.3, p.758-759; id. in: Sadie, Stanley, ed.: *The New Grove Dictionary of Music and Musicians*, second edition, London, Macmillan, 2001, vol. 5, p. 100-101.

Schwandt, Erich: 'March', in: Sadie, Stanley, ed.: *The New Grove Dictionary of Music and Musicians*, London, Macmillan, 1980, vol.11, p.650; id. in: Sadie, Stanley, ed.: *The New Grove Dictionary of Music and Musicians*, second edition, London, Macmillan, 2001, vol. 15, p. 816-817.

Schwandt, Erich: 'Tarantella', in: Sadie, Stanley, ed.: *The New Grove Dictionary of Music and Musicians*, London, Macmillan, 1980, vol. 17, p. 575-576; id. in: Sadie, Stanley, ed.: *The New Grove Dictionary of Music and Musicians*, second edition, London, Macmillan, 2001, vol. 25, p. 96-97.

Schwarz, Boris: 'Paganini, Niccoló', in: Sadie, Stanley, ed.: *The New Grove Dictionary of Music and Musicians*, London, Macmillan, 1980, vol.14, p.86-90.

Schwarz, Werner: *Guitar Bibliography*, München, Saur, 1984, p. 34, 35, 61-62, 153, 160, 166, 168.

Schwarz-Reiflingen, Erwin: 'Zur Neuausgabe der Gitarreschule von Fernando Sor', in: *Die Gitarre*, Berlin, 1922, Jahrgang III, Heft 11, p. 98-101.

Schwarz-Reiflingen, Erwin: 'Beiträge zur Geschichte der Gitarristik nach 1840', in: *Die Gitarre*, Berlin, 1923, Jahrgang IV, Heft 9 p. 65-68; Heft 10/11 p. 74-78; Heft 12 p. 90-93; 1924, Jahrgang V, Heft 1/2 p. 103-105; Heft 5/6 p. 35.

SchE3   Schwarz-Reiflingen, Erwin: 'Napoléon Coste', in: *Die Gitarre*, Berlin, 1927, Jahrgang VIII, Heft 7/8, [Coste-Heft] p. 43-47.

SchE4   Schwarz-Reiflingen, Erwin: 'Costes Bearbeitung der Sor-Schule', in: *Die Gitarre*, Berlin, 1927, Jahrgang VIII, Heft 7/8, [Coste-Heft] p. 51-52.

SchE5   Schwarz-Reiflingen, Erwin: 'Besprechungen. Napoléon Coste. op. 38....', in: *Die Gitarre*, Berlin, 1927, Jahrgang VIII, Heft 7/8, [Coste-Heft] p. 52-53.

Searle, Humphrey: 'Liszt, Franz', in: Sadie, Stanley, ed.: *The New Grove Dictionary of Music and Musicians*, London, Macmillan, 1980, vol.11, p.29-30.

Seguret, Christian: *l'univers des Guitares*, Paris, 1997, p. 16-17. [Lacôte, 1830]

ShaA   Sharpe, A.P.: *The Story of the Spanish Guitar*, London, Clifford Essex, 1954, 4 ed. e 1968, p. 18-19, 27, 61.

Shtokman, see Stockhausen, Stockmann

Singer-Kerel, J.: *Le coût de la vie à Paris de 1840 à 1954*, Paris, A.Colin, 1961 [LesF2 p. 440]

Sinier, Daniel & Françoise de Ridder: *La Guitare, Paris 1650-1950*, Cremona, Il Salabue, 2007, p. 56-60.

Smart, Mary Ann: 'Donizetti', in: Sadie, Stanley, ed.: *The New Grove Dictionary of Music and Musicians*, second edition, London, Macmillan, 2001, vol. 6, p. 471-475.

Smith, Richard Langham: 'Thomas', in: Sadie, Stanley, ed.: *The New Grove Dictionary of Music and Musicians*, second edition, London, Macmillan, 2001, vol. 25, p. 403-407.

Sor, Fernando: 'Über Gitarreschulen', in: *Der Gitarrefreund*, München, 1926, Heft 27, p. 79-82.

Soullier, Charles: *Nouveau dictionnaire de musique illustré...*, Paris, Bazault, 1855, p. 140-141.

SouC   Soullier, Charles: *Annuaire musical 1855*, Paris, Saint-Étienne, 1854, p. 16-22, 35, 36, 43, 44. [LesF2 p. 435]

Sparks, Paul: 'The origins of the classical guitar' in: James Tyler and Paul Sparks: *The guitar and its music*, Oxford, Oxford University Press, 2002, p. 193-283.

Stempnik, Astrid: *Caspar Joseph Mertz, Leben und Werk...*, Frankfurt am Main, Lang, 1990.

Stempnik, Astrid: 'Concertino oder Trois Morceaux?', in: *Gitarre und Laute*, Köln, vol. IV, 1982, no. 1, p. 25-33.

SteE1   Stenstadvold, Erik 'Napoléon Costes Beitrag zu den 20 Etüden von Fernando Sor', in: *Gitarre und Laute*, Köln, vol. VI, 1984, no. 3, p. 14-17.

Stenstadvold, Erik: 'Coste's contribution to the "20 Studies" by Sor', *Soundboard*, the journal of the Guitar Foundation of America, vol. XI, no. 2, 1984, p. 136-140.

SteE3   Stenstadvold, Erik: 'Coste, Napoléon', in: Sadie, Stanley ed: *The New Grove Dictionary of Music and Musicians*, Second edition, London, Macmillan, 2001, p. 534.

SE4   Stenstadvold, Erik: *An Annotated Bibliography of Guitar Methods, 1760-1860*, Organologia: Musical Instruments and Performance Practice no. 4, London, Pendragon Press, 2010, p. xi-xiv, 3-6.

Stockhausen (Stockmann?) [Shtokman] [i.e. Buek] see Makarow: 'Aus den Lebenserinnerungen des russischen Gitarrevirtuosen N. P. Makarow', in: *Der Gitarrefreund, Mitteilungen der Gitarristischen Vereinigung*, 11. Jahrgang 1910, Heft 6 p. 43-45; 12. Jahrgang, 1911 Heft 1 p. 1-3; Heft 2 p. 11-13; Heft 3 p. 23-25; Heft 4 p. 35-37; Heft 5 p. 45-47; .... [H. 6 fehlt im Bestand]

(Stockmann?) Stockhausen [Shtokman] [i.e. Buek] see Makarow: 'Aus den Lebenserinnerungen des russischen Gitarrevirtuosen N. P. Makarow', in: *Der Gitarrefreund, Mitteilungen der Gitarristischen Vereinigung*, 11. Jahrgang 1910, Heft 6 p. 43-45; 12. Jahrgang, 1911 Heft 1 p. 1-3; Heft 2 p. 11-13; Heft 3 p. 23-25; Heft 4 p. 35-37; Heft 5 p. 45-47; .... [H. 6 fehlt im Bestand]

StoJ	Stockmann [Shtokman], J.: 'Napoléon Coste', in: *Der Guitarrefreund, Mitteilungen des Internationalen Guitarristen-Verbandes*, München, 3. Jahrgang, 1902, Heft 5, p. 55-56.
	Summerfield, Maurice J.: *The Classical Guitar: It's Evolution, Players & Personalities since 1800*, Newcastle-upon-Tyne, Ashley Mark, 4th ed. 1996, p. 79.
	Tanno, John: 'the guitarist's bookshelf', in: *Guitar Review*, New York, The Society of the Classic Guitar, no. 66, 1986, p. 34-35; no. 88, 1992, p. 34.
	Tonazzi, Bruno: *Liuto, Vihuela, Chitarra e Strumenti similari nelle loro Intavolature*, Trieste, Bèrben, 1971, 2e ed. 1977, p. 142.
TorJ	Torpp Larsson, Jytte: *Catalogue of the Rischel and Birket-Smith Collection*, Columbus, Orphée, 1989, p. i, ii, 41-47, 95, 150-1, 175, 189, 198-203, 208, 212, 223, 241, 247, 249, 254, 257, 258, 263.
TorM	Torta, Mario: *Catalogo tematico delle opere di Ferdinando Carulli*, Lucca, Libreria Musicale Italiana, 1993.
TunD	Tunley, David: *Salons, singers and songs: a background to romantic French song, 1830-1870*, Ashgate, Aldershot, 2002, p. 230-249.
TurH1	Turnbull, Harvey: *The Guitar from the Renaissance to the Present Day*, London, Batsford, 1974, repr. 1976, p. 60, 84.
	Turnbull, Harvey: 'Guitar §5', in: Sadie, Stanley ed: *The New Grove Dictionary of Music and Musicians*, London, Macmillan, 1980, vol. 7, p. 835-838.
	Tyler, James: *The Early Guitar*, London, Oxford University Press, 1980, p. 52-58.
	Unverricht, Hubert: 'Serenade', in: Sadie, Stanley, ed.: *The New Grove Dictionary of Music and Musicians*, London, Macmillan, 1980, vol.17, p.159-160.
	Vannes, René: *Dictionnaire Universel des Luthiers*, Paris, 1951, 3rd ed. Bruxelles, 1988, p. 198.
	Viglietti, Cedar: *Origen e historia de la guitarra*, Buenos Aires, Albatros, 1976, p. 59, 77, 83-85.
	Vliet, Ari van: 'Gitaarmuziek in de tweede helft van de zeventiende eeuw', in: *De Tabulatuur*, Driebergen, Nederlandse Luitvereniging, 1995-1997.
	Wade, Graham: *Traditions of the Classical Guitar*, London, Calder, 1980, p. 98, 113, 128-130.
	Wade, Graham: *A Concise History of the Classic Guitar*, Pacific, Mel Bay, 2001, p. 72, 74, 85, 89-91.
	Walker, Alan: 'Liszt', in: Sadie, Stanley, ed.: *The New Grove Dictionary of Music and Musicians*, second edition, London, Macmillan, 2001, vol. 14, p. 755--760.
WalH	Walter, Horst: 'Fanny Elssler' v in: Sadie, Stanley, ed.: *The New Grove Dictionary of Music and Musicians*, London, Macmillan, 1980, vol.6, p.146; id. in: Sadie, Stanley, ed.:*The New Grove Dictionary of Music and Musicians*, second edition, London, Macmillan, 2001, vol. 8, p. 170-171.
	Warrack, Johns: 'Leitmotif', in: Sadie, Stanley, ed.: *The New Grove Dictionary of Music and Musicians*, London, Macmillan, 1980, vol.10, p. 644.
	Weber, William: *Music and the Middle Class, The Social Structure of Concert Life in London, Paris and Vienna between 1830 and 1848*, Ashgate, Aldershot, 1975, 2nd ed. 2004.
	Weber, William: *The Great Transformation of Musical Taste*, Cambridge, Cambridge University Press, 2008, p. 98.
	Webster, James: 'Sonata form', in: Sadie, Stanley, ed.: *The New Grove Dictionary of Music and Musicians*, London, Macmillan, 1980, vol.17, p.497-508; id. in: Sadie, Stanley, ed.:*The New Grove Dictionary of Music and Musicians*, second edition, London, Macmillan, 2001, vol. 23, p. 695-697.
	Wekerlin, J.B.: *Échos du Temps Passé*, Vol. I, Paris, Durand, 1971, p.43.
	Wennekes, Emmanuel Gerhardus Johannes: *Het Paleis voor Volksvlijt...*, Den Haag, SDU, 1999, p. 16-20.
	Weston, Pamela: 'Blaes, Arnold Joseph', in: Sadie, Stanley, ed.: *The New Grove Dictionary of Music and Musicians*, London, Macmillan, 1980, vol. 2 p. 772.
	Westrup, Jack: 'Cavatina', in: Sadie, Stanley, ed.: *The New Grove Dictionary of Music and Musicians*, London, Macmillan, 1980, vol.4, p.35.
	Whistling, Carl Friedrich & Friedrich Hofmeister: *Handbuch der musikalischen Literatur oder allgemeines systematisch geordnetes Verzeigniss...*' Leipzig, Whistling, 1828-1839; Hofmeister, 1844-1845; 1815, 1817-1829, 1834, 1839, 1844, 1852, repr. New York, Garland, 1975.
	Whittall, Arnold: 'Leitmotif', in: Sadie, Stanley, ed.:*The New Grove Dictionary of Music and Musicians*, second edition, London, Macmillan, 2001, vol. 14, p. 527-530.
	Will, Ethyl L.: 'Ludwig Wenzel Lachnith', in: Sadie, Stanley, ed.: *The New Grove Dictionary of Music and Musicians*, London, Macmillan, 1980, vol.10, p.350.
WynS2	Wynberg, Simon: '...zur Rettung Napoléon Costes', in: *Gitarre und Laute*, Köln, vol. III, 1981, no. 5, p. 29-32.
	Wynberg, Simon: 'Napoléon Coste', in: *Gitarre und Laute*, Köln, vol. IV, 1982, no. 1, p. 51.
	Wynberg, Simon: *Marco Aurelio Zani de Ferranti*, a biography, Heidelberg, Chanterelle, 1989, p. 37, 43, 62.
	Wynberg, Simon: 'Giulio Regondi' in: *Il Fronimo*, Milano, Suvini Zerboni, vol. XI, no. 42, 1983, p. 8-14.
	Young, Percy Marshall: *The concert tradition from ther Middle Ages to the twentieth century*, London, Routledge, 1965, p. 174-177.
	Zimmerschied, Dieter: *Thematisches Verzeichnis der Werke von Johann Nepomuk Hummel*, Hofheim am Taunus, Hofmeister, 1971. [cf Kroll]
	Zuth, Josef: *Simon Molitor und die Wiener Gitarristik*, Wien, Goll, 1920, p. 83.
ZutJ2	Zuth, Josef: 'Coste, Napoléon', in: *Handbuch der Laute und Gitarre*, Wien, Doblinger, 1926-28, repr. Hildesheim, Olms, 1978, p. 72-73.

Music

Adami, Vinatier: *Cavatine Italienne*, arr. Coste, Kk Rischel Ms. 58 mu 6701.0884.
Aguado, Dionisio: *Méthode Complète Pour la Guitare... Traduite en Français... par F. de Fossa*, Paris Meissonnier, 1826, repr. Genève, Minkoff, 1980.
Aguado, Dionisio: in: Jeffery, Brian: *The Complete Works for Guitar... Dionisio Aguado*, facsimile edition, Heidelberg, Chanterelle, 1994.
Andrade, Auguste: *Souffrir sans espérer*, arr. Carcassi, WoO, 1836, *Le Ménéstrel*, .II No.28(132) p.2-3.
Bailleux, Mr.: *Methode de Guitarre Par Musique et Tablature*, Parijs, 1773, repr. Genève, Minkoff, 1980.
Barroilhet, Paul: *La petite Savoyarde*, arr. Coste, c.1840, Lbl E.1717.l.(41).
Bellini, Vincenzo: *Norma*, partitura, Roma, Reale accademia d'Italia, 1935, p. 42, 57, 111, 131, 175.
Bellini, Vincenzo: *Il pirata, melodramma...*, reduzzione, Paris, Marquerie, 1840, p. 55.
Bobrowicz, Jan Nepomuk: in: Komarnicki, Krzysztof & Robert Coldwell: *Selected Works*, Vol. I & II, DGA Editions, 2005.
Carcassi, Matteo: *Méthode Complète op. 59*, Carli, Parijs, 1825, repr. Genève, Minkoff, 1988.
Carulli, Ferdinando: *Méthode Complète op. 27*, Carli, Parijs, 1809-10, Ancona, Bèrben, 1965.
Carulli, Ferdinando: *Supplement à la Méthode... op. 192*, Carli, Paris, 1822, Leipzig, Peters, 1930.
Carulli, Ferdinando: *Méthode Complète pour parvenir et pincer de la Guitare Op. 241*, Paris, Carli, 1825, repr. Genève, Minkoff, 1987.
Carulli, Ferdinando: *La Marseillaise Varié op. 330*, Mayence, Schott, 1830, Kk RiBS 0127.
Carulli, Fernando: *Les Trois Jours...*, op. 331. Mayence et Anvers, Schott, No. 3425, 1830, Kk RiBS 126.
Castellacci, Luigi: *Fantaisie sur la Marche favorite de Moïse de Rossini*, op.100, ed. Richard Long, Tuscany Publications, 1997.
Castellacci, Luigi: *L'Age de Quinze Ans* WoO, 1835, Lbl G.543.(65.)

WynS1	Coste, Napoléon, in: Wynberg, Simon: *The Guitar Works of Napoléon Coste*, facsimile edition, vol. I-IX, Monaco, Chanterelle, 1981, 1983; reprint 2006-7.
WynS1	Coste, Napoléon: 25 Etudes de Genre, facs. 2ᵉ ed. Richault c. 1880 ECH 1401

Coste, Napoléon: *Aux Parisiens*, chanson voc.pf, WoO 2, 1830, Pn [Vm7 44.830.
Coste, Napoléon: *L'Enfant au Berceau*, chanson voc.pf, WoO 7, 1864, Pn [Vm7 44.834.
Coste, Napoléon: *Lolla*, chanson voc.pf, WoO 10, 1878, Pn [Vm7 44.835.
Coste, Napoléon: *Le petit ange rose*, chanson voc.pf, WoO 11, 1878, Pn [Vm7 44.836.
Coste, Napoléon: *Fantaisie Sonate pour Violon ou Hautbois et Piano*, ob/pf, opus 34[b], Kk Rischel Ms. 35 b.
Coste, Napoléon: *Fantaisie de concert pour Deuz Hautbois avec Accompagnement de Piano*, 2ob/pf, opus 35, 1866, Pn Rch-08001729.
Coste, Napoléon: *Cavatine pour Hautbois ou Violon ou Flûte et Piano*, ob/pf, opus 37, 1869, Pn Rch-08001727.
Coste, Napoléon: *Méthode Complète pour la Guitare par Fernando Sor rédigée et augmentée... par N. Coste*, Paris, Schonenberger S.No.1726 [1851] Lbl b.1169
Donizetti, Gaetano: *Lucia di Lammermoor*, score, Boston, Ditson, 1854, p. 32, 39, 69, 140.
Escudier, Léon: *L'Esquif du Pêcheur*, arr. Coste, arr., c.1835, Br Mus 2.889 B1.
Giuliani, Mauro in: Jeffery, Brian: *The Complete Works..Mauro Giuliani*, facsimile edition, vol. I-XXXIX, London, Tecla, 1988.
Gluck, Christoph Willibald von: *Armide, drame héroique...*, partitur, Kassel, Bärenreiter, 1987-1991, p. 311.
Haydn, Joseph: *Armida, dramma eroico*, 1783, partituur, München, Henle Verlag, p.121-123.
Huerta, Trinidad in: Coldwell, Robert & Javier Suàrez-Pajares: *A.T. Huerta, Life and Works*, DGA Editions, 2006.
Legnani, Luigi: *Introduzione, Gran Variazioni e Coda op. 27*, Vienna, Sauer & Leidersdorf, RIBS 0492.
Legnani, Luigi: *Metodo per impare a conoscere la musica e suonare la Chitarra... op. 250*, Milano, RiBS 0496. (1840?)
Mertz, Caspar Joseph in: Wynberg, Simon, ed.: *Johann Kaspar Mertz, Guitar Works*, vol. I-X, Monaco, Chanterelle, 1982.
Meyerbeer, Giacomo: *Les Huguenots*, facs. ed. score, New York, Garland, 1980, p.2 61.
Meyerbeer, Giacomo: *Robert le Diable*, partition chant et piano, Paris, Deiss & Crépin, ca 1850.
Moine, Mr. le: *Nouvelle Méthode courte et facile Pour La Guitarre*, Paris, Imbault, 1802, repr. Genève, Minkoff, 1980.
Molino, François: *Grande méthode complète*, op. 33, Paris, c. 1823.
Molino, François: *Nouvelle Méthode pour la Guitare*, WoO, Leipzig, 1827, RiBS 0556.
Mozart, Wolfgang Amadeus: *Die Zauberflöte K620*, Wenen, 1791, Budapest, Könemann Music, 1993.
Paganini, Niccoló in: Gazzeloni, Giuseppe: *Niccolò Paganini, The Complete Works for Guitar Solo*, Heidelberg, Chanterelle, 2006.

WynS6	Regondi, Giulio in: Wynberg, Simon: *Giulio Regondi, Complete Works for Guitar*, Monaco, 1981.

Schubert, Franz: *Schlaflied (Abendlied, Schlummerlied)* op.24.2, D527, 1817, Neue Ausgabe sämtlicher Werke, Bd.2a p.20, arr Coste
La Berceuse WoO 33, 1834?, Hebe a12164.
Schubert, Franz: 'Das Fischermädchen' in: *Schwanengesang*, no. 10, WoO, D957, 1818, Neue Ausgabe sämtlicher Werke, Bd.14a p.148-151; arr Coste *La Fille du Pêcheur* WoO 34, 1836, Hebe a12172; arr. Mertz, *Das Fischermädchen* opus 13.3, 1847, Sk Boije 20862.
Schubert, Franz: *Wiegenlied* op.98.2, D498, 1819, Neue Ausgabe sämtlicher Werke, Bd.5a p.76; arr. Coste, *La Jeune Mère*, 1834, Hebe a12168.

JefB11	Jeffery, Brian, ed. Schubert, Franz: *Schubert Lieder*, London, Tecla, 2011.
SorF1	Sor, Fernando: *Méthode Complète pour la Guitare, Rédigée et augmentée.... par N. Coste*, Paris, c.1845, reprint Schonenberger no. 1726, ed. Lemoine.1893?.

SorF3	Sor, Fernando: *Méthode pour La Guitare* par Ferdinand Sor, Paris, L'Auteur, rue de Marivaux, no.1, 1830, reprint Genève, Minkoff, 1981.
	Sor, Fernando: *Method for the Spanish guitar*, translation by Merrick, ed. R. Cocks, London, c.1850, reprint New York, Da Capo, 1971.
	Sor, Fernando: in: Jeffery, Brian: *Fernando Sor, Complete Works for Guitar*, facsimile edition, New York, Shattinger, 1977.
	Sor, Fernando: *Le dernier cri des Grecs*, WoO, 1829, JefB1 p.140-141.
	Thomas, Ambroise: *Le Perruquier de la Régence*, arr. Coste, c.1840, Br 13.358 C52.
	Weigl, Joseph: *Die Schweizerfamilie*, Oper in 3 Akten, 1809, vollständiger Klavierauszug ca. 1809, No.7 Cavatine m.20-23.
	Zani de Ferranti, Marco Aurelio, in: Wynberg, Simon: *Marco Aurelio Zani de Ferranti, Guitar Works*, vol. I-XIV, Heidelberg, Chanterelle, 1989.
	Zani de Ferranti, Marco Aurelio: *Niaiserie musicale sur un air favori de la Famille Suisse* op. 21, Brussel, Kbr Fétis 2.917 C7 Mus.
	Zani de Ferranti, Marco Aurelio: *Smyrne est une Princesse*, chanson voc.pf, WoO, 1863, Lbl H.1774.j.(51.), (Digital Guitar Archive).
	Zani de Ferranti, Marco Aurelio: *Le Sylphe et la Rose*, chanson voc.pf, WoO, 1863, Lbl H.1774.j.(62.), (Digital Guitar Archive).

Bibliographies 287

Sources

The abbreviations are the sigla of the libraries with a given number.

A1	Århus, Statsbiblioteket, *Coste-Degen*, June 15, 1858, 4p., Søffren Degens Papirer, Manuscript no. 27b.
A2	Århus, Statsbiblioteket, *Coste-Degen*, October 17, 1863, 4p., Søffren Degens Papirer, Manuscript no. 27b.
A3	Århus, Statsbiblioteket, drawing: *Degen Heptachord Guitar*, Søffren Degens Papirer, Manuscript no. 27b.
A4	Århus, Statsbiblioteket, *Recommendation Degens Guitar*, N.P. Möller, 1847?, Søffren Degens Papirer, Manuscript no. 27b.
A5	Århus, Statsbiblioteket, *Royal permission to produce guitars*, Christian den Ottende, 1845?, Søffren Degens Papirer, Manuscript no. 27b.
B1	Besançon, Bibliothèque municipale, *Grotte de la Source du Léson*, lithography by Engelmann, Villeneuve, 1828, Est-Doubs-lison-2-a.
B2	Besançon, Bibliothèque municipale, *La Vallée d'Ornans*, lithography by Vernier, 1850?, after G. Courbet, Est-Doubs-lison-2-a.
Bad1	Besançon, Archives départementales, *acte de naissance Napoléon Coste*, État Civil, Amondans, N, 1793-1872, 5 Mi 177.
Br1	Bruxelles, Koninklijke Bibliotheek Royale, Section Musique, Concone, J. & Escudier, L: *L'Esquif du pecheur*, accomp.t de Guitare par Nap. Coste, Mus. 2.889 B1.
Br2	Bruxelles, Koninklijke Bibliotheek Royale, Section Musique, Masini, F. & Tastu, A: *La Pêche*, Mélodie Suisse, Accompagnement de guitare par Ledhuy, Mus. 2.889 B1.
Br3	Bruxelles, Koninklijke Bibliotheek Royale, Section Musique, Auber, D. & Schribe, E.: *L'Ambassadrice*, opéra comique en trois actes, avec accomp.t de Guitare par M. Carcassi, Mus. 2.857 B2.
Br4	Bruxelles, Koninklijke Bibliotheek Royale, Section Musique, Concone, J. & Escudier, L: *L'Esquif du pecheur*, accomp.t de Guitare par Nap. Coste, Mus. 2.889 B1.
Br5	Bruxelles, Koninklijke Bibliotheek Royale, Section Musique, Thomas, A. & Planard & Duport, P.: *Le perruquier de la régence*, avec accomp.t de Guitare par N. Coste, Mus. 13.358 C 52.
Br6	Bruxelles, Koninklijke Bibliotheek Royale, Section Musique, Carulli, Gustave: *les sept péchés capitaux*, Chant et Piano, Mus. 2.852 C.
Br7	Bruxelles, Koninklijke Bibliotheek Royale, collection des estampes, Portr. d'Henri Adan, J. Schubert, Vol. H, 7e60 - FF, 38953.
Br8	Bruxelles, Koninklijke Bibliotheek Royale, collection des estampes, Portr. Valentin Bender - plano, Litt. B., S II 64350.
Br9	Bruxelles, Koninklijke Bibliotheek Royale, collection des estampes, Portr. Joseph Blaes, SI 37503.
Br10	Bruxelles, Koninklijke Bibliotheek Royale, collection des estampes, Portr. 43 Kufferath, W. Stxeit, folio, SI 31630.
Br11	Bruxelles, Koninklijke Bibliotheek Royale, collection des estampes, Portr. Hubert Léonard - 8o, Litt. L., S V 15916.
Br12	Bruxelles, Koninklijke Bibliotheek Royale, collection des estampes, Portr. d'Adrien-François Servais, CR. Baugniet, Tome 4. 7e36, Vol. 1836-1842 - FF, s.no.
Dgh	Delfzijl, Gemeentehuis *Van het uittrekken der Franschen 23 mei 1814*, painting by Streun.
Kk1	Kopenhavn, Kongelige Bibliotek, Portraetsamlingen, *Coste, Napoléon*, 1806[sic]-1883, guitarspiller, by Disdéri (182-1889), Paris, 1867 fol. 150.867 (1939 Nr. 78) [i.e. Coste met vier gitaren]
Kk2	Kopenhavn, Kongelige Bibliotek, Portraetsamlingen, *Coste, Napoléon*,1806 [sic]-1883, guitarspiller, by Degen, fol. 184295 (1939 nr.138) [Coste met gitaar en hoed] [ME p.135] [RN p.31]
Kk3	Kopenhavn, Kongelige Bibliotek, Portraetsamlingen, *Degen, Søffren*, 1816-1885, guitarist, skuespiller, fotograf, DP008385. [ME p.127]
Kk4	Kopenhavn, Kongelige Bibliotek, Portraetsamlingen, *Degen, Søffren*, 1816-1885, guitarist, skuespiller, fotograf, DP008386, 1939 Nr.78.
Kk5	Kopenhavn, Kongelige Bibliotek, Portraetsamlingen, *Holm, Johan G.*
Kk6	Kopenhavn, Kongelige Bibliotek, Portraetsamlingen, *Schult, A.F.*, købmand, Sweden.
Kk7	Kopenhavn, Kongelige Bibliotek,, Portraetsamlingen, *Rischel, Thorvald*, 1861-1939, guitarist, driftsbestyrer.
Kk8	Kopenhavn, Kongelige Bibliotek, Portraetsamlingen, *Birket-Smith, Frederik*, 1880-1952.
Pan1	Paris, Archives nationales, Registres de Dépôt légal de musique, Musique, *Op.25 Consolazione*, F18* VIII 1 à 157, No. 20 January 3, 1856 - November 11, 1856, p.35 No.: 1641. June 19, 1856.
Pan2	Paris, Archives nationales, Registres de Dépôt légal de musique, Musique, *Op.30 Sérénade*, F18* VIII 1 à 157, No. 21 November 11, 1856 - August 5, 1857, p.122 No.: 1882. June 08, 1857.
Pan3	Paris, Archives nationales, Registres de Dépôt légal de musique, Musique, *Op.31 Le Départ*, F18* VIII 1 à 157, No. 22 August 5, 1857 - September 5, 1858, No.: 2686. September 05, 1857.
Pap1	Paris, Archives de Paris, *Acte de mariage Napoléon Coste & Louise Olive Pauilhé*, February 11, 1871, Série V2E 5Mi 3/210.
Pap2	Paris, Archives de Paris, *Acte de décès Napoléon Coste*, January 15, 1883, Série V2E 5Mi 3/1256. [JR p.78] [RN p.28]
Pap3	Paris, Archives de Paris, *Régistration des Actes de décès*, Napoléon Coste, March 2, 1883, DQ 2009 Ire partie No.52.
Pap4	Paris, Archives de Paris, *Déclarations de succession*, Napoléon Coste, May 1879 - May 1883, DQ 2009, I71, p.179, No.53.
Pbh1	Paris, Bibliothèque historique de la Ville de Paris, photo: *Rue du Vieux Colombier*, vue prise du coté de la rue Bonaparte vers la rue de Rennes, Marville, s.d. [vers 1876?] G.P. XXII, 29
Pbh2	Paris, Bibliothèque historique de la Ville de Paris, photo: *Rue du Faubourg St. Martin*, caputilation Prussiens, 1871, G.P. XXIX, 27.
Pbh3	Paris, Bibliothèque historique de la Ville de Paris, photo: *Rue du Faubourg St. Martin 65?*, caputilation Prussiens, 1871, G.P. XXIX, 26.
Pbh4	Paris, Bibliothèque historique de la Ville de Paris, photo: *Boulevard Poissonnière*, une file de petites voitures de marchands de quatre saisons, Cl. 1026.

Pbh5	Paris, Bibliothèque historique de la Ville de Paris, photo: *Rue du Faubourg St. Martin*, 462Cl.1041.
Pcdv	Paris, Service historique de la Défense, Château de Vincennes, *Dossier J.F. Coste*, cote 24ᵉ 815, item 1-81.
Pcm1	Paris, Cité de la Musique, *Coste Guitare Lacôte*, c. 1850, photo Anglès, E.995.26.I.
Pcm2	Paris, Cité de la Musique, *Coste Guitare Basse*, 18ᵗʰ c., photo Anglès, E.972 Chouquet no. C.280.
	Coffret Guillaume Berleur, *Pistolet d'Arçon*, An XIII. 1804-5, www.site.voila.fr.
Pn1	Paris, Bibliothèque nationale, Département de la Musique, Mr. Coste: *Aux Parisiens des 27, 28 et 29 juillet 1830*, Paroles de Harion, Paris, chez l'auteur, In.fol., 2 ex. [Vm7 44.830 et 44831.
Pn2	Paris, Bibliothèque nationale, Département de la Musique, Klosé, Hyacinthe Eleonore: *10.me Solo*, transcrit pour ob. pi. strq ad lib (without ob). P 1868, [Vm 19,23.
Pn3	Paris, Bibliothèque nationale, Département de la Musique, Coste, Nap.: *Schubert, Franz, La Sérénade*, adapt. chant & guitare, paroles françaises de Mr. Bélanger, accompagnement de guitare par Nap. Coste (s.d.) In: Recueil Repertoire de Chansons Tome III, [4eVm7 205 98 et 21.
Pn4	Paris, Bibliothèque nationale, Département de la Musique, Coste, Nap.: *Le Petit Ange rose* - Berceuse. Paroles de Pélan d'Angers, Paris, Katto, 1878, In. fol., [Vm7 44.836.
Pn5	Paris, Bibliothèque nationale, Département de la Musique, Coste, Nap.: *Lolla*, Mélodie, Paroles de Pélan d'Angers, Paris, Katto, 1878, In.fol., [Vm7 44,835.
Pn6	Paris, Bibliothèque nationale, Département de la Musique, Coste, Nap.: *L'Enfant au Berceau*, Paroles de Jules Adenis, Paris, Emile Chatot, 1864, In.fol., [Vm7 44.834.
Pn7	Paris, Bibliothèque nationale, Département de la Musique, Photothèque, *Berlioz, Hector, Concert au Cirque des Champs-Elysées*, 1845, Cliché: 73 C 60395, B.N. Mus.Est.
Pn8	Paris, Bibliothèque nationale, Département de la Musique, Photothèque, *Herz, Henri*, Cliché: C 93964, B.N. Mus.Est.
Pn9	Paris, Bibliothèque nationale, Département de la Musique, Photothèque, *Gluck, décor de Cambon pour Armide*, 2ᵉ tiers 19ᵉ s., Cliché: C 73716, B.N.Opéra.Esq.19.
Pn10	Paris, Bibliothèque nationale, Nadaillac Delessert, Baudry, Paul (1828-1886): portrait de Cécile Delessert, Comtesse de Nadaillac, NBA-095754.
Pn11	Paris, Bibliothèque nationale, Département de la Musique, Photothèque, *Martin, Nicolas, secrétaire du Théatre Royal de l'Opéra Comique*, Cliché: 87 C 178112, B.N.Mus.Est.1.
Pn12	Paris, Bibliothèque nationale, Département de la Musique, Photothèque, *Servais, Adrien François*, J.F. Servais, lithographie de Baugniet, 1838, Cliché: 65 C 26439, B.N. Musique, J.F. Servais, 4-5.
Pn13	Paris, Bibliothèque nationale, Département de la Musique, Photothèque, *Sor, Fernando*, lithography by Bordes/Engelmann, Cliché: 85 C 124519, Mus.Est.Sor.No.1.
Pn14	Paris, Bibliothèque nationale, Département de la Musique, Photothèque, *Triebert, Charles Louis, Hautboiste et facteur d'instruments*, Phot dans l'Album des membres de la Société Académique des Enfants d'Apollon, Photo par Trinquart, Paris, Cliché: 82 B 94850, Est.Mus.No.1.
VAL1	Valenciennes, Bibliothèque municipale, *Acte de décès Jean François Coste*, April 13, 1835, fonds modernes, série E: Etat civil, E1, R53.
VAL2	Valenciennes, Bibliothèque municipale, *Acte de décès Anne Pierrette Dénéria*, February 11, 1842, fonds modernes, série E: Etat civil, E1, R56.
VAL3	Valenciennes, Bibliothèque municipale, *Plan de Valenciennes*, 1837.

Letters [50] with annotations in original language

2 letters to Degen from: Århus, Statsbiblioteket, *Lettre Coste/Degen*, Søffren Degens Papirer, Manuscript no. 27b, copy original, June 20, 2006.
7 letters to Schult from: "Napoléon Coste - späte Briefe 1867-1882, aus dem Nachlass von Georg Meier/Willy Meier-Pauselius", I. und W. Holzschuh, Hamburg; acquisition by mediation of Andreas Stevens, Hilden; transcripts from the originals in an unkown handwriting and translations in German. November 21, 2014.
35 letters to Hallberg from: "Napoléon Coste - späte Briefe 1867-1882, aus dem Nachlass von Georg Meier/Willy Meier-Pauselius", I. und W. Holzschuh, Hamburg, acquisition by mediation of Andreas Stevens, Hilden; transcripts from the originals in an unkown handwriting and translations in German, and one copy of Coste's original manuscript September 22, 1880; November 21, 2014.
6 notes to Gruel from Norbert Fischer, Halen, acquisition by mediation of Andreas Stevens, Hilden, copy original, May 18, 2012.

1858_06_15   Coste-Degen, [A1] préfecture de la Seine petit emploi, souvent pas de leçons, emploi été supprimé, démarche humiliante, concert l'hyver prochain, regrette être revenu à mon poste après le concours, succès excellent passeport, port monté, Consolazione [i.e. op. 25 1855], gravure Fantaisie symphonique [op. 28b], dedication Degen

1863_10_17   Coste-Degen, [A2] Holm m'écrire, son Photographie [i.e. MølE p. 198], accident funeste six mois [i.e. Feb. 1863] bras gauche, commence à essayer poser les doigts sur le manche, guitare s'ennuye du long silence, Holm guitare à 10 cordes j'en suis fâché, Jái ajouté la 7ème, Le Montagnard absolument avec le hautbois [op. 34a 1861], je ne suis pas voyageur, j'ai bien vieilli, mon épaule peu mieux

1867_10_07   Coste-Schult, [S1] perte d'un ami, Triébert, concerts historiques, jouer archilute, Théorbe, Cystre, transcriptions anciennes tablatures, photographie 4 instruments, rayon de soleil brûlé ma figure, guitare 7 cordes le plus finis, Scherzer pas même égalité, 1835 ajouté corde, archiluh Louis XIV?, guitare négligéeHalévy instrument récompense pas la peine, je láime avec imperfections comme enfant malade, Mertz concertino, concours, Servais dit je mérite premier prix

1874_09_02   Coste-Schult, [S2] 25 etudes publiés, dédication, étendu les bornes

1874_12_08   Coste-Schult, [S3] Société, succès études, omoplate gauche décrochée, collection 100 morceaux, airs suédois, charmantes [i.e. op. 52 no. 17, 1880], Visée dans Méthode, Scherzer, 7 cordes suffit, attention notes aigués

18.._11_17   Coste-Gruel [G1] pouvez compter sur moi, ce soir aller vous voir

1874_12_12   Coste-Gruel [G2] à votre disposition mardi à partir de 8h

1875_04_17   Coste-Schult, [S4] Huerta, Ciebra, Sokolowski, Bosch ongles, 1862 guitarists Mikeli, 1830 à Paris, Sor, Aguado ongles, Carcassi, Molino, Carulli vieux, Legnani brillant, jeune Regondi, connaissance Sor, duos, amitié, son dernier concert [April 22, 1838], Sagrini 1828, plances morceaux détruites incendie Pacini, risque nouvelles publications

1875_04_22   Coste-Gruel [G3] venir voir ce soir, allons au concert Beaulieu, à dimanche

1876_07_20   Coste-Schult, [S5] femme et moi très malade, Sor duos exigent, femme remarquable amateur, piano que me veut tu, manie sans fin, amateurs fervents de guitare, mauvaise musique de Carulli et Carcassi, malheur quantité mauvaise musique, op. 41, op. 42, he combattrai

1876_10_15   Coste-Hallberg [H1] Tournoi op. 15 n'existe plus, Souvenirs op. 17-23 aussi, planches fondues [Challiot 1806-1868], mes anciennes compositions chez Richault médiocres, derniers ouvrages op. 39, 27, 28 & 40, 41, 42, 43 [1876], réaction en faveur de la guitare, beaucoup vendu, bonnes leçons, j'écrirai Schult incessamment

1876_11_02   Coste-Schult, [S6] Regondi, dépourvus d'idées et de charme, op. 23 meilleur, manque science contrepoint, Sor géant, Regondi pygmée, op. 44 gravé, je corrige épreuves, chifre somme, collection morceaux [i.e. op. 52, ed. 1880], collections guitares, vendu 5 ou 6, prix élevé, reprise instrument presque abandonné

1876_12_21   Coste-Hallberg [H2] Sor, graver musique à ses frais, ce que je fais, Regondi op. 19-23, mon avis pas gouté, op. 44 Andante et Polonaise [i.e. Souvenirs Jura 1876], premier fait graver famille Suisse op. 2 en 1829, succes à Paris concert avec Moscheles, Bohrer et Malibran, Armide op. 4 peu moins mauvaise, guitare reprend faveurs, élèves, collection instruments, vendre moins bonnes 300 fr.

1877_01_15   Coste-Schult, [S7] cordes graves plus longues, obtenir égalité du son, Regondi cherche se perd, éclairs de talent op. 22, 23, rester dans les bornes du possible, Sor main gauche admirable, tort d'écrire pour lui, ajouté 7me corde pour compléter diapason du violoncelle

1877_02_07   Coste-Hallberg [H3] bon 17fr, acheter oeuvres de Sor, plus de compositeurs pour la guitare, répertoire assez beau, Giuliani concerto's Rossiniani's, potpourri Hummel, Carcassi joli mais incorrecte, Regondi estime pas beaucoup, élèves, ajouté 7me corde pour compléter, en 1835, écrit Holm, envoyé op. 44 [Souvenir Jura], pas répondu

1877_02_23   Coste-Hallberg [H4] traduire poésie suédoise, dedié Jenny Lind, Schult a envoyé airs suédoises, intention faire une fantaisie, circonstances néfastes de 1870 et 71 perdre vue projet, point nouvelles de Holm

1877_03_01   Coste-Hallberg [H5] bnos lettres sont croisées, transcrire connaître harmonie, quintes quartes et octaves indispensables, mélodies Schubert il y a 30 ans [i.e. 1838], souvenirs forme nouvelle, faire paraître grand duo [i.e. WoO 8 pas publié], potpourri Hummel, duo Weber, Neuland, Sor, corrig;e épreuves Schonenberger duo Sor, Holm écrit

1877_03_07   Coste-Hallberg [H6] configuration chevalet, dessin pour luthier, seule exemplaire Souvenirs, nouvelle édition, 1 Zuyderzée, 2 Cloches, 3 Delfzil, 4 Meulan et petite étude fin Delfzil, photographie guitare Louis XIV qui en jouait, brûle par coup de soleil, barbe noire, drôlement fihure 80 ans, 70 bien

1877_05_01   Coste-Hallberg [H7] Schubert arr. il y a 30-40 ans, Grande Sérénade terminé, [i.e. op. 45?], nouvelles de Holm, Schult, connu Carcassi, beau son, compositions légères, harmonie négligé, Schubert arr. 1838-1840

1877_06_25   Coste-Hallberg [H8] lettre 3 mai, gravure nouvelle composition, [i.e. op. 45? Divagation], entendue jouer Carcassi il y a 30-40 ans [i.e. IV 1840?] très net et agréable, Schubert, Marguérite, Adieux, Plaintes jeune Fille, Sérénade meilleurs, études op. 38, observe doigté, commencer les moins difficiles

1877_08_23 Coste-Hallberg [H9] envoyé 11 melodies, pouce gauche mauvaise, Carulli, Giuliani école peu d'harmonie, mauvaises basses, Schult cette manière, fait entendre Divagation Enfants d'Apollon [i.e. August 12, 1877 op. 45] succès, manuscrit graveur

1877_09_30 Coste-Hallberg [H10] vues Upsala, dernier ouvrage sous presse, meilleure composition, Sor petite guitare, légué, médiocre instrument, déménagement 1847 brisée, Sor main gauche admirable, souplesse, malin plaisir écrire personne pouvait jouer, j'ai joué plus difficile op. 7 Pleyel sur guitare tierce, main petite, 12 décembre sur Le Départ [i.e. 29 dec] rappelle pas, Crimée

1877_10_15 Coste-Hallberg [H11] melodies Geijs [i.e. Gustaf Geijer, 1783-1847, musik för sång 1824?], enfin possession op. 45, donné planches op. 39-45 imprimeur, pas satisfait, réclamé, notes juridiques, nouveau retard, Degen visite Schult, duos

1877_11_15 Coste-Hallberg [H12] biographie Geijer, portrait Hallberg comme Schult et Holm, gravure ouvrages, cherche ouvrages Sor Heugel, doute résultat, Lemoine successeur Schonenberger, études Sor, solo's op. 7 et 30 à Aguado mieux que op. 7, Sor grandes beautés introductions, finissant médiocrement, passages impossibles, a fait plus de mal que de bien à l'instrument, études chef d'oeuvre

1877_12_07 Coste-Hallberg [H13] votre portrait, 10 fr prix trop élevé, ici diminution, petit nombre 'd'amateurs, Divagation, appréciation op. 45, op. 46 [Valse favorite] planches oeuvres Sor détruit, admiration Sor, Beethoven de la guitare, nouvelles Schult Holm touchées dernier ouvrage

1878_01_25 Coste-Hallberg [H14] votre portrait, 10 fr accompagnement de guitare, mon avenir sera court, mon nom oublié, duo Weber pf & gt, andante petit chèf-d'oeuvre, infortunes Schult, blesser façon penser de Regondi et Dubez, Schult adversité, je suis heureux, bonheur domestique

1878_02_20 Coste-Hallberg [H15] Très jeune mathématiques, algèbre et équitations, affreuse maladie quinze mois, perdu mémoire, père destinait je serais officier génie, intelligence vidée, pourquoi je suis musicien, tristes souvenirs

1878_03_03 Coste-Hallberg [H16] bon 25 fr. Nederlandse Bank, ignorance langue Deutsch, morceaux Carcassi, Sor à op. 30, passé ce numéro pas procurer, Degen, Schult, Holm négligé, vieillesse, me faire entendre, pas toujours refuser, 2 melodies [i.e. Lolla, Ange rose] médiocrité, femme voulu publ., pas accompagnement guitare

1878_05_28 Coste-Hallberg [H17] temps passe rapidité, compositions en train, demande me faire entendre, pas refuser, écrire Schult, duo hautbois-piano [i.e. Concertino WoO4?], envoyer un second [i.e.Le Montagnard op. 34a], oeuvres médiocres, terminer grand solo [i.e. op. 47 Source Lyson], jouerai dans huit jours Apollon [i.e. 2me dimanche 9 juin, Chant des Sylphes DecM p. 236] peine à trouver bonnes cordes, bonne soie difficile procurer, envoye un échantillon, provision

1878_06_27 Coste-Hallberg [H18] litho's reçu, Stockholm, bataille, lettre Degen, artiste de talent, exposition suédoise, bons amis Holm et Degen

1878_07_31 Coste-Hallberg [H19] entendu vos compatriotes, voix, public 6000 personnes, envoi La Consolation [i.e. op. 25 et 36?], échantillon cordes filées, soie pas bonne, persévérance étude guitare, Degen doit dire celà comme moi

1878_10_18 Coste-Hallberg [H20] visite Baldur Raven, amateur guitare, élève de Degen, Holm, Source du Lyson [op. 47], d'abord Fête villageoise [Chez l'auteur] voyage 1875 Franche=Comté, souvenir de ces lieux, leçons général espagnol [i.e. Pedro Segura?, op. 48 & 49]

1879_01_09 Coste-Hallberg [H21] mains saisies par froids, engelures, ne plier les doigts, plus écrire, éviter contact papier, douloureuse, peine poser sur cordes, Source du Lyson hommage [i.e. manuscrit Kk168], gravure op. 48 & 49

1879_03_22 Coste-Hallberg [H22] froid constant, mains agées, contact papier mal, retard correspondants Gênes, Livorno, Marseille, Stockholm, Copenhague etc., l'Encouragement Sor arrangé deux guitares égales, jouer avec ma femme, effet ravissant, graver, trouver 25 souscripteurs, coutera 160 à 180 fr., guitares Scherzer bons, poids énorme, dur à jouer, école Sor 11 cordes pas nécessaire, ressources doigts passer additions, ré seulement indispensable

1879_04_04 Coste-Hallberg [H23] bon 20 fr, 15fr musique, 5 souscription, Encouragement, pas graver, restituer

1879_06_16 Coste-Gruel [G4] vu marchand, céder théorbe pour 50 fr., demain matin

1879_09_17 Coste-Hallberg [H24] votre lettre de 12 sept., visiteurs pays lointains, pris beaucoup de temps, froid excessif, mains souffrent, Degen maladie, votre présence, gravure l'Encouragement, op. 50 Adagio, Scherzo, Menuet et Mazurka joué à Apollon 2me dimanche de ce mois [i.e. 14 sep. DecM p. 240], bien accueillis, poète

1879_11_07 Coste-Hallberg [H25] reçu 9 fr, était don, garde pour achats, attends épreuves l'Encouragement

1880_02_19 Coste-Hallberg [H26] accablé de travail, froid cruel [i.e. hiver -23,9 degrés], ramolissement doigts, accompagner romance Cherubini [i.e. Romance Essex, 1790], théâtre Français, 32 fois depuis novembre, demandé premier jour de l'année, foyer reception élite, Valse Favorite op. 46, grand succès, mauvaises mains

1880_09_22 Coste-Hallberg [H27] copy facs. original MS, arr. 24 sep.] souscription Livre d'Or, catalogue à Schult, ma femme malade, faiblesse, salutations à Wred

1880_10_05 Coste-Hallberg [H28] Holm relation club des guitaristes de Leipzig, influence avenir guitare, dédié Livre d'Or, Schroen Guitarre Geschichte, femme rétablie, faiblesse, j'accompagne et soutienne, épreuves Livre d'or [op. 52] corrections prendront 8-10 jours

1881_02_07 Coste-Hallberg [H29] trouvé oeuvres Sor, Fantaisie Pleyel op. 7, Rossini Neckens Polka, farceur, santé femme mieux, appui avec bras, mains saisies par froid, engelures, engorgées, contact papier fait mal

1881_03_25 Coste-Hallberg [H30] cherché vainement arr. Freischutz pour 2 gt de Diabelli, indiquer titre, joué toute musique de Sor

1881_04_29 Coste-Hallberg [H31] reçu 11 fr., conseils, oeuvres Giuliani un seul est bon l'allegro 3me concerto op. 70, joué tous oeuvres, connaissait pas meilleur, musique de Sor dans mes mains, juger Giuliani pauvre et vide, 3me concerto aide de Hummel, pas étudier mes ouvrages, Degen les joue guère, études succes élèves, guitaristes leipzig envie, envoyé cordes acier, pas satisfaisant, plus de bruit, exécutions mes oeuvres impossible, femme faible,

Bibliographies

1881_11_08   Coste-Hallberg [H32] gravement indisposé, congestion cérébrale, prends bromure de potassum, vis comme huitre, intelligence morte, sortir accompagné par ma femme, m'avait sauvé la vie en 1871, venu au monde 28 juin 1806 [i.e. 27 juin 1805], pas solide, mémoire manque, dédicace op. 53 vous agréable, amitié, Degen 2me guitare mes ouvrages, curieux

1881_12_16   Coste-Hallberg [H33] congestion cérébrale, bon médecin, soins femme, obéis comme ma mère, que j'adorais et vénérais, essai Degen 2me guitare inutile, essayé avec ma femme, pas satisfait, fatigue tête, bromier de potassum, autre drogues

1882_01_08   Coste-Hallberg [H34] santé passable, écris péniblement, compositions, renoncé leçons en ville, élèves chez moi, transformation instruments, élève aide, collection grand valeur, valent petit capital

1882_07_11   Coste-Gruel [G5] sommes à la campagne, peintre céramique, deux filles, donne leçons, pas annoncé absence, vous revoir fin du mois, pas cessé de pleuvoir

1882_09_01   Coste-Gruel [G6] reviendrons à Paris jeudi, Dimanche vous voir, séjour fait bien femme

1882_12_05   Coste-Hallberg [H35] il y a un an congestion cérébrale, avertissement ma fin approchait, santé rétablie, ferais plus rien, femme fluxion de poitrine, guitare abandonné, entreprendre travail Der Zweikampf pas courage, 2 mois à la campagne, temps détestable, revenu aussi malade, Degena écrit, pas moment répondre, lui écrirai

Magazines, 19th century with annotations in original language

BF   *Bibliographie de la France, ou Journal Général de l'imprimerie et de la librairie*, Paris, 1814-1856, samedi, repr. Nendeln, Kraus, 1966-1970; Uu

    1830   vol. XIX, no. 52, December 25, 1830, p. 834, *Aux Parisiens,* M. Coste, prix 2-0; chez l'auteur, rue Bleue, n. 28.

    1832   vol. XXI, no. 33, August 18, 1832, p. 472, *Fantaisie Armide,* Nap. Coste op. 4, prix 4-50; chez l'auteur, rue du Colombier, n. 25.

    1835   vol. XXIV, no. 28, July 11, 1835, p. 448, *Souvenir de Flandre,* [sic] Nap. Coste op. 5, prix 5-0; A Paris, chez Lacôte, rue de Louvois, n. 10.

    1837   vol. XXVI, no. 34, August 26, 1837, p. 424, *Fantaisie de concert,* Nap. Coste op. 6, prix 5-0; chez l'auteur, rue de l'Echiquier, n. 23.

    1841   vol. XXX, no. 44, October 30, 1841, p. 540, *Divertissement,* Nap. Coste, [op. 9] prix 4-50; chez Bernard Latte, boulevart [sic] des Italiens, n. 2.

    1843   vol. XXXII, no. 35, October 21, 1843, p. 452, *Fantaisie Norma,* Nap. Coste, [op. 16] prix 5-0; Chez Challiot, rue Saint-Honoré, n. 336.

    1852   vol. XLI, no. 29, July 17, 1852, p. 432, Nap. Coste, *Souvenirs Sept morceaux*, prix chaque morceau 4-0; [op. 17-23] chez Schonenberger. - L'auteur, rue de Calais, 11.
              vol. XLI, no. 31, July 31, 1852, p. 466, Nap. Coste, *Souvenirs No. 6 Meulan,* op. 22, prix 4-0; chez Schonenberger.

    1856   vol. XLV, no. 33, August 16, 1856, p. 862, N. Coste, *Consolazione,* op.25, prix 6-0, chez Colombier.

EdB   *L' Echo de Bruxelles,* Bruxelles, XVe Année; Br

    1856   Tuesday, October 14, 1856, no. 288, Nouvelles des lettres et des arts - matinee Makaroff; 18 XII 1856, no. 353, Prix du pain.

EFV   *L' Echo de la Frontière,* Valenciennes, 1829 - ? ; [continuation of *Petites Affiches*], VAL

    1829   8ᵉ Année, Wednesday, April 1, 1829, no. 767, On lit...Coste; [op. 2?]

    1835   14ᵉ Année, Tuesday, April 14, 1835, no. 1533, capitaine Coste;

    1840   19ᵉ Année, Tuesday, March 24, 1840, no. 2307, On se rappelle... ;

    1842   21ᵉ Année, Tuesday, April 5, 1842, no. 2623, M. Coste, jeune guitariste.

Fig   *Le Figaro*: journal non politique, Paris, 1826-1834, Pn

    1830   vol. V, No. 103, Tuesday, April 13, 1830, p. 2, Jules Regondi... virtuose trois pieds de haut; instrument ingrat;
              vol. V, No. 118, Wednesday, April 28, 1830, p. 3, concert du petit Jules.. matinée... hier;
              vol. V, No. 155, Friday, June 4, 1830, p. 3, Jules Regondi... admis devant le Roi... Sa Majesté;

    1831   vol. VI, No. 105, Wednesday, April 13, 1831, p. 4, M. Costes, jeune guitariste distingué...

    1877   vol. XXIII, série 3, no. 84, March 25, 1877, p. 3, Courrier des Théâtres, Aux variétés, à une heure et quart, réprésentation extraordinaire, au bénéfice de M. Coste. [??]

LFM   *La France musicale,* Paris, Escudier, journal hebdomadaire, dimanche, 1837-1870; DHnmi

    1838   vol. I, no. 4, January 21, 1838, p. 6, Concert Mll. Sardi...Sor & Coste Hôtel-de-Ville; [MosW3 p.97]
              vol. I, no. 9, February 22, 1838, p. 6, *La Cachucha,* par M. Czerny;
              vol. I, no. 14, April 1, 1838, p. 7, Monsieur Coste, un de nos meilleurs guitaristes; [MitA 1832!?] [MosW3 p.97]
              vol. I, no. 15, April 8, 1838, p. 8, 'Nouvelles publications musicales': Chez. M. Coste, 25 rue du Colombier. *Fantaisie Armide* op. 4; *Souvenirs de Flandre* [sic] op. 5; *Fantaisie de concert* op. 6; Mélodies de François Schubert, Avec accompagnement de guitare, par Coste. *Ave Maria, La Berceuse, La Jeune Mère, La Jeune Fille et la Mort, La Fille du Pêcheur, Les Plaintes de la Jeune Fille, La Barcarolle, Marguerite, Le Jeune Aveugle, La Poste, La Sérénade, Fais mes Amours, Adieu, Amour et Mystère*;
              vol. I, no. 16, April 15, 1838, p. 5-7, Soirée musicale [10 IV 1838] de M. Nap. Coste... duo avec Sor; [MitA 1832?!]
              vol. I, no. 19, April 29, 1838, p. 6-7, Concert Mlle Mazel huit jours... M. Sor et M. Coste; [MosW3 p. 98, 133]
              vol. I, no. 19, May 6, 1838, p. 8, *Le Perruquier de la Régence,* no. 3, Air... Si vous Voulez un Jour... avec acc.t. de guitare;
              vol. I, no. 50, December 9, 1838, p. 7, Carcassi *Fantaisie sur le Domino noir* op. 67, Chez Troupenas, 5F;

1839	vol. II, no. 45, July 14, 1839, p. 390, Le savant guitariste Sor vient de mourir... duo... Coste; [MosW3 p.103]
vol.II, no. 49, August 11, 1839, p. 451, La guitare de Sor... Rada 1801... Napoléon Coste; [MosW3 p.105]
1840	vol. III, no. 9, March 1, 1840, p. 9, M. Coste, guitariste, donnera, le 29 de ce mois, un concert dans la salle de M. Herz;
vol. III, no. 14, April 5, 1840, p. 147, Le concert donné... par M. Coste Rêverie, concerto Hummel, Jiuliani [sic]; samedi 11 salle Herz Levassor, Haumann, Huerta;
vol. III, no. 15, April 12, 1840, p. 155, M. Szizepanowski, célèbre guitariste polonais... donné un concert; 13 avril ... Huerta;
vol. III, no. 18, May 3, 1840, p. 177-180, Le joueur de guitare I, novelle de M. Cordelier Delanoue;
vol. III, no. 19, May 10, 1840, p. 189-191, Le joueur de guitare II;
vol. III, no. 20, May 17, 1840, p. 197-199, Le joueur de guitare III-IV;
vol. III, no. 21, May 24, 1840, p. 206-208, Le Joueur de guitare V-VI;
vol. III, no. 29, July 19, 1840, p. 276, *Zanetta*, opéra d'Auber, acc. de piano et de guitare;
vol. III, no. 30, July 26, 1840, p. 279, Omission... M. Coste, guitariste distingué... concert... salle de M. Herz;
vol. III, no. 38, September 20, 1840, p. 347, opéra *El Guittarero* [sic], Scribe / Halevy; [cf Courbet, 1844]
vol. III, no. 45, November 8, 1840, p. 404, Carcassi, Vimeux, *Zanetta* pour guitare;
1841	vol. IV, no. 3, January 17, 1841, p. 23, première Guittariste Opéra-Comique;
vol. IV, no. 4, January 24, 1841, p. 25-27, *El Guitarero* de M. F. Halévy;
vol. IV, no. 7, February 14, 1841, p. 55, guitariste Sczepanowski 1ᵉʳ mars chez M. Herz;
vol. IV, no. 10, March 7, 1841, p. 78, Un guitariste en 1841! M. Sczepanowski est un guitariste vraiment extraordinaire;
vol. IV, no. 15, April 11, 1841, p. 127, M. Sczepanowski... second concert... chez M. Herz;
1843	vol. VI, no. 15, April 9, 1843, p. 127, Nous avons entendu dans concert de M. Sczépanowski;
vol. VI, no. 17, April 23, 1843, p. 143, Concert de M. N. Coste, mardi 25, à 8 heures du soir, dans les salons de M. Soufleto, 171, rue Montmartre;
vol. VI, no. 32, August 6, 1843, p. 238, La guitare vient de trouver un chaud défenseur... Gozlan... novelle;
1844	vol. VII, no. 10, March 10, 1844, p. 76, La clé des modulations, Chaulieu;
vol. VII, no. 19, May 12, 1844, p. 146-148, Exposition de L'Industrie, guitares et harpes, le plus ingrat, guitare est abandonné, oublié de la haute classe, instrument mort, fleurs sur sa tombe, Pontécoulant;
vol. VII, no. 19, May 12, 1844, Plan exposition... facture instrumentale... Lacote; Pontécoulant: Guitares et Harpes, guitare ingrat, abandonné, oublié par haute classe, mort, fleurs sur la tombe;
1855	vol. XIX, no. 16, April 22, 1855, p. 122, concert historique, savant musicien Fétis, chant espagnol six voix de femmes accompagnement de guitares, Soto de Puebla;
vol. XIX, no. 18, May 6, 1855, p. 146, concert annuel Gouffé, Guerreau, Ney, Lebouc, Triebert, Paulin e.v.a.
vol. XIX, no. 34, August 26, 1855, p. 267, Coste, dimanche 12 août, Société Enfants d'Apollon, Mme Farrenc, MM. Cuvillon, Lebouc, Ney, duo deux guitares, Coste & anon., fantaisie harmonie piquante;
1856	vol. XX, no. 6, February 10, 1856, p. 47, Le célèbre guittariste Huerta... annoncé mort... est à Madrid;
1863	vol. XXVII, no. 46, November 15, 1863, p. 361, On joue encore de la guitare en Espagne... guitariste Areas;
1865	vol. XXIX, no. 11, March 12, 1865, p. 83, M. Mardi 14 à 8 h. 1/2 du soir, M. Sokolowski, guitariste... salle Pleyel;
1869	vol. XXXIII, no. 8, February 21, 1869, p. 59-60, L'impresario Ulman nous a enfin rendu les artistes....

GM	*Gazette musicale de Paris*, Paris, Schlesinger, paraît le dimanche de chaque semaine, 1834-1835; DHnmi	
	1834	vol. I, no. 13, March 30, 1834, Meyerbeer *À une jeune mère*;
vol. I, no. 27, July 6, 1834, p. 214-216, La Vina, Guitare indienne;
vol. I, no. 34, August 24, 1834, p. 276, maladie musicale;
vol. I, no. 41, October 12, 1834, p. 331, 'Instructions for playing on the enharmonic guitar';
	1835	vol. II, no. 16, April 19, 1835, p. 139, Le premier concert prétendu historique de M. Fétis, avait attiré fort peu de monde au Théâtre Italien;
vol. II, no. 18, May 3, 1835, p. 135-136, Concert historique de M. Fétis... pas eu lieu;
vol. II, no. 18, May 3, 1835, p. 154-156, De la situation des artistes et de leur condition dans la société, F. Liszt;
no. 19, May 10, 1835, p. 157-159, situation - Liszt 2ᵉ article;
no. 20, May 17, 1835, p. 165-166, situation - Liszt 3ᵉ article;
no. 30, July 26, 1835, p. 245-248, situation - Liszt 4ᵉ article;
no. 35, August 30, 1835, p. 285-292, situation - Liszt 5ᵉ article;
no. 41, October 11, 1835, p. 332-333, situation - Liszt 6ᵉ dernier article;

vol. II, no. 42, 18 X 1835, p. 336, Le guitariste Legnani... revenu parmi nous.;
vol. II, no. 48, 29 XI 1835, p. 395, M. Lagnani [sic] dont le concert était annoncé pour aujourd'hui... malheur... casser le bras... MM. Aguado et Sor... concert... salle Chantereine.;
vol. II, no. 49, 06 XII 1835, p. 403, au concert... M. Lagnani [sic] M. Sor a exécuté un solo.

LGM *Le Guide musical*, revue hebdomadaire des nouvelles musicales de la Belgique et de l'Étranger, Bruxelles, Schott, se publie tous les jeudis; Br

1856 2ᵉ Année, October 9, 1856, no. 32, Matinée de M. de Makaroff. [EDB 14 X 1856]

JdD *Journal des débats*, Paris, 1814-1944, DHnmi

1830 Monday, April 19, 1830, p. 3, Jules Regondi, ce joli petit bambin... concert mardi 27;

JT *Le Journal des Théâtres. Littérature, musique, beaux-arts,* Paris, 1843-1850; ed. Victor Herbin; DHnmi

1843 vol. I, no. 6, Thursday, May 4, 1843, p. 2 harpe et guitare tombées en vétusté;
vol. I, no. 57, Sunday, October 29, 1843, p. 1, l'éternel grincement de guitare...profondement ennuyeux;

1847 vol. V, no. 398, Wednesday, February 3, 1847, p. 1, amoureux, pinçant guitare, escalade balcons.

LaM *La Mélodie*, nouveau journal de chant, Paris, Troupenas, 1830; [LF2 p.342-3], DHnmi 1842-1843

1842 vol. I, no. 7, Saturday, September 10, 1842, p. 4, Guitare: Carcassi, *Fantaisie le Duc d'Orléans* Auber, ed. Troupenas, 5fr, also in theatre;
no. 14, Saturday, October 29, 1842, Küffner, *Souvenir de Naples*, motíf de Donizetti.

LM *Le Ménestrel*, Journal de Musique, Paris, Heugel, hebdomadaire dimanche, 1833-1940; DHnmi, Pn

1834 vol. II, no. 19, April 6, 1834, p. [1, 4], 'Guitare multicorde';
vol. II, no. 23, May 4, 1834, p. [4], Concert Hôtel de Ville, mardi 29 avril... Nous regrettons que Sor, le guitariste... morceau plus brillant;
vol. II, no. 36, August 3, 1834, p. [1- 4], Novelle 'Jack le Guitariste' singe à Ceylon joue de la guitare;
vol. II, no. 42, September 14, 1834, p. [1], La Guitare - Castil-Blaze: La guitare n'est point à dédaigner;

1835 vol II, no. 21 April 19, 1835, p. [4] concert historique Fétis, 14 IV 1835, Romanesca, Baillot;
vol. II, no. 23, May 3, 1835, p. [4] salons Pleyel, Sor, Listz [sic]
vol. II, no. 24, May 10, 1835, p. [4] salons Pleyel, Sor, Listz [sic]
vol. II, no. 29 June 14, 1835, [p. 4], Paganini de la rue, maêstro 10.000 Fr, 30 sous à moi;
vol. II, no. 37, October 18, 1835, Gymnase musical, Legnani, grande fantaisie original, dimanche dernier;

1836 vol. III, no. 11, February 14, 1836, p. [4] réorganisation de la société musicale, Zani de Ferranti;
vol. III, no. 15 (119), March 13, 1836, p. [4], concert merc. 16 III salle Pleyel, Ferranti; Lovy-red.;
vol. III, no. 27 (131), June 5, 1836, p. [4] annonce methode Carcassi, chez Troupenas, rue Neuve Vivienne, 5;
vol. III, no. 28 (132), June 12, 1836, p. [2-3], *Souffrir sans Espérer* romance, accompt. guitare par Carcassi;

1837 vol. IV no. 9, January 29, 1837, p. [4] concert donné, Sor le guitariste
vol. IV no. 31, July 2, 1837, p. [1] guitare à 25 cordes, pauvre, délaissé

1840 vol. VII, no. 12, February 16, 1840, p. [4], M. et Mme Laurelli, aujourd'hui matinée musicale, salons Petzold;
vol. VII, no. 13, February 23, 1840, p. [4], M. et Mme Laurelli, matinée musicale, salons Petzold; solo de guitare M. Coste;
vol. VII, no. 17, March 22, 1840, p. [3], M. Coste, le guitariste, 29 III 1840, grand concert salle Herz;
vol. VII, no. 19, April 5, 1840, p. [3], salle Herz, guitariste Coste, Hummel, Mme Widemann, MM. Verroust, Grard, Dancla jeune, Souvenirs de Russie Sor, une de ses élèves, talent précoce;
vol. VII, no. 21, April 19, 1840, p. [3], Concert historique, Fétis, salle Herz, musique ancienne, Carcassi, Coste, Roehder, Vimeux, Losset, Charpentier, *air de danse* guitare, Huerta
vol. VII, no. 22, April 26, 1840, p. [3], ce concert n'a pu avoir lieu * nieuwe datum] [cf 14 IV 1835 Aguado RM 12 IV 1835 p. 117, 125-126]
vol. VII, July 12, 1840, Huerta salle Vivienne;

1842 vol. IX, no. 18, April 3, 1842, p. [2], Coste, guitariste grand mérite, guitare sept cordes, soirée salons Duport, beaux succès;

Bibliographies 295

1843	vol. X, no. 19, April 9, 1843, Coste, annonce concert mardi 18 avril, Soufletot;
	vol. X, no. 21, April 23, 1843, p. [3], M. Coste, guitariste distingué, concert mercredi, 25 avril [sic i.e. 26 avril], salle Bernart, à 2 heures, M. Verroust, Coken, Coche, Dancla, Masone, Soler, et Mmes Masoue, Vavasseur et Nordet... trois morceaux inédits [MitA p. 184];
	vol. X, no. 26, May 28, 1843, p. [3], Société Enfans [sic] d'Apollon, mardi dernier, séance annuelle, Coste le guitariste [May 23, 1843];
	vol. X, no. 50, November 12, 1843, p. [3], cours piano Bodin, dimanche dernier, M. Coste l'habile guitariste [Novemeber 5, 1843];
	vol. X, no. 50, November 12, 1843, p. [3], Coste, l'habile guitariste, dimanche dernier, cours de piano E. Bodin, Mlle Bulté;
1857	vol. XXIV, no. 5 (580), January 4, 1857, p. [3], 'Un Concours de Guitare';
1860	vol. XXVII, no. 42 (740), September 16, 1860, p. 336, Huerta à Paris;
1861	vol. XXVIII, no. 16 (757), March 17, 1861, p. 127, Le beau concert du guitariste Huerta, merc. 20 mars;
1864	vol. XXXI, no. 13 (909), February 28, 1864, p. 102, La guitare, oubliée, délaissée, douce victime de l'injustice des hommes! ...M. de Folly... *Carnaval de Venise*;
1865	vol. XXXII, no. 19 (967), April 9, 1865, p. 152, 27 avril Salle Pleyel, M. Huerta, guitariste de S. M. la reine d'Espagne;
1879	vol. XXXV, no. 52 (2535), November 23, 1879, p. 411, Mariage de Figaro, Théâtre-Français;
1883	vol. XLIX, no. 9 (2708), January 28, 1883, p. 72 'Nécrologie', Heugel, ... mort de M. Napoléon Coste.

MHV *Mon Histoire*, Valenciennes, extrait de mon Histoire fonds Goube; [presscuttings and anonymus manuscript] VAL

1828	Wednesday, February 27, 1828, aujourd'hui concert... MM. Sagrini et Coste; [February 27, 1828]
	December 10, 1828, Nos concitoyens... jeune guitariste, M. Coste... salon Chinois; [December 14, 1828]
1838	April 19, 1838, p. 198, le 10 avril... M. Napoléon Coste... concert salon Duport, Paris, exécutans qui appartiennent à notre localité. MM. Tilmant frères, M. Lecointe, Mlle D'Hennin; [April 10, 1838]
1842	April 1842, annonce concert le dimanche 8 avril... Coste & Lecointe. [April 8, 1842]

OBA *L'Observateur des beaux-arts*, Paris, 1828-1829, semi hebdomadaire, Pn

| 1829 | vol. I, March 29, 1829, p. 419, Gymnase musical, ... Son exécution est à la fois savante, brillante et pure; et nous croyons que M. Costes. à peine âgé de 22 ans... |

OB *L'Observateur Belge*, Bruxelles, Coché-Mommens, 21ᵉ Année; Br

1856	no. 276, Friday, October 3, 1856, Beaux-arts-Littérature, M. de Makaroff donnera... matinée musicale;
	no. 278, Sunday, October 5, 1856, Beaux-arts-Littérature, M. Kufferath a eu l'honneur...orgue;
	no. 301, Tuesday, October 28, 1856, Beaux-arts-Littérature, concours ouvert pas M. de Makaroff;
	no. 340, Friday, December 4, 1856, Chemins de fer-Départs;
	no. 355, Saturday, December 20, 1856, Beaux-arts-Littérature, Le concours de guitares... a eu lieu.

PA *Petites Affiches*, Valenciennes; VAL

1823	2 Année, Saturday, July 19, 1823, no. 171, p. 231, fondation e Société Philharmonique;
1826	5ᵉ année, Saturday, May 20, 1826, no. 467, p. 165, lundi dernier... jeune guitariste de Valenciennes... manqué six pour compléter.. la douzaine; [May 15, 1826]
1827	6ᵉ année, Wednesday, March 14, 1827, no. 552, p. 526, concert Salon Chinois... M. Coste; [March 24, 1827]
	6ᵉ année, Wednesday, March 28 1827, no. 556, p. 545, variations de M. Coste... très grand plaisir... guitare triste rôle;
	6ᵉ année, Saturday, April 14, 1827, no. 561, p. 568, Salon Chinois... solo de guitare; [April 17, 1827]
1828	7ᵉ année, Wednesday, February 6, 1828, no. 647, p. 43, Bal du carvaval;
	7ᵉ année, Wednesday, Feburary 20, 1828, no. 651, p. 59, concert Sagrini... dans peu de jours;
	7ᵉ année, Wednesday, February 20, 1828, no. 651, p. 60, entendu M. Sagrini vendredi dernier; [February 15, 1828]
	7ᵉ année, Saturday, March 1, 1828, no. 654, p. 70, M. Coste a dignement rivalisé avec lui; [February 27, 1828]
	7ᵉ année, Saturday, December 6, 1828, no. 734, p. 480, Dimanche 14 décembre... concert M. Coste;
	7ᵉ année, Wednesday, December 10, 1828, no. 735, p. 486; Dimanche... concert M. Coste; [December 14, 1828]
	7ᵉ année, Wednesday, December 17, 1828, no. 737, p. 495, on s'est trouvé dans la ténèbre;
	continued as *Echo de la Frontière* (1829 - ..).

LP	*Pianiste, Le*, Paris, Delacour, 1833-1835, paraît le 5 et 20 de chaque mois; Pn	
	1835	2ᵉ année, no. 8, Friday, February 20, 1835, p.66 'Concert' Coste au théatre de Grenelle le 21 II 1835; 2ᵉ année, no. 9, Thursday, March 5, 1835, p.68, entendue avec plaisir; 2ᵉ année, no. 17, Sunday, July 5, 1835, p. 107, La Guitare simplifiée, méthode de Duverger, engagé par Fossa. [Aguado]
LPB	*La Presse Belge*, Journal politique, commercial et industriel, Bruxelles; Br	
	1856	1ᵉ année, no. 195, Friday, October 3, 1856, Nouvelles des lettres, des sciences et des arts - M. de Makaroff donnera... matinée musicale; 1ᵉ année, no. 197, Sunday, October 5, 1856, Nouvelles des lettres, des sciences et des arts - concert dirigé par M. Bender; 1ᵉ année, no. 221, Wednesday, October 29, 1856, Beaux-arts-Littérature, Concours ouvert par M. da Makaroff; 1ᵉ année, no. 274, Sunday, December 21, 1856, Beaux-arts-Littérature, Le concours... a eu lieu.
RP	*Revue de Paris*, journal critique, politique et littéraire, hebdomadaire, 1829-1845; Pn	
	1834	vol. VI, tome 6, June 1834, Malibran...Opéra Milan, 100.000 fr... vol. VI, tome 11, November 1834, Walter Scott de M. Defauconpret... immense succès... illustre auteur... 2.fr.50 à 3.fr.50 c. vol. VIII, tome 29, May 1836, soirée musicale, M. Mansui... salons Pape... M. Sor a eu une large part aux honneurs de la séance...
RM	*Revue musicale de Paris*, publ. par Fétis, fév. 1827 - nov. 1835; [1827-1831 tome I-VII; 1831-1835 vol.V-IX] Fétis in 1833 to Brussels [LH] son Édouard continues; [Fauquet Dictionnaire p.1062] DHnmi	
	1827	tome I, no. 1, February, p. 42-44, *Emmeline*, Weigl, Théatre [sic] de d'Odéon; tome I, March, p. 124, *Six nouveaux morceaux*... Sor... Meissonnier... oeuvres complètes ; tome II, p. 599, La guitare est... Carulli... Sor;
	1828	tome III, January, p. 40-41, facteurs de piano, soirée Dietz.. sam. 26 janvier... solo de guitare Sor; instrument trop peu sonore p. 142-143 salons Pape... Schultz & Hummel concerto de Giuliani; p. 155-157 salons Pape frères Schultz, guitare tierce, M. Léonard S. Ajax de la guitare; capodastre p. 302-303 concert 13-20 IV salle rue Chantereine, morceau de guitare Sor; Listz [sic] p. 303-304 concert dim 13 IV salle rue de Cléry, Sor a du talent; mauvais son; Listz [sic] p. 336 concert salons Dietz, Sowinski, Sor... 7 mai prochain; p. 402-403, concert salle rue de Cléry dim. 18 mai Sor... exécution étonnante;
	1829	tome IV, p. 527-528, Journal de guitare, Meissonnier, 10fr. par an; tome V, p. 115, concert salons Dietz, Sowinski, Sor, 11 mars 1829; p. 160-163, soirée Dietz, Herz, Malibran, Sowinski, Paër, p. 181, concert salons Dietz, Sowinski, Sor, 11 mars 1829, grand talent... petit instrument; p. 209-212, Malibran, Pape, Listz, p. 240, soirée musicale Panseron, Sor, sam. 11 avril 1829 hôtel Fesch; p. 276, concert Panseron, Sor not mentioned; p. 304, concert salons Dietz, Ch. Sor & Aguado, 14 IV 1829?, brillante exécution; p. 351, concert Mr. Herz 28 avril 1829, la Sentinelle, pi, vl, git, voc, Sor;
	1830	tome VI, p. 277-279, Harpolyre, nouvelle guitare, inventé par Salomon; [met tekening] vol. VII, tome I, March 27, 1830, p. 214-215, salons Pape, concert Sowinski & Sor, sam. 27 mars; salle Taitbout, concert Panseron & Sor; April 3, 1830, p. 266-267, concert Panseron & Sor, perfection rare... instrument ingrat! tome II, May 8, 1830, p. 16-18, concert salon Dietz, 1ᵉʳ mai, petit artiste haut de trois pieds... guitare; June 5, 1830, p. 150-153, première Famille suisse, Emmeline, Weigl; July 17, 1830, p. 346-347, salons Erard, soirée Mme Farrenc, solo de guitare Sor; July 24, 1830, p. 376-377, M. Sor a fait grand plaisir; December 18, 1830, p. 191, Bulletin d'annonces, p. 191 quadrilles et contredanses... Napoléon Coste op.5 3fr.75c. Romagnesi;
	1831	vol. VIII, tome IV, January 22, 1831, p. 330-332, M. Huerta, guitariste espagnol; compositions pas très bonnes; Vme année, no. 1, Saturday, Feburary 5, 1831, p. 1-4. Instrumens à cordes pincées, [DelM1 p.24]; no. 2, Saturday, February 12, 1831, p. 12-14, Méthode pour la guitare, Sor, 1830, 36 fr.; chez l'auteur, rue de Marivaux, no. 4; no. 3, Saturday, February 19, 1831, p.17-19, Instrumens à cordes pincées, deuxième et dernier article; no. 9, April 2, 1831, p. 71, soirée musicale salons Dietz, 27 mars, Sor & Aguado; no. 12, April 23, 1831, p. 96, M. Sor 19 avril, nouveau succès; M. Schmidt;

1832		VIme année, no. 49, January 14, 1832, p. 394, M. Huerta, merveilleuse agilité;
no. 3, February 18, 1832, p. 21, soirée musicale salons Dietz, February 15, 1832, Sor, très jolies choses;
no. 4, February 25, 1832, p. 31, autre soirée M. Sor, February 28, 1832;
no. 7, Saturday, February 17, 1832, p. 54, Aguado, mécanisme simple;
1833		VIIme année, no. 2, Saturday, February 9, 1833, p. 12, concerts historiques de M. Fétis 24 II... no. 4 luth;
no. 3, Saturday, February 16, 1833, p. 21, concert historique ne pourra avoir lieu, Société des concerts s'y est opposé;
no. 8, Monday, March 25, 1833, p. 60, concert historique, Sor, p. 61 concert Panseron salons Dietz, M. Huerta guitare; p. 63 Morceau de concert, Sor op. 54, Pacini;
no. 19, Saturday, June 18, 1833, p. 150, journal l'Europe littéraire, soirées, Sor a fait plaisir;
1834		VIIIme année, no. 4, Sunday, January 26, 1834, p. 27, La guitare et M. Zani de Ferranti;
1835		IXme année, no. 8, Sunday, February 22, 1835, p. 61-62, concert salons Duport, M. Sor et sa guitare ont été aussi bien applaudis;
no. 15, Sunday, April 12, 1835, p. 116-117, Concert historique, Aguado luth;
April 14, 1835, partie 2 no. 5 Vilhancico, acc.t de six guitares; La Romanesca Baillot;
no. 16, Sunday, April 19, 1835, p. 125-126, oeuvres guitare, 14 IV concert historique Baillot la Romanesca; M. Zani de Ferranti en Hollande.
RGMP	*Revue et Gazette musicale de Paris*, ed. Schlesinger, 1834 - 1880; DHnmi	
	1836	vol. III, no. 17, Sunday, April 24, 1836, p. 40, M. Zani de Ferranti arrive chez nous, Paganini de la guitare;
vol. III, no. 17, April 24, 1836, p. 136, M. Sor soirée musicale... Petzold, M. Aguado... piédestal;
vol. III, no. 23, June 5, 1836, p. 192-193, Vienne, virtuose anglais nommé Alwers... la guitare;
	1838	vol. V, no. 18, May 6, 1838, no. 18, Nouvelles, p. 190 'M. Coste marche'; [MosW3 p.98] [Norma]
	1839	vol. VI, no.31, Thursday, July 18, 1839, Sor vient de mourir; [MosW3 p.104]
vol. VI, no. 72, Sunday, July 29, 1839, p. 587, Toulouse M. Szczepanowski, guitariste polonais... concert;
	1840	vol. VII, no. 32, April 19, 1840, Nouvelles, p. 277 M. Coste, guitariste...concert Hertz Rêverie; [op. 24?]
vol. VII, no. 39, Sunday, June 7, 1840, p. 331, Mlle Lovrins, petite guitariste de dix ans; concert 4 juin;
	1841	vol. VIII, no. 15, Sunday, February 21, 1841, p. 120, Ferdinand Carulli... vient de mourir;
	1842	vol. IX, no. 16, April 17, 1842, p. 168, Nouvelles, 'M. Coste, l'héritier';
vol. IX, no. 40, Sunday, October 2, 1842, p. 395-396, Les Guitaristes... cet instrument ne figure plus que dans les mains de Figaro;
	1843	vol X, no. 17, April 23, 1843, p. 145, Concerts Annoncés... 25 avril à 8 heures M. Coste. Salons Soufleto.
	1845	vol. XII, no. 7, February 16, 1845, p. 52, M. Caceres...; [guitare? cf vol. XIX, no. 16, April 18, 1852, p. 123 Cibra & Caceres]
vol. XII, no. 22, June 1, 1845, p. 179-180, Le célèbre guitariste de la reine d'Espagne, don Francisco Huerta... concert 27 mai;
	1846	vol. XIII, no. 38, September 20, 1846, p. 304, New York... steamer... M. Zani de Ferranti;
	1847	vol. XIV, no. 19, May 9, 1847, p. 157-158, Mle Herminie Séron, petite virtuose de huit ans au moins... guitare; 30 mars;
	1849	vol. XVI, no. 41, October 14, 1849, p. 325, José Vignas... guitare; théâtre des Variétés;
	1850	vol. XVII, no. 23, June 9, 1850, p. 195, 'La Malibran noire'... s'accompagnant de la guitare; salon du directeur de l'opéra;
	1852	vol. XIX, no. 8, February 22, 1852, p. 58-59,'La salle de concerts... dimanche passé [i.e. February 15, 1852] congrès européen... violon et guitare... Hummel, Coste;
vol. XIX, no. 10, March 7, 1852, p. 73, Londres, exposition universelle 1851, Panormo... guitare enharmonique;
vol. XIX, no. 14, April 4, 1852, p. 110,... Zani de Ferranti donne pas des sérénades sous les balcons, mais il donne des concerts... tout ce qui a été fait avant lui sur la guitare n'était que jeu d'enfant.;
vol. XIX, no. 16, April 18, 1852, p. 123, la guitare est morte... Cibra et Caceres... concert;
vol. XIX, no. 49, December 5, 1852, p. 451, LaSociété académique des Enfants d'Apollon... cent dix-septième année... Henri Blanchard;
	1853	vol. XX, no. 4, January 23, 1853, p. 31, Carcassi... vient de mourir;

| | 1855 | vol. XXII, no.16, April 22, 1855, p.127, 'L'habile guittariste, Nap. Coste...'; [WynS1 VIII Intr.]
vol. XXII, no. 27, July 8, 1855, p. 312, M. Jean Wiesen... guitariste du roi de Bavière, salle Hesselbein;
vol. XXII, no. 32, August 12, 1855, p. 251, exposition universelle ... guitare... dans u coin... cercle musical est fort borné...;
vol. XXII, no. 33, August 19, 1855, p. 257, exposition universelle ... abandon de la guitare...;
vol. XXII, no. 43, October 28, 1855, p. 335, exposition universelle... regretter... guitares à double manche ... Autriche;
vol. XXII, no. 44, November 4, 1855, p. 348, Huerta... le Paganini de la guitare, vient de se suicider à Nice; |
| | 1856 | vol. XXIII no. 10, March 9, 1856, p. 79, M. Huerta, le célèbre guitariste... se trouve en bonne santé;
vol. XXIII, no. 26, June 29, 1856, p. 210, St. Petersbourg... Un amateur passionné de la guitare vient de mettre au concours...;
vol. XXIII, no. 43, October 26, 1856, Chronique Étrangère, p. 347 'Bruxelles.- M. de Makaroff';
vol. XXIII, no. 46, November 16, 1856, p.370, le célèbre guitariste J.H. Mertz est mort le 14 octobre à Vienne; |
| MN1 | 1857 | vol. XXIV, no. 1, January 4, 1857, no. 1, p. 6-7. Makaroff, Nikolai Petrovich de: 'Guitare et Guitaristes';
vol. XXIV, no. 21, May 24, 1857, p. 175; Meissonnier, compositeur et guitariste... vient de mourir à l'age de soixante-trois ans; |
| | 1858 | vol. XXV, no. 23, June 6, 1858, p. 190 M. José de Ciebra, noble espagnol et guitariste... salle Beethoven; |
| | 1859 | vol. XXVI, no. 14, April 3, 1859, p. 115 Herwyn... soirée musicale... mardi... Bosch, le guitariste;
vol. XXVI, no. 18, May 1, 1859, p. 142, Zani de Ferranti... infortunée guitare, victime du piano; atelier d'un peintre célèbre; |
| | 1860 | vol. XXVII, no. 6, February 5, 1860, p. 43-44, Zani de Ferranti... le plus étonnant guitariste du monde...concert sall Beethoven; lutter contre les ressources exiguës de son instrument; |
| | 1861 | vol. XXVIII, 1861 p. 2, Table Alphabétique, Concerts à Paris;
vol. XXVIII, no. 9, March 3, 1861, p. 70, M. Bosch, le célèbre guitariste est de retour à Paris;
vol. XXVIII, no. 19, May 12, 1861, p. 148, On sait que la guitare, aujourd'hui presque partout tombée en désuétude, ... en Espagne... partisans; |
| | 1862 | vol. XXIX, no. 20, May 18, 1862, p. 166, M. Zani de Ferranti a composé...mélodies bibliques vl & vlc; |
| | 1863 | vol. XXX, no. 15, April 12, 1863, p. 118, atelier Nadar... Vailati, l'aveugle...mandoline... Carnaval de Venise avec variations sur un seul corde...;
vol. XXX, no. 18, May 3, 1863, p. 141, L'aveugle M. Jean Vailati... salle Herz, pauvre mandoline;
vol. XXX, no. 30, July 26, 1863, p. 239, virtuose sur la guitarre [sic], Sokolowski; Wiesbaden; |
| | 1864 | vol. XXXI, no. 4, January 24, 1864, p. 26, M. Marc Sokolowski... cet instrument sourd et ingrat qu'on nomme une guitare... rabattre de nos préjuges;
vol. XXXI, no. 5, January 31, 1864, p. 35, Le nouveau guitariste Sokolowski... deux morceaux... bravos;
vol. XXXI, no. 14, April 3, 1864, p. 106, guitariste polonais Sokolowski... société Winnen-Orlowska.. merveilleux effets..guitare double... oublier la monotonie de cet instrument.. regretter que l'auteur n'ait pas donné un autre but à ses efforts.; |
| | 1865 | vol. XXXII, no. 12, March 19, 1865, p. 89, Mardi dernier... Sokolowski... instrument ingrat... |
| | 1866 | vol. XXXIII, no. 34, August 26, 1866, p. 271, Italienne pauvrement vêtue... devant café riche... superbe contralto... s'accompagnait de la guitare... Naudi, Verger, prendre adresse... |
| | 1867 | vol. XXXIV, no. 21, May 26, 1867, p. 165-166, exposition universelle, Espagne, Toute l'Espagne musicale est dans la guitare... envoyé de nombreux et beaux spécimens de son instrument national... Campo, Gonzalès, Fuentes...
vol. XXXIV, no. 26, June 30, 1867, p. 205, exposition universelle, Brésil... une guitare;
vol. XXXIV, no. 29, July 21, 1867, p. 231, guitariste Vailati; matinée musicale Théâtre International; |
| | 1870 | vol. XXXVI, no. 10, March 6, 1870, p.77, 'Nous n'avons pas manqué...matinée musicale... loge Frères Unis Inséparables'; [Coste niet genoemd] [CotR p.144] |
| | 1872 | vol. XXXIX, no. 8, February 25, 1872, p. 63, concert M. Bosch;
vol. XXXIX, no. 21, May 26, 1872, p. 167, mort de Giulio Regondi; |
| | 1873 | vol. XL, no. 14, April 6, 1873, p. 110, concert guitariste Bosch; |
| | 1874 | vol. XLI, no. 14, April 5, 1874, p. 110, guitariste Espagnol J. Bosch instrument aux ressources assez restraintes;
vol. XLV, no. 22, May 31, 1874, p. 174, Société des Enfants d'Apollon, 133ᵉ anniversaire; |

	1876	vol. XLIII, no. 47, November 19, 1876, p. 374, séance mensuelle des Enfants d'Apollon... [cf DecM p. 232 Sunday, November 12?, 1876]

	1878	vol. XLV, no. 3, January 20, 1878, p. 22, Le concert Cressonnois... dimanche dernier [i.e. January 14, 1878] ... musique antérieure de XIXe siècle... théâtre de la Porte-Saint-Martin ... puis, dans la partie moderne du programme, la valse de *la Nuit de Noël* de Reber (avec M. Coste), qui a été bissée, et enfin...
		vol. XLV, no. 23, June 9, 1878, p. 182, La Société des Enfants d'Apollon a donné, le jeudi 30 mai, son concert annuel à la salle Henri Herz. [i.e. Erard cf DecM p. 113]
		vol. XLV, no. 28, July 14, 1878, p. 217-220, exposition universelle, Espagne, 7 facteurs d'instruments de musique, une seule guitare reposant sur un piano de Barcelone;
		vol. XLV, no. 34, August 25, 1878, p. 266, exposition universelle, Argentine, Buenos Ayres, ces guitares, dont la mosaïque des tables se compose de plus de cinquante mille petits morceaux de pin, de bois, de jacaranda...;
		vol. XLV, no. 50, December 15, 1878, p. 407, A Pise est mort, le 28 novembre... Zani de Ferranti.

TdP *Les Tablettes de Polymnie, journal consacré à tout ce qui intéresse l'art musical*, Paris, 1810-1811; Pn

	1810	vol. I, .. February 1810, p. 1-2, Concert de M. Carulli, Salle Olympique 'Autrefois la guitare...; [Pistone p.86]

	1811	vol. II, no. 16, January 27, 1811, p. 255-256, Gatayes Plaisir d'Amour gt. & hrp, Carulli Etrennes;
		vol. II, no. 17, February 13, 1811, p. 272, de Call, musique pour la guitare;
		vol. II, no. 18, February 20, 1811, p. 287, Carulli, de Call, musique pour la guitare;
		vol. II, no. 19, February 27, 1811, p. 304, de Call, musique pour la guitare;
		vol. II, no. 20, March 20, 1811, p. 329, de Call, musique pour la guitare;
		vol. II, no. 23, May 13, 1811, p. 368, musique pour la guitare;
		vol. II, no. 28, July 20, 1811, Méthode complète de guitarre ou lyre, Carulli;
		vol. II, no. 29, August 5, 1811, p. 464 Carulli musique pour la guitare;
		vol. II, no. 33, October 5, 1811, p. 527 musique pour la guitare.

LTB *Le Télégraphe*, Journal politique, littéraire, commercial et industriel, Bruxelles; Br

	1856	3 Année, October 14, 1856 no. 288, Nouvelles des lettres et des arts, On e lit... Guide musical... Makaroff.

Dossier Coste, Jean-François, cote 24ᵉ 815.
Paris, Château de Vincennes, Service Historique de la Défense.

The items are annotated in the original language.

Coste, Jean-François, Capitaine adj. de place à Rochefort
En retraite (3 juin 1817)
Il jouit maintenant de la solde de
retraite de 1367 qui lui a été accordé le
3 Vend.re an 10.
Renseign.t jusqu'à S.D. le 18 9bre 1817.
01 * notice 12/08:(2p) 2 eme Division Etats-Majors. J.F. Coste, Capitaine ex-adjudant de place, demande la croix de St. Louis.
02 * 23 messidor an 2 (=11 VII 1794) Volontaires nationaux, levée du 5 août 1792, J.F. Coste, résident à Besançon, géomètre, élu Capitaine le 12 août 1792.
03 * 23 messidor an 2 (11 VII 1794) Extrait des Régistres des Baptèmes - 23 avril 1754 - a été baptésé le jour suivant.
04 *Retraite, Paris, le 19 juin 1817. Services.
05 * Campagnes / blessures / total des services: 20 ans, 11 mois, 5 jours (s.d.) quatre blessures dont une très grave à la machoire.
06 * Rapport (2p) au ministre le 20 mai 1817 - compte 16 ans, 10 mois et 20 jours de service - proposer 1. admettre à la retraite 2. ajourner sa demande de la Croix de St. Louis (aucun service Roi).
07 * Minute de la lettre de 19 juin 1817
08 * Etats Majors, Valenciennes le 1ᵉʳ mai 1817, le Capitaine Coste Ing.r Géomètre et Géographe - demi solde - demande le Croix de St. Louis - J'ai acquiser en pratiquant les eléments mathématiques de la géométrie et de la fortification etc.
09 * Etat de service Place de Valenciennes, le 4 mai 1817.
10 * Copies (2p) de quelques vues - Anvers, le 29 XI 1810 - etc. - Delfzil, 19 XI 1813.
11 * Extrait des régistres des actes civils, 28 nivose an neuf (=18 I 1801) acte de mariage J.F.Coste & Anne Pierrette Dénéria, 33 jr Extrait des régistres des actes civils, 28 nivose an neuf (=18 I 1801) acte de mariage J.F.Coste agé de quarante huit ans, né à Clairon Département du Doubs le vingt trois du mois d'avril mil sept cent cinquante quatre Capitaine au 5me Bataillon du Doubs, demeurant à besançon Dép.t de id. fils légitime de parent Etienne-François Coste, proprietaire cultivateur demeurant à Clairon Dépt.d'ici et de Jeanne-Françoise Drion son epouse natif de Clairon. et d'Anne Pierrette Dénéria agée de trente quatre ans née à Besançon la fille légitime de parent Claude-François Richard Dénéria Entrepreneur etc etc.
12* Brevet de capitaine Copie 24 IX 1816 du Brevet de capitaine au 5ᵉ bataillon du Doubs 12 germinal an 2 (1 IV 1793).
13 * Paris, le 6 vendemiaire an 10 (28 IX 1801), le ministre de la guerre à J.F.Coste: solde 1366 fr 88, brevet.
14 * Valenciennes, le 1ᵉʳ mars 1817, Coste à ministre de guerre, demande Décoration de l'ordre de St. Louis ou de l'ordre Royal de la légion d'honneur, ancienneté, conduite, dévouement, fidélité.
15 * Minute de la lettre demande décoration, le 24 avril 1817.
16 * Valenciennes, (3p) le 28 fefrier 1817, Coste à ministre secretaire d'etat de la guerre, - - la belle défense que j'ai fait au fort de l'Isle de Langeroge, place de la quelle elle avait bien voulut me confier le commandement - - ordre de l'evacuer - - maivais temps - - j'arrivai à Delfzil après huit jours de tempête, 7 mois bloqué dans cette place, ou j'été constamment jours et nuit emploié à l'amelioration de les fortifications pour la défense, pour ainsi être sans solde: il m'est encore dus 2 mois de 1813 et 2 mois de 1814 ensuite mis à demi solde en 1814 et 1815 ce qui existe encore actuellement et avec une famille de 5 personnes - -
(1) - - Langerooge en 1812 et 1813, à Delfzil en 1813 et 1814 - - leve et dressé la carte de siége dont une copie à été au ministere de la guerre en juin 1814.
17 * Lille, le 20 mai 1815 à Maréchal d'Empire - - nommé adjudant de première classe pour la place de Valenciennes - Je me mettrai en roule pour me rendre à mon poste au plutard le 22 du courrant.
18 * petit notice: demi solde.
19 * État des services 10 juin1817.
20 * Extrait du registre aux actes de l'Etat Civil de Besançon, Doubs: 24 décembre 1816 Acte de Naissance J.F.C.
21 * officiers en non activité, le 10 juin 1817 Que j'ai joui de la demi-solde attribuée au grqade de capitaine adjoint de place en non activité à partir de 1 X 1814 dans la place de Lille du 1 8bre 1814 au 16 mars 1815 dans celle de lille du 1 janvier 1816 au juin 1817.
22 * (cf. 74) Valenciennes, (2p) le 26 juin 1816, Coste à Ministre Secrétaire, solde 1366 fr 88, envoyé a Valenciennes en demi solde depuis 1 janvier, jour que les alliés vinrent? occuper ctte place, ce qui donne à cette officier 466 fr 88 centimes par an moins que la solde de retraite. + PS dur à cette officier ... quatre mois de solde arrière.. - - amélioré les fortifications de la place de l 'Ile de Langerooge... - - sort d'une famille respectable qui à donné à l'état, nombre de militaires marguants des hommes de barreau, et d'ecclesiastiques, il à même encore une cousine Germaine existante a Besançon qui à été la dernière abbesse de l'abbaye de Mirecourt (Loraine) etc. frére de son père... chevalier de St. Louis, frères de sa mère... cour de France comme ambassadeur, d'autres ingénieur etc. etc.
23 * Paris le 16 avril 1813 Ministère de la Guerre à J.F.Coste, Capitaine Command.t à l'Ile de Langeroge, dep.t de l'Ems Oriental, à Langeroge 24 jusqu'au 30 mars, attaques anglais.
24 * Récapitulation des services - Valenciennes, 26 juin 1816.
25 * copie Valenciennes le 26 juin 1816 de: Paris le 6 Vendémiaire an 10 (28 IX 1801) à J.F.Coste - solde 1366 fr 88 ct.
26 * Lille, (Nord) le 5 février 1815 Coste à Ministre de la Guerre - obligé d'évacuer l'Ile de Langeroge par ord\re supérieur le 11 9bre 1813 - amélioré des fortifications (Delfzil) - arrivant dans cette ville de Lille, faute de moyenne pécuniaire, il fut forcé de s'y fixer, provisoirement, avec sa famille, en attendant des ordres pour sa nouvelle destination ... se voit en proie à la plus grande détresse.
27 * État de services Lille (4p) le 16 septembre 1814 & Feuille individuelle.
28 A-I * Départ (9p) de l'Ems Oriental (Ile de Langeroge) Rapport Militaire, du 24 au 30 mars, relatis aux troubles de cet départ aux exutatives? des anglais ... (p2a2) cette flotte avançait toujours ... je crus devoir payer d'anglais pour empêcher un débarquement ... (p2a4) ... Nous sons alors au nombre de 5 combattants y compris (p3a1 different handwriting, cf.77-78) ... compris mon fils

Bibliographies

qui, agé de 8 ans seulement, s'est armé d'un bon pistolet d'arçon et a fort bien fait nous le service de suveillance et il continue chacun pur ansi dire en faction, pendant le jour mais surtout pendant la nuit en attendant l'ennemi de prez ferme: ce qui est bien nécessaire, car je ne peut guère compter sur les canonniers garder côtes, qui, tous du pays insurgé, étaient plus enclin de déserter qu'à faire une bonne défense (ce qu'ils auraient pu faire a marée basse).

29 * Ile de Langeroge le 20 avril 1813 (3p) Coste à Ministre de la Guerre coupe d'oeuil sur ma position 1366 fr 88 ct annuelle ... n'ayant que 1800 fr au lieu de 2400 fr comme capitaine ... en retenant ma solde je ne coute à l'état que 433 fr 12 ct pas an pour mon service actif.

30 * notice il existe une lettre...

31 *(cf.76) Copies des sieges desquelles le capitaine Coste...(2p)
   - Ministère de la guerre, Paris le 16 avril 1813 - - reçu le rapport - - de l'Ile de Langeroge, que vous commandez, depuis le 24 jusqu'au le 30 mars.-.-.Je ne puis, Monsieur, qu'applaudir à vôtre conduite dans cette circonstance...
   - Le commandant du Département de l'Ems Oriental, Aurich(?) le 10 mai 1813 - - parfaite considération
   - Place de Delfzil, le 21 mai 1814, Maufroy - - Mr le Capitaine Coste constamment occupé, comme adjoint a Mr le commdt du génie, aux travaux de construction pour la défense de la place - - levé et dressé la carte géometrique, représentant fidellement les ouvrages d'attaque et de défense des assiéger et des assiégeants &c
   - Le commandant d'armes de la place de Rochefort, le 31 juillet 1811, Srobst (?)
   - Place d'anvers, le 29 novembre 1810, le general de division - - Coste...y a été depuis le mois de septembre 1809.

32 * Groningue le 27 février 1813 (2p) lettre de service - Capitaine Bessat, nommé adjudant de place à l'Ile de Langeroge le 3 juin 1812 - remplacé par le Capitaine Coste, ex adjudant de place à Rochefort.

33 * Bois le Duc le 24 7bre 1812 (2p) le Capitaine Coste adjdt de Place - l'honneur nommé à l'adjudant de l'Ile de Langeroge - soit la longueur de la route, soit les obstacles qu'on y retrouve je ne me trouve encore qu'à Bois le Duc, d'ou je continue ma route pour me rendre le plustôt a ma destination...

34 * Rochefort le 28 juillet 1812 (2p) Coste à ministre de la guerre - changement de place capitaine Bessat de Langeroge occupe la place de Rochefort...et que j'occupe celle de Langeroge. 1 Rochefort e e tant un endroit très mal. - 2ᵉ Mais victime du mauvais air de ce pays ci, sav(?) trois mois de maladie la plus terrible, la mort d'une de mes filles du maladies réiteréer du restant de ma famille.

35 * Minute de la lettre écrite le 7 août 1812 (2p) Bessat - Coste - Rochefort - Langeroge.

36 * La Rochelle le 28 novembre 1811 Bureau de la Police Militaire à Ministre de la guerre - Coste, adjudant de place de Rochefort, qui avait de impliqué dans une affaire de vols de la succession - a été mis hors de cause par la cour impériale de Poitiers, qui a ordonné de poursuivre les autres accusés. J en'ai pas cru convenable de lui donner le commandemant de la place...

37 * copie La Rochelle le 28 novembre 1811.

38 * Rochefort le 16 avril 1811, Coste à ministre de la guerre - blessures - retirer - adresser des attestations ma conduite à Anvers employé extraordinairement à l état majore de cette place en 1809 et 1810.

39 * Anvers le 29 novembre 1810 (2p) le general de division - Coste secondé très utilement les officiers du génie Anvers le 24 9bre 1810 - Le maire de la ville d'anvers - Coste surveillé le logemens des gen de guerre.

40 * Anvers le 25 juin 1810 - Coste - pour aller jouir de ce congé près de ma famille, trop éloignée...

41 * Anvers le 24 7bre 1810 (3p) Coste à ministre de la guerre - je jouirais de la solde de retraite que j'ai obtenu en l'an 10 - - connaître le lieu que j áirai choisir pour ma residence. Cette malheureuse et j'ose dire juterressante(?) famille esperoit sur le dévouement de son chef qui... - Cette famille nombreuse espéroit dis(?) je qu'en continuant la carriere militaire - le père, la mère et les enfants se trouve à peut près agaux aus plusmalheureux; ma position est celle, que je me rouve même, hors d'état de retrouver près ma famille... - J'ai perdu par les assignats pres de 21000 francs par le remboursement de mes capitans de renter(?), a peut pres les trois quart et demi de ma petite fortune; ce me fut bien en comparaison de la parte de mon activité - que de me voir privé de de cette activité - emprunté 600 francs desquelles je dois encore 100 francs.

42 * Certificat de service, s.d.

43 * Minute de la lettre écrit le 13 de novembre 1810.

44 * Anvers 7 juillet 1810 (3p) Coste à ministre de la guerre - ma famille ne pouvant plus esubsister(?) que par le postage de mes appointeneurs que je fais avec elle. - ma famille comme moi dans le plus grand besoin - excellence a bien voulu sur la demande me remettre en service - m'envoyer au poste le plus éloigné, le plus fatigant le plus grand danger...demande qu'on me l'épargne.

45 * Anvers le 12 juillet 1810 (2p) Coste à Ministre de la guerre - vous pouvez rendre un grand service à moi et ma famille, elle est nombreuse et j'ose dire interressante, nous an\vons eprouvé de grande porter aux la révolution par celle de trois quart de notre fortune.

46 * Anvers le 12 7bre 1810 (2p) Coste à Ministre de la guerre 1800 francs au lieu de 2400 francs - congé limité jusqu'au 1 juillet - misère de ma malheureuse famille - en attendant la justice sans solde, sans argent, une famille languissante.

47 * au général à la Rochelle le 28 novembre 1810 - lettre de service de Coste.

48 * au général à la Rochelle le 20 novembre 1810 - lettre de service de Coste.

49 * Anvers le 21 9bre 1810 Coste à Ministre de la guerre - reçu la lettre nommé adjudant de 1ᵉʳᵉ classe de Rochefort.

50 * Anvers le 16 mai 1810 (2p) Coste à Ministre de la guerre - accorde un congé jusqu'au 1 juillet prochain - impossibilité d'en pouvoir profiter, me trouvant trop éloigné de ma famille, par un distance d'environ 78 miriamètres - je dois partager 150 francs pas mois d'appointement, avec une femme et quatre enfants - ou les vivres et les objets sont pour ainsi dire hors de prix.

51 * Minute de la lettre écrite le 20 de mars 1810.

52 * Rapport fait au ministre le 18 février 1810 - état de service.

53 * Anvers le 29 janvier 1810 (4p) - Coste à General chef de service - blessé 1ᵉ du 19 Vendémiaire an 4 dans la retraite de Mayenne sur les hauteur de Vorms 2ᵉ du 21 Messidor an 4 à Klinkheim pres Radstat 3ᵉ le 3 Vendémiaire an 8 au paysage de Lymath pres de Zurich 4ᵉ le 15 Vendémiaire même année pres de Constance. Porteur d'atestations de bons services - generaux gazan, Ste suzanne, De Caen(?) etc. Capitaine des 1792 de 1ᵉʳᵉ classe - solde annuelle 2400 francs pas an - ancienneté de mes services et mes blessures me forçeassent a prendre ma retraite - reprendre ma service...

54 * Ornans le 10 août 1809 (2p) Coste à Ministre de la guerre - je me troue\ve en état de pouvoir reprendre la service actif - fort bien guérit des infirmitiérs resultant de mes blessures...même de plusieurs performer des opérations Géometriques m'accessiblement à la distance de 25 kilomètres avec graphomètre sans lunettes...
55 * Besançon le 9 août 1809 Commissair de guerre.
56 * Copie collationnée et conforme (4p) aux originaux des certificats du citoyen Coste
    1ᵉ Je soussigné General ...depuis le 23 messidor an deux jusqu'à ce jourle e trois vendémiaire de l'année courante au paysage de Limath - Signé Gazan
    2ᵉ Je certifie ... de l'an 4 et de l'an 5 ... citoyen Coste servie siege de Kell ...
    3ᵉ Coste à été blessé le quinze Vendémiaire, a l'affaire qui eut lieu sur les hauteurs de Godlibeu(?) en tugovie(?)
    4ᵉ Coste servi a l'armee du Rhin et Mozelle Signé Bruneleau Ste Suzanne
    5ᵉ Ailzheim le 26 prairial an 7 ... Coste etc
    6ᵉ Coste etc. Strasbourg
    7ᵉ etc
    8ᵉ Officier de santé ... Coste a reçu un coup d'armes à feu qui a traversé les os maxillaires supérieures , avec un glaceer? considérable, qu'il en resulte des folules? que se dégorgent dans la bouche qu'il ne peut macheu des alimentaires. en conséquence nous estimons qu'il ne peut continuer son service, saulant(?) plus que depuis ce coup il à la vue tres assoiblie principalement de loeuil droit qui est presque nul.
    9ᵉ Je soussigne medecin de l'armée ... Coste ...à reçu un coup de feu qui lui a traversé les os maxillaires supérieures, les deus mollaires correspndanser au trajet de la Bâle ... impossibilité de manger des aliments de nature solide, enfin l'oeuil droit est resté doulourex et à perdu l'une partie de ses facultées. ... Besançon le 9 Brumaire 9ᵉ année ... signé ... Penotet.
57 * Coste, Capite retraite le 15 9bre 1817 répandu neg. le 10 8bre 1827 voir Makeréel(?) 2ᵉ(?).
58 * Valenciennes le 16 mei 1828 Coste a chancelier (3p) - obtenir les décorations de la légion d'honneur ou celle de St. Louis - pour récompense de mes long services, de mes blessures graves, actions &c - .
59 * copies conforme (4p) aux pièces originales Valenciennes le 8 mai 1828 (etat de services) - retraite le 6 vendémiaire an 10 solde fixé à le somme de 1366 fr. 88 centimes
    - Anvers ou il prendra la service le 18 août 1809 + certificat
    - Rochefort adjudant 1ᵉʳᵉ classe le 25 8bre 1810 + certificat
    - Ile de Langeroge le 7 juillet 1812 31ᵉ division militaire
    - applaudir conduite Langeroge
    - conduite l'Ems oriental 2x
    - certificat Delfzil dès 19 novembre 1813 capt Coste occupé aux travaux - Maufroy 21 mai 1814
    - Lille 11 mars 1815
    - Valenciennes 2x
    - retraite
    - registre civil de Clairon - acte de naissance.
60 * Paris, le 12 juin 1828 Coste désire obtenir la décoration de chevalier de l'ordre de la légion d'honneur.
61 * Valenciennes le 4 septembre 1827 - Coste a Charles X soit privé de décorations.
62 * Valenciennes le 15 avril 1822 (2p) - Coste a ministre de la guerre - service de 1792 jusqu'en 1817 - légion d'honneur.
63 * Etat de services. .
64 * Copies de pièces (5p) à l'appui de la c\demande du capitaine Coste No.1 brevet de capitaine No.2 certificat de service No.3 Anvers No.4 procéder l'inventaire des fournitures de lits militaires de la place No.5 le maire d'Anvers, conduite digne No.6 fortifications d'Anvers No.7 certificat Anvers No.8 Rochefort servi avec le plus grand zèle No.9 conduite No.10 belle conduite Ems No.11 Ems No12 Langeroge 24 - 30 mars 1813 No.13 Delfzil No.14 Jalousie Lille No.15 Valenciennes No.16 Clairon No.17 Maréchal
65 * Valenciennes le 10 9bre 1821 - Coste a ministre de la guerre - décoration.
66 * Copie Paris le 24 avril 1817 Ministére de la guerre a Coste - joindre acte de naissance.
67 * No. 6,194 Coste (Jean François) ancien Capitaine - Incompétence.
68 * No. 6, 194 Lille le 25 juin 1814 - Coste a ministre de la guerre (3p) - de lui accorder la continuation de son activité de service - décoration - etat de service - le 22 juillet 1812 il reçut sa nomination au commandant de la place de Langeroge ou il se rendit exactement et yrestait jusqu'au 11 9bre 1813. Epoque à laquelle il reçut, de Mr le Général Commandant en Chef la 31me di.on militaire, l'ordre d'evacuer cette place pour se rendre dans la forteresse de Delfzil; arriva le 19 du même mois.
    - arrivé pour cette place (Delfzil) pour lora bloqué; connaissant la fortification, il crut devoir offrir ses services dans cette partie, ce qui fut accepté et fut adjoint à M.r le commandant du génie, pour la construction sw défense de la place, ou il fut chargé de la construction des blindages de 10 magasins à sondre(?) d'une porte pour la faire servir de casemate & & ensuite de quoi il a eté occupé, et par ordre du commandant du génie et celui de la place, à lever géometriquement et dresser la carte topographique, représentant fidèlement la partie du paijs ou sont etés construits les ouvrages d'attaque et de défense, des assiegéants et des assiegés, ce qui la ocupé sans interruption jusqu'au 22 mai; epoque à laquelle les français ont dus evacuer cette place pour la remettre aux hollandais.
    - perdu petite fortune - blessé - défense de Langeroge - etc. attend les ordres ... Rue des Oyestr No.8 hotel d'Angleterre.
69 * Pour copie Paris le 16 avril 1813 - ministère de la guerre a Coste - Langeroge 24-30 mars - copie conforme.
70 * Lille le 18 juin 1814 Etat majors des places - Etat de services.
71 * Copie de sieces détaillés...(4p) - No.1 brevet, No.2 certificat, No.4 etc. - No.11.
72 * 6784 cher de St George Silvain.
73 * Coste Jean Pierre, adjudant de la Place de Valenciennes capitainde des géographes 1791-1847.
74 * (cf.22) (2p) Valenciennes le 2 décembre 1815 Coste a ministre secretaire - Le 23 8bre et le 28 9bre 1815, le Capitaine Coste, Décoré de la fleur de Lis, ex commandant - 23 ans et 4 mois de service - (1.) Dans la famille du supliant, son cousin Germain, off.ier, chevalier de St.Louis,

Mr Coste, ancien curé de Bregitte Faubourg de Besançon; Mr. Coste curé de Quingey; Mr. Varoud prêtre religieux, cousin de Germain; Mme Magdeleine Varoud, cousine Germaine, religieuse, et Mère de l'abbaye de Mirecourt & &. Dans la famille de son epouse Mme Dénéria, oncle paternel, capitaine de gendermerie et chevalier de St. Louis; Mr Siraud, oncle maternel, docteur en médicine…; Mr Giraud, ingénieur…aussi oncle maternel &. Cette famille etait aussi alliée à cette de Mnr Buliet(?), Evèque de Babilone &&.

75 * 17 janvier 1817 Coste a ministre de la guerre (4p) - reçu le décoration de la fleur de Lis - etat de service 22 années de grade de capitaine, blessures (1.) coup de feu…machoire supérieure privé d'autres allimenture tels que pain…une balle à l'épaule droite qui m'amis hors d'étatde m'habiller et deshabiller environ 4 ans… grandes douleurs environ 20 mois..(2.) Delfzil..carte ni finie ni signée…travaux de défense…je citerai seulement le fort de Langeroge, lorsque j'arrivai dans cette place tout y était dans le plus grand désordre; au lieu de m'en plaindre…etc. et lorsque attaqué par les anglais , et notammant au mois de mars 1813, secondés par des révoltés…ma conduit a été applaudi… demi solde…me faire obtenir la décoration militaire…p.s. appartenant à une honnête famille…

76 * (cf.31) Delfzil vingt et un mai 1814 Maufroy.

77 * Frais de bureaux Langeroge (cf.28C-I becomes more sloppy).

78 * Frais de bureaux Langeroge copie (cf.28C-I becomes more sloppy).

79 * Coste

80 * Rapport ecrit le 7 Germinal (2p) le citoyen Coste nommé adjudant général chef de brigade à l'armee du Rhin…absolument incapable d'occuper avec succès les fonctions de grade…on prie le ministre de faire connaître d'il accepte la démission de l'emploi d'adjudant général que donne le citoyen Coste et qu'il consent à ce qu'il rezte attaché au corps du génie.

81 * 2773 le 11 ventos 'an 2m (2p) adjudant e général armée du Rhin.

Websites: http://www.

ader-paris.fr: *Pistolet d'Arçon 1, 1760/1780*. July 2, 2007
answers.com: *Napoléon Coste*. March 4, 2007
armae.com: *Réproduction d'armures historiques - Napoléonien*. July 2, 2007
biblioline.nisc.com: RILM Abstracts of Music Literature; RIPM retrospective Index to Musical Periodicals; RISM International Inventory of Musical Sources. August 26, 2007
cndp.fr/themadoc/niepce/disderi.htm, October 30, 2007
csun.edu: *international guitar Research Archive (IGRA)*. January 5, 1999
delcamp.net: *Napoléon Coste (1805-1883)*. March 3, 2007
de.wikipedia.org: *Napoléon Coste*. March 4, 2007
ebookCafe.org: *The Guitar in Italy in the Nineteenth Century, sixty biographies of Italian composers and guitarists*, ed. Marco V. Bazzotti. February 7, 2008
fr.wikipedia.org: *Napoléon Coste*. March 3, 2007
fr.wikipedia.org: *Napoléon Coste*. February 12, 2008
fr.wikipedia.org: *Pistolet d'arçon*. July 2, 2007
geocities.com: *De geschiedenis van de gitaar in Vlaanderen*, Bart Van der Donck. February 4, 2007
ghs.be: *Le pistolet d'arçon*. July 2, 2007
guitarandluteissues.com: *Auprès de ma blonde, or The Makarov Guitar by Johann Gottfried Scherzer*. August 31, 2007
guitarandluteissues.com: *Bidrag till gitarristiken Part II*, Daniel Fryklund. August 31, 2007
guitarandluteissues.com: *Heinrich Albert and the First Guitar Quartet*, Allan Morris. August 31, 2007
guitarra.artelinkado.com: *Subasta de guitarras antiguas*. February 12, 2008
hebeonline.com: *Schubert songs with the piano accompaniments arranged for guitar by Napoléon Coste*, Marguerite, Adieu, la jeune fille et la mort, berceuse, Ave Maria, Sois touhours mes seuls amours, La meunier voyageur, La jeune mère, Sérénade de Shakespeare, Sérénade, La fille du pêcheur, 2003. March 4, 2007; February 5, 2008.
hebeonline.com: *Soffren Degen, A 19th century guitar virtuoso*, Jens Bang-Rasmussen. March 4, 2007
http://home.t-online.de/home/Rechtsanwalt.Joerg.Sommermeyer/ng3.htm, July 10, 2002.
hvanrongen.blogspot.com, February 12, 2008
icoldwell.com: *Napoléon Coste, guitarist and Composer*, by George C. Krick. March 4, 2007
justclassicalguitar.com/pen&nail/800/800minor.php: *Adami Vinatier Bella fiamma di gloria d'onore WoO21*, April 24, 2010
kresse.gitarren.de: *romantische Gitarren der Sammlung von Bernhard Kresse*, Originalinstrumente, Lacote, eigene Sammlung. February 7, 2008
learnclassicalguitar.com: *Napoléon Coste, French Guitar Master*. March 4, 2007
mediatheque.cite-musique.fr: *Guitare René Lacote, Paris, vers 1850*, "Guitare favorite de Monsieur Napoléon Coste", Numéro d'inventaire E.995.26.1. September 24, 2007; October 5, 2007
http://www.mvmm.org/m/docs/coste.html, November 10, 2014
naxos.com: *Guitar Recital: Anabel Montesinos*. March 4, 2007
naxos.com: *Coste, Napoléon Biography*. February 12, 2008
nl.wikipedia.org: *Franse Republikeinse kalender*, July 8, 2007
paulpleijsier.nl: *Nieuwe foto van Coste*. February 4, 2007
rsmits.com: *Raphaella Smits... Napoléon Coste*. March 4, 2007
seicorde.org: *Minor authors of 19th-Century Italian Guitar*, M. penny, transl. May 29, 2002
site.voila.fr: *Coffret 'Guillaume Berleur*. July 2, 2007

SomJ   Sommermeyer, Joerg: 'Noten, The Guitar Works of Napoléon Coste...', in: *Nova Giulianiad*, 1984 nr. 3, p. 167-169; http://home.tonline.de/home/Rechtsanwalt.Joerg.Sommermeyer/ng3.htm, July 10, 2002

tecla.com: *Napoléon Coste Compositeur*, 2005. February 5, 2008
tecla.com: *La Source du Lyson*, Op.47, the complete preface by Brian Jeffery. March 4, 2007; February 5, 2008
uakron.edu: *Stalking the oldest six-string guitar*, Thomas Heck. August 31, 2007
urfm.braidense.it/cataloghi/msselenco.php?Scatola=33&Progressivo=4 *Joseph haydn Armida Bella fiamma di gloria d'onore WoO21*, April 24, 2010
vrijmetselaarsgilde.eu/Maconnieke%20Encyclopedie/Franc-M/fra-f-03.htm, November 1, 2014

Discography

Albarello, Stefano: *Eco del Vesuvio*, Napoléon Coste: Barcarole op.51 no.1, Tactus TC 790001, 2004. Liner notes Stefano Albarello. Guitar: Pasquale Vinaccia 1889, Naples.

Ellipsis Duo, Alberto Cesaraccio & Alessandro Deiana: *Napoléon Coste*, Consolazione op. 25, Les Regrets op. 36, Marche et Scherzo op. 33, Le Montagnard op. 34, Feuilles d'Automne op. 41, Bongiovanni GB 5126-2, 2002. Liner notes Pierro Mioli.

Fischer, Ruth & Stephan Stiens: *Coste, Giuliani, Brouwer, Coates*, Napoléon Coste: Grand Duo, Academica 220959, 1990.

Fukuda, Shin-ichi: *19th Century Guitar*, Napoléon Coste: Rêverie op. 53 no. 1, Andante Fantaisie Symphonique op. 38 no. 14, Capriche sur l'Air Espagnol 'La Cachucha' op. 13, Denon CO-78950, 1995. Liner notes Shin-ichi Fukuda. Guitar: René Lacôte 1840?, Paris, diapason 63cm, nylon lute strings, a' = 430Hz.

Larousse, Florian: *Guitar Recital*, Coste le Départ op.31, Naxos Laureate Series 8.572565, 2010. Liner notes Graham Wade. Guitar: Hugo Cuviliez, Marsanne, Savarez strings.

Llobet, Miguel: *The Guitar Recordings 1925-29*, Napoléon Coste: Etude 23 op. 38, Chanterelle Historical Recordings CHR 001, 1993. Liner notes Ronald Purcell. Guitar: Antinio de Torres 1859 with tornavoz, Sevilla, gut-strings. [RJL p.18, 142]

Maccari-Pugliese Duo, Claudio Maccari & Paolo Pugliese: 'Sor-Coste' in: *The Classical Guitar Collection* Vol. 13, Brilliant Classics 9090/13, 2009. Liner notes Emma Baker. Guitars: René Lacôte 1824, 1825, 1827, Paris, Gaetano Il Guadagnini 1830, Italy, Joseph Pons 1825, France; gut-strings, a'= 430Hz.

McFadden, Jeffrey: *Guitar Recital*, Napoléon Coste: Rondeau de Concert Op. 12, Naxos Laureate Series Guitar 8.553401, 1994. Liner notes Michael Bracken, Jeffrey McFadden. Guitar: Manuel Contreras?, Madrid.

McFadden, Jeffrey: *Napoléon Coste [Vol. 1]*, Seize valses favorites de Johann Strauss op. 7, Divertissement sur Lucia di Lammermoor op. 9, Grand Caprice op. 11, Rondeau de concert avec introduction op. 12, Caprice sur l'air espagnol 'La Cachucha' op. 13, Naxos Guitar Collection 8.554192, 1997. Liner notes Richard Long. Guitar: Manuel Contreras, Madrid.

McFadden, Jeffrey: *Napoléon Coste Guitar Works Vol. 4*, Introduction & Allegretto, 25 Études op. 38, Rêverie Nocturne, Études from Complete Method for Guitar by Fernando Sor: Preludio (No. 11), Andante (No. 14), Preludio (No. 12), Estudio (No. 13), Naxos Guitar Collection 8.554354, 1998. Liner notes Richard Long. Guitar: Manuel Contreras, Madrid.

Metz, Andreas: *Coste & Regondi*, Napoléon Coste: Grand Solo op. 24, Andante et Polonaise op. 44, Fantaisie du Ballet d'Armide op. 4, Fantaisie de Norma op. 16, Born & Bellmann CD 980812, 1998. Guitar: Robert R. Ruck.

Montella, Nicola: *Sonata*, Napoléon Coste: Études de Genre op. 38 No. 4, 5, 6; Le Départ, Fantaisie dramatique op. 31; dotGuitar G1503, 2016. Liner notes Frédéric Zigante, guitars Marseglia 2013, Marín 2016.

Montesinos, Anabel: *Guitar Recital*, Napoléon Coste: Les Soirées d'Auteuil op. 23, Naxos Laureate Series Guitar 8.557294, 2003. Liner notes John W. Duarte.

Ratzkowski-Thomson Guitar Duo: *Scherzo*, Coste Scherzo et Pastorale op.10, Danachord DAOCD 373, 1993. Liner notes Mary Jane Vodicka. Guitars: G.K. Hannabach.

Riboni, Marco: *Napoléon Coste, 25 Études de Genre pour la guitare, op.38*, Etude 1 - 25, Nuova Era Records CD 7350, 2000. Liner notes Marco Riboni. Guitar: Anonymus 19th C., Russia, 7-string.

Sasaki-Holz duo, Bernd Holz & Tadashi Sasaki: *Duo Concertante*, Napoléon Coste: Le Montagnard op.34, Consolatione, Romance op.25, Les Regrets, Cantilène op.36, Marche et Scherzo op.33, HS 2 Plus, Kerpen, LC 6143, 1993. Guitar: Teruji Yamano 1983, 7-string.

Schneiderman, John: *Napoléon Coste*, Le Zuyderzée op. 20, Les Cloches op. 21, Meulan op. 22, Les Soirées d'Auteuil op. 23, La Vallée d'Ornans op. 17, Les Bords du Rhin op. 18, Delfzil & Etude op. 19, Récréation du Guitariste op. 51, Cantaur CRC 2609, 2002. Liner notes Peter Danner. Guitar: Tim Laughlin, 7-string.

Segovia, Andrés: *Guitar Etudes*, Napoléon Coste Allegretto no. 1 op. 38, Scherzando no.2 op. 38, Leccion 13, 9, 29 Méthode, MCA Classics The Segovia Collection Vol. 7 MCD 42073, 1990. Liner notes Eliot Fisk. Guitar: Hermann Hauser II?

Smits, Rafaella: *Fernando Sor - Napoléon Coste*, Rêverie op. 53 no. 1, Les Soirées d'Auteuil op. 23, Grande Sérénade op. 30, 2 Accent ACC2 9182 D, 1991. Liner notes Peter Andriessen.

Steidl, Pavel: *Napoléon Coste Guitar Works Vol. 3*, Deuxième polonaise op. 14, Le tournoi op. 15, Andante et Allegro (WoO), La romanesca op. 19b, Fantaisie op. 16, Introduction et variations (WoO), Deux Quadrilles, Naxos Guitar Collection 8.554353, 1998. Liner notes Richard Long.

Stenroos, Jouni: *Liebeslied*, Napoléon Coste: La Vallée d'Ornans op.17, Meulan op.22, Le Passage des Alpes op.27, 28 et 40, Clear Note 74327m 2007. Liner notes Pierre Tremblay. Guitar: Kauro Liikanen 2006, 10-string.

Teicholz, Marc: *Napoléon Coste Guitar Works Vol. 5*, La Ronde de Mai op. 42, Feuilles d'Automne Douze Valses op. 41, Marche Funèbre et Rondeau op. 43, Souvenir du Jura op. 44, Divagation op. 45, Naxos Guitar Collection 8.554355, 1998. Liner notes Richard Long.

Vallières, Jean: *Musique Française pour Guitare*, Napoléon Coste: La Vallée d'Ornans opus 17, Le Passage des Alpes, Rondo opus 40, Les Cloches, Fugue opus 21, Les Soirées d'Auteuil, Scherzo opus 23, Le Zuyderzée, Ballade opus 20, Étude No. 20 opus 38, La Chasse des Sylphes opus 29; Société Nouvelle d'Enregistrement SNE-554-CD, 1989.

Villa, Philippe: *Napoléon Coste 'Les Souvenirs'*, Fantaisie sur l ópéra Norma de Bellini op. 16, .Les Souvenirs, 7 morceaux épisodiques op. 17 - 23, Grande Sérénade op. 30, Mélancholie op. 51, Andantino op. 51, Barcarolle op. 51, Ligia Digital Lidi0102107-02, 2002. Liner notes Philippe Villa. Guitars: Coffe-Goguette 1838; Giuseppe Gualiardo 2001.

Viloteau, Thomas: *Romàntic*, Napoléon Coste: Le Passage des Alpes opus 27, La Vallée d'Ornans opus 17, Les Soirées d'Auteuil opus 23, Benicàssim LMG 2124, 2013. Liner notes Roger Altisent.

Vliet, Ari van: *Guitar Collection*, Napoléon Coste: Etude 20 op. 38, Cumuli Guitar Recital CGR 9609, 1996. Liner notes Ari van Vliet. Guitar: Manuel Contreras 1978, Madrid, diapason 66cm, Savarez-strings, a'=440Hz.

Vliet, Ari van: *N. Coste*, Napoléon Coste: Souvenirs op. 17-23, Fantaisie symphonique op. 28[b], Le Passage des Alpes op. 27, 28 & 40, Cumuli Guitar Recital CGR 1204. Liner notes Ari van Vliet. Guitar: Bernhard Kresse 2010, Köln, copy Lacôte heptacorde 1856, diapason 63cm, Damian Dlugolecki-strings a'=435Hz.

Wynberg, Simon & John Anderson: *Summertime, Music for Oboe and Guitar*, Napoléon Coste: Les Regrets op. 36, Chandos Collect CHAN 6581, 1984, 2006. Liner notes Noël Goodwin.
Zaczek, Brigitte: *Romantische Gitarre II Napoléon Coste 1805 - 1883*, Souvenir du Jura op. 44, Rêverie op. 53 Nr. 1, Fantaisie sur deux motifs de 'La Norma' op. 16, Le Zuyderzée op. 20, Caprice sur l'Air Espagnol 'La Cachucha' op. 13, Grande Sérénade op. 30, Valse favorite op. 46, 8 Walzer aus '16 Walses favorites de Johann Strauss 'op. 7, Extraplatte EX 652-2, 2005. Liner notes Alfred Komarek, Bruno Marlat, Brigitte Zaczek. Guitars: René Lacôte 1855, Paris, 7-string; Johann Stauffer 1837, Vienna. 8-string
Zaczek, Brigitte: *Romantische Gitarre*, Coste: Valse favorite op. 46, Grande Sérénade op. 30, Extraplatte EX 452-2, 2000. Liner notes Alfred Komarek, Brigitte Zaczek. Guitar: N.G. Ries c.1840, Vienna, 8-string.
Zanon, Fabio: *The Romantic Guitar*, Napoléon Coste: La Source du Lyson op. 47, Guitarcoop CGO2FZA/16, 2015. Liner notes Fabio Zanon, guitar Bouchet, 1964.
Zigante, Frédéric: *Napoléon Coste Guitar Works Vol. 2*, Variations et finale sur un motif favori de la famille suisse de Weigl op. 2, Deux Quadrilles de Contredanses op. 3, Fantaisie sur un motif du ballet d'Armide op. 4, Souvenirs de Flandres op. 5, Fantaisie de concert op. 6, Naxos Guitar Collection 8.554194, 1997. Liner notes Richard Long. Guitar: Masuro Kohno 1987.

Illustrations

Title page

Napoléon Coste, Kopenhavn, Kongelige Bibliotek, Portraetsamlingen, *Coste, Napoléon*, 1806 [sic]-1883, guitarspiller, by Disdéri (1819-1889), Paris, 1867 fol. 150.867 (1939 Nr. 78)

Chapter I

1	p.1	©2018 GeoBasis-DE/BKG (©2009), Google, Inst. Geogr. Nationale
2	p.1	Map data ©2018 Google
3	p.2	'La Vallée d'Ornans' - Vallée de la Loue, 2005, photograph author
4	p.3	Cléron Château, 2005, photograph author
5	p.5	La Source du Lison, 2005, photograph author

Chapter II

6	p.7	Genealogy Napoléon Coste (based on Roncet, exhibition Amondans, 2005)
7	p.8	Mairie Amondans 2002, photograph author
8	p.10	Ornans, 2005, photograph author
9	p.11	Holland, 1904, Bos Atlas
10	p.12	Report J.F. Coste, Paris, Service Historique de la Défense, Château de Vincennes
11	p.12	Report J.F. Coste, Paris, Service Historique de la Défense, Château de Vincennes
12	p.12	Signature J.F. Coste, Paris, Service Historique de la Défense, Château de Vincennes
13	p.13	*Van het uittrekken der Franschen 23 mei 1814*, by Streun, Delfzijl, Gemeentehuis

Chapter III

14	p.15	Valenciennes, plan 19th C., Bibliothèque municipale, photograph author 2007
15	p.18	Petites Affiches, May 20, 1826, Valenciennes, Bibliothèque Municipale, photograph author
16	p.20	Petites Affiches, April 14, 1827, Valenciennes, Bibliothèque Municipale, photograph author
17	p.21	Rue Askièvre, 2007, photograph author
18	p.22	Luigi Sagrini, New York, Public Library, Muller Collection, 1870198
19	p.24	Valenciennes, Place d'Armes, 2007, photograph author

Intermezzo I

20	p.26	Les Trois Jours, Carulli, Kk Rischel 126 mu 6621.1681 U48
21	p.27	Salon Herz, Paris, Bibliothèque nationale, cliché: C 93964, B.N. Mus.Est. n.d.
22	p.30	Berlioz, Paris, Bibliothèque nationale, 1845, cliché: 73 C 60395, B.N. Mus.Est. n.d.
23	p.33	Giuliani, by Stubenrauch/Jügel, c. 1815
24	p.33	Carulli, by Bouchardy, after Trioson, ca. 1820
25	p.33	Aguado, R. L. Ballesteros, lith. S. Darier, c.1840, Biblioteca Nacional de España
26	p.33	Sor, lith. Engelmann/Bordes, after Goubeau n.d.
27	p.34	Studio Giuliani, 1820, Vienna, Ataria, facsimile edition, London, Tecla, 1988
28	p.34	Méthode Carulli, 1825, Paris, Carli, repr. Genève, Minkoff, 1987
29	p.34	Méthode Aguado, 1826, Paris, Meissonnier, 1826, repr. Genève, Minkoff, 1980
30	p.34	Méthode Sor, 1830, Paris, L'Auteur, 1830, repr. Genève, Minkoff, 1981
31	p.34	Sor opus 7, *Complete Works for Guitar*, facsimile edition, New York, Shattinger, 1977
32	p.34	Sor opus 7, Oxford Guitar Music, 1974
33	p.35	Carcassi, by Jules David, Paris, Bibliothèque nationale, n.d.

34	p.37	Bibliographie de la France, 1828, facs. Nendeln, Kraus, 1966-1970
35	p.38	*La Guitaromanie*, lith. by Montoux, in: De Marescot, 1829, facs. Archivum musicum, 1985
36	p.39	Revue musicale 1827, The Hague, Royal Library
37	p.39	Le Ménestrel, 1838, The Hague, Royal Library
38	p.39	Gazette musicale, 1835, The Hague, Royal Library
39	p.39	Revue et Gazette musicale, 1852, The Hague, Royal Library
40	p.40	Harpolyre, Salomon, c.1830, Arthur Tracy Cabot Fund, Museum of Fine Arts, Boston
41	p.40	Lyre guitare, Pleyel, Paris, 1809, Cité de la Musique, E 23
42	p.40	Grobert, c.1830, Paris, Cité de la Musique, E 375
43	p.40	Lacôte, 1830, Paris, Cité de la Musique, E 986.5.1
44	p.42	*Discussion*, lith. by Montoux, in: De Marescot, 1829, facs. Archivum musicum, 1985
45	p.43	Rue Bleue, street sign, photograph author, 2007

Chapter IV

46	p.46	Boulevard Poissonnière, Paris, Bibliothèque Historique de la Ville de Paris, photo: *Boulevard Poissonnière*, une file de petites voitures de marchands de quatre saisons, Cl. 1026
47	p.48	Gymnase musical, Paris, Bibliothèque nationale, fol. I20 THE n.d.
48	p.51	Coste incipit Weigl-variations opus 2 1829
49	p.51	Zani de Ferranti incipit Niaiserie opus 21 c. 1832
50	p.52	Aux Parisiens, Coste, 1830, Bibliothèque nationale, Département de la Musique
51	p.53	Giulio Regondi, lith. Engelmann/Weber, 1831, London, Spencer collection
52	p.54	*La Contredanse*, lith by Montoux, in: De Marescot, 1829, facs. Archivum musicum, 1985
53	p.56	Paganini, miniature by Pommayrac, Genua, Palazzo Doria Tursi n.d.
54	p.58	Rue du Vieux Colombier c. 1876, Paris, Bibliothèque Historique de la Ville de Paris, photo Blancard: *Rue du Vieux Colombier*, vue prise du coté de la rue Bonaparte vers la rue de Rennes, Marville, s.d. vers 1876?] G.P. XXII, 29
55	p.59	Armide, stage design Cambon, Paris, Bibliothèque nationale, Département de la Musique, Photothèque, *Gluck, décor de Cambon pour Armide*, 2e tiers 19e s., Cliché: C 73716
56	p.61	Trinidad Huerta, Paris, Bibliothèque nationale n.d.
57	p.63	Coste, *Marche - Souvenirs de Flandres* opus 5, m. 15, facsimile edition, Monaco, Chanterelle, 1981, 1983, vol. 2 p. 44
58	p.66	Franz Liszt, 1837, Léon Noël, Source gallica.bnf.fr / BnF
59	p.69	Marco Aurelio Zani de Ferranti, daguerrotype ca. 1846
60	p.70	Bellini, 1835, Le Voleur, Source gallica.bnf.fr / BnF
61	p.71	Meyerbeer, 1836, Vigneron, Source gallica.bnf.fr / BnF
62	p.72	Strauss (Vater), 1835, lith. Kriehuber, 1835
63	p.73	*L'Esquif du Pêcheur*, title page, Bruxelles, Koninklijke Bibliotheek Royale, Mus. 2.889 B1.
64	p.74	*Ave Maria*, Schubert, arr. Coste, Copenhagen, RiBS 179 mu 6701.1182 U264
65	p.76	Hôtel de Ville, salle St.Jean, Guide pittoresque du Voyageur en France, 1838
66	p.79	Ambroise Thomas, Music Division, The New York Public Library
67	p.82	Rue de l'Échiquier, street sign, photograph author, 2007

Chapter V

68	p.84	Salle Herz, Paris, Bibliothèque Historique de la Ville de Paris, photothèque
69	p.89	François Fétis, photo Ghémar frères, Bruxelles n.d.
70	p.93	Fanny Elssler, 1837, Jerome Robbins Dance Division, The New York Public Library
71	p.94	La petite Savoyarde, Lb E 1717.I.(41.)
72	p.95	Donizetti, Naples, photograph author, 2010
73	p.97	Halévy, Paris, Bibliothèque nationale n.d.
74	p.98	Le Guitarrero, Courbet, 1844, Ornans, Musée Courbet
75	p.105	Salle du Conservatoire, engraving Germain, Paris, Photo Pic, n.d.

Illustrations

76	p.106	Concert May 25, 1843, in: Decourcelle, Maurice: *La Société des Enfants d'Apollon (1741-1880): programmes des concerts annuels...*, Paris, Durand, 1881, p. 78
77	p.108	Le Tournoi op. 15, manuscript Coste, Lam Spencer Collection
78	p.109	Grades Coste Loge maçonnique, http://www.mvmm.org/m/docs/coste.html
79	p.109	Registration Coste Loge maçonnique, http://www.mvmm.org/m/docs/coste.html
80	p.114	Title page *Méthode* Coste-Sor, *Méthode Complète pour la Guitare par Fernando Sor* rédigée et augmentée... par N. Coste, Paris, Schonenberger S.No.1726 [1851] Lbl b.1169
81	p.115	Sor *Méthode* Fig. 10, 11 Pl. IV, *Méthode pour La Guitare* par Ferdinand Sor, Paris, L'Auteur, rue de Marivaux, no.1, 1830, reprint Minkoff, Genève, 1981
82	p.115	Sor *Méthode* Fig.17, 18 Pl. VI, *Méthode pour La Guitare* par Ferdinand Sor, Paris, L'Auteur, rue de Marivaux, no.1, 1830, reprint Minkoff, Genève, 1981
83	p.115	Sor *Méthode* Fig. 14 Pl. VI, *Méthode pour La Guitare* par Ferdinand Sor, Paris, L'Auteur, rue de Marivaux, no.1, 1830, reprint Minkoff, Genève, 1981
84	p.115	*Étude* no. 11 *Méthode* Coste-Sor
85	p.115	Coste *Les Bords du Rhin* opus 18 m. 122
86	p.122	Title page *Souvenirs*, facsimile edition, Monaco, Chanterelle, 1981, 1983, vol. 3 p. 51
87	p.123	Rue de Calais no. 11, photograph author, 2007
88	p.124	*La Vallée d'Ornans*, lith. Vernier, c. 1850?, after G. Courbet, Besançon, Bibliothèque Municipale, Est-Doubs-lison-2-a
89	p.125	Les Bords du Rhin op. 18, manuscript Coste, Lam Spencer Collection
90	p.126	Delfzijl, 1814, by Streun, Delfzijl Gemeentehuis
91	p.126	Zuiderzee, Stadsmuseum Harderwijk, 1776
92	p.127	Cloches 'Les Trois Soeurs' St-Amand, Office du Tourisme, Valenciennes
93	p.128	Meulan op. 22, manuscript Coste, Lam Spencer Collection
94	p.132	Søffren Degen, Kopenhavn, Kongelige Bibliotek, Portraetsamlingen, *Degen, Søffren*, 1816-1885, guitarist, skuespiller, fotograf, DP008385
95	p.135	Napoléon Coste, photograph Søffren Degen, c. 1855, Kopenhavn, Kongelige Bibliotek, Portraetsamlingen, *Coste, Napoleon*,1806 [sic]-1883, guitarspiller, by Degen, 184295 (1939 nr.138)

Chapter VI

96	p.139	Nicolai de Makaroff, in: *Istorčieskij vestnik – Historic Gazette,* April 1910 (pages 89-116)
97	p.141	Henri Adan, Bruxelles, Koninklijke Bibliotheek Royale, collection des estampes, Portr. d'Henri Adan, J. Schubert, Vol. H, 7e60 - FF, 38953
98	p.142	Valentin Bender, Koninklijke Bibliotheek Royale, collection des estampes, Portr. Valentin Bender - plano, Litt. B., S II 64350
99	p.142	Joseph Blaes, Bruxelles, Koninklijke Bibliotheek Royale, collection des estampes, Portr. Joseph Blaes, SI 37503
100	p.143	Bertold Damcke, http://www.avemariasongs.org/aves/D/Damcke.htm
101	p.143	Hubert Kufferath, Koninklijke Bibliotheek Royale, collection des estampes, Portr. 43 Kufferath, W. Stxeit, folio, SI 31630
102	p.144	Hubert Léonard, Koninklijke Bibliotheek Royale, collection des estampes, Portr. Hubert Léonard - 8o, Litt. L., S V 15916
103	p.144	Adrien Servais, Bibliothèque nationale, Département de la Musique, Photothèque, *Servais, Adrien François*, J.F. Servais, lithographie de Baugniet, 1838, Cliché: 65 C 26439, B.N. Musique, J.F. Servais, 4-5
104	p.146	J. K. Mertz? in: Schwarz-Reiflingen, Erwin. *Altmeister der Gitarre: Johann Kaspar Mertz*. Magdeburg: Heinrichhofen's Verlag, 1924. Bickford Collection, VOB1802, Special Collections and Archives, Oviatt Library, California State University, Northridge
105	p.147	Concertino Mertz m. 35, in: Wynberg, *Johann Kaspar Mertz, Guitar Works*, Monaco, Chanterelle, 1982, vol. I p. 3
106	p.152	Nadaillac Delessert, Baudry (1828-1886): portrait de Cécile de Lessert, Comtesse de Nadaillac, Pn NB-A-095754
107	p.153	Fantaisie symphonique op. 28[b], transcript Kk Rischel & Birket Smith Collection
108	p.155	La Chasse des Sylphes, Coste op. 29 III m. 1-6, in: Wynberg, Simon, ed: *The Guitar Works of Napoléon Coste*, facsimile edition, vol. IV, Monaco, Chanterelle, 1983; reprint 2006-7
109	p.158	Crimean War, Art Archive, Rome
110	p.158	Royal Library, Brussels, photograph author, 2007

Intermezzo II

111	p.170	Olry & Lacôte heptacordes at auction 1995, photograph Sinier de Ridder, 2007

Chapter VII

112	p.173	Rue Blanche no. 100, photograph author, 2007
113	p.176	Johan G. Holm, Royal Danish Library, Photo Collection
114	p.177	Letter Coste-Degen, October 17, 1863, detail p. 4
115	p.179	Napoléon Coste, Disdéri, Kopenhavn, Kongelige Bibliotek, Portraetsamlingen, *Coste, Napoleon*,1806 [sic]-1883, fol. 150.867 (1939 Nr. 78)
116	p.183	Charles Triébert, Bibliothèque nationale, Département de la Musique, Photothèque, *Triebert, Charles Louis, Hautboiste et facteur d'instruments*, Photo dans l'Album des membres de la Société Académique des Enfants d'Apollon, Photo par Trinquart, Paris, Cliché: 82 B 94850, Est.Mus.No.1
117	p.189	Rue du Faubourg St-Martin, Paris, Bibliothèque Historique de la Ville de Paris, photo: *Rue du Faubourg St. Martin*, caputilation Prussiens, 1871, G.P. XXIX, 27.
118	p.191	*25 Études de Genre* op. 38 Lam Spencer Collection XX(159224.1)
119	p.201	Rue du Faubourg St-Martin, Paris, Bibliothèque historique de la Ville de Paris, photo: *Rue du Faubourg St. Martin*, 462Cl.1041.

Chapter VIII

120	p.209	Sor *Fantaisie Elegiaque* op. 59 II m. 3
121	p.209	Sor *Fantaisie Elegiaque* op. 59 II m. 52
122	p.209	Coste *Marche funèbre* op. 43 m. 4
123	p.209	Coste *Marche funèbre* op. 43 m. 22
124	p.211	*Jura, le Miroir d'Ornans*, Courbet, detail, Ornans, Musée Courbet
125	p.212	F. Schult, Royal Danish Library, Photo Collection
126	p.219	La Source du Lyson, lith. Engelmann, 1828, Besançon, Bibliothèque municipale, Est.-Doubs.Lison.2
127	p.223	Renault & Chatelain, Coste-guitar, courtesy of Erik Pierre Hofmann, 2016
128	p.223	Renault & Chatelain, Coste-guitar, courtesy of Erik Pierre Hofmann, 2016
129	p.223	Renault & Chatelain, Coste-guitar, courtesy of Erik Pierre Hofmann, 2016
130	p.227	Air Suédois, Coste-Schult, December 8, 1874
131	p.232	Rue du Faubourg St-Martin no. 50, 2007, photograph author

Chapter IX

The illustrations 132-154 in the conclusion are all musical examples made by the author and editor.

155	p.250	In honor of Napoléon Coste, based on photograph Søffren Degen, c. 1855, Kopenhavn, Kongelige Bibliotek, Portraetsamlingen, *Coste, Napoleon*,1806 [sic]-1883, guitarspiller, by Degen, 184295 (1939 nr.138)

Appendices

156	p.261	Paris map Garnier, 1864
157	p.267	Acte de naissance Napoléon Coste
158	p.268	Acte de mariage Coste-Pauilhé
159	p.269	Acte de décès Napoléon Coste
160	p.270	Enregistrement opus 30
161	p.270	Enregistrement opus 31
162	p.271	Coste-Degen, June 15, 1858 p. 1
163	p.272	Coste-Degen, October 17, 1863 p. 1
164	p.273	Coste-Gruel, June 16, 1879
165	p.274	Coste-Hallberg, September 22, 1880

The Author

166	p.318	Ari van Vliet, 2015

Index

Names (persons)

Abondance 180
Adam 32, 161, 236
Adan 141, 145, 147, 157, 166, 192, 200
Adenis 178
Adler xv
Aguado v, 21, 33-37, 39, 41, 42, 45, 46, 57, 60-63, 67, 80, 83, 90,
    100, 101, 112, 114, 116, 164, 211, 221, 235
Ajax 47
Alard 90, 159
Alberti 196
Alesi 84
Allorto v
Amant 109
Ambert 12
Anelli 39
Angers [see Pélan d=Angers]
Anjou 94
Arailza 36
Arcas 151
Arhusen 148
As(h)burnham 152, 166, 199, 235
Auber 69, 94, 95, 159, 161, 162
Aubert 34
Aubigny 185
Audéoude 226
Aulagnier 164
Aulnay 105
Aumont 106, 120
Azpiazu 233
Bach xi, 29, 39, 116, 162
Bagge 163
Baillie 93
Baillot 30, 32, 63, 67, 68, 100, 159, 236
Baliet 4
Balzac xi
Barroilhet 94, 109, 178
Batiste 120
Baudin 110
Bayer 33, 150
Beard xi, xv
Beck 102
Bédard 34
Beethoven xi, xii, 29, 31, 82, 90, 105, 162, 171, 183, 204, 206, 209,
    218-220, 227
Beilner 32
Bélanger 74
Bellini 19, 28, 29, 57, 58, 69-70, 78, 238
Bellon 121
Bellow 234
Benazet 62
Bender 140, 142, 146
Bent x
Berg x
Bériot 129, 143, 144, 183, 186, 235
Berlioz ix, xi, xii, xv, 26, 28, 29, 41, 50, 51, 56-58, 60, 71, 79, 107,
    109, 123, 131, 143, 153-156, 161, 162, 166, 169, 194,
    207, 218, 219, 220, 233, 235, 237, 240, 248
Bernard 104

Bertini 69
Berveling x
Bessat 11, 12
Beyle xi
Birket-Smith vii-ix, 69, 75, 92, 133, 141, 153, 155, 174, 176, 186
Blaes 140, 142, 146
Blainville 121
Blanc 130, 172
Blancard 59
Blanchard 99, 100-103, 110
Blume xi, xiii
Bobrovich 150
Bodin 110
Bödeker ix
Boehm 104
Bötticher xi, xii
Bohrer 48
Boieldieu 20
Boisson 231
Bolívar 102
Bonaparte, Napoléon vi, 4, 5, 9, 12, 13, 15-16 25, 27, 28, 49, 67,
    152, 179, 207
Bone 17, 22
Boquet 20
Bosch 110, 111, 151, 172, 180, 182, 203, 229
Bossuet 110
Bottesini 29
Boucher 23, 77
Braille 184
Brand 150
Brel 1
Bricqueville 95
Brion 3
Briqueville 95
Bruneleau 4
Buek 17, 59, 131, 191, 233
Buell x
Bulté 110
Burgmüller 68, 76-78, 236
Burzik 17, 65, 107, 220
Bussine 121
Buttigni 164
Caceres 110
Caillard 25
Calderón 111, 229
Call xxix, 182
Cambon 61
Campion 89
Candillon 231
Carcassi 21, 34-36, 41, 42, 45, 46, 50, 52, 69, 83, 90, 94, 95, 98,
    100, 101, 111, 112, 114, 119, 150, 151, 165, 193, 235
Carli 21, 64
Carulli 21, 25, 33-35, 42, 45-46, 52, 53, 58, 64, 69, 83, 98, 101,
    111-112, 116, 155, 164-165, 182, 193, 194, 221, 235,
    237
Carulli, G. 53
Castellacci 45, 83, 101, 111, 156
Castelli 62

Castil-Blaze 26, 38-39, 60, 61, 102, 103
Caudron 84
Cavaillé-Coll 161, 167
Cerclier 197
Challiot vii, 36-37, 56, 78, 79, 87, 107, 110, 123, 164, 236
Chanot 168
Chapalain 22
Charlemagne 154
Charles X 25, 27, 51
Charpentier 90
Chatelain 222-223
Chatot 164, 178
Chaulieu 62, 99
Chaulieu/Delacour 38
Cherubini ix, 2, 27, 29, 55, 56, 57, 78, 159, 216
Chollet 79
Chopin ix, xi, xii, 32, 57, 78, 157, 162, 175, 189, 194, 198, 209,
　　　　221, 233, 235, 237, 248
Choron 89, 121
Ciebra 110, 119, 137, 145, 146, 150, 171, 172
Clementi 32
Coche 104
Coffé-Goguette 168
Cokken 76, 104, 161
Colin 185, 186
Colombier 36, 129, 164, 174
Concone 72-73, 76-78, 80, 85, 89, 178
Constant 189
Cooper ix, 17
Coralli 92
Coste, Napoléon v-xvii, 1-5, 7-13, 15-26, 28, 30, 33, 35-38, 40,
　　　　41, 43, 45-65, 68-82, 83-134, 137-141, 145-162, 164-
　　　　201, 203-231, 233-249
Coste, Cathérine-Françoise 4, 7-8
Coste, Étienne-François 3
Coste, Jean-François viii, x, 1-5, 7, 9-13, 15, 64, 121, 173, 187,
　　　　231, 235
Coste, Jeanne-Étienne 3, 7-8, 10, 64
Coste, Jeanne-Pierrette 3, 7-8
Coste, Julie 3, 7, 189
Coste, M. (1851) 189
Coste, M. (1857) 189
Coste, A. (1870) 189
Coste, Mme 189, 211, 215
Costes (48), 57, (58)
Cotte 120
Coudray 164
Couperin 89
Courbet xiv, 1, 10, 98, 123, 161
Cruys vi, 151
Cuvillon 133
Czerny 32, 93, 236
Dahlhaus xi, xiv
Daly 218
Damcke 119, 140, 143, 145, 146
Dancescu 157
Dancla 29, 85, 99, 104, 121
Davids 126
Daza 89
Debain 167
Decombe 41
Decourcelle 28, 79, 99, 105, 106, 129, 133, 134, 172, 182, 184,
　　　　204, 205, 215, 216, 225
Defauconpret 28
Degen ix, 63, 69, 75, 92, 131, 132-134, 149, 166, 167, 171, 173-
　　　　179, 183, 196, 205, 207, 208, 212, 218, 235, 236

Degouve 187
Delaby 184, 186
Delacour 38, 99
Delanoue 96
Delessert [see Nadaillac]
Deligny 62
Dell=Ara 107, 118, 123, 152, 192, 219
Delle-Sedie 120, 186
Dénéria 4, 7, 9, 64, 99, 166, 188, 231, 235
Deshaulles 96
Devriès 91
Diabelli 21, 32, 151, 197
Dietz 30, 47, 53, 57, 60, 236
Disdéri vi, 166, 179, 222, 231, 236
Dömling xi, xii
Doisy (Doisi) 34-35
Donizetti 28, 57, 65, 86, 94-96, 171, 226
Doré 230
Dorus 29, 45, 46, 90, 120
Douillez 70, 86
Dubost 145
Dubouig 94
Ducis 100, 110
Dugot 180, 231
Dupin xiii, 189
Dupond 106
Dupont 105
Duport 46, 76, 78, 79, 100, 236
Durand 68
Dussek 35
Duverger 62
Duvernoy 120
Egasse de C. 191
Eglantine 9
Egrefeuille 38
Einstein xi, xiii
Elssler 92-93
Engebert 19
Érard 26, 27, 29, 30, 53, 103, 162, 168, 236
Ermel 106
Escudier 36, 72-73, 75, 76, 80, 81, 84, 100, 167
Espinel 90
Eulry 168
Exaudet 89, 206
Fack 17
Fallon 197
Farrenc 53, 133, 161
Fère 47
Féron 84
Ferranti [see Zani de Ferranti]
Fesch 60
Fétis v, ix, 26, 29, 32, 35-36, 38-40, 45, 48, 49-50, 53-54, 57, 60,
　　　　62, 63, 65, 68, 69, 72, 79, 81, 88-90, 103, 112, 116, 130,
　　　　140, 146, 147, 151, 161, 168, 180, 226, 231, 235, 237
Fischer 137, 150
Fischer, N. ix, 178, 204
Fokine 154
Folly 181, 182
Fontaine 41, 62
Fortoul xiii
Fossa 42, 62, 165
Franck 41, 121
Franz 151
Fuenllana 89
Gaccia 105
Garancelle 197

Index

Gardeton 41, 42
Gatayes 34
Gazan 4
Gelas 17, 131
Gérard 168
Germance 215, 217
Gide 92
Giordano 118, 192, 207, 208, 214, 233
Girard 29
Giraud 4
Girod vii, 36, 149, 150, 153, 155, 157, 164, 171
Giuliani v, 21, 22, 23, 33-34, 36, 47, 77, 80, 85, 90, 148, 164, 165, 193, 194, 219, 237, 242
Gloag xi, xv
Gluck 19, 50, 58, 60
Goethe xii, xiii, xiv
Gossec 2
Gouffé 99, 131
Gounod 161
Gozlan 102, 182
Gozzoli 166, 199, 214
Granata 89
Grard 85
Grijp x
Grobert 41, 168
Grove 163
Gruel ix, 178, 204, 205, 208, 222, 230
Grus 95, 110
Guerau 89
Guerreau 130-131
Habeneck 29, 31, 99, 144, 161
Haendel 29, 89, 116
Halévy 43, 96, 97-98
Hallberg ix, 16, 48, 50, 56, 63, 74, 81, 167, 178, 179, 180, 188, 210, 212, 214, 216, 217, 218, 221, 222, 224, 225, 228, 229, 230, 231, 235
Hanslick xv, 169
Harion 51
Harris 166, 198
Haumann 91
Haussmann 25, 160, 171, 173
Haydn xi, 29, 90, 105, 206
Heck v, vi, x, 22
Hegel xv, 169
Hennin 46, 72, 77
Henri, L= 38
Herbin 110, 111
Herder xiii
Hermann 20
Hervé 214
Herwyn 172
Herz 30, 69, 84-86, 88, 91, 103, 161, 236
Heugel 38, 230
Hirsch 164, 175
Hitz 196
Hoek 118, 192
Hoffmann xi-xv
Hofmann 222-223
Holm 69, 166, 167, 175-176, 178-179, 196, 206, 221, 227
Huel 168
Huerta 45, 53, 54, 60, 61-62, 83, 90, 91, 93, 101, 103, 110, 133, 151, 156, 171, 172, 181, 182, 203
Hugo xii, 111, 207, 229
Hullin 41, 75
Hummel 32, 47, 53, 77, 85, 99, 100, 121, 214
Husson 41

Jancourt 120
Janicot 195
Jansen 150
Jaworski vii, x, 17, 131, 177, 231, 234
Jeffery v, vi, vii, x, 8, 9, 41, 74, 80, 107, 118, 123, 124, 210, 218, 219, 221, 224, 234
Joachim 162
Johnson ix
Kalkbrenner 32
Kamberger 150
Kant xv
Katto 59, 164, 216, 217, 218
Kepper 60
Klier 118
Kloe x
Klosé 79, 120, 129, 130, 161, 183, 185
Knaffl 33
Knudsen 132
Koechlin xv, 234
Kontski 105
Komarny 146, 147
Kresse vi, x
Kreutzer 32, 46, 143, 236
Krüger 169
Kufferath 140, 143, 146
Küffner 150, 182
Kühnel 146, 147
Labarre 69, 90
Lacôte vi, x, 33, 41, 45, 63, 64, 80, 103, 110, 114, 116, 123, 126, 132, 146, 164, 168, 189, 197, 222-223, 236
Lacoux 41
Läpke vii, 17, 131, 191, 227, 233
Lalo 162, 207
Lamoureux 162
Laprévotte 168
Larmande 68
Larrieux 184, 186
Lasalle 55, 162
Lassus 9
Latte 36, 95, 123, 164
Laurelli 83, 110
Laurent 9
Lebouc 130-131, 133
Lecocq 214
Lecointe 45, 46, 76, 77, 100
Ledhuy 45, 112
Leduc 182
Lefèvre 58
Lefort 217
Legnani 21, 35, 66, 93, 111, 133, 151, 165, 211-212
Lelorin 86, 92
Lemoine 34-37, 89, 164, 165
Léonard 140, 143, 144, 147
Leopold I 142, 165
Lepeintre 111
Levien 41
Lesueur 28, 56
Levasseur 91
Levoisseur 29
Lintant 34, 35
Lissajous 43
Liszt v, ix, xi, xii, xiv, 27-28, 31-32, 47, 57, 63, 65-68, 72, 78, 83, 90, 91, 99, 142, 143, 157, 163, 194, 207, 221, 235, 236-237, 248
Llobet vi, 157, 191, 249
Longyear xi

Losset 90
Louis XIV 117, 180, 231, 236
Louis XVI 2
Louis XVIII 27
Louis Philippe I 25, 51, 161
Louis Napoléon 12
Lovrins 91
Lovy 104, 149
Lozano 110
Lully 60
Lunebourg 10
Luther 71
Maelzel 40
Makaroff vii, viii, xv, 68, 119-120, 132, 137-143, 145-151, 153, 155-157, 159, 164, 166, 171, 172, 191, 193, 200, 206, 207, 249
Malibran 48, 57, 78, (111)
Marchélie 219, 220
Marescot 33, 38, 42, 55
Marmontel 181
Marsoudet 196, 210
Martinez 111
Masone 104
Massenet 209
Massimino 38
Maufroy 12
Mayaud 95
Mayerhofer 74
Mayseder 85
Mazel 78
McFadden 191
McPherson xiv
Méhul 2
Meier ix, 56
Meier-Pauselius 56
Meissonnier 37, 38, 41, 112
Meissonnier/Heugel 38
Mendelssohn 29, 143, 154, 162
Merchi 34
Mertz vi, xvii, 40, 69, 119, 120, 137, 139, 140, 145-151, 156, 157, 164, 165, 194, 212, 249
Meyerbeer 29, 58, 70-71, 82, 96, 99, 120, 161, 207
Miel 26
Milan 89
Miró 57
Molard 186
Møldrup viii, ix, x, 132, 175
Molière 28
Moline 20
Molino (20), 34-35, 42, 45-46, 83, 98, 111-112, 116, 168, 182
Monk 275
Monteverdi 89
Montigny, P(aul de) 59, 87, 88, 101
Montigny, Caroline (de) 59, 86, 87, 101, 112, 133, 166, 198
Montoux 55
Moretti 36, 165
Moschelès 32, 48, 85, 162
Moser v, 75
Moucelot 155, 157
Mozart xi, 29, 39, 49, 90, 133, 197, 204
Mudarra 89
Nadaillac-Delessert 152, 166, 206, 235
Napoléon [see Bonaparte]
Napoléon III 160, 162, 187
Narváez 89
Neubauer xi, xiv

Neuland 182
Ney 130-131, 133, 172
Nietsche xv
Nightingale 158
Nilsson 186, 187, 227
Nordet 104
Offenbach 161, 211
Ophee vii, x, 137, 141, 146, 148, 192
Ordinaire 9
Ortigue 26
Ossian xiv
Oudet 210
Ourika 111
Outhoorn 152, 225, 235
Padovetz 150
Paganini ix, xi, 41, 56, 57, 66, 69, 83, 111, 163, 172, 181, 235
Page 197
Panco 196
Panormo vi
Panseron 47, 53, 79, 99, 104, 109, 120, 121, 161, 187, 235
Pape 47, 53, 78, 103
Paracelsus 154
Pascal 51, 198
Pasdeloup 161, 162, 163
Pauilhé (wife) 7, 86, 92, 166, 171, 187-190, 197, 205, 209, 228, 229, 231, 235
Pauilhé, A 189
Paulin 130
Pélan d=Angers 216, 217
Pérez-Diaz v
Pénotet 4
Perriquet 19, 22
Petetin 64, 189, 190, 195
Petiteau 178
Petiton 121
Pettol 150
Petzold 54, 57, 60, 83, 236
Philip II 90
Pilate 217
Piris 75
Pisador 89
Pius VII 5
Planard 79
Planque 45, 70
Pleyel 30, 41, 63, 69, 81, 103, 131, 162, 168, 181, 236
Pollet 35, 99
Ponchard 121
Ponchita 20, 21
Pontécoulant 103
Potier 105
Powroïniak 234
Pretet 3, 7
Promayet 98
Prumier 109, 120, 235
Pujol vi, 41, 111, 249
Rada 81
Radole 192, 218
Ragossnik 192
Rambuteau 25
Rameau 29
Ravina 120
Realino 155, 220
Reber 215
Regnault 67
Regondi 35, 53, 91, 111, 119, 137, 151, 164, 181, 194
Reicha 28, 56

Index

Renault 222-223
Reussner 124
Riboni x, 191-199
Ribouillault 41, 118
Richardière (Bourgeois de la) 134, 166, 182, 195, 204
Richault vii, 28, 36-37, 45, 49, 59, 63, 68, 70, 72, 74, 79, 91-93, 101, 110, 123, 152, 164, 185, 190, 205-207, 236
Ridder 189
Rilling 150
Rischel vii, viii, ix, 5, 56, 68, 69, 75, 92, 131, 133, 141, 153, 141, 153, 174-176, 186, 212, 218, 227, 231
Rivière 83, 231
Rochefoucauld 29
Rode 32, 236
Roehder 90
Roger 120
Romagnesi 38, 48, 49, 52, 54, 110, 123, 164
Romani 20, 21
Roncalli 89
Roncet vii, viii, x, 4, 8, 17, 173, 177, 217, 231
Rosen xi
Rossi 105
Rossini 19, 20, 28, 57, 69, 78, 85, 94, 96, 182
Rousseau 65, 68
Rubinstein 142, 162
Sagrini 21-23, 37, 46
Saint-Saëns 162, 207
Salomon 41, 112
Sand [see Dupin]
Sanz 89
Sapho 163
Sardi 75
Sasser v, vi
Sax 167
Scarlatti 198
Scherzer 119, 137, 139, 140, 148, 151
Schick 227
Schiller xiii
Schlesinger 37, 38, 40
Schmidt 60
Schonenberger vii, 28, 36, 110, 113, 123, 164, 236
Schopenhauer xv, xvii
Schott 52, 138, 141, 144, 145, 147, 151, 160
Schubert vii, xii, 27, 28, 70, 72-74, 80, 162, 178, 236, 237, 248
Schult ix, 97, 116, 147, 166-167, 172, 179, 181, 185, 190, 200, 204, 207, 208, 210, 212, 218, 222, 226-228, 235
Schultz 47, 77, 119, (212)
Schumann 162, 194
Schumann, Clara 143
Schwarz-Reiflingen vii, 17, 59, 117, 118, 131, 192, 224, 233
Scott 28, 96, 107, 121
Scribe 71, 95, 97
Seghers 162
Segovia vi, 117, 118, 191, 204, 249
Segura 221
Serral 92
Servais 68, 140, 143-147
Sévelinges 26
Shakespeare 154, 215
Sharpe 192
Shtokman 16, 17, 131, 191, 233
Sinier 189
Sokolowski 172, 181, 182
Soler 104, 105, 129
Sommermeyer 107, 123, 152, 155, 208, 214, 226

Sor v, vi, xv, xvi, 21, 23, 25, 29, 30, 33-37, 39, 41, 42, 45, 46, 47, 52-57, 60, 61-64, 67, 68, 72, 74-78, 80-83, 85, 86, 89, 90, 98, 100, 101, 111-119, 124, 156, 164, 165, 181, 190-192, 197, 209, 211, 213, 214, 223-224, 231, 233, 235, 237, 242, 243, 247, 248
Sor, Caroline 75
Sor, Charles 41
Soto 90
Souffleto 103, 104
Soulié 26
Soullier 168
Soussman 150
Sowinski 47, 53
Spencer 79, 206, 221, 224, 225, 228
St-Albin 53
Stauffer 119, 137
Steenkiste 90
Steffe 257
Stempnik vi, 146, 156
Stendhal [see Beyle]
Stenstadvold x, 17, 118
Stevens ix, x
Stockmann [see Shtokman]
Stradivarius vi, 144, 168
Strauss 70, 71-72, 80, 91, 208, 236
Streun 13
Suzanne 4
Szczepanowski vi, 91, 145, 150, 171
Taitbout 53, 60,
Tárrega vi, 111, 203, 229, 249
Thalberg 32
Thomas 79, 80, 92, 99, 109, 178
Thys 106, 107, 109
Tillemont 121
Tilmant 28, 29, 45, 46, 76, 77, 99, 161
Torta 53, 98
Triébert 99, 103, 105, 107, 109, 120, 121, 129-131, 164, 166, 174, 183-186, 235
Troupenas 38, 95
Ulenbrock 123, 166, 198
Vailati 181, 182
Valance 170
Valderrábano 89
Valentin 51
Vandenberghe 99
Vanrycke 188
Varoud 3
Varoux 3
Vavasseur 104
Verhagen x
Véron 29, 30, 53, 56, 67, 71
Verroust 85, 104, 129, 161
Vialon 123
Viardot 162
Vidal 34, 35
Vierne 207
Vignas 110
Vimeux 90, 95
Visée 89, 116-118, 198, 206, 226
Vliet x, xvii
Vliet-Voordouw x
Vuillaume 132
Wagner 161, 163, 169, 200
Wal x
Wartel 121

Watteau 16
Weber, William ix, 32, 162
Weber, C.M. von 154
Weigl 19, 21, 48-50, 65, 198
Wekerlin 68, 189
Wennekes x
Whistling viii
Wideman(n) 85, 86, 90, 91
Wieland 154
Wieniawski 143, 233
Winter 50

Wilhem 27
Winkel 40
Wittmann 151
Wynberg vi, vii, 8, 17, 68, 69, 79, 131, 149, 151-153, 171, 175,
    184, 186, 193, 218, 221, 225, 227, 228, 249
Yradier 145
Zani (de Ferranti) vi, xvii, 19, 40, 48, 49, 50, 52, 69, 111, 119, 133,
    137, 145, 150, 151, 164, 165, 171, 172, 182, 212, 249
Zola 161
Zuth v, 17, 22

Works (Coste)

Méthode (xvi, 64, 68, 72, 75, 86, 89, 107, 111 118, 123, 164, 174, 191. 204, 206, 226, 228, 242, 243, 246, 248)

opus 1 (51, 52)
opus 2 (19, 48 51, 60, 65, 86, 198)
opus 3 (51, 52, 54, 59, 111, 112, 152, 166, 199)
opus 4 (19, 37, 50, 58 60, 65, 70, 82, 101, 207, 243)
opus 5 (16, 54, 63, 65, 82, 121, 158, 166 210, 214, 220)
opus 6 (19, 50, 59, 63, 70 71, 82, 86, 99, 207, 241)
opus 7 (72, 91, 99, 208)
opus 8 (86, 87, 88, 104, 211, 238, 240, 244)
opus 9 (28, 86, 92, 95, 99, 238, 246)
opus 10 (59, 86, 87, 91, 101, 112, 133, 176, 177, 198 205)
opus 11 (59, 86, 87, 88, 101, 104, 238, 245)
opus 12 (86, 91, 92, 93, 133, 174, 207, 218)
opus 13 (86, 91, 92, 93, 156, 166, 171, 176, 188)
opus 14 (86, 87, 88, 104, 149, 152, 156, 204, 211, 239, 240, 245)
opus 15 (28, 45, 56, 79, 86 88, 99, 104, 106 110, 121, 153, 158, 166, 183, 191, 196, 216, 239, 240, 244, 246, 247)
opus 16 (69, 70, 76, 78 79, 82, 84, 99, 105, 107, 110, 213, 238, 246)
opus 17 (vi, vii, 1, 10, 121, 123 125, 129, 183, 191, 192, 195, 197, 198, 210, 234, 244, 245, 247, 248)
opus 18 (2, 68, 116, 124 125, 129, 196, 235, 242, 247)
opus 19 (12, 125, 129, 204, 205, 228, 235, 239)
opus [19b] (68)
opus 20 (12, 126 127, 129, 213, 235, 245, 247)
opus 21 (122, 127, 129, 248)
opus 22 (121 123, 127 129, 220, 239, 240, 247)
opus 23 (121, 128 129 160, 192, 205, 210, 234, 238, 239, 243, 244, 247)
opus 24 (19, 50)
opus 25 (129, 155, 166, 167, 174, 183, 184, 186)
opus 26 (150, 152, 247)
opus 27 (vi, 2, 5, 86 88, 133, 149, 152, 157, 166, 174, 196, 206, 207, 212, 213, 218, 220, 239, 241, 244, 245)
opus 28 (150, 152, 153, 158, 246, 247)
opus 28[b] (vi, vii, 88, 134, 149, 152 154, 156, 166, 167, 174, 196, 197, 205, 208, 213, 220, 238, 240, 241, 246, 247, 249)
opus 28[c] (152)
opus 29 (149, 150, 152 155, 157, 171, 178, 215, 220, 228, 238, 241, 242, 244, 246)
opus 30 (129, 147 149, 152, 155 157, 166, 171, 200, 218, 241, 244, 245, 246, 247)
opus 31 (5, 138, 141, 145, 149, 150, 155, 157 158, 160, 166, 171, 172, 200, 228, 235, 239, 241, 243, 244, 245)
opus 32 (175, 183)
opus 33[a] (175, 198)
opus 33[b] (175, 184, 186)
opus 34[a] (124, 166, 175, 178, 183, 184, 186)
opus 34[b] (130, 175, 184)
opus 35 (19, 129, 184, 186)
opus 36 (129 130, 166, 186)
opus 37 (186)
opus 38 (viii, xvi, 59, 64, 69, 101, 117, 123, 133, 134, 141, 153, 157, 158, 165, 166, 167, 174, 175, 182, 189 201, 204. 205, 206, 207, 208, 210, 212, 228, 231, 235, 238, 241, 242, 243, 244, 246, 249)
opus 39 (69, 167, 175, 196, 205 206, 214, 239, 245)
opus 40 (vi, 2, 5, 133, 149, 150, 152, 166, 174, 206 207, 212, 214, 218, 220, 241, 244)
opus 41 (59, 133, 149, 166, 167, 196, 207 208, 214, 218, 226, 238)
opus 42 (191, 204, 208, 214, 245)
opus 43 (158, 166, 167, 190, 206, 209, 214, 245)

opus 44 (1, 156, 158, 196, 204, 205, 206 210, 214, 226, 238)
opus 45 (158, 166, 174, 200, 205, 210, 212 214, 218, 221, 226, 246)
opus 46 (65, 199, 214, 216)
opus 47 (1, 59, 133, 158, 192, 194, 207, 210, 216, 217 221, 226, 242, 247)
opus 48 (221, 245)
opus 49 (222, 238)
opus 50 (40, 152, 223 226, 245)
opus 51 (40, 225, 226, 245)
opus 52 (ix, 72, 89, 90, 166, 187, 192, 203, 206, 226 227)
opus 53 (86, 165, 166, 167, 204, 227 228, 239)

WoO 2 (51, 59, 166, 178, 184, 207, 235)
WoO 3 (129, 186)
WoO 4 (166, 184, 186)
WoO 5 (55, 111, 162)
WoO 6 (133, 167, 176, 177, 212, 228)
WoO 7 (51, 178, 189)
WoO 8 (56, 133 134, 174, 177, 182, 195, 231)
WoO 9 (19, 50, 60, 69 70, 82, 104, 176, 239)
WoO 10 (51, 178, 217, 218)
WoO 11 (51, 166, 178, 189, 215, 216 217, 218)
WoO 12 (184, 186)
WoO 13 (129, 175, 183, 185, 186)
WoO 14 (184, 186)

The Author

Dr. Ari van Vliet is both a musician and a musicologist. He has made his career as a concert guitarist, giving many recitals with a Spanish, Latin-American and French repertoire, which he has also released on compact disc: *Latin Recital, Iberia, Guitar Collection, Collector's Item, Atahualpa Yupanqui Instrumental, Napoléon Coste*. He completed his master as a guitarist at the Royal Conservatoire in the Hague, studying with his friend and teacher Antonio Pereira Arias, under whose tutelage he mastered the lyrical interpretation of guitar music. As a guitar teacher, he has succeeded in training many pupils to a high standard of artistry. He received his master's degree in Musicology in 1992 with a thesis entitled *The Italian, Spanish and French style in guitar music in the second half of the seventeenth century*, at the University of Utrecht. He has published articles based on this work in *De Tabulatuur*. He is the author of several methods for guitar and music education. Van Vliet draws upon his scholarship and extensive knowledge of music, as well as his insight and experience, in his doctoral research on the life and works of 19th-century French guitar composer Napoléon Coste. His compact disc of Coste's most important works, including the first known recording of the *Fantaisie symphonique* opus 28[b], appeared in 2012 as the historical performance practice part of his dissertation, on the basis of which he received his doctorate in 2015 with the biography: *Napoléon Coste: Composer and Guitarist in the Musical Life of 19th- Century Paris*. at the university of Utrecht.

166 Ari van Vliet, 2015

CD Notes

Napoléon Coste was born in the French village of Amondans on the 27th of June 1805 as the first and only son of Jean François Coste, an officer in the Napoleontic army, mayor of the village at the time. His mother, Anne Pierrette Dénéria, was the second wife of Jean François, who had two daughters from his first marriage and a daughter Cathérine, the older sister of Napoléon Coste. Soon the family moved to Ornans, a greater village, close to Amondans, in the Jura. When his father reentered the army and was offered a post in the North in 1812, the little Napoléon went with him to Langeoog, a 'waddeneiland' near the Eems between Holland and Germany. An evacuation report states that, as a boy of only 8 years, armed with a saddle pistol, he stood guard with the soldiers under the attack of the English. Later he stayed in Delfzijl until the French army, and so his father, had to leave the fortress as a result of the defeat of Napoléon Bonaparte at Leipzig. Then he must have passed the Zuiderzee, the large and dangerous inner sea of Holland.

He was united with his family and lived in Valenciennes in the North of France, where he grew up. The story goes that he fell seriously ill and could not fulfill the ambition his father had for him in a military career. Instead, he turned to music and learned to play the guitar, at first by his mother. At the age of 18 he gave his first concerts in Valenciennes, one in a duet with the traveling virtuoso Sagrini in the *Gran Variazioni Concertanti* opus 35 that Giuliani wrote in cooperation with Hummel. Coste also must have played the piano, as he was a teacher of music in Valenciennes and later composed several works for the instrument.

In 1828/29 he moved to Paris to start a career as a guitarist/composer. There he met other guitarists such as Carulli, Carcassi, Aguado and Sor, with whom he probably studied counterpoint and harmony. If not so, he might have studied these skills with a professor of the conservatoire. In 1851 he became a member, and even the secretary in 1870, of the Freemasons lodge 'Les Frères Unis Inséparables' in which many musicians and composers participated, as Klosé, Meyerbeer, Panseron and Triébert did.

Paris was on the threshold of important developments in romantic music with Berlioz, Chopin, Liszt, and Coste fulfilled his role in the heritage of Sor, composing an important oeuvre for the guitar. He took music for guitar a step further into romanticism in Paris, as did Mertz in Vienna and Zani de Ferranti in Brussels. He made a successful career as a guitarist, performing in many concerts, despite the declining interest for the instrument in recitals in favor of the piano. This ended when he injured his left arm in 1863 and again in 1874. By then he already had published a voluminous oeuvre of compositions for guitar solo, but nevertheless he had to accept a post as administrator at the Paris community in 1855 for a living, from which he was pensioned in 1875.

Around 1850 the Paris luthier Lacôte developed a heptacorde guitar, as said under instruction of Coste, with the seventh string in D as a bourdon aside the fingerboard. Several of the guitar works of Coste cannot be played otherwise than on such an instrument.

The Russian nobleman Makaroff, who traveled through Europe visiting important guitarists/composers, organized a guitar construction and composition contest in 1856 that took place in Brussels, a quite neutral place at the time of the Crimean war. Coste and Mertz entered this contest with many compositions, and Mertz won the first prize with his *Concertino*. As he had just died, this could have been out of pity for his widow. Coste went to Brussels, played his compositions in the apartment of Makaroff at the Houtmarkt for the jury that consisted of professors of the conservatoire and achieved the second prize for his *Sérénade* opus 30. On the occasion of this contest he composed his most important works *Le Passage des Alpes* opus 27, 28 & 40, *Fantaisie symphonique* opus 28[b], *La Chasse des Sylphes* opus 29 and *Le Départ* opus 31.

In 1871, two weeks after the capitulation of Paris in the war against the Prussian army that destroyed most of the city, he married his much younger pupil Louise Olive Pauilhé.

After having published most of his works with the publishers Richault, Challiot and Schonenberger, from 1876 on he published his own works from opus 43 to 53. In Europe he had many admirers with whom he had a regular correspondence. One was Degen from Denmark who made the first known photo of Coste, probably on the occasion of his visit to Paris in 1855. The other most well-known photo was taken many years later by the commercially active photographer Disdéri in Paris. The fame of Coste even went to Germany where he became an honorary member of the Club des Guitaristes de Leipzig, to which he dedicated his famous *Livre d'Or du Guitariste* opus 51. In 1883 Coste fell ill and died January 14th, the same day as Gustave Doré.

As a composer he composed some 53 opus numbers, mostly works for guitar solo, but also transcriptions of Schubert songs, guitar duets, works for oboe and guitar in many genres. Two of his guitars are now in the Cité de la Musique museum in Paris. His importance for the romantic guitar cannot be underestimated, as he is the key figure in the transition from classical towards romanticism. His compositions appear more and more in recitals and in recordings all over the world.

Souvenirs

The set of seven souvenirs, composed around 1852, is a journey through the memories of Coste, the landscapes of his childhood, the sounds in his youth and the romance of his adolescence.

First it leads to Ornans, the village of his childhood in the Jura, in the East of France with its grassy fields, corn, woods, rivers and waterfalls, but also rough highlands, where mountaineers travel in their special outfit and finally vanish in the distance.

The river Rhine is mainly the border between France, with its elegant waltzes and Germany, which the French never liked because of its assumed rudeness and lack of refinement. But the flow of the sparkling water is reflected on both sides of the river and in both parts of the composition.

In Holland the people must have been kind to the young Coste, as *Delfzil* breathes a gentle atmosphere. It is a waltz with sad and happy memories, the composition varies these feelings in quiet and violent movements, sometimes even imitating the abrupt speech of Groningen.

The Zuyderzée was very impressive to the young boy. In the music one can hear the movement of the waves, a tumultuous storm coming up, even lightning and thunder. Then a fine waltz shows folkloristic features, people dancing and an exciting finale.

Les Cloches is clearly imitating the carillons of Flanders, after the polyphonic introduction of the *Fugue*, the only one Coste composed. The *Rondeau* is very emblematic with the returning sounds of chimes, alternating warming melodies and fast movements of chords.

Meulan is a small city near Paris where, according to this music, Coste might have met his wife and spent happy times with her. The piece starts with an amorous and charming melody, moves to a striking moment of falling in love, and then turns to a gripping waltz, ending in enthusiastic happiness.

Finally, in *Les Soirées d'Auteuil*, also a village close to Paris, a *Sérénade* brings a tribute to loving memories and a Scherzo refers to merry moments Coste must have waltzed with his wife. The *Souvenirs* show the great musical abilities of Coste as a composer in an intense and sensible musical style, romanticism referring to nature, cities, sentiments, folklore and, why not, love.

Fantaisie symphonique

This piece was composed for the Makaroff guitar composition concours in 1856 and part of the five pieces that Napoléon Coste submitted to the competition. It was not published at the time.

Until now it has not been recorded, probably because of the intensive use of the seventh string in D, adjacent to the sixth in E for which a seven string guitar is indispensable. Here, finally is the first recording of this important work of Coste.

The title might refer to the *Symphonie Fantastique* of Berlioz 36 years earlier, Coste was an admirer of this composer, but the programmatic reference of the music is not very clear. The five parts are episodic as a compilation in themselves. The moods differ many times from strong rhythmic motives and themes to lovely lyrical melodies, always set in rich harmony and polyphonic passages. The beautiful Andante with its very romantic and lyrical melody also appears in the *Etudes* as no. 14, which is dedicated to his wife. The final *Scherzo* shows interesting guitaristic and musical inventions, with humor in a during movement of a waltz, the personal preference of Coste.

LE PASSAGE DES ALPES

The music opens in a *Maestoso* that, by the atmosphere and even the tempo, pictures the journey through the Alps of the great Napoléon Bonaparte, admired by Coste. Another possibility for the program of the music is the passage over the Alps by Hannibal, as written in the book of Jean André de Luc. But the event of Napoléon himself in 1800 is closer to the truth. The many hardships the famous traveler experiences pass in revue in this programmatic piece in the many gradations of musical passages, rhythms, spherical sketches, abrupt changes and lyrical melodies. The *Marche* refers to the heroic intentions of Napoléon, with trumpet sounds, echoes in the valleys, marching troops and the local people looking at the passing army in adoration. Then the arrival in Italy follows, a *Rondo*, even with references to the most famous Italian musician in his violin concerto, Paganini of course, and also there is a trio with folk music elements. The composition ends in a majestic tarantella movement, with both classic and romantic references to the greatness of an honored monarch from Corsica.

PERFORMER

Ari van Vliet is a guitarist and a musicologist. He studied the guitar with Antonio Pereira Arias at the Royal Conservatoire in The Hague. In the tradition of Segovia he developed a lyrical style of playing. He gives concerts, lectures and lessons in music and recitals with classical, Spanish and Latin-American repertoire. His interpretation of guitar music can be heard on his recital CD's Iberia, Guitar Collection, Collector's Item, Latin Recital and Atahualpa Yupanqui Instrumental. He graduated in musicology at the University of Utrecht on the subject 'Guitar music in the second half of the 17th century: the Italian, Spanish and French style'. Currently he is writing the biography of Napoléon Coste that includes a thematic catalogue. As musical practice always comes first, he studied the most important works of Coste as a performer and now presents this program in a recital played on a Kresse copy of the Lacôte seven-string guitar that was developed under the instruction of Coste.

GUITAR

To experience the way Coste himself played, Ari van Vliet searched for a copy of this guitar. Unfortunately, the instrument was in the Cité de la Musique in Paris and there were no construction drawings available. Luckily Bernard Kresse in Köln had obtained another Lacôte heptacorde, and he ordered a copy of the instrument in 2010. To come even closer to the way Coste may have played and how his music could have sounded, the next step was to turn to gut-strings that were in use at the time. These strings are tuned in the 19th century pitch of a' = 435 Hz. The playing technique and sound differs from that of the modern guitar, but nevertheless has its own quality and character. The strings are somewhat less direct in producing the tone after the stroke, which influences the way of phrasing. The sound acoustics are deeper, more rounded and terse. All this means a development of different aesthetics in the way of the production of the sound and in the interpretation of the music. The experienced listener and player can abandon modern aesthetics of sound to give way to this interpretation of the 19th century romantic guitar music of Napoléon Coste.

Tracklist

Souvenirs, Sept Morceaux Episodiques pour la Guitare 1852

La Vallée d'Ornans opus 17
    1 Cantabile — 2:15
    2 Les Montagnards, Rondo — 3:20

Les Bords du Rhin opus 18
    3 Valse — 5:31

Delfzil opus 19
    4 Scherzo — 3:23

Le Zuyderzée opus 20
    5 Ballade; Allegretto grazioso — 5:19

Les Cloches opus 21
    6 Fugue — 1:24
    7 Rondeau — 3:40

Meulan opus 22
    8 Andantino — 6:21

Les Soirées d'Auteuil opus 23
    9 Sérénade — 2:57
    10 Scherzo — 4:03

Fantaisie symphonique en deux parties pour la guitare opus 28[b] 1856

Première Partie:
    11 Allegro — 1:28
    12 Andantino grazioso — 2:30
    13 Rondo — 2:06

Deuxième Partie:
    14 Andante — 3:50
    15 Scherzo — 4:55

Le Passage des Alpes, Trilogie pour la Guitare 1856
    16 Maestoso opus 27 — 4:44
    17 Marche opus 28 — 7:46
    18 Rondo opus 40 — 5:05

This recital was recorded in 2011 and played on a copy of a Lacôte heptacorde guitar from 1856 made by Bernhard Kresse in Köln 2010, with gut strings made by Damian Dlugolecki tuned in a' = 435Hz. The original editions and manuscripts of the music come from the Rischel Birket-Smith collection in the Kongelige Bibliotek in Kopenhagen.

CUMULI   GUITAR   RECITAL   CGR 1204

All rights of the producer and the owner of the work reproduced reserved.
Unauthorized copying, hiring, lending, public performance and broadcasting of this recording prohibited.
Alle Urheber- und Leistungsschutzrechte vorbehalten.
Kein Verleih. Keine unerlaubte Vervielfältigung, Vermietung, Aufführung, Sendung.

www.ingramcontent.com/pod-product-compliance
Lightning Source LLC
Chambersburg PA
CBHW080842010526
44114CB00017B/2354